THE
MARX–ENGELS
CYCLOPEDIA

SYMBOLS

→ The **arrow** refers to entries in Volume I (*Marx–Engels Chronicle*). It points to a specific **year and paragraph** in the chronology. In Volume I it points right (→) or left (←) depending on whether it refers ahead or behind. In Volumes II and III it points right only.

\# The **"number"** symbol refers to entries in Volume II (*Marx–Engels Register*), in conjunction with "ME," "M," or "E." For example, #ME74 = Marx and Engels' *Holy Family*; #M129 = Marx's *Capital*; #E23 = Engels' *Anti-Dühring*; etc.

* The **asterisk** refers only to the entries in Volume III (*Marx–Engels Glossary*). Marking a name (person, periodical, etc.), it means that there is an entry for this name in the *Glossary*; it is used only when there is special reason to signal the entry.

\+ The **plus** symbol following a date means indefinite continuance; e.g., 1834+ means "From 1834 on. . . ."

/ The **solidus or slash mark** generally means "or," as in "M/E" (Marx or Engels). Similarly, "1834/35" means "1834 or 1835."

% The **percent sign,** used in Volume II (*Marx–Engels Register*), indicates a *partial* translation.

++ The **double plus sign,** used in Volume II (*Marx–Engels Register*), indicates additional information or notes.

DATE ABBREVIATIONS

Months: Months may be abbreviated with a three-letter form, without a period, except for June and July, which are spelled out; e.g., Jan, Feb, Mar, Apr, May, Aug, Sep, Oct, Nov, Dec.

Parts of the Month: In the absence of exact information, parts of the month may be indicated using the letters A, B, C, and D to stand for the four quarters of the month. For example,
Mar A = beginning of March
Mar AB = first half of March
Mar M = middle of March

Mar CD = last half of March
Mar D = end of March

"About" Dates: Before a date or its symbol, the word *about* may be represented by "c." (for "circa"). For example,
Mar c.7 = about Mar 7
c.1853 = about 1853
Mar c.A = about the beginning of March
Mar c.CD = about the last half of March
But the common abbreviation "ca." (also for "circa") may be used with the same meaning in other circumstances.

ABBREVIATIONS FOR MARX, ENGELS

The letters M and E (without periods) are often used for the names Marx and Engels, especially in concise presentations of information; ME = Marx and Engels (in *Register* titles), M–E = Marx and Engels (in certain other contexts), M/E = Marx or Engels.

For the full list of abbreviations, see page xvii.

VOLUME I
of the Marx–Engels Cyclopedia

THE
MARX–ENGELS
CHRONICLE

A Day-by-Day Chronology of
Marx and Engels' Life and Activity

By HAL DRAPER

with the assistance of the Center for Socialist History

SCHOCKEN BOOKS • NEW YORK

9 - 3 - 87

First published by Schocken Books 1985
10 9 8 7 6 5 4 3 2 1   85 86 87 88

Library of Congress Cataloging in Publication Data
Draper, Hal.
   The Marx–Engels chronicle.
   (The Marx–Engels cyclopedia ; v. 1)
   1. Marx, Karl, 1818–1883—Chronology. 2. Engels,
Friedrich, 1820–1895—Chronology. 3. Communists—
Biography. I. Center for Socialist History (Berkeley, Calif.). II. Title.
III. Series: Draper, Hal. Marx–Engels cyclopedia; v. 1.
HX39.5.D69 1984   vol. 1 335.4s 84–3013[335.4′092′4] [B]

Designed by Nancy Dale Muldoon
Manufactured in the United States of America
ISBN 0–8052–3909–X (v. 1)

Contents

THE MARX–ENGELS CHRONICLE

General Introduction

The *Marx–Engels Cyclopedia* (MEC) comprises three reference works made one by interreference and interindexing:

Volume I: The *Marx–Engels Chronicle*. A day-to-day chronology of Marx and Engels' lives and activities.

Volume II: The *Marx–Engels Register*. A bibliography of Marx and Engels' individual writings.

Volume III: The *Marx–Engels Glossary*. A dictionary of all proper names mentioned in Volumes I and II: persons, periodicals, parties, organizations, etc.

Each volume can be used independently. At the same time, its usefulness is enhanced by the fact that the other volumes offer additional channels of access to its contents.

For example, Volume I, the *Marx–Engels Chronicle*, refers under the appropriate dates of composition and publication to the individual writings, by *Register* number if not title. Thus it offers a *chronological* mode of access to the entries in the *Marx–Engels Register* (Volume II), which are organized there alphabetically. Contrariwise, the entries in the *Register* are indexed to locations in the *Chronicle* (Volume I). The *Marx–Engels Glossary* (Volume III) indexes references to a given name occurring in Volume I or II.

In short, whether you start with a title, an event, or a name, you can work your way from the known fact to other sources of information. As additional aids, there are a number of special lists, particularly in Volume II, directed to the bibliographical control of Marx and Engels' contributions to certain periodicals, notably the *New York Daily Tribune*.

Not included in this *Cyclopedia* is another kind of work: a dictionary of ideas and terms, an exposition of Marx's thought in alphabetical format. This would be a laudable enterprise, but of a different sort altogether. Rather, this *Cyclopedia* is dedicated to hard facts. In an area as inevitably ideological as that of Marx studies, hard facts are not less but more important: they are moorings. True, one cannot hope to eliminate all ideological reflections from such a work; but at any rate the facts are here.

SOURCES

The main source of the information contained in this *Cyclopedia* is the scientific output of the Institute of Marxism-Leninism (IML) of Moscow, together with its predecessors and its collaborating institutions. Its most important predecessor was the original Marx–Engels–Lenin Institute founded by D. Ryazanov; its present main collaborator is the IML of East Germany.

These institutes, with their publishing affiliates and associates, have over the years accomplished a prodigious work. At the same time, like all scholarly work in the world of the Communist bureaucratic-collectivist states, this job has been done under well-known political constraints, which need not concern us except to explain that the IML output must be subjected to constant checking. In addition, the material quarried from IML sources must be compared with and supplemented by information available from other sources, as far as possible.

The principal IML sources, often referred to in the volumes of this *Cyclopedia*, are the following four editions of Marx and Engels' work:

1. The *Marx-Engels Werke* (*MEW*), published in East Germany. As this is written, it is still the only near-complete, or the nearest-complete, edition of Marx and Engels' works—in German only. Its notes and appendices are a mine of information.

2. The so-called *MEGA*—customary name for the old and original *Marx-Engels Gesamtausgabe* of 1927–1935—is still useful for some purposes; but of course it covered only up to 1848, and it has been largely superseded even for that period.

3. The *New Mega* (to use our own designation) got started in 1975, and as this is written, it has gone only about a seventh of the way toward its planned 100 volumes, which may not be completed until some time after the year 2001. Though it was given the old *Gesamtausgabe* name by the IML, it is really an independent project, not a continuation of the old *MEGA*.

4. The new English edition of Marx and Engels' *Collected Works* (*MECW*), likewise in process of publication, is little more than a quarter of the way to its final Volume 50, perhaps due also in the next century.

Smaller-scale publications have made some limited contributions as well; see the Sources and Translations ("ST") List in Volume II.

A definitive summing-up of the field covered by *MEC* is still some distance away. All we can do is give the state of information as of now—with many lacunae and a sprinkling of question marks.

A reference work of this sort is not by nature a one-man project, and there are bound to be errors of omission and commission. Alas, in the course of the present work I have found not a few mistakes even in the *Marx-Engels Werke*, which is usually a reliable source of raw facts; and the *New Mega* apparently suffers from even more. Alert users of this *Cyclopedia*, I am afraid, may find some here too; and I request that these be communicated to me through the publisher, with an eye to a revised edition.

TECHNICAL POINTS

Spelling. American spelling is used throughout, except in direct quotes from British sources and in British names. Thus there was a *Labor Standard* in New York and a *Labour Standard* in London; the group that met in Manchester called itself a Labour Parliament, but Marx's article on it in the *New York Daily Tribune* called it the Labor Parliament; and so on.

Good English. I am a militant proponent of using *contact, enthuse,* and *feature* as verbs, of splitting infinitives at will, of using *hopefully* like the best English writers, and of other practices condemned by certain misguided literati. I mention this only to absolve the publisher and its editors of any responsibility for these alleged deviations.

German Spelling. When using indexes and other alphabetized lists, readers should know that in German *Carl* and *Karl*, or *Conrad* and *Konrad*, are often interchangeable, and that therefore many names appear in both forms in different places. The same applies to some place names (Carlsbad, Coblenz, etc.). I have tended to give the right of way to the K. Also, there are some cases where the common English name of a place differs from the native name (for example, Hanover/Hannover); our text uses the English form, though alternative forms are explained in the *Glossary*.

Alphabetization. All alphabetization in this work follows the so-called Anglo-American rules, used in library catalogs. German alphabetization, which is different in several respects, has influenced some American publications (especially translations), creating some technical confusion. The following points should be noted: (1) Alphabetization is word by word, not letter by letter—except perforce in the "List of Abbreviations." (2) The German umlauted vowel is treated as if followed by an e: that is, ä = ae, ö = oe, ü = ue; just as "Mc" or "M'" is treated as if spelled out "Mac" no matter how a given name is written. (3) An initial definite or indefinite article is ignored for alphabetizing purposes, in English as in other languages. This pertains to the English *the, a, an;* the German *der, die, das, ein, eine,* etc.; the French *le, la, les, l', un, une;* and so on, including the Portuguese article *O.*

Manuscripts. Information given here on a number of unpublished manuscripts by Marx or Engels is necessarily tentative, and probably defective, being based on incomplete descriptions. This cannot be fully remedied until, and unless, these manuscripts are published in the *New Mega.* Present information often comes from excerpts published in some collection by the IML. In some cases available references to some manuscripts are so fragmentary that I have preferred to include nothing at this time.

Number Interpolation. The *Register,* also the "ST" List (both in Volume II), is numbered from 1 on, in alphabetical order; but provision has had to be made for revisions, requiring the insertion of new numbers into the sequence. This has already proved necessary in the course of work on this *Cyclopedia,* and will no doubt continue to be necessary for future revisions. For this reason I have used a flexible decimal system. For example, between 150 and 151, the first interpolated number is 150.5; a future interpolation between 150 and 150.5 may be 150.3. Thus the revised list remains in numerical order.

THE CENTER FOR SOCIALIST HISTORY

The Center for Socialist History in Berkeley, California, has assisted this project in its later stages, since the Center itself was only recently established. Its help has been invaluable, and I am happy to acknowledge it. Steve

Diamond, who has been associated with me throughout the work on the *Cyclopedia*, is also a director of the Center.

The Center's interest in this project will postdate publication too. This *Cyclopedia* is published without a comprehensive subject index; still, some users may want to trace, say, Marx's views on party organization, war, anarchism, or some other theme. A "Selected Subjects Index" is planned by the Center, and possibly also other research aids. Inquiries should be directed to the Center for Socialist History, 2633 Etna, Berkeley, CA 94704.

H.D.

Preface to Volume I

The *Marx–Engels Chronicle* is a chronology, not a biography. A good biography gives a balanced view of a life; in a chronology, relatively trivial events may jostle some of the most important dates in political history.

In the *Chronicle* the qualities that make for a good biography have been sacrificed in favor of the accurate assemblage of more or less raw data—that is, unevaluated facts. Above all, a chronology should provide specific dates, and indeed this has been one of the major concerns.

Like the *Marx–Engels Cyclopedia* as a whole, this chronology covers both Marx and Engels, up to the year of Engels' death (1895). All previous chronologies, with one exception, have focused on Marx. In principle *MEC* devotes equally detailed attention to both men, but possibly the reader may detect somewhat greater emphasis on Marx.

THE TWO FOUNDATION CHRONOLOGIES

This chronology did not start from scratch: it was based on two great chronologies already available, both in German.

1. The first, in point of time, was *Karl Marx, Chronik seines Lebens* (abbreviated *KMC*—see ST/36) published in 1934 by the Marx–Engels–Lenin Institute of Moscow, largely based on the earlier research of the staff organized by D. Ryazanov. For almost a half century it has been one of the most important resources for Marx studies. For almost as long, there have been reports that an English translation was under way, but none ever appeared. Now we can say: just as well. Much of this great work is now out of date; in the light of several decades of research, it is clear that it is peppered with errors. It is important to point these out, since the *Chronik* is still being used as an authority; and accordingly the most important errors are mentioned in the following pages. But it is just as important to preserve, and pass on, the positive content of this work.

2. The more modern basic chronology winds through 19 volumes of the *Marx–Engels Werke* (*MEW*—see ST/ME69) in the form of a section titled "Daten aus ihrem Leben und ihrer Tätigkeit" [Dates in Their Lives and Activities]. It is referred to here as *MEW Daten*. The 19 sections add up to a work of 352 pages. It covers both Marx and Engels, often in great detail.

The *Marx–Engels Chronicle* started with the idea of conflating *KMC* and *MEW Daten*, a combination that would automatically be the most useful chronology available. Two other steps have been taken: enrichment with added material, and the excision of extraneous matter. First, on the enrichment process:

New material has been drawn from a variety of sources, which need not be listed here since they constitute most of the Sources and Translations ("ST") List found in Volume II. Four special campaigns of the enrichment process may be described as follows:

1. Special notice was taken of Marx and Engels' reading and study patterns, including the listing of many of the specific books they read and annotated. In order not to overload the *Chronicle* dates with long lists, the book titles or authors are often detailed in a "Year Appendix" section (following December), and are sometimes reserved to the author's name in the *Glossary* (Volume III). In any case, the *Glossary* indexes all mentions of a given name.

2. The chief source for the enrichment process was the body of the Marx–Engels correspondence: letters by them to each other or to third persons. The correspondence has also functioned as a check on the *KMC* and *MEW Daten* entries, and as a source of specific dates not otherwise mentioned.

3. The next great source was the minutes and documents of the General Council of the International (see especially ST/21 and ST/26, 27). The *Chronicle* now provides full access to *all* of Marx and Engels' participations in General Council meetings and International conferences, connected up with their correspondence.

4. Another special project embodied in the *Chronicle* is the tracing of Marx's "road to *Capital*," that is, the steps and events in the development of his views on political economy (insofar as this can be done in terms of a chronology). All the essential entries have been placed under two rubrics, which identify them. Up through December 1862, when Marx adopted the title *Capital*, the rubric is (or contains) the key word "Economica"—a term used by Marx for the work he was preparing. (By analogy it is also used for Engels, when necessary.) From 1863 on the rubric is "Capital." If you follow these two signposts from month to month, you are on the "Road to Capital"—which heading has indeed been placed on a special periodization/chronology found in the Appendix to this volume.

On the other hand, in the course of conflating *KMC* and *MEW Daten*, certain material has been digested *out*. I want to call these extruded elements to the reader's attention, in the case of both of the older works.

Karl Marx, Chronik. In this work, each dated entry is followed by a small-type note giving a list of the sources on which the entry is presumably based: very often, letters by or to Marx and Engels. I have not taken over these notes as such, though much of their content has been used. Many of these references are to letters sent to Marx or Engels by others, mostly unpublished, hence available chiefly in the archives of the Institute of Marxism-Leninism in Moscow or the International Institute for Social History in Amsterdam. But *nota bene:* for some purposes this material may still be useful to certain researchers; to this extent *KMC* is not completely superseded by the present *Chronicle.*

MEW Daten. All of the factual material in this chronology has been carried over to the present *Chronicle* (apart from errors, of course). What has been omitted are the frequent homilies and party-line statements on various points of doctrine and interpretation inserted by the IML editors to sanitize whatever material would otherwise taint the pages. However, it should be said, as strongly as possible, that I have found no clear instance where the party-line predilections of the editors have led to the falsification of hard facts or of published texts; acts of omission, and omitted texts, are another matter, as is well known. Not only in *MEW Daten* but also in *MEW* editorial notes, peculiar interpretations are legion, but there is no problem about distinguishing between these and the line separating hard facts from factual errors.

Since I have explained what has been dropped from *KMC* and *MEW Daten*, I must now emphasize the other side of this coin: special effort has been made to carry over all other details given in these works, *even those I might otherwise have considered too minor to include.* In fact this explains why certain entries appear while equally unimportant items have been left out: the former were already in *KMC* or *MEW Daten* and therefore could not be omitted by the above rules. Put in another way, one aim of the *Chronicle* is to supersede the two foundation works to the fullest extent possible.

OTHER PUBLISHED CHRONOLOGIES

Many books about Marx include short chronologies of a few pages; these need not concern us here. Noteworthy chronologies on a larger scale have been produced by Maximilien Rubel, singly or with an associate. Readers may find these useful. They are mainly concerned with Marx alone, and are mostly based on *KMC* plus a survey of Marx's writings and letters. They tend to be organized mainly by month only, deemphasizing specific day dates, and often offer discursive passages in which Rubel expresses his special views on Marxism. Here is a chronological list, each publication being a revised form of the preceding:

1. "Chronologie," by M. Rubel, in Marx's *Oeuvres. Economie*, edited by Rubel, Tome I, pages lvi to clxxvi (Paris: Gallimard, Bibliothèque de la Pléiade, 1963; 2d ed., 1965). In French.

2. M. Rubel, compiler, *Marx-Chronik. Daten zu Leben und Werk* (Reihe Hanser 3) (Munich: Carl Hanser Verlag, 1968). 163pp. In German.

3. M. Rubel and M. Manale, *Marx without Myth. A Chronological Study of His Life and Work* (Oxford: Blackwell, 1975). 368pp. In this version the Marx chronology is embedded in parallel chronologies of general events and "Technological Progress," plus bibliographical appendices, and is organized by year, but not by month or day (month/day dates are scarce). Indeed this work is halfway between a chronology and a sort of biography, with frequent political essays by the authors on their views.

FORM OF PRESENTATION

In principle the *Marx–Engels Chronicle* is a day-by-day chronology, with compromises here and there. Within the year the basic division is the month but unfortunately not everything fits neatly into this framework. Below we list several ways in which this framework has been rubberized.

Thematic Rubrics. Related events that occur within a month or part of a month—usually within a few days—have been grouped together under topical rubrics, thereby combining the chronological with the thematic. Rubrics pertaining to Marx, or to both Marx and Engels, do not necessarily include Marx's name; but Engels' name always appears in rubrics pertaining to him. Some rubrics are used repeatedly as standard tags, in particular "W&P" (Writing and Publication), referring to the activities covered by (W) and (P) in the *Register*; but this rubric also covers plans and intentions. In any case the rubrics are not necessarily exact descriptions, being limited by the compulsions of brevity.

Conspectus. At the beginning of most years, an overview of events and activities is given, in the first place as a summary of the period. This Conspectus also points to material that cannot be pinpointed in a specific month, either because it extends over part of the year or because its dating is indeterminate. It includes *broad dates*: events extending over more than one or two months or outside the current year. These events may also be noted in the month-by-month chronicle at the beginning and ending dates. It includes *indefinite dates*, lacking sufficient information to fix their place: e.g., "sometime in 1853," or "the first half of 1871."

Year Appendix. This section, located after December at the end of a year, is mainly a device for removing long lists of authors read and studied by Marx or Engels, from the other sections of the *Chronicle*. However, short references under the rubric "Reading and Study" are still found in the Conspectus or elsewhere, especially if limited to a particular month.

Relation to the *Register*. While the *Register* is organized alphabetically, the *Chronicle* provides a systematic chronological access to Marx and Engels' writings: this is why the *Register* numbers (#) pepper the text. Major writings are mentioned by title; minor writings may be indicated by subject; others may be listed by place of publication (like *New York Daily Tribune* articles); but in all cases the *Register* number provides a bridge to the bibliography. Journalistic writings are located in accordance with the publication date—(P) in the *Register*—and unless otherwise specified the date of writing (W) may be assumed to be within a couple of days. Writing dates are given for major works, for unpublished writings, and in most cases where there is a substantial gap between the dates of writing and publication. See the remarks on "broad dates" and "indefinite dates" under Conspectus, above.

Multimonth Dates. If the date of an event is, say, "Jan-Mar," the entry will appear in the earliest month, with a back-reference probably added at the end-date. Such an "indefinite date" would appear toward the end of the January listings, in order to point ahead.

Season Dates; Parts of Years. Given dates are sometimes formulated in terms of seasons rather than months. While "summer 1868" may be used in the text, it is in practice interpreted to mean "July-Aug." Similarly: "winter" = Jan-Feb; "autumn" = Oct-Nov; "spring" = Apr-May. The words "beginning of 1870" are interpreted to mean Jan-Feb; "end of 1870" = Nov-Dec. In such cases the exact dates are probably unknown.

Dating from Letters. As mentioned, many entries derive from letters, which do not always give exact dates. Suppose that on November 20 Marx writes Engels that he has read a certain book; the frequent practice of *KMC* and *MEW Daten* is to make a guess and state: "First half of Nov: M reads X's book. . . ." Actually it is not known whether he read the book that month or before. Instead of guessing, it is preferable to state the known fact, namely, "Nov 20: Marx writes Engels he has read. . . ." This may make the *Chronicle* read in part like a record of correspondence, but it has the advantage of stating the truth rather than unacknowledged speculation.

Here is a second problem: *KMC* and *MEW Daten* often list letters by the date putatively *received* by Marx or Engels, rather than the date on the letter itself, the date sent. This practice has been changed wherever possible, in any case making clear which date is involved. In some cases both dates are given, e.g., "Oct 4 (rec'd 7) . . ."—especially in the case of letters from America, since here the gap was nearly two weeks. Let us note that letters between London and, say, Germany seem to have taken two or three days; and letters between London and Manchester could be depended on to be delivered the following morning, sometimes even the same day. (It has taken a century of triumphant technological progress to bring it about that a first-class letter from one side of Manhattan to another can take anywhere from days to weeks.)

No-Day Dating. If our date is the name of the month only, this may be ambiguous. The dating "Nov" by itself may mean either "the whole month of Nov" or "sometime during the month." In some cases the context makes the case clear; if it does not, the case is probably that we simply don't know.

Dating Abbreviations and Short Forms. The reader is referred to the material facing the title page of this volume for a summary of the most important dating abbreviations: the months (Jan, June, Oct, etc.); the quartering of the month (Jan A, Jan AB, Jan CD, etc.); and the use of "c." as "circa" (about). This material also lists all symbols used. For other abbreviations and short forms, see the "List of Abbreviations" (which follows this Preface), including abbreviations for periodicals. Periodical names are often given without a definite article (e.g., *Volksstaat* instead of *Der Volksstaat*); the complete name is available in the *Glossary* (Volume III).

Arrow Symbol. The arrow symbol (→) is always a reference to the *Chronicle*, to a particular year and paragraph. Thus [→ 62:4] refers to the year 1862, paragraph 4. Inside the *Chronicle* the arrow points right or left, ahead or behind, depending on whether it is pointing to the future or to the past: thus under the year 1880 the same symbol would point left: [← 62:4]. (But outside the *Chronicle*, that is, in Volumes II and III, only the right-pointing arrow is used.) *Inside* a year, an arrow reference will omit the year's number; for example, in the course of 1862, the mentioned reference would look like this: [→ :4]. The colon always introduces the paragraph number and the year is printed in italics.

H.D.

Abbreviations

This list covers all volumes of the *Marx–Engels Cyclopedia*. Alphabetization is letter-by-letter. Some standard abbreviations in general use may not be included.

Many of these abbreviations are used only in certain limited contexts, where their meanings are probably clear anyway. There is one extreme case, the letter E, which is used in three ways: for "Engels," throughout the *Cyclopedia;* for "English" *only* after the entry titles in the *Register;* and for "East" in common geographical names.

For symbols and the main date abbreviations, see the material facing the title page of this volume.

A	*In dates:* early part (first quarter) of month
AB	*In dates:* first half of month
Addr	*Esp in titles:* Address
AFL	American Federation of Labor
Angl.	Anglicized (form)
App.	Appendix
Apr	April
assoc(s)	association(s)
Aug	August
AZ	*Allgemeine Zeitung* (of Augsburg)
b.	born
Bd.	Band (Ger. = volume); or Board
betw	between
bk	book
BM	British Museum (Library)
BM Cat.	British Museum Library catalog
BN	Bibliothèque Nationale (Paris)
BN Cat.	Bibliothèque Nationale catalog
Brit.	British
c.	*With dates:* circa, about
ca.	*In text:* circa, about
CC	Central Committee
CC/CL	Central Committee of the Communist League
CCC	Communist Correspondence Committee (Brussels)
CC/NG	Central Committee of the National Guard (in Paris Commune)
CD	*In dates:* second half of month
cf	compare
Ch.	Chapter
Chron.	*Marx–Engels Chronicle* (Vol. I of this *Cyclopedia*)
CL	Communist League
CL/CC	Same as CC/CL, q.v.
com	communist
comm	committee
commsn	commission
cont'd	continued

contribd	contributed
corr secy	corresponding secretary
CP	Communist party
CPC	Communist publishing complex. (See Preface to Vol. II.)
CPSFW	Cooperative Publishing Society of Foreign Workers in the USSR. (See Preface to Vol. II.)
(D)	*In Register:* date; dateline
d.	dated
DB	See *DBMOF*
DBMOF	Jean Maitron, ed., *Dictionnaire biographique du mouvement ouvrier français*
DBZ	*Deutsche-Brüsseler-Zeitung* (Brussels)
Dec	December
Demo	Democratic
Demo Wochenblatt	*Demokratisches Wochenblatt.* (See *Glossary.*)
DFJ	*Deutsch-Französische Jahrbücher* (Paris)
do.	*In Register:* ditto (i.e., same translation title as the preceding)
D&A	Dubiosa and Apocrypha. (See Preface to Vol. II.)
E	Engels
E.	*In geog. names:* East
[E]	*In Register, after entry title:* English
ed	editor
ed bd	editorial board
ed by	edited by
ed note	editorial note
edit	editorial
edn	edition
Eng.	England
erron.	erroneous(ly)
esp	especially
et al	and others
Exec	Executive (Committee, Board)
Feb	February
FLPH	Foreign Languages Publishing House (Moscow)
FP	*Free Press* (London)
Fr.	French; France
GC	General Council (of the IWMA)
GC/IWMA	General Council of the IWMA
GCFI	The set titled *General Council of the First International.* (See ST/21.)
Gen.	General
gen secy	general secretary
Ger.	German; Germany
GGWA	General German Workers Association (Lassalleans). (See *Glossary.*)
Gr Brit	Great Britain
GWEA	German Workers Educational Association. (See *Glossary.*)
i.a.	inter alia, inter alii; among others, among other things
IISH	International Institute for Social History (Amsterdam)
ILP	Independent Labour party (Brit.)

IML	Institute of Marxism-Leninism (Moscow or E. Berlin). (See *Glossary* for name variation.)
incl	including
ind	independent (translation)
info	information
installs	installments
int'l	international
Int'l Pub	International Publishers (New York)
intro	introduction
intro note	introductory note
irreg.	irregular
It.	Italy; Italian
Ital.	Italian
IWMA	International Working Men's Association (the First International)
IWMA/GC	General Council of the IWMA
J.	*In titles:* Journal
Jan	January
Kerr	Charles H. Kerr, publishers (Chicago)
KMC	The book *Karl Marx, Chronik seines Lebens* (Moscow, 1934). (See Preface to Vol. I.)
KZ	*Kölnische Zeitung* (Cologne)
Labour Mo.	*Labour Monthly* (London)
L., Laura	Laura (Marx) Lafargue. (See "*Marx, Laura," in *Glossary*.)
Lib	Library
Lon	*In imprints:* London
ltr	letter
L&W	Lawrence & Wishart, publishers (London)
M	Marx
M	*In dates:* middle of month
M&E	Marx and Engels
Mar	March
ME	Marx and Engels (as joint authors, etc.)
M–E	Marx–Engels
M/E	Marx or Engels
MEC	*Marx–Engels Cyclopedia*
MECW	Marx–Engels, *Collected Works.* (See the General Introduction.)
MEGA	*Marx–Engels Gesamtausgabe* (1927–35), the old *MEGA*. (For the new edition, see *New Mega*, below. See also the General Introduction.)
ME:SW	Marx–Engels, *Selected works in three volumes* (Moscow, 1969–70). (See ST/ME64.)
MEW	*Marx–Engels Werke* (Berlin, 1956–68). (See the General Introduction.)
MEW Daten	The Chronology section in *MEW*. (See the Preface to Vol. I.)
Min	*In cabinet titles:* Minister
Mos	*In imprints:* Moscow
ms	manuscript
mss	manuscripts
NAC	*New American Cyclopaedia* (New York)

NB	Nota bene
n.d.	no date
NDZ	*Neue Deutsche Zeitung* (Darmstadt, Frankfurt)
Neth.	Netherlands
New Mega	New edition, *Marx–Engels Gesamtausgabe* (Berlin, 1975+), in progress. (See the General Introduction.)
NG	National Guard (Paris)
NMW	*New Moral World* (London), Owenite organ
N.	north
no.	number
Nov	November
NOZ	*Neue Oder-Zeitung* (Breslau)
NRZ	*Neue Rheinische Zeitung* (Cologne, 1848–49), ed by Marx
NRZ-Revue	*Neue Rheinische Zeitung, politisch-ökonomische Revue* (London, 1850), magazine, ed by Marx
NS	*Northern Star* (Leeds, London)
n.s.	*In periodical dating:* new series
N/s	Not signed; no signature
N/t	No title
NUC	National Union Catalog
NY	New York
NYC	New York City
NYDT	*New York Daily Tribune*
NYLNCo	New York Labor News Company (SLP publishers)
NYSWT	*New York Semi-Weekly Tribune* (edition of *NYDT*)
NYWT	*New York Weekly Tribune* (edition of *NYDT*)
NZ	*Neue Zeit* (Stuttgart)
N-Ztg	*National-Zeitung* (Berlin)
Oct	October
organizn	organization
orig	original; originally
(P)	*In Register:* published; publishing data
para	paragraph
PMG	*Pall Mall Gazette* (London)
polit	political
polit eco	political economy
PP	*People's Paper* (London)
(P/P)	*In Register:* posthumously published
Pr	*In imprints:* Press
pres	president
prob	probably
Prof	Professor
Prog Pub	Progress Publishers (Moscow)
Prov Government	Provisional Government
pubd	published
publ	publication
pub'r	publisher
pubs	publishes
q.v.	which see
re; in re	regarding; in regard to

(Re)	*In Register:* reprint, republication
rec'd	received
reorganizn	reorganization
repr	representative
repr'd	reprinted
repubd	republished
republ	republication
repubs	republishes
resp	respectively
retrans	retranslation
retransd	retranslated
retrotrans	retrotranslation
rev	revised (edition)
Rev	*In titles: Review*
Revol. Zent.	Revolutionäre Zentralisation (group)
RZ	*Rheinische Zeitung* (Cologne), ed by Marx
S.	South
(S)	*In Register:* Source. (See Vol. II, "Guide to Register Entry.")
S-D	Social-Democratic
SDF	Social Democratic Federation (Brit.)
SDWP	Social-Democratic Workers party. (See *Glossary*.)
secy	secretary
Sep	September
SL	Socialist League (Brit.)
SLP	Socialist Labor party (U.S.)
SP	Socialist party
Sp.	Spain
[Sp.]	*In Register:* Spanish
specif	specifically
SPGB	Socialist Party of Great Britain
ST	Sources & Translations: see the "ST" List in Vol. II.
Sub-Comm	Sub-Committee (of the IWMA/GC); see → 64:30, note, in the Chronicle.
subseq(ly)	subsequent(ly)
SUCR	Société Universelle des Communistes Révolutionnaires. (See #ME80 or *Glossary*.)
SWT	See *NYSWT.*
t.	tome (Fr. = volume)
TfD	*Telegraph für Deutschland* (Frankfurt, Hamburg)
t.p.	title page
(Tr)	*In Register:* translation(s) into English
trans	translation
transd	translated
TU	trade union
U.	University
UGWA	Union of German Workers Associations. (See *Glossary*.)
unanim	unanimously
Univ.	University
unpubd	unpublished
US	United States

v.	volume
vice-pres	vice-president
VJ	*Volunteer Journal*
vol.	volume(s)
vs	versus
W.	West
(W)	*In Register:* written; data on composition
WA	Workers Association
WEA	Workers Educational Association
WP	Workers party. (See "French Workers party" in *Glossary*.)
WT	See NYWT
W&P	*In Chronicle rubrics:* Writings and Publications
Ztg	*Zeitung* (in German newspaper titles)

THE
MARX–ENGELS
CHRONICLE

1818–1834

1818

BIRTH (M). **May 5:** Marx is born at 2 A.M. in Trier, at Brückergasse 664 (now Brückenstrasse 10), into which the family had moved only days before, on May 1.

1819

RESIDENCE. **Oct 1:** Heinrich Marx (father) buys the house at Simeonsgasse 1070 (now Simeonstrasse 8). The family moves in later in the year or perhaps early next year.

1820

BIRTH (E). **Nov 28:** Engels is born at 9 P.M. in Barmen.

1821

BAPTISM. **Jan 18:** E is baptized in the Reformed Evangelical Parish in neighboring Elberfeld. Godparents: grandfather Caspar E and grandmother Franciska Christina van Haar.

1823

GRANDMOTHER. **May 13:** M's paternal grandmother, Eva Moses Lvov Marx, dies in Trier.

1824

MARX FAMILY BAPTISM. **Aug 26:** The children of the M family—Sophie, Hermann, Henriette, Louise, Emilie, Caroline, as well as Karl—are baptized in the Evangelical church. (For the father's baptism, see *Marx, Heinrich.)

1825

MOTHER'S BAPTISM. **Nov 20:** M's mother Henriette is baptized in the Evangelical church.

1826

BROTHER. **Apr 17:** M's brother Eduard is born.

1827

UNCLE. **Date uncertain:** M's paternal uncle, Rabbi Samuel M—the city's rabbi—dies in Trier.

1829

SCHOOL (E). E enters the Barmen municipal school (*Stadtschule*) which he will attend until 1834.

1830

SCHOOL (M). **Oct:** M enters Trier's Friedrich-Wilhelm-Gymnasium (high school) [→ 35:3].

1832

SCHOOL CLUB. **1832–34:** M may well have become a member of a "Young German Literary Circle" which exists at the high school.

1833

POETRY. M's sister Sophie starts a poetry notebook, which she will work on until 1837; it contains some poems by young M, incl his earliest known (see #M661). **Dec 20:** Young E writes a poem "To my grandfather" (#E811).

1834

1. FATHER AS LIBERAL. **Jan 18:** M's father Heinrich participates in, and gives a political toast at, a liberal banquet in favor of representative government, held by the Casino Society; as a result he comes under surveillance by the Prussian government. **Jan 25:** A similar banquet leads to government harassment of many participants.

2. CONFIRMATION. **Mar 23:** M is confirmed in the Evangelical church, by Pastor J. A. Küpper, religious instructor at M's high school. The godfathers include three of Heinrich M's fellow lawyers and a government official.

3. SCHOOLDAYS (E). **Sep 25:** E graduates from the Barmen municipal school [← 1829]. **Oct 20:** He enters the Elberfeld Gymnasium (high school) [→ 37:12]. For some indications about E's work there, see #E472.5.

1835

CONSPECTUS

1. M graduates from high school [← 30:1] in autumn, and goes on to Bonn U. His address there is Stockenstrasse 1, later Josephstrasse 764. —Poems written by M during 1835–36 will later be compiled by his sister Sophie in a notebook (#M664).

AUGUST

2. FINAL EXAMS. Aug 10–17: M takes final examinations at the Trier Gymnasium and writes examination exercises (*Abiturientenarbeiten*). **Aug 10** (prob): Religious essay (#M956); also Greek trans (of Sophocles' *Trachiniae*, verses 140–76, passage headed "Deianira"). **Aug 12:** German essay (#M729). **Aug 13:** French trans (of passage headed "Exemples, qui servent à prouver, que l'homme peut motiver les influences du climat, qu'il habite"). **Aug 14:** Mathematics exercise (one each in geometry, trigonometry, and algebra). **Aug 15:** Latin essay (#M251). **Aug 17:** Extempore Latin trans (of passage headed "De Hemsterhusii moribus"). (For the text of all exercises, incl those not in the *Register*, see MEGA I, 1.2:164 or *New Mega* I, 1:449.)

SEPTEMBER

3. GRADUATION. Sep 24: M graduates from the Trier Gymnasium [← 30:1]; receives his graduation certificate, with a summary of his schoolwork.

OCTOBER

4. UNIVERSITY. Oct c.13: M leaves Trier for Bonn, to begin studies at the university there. **Oct 15:** M matriculates at the university, beginning studies in the Law Department (jurisprudence).

5. WINTER SEMESTER. Oct to Mar: M attends the following lectures: jurisprudence, with Puggé; institutions, with Böcking; history of Roman law, with Walter; mythology of Greece and Rome, with Welcker; Homer, with Schlegel; modern art history, with D'Alton.

6. HIGH SCHOOL (E). Oct 19: E enters the second form (*Sekunda*) at the Elberfeld Gymnasium. (For some extant schoolwork, notebooks, and exercises, etc., see #E351.5, 528.5.)

NOVEMBER

7. POLONIUS TIME. Nov 18–29: His father writes M his first long letter, full of advice and encouragement.

8. UNIVERSITY LIFE. Nov-Dec: M is a member of the Assoc of Trier Students. He participates, together with E. Geibel, Karl Grün, et al, in a poetry circle, which enters into competition with a Göttingen circle (whose members include Bernays, H. B. Oppenheim, Creizenach, etc.).

DECEMBER

9. DUTCH TRIP. Dec D: During the Christmas holidays, M journeys to Nijmegen (Neth.) to visit his mother's Dutch relatives, till Jan A.

1836

CONSPECTUS

1. M stays at Bonn through the summer semester, then transfers in autumn to the U. of Berlin. For his Bonn lectures, see ← 35:5.

2. *Indefinite Dates.* At Bonn, M becomes one of the five chairmen of the Assoc of Trier Students. —M's poems of 1835–36 will later be compiled in sister Sophie's notebooks (#M664). —E also has a poem dated this year (#E588).

3. *Engels in High School.* For some indications about E's schoolwork, see #E351.5, 528.5, 728.5.

MARCH

4. AT BONN. Mar M: M gets involved in debts; his father sends extra money to cover them. **Mar D to Apr A:** M spends the Easter holiday at his parents in Trier.

MAY

5. BONN: SUMMER SEMESTER. May to Aug: M attends lectures on history of German law, with Walter; Propertius, with Schlegel; European international law and natural law, with Puggé.

JUNE

6. SHENANIGANS. June 13: M is charged with "making a row at night, and drunkenness"; sentenced by the university proctor to one day's detention (June 16–17).

JULY

7. TRANSFER. July 1: M's father signs the consent form for his transfer from Bonn to the U. of Berlin.

AUGUST

8. DUEL. c.Aug: Still at Bonn, M is involved in a duel and wounded above one eye.

9. WINDING UP BONN. Aug 22: The Bonn administration issues M's Certificate of Release, summarizing his record. It mentions that a charge of carrying prohibited weapons in Cologne is still under investigation; but M is not suspected of involvement in "any forbidden assoc" of students. **Aug D to Oct M:** M spends the summer holiday in Trier. He gets secretly engaged to Jenny von Westphalen.

SEPTEMBER

10. ENGELS IN HIGH SCHOOL. **Sep 13:** E finishes the second form (*Sekunda*) at the Elberfeld Gymnasium [← 35:6].

OCTOBER

11. TO BERLIN. **Oct M:** M moves to the capital; address, Mittelstrasse 61. **Oct 22:** M matriculates in the Law Department of the university (Friedrich Wilhelm Univ.; today, Humboldt Univ.).
12. WINTER SEMESTER. **Oct to Mar:** M attends lectures in the Pandects, with Savigny; criminal law, with Gans; anthropology, with H. Steffens.

NOVEMBER-DECEMBER

13. POETRY. M puts together three notebooks of poems (*Book of Songs; Book of Love*, Parts I and II) (#M662), and sends them to Jenny (Trier).
14. JENNY. Concerned by Jenny's difficult position re the secret engagement, M's father and sister Sophie press M to plan how to resolve the situation. **Nov 9:** Father urges M to face up to the duty of straightening the situation out, presumably by getting a commercial job. **Dec 28:** Father writes M of his concern that the son should quickly fit himself to earn a living so that marriage can solve the sticky situation; he urges getting an academic post fast, even if a low one. He warns: "Your views on law are not without truth, but are very likely to arouse storms if made into a system. . . ."
15. THEORY. **Winter 1836/37:** M tries to work out a new theory of law and jurisprudence (cf #M61), which he will outline in a letter (#M455).

1837

CONSPECTUS

1. For M this is a year of study and intellectual crises at the U. of Berlin, accompanied by tension with his family, esp his father, over the secret engagement to Jenny—a problem whose solution requires preparations for earning a living. Re intellectual crises, see ← 36:15, and cf M's letter to his father (#M455).
2. E is taken out of school by his father, to learn the family business. *Indefinite Dates:* E tries his hand at a narrative tale (#E585), and early in the year, another poem (#E589). For some indications about E's schoolwork, see #E528.5, 728.5.

JANUARY-FEBRUARY

3. UNIVERSITY OF BERLIN. **Winter 1836/37:** M continues working on his new philosophical presentation of law and jurisprudence (#M61) [← 36:15]; it remains unfinished. He carries on philosophical and historical studies, incl studies on Hegel. He establishes his lifelong habit of filling notebooks with excerpts and notes on books read.

FEBRUARY-MARCH

4. POETRY. **Feb-Mar:** M puts together a poetry album dedicated to his father on his birthday (#M663), incl a "comic novel" *Scorpion and Felix* (#M811) and a drama *Oula-*

nem (#M623) [→ :6]. —Around this time M writes the two poems which will later be pubd as "Wild Songs" (#M992) [→41:4].
5. PATERNAL LETTERS. **Feb 3:** Father writes M approvingly on his adjustment to the university, etc. **Mar 2:** Father's letter wonders whether M's "demon" is "heavenly or Faustian," and expresses forebodings about his course.
5.5 ENGELS: CONFIRMATION. **Mar 12:** E is confirmed at the United Evangelical church in Lower Barmen. The biblical motto selected by local pastors is Phil. 3:13–14: ". . . forgetting those things which are behind, and reaching forth unto those things which are before, I press toward the mark. . . ."

APRIL

6. UNIVERSITY. **Apr:** M makes an intensive study of Hegel's philosophy and the Hegelian school, and makes the acquaintance of the Young Hegelian circle. **c.Apr:** M moves to Stralau, near Berlin, on his doctor's advice, because of overwork. **Apr A:** M presents the poetry album (#M663) [← :4] to his father.

JUNE-AUGUST

7. WRITING. About this time (summer) M writes a philosophic dialogue "Cleanthes" (#M149) on "the starting point and necessary progress of philosophy." Also, around summer-autumn he writes a piece called "The visit" (#M967), which his father later calls an extract from Karl's diary.

8. STUDIES. In the summer semester M attends lectures on church law, common German lawsuits, and Prussian lawsuits, all with Heffter. He carries on studies in jurisprudence, reads i.a. Savigny's *Right of ownership*, Feuerbach's *Penal law*, Grolmann's *Principles of criminal science*; he translates Aristotle's *Rhetoric*, reads Bacon's *Advancement of learning*, and Reimarus's *Von den Kunsttrieben der Tiere*.

9. DOCTORS CLUB. M enters the circle of the Doctors Club (Young Hegelians) and makes the acquaintance of Bruno and Edgar Bauer, Rutenberg, Köppen, et al.

10. FATHER'S LETTERS. Aug 12: M's father, who is quite ill and staying at Bad Ems for his bad health, writes chidingly, urging more consideration for the parents. **c.Aug 20:** Father sends more advice on studies and preparations to enter the legal profession.

SEPTEMBER

11. LOOKING TO THE FUTURE. Sep 16: Father's letter to M weighs alternatives on what field to prepare for—law, writing, academia, etc. **Sep to Nov:** M participates in plans to publish a magazine on theater criticism, with contributions from the Hegelian school.

12. ENGELS LEAVES SCHOOL. Sep: On his father's insistence, E leaves high school (Gymnasium) before completing it, to begin work as a commercial assistant in his father's firm in Barmen. **Sep 15:** At the school's public ceremony, E reads a Greek poem of his composition in epic verse (#E745). **Sep 25:** A school-leaving certificate is issued to E as of this date.

OCTOBER

13. REJECTIONS. c.Oct: M sends some poems for publ to Chamisso's *Deutsche Musen-Almanach*; they are rejected.

NOVEMBER

14. UNIVERSITY. Winter semester: M attends only the lectures on criminal trials, by Heffter.

15. LETTER TO FATHER. Nov 10: M writes a long letter (the only extant letter to his father) reviewing his university life, intellectual crises, and strivings during this first year in Berlin, esp his conversion to Hegelianism (#M455). **Nov 17:** His father, in reply, chides him for this letter "without form or content. . . ."

DECEMBER

16. FATHER'S LETTER. Dec 9: Father writes with irritation and apprehension about M's failure to ensure earning a living instead of "misty excursions" and "brooding."

17. BROTHER DIES. Dec 14: M's brother Eduard, 12, dies of tuberculosis, in Trier.

1838

CONSPECTUS

1. M continues at the Univ. of Berlin, still associated with the Doctors Club [← 37:9]. His father dies in May.

2. E takes a trip through the Netherlands to the family business in Manchester, then returns to Germany to become a commercial apprentice in Bremen, as arranged by his father—a life that will continue until Mar 1841, over two and a half years. During this Bremen period E concerns himself with reading literature, writing prose and verse, contributing to periodicals; he makes a beginning at breaking into the liberal-leftist politico-literary press. He also studies Hegel and the literature of current religious controversy, esp Strauss's *Life of Jesus*. His views are liberal-democratic, close to the Young Germany tendency.

FEBRUARY

3. FATHER'S LETTER. Feb 10: M's father, beset by sinking health, sends a somewhat milder version of previous criticisms [← 37:16], ending on a note of perplexity and resignation.

4. HEALTH. Feb 15–16: M's mother writes urging him to avoid the year of military service on medical grounds. Around this time M suffers from heart trouble (cardiac dilation), also eye trouble. **Feb c.18:** M receives a medical certificate, sent on to him by his mother, releasing him from military service for medical reasons ("chest weakness and periodic coughing-up of blood").

MARCH-APRIL

5. FATHER'S PAMPHLET. Mar to prob May A: M revises, with corrections and additions, a pamphlet written by his father on the Cologne church dispute (#M252).

MAY

6. DEATH OF FATHER. **May 10:** M's father dies in Trier, of tuberculosis and liver ailments.
7. UNIVERSITY: SUMMER SEMESTER. **May to Aug:** M attends lectures on logic, with Gabler; general geography, with Ritter; Prussian common law, with Gans. Gabler and Gans mark him "very diligent."

JULY

8. ENGELS' TRIP. **July 22:** E, prob with his father, goes on a trip to the Netherlands and England; first, down the Rhine to Rotterdam. **July 23–24:** E stops in Rotterdam. **July 24–26:** E goes by paddle steamer from Rotterdam to London, then by railway to Manchester.

AUGUST

9. ENGELS' TRIP (CONT'D). **Aug 1:** E is in Manchester, where the firm of Ermen & Engels is established by a merger with Peter Ermen. **Aug c.10–14:** E goes to Bremen, either direct from London or via Amsterdam.
10. ENGELS IN BREMEN. **Aug 15:** E takes up life [cf ← :2] as a clerk in training in the commercial house of Heinrich Leupold, boarding with the minister G. G. Treviranus (SOURCE: ST/56; but *MEW Daten* puts arrival for duties in Bremen at July M).

SEPTEMBER

11. ENGELS PUBLISHES. **Sep 16:** E's first pubd writing is a poem in a Bremen paper (#E73).

OCTOBER

12. UNIVERSITY. **Winter semester:** M attends lectures only on inheritance law, with Rudorff; he is marked "diligent."

1839

CONSPECTUS

1. M continues his studies at the U. of Berlin, still associated with the Young Hegelian circle; he often visits the Bauer brothers (Bruno, Edgar) in Charlottenburg. Early in the year he starts work on a doctoral dissertation on Greek philosophy, beginning with notebooks on Epicurean philosophy (#M576). KMC has him working further on this material in the period May-Aug and from Oct into 1840. Included in these notebooks of 1839 is also a set of notes on Hegel's philosophy of nature (#M658)—assigned by KMC to c.Nov. *Indefinite Date:* From various collections, M puts together a collection of folk songs, handwritten for Jenny (#M319).
2. E, still a commercial apprentice in Bremen, starts getting his politico-socio-literary journalistic work pubd in Bremen papers and also in the Young German organ *Telegraph für Deutschland* (TfD), where he signs himself "Oswald." This association will start petering out in 1841.

JANUARY

3. INDIANS (E). **Jan 20:** In a letter to a friend, E includes a poem "Florida" (#E281) on the American Indians as freedom fighters.

FEBRUARY

4. ENGELS: POETRY. **Feb 19:** E sends a friend an unpubd poem, "The Pietist declares

his love" (#E211). **Feb 24:** He gets a second poem (#E840) into a Bremen paper.

MARCH

5. ENGELS IN PRINT. **Mar 24:** E pubs a third poem in a Bremen paper (#E94), signed "Theodor Hildebrandt." **Mar-Apr:** E writes and pubs his first article, "Letters from the Wuppertal," in the Young Germany organ *TfD*, in six installs (#E452).

APRIL

6. ENGELS: POEMS AND PROSE. **Apr 23–28/30:** In personal letters, E includes other poems of his (#E231, 357, 590A). **Apr 27:** He gets a fourth poem into a Bremen paper (#E816), also by "Hildebrandt." **Apr:** For his *TfD* article, see ← :5; this article scandalizes the Barmen-Elberfeld (Wuppertal) district.
7. MARX AT THE UNIVERSITY. **Apr to Aug:** During the summer semester M attends lectures in only one course, on Isaiah, with Bruno Bauer. He is prob also continuing his dissertation work on Greek philosophy.

MAY

8. ENGELS IN PRINT. **May 9:** In response to attacks on his Wuppertal article (#E452), E pubs a reply in an Elberfeld paper (#E572). **May:** He pubs another article in *TfD*, on F. W. Krummacher (#E263).

8.5 ENGELS: POETRY. **July D or Aug A:** E sends a friend a poem titled "German July days, 1839" (#E332); it looks to a revolution against the German kings and princes, like the French "July revolution" of 1830.

OCTOBER-NOVEMBER

9. UNIVERSITY. **Oct-Nov:** After B. Bauer departs from Berlin for a post in Bonn, M becomes close friends with Köppen. He now plans to cover all of Epicurean, Stoic, and Skeptical philosophy in his dissertation, and looks forward to qualifying for the Bonn faculty after graduation [→ 40:6]. **Nov to 1841, c.Apr:** M corresponds with B. Bauer in Bonn. He works on logic studies, reads and excerpts Aristotle's *De anima*, and plans a work polemizing against F. A. Trendelenburg. [→ 40:4].

10. ENGELS IN PRINT. **Nov:** E pubs two more articles in *TfD* (#E300, 330), the first signed "S. Oswald," the second "Friedrich Oswald" (which will be his pen name for the next period). **Nov to Dec A:** He writes another article, "Karl Beck" (#E404) [→ :11], and begins "Retrograde signs of the times" (#E683) [→ 40:5].

DECEMBER

11. W&P (E). **Dec:** E pubs "Karl Beck" in *TfD* (#E404) [← :10]. He writes "Platen" (#E586) [→ 40:5].

1840

CONSPECTUS

1. M works on his doctoral dissertation (#M235), which is not limited to Democritus and Epicurus [cf ← 39:9], from the second half of 1840 to Mar D 1841. For M's notes on Aristotle, prob in the first half of the year, see #M79. He is still associated with the Young Hegelian Doctors Club, esp friendly with Köppen.

2. E continues to write and publish verse; his first publ in his own name is a verse trans from the Spanish (#E559), written in the first half of this year (indefinite date). He continues writing for the Young Germany organ *Telegraph für Deutschland* (*TfD*), and begins publishing specifically literary articles in the politico-cultural periodicals *Morgenblatt für gebildete Leser* and *Mitternachtzeitung für g. Leser*.

3. *Reading and Study:* See → :19.

JANUARY

4. W&P. **Jan-Feb:** M works on a satire directed against K. P. Fischer's *Idee der Gottheit*, to be called "Fischer vapulans": not finished, not extant. He also continues, or perhaps begins, working on his anti-Trendelenburg polemic [← 39:9] **Jan to Mar:** E works on two articles for *TfD* (#E400, 677) [→ :8].

FEBRUARY

5. W&P. **Feb:** For M, see ← :4. E pubs more articles in *TfD*, "Retrograde signs . . . " (#E683) and "Platen" (#E586) [← 39:10, 11].

MARCH

6. W&P. **Mar:** M works with B. Bauer on the latter's edition of Hegel's *Philosophy of* religion, and intends to write a work on the subject itself. —E pubs his first article of literary criticism (#E491).

APRIL

7. KÖPPEN. **Apr M:** M's friend pubs *Friedrich der Grosse und seine Widersacher*, with a dedication to "my friend Karl Heinrich Marx of Trier."

8. ENGELS IN PRINT. **Apr:** E pubs more articles in *TfD* (#E400, 677, 536) [← :4 for the first two].

MAY

9. WESTPHALEN FAMILY. **May 29:** M's mother writes him that since her husband's death the Westphalen family has become less friendly.

10. ENGELS ON TOUR. **May to June AB:** E travels around Westphalia, visits Münster, and meets Levin Schücking.

JUNE

11. W&P (E). **June D to July:** E writes a travel piece (#E414) [→ :12].

JULY

12. W&P. **July AB:** E takes a trip (July 5) to Bremerhaven, and soon afterward writes it up as an article (#E575) for the *Morgenblatt*, which, however, will publish it only a year later [→ 41:15]. **c.July to Dec:** M plans a book criticizing Georg Hermes' ideas, and through Bauer tries to get a publisher in Bonn. **July 30–31:** E pubs the first two articles (#E804, 454) in a series (#E674) of socioliterary essays on Bremen life, in the *Morgenblatt*. **July-Aug:**

E's travel piece (#E414) [← :11] is pubd in *TfD*.

AUGUST

13. W&P (E). **Aug 20:** E breaks into the prestigious *Allgemeine Ztg* of Augsburg (*AZ*) with reportage (#E506). **Aug:** He pubs a poem "An evening" (#E256) in *TfD*, and offers satirical verse in a letter (#E590B).

SEPTEMBER

14. W&P (E). **Sep A:** E writes an article on Krummacher (#E881), pubd in *TfD* this month. He also writes four pieces pubd in Oct, q.v.

OCTOBER

15. W&P (E). **Oct 7–8:** *AZ* pubs another piece of reportage (#E729). **Oct 10, 17–19:** *Morgenblatt* pubs a literary essay (#E550), and two more in the series on Bremen life (#E651, 737). **Oct:** He offers an ode to mustaches (#E590C) in a letter, and begins writing a long essay on Arndt (#E248) [→ :18].

NOVEMBER

16. W&P (E). **Nov 7, 13:** *AZ* pubs two reportage pieces (#E184, 780). **Nov:** *TfD* pubs a poem on Napoleon (#E721); E writes a poem on Siegfried (#E743) [→ :18].

17. UNIVERSITY (M). **Nov:** M takes only one course, on Euripides with Geppert— "diligent attendance."

DECEMBER

18. W&P (E). **Dec:** Besides publishing the Siegfried poem (#E743) [← :16] in *TfD*, E works, around the turn of the year, on an opera libretto "Cola di Rienzi" with a political-historical theme; unfinished (#E149). Around the end of the year E writes the poems "Night journey" (#E524) [→ 41:5] and "Imperial cortege" (#E370) [→ 41:6]; also around the turn of the year, an article on Immermann (#E368) [→ 41:10]. He finishes the article on Arndt (#E248) [← :15; → 41:5].

YEAR APPENDIX

19. For 1840–41, see the list of works excerpted in M's "Berlin notebooks" given in #M79.

1841

CONSPECTUS

1. This is a turning-point year for both M&E. M finishes his doctoral dissertation (#M235), and by the end of the year orients away from academic life. E finishes his stint as commercial apprentice in Bremen, and in Berlin on military service, gets involved with the Young Hegelians.

2. In about the first quarter of the year M is associated with the radical literary circle around the magazine *Athenäum*, deriving from the Doctors Club personnel. Then he plans to participate in a radical philosophical periodical *Archiv des Atheismus*. *Indefinite Date:* In the first quarter M studies, or begins to study, Italian. *Reading and Study:* For 1840–41, see ← 40:19.

3. E continues his collaboration with the Young Germany movement and its organ *Telegraph für Deutschland* (*TfD*). *Indefinite Date:* E leaves his opera libretto "Cola de Rienzi" (#E149) unfinished [← 40:18]. For E's "Studies on the critique of New Testament writings" (betw Sep 1841 and Oct 1842), see #E787.5.

JANUARY

4. MARX. **Jan c.A:** M gets acquainted with Eduard Meyen. **Jan 23:** *Athenäum* pubs two of his poems, "Wild songs" (#M992)—his first pubd work. **Jan to Mar:** For M's notes on Leibnitz and Hume, see #M79.

5. W&P (E). **Jan:** E pubs the long Arndt article (#E248) in *TfD* [← 40:15, 18], also the poem "Night journey" (#E524) [← 40:18] in *Deutscher Courier*. **Jan 15–19:** E pubs three articles (#E233, 663, 456) in the ongoing Bremen series (#E674).

FEBRUARY

6. W&P (E). **Feb 9:** The Augsburg *AZ* pubs its last E article (#E425). **Feb:** E pubs the poem "Imperial cortege" (#E370) [← 40:18] in *TfD*.

MARCH

7. UNIVERSITY. **Mar D:** M finishes his doctoral dissertation [← 40:1]. **Mar:** In preparation for publishing it, M writes a dedication, a foreword, and some notes (#M236–37, 240). **Mar 30:** This is the date on M's leaving certificate from the U. of Berlin. **Mar-Apr:** For M's notes on Spinoza and on Rosenkranz's book on Kant, see #M79.

8. ENGELS GOES HOME. **Mar D:** E leaves Bremen and returns to Barmen.

APRIL

9. PH.D. Apr 6: M sends his dissertation to Prof. Bachmann, philosophy dean at the U. of Jena (application form, #M475; curriculum vitae, #M210). **Apr 13:** Prof. Bachmann praises the dissertation and recommends granting the degree. **Apr 15:** M receives the Ph.D. degree from Jena (the document is so dated). **Apr M:** M travels from Berlin, via Frankfurt, to Trier, where he will stay till July A.

10. W&P (E). Apr: Since E attacked Paniel in the *Morgenblatt* (#E233), when the paper praises Paniel, E sends a polemical "Statement" (#E774) which is rejected; E ceases contributions to the paper. —E pubs an article on Immermann in *TfD* (#E368) [← 40:18].

MAY

11. ENGELS ON TOUR. May 6: With his father, E leaves on a trip to Switzerland and northern Italy. **May 8–10:** They stay at the Three Kings Hotel in Basel. **May 10–13:** At the Hotel Baur in downtown Zurich. **May c.14–15:** At the Red Lion Inn in Chur. **May c.16:** They travel through the Splügen Pass and Chiavenna to Milan.

JUNE

12. ENGELS ON TOUR. June: Details on E's tour through northern Italy in June-July are not available. Perhaps E now drafted his "Wanderings in Lombardy" (#E897), which he began publishing in Dec [→ :23]; see *Register*.

JULY

13. ENGELS ON TOUR. July c.28: E and his father return from Italy to Barmen.

14. MARX IN BONN. July A: M moves from Trier to Bonn to seek a post at the university. Here M remains close to Bauer until the latter leaves for Berlin (May A, 1842). **c.July:** M studies Feuerbach's *Essence of Christianity*.

AUGUST

15. W&P. Aug 17–21: E's article on his trip to Bremerhaven (#E575)—which he wrote over a year ago [← 40:12]—is at last pubd in the *Morgenblatt*, as the last-pubd part of E's series on Bremen life (#E674). **c.Aug to Sep:** M helps Bauer as the latter writes the polemical pamphlet *The trumpet of the last judgment on Hegel* . . . (pubd Nov A).

SEPTEMBER

16. COLLABORATION. Sep 2: Hess writes a friend that young M is the greatest living philosopher. **Sep:** M is drawn into the work of founding the *Rheinische Ztg*, through G. Jung and Hess in Cologne. **c.Sep to Feb:** M and Bauer plan a joint Part 2 of *The trumpet of the last judgment. . . .* In this connection M studies the history of art and religion, and starts a critical examination of Hegel's political theory (*Rechtsphilosophie*); cf #M204.

17. ENGELS TO BERLIN. Sep c.19: E leaves Barmen for Berlin as a one-year volunteer in the artillery to do his required military service. For his sojourn in Berlin, see → 42:1. **Sep c.21–22:** En route, E stops over in Brunswick, possibly looking up the pub'r G. C. E. Meyer. **Sep c.24:** E arrives in Berlin.

OCTOBER

18. ENGELS IN BERLIN. Oct 1: E begins military service. **Oct-Nov** (autumn): E begins to attend lectures at the U. of Berlin and frequents the Berlin circle of Young Hegelians; begins studying Feuerbach's *Essence of Christianity* (sometime in the second half of 1841).

19. MARX AND ACADEMIA. Oct-Nov (autumn): After Bauer is suspended from the Bonn faculty, M abandons hope of getting a university post.

NOVEMBER

20. PLANS. Nov: M begins working on a critique of Hegel's philosophy of right (*Rechtsphilosophie*, legal and political theory), esp his theory of constitutional monarchy (cf #M204) [→ 42:8]; also on an essay on religion and art (cf #M595).

21. ENGELS AND SCHELLING. Nov 15: E attends an important lecture by Schelling at the university, and writes a polemic, "Schelling on Hegel" (#E727) [→ :23].

DECEMBER

22. DISSERTATION. c.Dec and turn of the year: M once again plans to publish his dissertation (#M235) [← :7] and to this end drafts a new foreword (#M238).

23. W&P (E). Dec 4, 11: E pubs travel sketches of his trip [← :11–13] in a Young Hegelian magazine (#E897). **Dec:** E's first polemic against Schelling is pubd in *TfD* (#E727) [← :21]. He also begins working on an anti-Schelling pamphlet (#E726), continued after the turn of the year [→ 42:9].

1842

CONSPECTUS

1. In the first part of 1842 M gets more and more involved with the newly founded *Rheinische Ztg*, both in writing for it and in influencing its editorial administration. Finally, in Oct he becomes editor-in-chief. He is soon in the midst of conflict with the government censorship, with the RZ shareholders who want a moderate (and profitable) policy, and with leftist groups whom he considers mere phrasemongers but who want to use RZ as their outlet. M is thrown more than ever into socioeconomic questions, and begins to study the new ideas of socialism. He has to put aside the writing projects previously contemplated [← 41:20; → :8].

2. E continues his politico-literary writings for the periodical press, as well as occasional unsigned pamphlets: for example (*indefinite dates*) two on Schelling, one written around the turn of the year, a second written subseqly, resp pubd Mar and May (#E726, 728). For E's studies on New Testament critiques, see #E787.5. With the end of his military service, he returns to Barmen in Oct. By Nov M, he is on his way to England to learn the family business in its Manchester branch; he will stay there until Aug 1844. On arrival he immediately starts writing on English affairs for RZ.

3. *Reading and Study:* See → :37.

JANUARY

4. IN TRIER. **Jan to Mar:** M stays in town with Ludwig von Westphalen, who is very ill [→ :7]. **Jan A:** Re M's plans for his dissertation at the turn-of-the-year period, see ← 41:22. **Jan M:** Rutenberg, whom M has recommended for the post of RZ editor, gets the job.

5. W&P. **Jan 15 to Feb 10:** M writes his first political article, on censorship and freedom of the press (#M156); but it will not be pubd for over a year [→ 43:6].

FEBRUARY

6. W&P: PLANS. **Feb A:** M contemplates writing two critical articles for the *Deutsche Jahrbücher*, on W. Vatke and K. Bayer. **Feb 10:** M informs Ruge of this intention, and also sends the now-finished article on freedom of the press (#M156), for the *Deutsche Jahrbücher* [← :5].

MARCH

7. WESTPHALEN FAMILY. **Mar 3:** Ludwig von Westphalen dies in Trier.

8. STUDIES; W&P. **Mar:** M resumes his study of the history of religion and art, begun last Sep [← 41:16]. He has apparently drafted, or outlined, an essay on "Christian art." **Mar 5:** M writes Ruge that this essay should be pubd in the *Anekdota*. He also begins to rewrite his critique of Hegel's political theory (#M204) [← 41:20] as a contribution to the *Anekdota*. **Mar 20:** M writes Ruge that the essay on Christian art is to be rewritten as one "On religion and art, with special reference to Christian art." He promises it for Apr M; but he cancels his plan for an article on Hegel's philosophy of right. **Mar to May:** For M's "Bonn notebooks" on the history of art and religion, see #M93.

9. W&P (E). **Mar:** E's first pamphlet against Schelling (#E726) [← 41:23] is pubd. E writes his first article for RZ, on liberalism (#E526) [→ :12].

APRIL

10. TO BONN. **Apr A:** M first moves to Cologne, but finds the atmosphere unconducive to work. **Apr c.10:** He moves to Bonn, where he resumes close assoc with Bauer. **Apr 26:** M receives a visit from the theologian F. R. Hasse of Greifswald, who is prob at the U. of Bonn. **Apr-May:** For M's "Bonn notebooks" on art and religion, see #M93 and ← :8.

11. W&P. **Apr 27:** Writing to Ruge, M now promises four essays: on religion and art [← :8], "On the romanticists" (cf #M613), "The positive philosophers" (#M680), and (the only one actually written and pubd) on the historical school of law. **Apr to Aug A:** M writes the last-listed article as "The philosophic manifesto of the historical school of law" (#M655) [→ :22]. **Apr:** M writes his first article for RZ, a second article on freedom of the press (#M216) [→ :14]; it deals with the proceedings of the Rhineland Diet of May-July 1841.

12. W&P (E). **Apr 12:** E pubs his first RZ article (#E526) [← :9].

MAY

13. TO TRIER. **May D:** M comes home because of the death of a younger brother, Hermann; he will stay until July M.

14. RZ ARTICLES. **May 5–19:** M pubs his first article in RZ, dealing with the Diet debates on freedom of the press (#M216) [← :11], first of a series on Diet proceedings. **May (or June):** M writes the second article in this series (#M217), which never appears because of the censorship. **May CD:** M begins a reply to a Hess article on centralization; it remains an unfinished fragment (#M722).

15. W&P (E). **May A:** E pubs a second pamphlet against Schelling (#E728). **May 10–25:** He pubs three more articles in RZ (#E224, 703, 467), and writes another (#E591) [→ :18].

JUNE

16. FAMILY AFFAIRS. **June to July M:** M's mother blocks his getting any money from his father's estate; she deplores his refusal to embrace an academic or governmental career; M has to postpone his marriage plans.

17. W&P. **June:** Re the censored second article in the Rhineland Diet series (#M217), see ← :14 [→ :20]. **June 29 to July 4:** M writes a polemical article against K. H. Hermes in defense of the Young Hegelians (#M448) [→ :20].

18. W&P (E). **June 10–30:** E pubs four articles in RZ (#E591, 577.5, 453, 240), and writes another (#E549) [→ :21]. **June c.15:** E writes a long article on Alexander Jung (#E684) [→ :21]. **June-July:** E works with Edgar Bauer on the satiric "epic" *The triumph of faith* (#E872) [→ :36].

JULY

19. TRIER TO BONN. **July 12:** M's sister Sophie is married to a Maastricht lawyer, W. K. Schmalhausen. **July M:** M moves from Trier back to Bonn.

20. W&P. **July 9:** M writes Ruge that he plans to publish the censored article (#M217) [← :14] on the Cologne church dispute as a brochure if necessary. He also criticizes the Berlin group "Die Freie" (The Free) as empty phrasemongers. **July 10–14:** M's polemic against Hermes (#M448) [← :17] is pubd in RZ.

21. W&P (E). **July 14:** E pubs another article (#E549) [← :18] in RZ. **July:** E pubs the long article on A. Jung (#E684) [← :18] in *Deutsche Jahrbücher*.

AUGUST

22. W&P: RZ. **Aug 9:** M's article on the historical school of law, written for the *Anekdota* (#M655) [← :11], is pubd in RZ. **Aug c.25:** Writing to D. Oppenheim, M says he plans to write a number of articles for RZ, including one on civil rights for Jews (attacking K. H. Hermes), a critique of Edgar Bauer's antiliberal articles in RZ, and one on the system of Rhenish municipal government. **Aug-Sep:** M influences the editing of RZ through his letters to Oppenheim and G. Jung.

23. ENGELS IN BERLIN; W&P. **Aug 2–8:** E includes light verse in a letter to his sister

(#E590D). **Aug 15:** E ends his (unofficial) attendance at the university, in anticipation of the end of his military service. **Aug 29:** E has two articles pubd in RZ (#E262, 77).

SEPTEMBER

24. W&P. **Sep A:** M writes an article on Bauer and academic freedom (#M995) [→ :31].

25. ENGELS IN BERLIN; W&P. **Sep 18:** E pubs an article on "Centralization and freedom" (#E132) in RZ. **Sep 30:** E's period of military service ends.

OCTOBER

26. MARX BECOMES RZ EDITOR. **Oct AB:** M accepts the editorship and moves to Cologne. **Oct 15:** M is installed as editor-in-chief. The same day, he writes a rejoinder to the Augsburg AZ on communism and the RZ position (#M165), pubd Oct 16; a follow-up comment is pubd Oct 23 (#M166). **Oct CD** (prob): M writes the third article in the Rhineland Diet series, on the debates over the wood-theft law (#M218); pubd in RZ, Oct 25 to Nov 3. Around this time M participates in a weekly gathering of the RZ circle discussing the "Social Question" and tariff policy, which will continue meeting into 1843. M studies French socialism: Fourier, Cabet, Dézamy (*Calomnies et politique de M. Cabet*), Leroux, Considérant, Proudhon (*What is property?*). **Oct CD:** M gets acquainted with Karl Heinzen.

27. ENGELS GOES HOME. **Oct A:** With the end of his military service [← :25] E leaves Berlin. **Oct c.3:** E arrives in Frankfurt; perhaps visits his brother Hermann, who is in training in a bank. **Oct 7:** E stays in Cologne at the Bonn Inn; meets Hess, prob also Peter Ermen (of the Manchester firm), but he is unable to meet with RZ editor Marx. **Oct 9/10:** E arrives home in Barmen.

28. W&P (E). **c.Oct:** E writes a programmatic article on Prussian politics (#E299) which will be pubd some months later [→ 43:19].

NOVEMBER

29. WITH THE RZ. **Nov 8–30:** M pubs a number of articles in RZ (#M164, 188, 123, 669), also ed notes (#M473, 601, 64); for Dubiosa, see #M265. A sharp conflict starts developing with the government censorship. **Nov 17:** In reply to a Nov 12 threat from the government, M sends a letter to the governor on behalf of the RZ pub'r (#M456), defending the right to independent expression. The RZ shareholders are also pressing for "moderation."

30. MARX AND *DIE FREIE*. **Nov:** This Berlin Young Hegelian circle ("The Free") is dissatisfied with M's treatment of their contributions. **Nov c.24:** M receives a letter from Herwegh on his and Ruge's conflict with the Berliners, also a letter from E. Meyen on behalf of the group. **Nov c.25:** M writes the Berlin group his own criticism of their radical phrasemongering. **Nov 29:** M pubs a piece in *RZ* (#M64) reporting Herwegh's and Ruge's attitude, ed by M. This public rebuff, plus others, produces a definitive break. **Nov 30:** M writes Ruge that he has replied sharply to Meyen and expects a break.

31. W&P. **Nov 16:** M's article on Bauer and academic freedom (#M995) is pubd in *Deutsche Jahrbücher* [← :24].

32. ENGELS TO ENGLAND. **Nov M:** E sets out to take up a post in the family firm in Manchester. **Nov 16:** En route, with a friend K. A. Erbslöh, E stops in Cologne, staying at the Wiener Hof Hotel. Here he visits the *RZ* office and meets M for the first time, a cool meeting since M thinks E is associated with the "Free" group (SOURCE: ST/56; KMC says Nov c.24; *MEW Daten*, Nov CD). **Nov 17–19:** E takes the ship *Sir Edward Banks* from Ostend to England. **Nov 19–c.30:** E spends some days in London before going on to Manchester. **Nov 29–30:** E writes two articles on the "internal crises" in England for *RZ*, without even unpacking all his bags (#E247, 379) [→ :36]. (Note: E will later write in a letter that he arrived in Manchester "at the end of Nov"; perhaps.)

DECEMBER

33. WITH THE *RZ*. **Dec 11–31:** M pubs a long three-part article on the estates-commit-

tees (#M869). **Dec 18–19:** M writes and pubs an article exposing the government's divorce bill (#M249). **Dec c.23:** M is informed that the Moselle correspondent Peter Coblenz, who had pubd three articles on the plight of the wine-growing peasants (Nov 15 to Dec 18) which had displeased the governor, is the recipient of official charges, and Coblenz has declared himself unable to write an effective reply; therefore M himself must undertake it. He begins on it (#M965) Dec D or Jan 1 [→ 43:4]. **Dec 26:** M perhaps begins writing #M667; see → 43:5. **Dec 31:** M works on the first of a number of polemical articles against other papers on the issue of the government ban against the *Leipziger Allgemeine Ztg* (#M72) [→ 43:4].

34. PERSONAL. **Dec D:** M goes to Kreuznach to visit Jenny.

35. ENGELS IN MANCHESTER. **Dec 1:** E arrives to complete his commercial apprenticeship in the office of Ermen & Engels; for an overview, see → 43:2. **Dec:** In Manchester E becomes acquainted with Mary Burns; they become lovers (time uncertain).

36. W&P (E). **Dec 8–10:** E's first articles on England (#E247, 379) [← :32 (Nov 29–30)] are pubd in *RZ*, ed by M. **Dec CD:** E pubs three more articles in *RZ* (#E597, 170, 186) on English politics and economics, incl his first "condition of England" article (#E170). **Dec:** The anonymous pamphlet *The triumph of faith* (#E872) [← :18] is pubd in Germany.

YEAR APPENDIX

37. M's plans to write on religion and art [see ← :8, 10] are reflected in the so-called Bonn notebooks. See the list of works studied in #M93.

1843

CONSPECTUS

1. The conflict between the *RZ* under M's editorship and the Prussian government censorship comes to a head: the government bans the paper as of Apr 1, despite M's resignation. M looks to editing another periodical outside of Germany; after discussions with Ruge lasting from Mar to Sep, he accepts a partnership with Ruge to publish *DFJ*. He marries Jenny in June, and stays in Kreuznach until Oct, writing, reading, and studying. In Paris he gets acquainted with the leftist and workers' groups, and prepares to publish *DFJ*.

2. E establishes himself in Manchester, where he is finishing his commercial training in the office of Ermen & Engels (cotton

business). Until his return to Germany in Aug 1844, E studies polit eco and English conditions, esp the socialist (Owenite) and Chartist movements; he gets acquainted with their leaders and writes for their organs, mainly about the Continental movement. En revanche, he writes for the German press (later the French press too) as a reporter on English affairs. He studies the writings of the bourgeois economists, Adam Smith, Ricardo, J. B. Say, McCulloch, James Mill, et al, and reads the writings of Saint-Simon, Fourier, Owen, Babeuf, Cabet, Weitling, Proudhon, and other socialists, completing his transition to materialism in philosophy and communism in social ideology.

3. *Reading and Study:* During the Kreuznach (honeymoon) period of c.June-Oct, M reads esp intensively in the history of the French Revolution and related subjects (cf #M436). His notes include an extensive section on Levasseur's *Mémoires* (#M338), done at the end of 1843 and after. For the list, see → :32, 33.

JANUARY

4. AGAINST PRUSSIAN CENSORSHIP. **Jan 1–16:** M writes [← 42:33] and pubs a series of polemical articles on the government ban against the *Leipziger Allgemeine Ztg* (#M72, 431, 352, 741, 742, 233, 781). He researches the situation of the Moselle peasants in order to reply to the governor's charges against RZ [← 42:33]. **Jan 3–20:** M announces (#M41) and then pubs the first two parts of his "vindication" of the Moselle articles (#M965) [→ :6]. **Jan 19:** The Prussian government decides to ban RZ as of Apr 1 and to put it under stricter censorship till then. (This decision is dated Jan 21 in some places.) **Jan 24:** RZ is officially informed of the ban. **Jan 25:** Writing to Ruge, M says he is eager to leave RZ and quit the stifling atmosphere of Germany; he intends to get married and work with Herwegh in Zurich on editing a new periodical. **Jan 30:** A Cologne protest meeting of about 100 condemns the RZ suppression, with a petition to the king (text: *MECW* 1:710) [→ :6 (Feb 18)].

5. RZ ARTICLES. **Jan 3, 12:** M pubs ed notes polemizing against the Augsburg *Allgemeine Ztg* (#M667, 668). **Jan 7:** For an example of M's editing of a correspondent's article, see #M187.

FEBRUARY

6. AGAINST PRUSSIAN CENSORSHIP. **Feb 4–7:** M drafts notes for replying to the ban on RZ (#M585); perhaps also drafts a memorandum (#M507?). **Feb 10:** The censor bans M's Part 3 of the Moselle article (#M965; cf #M966) [← :4 (Jan 3–20)]; M abandons the project. **Feb 12:** A special meeting of RZ shareholders votes for moderating the paper's policy, M voting with the minority. The meeting adopts a petition (signed also by M) promising a more moderate tone but not repudiating past policy. (This petition will be pressed on the government by Oppenheim et al during Feb-Mar.) **Feb M:** M's article on freedom of the press (#M156) written in early 1842 [← 42:5] now appears in the *Anekdota*. **Feb 18:** The Jan 30 petition is sent to Berlin with 911 signatures. **Feb c.20:** M, who aims to persuade the government to lift the RZ ban if he ceases to be editor, works at getting an article pubd in the *Mannheimer Abendzeitung* which portrays him as the "evil spirit" of RZ; this article is pubd Feb 28. **Feb D to Mar A:** M persuades the censor Saint-Paul, in the course of discussions, to recommend to the government that the RZ ban be lifted after M resigns.

7. PLANS. **Feb 1:** Ruge proposes that M become coeditor of a new periodical replacing the suppressed *Deutsche Jahrbücher*, to be pubd in Switzerland [→ :11]. **Feb c.19:** M is pressed by Herwegh to collaborate on the planned *Deutsche Bote aus der Schweiz*.

MARCH

8. MARX AND RZ. **Mar 9–14:** M pubs his last three articles in the paper (#M477, 782, 866). **Mar 17–18:** M formally resigns as editor, and pubs a statement (#M38).

9. END OF RZ. **Mar 21:** The king decides to confirm the RZ suppression. **Mar 27:** The shareholders' petition of Feb 12 is officially denied. **Mar 31:** Ditto the citizens' petition of Jan 30.

10. PERSONAL. **Mar A:** M visits Jenny in Trier. **Mar D:** M goes on a trip to the Netherlands, presumably to discuss the matter of his inheritance with his mother's Dutch relatives.

11. PLANS. **Mar 3:** M writes Ruge proposing that the new magazine [← :7] be jointly ed by them and be pubd in Strasbourg (France) together with French leftist Democrats. **Mar 13:** Writing to Ruge, M is enthusiastic about their plans for the magazine, to be called the *Deutsch-Französische Jahrbücher* (*DFJ*), pubd outside of Germany (Strasbourg or Switzerland); he announces his coming marriage ("head over heels in love"). Shortly before Mar 13 he has received from Ruge the *Anekdota* issue containing his article (#M156) [← :6], in which he reads Feuerbach's latest essay "Preliminary theses toward the reformation of philosophy"—which, he comments to Ruge, is insufficiently concerned with politics. **Mar D:** While traveling in Holland (see ← :10) he writes Ruge on the necessity of revolution in Germany; this letter will later be pubd in *DFJ* (#M471); Ruge's pessimistic reply will be pubd in the same exchange of letters.

MAY

12. RUGE. **May:** M replies to Ruge's pessimistic letter [← :11] with the second of his programmatic *DFJ* letters (cf #M471). **May c.20–25:** M goes to Dresden for a few days to discuss the planned *DFJ* with Ruge.

13. PERSONAL. **May c.D:** M moves to Kreuznach where Jenny is living with her mother.

14. ENGELS IN ENGLAND. **May:** Continuing the reports on England he had done for the now banned *RZ*, E starts publishing a series of four articles on England in a Swiss paper (#E447); the first two are pubd May 16 and 23 [→ :17]. **c.May-June:** E enters into relations with the leaders of the League of the Just—Schapper, Moll, H. Bauer, et al.

JUNE

15. MARRIAGE. June 12: M and Jenny sign the marriage contract. **June 19:** M, 25, marries Jenny von Westphalen, 29, in Kreuznach at 10 A.M. (cf *MECW* 3:571); they stay in Kreuznach for their honeymoon.

16. TEMPTATIONS. c.June CD: M receives and rejects an offer, made via J. P. Esser (Prussian official, friend of M's father), to enter into the state's service as editor of a government publ.

17. W&P (E). June 9, 27: E pubs the last two articles of a series on England (#E447) [← :14] in a Swiss paper.

JULY

18. IN KREUZNACH. July-Aug: M works on his critique of Hegel's political theory (#M206; cf preliminary work #M204), along with extensive reading and note-taking (see → :32). **July D:** Ruge comes to visit, to discuss problems of issuing *DFJ*.

19. W&P (E). July: E's important article on Prussia (#E299) [← 42:28] is pubd in the collection *Einundzwanzig Bogen* (ST/31).

AUGUST

20. IN KREUZNACH. Aug: Still on honeymoon, M prob works on his critique of Hegel (#M206) [← :18] and on a draft program for *DFJ* (#M254). Ruge's reply [← :12] continues the programmatic exchange of correspondence (#M471).

SEPTEMBER

21. PREPARING *DFJ*. Sep: M addresses a final letter to Ruge [← :20] in the programmatic exchange of letters for *DFJ* (#M471). **Sep A:** M and Ruge finally fix on Paris as place of publ. **Sep D:** Perhaps M starts work on his essay on the Jewish question (#M609)—see → :22.

OCTOBER

22. IN KREUZNACH. Oct: M works on his essay "On the Jewish question" (#M609), prob finished later in autumn in Paris (pubd in *DFJ*, → 44:6). **Oct 3:** M writes Feuerbach asking him to collaborate on *DFJ*, suggesting an article against Schelling. **Oct 25:** Feuerbach declines.

23. MOVE TO PARIS. Oct D: M and his wife move from Kreuznach to Paris (rue Vanneau, in the Faubourg St-Germain, first at no. 23, then no. 31, finally settling at no. 38).

24. ENGELS AND THE ENGLISH MOVEMENT. Oct-Nov: E visits the office of the *Northern Star* in Leeds, perhaps referred by James Leach, and gets acquainted with editor Harney. **Oct 23:** E begins writing his first article for the Owenite *New Moral World*, marking the start of his collaboration with this movement [→ :27].

25. ECONOMICA (E). Oct-Nov: E writes his seminal article on polit eco (#E576) for *DFJ*, and sends it off (*MEW* dating: end of 1843 to Jan) [→ 44:6].

NOVEMBER

26. MARX IN PARIS. Nov: M makes connections with the French Democrats and socialists and leaders of workers' secret societies; he attends meetings of German and French workers' groups. **Nov 21:** By this date (as M informs *DFJ* pub'r Fröbel) M has gotten busy on the editorial work, held "protracted discussions" on rejected articles with Hess and others, and carried on editorial correspondence, while awaiting Ruge's arrival in Paris.

27. ENGELS AND THE ENGLISH MOVEMENT. Nov 4, 18: E pubs his first article in the Owenite *NMW* (repr'd Nov 11, 25 in the Chartist *NS*), reporting on the state of the Continental movement (#E623).

DECEMBER

28. PREPARING *DFJ*. Dec 11: M and Ruge publish a statement on Lamartine and *DFJ* (#M459) in *Démocratie Pacifique*. **Dec c.M:** M begins work on his intro to a critique of Hegel for *DFJ* (#M205) [→ 44:4].

29. STUDIES. Dec: Around the end of this year (perhaps Nov-Dec) M begins an intensive study of the history of the French Revolution, with the idea of writing a history of the Convention; M reads such works as Blanc's *Histoire de dix ans*; see → :32, 33, for a list of authors. At the same time M also reads in polit eco, taking notes on Adam Smith, Say, Skarbek, et al.

30. HEINRICH HEINE. Dec D: M becomes acquainted with Heine through Ruge; Heine soon becomes a close friend and regular visitor.

31. ENGELS IN MANCHESTER. Dec 9: E continues writing on the Continental movement, with an article (#E622) pubd in *NS* and repr'd in *NMW*. **c.Dec:** E makes the acquaintance of Georg Weerth, the revolutionary German poet; they become friends.

YEAR APPENDIX

32. M's reading on the French Revolution and other historical subjects [cf ← :3] includes the following writers: J. C. Bailleul, Brougham, Chateaubriand, Daru, E. G. Geijer, Thomas Hamilton, C. G. Heinrich, C. G. Jouffroy, J. C. Lacretelle, K. W. von Lancizolle, J. M. Lappenberg, J. Lingard, C. F. E. Ludwig, Machiavelli, J. Möser, Montesquieu, Pfister, L. von Ranke, Rousseau, Lord John Russell, Savigny, E. A. Schmidt, W. Wachsmuth.

33. M's end-of-the-year reading [← :29] includes writings of: Babeuf, Desmoulins, Louvet, Montgaillard, Mme Roland, and official parliamentary reports and periodicals. For Levasseur, see ← :3.

1844

CONSPECTUS

1. *Paris:* M's editorial project, the *Deutsch-Französische Jahrbücher,* is pubd in Feb and sinks quickly; his assoc with Ruge breaks up. He makes new contacts in Paris, among French and émigré workers; from c.May to next Jan D he frequently attends public meetings of German artisans in Paris, and enters into relations with the Paris leaders of the League of the Just. M and E meet again, and set about writing the *Holy family* (#ME76) as a critique of Bruno Bauer's tendency. M also works on the so-called *Economic and philosophical manuscripts* (#M261) during the year (Apr to Aug), and does extensive reading in the literature of polit eco. (For details, see → :48, 49.) His early economic views take form in a note on a book by James Mill (#M303) [→ :10], which is more indefinitely dated by *MECW* as "first half of 1844." The outbreak of the Silesian weavers' revolt in June affects him strongly, and is involved in his break with Ruge. On the personal side, his first child is born.

2. *Manchester:* E contributes two important articles to *DFJ,* and follows with more articles on England for the press. Besides writing occasionally for the Owenite paper *NMW,* he becomes a more regular correspondent for the Chartist *Northern Star.* Then in Aug E leaves England; on the way home he meets M, and writes his small part of the *Holy family.* In Barmen he starts work on a book about England (#E171).

3. *Reading and Study:* Esp stimulated by E's essay on polit eco in *DFJ* (#E576), about Mar, M enters on a course of reading and excerpt-making on the literature of economics; esp noteworthy are his passages on James Mill's *Elémens d'économie politique* (1823) (#M303) and on E's *DFJ* essay (#M867). (The English writers are being read in French.) For other titles, → :48.

JANUARY

4. PREPARING *DFJ;* STUDY. **Jan:** M completes his intro to Hegel's political theory (#M205) for publ in *DFJ* [→ :6] and receives E's two articles for *DFJ* (#E576, 169). He continues his reading on the French Revolution, e.g., his notes on Levasseur (#M338).

5. W&P (E). **Jan:** E writes an important article reviewing Carlyle's *Past and present* (#E169) for *DFJ.* **Jan 20:** E pubs a note on the *Times* and the German movement (#E808) in the Owenite *NMW.* **Jan 28:** E sends *NMW* a correction on this note (#E296) [→ :7].

FEBRUARY

6. PUBL OF *DFJ.* **Feb D:** The first (and last) issue, a double number, appears in Paris, in about 1000 copies (800 of which will be confiscated by the German police). Besides the programmatic letters by M (#M471), it contains four important articles: M's essay on the Jewish question (#M609) [← 43:22] and his introductory critique of Hegel (#M205) [← :4]; E's article on polit eco (#E576) [← 43:25] and his review of Carlyle (#E169) [← :5].

7. W&P (E). **Feb 3:** Three pieces by E are pubd in one day—two in *NMW* (#E296, 182), one in *NS* (#E618)—all dealing with reports about the Continental movement. **Feb:** E begins work on a series of articles on the "condition of England," originally intended for *DFJ;* he completes the first one (#E167) [→ :29].

MARCH

8. MARX AND RUGE. **Mar c.A:** Relations become strained as a result of business friction over *DFJ* and Ruge's hostility to communist ideas, which M is now espousing. **Mar 26:** M writes a letter to Ruge breaking relations; the immediate trigger is Ruge's attacks on Herwegh, with whom M enters a close friendship this spring.

9. FRIENDS AND ACQUAINTANCES. **Mar 13:** H. J. Claessen (in Cologne) sends M the sum of 1000 talers, a fund collected from former *RZ* supporters on G. Jung's initiative as financial subvention for M's activities in the Paris movement. **Mar 23:** At an international Democratic "banquet" (political meeting), M meets a number of Russian émigrés and travelers, incl Bakunin, V. P. Botkin, G. M. Tolstoy, and French Democrats and socialists, incl Leroux, L. Blanc, F. Pyat, V. Schoelcher, as well as other émigrés, Bernays, Ribbentrop, et al; they all discuss questions of theory and politics. **Mar:** M receives a visit from Count Cieszkowski.

10. ECONOMICA. **c.Mar to June:** In the course of his economic readings, M reads James Mill's *Elements of political economy* (in French) and sets down a comment which turns into his first significant statement on economics (#M303).

11. W&P (E). **Mar:** E writes the second article (#E168) [← :7] in the "condition of England" series [→ :36].

APRIL

12. AFTER *DFJ*. **Apr 14:** To counter press rumors, M sends the Augsburg *AZ* a statement on the suspension of *DFJ* (#M460); pubd Apr 20. **Apr 16:** On the basis of M's *DFJ* articles, the Prussian government charges him with "high treason and lèse majesté," and issues a warrant for his arrest if he enters Prussia. (Under June D, *KMC* says that this news and press reports about it reach M in Paris.)

13. FRIENDS. **Apr:** Roland Daniels of Cologne visits M. —Around this month M enters into personal relations with the Paris leaders of the League of the Just (e.g., Ewerbeck) and of secret workers' societies, without joining any group.

14. ECONOMICA. **Apr to Aug:** M begins drafting the *Economic and philosophical mss* (#M261), the "first ms" being written c.Apr-May.

15. W&P (E). **Apr:** E continues his study of English economics and workers' conditions, collecting material for his planned work on English history and workers' conditions; this preparatory work will continue till Aug. **Apr D:** E comes to an agreement with *NS* to send regular articles on Continental affairs [→ :17].

MAY

16. PROGENY. **May 1:** M's first child is born, named Jenny.

17. W&P (E). **May 4:** *NS* pubs an announcement, in the form of an unsigned letter by E, promising regular articles on the Continental movement (#E441). **May 4–25:** *NS* pubs six pieces by E, mainly on Germany (#E750, 515, 273, 74, 577), one on Russia (#E518).

JUNE

18. SILESIAN WEAVERS' REVOLT. **June 4–6:** Mass actions by hungry weavers against their local exploiters are bloodily repressed by military force [→ :25].

19. CORRESPONDENCE WITH G. JUNG. **June D:** M and Jung plan the smuggling of *DFJ* into Germany; M also criticizes B. Bauer's *Allgemeine Literatur-Ztg*. **June 26:** Jung writes M that the Silesian revolt is a brilliant confirmation of M's thesis in *DFJ* on the role of the proletariat (#M205).

20. MRS. MARX. **June M:** She takes the baby ("Jennychen") to Trier, to be shown to the two grandmothers; soon after arrival, the baby falls ill, but is pulled through [→ :34].

21. W&P (E). **June 15–29:** *NS*, as promised in May, pubs four articles by E, on Switzerland (#E145), France (#E514), and Prussia (#E517, 318).

JULY

22. POLITICAL CONTACTS. **c.July:** M gets acquainted with Proudhon and begins discussions with him, i.a. on Hegelianism. —M begins to associate, until c.Sep, with the physician Georg Weber of Kiel, and helps him write for *Vorwärts*, with which M is also beginning to collaborate; M enters into closer relations with the *Vorwärts* circle, incl Bernays, Börnstein, Weill, et al. **July M:** Writing to G. Jung, M again [← :19] criticizes Bauer's *Allgemeine Literatur-Ztg*; Jung sends recent issues, incl a review of Sue's *Mystères de Paris*.

23. AGAINST RUGE. **July 27:** *Vorwärts* pubs an article signed "A Prussian" (Ruge) on "The king of Prussia and social reform," in which Ruge poohpoohs the Silesian revolt and retreats from revolutionary oppositionism. **July 31:** M writes a reply to Ruge (#M203) [→ :25].

24. PLANS. **July:** M abandons his intention of writing a critique of Hegel's political theory as a single work, aiming instead to write separate brochures on "law, ethics, politics, etc.," and link them up later.

AUGUST

25. MARX AND *VORWÄRTS*. **Aug 7–10:** M's reply to Ruge [← :23], titled "Critical notes on the article [etc.]" (#M203), is pubd in *Vorwärts*. It is M's first article in that paper; he gets increasingly involved with its editorial work. **Aug 17:** M pubs a minor article in *Vorwärts* (#M383).

26. MARX AND BRUNO BAUER. **Aug c.3:** M hears further from G. Jung [← :22], who sends recent writings by Bauer and by Szeliga and Stirner on E. Sue, and urges M to write a criticism of the Bauer school. **Aug D:** M receives another issue of Bauer's paper containing an anti-M article; he decides to come out against Bauer; he plans to publish a part of his Paris mss (#M261), prob the "First ms," together with a discussion of Hegel's dialectic, as a brochure, and writes a preface for it (unfinished) attacking Bauer and defending Feuerbach.

27. MARX AND FEUERBACH. **Aug 11:** M sends Feuerbach his *DFJ* essay on Hegel (#M205), expresses his high opinion of Feuerbach's writings, and invites him to correspond. M also describes the great impact of the workers in the Paris communist clubs.

28. MARX AND BAKUNIN. **Aug to Dec:** During this period they often meet and discuss.

29. ENGELS MEETS MARX: THE ALLIANCE BEGINS. **Aug c.21:** E leaves Manchester for Paris (SOURCE: ST/56; MEW's date is Aug c.26). **Aug c.23 to Sep c.2:** E sojourns in Paris and gets acquainted with M; in discussions they find that they agree on basic questions. E is persuaded to collaborate with *Vorwärts*, and acquaints himself with the French leftist and workers' movement. **Aug 31 to Sep 11:** E pubs in *Vorwärts* the first of a pair of "condition of England" articles (#E167) [← :7; → :36].

30. HOLY FAMILY. **Aug D to Sep A:** M&E plan the writing of this critique of the Bauer school (#ME76); the few sections by E are written before he leaves Paris. M quits working on the unfinished *Economic and philosophical mss* (#M261) [← :14].

SEPTEMBER

31. HOLY FAMILY. **Sep to Nov:** M works on the book *Holy family* (#ME76), extending its scope. The foreword is written in Sep.

32. HEINE. **Sep 21** (rec'd c.24): Heine writes M (from Hamburg) that he is sending, under separate cover, his new poem "Germany, a winter's tale" and other political parts of his forthcoming book *Neue Gedichte*, requesting that M get *Vorwärts* to publish whatever he thinks advisable, and also write an "introductory word" for the "Winter's tale." (M will get some of the poems pubd in *Vorwärts*, esp the "Winter's tale," but will not write an intro.)

33. ECONOMICA: A NOTE. **Sep to Nov:** Since the *Holy family* (#ME76) contains only incidental reference to polit eco, the writing of this book represents a hiatus in M's work on the economics opus.

34. MRS. MARX. **Sep:** She returns from Trier [← :20] with baby Jenny, also with a wetnurse named Gretchen from her mother's household.

35. ENGELS: PARIS TO BARMEN. **Sep A:** Before leaving Paris, E meets M's Russian

acquaintances, G. M. Tolstoy and Bakunin. **Sep c.2:** E departs from Paris (SOURCE: ST/56; MEW's date is Sep c.6). **Sep 3 to c.6:** E stays over in Aachen, at Im Mainzer Hof. **Sep c.7:** E arrives home in Barmen. **Sep 16, 27:** E makes trips to Cologne. **Sep D to next Mar:** E works in his father's firm in Barmen and Engelskirchen, also doing socialist propaganda work in the district and contacting other Rhenish socialists; he works on his book on the English working class (#E171).

36. W&P (E). **Sep 11:** *Vorwärts* finishes publishing E's first of two "condition of England" articles (#E167). **Sep 18 to Oct 19:** *Vorwärts* pubs E's second of this pair (#E168) [← :7, 11].

OCTOBER

37. MARX–ENGELS CORRESPONDENCE BEGINS. **Oct A:** E writes M on the needs of socialist propaganda work in Germany, esp for books of basic theory. In this, E's first (extant) letter to M, he is *already* urging M to finish his book on polit eco.

38. WEITLING. **Oct CD** (after Oct 18): Weitling (in London) writes to M, proposing correspondence.

39. W&P (E). **Oct 5:** E pubs a short piece on the Continental movement in *NMW* (#E183). **Oct M:** E writes an article for a yearbook on existing communist colonies (#E218) [→ :47].

NOVEMBER

40. W&P. **Nov CD:** M finishes work on the *Holy family* (#ME76) [→ 45:15]. Unbeknown to M, Ruge blackmails Fröbel into refusing to publish it; Börnstein, the *Vorwärts* pub'r, also turns it down. **Nov c.D:** The book is accepted for publ by J. Rütten (see ST/ME25). **Prob Nov:** In his notebook, M sets down an outline for a book on the state (#M253) and notes on Hegel's *Phenomenology* (#M368)—both possibly dated Jan 1845.

41. CONTACTS. **Nov M to Jan D:** M associates with Karl Grün and H. Bürgers, who have moved from Cologne to Paris.

42. ENGELS AND STIRNER. **Nov 19:** Having read Stirner's new book *The ego and his own* in advance proofs sent by the pub'r, E discusses it in a letter to M.

43. W&P (E). **Nov 9:** E starts writing an article—the first of three—on the progress of communism in Germany (#E649) [→ :47].

DECEMBER

44. W&P. **Dec:A:** M receives 1000 francs from the pub'r for the *Holy family* (#ME76).

Dec: M reads Stirner's book [← :42] and plans to write a critique for *Vorwärts*.

45. *VORWÄRTS.* **Dec:** The paper suspends publ, as a result of Prussian-inspired government harassment.

46. ECONOMICA. **Dec to Jan:** M continues his study of English and French political economists.

47. W&P (E). **Dec 13:** E's first article on the progress of communism in Germany (#E649) [← :43] is pubd in *NMW*; for two more, see → 45:17. **Dec:** E's article on communist colonies (#E218) [← :39] is pubd in a yearbook.

YEAR APPENDIX

48. M's reading on polit eco [← :3] includes writings by the following: Buret, Destutt de Tracy, Lauderdale, F. List, J. R. McCulloch, H. F. Osiander, Ricardo, J. B. Say, C. W. C. Schüz, F. Skarbek, Adam Smith, and Xenophon; also a collection edited by Daire, 1843, in which M reads essays by John Law and Boisguillebert.

49. KMC adds the following writers to this list: Pecqueur, Wilhelm Schulz, and Sismondi. —Also studied in 1844–47: Cherbuliez, Sismondi, Cantillon, J. Child.

1845

CONSPECTUS

1. M, expelled from France, goes to live in Brussels in Feb; E joins him in Apr.

2. At first M works on his Economica; during the summer he and E take a trip to England, where they study polit eco and meet the movement's leaders. Around autumn M turns toward settling accounts with his philosophic past, and (with E) starts on his *German ideology* (#ME66), which had been preceded by his "Theses on Feuerbach" (#M878) in the spring.

3. In Brussels, M corresponds with German leftist leaders in Paris, esp the Paris circle of the League of the Just, and at home starts entering into relations with Belgian leftist (Democratic and socialist) leaders and Polish revolutionary émigrés. (*MEW* dates this Apr-Dec.) *Indefinite Date:* Prob around the last quarter of the year, M writes an article on Peuchet and suicide (#M653).

4. E works on finishing his book on England (#E171) until Mar M; before moving to Brussels he is also involved in local propaganda activities. His important book on England (#E171) is pubd in May. Besides joining M on the trip to England, he continues to work on English affairs; his overall plan is to produce a social history of England (of which #E171 is only a part)—an intention he will not give up till late 1847. *Indefinite Dates:* Around summer-autumn, E works on "supplementary material" to the subject of the book [→ 46:7]. He writes an article on "The Festival of Nations" (#E277) around the end of the year (entered here under Nov-Dec).

5. E also initiates a plan for M&E to edit a "library" (publisher's series) of socialist works; they take it up Mar-May [→ :19]; and (*indefinite date*) sometime during this year, in this connection, E translates a piece by Fourier (#E288).

6. *Reading and Study.* M's notebooks for this period show a long list of works read and excerpted; see → :50–52.

JANUARY

7. NOTES ON THEORY. **Jan:** See ← 44:40 for two notebook jottings by M which may possibly belong to this month: an outline for a book on the state (#M253) and notes on Hegel (#M368).

8. FRANCE ORDERS EXPULSION. **Jan c.11:** Min of the Interior Guizot orders the expulsion from France of M and other *Vorwärts* collaborators, under pressure from Prussia. **Jan 12:** M writes to Heine that leaving him behind will be the worst part of being expelled [→ :12].

9. LAST DAYS IN PARIS. **Jan 12, c.19:** M receives—first from Leske, then from Hess— an invitation to collaborate on the *Rheinische Jahrbücher* planned by Püttmann. **Jan M:** M sends E a criticism of Stirner [← 44:42], with which, **Jan 20,** E says he agrees; this discussion will lead to the writing of the *German ideology* (#ME66). **Jan D:** M meets with Louis Blanc.

10. ECONOMICA. **Jan:** M continues his study of polit eco [← 44:46], at least till his expulsion on Feb 3. **Jan c.19:** M plans to write a critique of F. List [→ :19]. **Jan D:** M negotiates with pub'r Leske for a contract for his Economica [→ :14]. **Jan 20:** Once again [← 44:37] E urges M to finish his book on polit eco, as he will continue to do for the next few decades.

11. ENGELS IN BARMEN. **Jan 20:** E announces he will work with Hess in establishing a new monthly, *Gesellschafts-Spiegel*, in Hagen, beginning Apr 1. **Jan D:** E collaborates with Hess in drawing up the editorial statement for the new monthly (#E862).

FEBRUARY

12. LAST DAYS IN PARIS. Feb 1: M makes a contract with pub'r Leske; see → :14. **Feb c.2:** M meets with Cabet. **Feb 3:** In accordance with the government expulsion order [← :8] M quits Paris for Brussels.

13. IN BRUSSELS. Feb 3: M goes to Brussels, via Liège, with H. Bürgers. After stopping at the Hôtel de Saxe, his first address is 35 rue Pacheco "vis-à-vis du hôpital St-Jean." **Feb A to Mar D:** M receives money from a fund initiated by E in Barmen to help the M family resettle after expulsion; he gets about 50 talers this month, 122 francs in Mar [→ :21]. **Feb c.5:** M gets acquainted with Freiligrath, who has recently pubd his poetry, and at his home again meets Karl Heinzen, who has fled from Germany. **Feb 7:** M sends the Belgian king a formal request for permission to reside in the country (#M887). **Feb D:** Hermann Kriege, recommended by E and Julius Meyer, comes to see M.

14. ECONOMICA. Feb 1: The Darmstadt pub'r H. Leske (who is visiting Paris) signs a contract with M for publ of a two-volume work on polit eco, *Critique of politics and polit eco.* (For the contract, see *MECW* 4:675.) **Feb to July:** Settled in Brussels, M continues his study and work on polit eco; see → :50 for details.

15. PUBL. Feb c.24: The *Holy family* (#ME76) is pubd in Frankfurt [← 44:40].

16. ENGELS: PROPAGANDA ACTIVITY. Feb 8, 15: E gives talks at two meetings he helps to organize in nearby Elberfeld, to popularize socialist ideas (#E770) [→ :34]. **Feb 22:** E participates in a third meeting. **Feb 28:** E receives an official order from the Elberfeld mayor banning further socialist meetings. **Feb c.28 to Mar 6:** E spends a week in Bonn and Cologne (staying at friends' houses) organizing propaganda activities (on which he reports to M, Mar 7).

17. W&P (E). Feb 2: E writes the second of three articles on the progress of communism in Germany (#E649) [← 44:47; → :27].

MARCH

18. IN BRUSSELS. Mar c.10: M's house is the scene of a farewell party for Freiligrath, with Bürgers and Heinzen. **Mar 22:** M signs the required pledge not to publish in Belgium on current politics (cf text, *MECW* 4:677).

19. W&P. Mar: M writes a critique of F. List's polit eco, unfinished, apparently for Püttmann's planned *Rheinische Jahrbücher* (#M591). **Mar to May:** M&E plan [← :5] the publ of a series of edns of the major socialist/communist writings, with the collaboration of Hess (cf #M659); but pub'r Leske turns the project down.

20. ENGELS. Mar A: For E's propaganda activity, see ← :16. **Mar M:** E finishes writing his book on England (#E171) [← :4; → :27]. **Mar 15:** E writes, and dates, his English-language Dedication (#E173) to be included in the book.

APRIL

21. IN BRUSSELS. Apr c.9: M receives more money (750 francs) from the resettlement fund [← :13] sent by G. Jung, from Bielefeld and Cologne. **Apr c.30:** M goes to Hamburg on a visit (SOURCE: KMC, based on newspaper reports; no further info).

22. NOTES ON THEORY. Prob Apr: M sets down a short note on the state (#M565). **c.Apr-May** (spring): M writes down his "Theses on Feuerbach" (#M878) as a seminal statement of his new views of society.

23. HELENE DEMUTH ARRIVES. Apr: Mrs. M's mother sends her own maidservant to join the M family in Brussels; from this time on Helene Demuth stays permanently with the family as a key member of the household.

24. ENGELS MOVES TO BRUSSELS. Apr 7: In Barmen, E submits a request to the mayor for permission to emigrate to England. **Apr c.M:** E sojourns in Bonn; on Apr 15 he stays there with his father, who may have been returning from a quick trip to England. **Apr 24–25:** E is in Düsseldorf. **After Apr 25:** E moves to Brussels, near the M family. (This account follows ST/56; MEW dates E's move "after Apr 5.")

25. W&P (E). Apr 5: E writes, or finishes writing, the last of three articles (#E649) [← :17] for the Owenite *NMW*, this one reporting the Elberfeld meetings [← :16]. This is his last piece before moving to Brussels.

MAY

26. NEW RESIDENCE. May 1–3: The M family moves from Plaine Ste-Gudule to 5 rue de l'Alliance, in the Brussels suburb Saint-Josse-ten-Noode, "hors de la Porte de Louvain." E lives nearby, at no. 7 on the same street.

27. PUBL (E). May 8–10: *NMW* pubs the last two articles of E's report on the German movement (#E649) [← :25]. **May D:** E's book *The condition of the working class in England* (#E171) is pubd in Leipzig.

JUNE

28. ECONOMICA. June: M's reading of E's new book on England (#E171) [← :27] makes a significant contribution, often overlooked, to M's orientation in the field of polit eco.

JULY

29. ECONOMICA. **July A:** M receives an advance of 1500 francs from pub'r Leske for his planned book [← :14].

30. TRAVELS. **Prob July to Sep M:** Mrs. M goes to her mother's house in Trier for the summer, along with little Jenny and Helene Demuth. **July:** M&E are visited by G. Weerth, who stays for some weeks (SOURCE: *KMC*, on basis of Weerth's letters; but it is not clear how this jibes with the next item; cf → 46:21). **July c.12:** M&E depart together for a trip to England (London, Manchester), to get acquainted with the English workers' movement and to study English conditions and polit eco in the libraries. See → :32.

31. ECONOMICA: ENGLAND. **July CD to Aug:** M's study of polit eco in London's BM and Manchester libraries is extensive; it is in this period that M studies the "socialist Ricardians" (for M's reading, see → :51).

AUGUST

32. TRIP TO ENGLAND. **Aug:** M&E spend much time in library study of economic sources [← :31] as well as in meeting and talking with labor and socialist leaders in London and Manchester. **Aug M:** They meet with Harney, and with the London leaders of the League of the Just (Schapper, Moll, et al). **Aug c.20:** They participate in a conference along with Chartist leaders, League of the Just people, and other Democratic émigrés. A resolution is passed (E supporting) to establish in London an international organizn of Democrats for exchange of info. (This will be founded next month as the Fraternal Democrats.) **Aug c.24:** M&E return to Brussels (SOURCE: *MEW*; the chronology in ST/56 dates this return Aug c.14, without explanation of discrepancies).

33. EWERBECK. **c.Aug-Nov:** In correspondence with Ewerbeck (in Paris), M convinces him to come out against Karl Grün's activity among the German workers in Paris.

34. PUBL (E). **Aug:** E's Elberfeld speeches (#E770) [← :16] are pubd in *Rheinische Jahrbücher*.

SEPTEMBER

35. SECOND DAUGHTER. **Sep M:** Mrs. M returns from Trier [← :30]. **Sep 26:** She gives birth to a daughter, Laura.

36. GERMAN IDEOLOGY. **Sep A:** M&E read the new Vol. 3 of *Wigand's Vierteljahrsschrift*, with polemical essays by Bauer and Stirner, and they plan to write a critique—which will later become part of the *German ideology* (#ME66). Possibly they start writing it in Sep

(so according to *MEW*, but see → :43 for *MECW* estimate).

37. ECONOMICA. **Sep to Nov:** Back in Brussels, M continues his reading and study in polit eco [→ :44] (for details, see → :52).

38. PUBL (E). **Sep 13–27:** E pubs three articles (#E420, 887, 924) in *NS* on Germany and the Continental movement.

OCTOBER

39. PRUSSIAN CITIZENSHIP. **Oct 17:** M sends to the Trier burgomaster a request (#M885) for a certificate for emigration to the US, thus entailing release from Prussian citizenship [→ :42]. It is not certain whether M actually contemplates emigration at this time or whether this is a device to block Prussian government pressure on the Brussels authorities.

40. PLANNED BOOK. **Oct:** M&E plan to write a work on the tariff question, protection vs free trade; they offer the project to pub'r Campe (SOURCE: *KMC*).

41. PUBL (E). **Oct 25:** E pubs two more articles in *NS* on the Continental movement: a report on anticommunist persecution (#E582) and E's first article on the "state of Germany" (#E772) [→ :45].

NOVEMBER

42. PRUSSIAN CITIZENSHIP. **Nov 10:** In response to a query from Trier [← :39] on whether his request applies to his family, M answers yes *if* necessary for granting consent (#M886). There is no record that the request is granted [→ :46].

43. JOINT WORK. **Nov 20:** M&E write a reply to B. Bauer's criticism of the *Holy family* (#ME129) [→ 46:7]. **Nov:** M&E start writing the *German ideology* (#ME66)—according to *MECW* (but see dating in Sep from *MEW*). — Around this time (autumn) E makes notes on "Feuerbach" (#E278), prob for the joint book.

44. ECONOMICA. **Nov:** The *German ideology* project means the interruption of M's work on polit eco, though he may have continued some reading in the field. **Nov 24:** G. Jung writes M that he and his friends are looking forward to the coming work on polit eco.

45. W&P (E). **Nov 8:** E pubs the second article of the series "The state of Germany" (#E772) [← :41; → 46:10]. **Nov-Dec** (end of the year): E writes the article "The Festival of Nations" (#E277). Around this time, perhaps as early as Sep, M writes a piece on Peuchet and suicide (#M653).

DECEMBER

46. PRUSSIAN CITIZENSHIP. **Dec 1:** As a result of his harassment in Brussels by the

Prussian government, M sends an official request to be relieved of Prussian citizenship.

47. ECONOMICA. **Dec 6:** The pub'r Leske [← :14] presses M to finish his book on polit eco.

48. PUBL (E). **Dec:** The *Telegraph für Deutschland*, for which E has not written since 1841, pubs his article on the English corn laws (#E354), sent to it by a press bureau commissioned by E.

YEAR APPENDIX

49. Following are a list of writers whose books were annotated by M in his ten notebooks of this period, divided into three groups. However, there is no certain dividing line separating the reading of 1845 from that of 1846. (Cf → 46:51–53. Also see ← 44:49.)

50. *Brussels Notebooks (Feb–June).* **Notebook 1:** C. G. de Chamborant, Louis Say, Sismondi, A. de Villeneuve-Bargemont. **Notebook 2:** E. Buret, N. W. Senior. **Notebook 3:**

F. L. A. Ferrier, Théodore Fix, A. de Laborde, A. Moreau de Jonnès, Ramon de La Sagra, L. F. B. Trioen. **Notebook 4:** J. A. Blanqui, C. Ganilh, J. R. McCulloch, Pecchio, F. Villegardelle, John Watts. **Notebook 5:** C. Babbage, E. de Girardin, Péreire, P. Rossi, Andrew Ure, Isaac Pinto.

51. *Manchester Notebooks (July–Aug).* **Notebook 6:** Th. Cooper, T. R. Edmonds, J. W. Gilbart, Th. Jarrold, M. T. Sadler, T. Tooke. **Notebook 7:** James Anderson, G. Browning, C. D'Avenant, E. Misselden, W. Petty. **Notebook 8:** W. Cobbett, D. North, N. W. Senior, W. Thompson.

52. *Brussels Notebooks (Sep to Dec and perhaps early 1846).* **Notebook 9:** J. Aikin, W. Atkinson, Th. Carlyle, Daniel Defoe, F. M. Eden, Th. Gisborne, J. R. McCulloch, J. S. Mill, John Wade. **Notebook 10:** R. Hilditch; and essays by W. R. Greg, G. Hope, and A. Morse, in *Three prize essays on agriculture and the corn law*, pubd by the Anti-Corn-Law League (1842).

1846

CONSPECTUS

1. In Brussels, M&E establish a Communist Correspondence Committee early in the year [→ :8]. During the year there are a series of tensions between this Brussels circle and the communist artisans of the League of the Just in London. The CCC tries to extend its contacts in Paris; E goes there in Aug for a stay. In Brussels the Marx circle comes to a break with Weitling and his tendency, esp Kriege in the US. Proudhon (in Paris) rejects the CCC's overtures, and M&E move to combat Proudhonist ideas.

2. M&E work on the *German ideology* (#ME66); their last work on the ms is done in Aug. But they find there is no chance of publ, and abandon the project; M goes back to working on polit eco.

3. *Economica:* While the subject of polit eco is incidental to the *German ideology*, it is here that M first explicitly accepts the labor theory of value; it is conjectured that M adopts it between July 1845 and the end of work on this book. For M's readings in economics during this year, see → :51–53.

4. *Indefinite Dates:* Sometime toward the end of the year E's article "The Festival of Nations" (#E277) [← 45:45] is pubd in the *Rheinische Jahrbücher*. Prob during the first half of the year, E writes Part 1 of his "German socialism in verse and prose" (#E337); Part 2, after Aug M. For its publ, see → 47:31.

JANUARY

5. PHILANTHROPISM. **Jan 18:** M sends a statement to *Trier'sche Ztg* repudiating his alleged assoc with that paper, as it is "bourgeois-philanthropic," not communist (#M847); pubd Jan 26.

6. GERMAN IDEOLOGY. **c.Jan:** M&E fix on the book's framework and contents, as well as title and subtitle [→ :17, 19].

7. PUBL. **Jan:** Previously written pieces appear in print: M&E's reply to Bauer on the *Holy family* (#ME129); M's article "Peuchet: On suicide" (#M653); the first part of E's supplementary material on England (#E792) [← 45:4].

FEBRUARY

8. COMMUNIST CORRESPONDENCE COMM. **Feb:** Around this time (perhaps in Jan) M&E establish this attempt at a political center in Brussels. **Feb M:** M informs Ewerbeck (in Paris) of the CCC project—"a new system of propaganda"—and asks him to collaborate. M&E also inform Harney and request his support, esp of a planned periodical [→ :11].

9. PERSONAL. **Feb c.12:** M receives from Bürgers (in Cologne) a loan of 370 francs. **Feb 19–21:** M accompanies his wife partway as she goes to visit her sick mother in Trier; he stops in Arlon.

10. W&P (E). **Feb:** E pubs the rest [← :7]

of his supplementary material on England (#E792). **Feb 20:** He writes the third article in his series on Germany for *NS* (#E772) [← 45:45; → :18].

MARCH

11. COMMUNIST CORRESPONDENCE COMM. **Mar 25:** The Brussels circle adopts a resolution against Thomas Cooper for deserting Chartism. **Mar 30:** Harney writes from London that he will collaborate with the Brussels circle if the London group of German communists (esp Schapper) does. —The Brussels group holds a discussion meeting at M's house with Weitling, newly arrived from London, on propaganda work in Germany; there is a sharp conflict. Present are Gigot, Weydemeyer, Seiler, Edgar von Westphalen, Heilberg, plus Annenkov as guest, besides Weitling and M&E. **Mar D:** M is visited by P. V. Annenkov, a Russian traveler who comes with a recommendatory letter from G. M. Tolstoy.

12. ECONOMICA. **Mar 31:** Pub'r Leske abrogates the agreement to publish M's work [← 45:14] in view of its probable banning in Germany. (But see → :28.)

13. OPTIMISM. **Mar 5:** Writing to Harney to ask his support for the Brussels CCC (see his reply ← :11), E says he expects the speedy coming of a revolution in England, the winning of the Charter by the end of the year, and the abrogation of private property within three years. E criticizes O'Connor's leadership of the Chartist movement and praises Harney's.

APRIL

14. HEINE. **Apr c.5:** M writes Heine (in Paris) introducing Annenkov; he also mentions an intention to write an article defending Heine's book against Börne, which has been attacked in the press. (No such article is extant.)

15. WEITLING. **Apr M:** Writing to Ewerbeck (in Paris) to introduce Annenkov, M reports the conflict with Weitling [← :11] and warns against Karl Grün. **Apr 20:** M&E begin working on a circular repudiating the US activities of the Weitlingite, H. Kriege (#ME28) [→ :20].

16. WILHELM WOLFF. **Apr D:** Wolff, a recent émigré from Germany, looks up M&E in Brussels. They become acquainted, then close friends; Wolff joins the CCC.

17. *GERMAN IDEOLOGY.* **c.Apr:** M writes a critique of Grün's book which will later be included in the *German ideology* (#ME66) and also pubd separately [→ 47:16]. **Apr D:** M&E are finished in the main with the first vol. of the work. Weydemeyer takes the ms

with him back to Westphalia where he expects to finance publ through a couple of affluent socialists.

18. PUBL (E). **Apr 4:** E pubs the third article in his *NS* series on Germany (#E772) [← :10].

MAY

19. *GERMAN IDEOLOGY.* **May 14:** M writes Weydemeyer that the second vol. is almost finished, and the rest of the first vol. is en route to him; he should start publ immediately. **May CD:** M learns from Weydemeyer that his "angels" [← :17] will not finance the book [→ :27].

20. COMMUNIST CORRESPONDENCE COMM. **May 5:** M writes Proudhon (in Paris) requesting that he be French correspondent; M also warns against K. Grün. **May 11:** The Brussels CCC in session votes to criticize Kriege's noncommunist activities in the US and adopt M&E's circular on him (#ME28), only Weitling voting against. The circular, lithographed, is sent out to CCC contacts and to Kriege's paper in America. **May M:** Sending the circular against Kriege, the CCC proposes to the League of the Just and GWEA in London (led by Schapper) to form a London CCC and correspond regularly with the Brussels group. **May 17** (rec'd c.19): Proudhon replies [← May 5] rejecting M's proposal because he is against revolutionary action, and defending Grün. **May 19:** M writes to Hess, sharply criticizing Weitling's politics. **May 20, 29:** Hess says he separates himself from the "Marx tendency" but assures M of his personal regard.

21. PERSONAL. **May AB:** The M family moves to an inn, Au Bois Sauvage, Plaine Ste-Gudule, no. 19 (or 19–21). **May M to June D:** Weerth visits and stays at M's address [→ :44.5].

22. PUBL (E). **May 30:** E pubs an article on Prussia in *NS* (#E889).

JUNE

23. *GERMAN IDEOLOGY.* **June A:** M&E finish the second vol., and return to Ch. 1 for redrafting.

24. COMMUNIST CORRESPONDENCE COMM. **June:** It asks G. Weber (in Kiel) to act as correspondent for northern Germany. **June c.8:** M receives a favorable reply from the London communist group [← :20]; they will form a Correspondence Comm; they approve the break with Weitling [← :11] but criticize the sharp tone of the circular against Kriege [← :20]. **June 15:** CCC sends a communication to the communists in the Wuppertal (Barmen, Elberfeld), addressed to Köttgen (#ME86), discussing propaganda and organization measures, but opposing an immediate congress of German communists as premature. **June 22:** CCC writes the London comm urging a fight against "philosophical and sentimental communism"; it suggests holding a general communist congress in England.

25. VISITOR. June D: M is visited by a German worker from Paris, Adolph Junge (introduced by Daniels and Bürgers), who reports on the movement in France.

26. W&P (E). June D: E writes an article on Prussia for NS (#E641) [→ :30].

JULY

27. GERMAN IDEOLOGY. July c.13: M receives final word that Weydemeyer's publishing angels [← :19] refuse financial support. **July M:** M&E end work on their redraft of Ch. 1 [← :23], leaving it unfinished.

28. ECONOMICA. July 29: Pub'r Leske [← :12] writes M asking him to return the advance or else immediately deliver the ms [→ :33].

29. COMMUNIST CORRESPONDENCE COMM. July M: CCC sends further suggestions for propaganda to Weber (in Kiel) [← :24]. **July 17:** M&E, signing "Democratic Communists of Brussels," send greetings, via Harney, to Chartist leader O'Connor for his election victory in Nottingham (#ME4); pubd in NS, July 25. **July 17** (rec'd c.19): Schapper replies for the Londoners [← :24] complaining of "intellectual arrogance," advocating a softer attitude on "sentimental communism" and on Kriege, and proposing London for a communist congress. **July 20:** Harney [← :11] writes M&E that he will support the CCC project in view of the agreement reached with the London communists (Schapper et al). **July 27** (rec'd c.29): Ewerbeck (in Paris) promises to be active in Paris on behalf of the CCC. **July 29:** M proposes to Bürgers the formation of a CCC in Cologne [→ :34]. He writes Ewerbeck that E will go to Paris soon.

30. PUBL (E). July 4: E pubs an article on Prussia in NS (#E641) [← :26].

31. PERSONAL (M&E). July c.M: M has an attack of asthma. **July c.20 to Aug c.12:** E takes a seaside holiday in Ostend with his mother and sister [→ :35].

AUGUST

32. GERMAN IDEOLOGY. Aug AB: M drafts the preface; this is the last work done on the ms.

33. ECONOMICA. Aug 1: M replies to Leske [← :28] with a promise to supply the ms of the first vol. by Nov D.

34. COMMUNIST CORRESPONDENCE COMM. Aug 11: Bürgers replies [← :29] that formation of a CCC in Cologne would be premature.

Aug D: CCC, via W. Wolff, makes contact with Silesian communists, who begin sending reports on the working-class situation.

35. HOLIDAY IN OSTEND. Aug c.2: M joins E in Ostend [← :31]. **Aug c.12:** E leaves. **Aug c.14:** M leaves.

36. ENGELS: TO PARIS. Aug 15: E moves to Paris, to carry on CCC work esp in the League of the Just, aiming to form a CCC branch. **Aug 15–19:** E makes the acquaintance of Cabet. **Aug 19:** E sends his first report (letter) to the Brussels CCC on the situation in Paris (#E439).

37. W&P (E). Aug 15 to next Jan 15: Sometime in this period E writes the second part of his "German socialism in verse and prose" (#E337) [← :4; → 47:31].

SEPTEMBER

38. ECONOMICA. Sep: M resumes work on polit eco, till the end of the year (for his reading, see → :51–53).

39. G. M. TOLSTOY. Sep D: M inquires from Annenkov (in Paris) whether the Tolstoy exposed in the German press as a Russian secret agent is the G. M. Tolstoy they both know [→ :43].

40. ENGELS IN PARIS. Sep: E argues against the views of Grün and Proudhon in the League of the Just [→ :44]. **Sept 16:** E sends a second report (letter) to the Brussels CCC (#E439), i.a. criticizing Proudhon's new book, as also in a letter to M, Sep 18. E has made extensive notes for himself on Proudhon's book [→ :48].

41. W&P (E). Sep c.1: E writes an article on France for NS (#E339); pubd Sep 5.

OCTOBER

42. COMMUNIST CORRESPONDENCE COMM. Oct 13: M and the Brussels comm send the London comm (Schapper et al) a report on the progress of the movement in Germany. **Oct c.20:** M draws up a second circular against Kriege, which is issued over his signature only (see #ME28, note). **Oct to Dec:** Bürgers sends M reports on Cologne, incl the work of d'Ester in the city council.

43. G. M. TOLSTOY. Oct 2: In reply to M's inquiry [← :39], Annenkov answers that the secret agent is not G. M. Tolstoy.

44. ENGELS IN PARIS. Oct 18: E writes M a critique of Feuerbach's Essence of religion, which he has just read. **Oct 23:** In a third report (letter) to the Brussels CCC (#E439), E says he has won over a majority of the Paris branch of the League of the Just against "True Socialism" and Proudhonism, after three meetings of discussion in which E described the principles of communism.

44.5 PERSONAL. **Oct:** The M family moves to 42 rue d'Orléans, Faubourg de Namur (but M also writes: Faubourg d'Ixelles). The street will later be renamed rue du Président [→ 48:9].

NOVEMBER

45. LONDON VS BRUSSELS. **Nov:** London leaders of the League of the Just (Schapper et al) send out, without consulting Brussels, a circular to League branches proposing a communist congress in May and suggesting distrust of the Brussels "intellectuals."

46. WEYDEMEYER. **c.Nov:** M writes him about the conflict with Weitling.

DECEMBER

47. COMMUNIST CORRESPONDENCE COMM. **Dec c.A:** M informs E (in Paris) of the new tension with the London communists [← :45]. E replies, discussing possible alternative courses. —In Paris, the police begin surveillance on E.

48. ON PROUDHON. **Dec c.20–28:** Stimulated by E's letter [← :40], M reads Proudhon's new book. **Dec 28:** In reply to an inquiry from Annenkov, M sends the Russian a long letter analyzing Proudhon.

49. ECONOMICA. **Dec:** M's reading of Proudhon's book (see ← :48) moves him to reply in the arena of polit eco; his refutation will lead to his writing a book against Proudhon (#M681). In his Dec 28 letter to Annenkov (see ← :48) M reports he has not been able to get his Economica published.

50. PERSONAL. **c.Dec:** M's son Edgar is born (either this month or next, Jan 1847).

YEAR APPENDIX

51. As M returns to working on polit eco [← :38] he resumes filling his notebooks. The following list picks up from 1845; there is no certain dividing line. These titles represent the continuation of the works listed in the *MEGA* for the period "Brussels: Sep 1845 to 1846."

52. **Notebook 10** (cont'd): Robert Owen. **Notebook 11:** J. F. Bray, Robert Owen, R. Parkinson. **Notebook 12:** F. Quesnay.

53. See also the reading list for 1847 (→ 47:58), some of which may possibly apply to the end of 1846.

1847

CONSPECTUS

1. The League of the Just (Schapper et al) decides to merge with Marx's circle, on the basis of M's views; the resulting Communist League is established in June. M&E form a CL in Brussels and reorganize their work there; they also help found a Democratic Association in Brussels. After the CL's second congress in Dec, they work on drafting a Communist manifesto.

2. M's readings in polit eco continue [← 46:38] into 1847, and merge with his work on his book criticizing Proudhon (#M681), which focuses on polit eco. There is some follow-up on the unpubd *German ideology* (#ME66): one chapter is pubd [→ :25], and E writes a continuation on "True Socialism" [→ :9].

3. A free-trade congress of economists, held in Brussels in Sep, stimulates M to write and publish on the tariff issue [→ :33]; this is also one facet of his continuing work on polit eco.

4. On the personal side, M is in financial straits; from autumn on [→ :38] M negotiates through a Dutch relative for payment of a part of his father's legacy.

5. E is active in Paris at the beginning and end of the year, but spends July D to Oct M in Brussels, helping M on the reorganizn of the movement. On his return to Paris he enters into new relations with the important leftist organ *La Réforme*. Besides writing for this paper, he also publishes in the Chartist *NS* and the Brussels *DBZ*. Among his important productions are two preliminary drafts for the *Com Manifesto* [→ :20, 43].

6. *Indefinite Dates:* M writes his anti-Proudhon *Poverty of philosophy* (#M681) during the first half of the year; it is pubd in July. E's article on "The True Socialists" (#E873) is listed as "c.Jan to Apr."

7. *Reading and Study:* See → :58 for a few authors additional to the 1846 list.

JANUARY

8. TOWARD UNITY. **Jan 20:** The London comm of the League of the Just empowers Moll to go to Brussels and Paris to invite M&E to join, with the assurances that the League is ready to change its organizn and program in accord with their views.

9. W&P. **c.Jan-Feb:** M begins work early in the year on his book against Proudhon (#M681). **c.Jan-Apr:** E writes an essay on the "True Socialists" (#E873), unfinished, continuing the subject from the *German ideology* (#ME66).

10. PERSONAL. **Jan 13:** M's sister Caroline dies, in Trier. **Possibly Jan:** M's son Edgar is born (or see ← 46:50).

FEBRUARY

11. TOWARD UNITY. **Feb:** Discussions take place in Brussels between Moll [← :8] and M, as Moll urges him to join the League of the Just and recast it in accord with his "critical communism."

12. ECONOMICA. **Feb 2:** Pub'r Leske [← 46:33] definitively abrogates the publishing agreement, and requests speedy repayment of the advance with threats to take measures.

13. W&P (E). **Feb D:** E writes "The Prussian constitution" (#E642) for NS [→ :15].

MARCH

14. COMMUNIST CORRESPONDENCE COMM. **Mar 3, 7:** M writes to Daniels and Bürgers (in Cologne) that one of them must come to Belgium (to meet at Malines, not Brussels) because there are matters that cannot be discussed by mail. **Mar 27:** Weerth comes from Paris to visit M.

15. W&P (E). **Mar 6:** E's article on Prussia is pubd in NS (#E642) [← :13]. **Mar-Apr:** E writes an important pamphlet on German politics and the constitutional question (#E779), directed against profeudal "True Socialism" [→ :18].

APRIL

16. KARL GRÜN. **Apr 3:** M sends in a statement attacking Grün (#M220) for a piece in Trier'sche Ztg of Mar 25 on M's forthcoming anti-Proudhon book. **Apr 8–9:** The statement is pubd in DBZ and Trier'sche Ztg. (This is M's first contribution to DBZ.) **Apr to June:** M makes efforts to publish his critique of Grün's book [← 46:17] as a brochure; Bürgers and Daniels in Cologne look for a pub'r [→ :25].

17. W&P (E). **Apr:** For E's pamphlet on Germany (#E779), see ← :15 [→ :18].

MAY

18. ENGELS' PAMPHLET. **May 15:** In his first extant letter to E (in Paris), M writes that the recent arrest of Brussels pub'r Vogler in Aachen prevents publ of E's pamphlet on Germany (#E779) [← :15]. M says the first third of the ms is very good, but the other two (parts or thirds?) will need changes. (This may indicate that the ms contained three numbered parts; the extant ms ends before the end of Part 2.) In fact the pamphlet will remain unpubd.

19. CARICATURE. **May 6:** DBZ pubs a special supplementary page reproducing a caricature by E, given to the paper by M, of the Prussian king's speech from the throne of Apr 11. (For the caricature, see MEW 4: opp. 32.)

JUNE

20. COMMUNIST CONGRESS. **June:** The congress in London has been organized by the London comm of the League of the Just in agreement with M&E, who are ready to join [← :11]; it will be the first congress of the new Communist League. M is unable to go to London, mostly for lack of money; E goes from Paris, Wolff from Brussels. **June 1:** E and Wolff meet in Ostend and take the ship Belgian Railway to Dover. **June 2–9:** E takes an active part in the congress. **June A:** E writes a draft of a communist credo (#E229) for the program of the new Communist League. **June 9:** At its last session the congress adopts E's draft, to be sent to the branches for discussion. **June M:** E returns to Paris.

21. VISIT. **June:** M is visited by Herwegh, in Brussels.

22. W&P (M). **June 15:** M finishes his book on Proudhon, Poverty of philosophy (#M681); at any rate, this is the date of the preface [→ :24].

23. W&P (E). **June A:** E writes an article on the tariff question for DBZ (#E638); pubd June 10. **June 26:** E writes an article on French politics and Guizot's decline (#E212) for NS [→ :27].

JULY

24. ANTI-PROUDHON. **July A:** M's Poverty of philosophy (#M681) is pubd in Brussels in 800 copies [← :22].

25. MORE PUBL. **July c.5:** Unable to publish his critique of Grün's book (Ch. 4 of German ideology—see #ME66) as a brochure [← :16], M sends the ms to Weydemeyer (in Hamm) for publ in Westphälische Dampfboot [→ :29].

26. ENGELS: TO BRUSSELS. **July c.27:** E leaves Paris to return temporarily to Brussels, where he will consult with M on CL affairs. (He will stay in Brussels till Oct M.)

27. W&P (E). **July 3:** E pubs his article on French politics (#E212) in NS [← :23].

AUGUST

28. REORGANIZATION IN BRUSSELS. **Aug 5:** M&E establish a Brussels branch of the CL, with M as chairman (Präsident); also a district exec (M, Gigot, Wolff, Junge). For M's minutes of this meeting, see #M564. **Aug D:** M and the Brussels CL set up a German Workers (Educational) Assoc, like the London GWEA;

its exec includes Wallau, Hess, Wolff, Riedel. **Aug:** M plans to publish a monthly, with a printshop and publishing house. **Aug 28:** M writes Cologne friends to subscribe shares. **29.** W&P. **Aug A:** *DBZ* editor Bornstedt agrees to print all material supplied by M&E. **Aug-Sep:** M's critique of Grün [← :25] is pubd in *Westphälische Dampfboot*, under M's name, for 27½ Reichstaler. **30.** ENGELS: TO ENGLAND. **Aug 8:** E arrives in Dover, from Ostend (SOURCE: ST/56, which does not explain what E is doing there).

SEPTEMBER

31. *DBZ* COLLABORATION. **Sep:** In line with the agreement [← :29], M&E begin publishing regularly in *DBZ*; M exercises a growing influence on the editorial management of the paper. (*KMC* dates this Sep M to Feb.) **Sep 5:** M writes "The communism of the *Rh. Beob.*" (#M167). **Sep 12:** *DBZ* pubs two major articles: the preceding (#M167) against feudal socialism, and E's "German socialism in verse and prose" (#E337), which is pubd in eight installs till Dec 9. **Sep 23:** E pubs an article on the free-trade congress (#E234) in *DBZ* (→ :32). **32.** FREE-TRADE CONGRESS. **Sep 16–18:** The International Congress of Economists meets in Brussels; M&E take part, and develop arguments on the issue defending working-class interests. M prepares a speech but is prevented from delivering it. **Sep c.18:** M begins to write up his undelivered speech from notes (for part of which, see #M705). **Sep CD:** M attempts to get the speech pubd; the Brussels *Atelier Démocratique* pubs it (or part of it) on Sep 29. For E's report of the speech (#E291), see → :40. The first part of the speech will later be pubd in pamphlet form (#M706). **Sep 19–22:** E writes an article for *DBZ* on the congress (#E234); pubd Sep 23. **33.** ECONOMICA. **Sep-Oct:** M's attention to the free-trade and tariff question during this period must be considered part of his continuing work on polit eco; note that it will lead [→ :53] to lectures on the subject. **34.** W&P. **Sep A:** The second part of M's critique of Grün [← :29] is pubd in *Westphälische Dampfboot*. **35.** TRIP TO THE NETHERLANDS. **Sep D to Oct A:** M goes off to visit his Dutch relatives, on financial matters (SOURCE: KMC). **36.** DEMOCRATIC ASSOC. **Sep 27:** While M is away, E attends a Democratic political banquet at which the Democratic Assoc of Brussels is founded. E agrees to accept the vice-presidency as a stand-in for M. **Sep 28–**

30: E writes to M describing the complex intrigues accompanying the affair. **37.** W&P (E). **Sep 26:** E writes the first part of a polemic against Heinzen (#E152) [→ :41].

OCTOBER

38. RETURN HOME. **Oct A:** M returns from the Netherlands. From now till Dec, M will continue negotiations with his mother regarding payment of part of his paternal inheritance, through the mediation of his brother-in-law Schmalhausen of Maastricht. **39.** BRUSSELS: MOVEMENT AFFAIRS. **Oct c.1:** M, still in the Netherlands, receives E's long letter [← :36] on the founding of the Democratic Assoc. **Oct 18:** The London CC of the CL asks the Brussels branch to send a delegate to the CL second congress, urges M to come himself. **Oct D:** Stephan Born arrives from Paris and visits M, on E's recommendation. —M and Jottrand, the editor of *Débat Social*, discuss problems of organizing the Democratic Assoc. —M writes A. Gottschalk (in Cologne) to push the sales of shares for the planned monthly organ [← :28] in order to finance the project. **Oct 26:** M asks Herwegh to support the plan to publish this monthly; in this letter M writes enthusiastically about the prospects of revolutionary activity in "little Belgium" even as compared with France. **40.** FREE-TRADE QUESTION. **Oct A:** M plans to write an essay on the issue. **Oct c.3:** To Lüning, M proposes publ of this essay in *Westphälische Dampfboot*. **Oct 9:** E pubs a report on the free-trade congress (#E291) in *NS* [← :32]. **41.** AGAINST HEINZEN. **Oct 3:** E writes the second part [← :37] of a polemic against Heinzen on some basic political issues (#E152); the article is pubd Oct 3, 7, in *DBZ*. **Oct 21:** Heinzen replies in *DBZ* with an abusive anticommunist blast. **Oct D:** M continues the argument with a long analysis of Heinzen's politics, "Moralizing criticism [etc.]" (#M531), which is pubd in *DBZ*, Oct 28 to Nov 25. **42.** ENGELS: TO PARIS. **Oct M:** E returns to Paris, to begin building a CL branch. **Oct CD:** E enters into relations with the Democratic left around *La Réforme*. **Oct 23:** E writes his first article for *La Réforme*, on England (#E151); pubd Oct 26. **Oct c.25:** E visits the office of the Christian Socialist organ *L'Atelier*, whose editors urge him to contribute; he gives them for publ a letter on the class struggle in England (#E472) [→ 49]. **Oct 30:** E writes an article on the Chartists for *La Réforme* (#E8) [→ 49]. **Oct D:** E tries unsuccessfully to persuade L. Blanc and Flocon that *La Réforme* should publish M's undelivered speech on the tariff issue [← :32].

43. ENGELS DRAFTS THE "PRINCIPLES." **Oct 22:** At a session of the Paris CL district exec, E criticizes Hess's draft of a communist credo; the exec charges E with writing a new draft. **Oct D:** E works on a new draft program for the CL, later called "Principles of communism" (#E620), in catechistic form, for consideration by the CL [→ :45]. Note: Andréas has argued that E drafted it during the summer.

NOVEMBER

44. BRUSSELS DEMO ASSOC. **Nov 15:** M is elected vice-pres, replacing the departed E [← :36], at the assoc's second membership meeting; J. Imbert is president.

45. PREPARING THE CL CONGRESS. **Nov 14:** The Paris district exec elects E as its delegate. **Nov 23/24:** In a letter to M, E suggests dropping the catechistic form of the communist credo [← :43] and calling it "Communist manifesto." **Nov c.26:** Before leaving Brussels, M commissions S. Born to speak for the Brussels Workers Assoc at the international fête for Poland taking place in Brussels on Nov 29. **Nov 27:** M travels with Victor Tedesco from Brussels to London as delegate to the CL congress. They meet E, coming from Paris, in Ostend, and spend the night there, discussing congress problems. **Nov 29:** They arrive in London (SOURCE: *MEW, KMC;* according to ST/56, M arrives in London on Nov 28 and E on Nov 29 after traveling Ostend–Dover on the ship *Onyx*).

46. CL SECOND CONGRESS. **Nov 29:** In London, M&E attend the international meeting organized by the Fraternal Democrats to celebrate the anniversary of the 1830 Polish uprising; both give speeches on Poland (#M833, #E768) [→ :54]. M gives the Fraternal Democrats a communication from the Brussels Demo Assoc urging closer relations. At a banquet, in the name of the Demo Assoc, M invites those present to an international Democratic congress to be organized next year [→ :52]. **Nov 29 to Dec 8:** CL holds its second congress, with M&E taking an active part (see → :50). **Nov 30:** M&E give talks at a meeting of the London GWEA (for minutes, see #M749, #E430A). M reports on the Brussels Workers Assoc and discusses leftist literature in France and Germany, esp Blanc's history of the French Revolution; E talks on the socioeconomic consequences of the discovery of America.

47. PERSONAL. **Nov 9:** M asks his brother-in-law Schmalhausen [← :38] for a loan. **Nov c.15:** He receives 150 francs.

48. W&P (M). **Nov 11–25:** *DBZ* pubs the last parts of M's polemic against Heinzen (#M531) [← :41].

49. W&P (E). **Nov 1–30:** Work for *La Réforme:* E pubs his article on Chartism (#E8) [← :42], and writes another on the Chartist electoral banquet (#E137), pubd Nov 6; Nov 21, he writes again on Chartism (#E138), pubd Nov 22; and Nov 30 E writes a report of the Poland meeting of Nov 29 (#E20) [→ :54]. **Nov 6–D:** Work for *NS:* It reprints Nov 6 the article in *La Réforme* on Chartism (#E8) [← Nov 1]; Nov A, E writes an article on Lamartine (#E466), pubd Nov 13, and also an article on the French reform movement (#E657), pubd Nov 20; Nov D, he writes an article on the split in the French left (#E771) [→ :57]. **Nov c.10:** E writes an article for *DBZ* on Switzerland (#E144); pubd Nov 14. **Nov:** E's article on England (#E472) [← :42] is pubd in *L'Atelier.*

DECEMBER

50. CL SECOND CONGRESS. **Dec A:** As the congress continues [← :45], M&E are commissioned to write the programmatic manifesto of the movement; the Rules are changed in the direction of an open, democratic structure in accord with M&E's proposals. M carries on discussions with Chartist leaders also: Harney, Jones, et al. **Dec 7:** E gives a lecture at the London GWEA on economic crises and overproduction (#E430B). **Dec 9:** Finding himself in bad financial straits, M asks Annenkov (in Paris) to lend 100–200 francs, to be sent to Brussels. **Dec c.13:** M leaves London to return to Brussels. **Dec 17:** Ditto E.

51. *COMMUNIST MANIFESTO.* **Dec 9–c.13:** M&E work on the *Manifesto* [see ← :50] while still in London. **Dec CD to Jan CD:** M works on it in Brussels. (Besides #ME33, see also #ME34, 35.)

52. ACTIVITY IN BRUSSELS. **Dec 18:** Harney writes M that his proposal for an international Democratic congress [← :46] has been unanim approved by the Fraternal Democrats, London GWEA, and Chartists. **Dec 20:** At the Demo Assoc, M reports on the Polish meeting of Nov 29 in London, and Harney's acceptance of the congress proposal. The Assoc names E as its representative in Paris. **Dec 23:** M and Bornstedt protest at the office of the *Journal de Bruxelles* against that paper's attacks on foreigners in Brussels. **Dec 26:** At the Demo Assoc, M supports the admission to membership of Bakunin and d'Ester. **Dec 31:** At the New Year's Eve celebration by the German Workers Assoc, M gives a short talk in the form of a toast, stressing appreciation of Belgium's democratic freedoms (see *MECW* 6:639).

53. ECONOMICA. **Dec CD:** M gives lectures at the German Workers Assoc on polit eco, and prepares the lectures for publ [→ 48:8] as a pamphlet on "Wages" (#M970; see also #M968–969, and notes on #M231).

54. PUBL: SPEECHES ON POLAND. **Dec 3–4:** Reports on M&E's speeches of Nov 29 appear in *Deutsche Londoner Ztg* and NS. **Dec 5:** E's report of the Nov 29 meeting (#E20) is pubd in *La Réforme* [← :46]. **Dec 9:** The speeches (#M833, #E768) are pubd in *DBZ*.

55. PUBL: DEFENSE OF COMMUNISM. **Dec c.17:** M writes an article defending the communists against Bartels (#M732); pubd in *DBZ*, Dec 19. **Dec 24:** M writes in defense against attacks by Lamartine (#M441); pubd Dec 26.

56. ENGELS: BRUSSELS TO PARIS. **Dec c.20:** The London Fraternal Democrats ask E to be their representative in Paris. **Dec 20:** M

Ditto the Brussels Demo Assoc (see ← :52). **Dec D:** E goes to Paris. **Dec 31:** E gives a talk at the New Year's Eve celebration of the German émigrés in Paris.

57. PUBL (E). **Dec 4:** NS pubs E's article on France (#E771) [← :49]. **Dec AB:** E writes two articles on the French reform movement (#E656, 658) for NS; pubd Dec 18. **Dec 30:** E pubs articles on France (#E659, 455) in *DBZ*, and an article on England (#E136) in *La Réforme*.

YEAR APPENDIX

58. In the course of his studies (see the reading list for 1846: ← 46:51–53), M seems to have read G. von Gülich during 1847, though the dividing line is uncertain; also D. Macpherson. One should also check the works mentioned by M in *Poverty of philosophy* (#M681), e.g., the list in *MECW* 6:739–46.

1848

CONSPECTUS

1. The beginning of this fateful year finds M in Brussels and E (till Jan D) in Paris. The *Com Manifesto* is pubd just before the "February Revolution" breaks out in France. After a short preparatory period in Paris, M&E return to Germany Apr A, and begin publishing the *Neue Rheinische Ztg* in Cologne on June 1. Until the NRZ's last issue on May 19 of next year, both M&E are intensively involved in writing for and editing the paper, and in activity in Cologne's Democratic Assoc and Workers Assoc, while resisting harassment by the Prussian authorities. Threatened by arrest, E and some other NRZ editors have to flee Cologne Oct A (till next Jan). Most of this time E is in Switzerland, while M carries on the NRZ work nearly singlehandedly, in the face of increasing repression.

JANUARY

2. *COM MANIFESTO.* **Jan 24:** The Communist League's Central Comm (CL/CC) in London sends M a warning that he has until Feb 1 to finish the *Manifesto*, or measures will be taken. **Jan CD:** M finishes the *Manifesto*. **Jan D:** He sends it to the printer in London, prob right after receiving the CL/CC's warning. (This may be dated Feb A.)

3. FREE TRADE. **Jan 9:** M gives a lecture on this subject at a public meeting of the Demo Assoc, which votes to publish it as a pamphlet (#M836) [→ :8].

4. DEMOCRATIC ASSOC. **Jan c.17–c.23:** M

goes to Ghent with a delegation to establish a branch.

5. PUBL (E). **Jan 8, 10, 19:** E pubs articles on the Chartist movement in England (#E148, 140, 139) in *La Réforme*. **Jan 9:** E pubs an article on O'Connor and the Irish (#E275) in *DBZ*.

6. PUBL ON THE EVE OF REVOLUTION. **Jan 8, 22:** E pubs two articles on France (#E723, 261) in NS. **Jan 16:** M sums up the French situation (#M820) in *DBZ*. **Jan 19:** *La Réforme* reprints this piece (#M820) in Paris. **Jan 23:** E pubs an important survey of Europe on the eve, "The movements of 1847" (#E497). **Jan 27:** Ditto on Austria (#E75).

7. ENGELS EXPELLED FROM FRANCE. **Jan 29:** The tottering government expels E for revolutionary activity in Paris workers' circles. **Jan 31:** E returns to Brussels (*KMC* dates this Feb M).

FEBRUARY

8. ECONOMICA. **Feb:** M prepares his lectures on "Wages" [← 47:53] for pamphlet publ, and gives the ms to the Brussels printer Callewaert (#M969); but publ will be aborted by the outbreak of revolution [→ 48:31]. **Feb A:** M's pamphlet on free trade (#M836) [← :3] is pubd.

9. PERSONAL. **Feb c.10:** M receives from his mother a part of his paternal inheritance, 6000 francs [← 47:38]. **Feb 19:** M moves from the rue d'Orléans [← 46:44.5] back to Brussels proper, Plaine Ste-Gudule. **Feb 26:** He so notifies the police.

10. BRUSSELS DEMO ASSOC. **Feb 6:** *Débat Social* (Bartels) attacks communist influence in the Assoc. **Feb c.10:** M writes a polemical reply (#M213); pubd in *DBZ*, Feb 13. **Feb 13:** M takes part as the Assoc decides to convene an international congress of Democrats as previously suggested [← 47:46]. The Assoc adopts a reply to the London Fraternal Democrats [← 47:52], signed by M as vice-pres, which includes a report on the progress of the Assoc (#M57) [→ :17]. **Feb 20:** At a meeting with M in the chair, E tells of his expulsion from France and refutes the *Moniteur Parisien* (government version) news report pubd Feb 24 (cf *MECW* 6:643). **Feb 22:** M&E give speeches at a public meeting held by the Assoc on the anniversary of the Polish uprising of 1846 in Cracow (#M825, #E769) [→ :21]. At this meeting a controversy between M and Jottrand leads M to hand in his resignation as vice-pres, but he withdraws it after Jottrand's letter of Feb 25.

11. PUBL ON THE EVE: ENGELS IN *DBZ*. **Feb 20:** E pubs an article on the overthrow of three absolutisms (#E807). **Feb 24:** Ditto in defense of Italian liberation from Austria (#E920).

12. *COM MANIFESTO* PUBD. **Feb c.24:** The *Manifesto* (#ME33) comes off the press in London.

13. REVOLUTION IN PARIS. **Feb 22:** Demonstrations and barricades: fighting begins in the streets. **Feb 23:** The king dismisses Guizot; the workers continue fighting, and by morning are winning. **Feb 24:** Louis Philippe abdicates; a republic is proclaimed by the Provisional Government in response to mass demand.

14. IMPACT IN BRUSSELS. **Feb 25–26:** The news from Paris galvanizes the Belgian republican movement; M&E take an active part. E writes the article "Revolution in Paris" (#E700), greeting the outbreak; pubd in *DBZ*, Feb 27. **Feb 27:** The Demo Assoc, following M's lead, decides to propose to the City Council that the regular Civil Guard be supplemented by an armed force of workers to "maintain public peace and avoid all bloodshed." **Feb 27–28:** M is involved in drawing up two addresses by the Assoc: one, directed to *NS* and the Fraternal Democrats, reports on the Assoc's activities, esp its proposal to arm the Brussels workers (#M888); a second one greets the Prov Government of the new French republic and congratulates France on the revolution (#M892) [→ :16].

15. COMMUNIST LEAGUE. **Feb c.27:** The CL/CC (London), seeing that the focus of revolution has shifted to the Continent, transfers its powers to the Brussels district Exec led by M.

MARCH

16. LAST DAYS IN BELGIUM. **Mar 1:** The French Prov Government (Flocon) writes M, voiding the Guizot regime's previous expulsion order: "free France opens its doors to you" (text: *MECW* 6:649). The address by the Brussels Demo Assoc to the Prov Government (#M892) [← :14] is pubd in Brussels. **Mar 2:** A Belgian royal decree orders M to leave the country in 24 hours (text: *MECW* 6:650). **Mar 3:** M receives this decree at 5 P.M.; also Flocon's communication prob the same day. The Brussels CL Exec decides to use its authority [← :15] to transfer the League seat to Paris (#ME45), and charges M to form a new CL/CC in Paris, with "full discretionary powers."

17. EXPULSION. **Mar 3–4** (night): The police break into M's house about 1 A.M. while he is busy with going-away preparations, and arrest him; later on Mar 4 his wife is arrested too. After 18 abusive hours in jail M and his family are forced to leave Belgium instanter (travel document: *MECW* 6:653). **Mar 4:** The Demo Assoc's address to the Prov Government (#M892) [← :16] is reprinted in Paris. The Assoc's report to London (#M57) [← :10] is pubd in *NS*. **Mar 5:** E, in Brussels, is active in the protest campaign against government harassment of M and other émigrés; he writes it up for *NS* (#E825), where after some delay it is pubd Mar 25. **Mar A:** M makes notes on police abuse of W. Wolff, Feb 27 to Mar 1 (#M584).

18. *COM MANIFESTO*. **Mar 3:** *Deutsche Londoner Ztg* begins printing the *Manifesto* in 13 installs, ending July 28. **Mar:** The pamphlet goes through three different printings of the first edn.

19. MARX IN PARIS. **Mar 5:** M arrives and takes lodgings (at least by Mar 12–13) at 10 rue Neuve-Ménilmontant. **Mar 6:** M takes part in a meeting of German workers in Paris on the revolutionary crisis in France. **Mar c.6:** M writes an open letter for *La Réforme* on his expulsion from Belgium and the police brutality against his wife (#M895); and writes the London CL of the Brussels decision to transfer the Exec to Paris [← :16]. **Mar 8:** The open letter (#M895) is pubd in *La Réforme*. The Londoners approve the decision to transfer. **Mar c.6 to Mar M:** M and the Paris CL combat the plan of the German Demo Assoc in Paris (Herwegh, Bornstedt, et al) to form an adventurist "German Legion" of émigrés to march from France into Germany and import the revolution; M instead proposes an unadvertised return to Germany and activity to form workers' assocs throughout the country; meanwhile they should participate in Paris in the expected uprising. **Mar 6–c.10:** M meets with English Chartists (Harney, Jones) and German comrades (Schapper, H. Bauer, Moll, etc.) to plan activity.

20. CL ACTIVITY. **Mar 8:** The four CL branches in a joint meeting (Schapper as chair, M as secy) merge into a unified Paris district organizn, which decides to set up a German Workers Club as a public organizn, H. Bauer as pres. M is commissioned to draft its by-laws immediately (M's minutes: *MECW* 6:654). **Mar 9:** A follow-up CL meeting adopts M's draft by-laws unamended. On M's proposal it resolves that every member is to wear a red ribbon, and all must give the secy their (preferred) name and address (M's minutes: *MECW* 6:656). **Mar 10:** The press announces that the German Workers Club will hold its first public meeting on Mar 14; M's name is on its exec. **Mar c.10:** M writes a piece for *La Réforme* on Belgian police persecution of foreign radicals (#M650), using his notes on Wolff (#M584) [← :17]; pubd Mar 12.

21. MEANWHILE BACK IN BRUSSELS. . . . **Mar 11:** In parliament, Deputy Bricourt interpellates the min of justice on M's expulsion and police abuse of Mrs. M. **Mar c.15:** The pamphlet with M&E's speeches on Poland (#M825, #E769) [← :10] is pubd. **Mar 18:** Before leaving Brussels for Paris, E writes an article for *La Réforme* on the Belgian situation (#E746); unpubd. **Mar 25:** The Brussels City Council resolves to dismiss the assistant police commissioner G. Daxbeek for his harsh tactics in carrying out the expulsion decree against the Marxes.

22. THE CL IN PARIS. **Mar 11:** The CL's new CC is set up in Paris, as previously decided [← :16]; M is chairman, Schapper secy; members are H. Bauer, Moll, Wallau, W. Wolff, also E in absentia. **Mar c.14:** M visits Flocon at the office of *La Réforme*. **Mar c.15:** M begins preparations to organize the return of CL members and others to Germany and to publish an organ there. **Mar 16:** In the CL, M moves to expel Bornstedt, who is publicly helping to form the "German Legion" in opposition to the CL.

23. REVOLUTION IN BERLIN ("MARCH REVOLUTION"). **Mar 18–19:** Excited demonstrations, fired on by troops, turn into barricade fighting. On the second day King Friedrich Wilhelm IV of Prussia capitulates and agrees to grant a constitution someday. **Mar 29:** The Camphausen government takes office in Prussia.

24. ENGELS: TO PARIS. **Mar c.21:** E leaves Brussels for Paris.

25. CONTACTS WITH LONDON. **Mar 19:** The London CL sends 1000 copies of the *Com Manifesto* to the Paris organizn; it also apprises M of negotiations in London with the ex-duke of Brunswick for material aid to the revolution. **Mar 22:** It reports to M that nothing has come of these negotiations; it also announces the big Chartist demonstration planned in London for Apr 10. **Mar c.26:** M sends Schapper to London to resume negotiations with the ex-duke. **Mar 28:** Schapper writes back that the negotiations have fallen apart.

26. PREPARING THE RETURN TO GERMANY. **Mar 18, 25:** Daniels and Weerth send M reports on the situation in Cologne. **Mar 21–24:** M&E draft the "Demands of the Communist party in Germany" (#ME47) for a flysheet, to distribute with the *Manifesto*. **Mar c.23:** M requests Weydemeyer to report the work of the German Workers Club in Paris in the German press and to propagandize against the German Legion being formed in France. **Mar 24–25:** The "Demands" (#ME47) come off the press as a flysheet, for use with the *Manifesto* by CL supporters returning to Germany. **Mar 30:** The Préfet de Police issues M a French passport, good for a year.

27. LAST DAYS IN PARIS. **Mar D:** M&E, visiting Flocon, are offered money for the German paper they plan; they decline to take any. —M meets Annenkov once again. — The press attacks by M and the CL on the German Legion anger Herwegh and Bornstedt into sharper conflict (cf #ME175). M sends statements to the Paris press to publicize Communist disavowal of the Legion; one such statement (#ME87) is sent to Cabet for his *Populaire*. —The CL begins sending advance organizers into Germany, esp Wallau to Mainz, to establish workers' assocs, with Mainz as center of a projected network. The CL mobilizes about 300–400 people associated with the German Workers Club for the return, most of whom will leave Paris Apr 1. To finance these activities, M puts more of his own legacy money [← :9] at the disposal of the organizn.

APRIL

28. FROM PARIS TO COLOGNE. **Apr c.1:** The bulk of the CL supporters in Paris leave for Germany by different routes. **Apr c.4:** M meets with Venedey to discuss the German Legion. **Apr c.6:** M&E leave Paris and set out for Germany, together with W. Wolff, Dronke, et al. **Apr 8:** M&E, in Mainz, consult with the CL members there, esp Wallau, on the plans to form a network of workers' assocs. (*KMC* dates this stay Apr 7–9.)

29. IN COLOGNE. **Apr 11:** M&E, with Dronke, arrive from Mainz, putting up at the hotel Im Laacher Hof. They immediately begin making preparations to publish a daily paper. M will move to Apostelstrasse 7. **Apr**

13: The Cologne Workers Assoc is formed at a meeting called by A. Gottschalk. —M formally requests (#M51) the Cologne police authorities to reinstate his Prussian citizenship (for renunciation, see ← 45:46). **Apr c.M:** A friend of Prime Min Camphausen makes M an offer to join Camphausen in Berlin; it is immediately rejected. —The Cologne City Council grants M's petition for domiciliary permission in the city (in view of the Prussian citizenship problem). —The CL/CC under M's direction sends out organizers (Dronke, Wolff, Schapper, et al) to different cities to form workers' assocs and CL branches (*KMC* dates this Apr c.19). **Apr 19:** Police Inspector Hünermund interviews the "politically unreliable Dr. KM" re his citizenship application; the police begin to stall the application (cf *MECW* 7:538).

30. PREPARING THE *NRZ*. **Apr c.24:** Bürgers issues a prospectus for the *Neue Rheinische Ztg* (cf *MECW* 7:539). M calls Dronke and F. Wolff back to Cologne to join the ed board; he also asks Heine, via Ewerbeck, to write for it. **Apr D to May:** M carries on correspondence with the CL organizers in other cities, on CL work and on the campaign to get subscriptions to *NRZ* shares.

31. PUBL. **Apr 5 & later:** The "Demands" (#ME47) are reprinted in Düsseldorf, Berlin, Cologne, etc. **Apr 24:** M is informed by pub'r Vogler that the Brussels printer Callewaert [← :8] wants more ms and more money for the brochure on wages (#M969) which is standing in type, or he will break up the type. (But M is too busy to ensure publ and the printing will not take place.) **Apr or May:** The second pamphlet edn ("30-page edn") of the *Com Manifesto* is pubd in London.

32. ENGELS: TO BARMEN. **Apr c.14:** E goes to towns in the Rhineland, incl in Wuppertal, to sell shares for *NRZ* financing, also to build CL branches where possible. **Apr CD:** In Barmen, E works at translating the *Com Manifesto* into English. **Apr 25:** E writes M that he has finished over half the *Manifesto* (not extant).

MAY

33. REPORTS AND PERSPECTIVES. **May A:** M asks S. Born (in Berlin) to report on the city's CL branch, general press, and political situation. **May c.3:** M receives from Ewerbeck a report on the Paris CL and its relations with French workers. **May c.6–8:** M and Weerth go to Elberfeld, and talk with E (in Barmen) about *NRZ* finances and the formation of a CL branch locally. **May 11:** At the Cologne CL, with M presiding, M asks Gottschalk his attitude toward the CL; Gottschalk says he is resigning but is willing to help

League work (cf *MECW* 7:542). —From Berlin, Born, who is drifting away from communist views, reports on his own moderate role in the workers' movement. **May D:** On the basis of reports during this month from CL organizers around Germany (W. Wolff in Breslau, Stumpf in Mainz, Dronke reporting from Coblenz, Frankfurt, Nassau, etc.), M and the CL conclude that the League is still too weak, and the organizn of workers' assocs too difficult, for the League to affect the mass movement that is coming into existence. M turns toward concentrating on the Demo Assocs and the existing workers' assocs: M himself will join the Demo Assoc, and the Cologne CL will divide its forces between the Democratic movement and the Cologne Workers Assoc.

34. PREPARING THE *NRZ*. **May c.3:** M hears from Ewerbeck [← :30] that Heine is willing to write for *NRZ*. **May M:** M informs Jottrand (in Brussels), via Weerth, about the coming publ of *NRZ*. **May 19:** Jottrand replies that he is willing to work for the paper's distribution in Belgium, and asks M to maintain regular correspondence. **May 20:** E returns to Cologne [← :32] from Barmen and plunges into *NRZ* preparatory work. **May CD** (after May 20): M&E decide to advance the date of publ from July 1 to June 1, in view of the tense situation. **May D:** M writes (#M912) to the leftist Florence daily *L'Alba*, for relations with *NRZ*; it will be pubd June 29. —A meeting of *NRZ* shareholders elects a provisional comm for final editing of the Articles of the *NRZ* Company [→ :38]. **May 31:** M drafts the *NRZ*'s editorial statement (#M855) for publ in the first issue, which appears this evening, dated June 1.

JUNE

35. *NRZ* BEGINS PUBLICATION. **June 1:** This is the date of the first issue (out the previous evening). Throughout the life of *NRZ* (June 1 to Sep 27, Oct 12 to next May 19) M will be overloaded with editorial responsibilities, with E doing much of the writing. This first issue carries a sharp criticism of the National Assembly in Frankfurt by E (#E44, 362); also E on the repression in Naples (#E424). **June 2:** M's first article, "The Democratic party" (#M232) is pubd. **June A:** The first week of the paper sees other articles spelling out a radical policy on the revolution and the government (#M128, 127; #ME90, 126, 32, and esp 117); also articles by E on the conflict with Denmark over Schleswig-Holstein (#E213, 270), and on Italy's liberation (#E647). —As a result of the sharp line of antigovernment criticism taken in *NRZ*, a large number of shareholders pull out.

36. SHELVING THE COMMUNIST LEAGUE.

June A: The NRZ office sees a lively discussion by the CL group over the question of continued League activity as such. M&E put through the policy that under existing conditions the CL should be shelved in favor of operating through NRZ as the communist political center. (It is not certain whether the CL is *formally* disbanded at this point.) Henceforward the communist tendency organizes through NRZ, the Cologne Workers Assoc, and the Demo Assoc.

37. NRZ: SECOND WEEK. June 8–14: M&E concentrate on revolutionary criticism of the Berlin (Prussian) Assembly and the Camphausen government's policy of conciliating the crown by a deal (see *Vereinbarung policy). Main articles: #E160, 156, 76; also #ME125, 153, 46; article on the situation in Cologne, #E150; on Prussian Poland, #E512. **June 14:** The end of the second week is marked by the mass storming of the Arsenal in Berlin.

38. NRZ: THIRD WEEK AND AFTER. June 15–20: The paper continues its attacks on the Berlin Assembly. Main article: #E165; also #ME38, 189, 168; on the situation in Cologne, #ME115; on foreign events, #E513 (Prussian Poland), #E599 (Czech revolution). **June 18, 21:** Meetings of NRZ shareholders [← :34] settle the Articles of the Company (cf MECW 7:543), which will be pubd in July. **June 19–26:** The NRZ's feuilleton section offers the proceedings of the French National Convention of 1792–93 which condemned Louis XVI to death. **June 20:** The Camphausen government falls (#ME51, 57). **June 25:** It is replaced by the Hansemann cabinet (so-called Government of Action). **June 23–26:** NRZ's main articles include pieces on the Frankfurt (National) Assembly, #E280, also #ME170; on the Berlin government, #ME73, 128; on England, #ME98; on the Czech revolution, #E216; and an important first article on the demands of the peasantry against feudal obligations, #ME113 (June 25).

39. THE DEMOCRATIC ASSOC. June 14–17: The First Democratic Congress in Frankfurt is attended by Schapper, Moll, and others of the NRZ group, but not M. **June c.23:** M is elected a delegate of the Cologne Demo Assoc to a conference discussing coordination of the three Democratic organizations in the Rhineland; Schapper and Moll represent the Workers Assoc. **June 24:** M takes part in the conference, which sets up a Rhineland district comm or exec of the Democrats, to which he is elected.

40. JUNE UPRISING IN PARIS ("JUNE DAYS"). Jan 23: Workers build barricades and prepare for a desperate armed resistance to the government's attack on the National Workshops. **Jan 24:** The Assembly appoints Gen. Cavaignac dictator to suppress the revolt. **June 25:** Heavy fighting; the workers hold the right bank. **June 26:** The workers' last stronghold, in the Faubourg Saint-Antoine, is overcome. The government begins a systematic massacre of prisoners.

41. NRZ ON THE JUNE UPRISING. June 25: NRZ prints first reports (#ME102). **June 26–29:** E's articles describe the revolt as a working-class insurrection (#E219, 879, 876, 875; also #ME103, #M558). **June 29:** M pubs an important programmatic analysis, "The June revolution" (#M425).

JULY

42. NRZ: MORE ON PARIS. July 1–3: E summarizes the events of the uprising (#E410, 403); M&E discuss Marrast and Thiers (#ME93).

43. NRZ: ON THE EUROPEAN REVOLUTION. July 3: It expresses support to revolutionary aims abroad (#E331). **July 12:** Article on the Czech revolution (#ME65). **July 25:** Article on Italy (#ME188). **July 21–28:** It discusses the conflict with Denmark (#E265, 35, 33, 34).

44. NRZ: CRITIQUE OF ASSEMBLY AND GOVERNMENT. July 4–15, 26: E continues his detailed analysis of how the Berlin parliamentarians are voiding the revolution (#E157, 158, 161, 154, 164, 162, 159, 163). **July 9–10:** Articles on cabinet crises (#M354, 513). **July 14, 26–30:** Articles on financial policy (#ME75, 22). **July 18–25:** E pubs a major article on the Frankfurt Assembly (#E206). **July 30:** M defends the peasant demands for the abolition of feudal obligations (#M84).

45. GOVERNMENT HARASSMENT. July 4: NRZ reports the arrest of Gottschalk and Anneke on July 3 (#ME13). **July 5:** NRZ describes the arrest of Anneke and attacks the authorities responsible, esp Chief Public Prosecutor Zweiffel and Public Prosecutor Hecker, in an article "Arrests" (#ME14). On the ground of this article, Hecker accuses NRZ of "defamations and insults" against Zweiffel and announces legal proceedings. **July 6:** M is haled before an examining magistrate for interrogation; he and Korff (NRZ's responsible editor) are charged with slander against Zweiffel. Then, searching the NRZ office, the police seize a ms written in an unidentified hand; M refuses to name its writer. The authorities remand M and Korff for trial, also E and Dronke. **July 7:** NRZ reports this case (#M450; cf MECW 7:554). **July 11:** Eleven NRZ typesetters are questioned by a magistrate about the unidentified ms; in an article M analyzes Prussian law on "defamation" (#M451). **July 22:** M is again interrogated by a magistrate on the alleged defamation (cf *MECW* 7:555).

46. NRZ: THE BAKUNIN RUMOR. **July 6:** NRZ prints a Paris dispatch from Ewerbeck saying that George Sand has evidence that Bakunin is a Russian agent. **July 16:** NRZ reprints from a Breslau paper Bakunin's statement against this Paris report [→ :50].

47. NRZ: FINANCES. **July M:** M vainly tries to get money for the paper from Gigot and pub'r Vogler (Brussels).

48. REPRESSION OF THE DEMOCRATIC CLUBS. **July 20:** NRZ attacks the suppression of the Demo Clubs in Stuttgart and Heidelberg (#E793) and the Prussian bill against freedom of the press (#M712). **July 21–24:** NRZ criticizes the bill to straitjacket the militia (#ME94). **July 28:** NRZ attacks the ban on the clubs in Baden (#E226).

49. THE MOVEMENT IN COLOGNE. **July 6:** The Workers Assoc elects Moll as pres, Schapper as vice-pres; the NRZ group is in control. **July 21:** At the Cologne Demo Assoc, M is elected a member of the Rhineland district Exec. —Weitling gives a speech advocating a personal dictatorship in the revolution; M postpones taking the floor [→ :55], and meanwhile arranges distribution of the *Com Manifesto*.

AUGUST

50. THE BAKUNIN RUMOR. **Aug 2:** The Polish Democrat, W. Kościelski, calls on M on Bakunin's behalf [← :46]; M convinces him that NRZ had no alternative on receiving the report sent from Paris by a collaborator (Ewerbeck) but to print it. Kościelski writes Bakunin he will no longer act as his second. **Aug 3:** M prints in NRZ a letter by George Sand (cf #M71) repudiating the accusation against Bakunin.

51. NRZ: ON REVOLUTION AND COUNTER-REVOLUTION. **Aug 2:** Article on the Berlin Assembly (#E155). **Aug 3–4:** On the worsening of criminal penalties in Prussia (#M515, #ME74). **Aug 4:** On state finances (#ME82). **Aug 6:** On the peasantry and feudal obligations (#E209). **Aug 27:** For Rhenish independence from Prussia (#E925).

52. NRZ: ON REVOLUTION IN EUROPE. **Aug 1:** Article on the class struggle in England (#E408). **Aug 2–27:** Articles supporting the Italian liberation struggle (#E481, 396, 135, 409). **Aug 3:** Against Russian aims in Europe (#ME148). **Aug 5:** On Proudhon vs Thiers in France (#ME121). **Aug 7:** On pauperism in Belgium (#M523). **Aug 9 to Sep 7:** A long series of articles on the Frankfurt Assembly and the Polish question (Prussian Poland) (#E205). **Aug 11:** A note on Denmark

(#E202). **Aug 26:** Prussia and Denmark sign an armistice at Malmö [→ :60].

53. MARX AND CITIZENSHIP. **Aug 3:** Police Chief Geiger informs M that the Rhineland Province government has denied his application for restoration of citizenship [← :29] and continues to regard him as a foreigner. **Aug 4:** At a Demo Assoc meeting, E reports that the Prussian government is not only denying M's citizenship but also threatening expulsion. **Aug 5:** M informs Geiger he is appealing to the min of the interior, and still regards himself as a German citizen (#M889). **Aug 11:** The Cologne Demo Assoc forms a delegation to protest police measures against M and Schapper. M explains that the government authorities recently tried in vain to win him over [← :29] and now deny him citizenship when they have failed (cf *MECW* 7:562). **Aug 22:** M sends a communication to Interior Min Kühlwetter (cf #M174) requesting nullification of the provincial decision and restoration of his Prussian citizenship [→ :60].

54. MORE HARASSMENT. **Aug 3:** E is called for interrogation before a magistrate in re the legal proceedings instituted against NRZ [← :45] (cf *MECW* 7:560). **Aug 5:** NRZ protests the inquisitorial treatment of Gottschalk (#ME50). **Aug 11:** Dronke is called for interrogation (cf *MECW* 7:566). E reports to the Demo Assoc on the harassment of Schapper. **Aug 12–24:** NRZ pubs repeated attacks on the government's attempts to expel Schapper as a noncitizen (#ME16, 63, 64).

55. COLOGNE DEMOCRATIC ASSOC. **Aug 4:** The Democratic CC (incl M) issues a call for a Rhineland congress of Democratic organizations, to be held in Cologne on Aug 13 (#M40). —At a meeting of the Cologne Assoc, M sharply replies (#M748) to Weitling's speech for dictatorship [← :49]. E speaks on the government's refusal to restore M's citizenship (#E670). **Aug 11:** The Assoc adopts a protest to the Frankfurt Assembly against the incorporation of Posen (Poland) into the German federation (cf *MECW* 7:564; see also ← :54, Aug 11). **Aug 13–14:** The First Rhenish Democratic Congress, held in Cologne with 17 organizations represented, confirms the existing Rhenish district exec (incl M). **Aug 13:** E's speech at the congress stresses the Rhineland's hatred of Prussianism and Prussian officialdom (cf *MECW* 7:567). **Aug 14:** The congress decides to expand work among factory workers and peasants and to form branches in the villages. M (who does not make a speech) gets acquainted with Kinkel, Schily, Imandt.

56. BEGINNING OF PEASANT WORK. **Aug 26:** Workers Assoc members go to Worringen, near Cologne, to organize the countryside, esp peasants; a branch is formed [→ :64].

57. TRIP TO BERLIN AND VIENNA. **Aug 23:** M goes off to raise funds for NRZ and improve contacts with other workers' groups and the Democratic movement (cf MECW 7:568). **Aug 25–26:** In Berlin, M has discussions with d'Ester, Jung, G. Julius, et al; he meets with Köppen, and encounters Bakunin. **Aug 27:** M arrives in Vienna (cf MECW 7:569). **Aug 28:** M gives a talk at the Vienna Demo Assoc on problems of the revolution (#M832). **Aug 30:** M gives a talk at the First Vienna Workers Assoc, in the Josefstadt, on the role of the proletariat in the revolution (#M831).

SEPTEMBER

58. MARX'S TRIP (CONT'D). **Sep 2:** M gives a lecture on wage-labor and capital at the First Vienna Workers Assoc (#M449). **Sep A:** M has a conversation with Borroš on the national question in Austria and relations between German and Czech workers. **Sep 6:** M decides to break off his trip because of the tense situation in Cologne (see → :60); he leaves Vienna. **Sep c.7:** M stops off in Dresden. **Sep c.8–10:** M stops in Berlin: he attends a meeting of the Assembly, and meets leftist leaders, incl August Brass, J. Berends, and Polish Democratic leaders (of whom W. Kościelski will send him 2000 talers for NRZ on Sep 18). **Sep c.11:** M returns to Cologne.

59. NRZ: ON REVOLUTION IN EUROPE. **Sep 1, 3:** Articles on Italy and Belgium (#E478, 30).

60. COLOGNE: CRISIS AND REPRESSION. **Sep 4:** E is again interrogated by the examining magistrate (cf MECW 7:576), this time as a codefendant in the case against NRZ based on the "defamatory" article of July 5 ("Arrests," #ME14) [← :45]. **Sep 5:** NRZ pubs letters of Police Chief Geiger on M's citizenship and M's reply (#M174) [← :53]. **Sep 7:** The Cologne Demo Assoc calls a meeting in the Reitbahn (riding academy arena), where some thousands adopt protests against the armistice with Denmark [← :52] and the antidemocratic Militia Bill. The "Address" to the Frankfurt Assembly on the Danish question, which E has helped draft, is pubd in NRZ, Sep 9 (cf MECW 7:577). **Sep 8:** At the regular meeting of the Demo Assoc, several hundred new members join. **Sep A:** The "Demands" (#ME47) are reprinted in Cologne as a flysheet. **Sep c.10:** The "Demands" are distributed in several places in the Rhineland. **Sep 10:** A new leftist paper, the Neue Kölnische Ztg (subtitled "For citizens, peasants, and soldiers"), starts publishing, ed by Beust and Anneke, after being announced Sep 8. **Sep 11:** At a committee session of the Workers Assoc, E gives a long talk on the National Workshops' experience in France to refute the claim that their failure invalidates the "organization of labor" idea behind them; his speech gets great applause. Dronke gives an analysis of the cabinet crisis in Berlin (cf MECW 7:579). **Sep 12:** Interior Min Kühlwetter's letter to M rejects his appeal on citizenship (cf MECW 7:581). For more on the crisis, see → :62.

61. GERMANY: REVOLUTION AND COUNTER-REVOLUTION. **Sep 8:** The Hansemann government falls (resignation accepted Sep 10). **Sep 9–10:** E analyzes the new turn in NRZ (#E268, 350), and hints at refusal of funds to the government (#E235). **Sep 10:** New arrests: the government jails organizers in Wesseling; the threat of repression grows. **Sep 12:** Article on this threat in NRZ (#E39). **Sep 12–16:** NRZ prints a major series of articles by M on "The crisis and the counterrevolution" (#M197). **Sep 16:** The Frankfurt Assembly ratifies the armistice with Denmark [← :52], in what the left sees as a betrayal of national interests. (NRZ articles discuss this issue Sep 8–22: #E201, 203, 37, 650, 264.) As for consequences, see Frankfurt uprising [→ :63]. **Sep 17:** NRZ defends the right of the Berlin populace to exert pressure on the Assembly (#ME61), esp in reply to attacks (Sep 12) by the Kölnische Ztg against "mob pressure."

62. COLOGNE: THE CRISIS CONTINUES. **Sep 11** (evening): Soldiers of the Prussian garrison viciously provoke a brawl with civilians. **Sep 12:** A protest meeting by Democrats and radicals at city hall demands removal of the garrison regiment from the city; the military commander yields. The militia, comprising 5000 armed men, is mobilized, incl its Ninth Company (the "Red Company"), commanded by Karl Wachter, a Democrat, and including Schapper and other NRZ people. The leftists propose a Comm of Public Safety but the military reject it; Democratic and Workers Assoc leaders decide to call a mass meeting next day. Placards and announcements are printed up and posted all over the city during the night. **Sep 13** (noon): NRZ and the two assocs organize a midday mass meeting of several thousand on the Frankenplatz; W. Wolff acts as convenor, Bürgers as chairman; E and Dronke are among the speakers. The "Demands" (#ME47) are distributed. Wolff proposes, and E supports, the election of a Comm of Public Safety of 30, which includes M&E. The meeting also adopts an "address" to the Berlin Assembly, proposed by E, calling on deputies to resist forcible dissolution and to "defend their seats even against the force of bayonets." In the evening the Comm of Public Safety meets, with M&E and many other NRZ people present; H. Becker is elected chairman. **Sep 15:**

NRZ explains that the Comm of Public Safety will operate legally, that it is not a "Red conspiracy," and will usurp no power (cf MECW 7:582). **Sep M:** The Rhineland district comm of the Demo Assoc makes preparations for the second Rhenish Democratic Congress, scheduled for Sep 24 (but see → :65).

63. GERMANY: FRANKFURT UPRISING. **Sep 17:** In reaction to the Frankfurt Assembly's vote [← :61] for the Danish armistice, a huge mass meeting of protest covering the Frankfurt region takes place in a meadow. The people go back to the city and start raising barricades. The government summons troops to Frankfurt. **Sep 18:** The insurrection spreads in Frankfurt and environs. **Sep 19–20:** The uprising, supported by peasants from the surrounding countryside, is quelled by troops. **Sep 20–21:** E discusses the uprising in NRZ (#E884). **Sep 21:** Abortive attempt at an uprising in Baden. The Pfuel cabinet is formed in Prussia, representing a new turn to reaction.

64. COLOGNE AND THE RHINELAND: REPRESSION. **Sep 17:** A mass meeting in Worringen, near Cologne, called by the Cologne movement [← :56], rallies about 8000 people, with delegations from other Rhenish towns; Schapper is chairman, E secy. It declares for a Democratic and Social Republic, and recognizes the Cologne Comm of Public Safety, among other resolutions (cf MECW 7:586). **Sep 20:** A mass meeting in Cologne's Eisersche Saal (Eiser Hall), called by the Comm of Public Safety with the Demo Assoc and Workers Assoc, on the Danish armistice and the Frankfurt uprising, adopts a proclamation supporting the Frankfurt people and declaring the pro-armistice deputies to be traitors; E gives one of the speeches. **Sep 23:** The proclamation is printed in NRZ, and on placards and flysheets; the NRZ office declares its readiness to accept contributions for the Frankfurt fighters and their families (cf MECW 7: 588). NRZ pubs a leading article on the new Pfuel cabinet and the counterrevolution (#ME70).

65. COLOGNE: COUNTERREVOLUTION. **Sep 23–24:** The government makes preparations for its police action to arrest Cologne's left leaders. **Sep 25:** The Cologne police action is launched at 6 A.M. on this day which is scheduled to see the opening of the Democratic Congress [← :62]. The Cologne public prosecutor institutes court actions against E, W. Wolff, and Bürgers for conspiracy against the existing order and participation in the Sep 20 mass meeting. The Imperial Ministry of Justice instructs the Cologne prosecutor's office to institute proceedings against the Comm of Public Safety (cf #ME30), also against the

Demo Assoc and Workers Assoc as well as NRZ. Public Prosecutor Hecker is investigating participants in the Worringen meeting of Sep 17 (see NRZ article of Sep 26, #ME124). In the morning the police arrest Schapper and Becker; they seize Moll and Wachter but are forced to release them by the assembled crowd; they fail to find W. Wolff and E (cf #ME41, 15). The Second Rhenish Democratic Congress fails to open as scheduled because of the arrests, but M does come to the hall. At 1 P.M. a mass meeting in the Altenmarkt (Old Marketplace) is opened by Imandt, chaired by W. Wolff. M speaks to a Workers Assoc meeting in the Gasthaus Im Kranz, warning against police provocations to isolated actions; the moment for an armed uprising has not yet come; a premature action would end in a putsch, which would rob the working class of its fighting strength for the decisive day. In the afternoon there is a joint meeting of the Demo Assoc and Workers Assoc in the Eiersche Saal; M and his supporters again warn against premature actions. In face of threatened arrest, E, Dronke, W. Wolff, and F. Wolff leave Cologne. Prussian troops start to move into the city. A workers' meeting in the Altenmarkt disperses, and some begin building barricades. The Prussian commander decides to wait for daylight before attacking. But during the night the barricades are silently abandoned, in line with the warnings against putschist action which had been repeated all day.

66. NRZ BANNED. **Sep 26:** The government declares a state of siege (martial law) in Cologne. The military commander indefinitely suspends the publ of NRZ and other Democratic organs in the city. Printing of NRZ's issue of Sep 27 had already been started in haste (cf #ME159); this is the last issue before suspension of the paper. **Sep 28:** In a leaflet, NRZ informs subscribers of the ban, states it will reappear in a few days, and asks for subscriptions (cf MECW 7:590). **Sep D:** The fifth 10% installment is due from shareholders, but many of them withhold it, aggravating NRZ's money troubles. **Sep 30:** NRZ sends a communication to subscribers: it expects that the state of siege will be lifted on Oct 4 and that the paper will reappear Oct 5 (cf MECW 7:591). **Sep D:** Since the Neue Kölnische Ztg [← :60] is suspended too, an attempt is made by Mathilde Anneke (F. Anneke's wife), a militant feminist writer, to put it out as the Frauenzeitung (Women's Gazette), but this is quashed by the authorities.

67. ENGELS IN HIDING. **Sep 25 to Oct c.3:** After leaving Cologne a jump ahead of the police [← :65], E goes to Barmen and stays with his family. During this period he prob destroys many of his papers, incl letters from M.

OCTOBER

68. ENGELS: ON THE MOVE. **Oct 3:** In Cologne, Public Prosecutor Hecker issues a warrant for the arrest of E and Bürgers as fugitives (cf *MECW* 7:593). **Oct 4:** E, with Dronke, arrives in Brussels; he is arrested and jailed overnight. **Oct 5:** Brussels police expel them over the French border; they go to Paris (cf #ME84; also see *MECW* 7:594). **Oct c.10:** E leaves Paris and goes on a walking tour through France to Switzerland; this is the journey which E describes in "From Paris to Bern" (#E301) (dating from *MEW*; ST/56 dates the start Oct c.20). **Oct c.24:** E arrives in Geneva [→ :75].

69. COLOGNE: MORE REPRESSION. **Oct 1:** The public prosecutor's office institutes legal proceedings against M, E, and other *NRZ* editors for publ of an unsigned feuilleton, "Life and deeds of the famous knight Schnapphahnski" (a satire by Weerth). **Oct 3:** The state of siege is lifted, under pressure from Berlin, but the militia is not reconstituted nor are prisoners released. **Oct M:** Public Prosecutor Hecker objects to *NRZ*'s publ on Oct 14 of an article by the republican Friedrich Hecker. *NRZ* comments Oct 29 (#M718).

70. *NRZ* IN DISTRESS. **Oct:** With so many of the *NRZ* editors out of the city or in jail, M is left to hold the fort almost alone, at the same time suffering acutely from lack of money for the paper. **Oct 1:** At this due date for the autumn quarter's renewal of subscriptions, returns are slow. M sends out notices again [← :66] on Oct 3, as martial law ends, announcing the coming reappearance of the paper (cf *MECW* 7:592). **Oct 3–c.5:** Freiligrath, acquitted on Oct 3 in Düsseldorf on a charge of treason, accepts M's invitation to join the *NRZ* ed board. **Oct 10:** M issues loan certificates to raise money for *NRZ*. **Oct 12:** *NRZ* reappears, the first issue pubd since Sep 27. A statement (#M266) announces Freiligrath's accession. **Oct 13:** A retrospective article explains what happened in Cologne during the Sep crisis, "The 'Cologne revolution' " (#M152).

71. COLOGNE MOVEMENT UNDER PRESSURE. **Oct 1:** There is a successful organizing meeting at Wesseling (Wesslingen), outside Cologne. **Oct 5:** The Workers Assoc resumes meeting; its organ reappears, ed by W. Prinz. **Oct c.10–12:** A Workers Assoc delegation asks M to take over the presidency in the absence of Schapper and Moll; M hesitates because of his workload. **Oct 15:** The Workers Assoc holds another big rally in Worringen despite a ban by the authorities,

who however refrain from suppressing the meeting. **Oct 16:** At a committee session M agrees to become temporary pres of the Workers Assoc. He gives a talk on the revolutionary role of the working class, esp in the Vienna uprising. He proposes an address of greetings to the Vienna Workers Assoc, the election of delegates to the Second Democratic Congress in Berlin [→ :72], and devotion of the second hour of Assoc meetings to educational programs (cf *MECW* 7:595). **Oct c.21:** Deputy Bassermann attacks the Worringen meeting of Sep 17, in the Frankfurt Assembly (reported in *NRZ*, Oct 22). **Oct 22:** The Cologne Workers Assoc membership meeting, in Gürzenich, confirms M as pres, Röser as vice-pres, and elects Beust as delegate to the Democratic Congress in Berlin, where he is to make proposals based on the "Demands" (#ME47). M gives a talk on the undemocratic system of indirect voting in Germany (cf *MECW* 7:597). **Oct 24–25:** The responsible editor and printer of the Workers Assoc organ, Brocker-Everaerts, is tried and condemned for "defamation" of the public prosecutor and police who arrested Gottschalk and Anneke [← :45]; he is sentenced to a month in jail and the paper is ordered to post a big bond. **Oct 26:** The Workers Assoc starts an organ under another name, *Freiheit, Brüderlichkeit, Arbeit*, instead of posting the bond, with Röser as pub'r. **Oct-Nov:** New branches of the Assoc are organized in small towns and among the peasantry of the region; the "Demands" are distributed.

72. BERLIN AND VIENNA. **Oct 6–7 to 31:** A revolutionary uprising breaks out in Vienna, and is eventually suppressed by Windischgrätz's "Croat" troops; *NRZ* articles discuss it on Oct 12, 19 (#M777, 329). **Oct 16:** In Berlin, a violent clash takes place between the populace and the militia. **Oct 20:** Funeral demonstrations for the victims take place. **Oct 26–30:** At the Second German Democratic Congress, in Berlin, after lively conflicts the right wing walks out; the left elects the new CC headed by d'Ester, and adopts Beust's programmatic report. **Oct 29:** The congress issues a weakly worded appeal to the people [→ :77]. **Oct 30:** The congress left-wingers help to organize a large popular rally. **Oct 31:** A continuing huge demonstration presents a petition to the Assembly for aid to revolutionary Vienna. In the evening the crowd besieges the Assembly, which is rescued when the militia attacks the people; the Assembly then votes the proposal down. —In Vienna, Windischgrätz bombards the city into submission.

73. *NRZ*: OTHER ARTICLES. **Oct 14, 19, 20:** Articles on German affairs (#M654, 736, 735). **Oct 14, 22:** On French politics

(#M879, 730, 35). **Oct 22:** On Italy and Belgium (#M35, 522).

74. PERSONAL. Oct 26: M writes to E (in Geneva) about NRZ's reappearance, asks him to send articles, and transmits money and other info. **Oct D:** Through Vogler and Gigot, M receives the books and household things he had left behind in Brussels. **Oct:** M is visited by Bruno Bucher, brother of Lothar Bucher. **Oct-Nov:** There are attempts by Hess, Ewerbeck, and d'Ester to alienate M from the absent E.

NOVEMBER

75. ENGELS: IN SWITZERLAND. Nov A: After staying a few days in Geneva [← :68], E goes to Lausanne; there he enters into relations with the Lausanne Workers Assoc. **Nov c.7:** E goes from Lausanne to Neuchâtel; he writes an article on the canton for NRZ (#E259), pubd Nov 11. **Nov c.9:** E leaves Neuchâtel for Bern. **Nov M:** M writes to E about the money he has sent E and other fugitives from Cologne; assures him of continued regard despite malicious reports (see ← :74); and suggests that E go to Bern. **Nov 15:** In Bern, E applies to the canton authorities for residence permission as a political refugee (#E583.5) [→ :82] **Nov 20:** Dronke writes M from Paris that he has not received moneys due. **Nov 21:** Back in Cologne, a court hints that the fugitives (e.g., E and Dronke) might be acquitted if they give themselves up (cf MECW 8:499, 500). **Nov 29:** M writes E to send articles on Proudhon's activity, on Hungary, and on Swiss federalism. **Nov CD:** E pubs a dozen articles in NRZ on Swiss political affairs. Of these, the longest are #E505, 238, 237, 584, and an article on tension with Berlin, #E329. (Others: #E734, 520, 680, 204, 652, 735, 402.)

76. REACTION IN BERLIN. Nov 1–2: The king of Prussia ends constitutional pretenses and dismisses the Pfuel cabinet. **Nov 4:** The king appoints Count Brandenburg to head a new cabinet, without consulting the Berlin Assembly; popular hostility to the government mounts. **Nov 9:** Count Brandenburg adjourns the Assembly to Nov 27, when it is to reconvene outside Berlin, in the town of Brandenburg; a majority of the Assembly defies the order. —In Vienna, Robert Blum, a leader of the Frankfurt Assembly left who aided the Austrian fighters, is shot by order of a court-martial. **Nov 10:** Gen. von Wrangel enters Berlin with 10,000 troops and orders recalcitrant deputies to adjourn under the threat of bayonets. **Nov 11:** The Assembly declares Count Brandenburg guilty of high treason, and appoints a commission to discuss

tax refusal as a weapon. **Nov 14:** A state of siege is declared in Berlin.

77. NRZ AGITATION. Nov: At this juncture M is still bearing the editorial work of NRZ, responsibility as pres of the Workers Assoc [← :71], and work as a leader of the Demo Assoc and the Rhenish Democratic district comm. **Nov 1:** NRZ pubs an appeal for the organizn of a partisan corps to support revolutionary Vienna. **Nov 3:** In NRZ, M sharply criticizes the weakness of the Oct 29 appeal issued by the Democratic Congress in Berlin (#M46) [← :72]. **Nov 6:** At a session of the committee of the Workers Assoc, M reports on the fall of Vienna; he stresses the betrayal of the bourgeoisie (cf MECW 7:598). **Nov A:** M pubs a number of NRZ articles on the Vienna revolution (#M964, 445, 559, 961), and articles on other subjects (#M633, 624, 78).

78. TAX-REFUSAL CAMPAIGN. Nov 11: M picks up the idea tentatively suggested in Berlin—tax refusal as a mass weapon against the government. In two articles he raises it as a slogan (#M191, 219); both articles are pubd on Nov 12, inaugurating the campaign. —A mass meeting is held in the Eisersche Saal and adopts a resolution condemning the government. **Nov 11–12:** Over 7000 signatures are quickly appended to this resolution. The meeting decides to remain "in permanence" as a continuing body. **Nov 12–14:** NRZ pubs M's articles on "The counterrevolution in Berlin" (#M191). **Nov 13:** The meeting in permanence elects an exec comm of 25, soon called the People's Comm, incl M&E and other NRZ editors, and also a spectrum of other elements indignant against the Brandenburg government. M is maintaining close contact with d'Ester, head of the Demo Assoc CC in Berlin; he writes Lassalle to raise the tax-refusal campaign in Düsseldorf, esp in the countryside.

79. MARX AS AGITATOR. Nov 13: M receives a summons to appear before the examining magistrate in Cologne (reported in NRZ, Nov 14). —At a meeting of the Cologne Demo Assoc, M reads a telegram just received from Vienna on Blum's execution [← :76], evoking a storm of indignation. **Nov 14:** M is interrogated by an examining magistrate on the "defamation" against Prosecutor Hecker [← :45]. A mass sympathy demonstration for M takes place before the courthouse; when he emerges, with loud applause the crowd accompanies him to the Eisersche Saal, where he explains what happened (cf MECW 8:495-96). —In the name of the Rhenish Democratic district comm, M and Schneider send an appeal to the associated groups, proposing mass meetings and tax refusal, and scheduling a Rhenish Democratic Congress for Nov 23

(#M47); pubd Nov 15. —NRZ pubs a short piece by M on the June uprising in Paris (#M137). **Nov c.14–15:** Ewerbeck, en route from the Berlin Democratic Congress to Paris, visits M and reports on the Congress. M commissions him to publish a French edn of the *Com Manifesto* in Paris and to contact the Polish Demo Comm there. **Nov 15:** Schapper, released from prison, is elected first vice-pres of the Cologne Workers Assoc and resumes its practical leadership; educational programs are inaugurated.

80. "NO MORE TAXES!" **Nov 15:** The Berlin Assembly unanim adopts an appeal for tax refusal against the government, to go into effect Nov 17. —Beust drafts a plan to create a revolutionary fighting force out of the Landwehr (National Guard reserve). —NRZ pubs M's article "The cabinet is put on trial" (#M122) on tax refusal, in addition to the appeal of Nov 14. **Nov 17:** NRZ starts featuring the watchword "No more taxes!" (#M562), and this appears as a banner headline every day till Dec 17. In an article M argues against half measures (#M171). Other articles: #M848, 430. **Nov 18:** The Rhenish Democratic district comm (M, Schneider, Schapper) issues another appeal calling for resistance by every means to forcible collection of taxes, and the formation of a people's militia and local comms of public safety (#M48). **Nov 19:** This appeal is pubd in NRZ, plus two articles by M on tax refusal (#M225, 874). **Nov 20:** The three signers (M, Schneider, Schapper) are charged with "public incitement to rebellion." M writes another appeal (#M49) about their summons to appear Nov 21, warning that the government hopes to provoke a putsch. **Nov 21:** The new appeal (#M49) is pubd in NRZ. The three men are interrogated on their authorship of the appeal. But first a delegation from the People's Comm [← :78] had gone to the office of Chief Prosecutor Zweiffel and obtained assurances that the three would not be arrested (articles in NRZ: #M142, 49; also cf MECW 8:501). —Beust is elected commander of various military-revolutionary formations that have sprung up this month; e.g., the Workers Assoc has set up a "Flying Corps"; the Turnverein, a "Free Corps"; efforts had been made to revive the militia.

81. COLOGNE IN FERMENT. **Nov 22:** The Frankfurt Assembly issues an appeal against the tax-refusal campaign, thereby taking sides with the developing reaction. —In Cologne there are mass demonstrations, in which VIPs' windows are broken (articles in NRZ: #M611, 139, 719). **Nov 23:** NRZ repeats its call for a "Free Corps" (revolutionary militia). — Beust's forces clash with the regular troops; Beust shortly flees Germany. —At the Sec-

ond Rhenish Democratic Congress (M attending) there is a debate on the tax-refusal campaign; the congress confirms the district comm's policies, and promotes work among the peasants (articles in NRZ: #M327, 845, 679). **Nov 25:** Interrogation of the three defendants (M, Schneider, Schapper) [← :80] is concluded by the examining magistrate (cf MECW 8:503). **Nov 26:** NRZ attacks Gen. Drigalski's "communist" pretenses (#M255). **Nov 27:** The Prussian Assembly convenes in Brandenburg [← :76] with no quorum [→ :83]. **Nov 29:** M writes E (in Bern) with optimism about the growing influence of NRZ: "La révolution marche." **Nov D:** More NRZ articles: #ME92, 130, 101, 109, 67; #M883, 472, 779. **c.Nov:** Around this time M is visited by NYDT editor Charles A. Dana, on tour, who sees M as "the leader of the people's movement" in the area; Freiligrath is also present at this meeting.

DECEMBER

82. ENGELS IN SWITZERLAND. **Dec 1–6:** E pubs a number of articles on Swiss political affairs in NRZ (#E732, 731, 79, 521, 232, 146, 276); also one on the Vienna revolution as seen in the Swiss press (#E795). **Dec A:** E writes the article on Proudhon that M requested (#E639), also an account of political issues in France (#E298); both remain unpubd. **Dec 8:** The Lausanne Workers Assoc names E its delegate to the first congress of German workers' assocs in Bern, Switzerland, Dec 9–11. **Dec 9:** E receives a sojourn permit for Bern from the Swiss authorities [← :75]. **Dec 9–11:** E participates in the German workers' congress in Bern. **Dec 10–28:** E pubs more articles on Swiss affairs in NRZ (#E477, 503, 885, 812, 476). **Dec 14:** E is elected a member of the CC of the German Workers Assoc in Switzerland. **Dec M:** E drafts the CC's address to the March Assoc of Frankfurt (#E843). **Dec 28:** E writes M asking if he should return to Cologne.

83. GERMANY: COUNTERREVOLUTION. **Dec 5:** The king issues a decree dissolving the Prussian Assembly in Brandenburg, and imposes ("octroys") a constitution that keeps all state power in the hands of the crown. **Dec 6:** The crown issues an electoral law providing for a two-stage election, excluding most workers. **Dec 7–8:** In NRZ, M calls these moves a new stage of the counterrevolution (#M245, 193; also #M371). **Dec 10–31:** In a major four-part article M analyzes "The bourgeoisie and the counterrevolution" (#M95). He also pubs an article on the international aspect of the European reaction (#ME100), and ancillary articles (#ME99, #M125, 241).

84. REPRESSION AGAINST THE NRZ. **Dec**

c.2: M is again called for interrogation because of a number of NRZ articles (for details, see MECW 8:504). **Dec 20:** The scheduled trial of M, E, and Korff on the "defamation" charge [← :79] is postponed to Feb 7 when the defense counsel points out the required ten-day notice was not received (cf MECW 8:511). **Dec 21:** M is called before the examining magistrate for alleged slander of the Düsseldorf commander Gen. Drigalski [← :81] (cf MECW 8:512). **Dec 21–23:** Trial of Gottschalk, Anneke, and Esser in Cologne: they are acquitted (cf #M944). **Dec 23:** The authorities deny the Workers Assoc's request for permission to hold a torchlight procession to celebrate the acquittal (M's note on it: #M698). **Dec 24:** M discusses the need to revolutionize the Prussian judicial system (#M709).

85. NRZ AND MARX: MISCELLANEOUS. **Dec 12:** Ewerbeck (in Paris) sends M a report on his dealings with the Polish Democratic émigrés and on the projected French trans of the Com Manifesto [← :79] **Dec 19:** NRZ launches its subscription drive for the first quarter of 1849 with a front-page appeal (running till Jan 14) which calls NRZ "the organ not only of the German but of the European Democracy" (cf MECW 8:509). **Dec 24:** NRZ pubs a Frankfurt dispatch exposing the Berlin police chief, Stieber, as a spy hiding behind a Democratic mask. **Dec 25:** NRZ advertises in its rival, the Kölnische Ztg, claiming a wider distribution than any other German paper. (For a jibe against the KZ, pubd Dec 27, see #ME127.) **Dec 26:** Stieber demands that the NRZ publish his reply to its Dec 24 dispatch. **Dec c.29:** M refuses to do so (cf #M890). **Dec 31:** M, Freiligrath, and Alfred Meissner (according to Meissner's autobiography) celebrate New Year's Eve at the home of the London Daily News correspondent Keene. **Dec D:** The Workers Assoc's paper suspends publ [→ 49:6].

1849

CONSPECTUS

1. As the revolutionary climate declines in all of Germany, governmental pressure on M and the NRZ increases, until the authorities finally judge the time opportune for M's expulsion from Prussia; this also means the end of the paper, whose last issue comes out May 19. M&E spend the rest of the month vainly urging a revolutionary policy on the Baden-Palatinate insurrectionary forces. Then M goes to Paris; E joins the fighting, in Willich's corps, until July, when he becomes a political refugee in Switzerland. M's expulsion from Paris sends him to (permanent) exile in London, where he is joined by E in Nov. In London, M makes preparations to launch a magazine, helps to organize a refugee-aid committee, revives the Communist League, and gives lectures on polit eco.

2. Economica: M's renewal of work in this field is signalized in Apr by his publ of Wage-labor and capital (#M968) in NRZ, and by educational lectures to the Workers Assoc. However, the turmoil of revolution and counterrevolution breaks this off until, settled in London, M renews his educational activities [→ :41] with lectures on economics.

JANUARY

3. ARTICLES IN NRZ. **Jan 1:** An important programmatic article by M, "The revolutionary movement" (#M778), stresses the international interdependence of the revolution and England's role. **Jan 5–9:** Two more significant articles: on the oppressive "workers' card" used for police control and on the Prussian army (#M94, 556). **Jan 14:** NRZ features Lassalle's protests from prison against his police persecution. **Jan 15:** M invites Müller-Tellering, NRZ's expelled Vienna correspondent, to become correspondent in Breslau. **Jan 31:** NRZ sounds the alert on a possible reactionary coup d'état in France, and stresses that the only alternative is the "red republic" (#ME154, 155).

4. MISCELLANEOUS. **Jan 1:** A. Meissner [← 48:85], who is going to Paris, is given by M a package, received four days before from Leghorn, to be conveyed to an Italian named Sarpi in Paris (this according to Meissner's autobiography). **Jan c.A:** M and his wife visit Gottfried and Johanna Kinkel in Bonn. **Jan 14:** M sends money to Dronke (25 talers) and F. Kapp (15 talers). **Jan 26:** Ewerbeck requests biographical material on M&E for the French edn of the Com Manifesto; he reports on the trans being done by the French Democratic journalist Paya (which will not in fact be pubd).

5. ENGELS RETURNS. **Jan 13–17:** In addition to an article pubd Jan 3 (#E796) E pubs several articles on Swiss affairs (#E348, 419, 108, 619, 637, 499), esp one on the Swiss press (#E797). More important is his programmatic article, requested by M [← 48:81 (Nov 29)] on the Hungarian revolution (#E461), followed up Jan 28 by #E646. **Jan M:** E leaves Switzerland and rejoins the NRZ staff in Cologne. **Jan 26:** The examining magistrate briefly interrogates E on the Sep events in Cologne, and states there is no case against him (cf *MECW* 8:516).

6. THE WORKERS ASSOC. **Jan 14:** The organ of the Assoc [← 48:85] resumes publ under the name *Freiheit, Arbeit*, with pub'r Brocker-Everaerts. **Jan 15:** At a committee session of the Cologne Workers Assoc, chaired by Röser, M proposes electing an ed board for the organ to supplement the editor, Prinz; Schapper, Röser, and Reiff are named (cf #M830). **Jan 29:** Another comm session decides that *Freiheit, Arbeit* as ed by Gottschalk's supporter Prinz should be supplanted by a new Assoc paper, ed by Esser, since Prinz refuses to submit to the ed board; the new title is to be *Freiheit, Brüderlichkeit, Arbeit* (a former title). **Jan D or Feb A:** M&E meet at the *NRZ* office with the leader of the Workers Brotherhood of Berlin, S. Born, who is visiting Cologne; M aims to convince him to follow the *NRZ* line instead of the conservative policies he has been pursuing.

7. ELECTION POLICY. **Jan 15:** At the Cologne Workers Assoc, M advocates supporting, in the first-stage elections scheduled for Jan 22, good Democrats who are opposed to the government even if not necessarily revolutionaries, in order to unite all forces against absolutism (esp since most workers could not vote anyway) (cf #M830). **Jan 21–22:** M pubs a major article on election policy, "Montesquieu LVI" (#M530). **Jan 26–28:** He follows up with a supplementary article on policy in the election, the second stage of which is due Feb 5 (#M80).

FEBRUARY

8. MARX AND ENGELS ON TRIAL. **Feb 7:** Court trial of M, E, and Korff for "defamation and insults" against the public prosecutor and police [← 48:45]: M&E give political defense speeches attacking the government; the jury acquits them after brief deliberation; a sympathizing crowd is present (cf *MECW* 8:517–19). **Feb 8:** Trial of the Rhenish Democratic district comm—M, Schapper, Schneider—for their tax-refusal incitation of Nov 18: M's defense speech indicts the government and explains revolutionary policy, before a crowded courtroom; the jury acquits all defendants (cf *MECW* 8:520–21). **Feb 10:** NRZ comments on the acquittal (#M875, #ME114). **Feb 14:** *NRZ* pubs M&E's defense speeches of Feb 7 (#M946, #E871; also cf draft, #M946.5). **Feb 17:** The Cologne military commander writes Rhineland Gov. Eichmann that, after acquittal, M is becoming "increasingly audacious" in his "increasingly popular paper," and is indirectly calling on the people to revolt; he wants the police to

deport M, to restore respect for the police (cf *MECW* 8:527). **Feb 25, 27:** *NRZ* pubs M's defense speech of Feb 8 (#M947). **Feb 28:** The *NRZ* office pubs a pamphlet, "Two political trials," containing the speeches at the trials of Feb 7–8 (ST/74).

9. THE COLOGNE MOVEMENT. **Feb 4:** M&E propose to a Workers Assoc membership meeting the holding of regular, free educational programs on "social subjects." The Assoc takes reorganization measures toward a stronger stable structure. **Feb 8:** The Assoc paper *Freiheit, Brüderlichkeit, Arbeit* reappears under this title, ed by Esser [← :6]; the Gottschalk–Prinz paper *Freiheit, Arbeit* continues to appear (until June 17). **Feb 11:** M&E attend a Democratic banquet held by the Workers Assoc of Mülheim. M gives a talk on the role of German workers in revolutions abroad, and offers a toast to Mülheim deputy A. Gladbach of the Berlin Assembly left wing. E's talk greets the Hungarian revolutionary fighters; he offers a toast to the Hungarians and Kossuth. Lucas of the Mülheim Assoc offers a toast to Democrats like M who espoused the rights of the working class long before the revolution. This is the first such Democratic banquet in the Rhineland, intended to initiate others (cf *MECW* 8:522). **Feb M:** At a membership meeting of the Cologne Workers Assoc, on reorganizn plans, Schapper announces that M&E plus Schapper will deliver fortnightly free lectures on social questions (cf *MECW* 8:523). **Feb 15:** The Assoc's comm meeting adopts E's proposal to hold a banquet for the anniversary of the February Revolution in France (cf *MECW* 8:525). **Feb 23:** Gottschalk pubs an unsigned virulent attack on M in his own organ [← :6]. **Feb 24:** M&E take part in the anniversary banquet, with a capacity crowd of 2000–3000; M is elected chairman by acclamation but hands the chair to Schapper. E offers a toast to the Italian liberation struggle and the Roman republic. (Cf *MECW* 8:529). **Feb 28:** Schapper takes over the presidency of the Workers Assoc (until May D).

10. NRZ: IMPORTANT ARTICLES. **Feb 1:** NRZ pubs a political summary of the elections (#M432). **Feb 3:** E begins writing reports on the military progress of the revolutionary struggle in Austria-Hungary and the Balkans (#E786), and he will continue publishing such reports for the next three months (cf the list in #E308, et al). **Feb 4:** NRZ pubs M's summary of the Camphausen period (#M126). **Feb 11:** NRZ pubs the first of many articles on the government's prosecution of Lassalle in Düsseldorf (#M442), also one on the prosecution of Kinkel (#E719). **Feb 15–16:** NRZ pubs E's major article criticizing Bakunin's pamphlet on Pan-Slavism (#E217).

Feb 17, 23: Articles on Prussian state finances (#M710, 339). Feb 18: Article on policy in Germany (#ME167; cf also #M248). In #M882, M needles the *Kölnische Ztg.* Feb 22: On revolution abroad: in Italy (#ME116), Austria (#E919). 11. REVIVE THE CL? c.Feb: Moll arrives as emissary of the London CL/CC to discuss this with M&E and the NRZ group, incl W. Wolff, Schapper, Röser, Esser, Bedorf, Nothjung, Haude. M rejects the revised by-laws brought by Moll because they propose not a communist aim but a "social republic" and because they tend to conspiratorialism (SOURCE: KMC). 12. MISCELLANEOUS. Feb A: M fights for the continued existence of the NRZ against stringent financial difficulties, pressure from creditors, etc. Feb 12: D'Ester (in Leipzig) asks M to suggest an editor for the planned organ of the Democratic Exec in Berlin. Feb 23: Lelewel (in Brussels) writes M to print a warning against Prussian police spies in Brussels; this is pubd in NRZ on Feb 28. Feb 28: Lassalle, in jail in Düsseldorf [← :10], writes M asking him for measures of support to speed up his trial, esp by sending a delegation to exercise pressure [→ :13].

MARCH

13. LASSALLE CASE. Mar c.1: M receives Lassalle's request for help [← :12]. Mar 3: M&E go with a delegation to the office of the Rhineland prosecutor, G. H. F. Nicolovius (in Cologne), to demand the speeding-up of the court proceedings against Lassalle. Mar 4, 6: NRZ pubs M's articles on the Lassalle case (#M443, 694). 14. COLOGNE: UNDER PRESSURE. Mar 2: Two NCOs of the Cologne military garrison appear at M's house and, with threats, demand he name the author of an NRZ piece on Capt. von Uttenhoven; M refuses [→ Mar 15]. Mar 3 and c.5: M registers a sharp protest against this action with the military commandant of Cologne (#M453). Mar 9: NRZ rejects a protest made by the military commandant against its alleged insult to Prince Waldemar of Prussia in its Feb 23 issue. Mar 10: The Cologne authorities report to Interior Min Manteuffel that the military commandant has asked for M's deportation [← :8], and say they agree "if he [M] gives any specific cause," but it is not expedient right now because it may "provoke a demonstration," esp because NRZ's "impertinence and humor" constantly attract new readers (cf *MECW* 9:487). Mar 11: At the meeting of primary voters in Cologne's Gürzenich Hall, M is elected to the comm that will establish permanent relations with the deputies of the

Prussian Diet, second chamber. The meeting adopts an address asking the deputies to get the state of siege abolished in Berlin and end the "dictatorship of the saber." —The Demo Assoc of Solingen invites M&E and the NRZ staff to participate in a celebration of the March 18 revolution in Berlin (cf *MECW* 9:489). About this time many other such invitations come in. Mar 15: M receives a threatening letter signed only "The soldiers of the 34th Infantry Regiment." Mar 18: On this anniversary, M pubs a short piece saying that the NRZ prefers to celebrate the anniversary of the Paris June uprising (#M269, also #M538); and NRZ explains that the staff is not accepting any of the invitations received from neighboring towns to attend Mar 18 banquets. Mar 19: The NRZ and the Workers Assoc hold a banquet meeting in Gürzenich Hall, as a counterdemonstration to the Mar 18 celebrations held elsewhere; it celebrates the Berlin barricade struggle of Mar 1848; a crowd of 5000–6000 attends, plus a large overflow. E offers a toast to the June insurgents of Paris (cf *MECW* 9:490). Mar 29: The Prussian min of the interior proposes M's expulsion, but Rhineland Gov. Eichmann regards this as premature: he fears disturbances and counsels waiting for a more favorable moment. 15. NRZ: ON THE REACTION. Mar: Articles on the international scene (#E255; #ME161, 190), in particular Italy (#E906, 214); on the advance of reaction in Germany (#ME158, 71; #E228, 207); on the fight for democratic rights (#ME55, 27; #M881, 378, 379); on the compromising Democrats (#ME146; #M496, 328); E's article on military dictatorship in Austria (#E484) remains unpubd. Mar 16: On the peasant question, an article (#ME95) introduces an important series of studies by W. Wolff on "The Silesian billion," pubd Mar 17 to Apr 25, portraying the feudal exploitation of the countryside. Mar to May: E pubs a stream of reports on the military side of the revolutionary wars going on in Europe. 16. MISCELLANEOUS. Mar 12, 30: M receives offers from G. A. Schlöffel, Jr., to write for NRZ. (Schlöffel will start sending correspondence from Frankfurt in Apr.) Mar 19: Harney (in London) writes E about his "death struggle with O'Connor" in the Chartist movement. He urges E to write for his planned paper, which will be "not merely Chartist" but "the organ of *European* Democracy." Mar D: M is suffering from a liver ailment, and plans to take the waters as treatment.

APRIL

17. THE REVOLUTION IN DECLINE. Apr: By order of the Berlin police, the Cologne

police hold up all letters sent to M&E and other NRZ editors; a Berlin police official comes to Cologne to carry this measure out. **Apr 7:** Interior Min Manteuffel tells the Cologne authorities they have a free hand in finding a pretext to expel M (cf MECW 9:492). **Apr 19:** The Cologne authorities give Police Chief Geiger instructions to carry out the expulsion of M "when direct cause is next given by an unequivocal offence" by him (cf MECW 9:496). **Apr 27:** The Berlin government dissolves the Prussian Diet (Second Chamber) because it votes for the Frankfurt Assembly's constitution; discussed by #E227. **Apr:** NRZ articles discuss the events in Germany and abroad (#E271, 260, 733; cf an unpubd article #E112); articles discuss the attack on civil liberties (#E239, 208); Lassalle case (#E415); events in Italy (#E214), France (#ME62), Poland and Russia (#E507, 594). For E's military reportage, see ← :15; a number of his articles cover Austria-Hungary.

18. *WAGE-LABOR AND CAPITAL.* **Apr A:** M prepares his 1847 Brussels lectures on polit eco for NRZ publ [← 47:53]. **Apr 5:** In an introductory statement to his series of articles (#M968), M draws the lesson that every revolution today depends on the victory of the working class, that every social reform depends on proletarian revolution. **Apr 5–11:** The series runs for five installs, ending "To be continued," but it is interrupted by M's trip (see → :20) and will not be resumed. **Apr 11:** The Workers Assoc comm decides to devote the educational programs at its branches' meetings to discussion of this series of articles. **Apr 20:** An ed note in NRZ explains the author's "temporary absence" and promises resumption of the series shortly.

19. POLITICAL TURN. **Apr 14:** M, Schapper, W. Wolff, H. Becker, and Anneke resign from the Rhenish district comm of the Demo Assocs, stating that they prefer to work for a "closer union" of the Workers Assocs, which comprise more "homogeneous [class] elements" (#M854); pubd in NRZ Apr 15. This is M's turn in orientation: focusing on organizing a specifically workers' movement in Germany instead of the (socially heterogeneous) organizn of Democrats of various hues. **Apr 16:** A membership meeting of the Cologne Workers Assoc unanim votes to drop its affiliation with the Demo Assocs and to help organize a Rhenish congress of all workers' assocs, looking to a national workers' congress to follow, in Leipzig (cf MECW 9:494) [→ :22]. **Apr 17:** The comm of the Workers Assoc elects M to a provisional commission to prepare the congress of workers' assocs of the Rhineland and Westphalia, which is set for May 6 (cf MECW 9:495). **Apr 23:** The Assoc's membership approves the membership of this

commission: M, Schapper, W. Wolff, Anneke, Esser, Otto (cf MECW 9:501). **Apr 24:** This convening commission (minus M, who is out of town) adopts a call and an agenda for the May 6 congress, which is to found a Rhenish organizn of workers' assocs; pubd in NRZ on Apr 26 (cf MECW 9:502). **Apr D:** Branch No. 1 of the Workers Assoc adopts a detailed resolution indicting Gottschalk, under 11 counts, for his reactionary political line and his slanders against M; pubd in the Assoc's organ on Apr 29 (cf MECW 9:498).

20. MARX ON TOUR. **Apr c.14 to May 9:** M undertakes a politico-organizational trip through northwest Germany; visits Bremen, Hamburg, Bielefeld, Hamm; meets with communists and Democrats; surveys the revolutionary situation; and also concerns himself with raising money to continue NRZ. E is in charge of the paper during M's absence. **Apr c.15–18:** In Bremen, M makes an unsuccessful attempt to get financial help for NRZ from J. Rösing, a Democratic leader. **Apr c.19 to May c.6:** In Hamburg, M meets with the communists Bruhn, Grübel, K. Schramm, T. Hagen, Strohn, and with several Democrats also; he sends Bruhn and Schramm as emissaries to central and eastern Germany—all this to raise funds for NRZ.

MAY

21. MARX ON TOUR (CONT'D). **May 6:** In Harburg (near Hamburg) [← :20], M gets a loan from one Herr von Frisch. **May c.7–8:** M travels from Hamburg to Bielefeld, where he visits Rempel to get NRZ funds; Rempel refers him to a contributor who lends 300 talers. **May 9:** M returns to Cologne.

22. WORKERS' CONGRESS. **May 6:** The congress of Rhenish workers' assocs [← :19] takes place in Cologne as scheduled; it holds a joint session with a simultaneous congress of Demo organizations. Schapper presides over the workers' congress; M is out of town; E's name does not figure in the press report (cf MECW 9:506).

23. NRZ UNDER ENGELS. **May 1–9:** During M's absence, E, in charge of NRZ, continues its analysis on the advance of reaction (esp #E189, 632, 643, 200, 225, 805); on the signs of a revolutionary explosion (#E640, 31; also #E535, pubd May 11). His articles warn against government provocations in Cologne and against premature outbreaks (#E347, 702, 648); and continue agitation on Lassalle's case (#E416, 417). E also continues his military reportage on revolutionary battles in Europe (his last report is pubd May 10).

24. UPRISINGS IN GERMANY. **May AB:** Uprisings and barricade fights break out around Germany in response to the government's rejection of the Frankfurt Assembly's draft of a constitution [← :17]. An uprising in Dresden (with participation by S. Born, Bakunin, and Richard Wagner, i.a.) lasts May 3–9; barricades in Breslau, May 6–7; these and other explosions are put down by Prussian troops. **May 8:** An uprising breaks out in Elberfeld (reported in *NRZ*, May 10—see #E747); there are other clashes and barricades in Iserlohn, Solingen, Düsseldorf, Hagen, and other Rhineland towns, soon suppressed. **May c.10:** E draws up some guidelines on military policy in aid of the Rhenish rebellions (apparently in nonextant notes: summarized in #E328, *MECW* 10:163); he writes a report for *NRZ* on the uprisings in Elberfeld and Düsseldorf (#E883), pubd May 11.

25. ENGELS AND THE ELBERFELD UPRISING. **May 10:** E leaves Cologne for the Wuppertal; he stops in Solingen, gathers a workers' detachment, and continues on to Elberfeld. **May 11:** E arrives in Elberfeld with the Solingen workers. The Comm of Public Safety puts him in charge of fortifications and barricades; he assures the comm that he will concern himself only with military matters, not with the political character of the movement. **May 12:** E is put in charge also of artillery installation. **May 13:** Prob while he is involved in trying to win over the civil guard of neighboring Barmen (his hometown), E meets his father near the connecting bridge, his father being on his way to church; there is a painful scene. **May 14:** The Comm of Public Safety, under pressure from the Elberfeld bourgeois Democrats who are afraid E will "proclaim a red republic," asks E to leave the area even though they "appreciate" his work, in order to tranquilize the Democrats' alarm. E insists the request be publicized in writing and approved by Commandant Mirbach. **May 15:** Mirbach reluctantly signs the statement and it is publicized. Though indignant workers ask E to stay, he refuses to flout the authority of the military-revolutionary authorities and split the insurrectionary camp. Before leaving for Cologne, he heads a detachment which liberates a quantity of matériel for the insurgents from the Gräfrath arsenal (cf *MECW* 9:508, 10:602f). **May 16:** The Comm of Public Safety of Elberfeld, after ousting E, also ousts workers' detachments which had come from other towns (yielding to the same pressures), and this policy helps to seal its fate. **May c.17:** The government issues an order for E's arrest because of his Elberfeld activities. **May 17:** E is forced to leave Cologne to avoid arrest. *NRZ* pubs his account of the Elberfeld episode (#E236; also #E923; note also E's later account in #E328).

26. EXPULSION; END OF THE NRZ. **May** 10–17: M pubs a notable indictment of the Prussian dynasty, "The deeds of the House of Hohenzollern" (#M226); also, continued attacks on the reaction (esp #M552, 553, 549), on the reactionary press (#M960, 437), and reports on the revolt (#M805, 958). **May 11:** The Prussian government orders M's expulsion from Prussia, which will shut down *NRZ*. (By this time the government has accumulated 23 separate charges against M, not yet used.) **May 16:** The expulsion order is served on M. **May c.16–19:** The M family sells its furniture to avoid their legal attachment. M uses all available moneys, his own and the proceeds of selling the press, to settle obligations owed by *NRZ* to employees, printers, creditors, etc. **May 18:** The last issue of *NRZ*, no. 301, appears this evening, dated May 19: it is printed in red ink, in an extra press run distributed during the following days. M's summary article (#M870) reviews the revolutionary course of the paper; E pubs a last survey of the Hungarian scene (#E366); M&E take a last cockshy (#ME172) at the Prussian king, and publish a last statement (#ME186) warning Cologne workers against a putsch. The issue features a farewell poem on *NRZ* by Freiligrath. (For press reactions, see *MECW* 9:509.)

27. MARX–ENGELS AND THE SOUTHWEST UPRISING. **May 19–20:** M&E go to Frankfurt, where they vainly try to persuade the left deputies of the National Assembly to put themselves at the head of the uprising in southwest Germany, call the revolutionary army of Baden and the Palatinate to Frankfurt, and establish an all-German assembly under the aegis of the insurrectionary forces and population. **May c.20:** M&E depart for Baden, leaving Mrs. M and the children with the Weydemeyers in Frankfurt, where Mrs. M pawns the Westphalen family silver in order to live. (But by another account [Dornemann], Mrs. M separates from M in Bingen; see → :28.) **May 20–21:** In Baden (Mannheim, Ludwigshafen, Karlsruhe) M&E vainly try to persuade the leaders of the insurrectionary movement to send their armed forces to Frankfurt in order to give their now-regional movement an all-German character. **May 23-24:** In Karlsruhe, M&E meet with members of the Regional Exec (*Landesausschuss*), whose irresoluteness and foot-dragging they deplore; only Karl Blind and A. Goegg agree with them. **May 24:** M&E go to the Palatinate; in Speyer they want to see d'Ester and the Prov Government, who have left; they meet Willich and his partisan corps. **May c.25–26:** M&E go with Willich to Kaiserslautern, where they meet d'Ester and the Prov Government; they have private discussions with d'Ester. M&E decline to participate in the leadership of this

movement since they would inevitably clash with the petty-bourgeois Democrats who head it. **May c.26–27:** En route to Bingen, M&E with several friends are arrested by Hessian soldiers on suspicion of participation in the uprising; they are brought to Darmstadt, then Frankfurt, and released in Frankfurt. There M meets with G. Jung, from whom he gets a passport made out to E. Meyen.

28. IN BINGEN. May c.28: M&E continue on to Bingen (where they will stay until June 1). **May 29:** Back in Cologne, a police court, hearing the case in the absence of the defendants, acquits M, Dronke, Weerth, et al of charges of libeling the Frankfurt Assembly deputies in *NRZ*, although Korff gets one month for "insulting" a deputy (cf *MECW* 9:516–20). **May 30:** On a different charge Korff is acquitted when brought before the police court. **May 31:** In Bingen, M sends out a statement (#M853 and covering letter #M463) repudiating any connection with the *Westdeutsche Ztg* (Cologne), which claimed to be *NRZ*'s successor; pubd June 2–7, 3. **May D:** According to Dornemann's account [cf ← :27] Mrs. M stays in Bingen for a week, during which time she makes an excursion to Frankfurt, staying with the Weydemeyers, to sell the family silver in order to live; from Bingen she goes to her mother in Trier [→ :31].

JUNE

29. BACK TO PARIS. June c.2: M, who expects a revolutionary outbreak in France, gets a mandate, made out by d'Ester for the Palatinate CC of the Democrats, to represent the German revolutionary movement to the French Democratic-Social party in Paris. **June c.3:** M departs for Paris. **June A:** In Paris, M establishes relations with leaders of the leftist clubs and secret societies of workers, as well as with the Democrats and the Social-Democratic tendency. M also contacts Schütz, the official representative of the Baden Prov Government. **June 7:** M writes E (in Kaiserslautern) that a volcanic explosion is near in Paris. **June 11:** In the Assembly, Ledru-Rollin's motion to impeach Bonaparte and his ministers is rejected; leaders of the secret workers' societies urge the launching of an uprising that same evening, but Ledru-Rollin rejects any unconstitutional action. **June 13:** An indecisive demonstration by Ledru-Rollin's supporters becomes an abortive semi-revolt, and is turned by Bonaparte into a catastrophic defeat for the left, inaugurating an accelerated slide to reaction (June Days of 1849). **June 21:** M writes an article on the June 13 events (#M880), pubd June 29 in a German paper. **June 29:** Mrs. M writes from

Trier, to a friend, about her old mother's sad situation. **June to Aug:** Besides the persons mentioned above in Paris, M meets Ewerbeck, Weerth, Dronke, Seiler, K. Blind, F. Wolff, N. Sazanov, and (several times) Heine and his secy R. Reinhardt.

30. ENGELS JOINS THE FIGHTING. June c.2: E goes to Kaiserslautern, where the Palatinate Prov Government offers him various civil and military posts, which he refuses. He agrees to write articles for their organ, and immediately does write one on the uprising (#E701), dated June 2; pubd June 3. **June A:** When the editors object that E's second article is too "seditious," E abandons further collaboration with them. **June 6:** Back in Cologne, the prosecutor's office issues a warrant for the arrest of E as a fugitive (cf *MECW* 9:524). **June c.13:** E goes via Neustadt to Offenbach, to join the Baden-Palatinate insurrectionary army, as a soldier in Willich's volunteer detachment. **June 13 to July 12:** E participates in the fighting, in four battles incl the engagement at Rastatt; he becomes Willich's adjutant, jointly works out with him the plans for military operations, and directs the carrying out of various military measures.

JULY

31. MARX IN PARIS. July c.13: Mrs. M, with the children and Helene Demuth, arrives in Paris; the family moves into a house at 45 rue de Lille, where F. Wolff is also living. They are "penniless" (M to Weydemeyer, July 13); Mrs. M has already pawned all jewelry. (*KMC* dates Mrs. M's arrival as July 7.) **July 19:** Police come to the M residence with a government order for his expulsion from Paris, to the marshy département of Morbihan (Brittany) (cf *MECW* 9:526). On M's protest to the Interior Ministry, the order is held in abeyance. **July c.20:** In desperate need of money for living expenses, M turns to Freiligrath, Daniels, Strohn, Lassalle. Lassalle (in Düsseldorf) raises about 200 talers among Rhenish friends. **July 27:** M receives 439 francs from Lassalle. **July 30:** M pubs a letter in *La Presse* correcting its erroneous account of his recent movements (#M894).

32. ENGELS IN SWITZERLAND. July 12: Following the defeat of the Baden-Palatinate uprising, the Willich detachment (incl E) is the last to cross the border into Switzerland, covering the retreat. **July 24:** E arrives in Vevey (canton of Vaud). **July 25:** E writes Mrs. M (for the first time since separating June A); he reports on his experiences as a soldier and suggests that M may be safer in Switzerland than in Paris. **July 26:** On behalf of a number of men in Willich's corps, E drafts a statement refuting certain slanders circulated against the corps by political enemies (#E676); not pubd.

AUGUST

33. MARX IN PARIS. Aug c.1: M writes E (in Vevey) urging that he write an account of the insurrectionary movement; M reports on negotiations to establish a politico-economic monthly in Berlin. —M writes Weydemeyer (in Frankfurt) for help in getting a publisher for a brochure containing the whole series on *Wage-labor and capital* (#M968), only part of which had been pubd in Apr, to be supplemented by a "short political preface on the present status quo." He promises to send an article on "the present situation in England" for *NDZ*, of which Weydemeyer is coeditor. **Aug A:** The whole M family is ill. **Aug 16:** The Paris police commissioner, Dourlens, notifies M that the interior min has denied his appeal [← :31] and that M is to leave for Morbihan forthwith (cf *MECW* 9:527). **Aug 17:** Before receiving this notification from the police, M (using the cover address "Monsieur Ramboz") writes E (in Vevey) that the Morbihan climate would be deadly. M reviews the bad situation on the Continent, esp in Prussia, but seems optimistic about England. He suggests launching "a literary and commercial enterprise" of some sort. **Aug 23:** M writes E (in Lausanne) that instead of going to Morbihan (which would be "disguised murder") he will leave France. Switzerland is not feasible; hence he is leaving for London tomorrow, with a "positive" prospect of founding a German journal there. He urges E to go to London immediately. **Aug 24:** M leaves Paris, accompanied by Seiler and K. Blind; Mrs. M and the family provisionally remain in Paris. **Aug 26:** M embarks at Boulogne for England.

34. MARX IN LONDON. Aug 26 or 27: M arrives in London. **Aug D to Sep A:** M helps to reconstitute the Communist League's CC.

35. ENGELS IN SWITZERLAND. Aug c.20: After a month's stay in Vevey, E goes to Lausanne. **Aug M to Sep:** In Lausanne, E begins work, as suggested by M [← :33], on his account of "The German campaign for a Reich constitution" (#E328), which will be finished next Feb. **Aug 25:** E writes Weydemeyer (in Frankfurt) about getting a publisher for this work; he mentions he was recently in Geneva, where he saw H. Becker. In Geneva, E also met with W. Liebknecht, who soon afterward joins the CL.

SEPTEMBER

36. MARX IN LONDON. Sep: M begins on intensive preparations of a magazine; he writes to friends and acquaintances every-

where to get finances, a publisher, and writers. **Sep A:** M becomes a member of the London GWEA, which is led by the local CL. —M suffers for some days from "a sort of cholera." **Sep M:** M begins working with K. Blind, Seiler, et al to organize aid to German refugees in London. **Sep c.17:** Mrs. M and the children arrive in London from Paris. The M family moves into a furnished room in Leicester Square, temporarily [→ :39]. **Sep 18:** A GWEA membership meeting elects M to a Comm to Aid German Refugees in London, along with Blind, H. Bauer, Pfänder, Füster. This refugee-aid comm includes noncommunists also [→ :40]. **Sep 20:** M is among the signers of the refugee-aid comm's Appeal (#M163A); pubd in several German papers during Sep.

37. ENGELS IN SWITZERLAND. Sep 11: The Swiss authorities issue E a permit to leave the country (cf *MECW* 10:595). **Sep 15:** E meets with W. Wolff in Bern.

OCTOBER

38. ENGELS: EN ROUTE. Oct A: E leaves Switzerland and sets out for England. Since France refuses him passage, he goes via Italy and the sea. **Oct 5:** E arrives in Genoa and writes Harney that on Oct 6 he will take ship on the vessel *Cornish Diamond*, for a four- or five-week voyage to England. (Harney informs M, on receiving the letter.) (For sketches made by E during the voyage, see #E751.5.)

39. MARX IN LONDON. Oct c.M: M meets Willich, who has arrived from Switzerland with a recommendation from E. On M's proposal, Willich is taken into the CL/CC. **Oct:** The M family moves to Chelsea, 4 Anderson Street.

NOVEMBER

40. LONDON ACTIVITIES. Nov c.8: M receives news of CL activities in Cologne through a letter of Nov 5 sent by Lessner to H. Bauer. **Nov 12:** E arrives in London after 38 days at sea (SOURCE: ST/56 and *New Mega*; *MEW* dating is Nov c.10). He is taken into the CL/CC and GWEA, and begins working on the preparations for the new magazine. **Nov 18:** At a GWEA membership meeting M and his CL supporters change the name of the refugee-aid comm [← :36] to Social-Democratic Aid Comm for German Refugees, in order to differentiate it, as a socialist group, from a rival refugee organizn founded by bourgeois-liberal émigrés (Struve, Heinzen, et al). The meeting approves the membership of the refugee comm (all CL), incl not only M but also E and Willich, who replace K. Blind and Füster (who have left London); it also approves the comm's financial accounts (#M163B). **Nov 20:** T. Hagen (in Hamburg) writes M that he has lined up a printer for the projected magazine (Köhler) and a commission pub'r (Schuberth & Co.). Subsequently, M names K. Schramm as responsible manager (*gérant*). **Nov 30:** Since the M family's doctor, Dr. L. Bauer, is a political leader of the antisocialist refugee-aid comm and has publicly attacked M's tendency, M writes him a cordial note saying that, to avoid "ambiguous interpretations," their medical relations had better cease.

41. ECONOMICA. **Nov to next Sep:** M begins a course of lectures at the GWEA on polit eco and the ideas of the *Com Manifesto*. He also gives a number of more intensive classes in the same field for CL activists, in his home. M plans to publish some of these lectures in the projected magazine, but this aim will not be realized. (KMC dates these lectures as Dec to c.Jan, and gives the subject as: "What is bourgeois property? I. Capital. II. Landed property." But for dating, cf #M454.)

42. PERSONAL. **Nov 5:** A son, Heinrich Guido, is born to the Marxes, on the anniversary of the Guy Fawkes Gunpowder Plot.

DECEMBER

43. PREPARING THE *NRZ-REVUE*. **Dec AB:** The contract for the magazine is finally settled

between Schramm as manager and the pub'r Schuberth. (For some cost figures, see #E279.5.) **Dec 15:** M&E issue the announcement (#ME11): "The *Neue Rheinische Zeitung, politisch-ökonomische Revue*, edited by Karl Marx, will appear in Jan 1850." **Dec c.M:** M writes Lassalle to get subscriptions for the magazine. **Dec 19:** M writes Weydemeyer regarding publicity for the *Revue* in Germany. **Dec 27:** The announcement is pubd in a Bern paper. **Dec 28:** Goegg, via K. Blind, sends M a contribution of 100 francs for the *Revue*.

44. POLITICAL ACTIVITIES. **Dec 1:** E pubs a piece on Heinzen in NS (#E336). **Dec 3:** M is one of the signers of the first public financial statement of the refugee-aid comm (#M163C). **Dec 6:** Sazanov (in Paris) asks M to send him articles for *La Réforme* on Germany or on the workers' movement in England, and to recommend a German Democrat as collaborator on the German Democratic correspondence he is planning to publish. (M recommends Reinhardt.) **Dec c.25:** M&E attend the Christmas celebration of the GWEA. **Dec 31:** M&E and other CL/CC members attend a New Year's Eve affair held by the Fraternal Democrats, with Harney presiding; a number of revolutionary émigrés of various countries are present, incl French Blanquists. **Dec:** For M's lectures on economics, see ← :41.

1850

1. This year is dominated by two parallel enterprises, both of which go under by autumn: the reorganization of the Communist League, which splits in Sep over irreconcilable political differences; and the magazine Neue Rheinische Zeitung, politisch-ökonomische Revue (NRZ-Revue), which staggers through five delayed issues, beset by lack of funds and of copy, before it is suspended. At the same time M&E are deeply involved in providing material aid to German refugees in London, through an aid committee established by the German Workers Educational Assoc (GWEA), which in turn is dominated by the CL. As M's funds are exhausted in supporting the NRZ-Revue, E makes the fateful decision in November to go back to a desk in the family cotton firm in Manchester, largely in order to support M.

2. Outside of a major political document on the lessons of the revolution ("Address to the CL," #ME2), most of M&E's important writing is done for the NRZ-Revue, esp two surveys of the revolution that had just failed (#M148, #E328) and one of a revolution in

the past (#E579)—ventures in summing up the lessons of historical experience.

3. Economica: In the course of the year, M resumes his study of polit eco in the British Museum Library [→ :24], comes to the conclusion that the end of the economic crisis has entailed an end to the revolutionary situation [→ :28], and by around Sep or Oct plunges into intensified reading in the field. Reading and Study: From around Sep 1850 to Aug 1853—that is, from the breakup of the CL to the outbreak of the Crimean War [→ 53:37]—M will fill a series of 24 notebooks, numbered with roman numerals, on a variety of economic subjects. (For details, see → :50, 51.)

JANUARY

4. THE *NRZ-REVUE*. **Jan to Feb 2:** For the first issue of the new magazine M writes Part I of his study of the failed revolution in France, which will later be entitled *Class struggles in France, 1848–1850* (#M148). **Jan-Feb:** M&E write two book reviews, one of a book by

Daumer on religion (#ME142), the other of a book by Ludwig Simon of Trier (#ME142), and possibly also a third review (#ME138; see → :6). These reviews will appear in no. 2 of the *Revue*. **Jan 1:** An appeal for stock subscription is issued, signed by K. Schramm as manager (*gérant*) (cf *MECW* 10:605). **Jan 8:** M&E's announcement of the magazine (#ME11) starts appearing in the German press. **Jan CD:** M is ill the last week and a half of the month, and does not finish his Part I of the *Class struggles* [→ :6]; mss are slow in coming in. M wants to postpone publ for some weeks and then begin with a double number, but pub'r Schuberth protests on Jan 18. On Jan 25 M's Hamburg agent Hagen demands the mss for the first number, which, however, is delayed. **Jan 31:** M&E write, and date, the "Review" of the month (#ME134), but it will be pubd in no. 2 of the *Revue*, with a part added in Feb.

5. CL AFFAIRS. **Jan:** The CL/CC, incl M&E, begins reorganizing the League. **Jan A:** M writes to Röser (in Cologne) urging establishment of a CL branch in the city and elsewhere in the Rhineland, necessarily illegal because of the de facto suppression of civil liberties. —Leaders of the German Democratic emigration (R. Schramm, Struve, etc.) call a meeting for Jan 3 to organize the émigrés; they exclude M's supporters (e.g., F. Wolff, K. Schramm) while inviting M&E on Jan 2; M&E refuse to participate. **Jan 10:** On M's proposal, the CL/CC decides to send K. Schramm as emissary to America—representing the left Chartists and the French Blanquist emigration as well—to raise money and support for NRZ-Revue and for other propagandist purposes. **Jan 10–c.11:** M calls on CL supporters in Germany to raise funds for Schramm's mission; Freiligrath sends 40 talers on Jan 26. (The trip will not take place for lack of funds.)

FEBRUARY

6. THE *NRZ-REVUE*. **Feb 2:** M finishes writing Part I of his *Class struggles* (#M148) [← :4]. **Feb c.2:** M&E send the ms copy for no. 1 to the Hamburg printer. The printing will be drawn out because of M's difficult handwriting and pub'r Schuberth's worry about government harassment [→ :10]. **Feb to Mar 7:** M writes Part II of his *Class struggles* (#M148). **Feb 7:** M writes G. Bergenroth (in Berlin) for an article on Prussian finances, and asks him to look for other contributors. **Feb 12:** Lassalle writes M about his activity on behalf of the *Revue*, and about the Hatzfeldt case. **Feb M:** On M's behalf, E asks Dronke (in Paris) to supply a contribution on France. **Feb 28:** Issue no. 1 is printed and

goes to the bindery (till Mar 7). **Feb D:** M&E write an announcement about the magazine's delay (#ME54A), for publ in no. 1. **Feb:** M&E add a section to the "Review" of the period (#ME134) [← :4], for no. 2 —They write a book review on Guizot's brochure about England (#ME138), also for no. 2. —E finishes his study of the German armed campaign of 1849 (#E328) [← 49:35; → :10].

7. POLITICAL AFFAIRS. **Feb A:** M replies to a question from Röser that the CL should base its propaganda on the *Com Manifesto*, and that the coming League congress will work out new statutes to replace the obsolete ones of 1847 or 1848. **Feb 13:** R. Schramm [← :4] again asks M for collaboration in émigré organizn. **Feb 25:** E speaks at a banquet of the French Blanquist émigrés celebrating the February 1848 revolution; he ends with a toast to the Paris June insurgents, "amidst thunderous applause" (cf *MECW* 10:607). **Feb D:** For an example of day-to-day problems in refugee comm work, see #E855—a case requiring liaison with the Hungarian refugee comm in London.

8. ECONOMICA. **Feb c.D to Mar:** M gives several lectures on polit eco, at home, for friends (Pfänder, Eccarius, et al).

9. W&P. **Feb 8–20:** E writes the article "The ten hours' question" for Harney's *Democratic Review* (#E800) [→ :11]. **Feb 14:** Bruno Bucher (in Köslin) proposes that M write a popular almanac (*Kalender*) on polit eco, esp intended for peasants, to be pubd by Bucher.

MARCH

10. THE *NRZ-REVUE*. **Mar c.4:** M finishes Part II of his *Class struggles* (#M148). **Mar c.7 to Mar CD:** M writes Part III of the same. **Mar c.8:** The first number of the magazine appears in Hamburg and is sent out, dated Jan. Main contents: Part I of M's *Class struggles in France* (#M148); Part I of E's "German campaign [etc.]" (#E328), and an article by K. Blind on "Austrian and Prussian parties in Baden." **Mar 19:** M sends a letter to Naut (in Cologne) about his financial crisis: 30 talers are urgently needed. **Mar c.27:** M receives 30 talers from Naut, borrowed from a bookseller. **Mar D:** For two articles which are perhaps begun by M&E (#M489, #ME69), see → :14. **Mar c.22:** The second number of the magazine is pubd in Hamburg, dated Feb. Main contents: second installment of the ongoing series by M (*Class struggles*, #M148) and by E ("German campaign [etc.]" #E328); three book reviews (#ME137, 142, 138), and the "Review" of Jan-Feb (#ME134). **Mar CD:** E writes an article on the English ten hours' bill for the *Revue* (#E246); it will be pubd in no. 4. **Mar to Apr:** M&E write book reviews of Carlyle's *Latter-day pamphlets* (#ME139) and of two books by French police agents [#ME141]—to be pubd in no. 4.

11. W&P (E). **Mar:** *Demo Review* pubs E's article on the ten hours' question (#E800) [← :9].

12. POLITICAL AFFAIRS. **Mar 4:** The financial statement of the S-D Refugee Comm [← 49:40], signed i.a. by M&E, is approved at a GWEA meeting (#ME157A). **Mar M:** There is a sharp break between M&E and Müller-Tellering, former *NRZ* correspondent in Vienna, accompanied by Tellering's personal attacks on M&E. **Mar 27:** Bürgers (in Cologne) writes M for advice on political management of the Cologne *Westdeutsche Ztg*, of which he is to become an editor. (In subsequent letters, M disapproves of collaboration with that paper.) **Mar D:** M&E write a circular to the League membership ("Address to the CL," #ME2) in which they analyze the basic lessons of the failed revolution of 1848–49 and advocate a "Permanent Revolution" policy. **Mar D to Apr A:** The CL/CC sends H. Bauer as an emissary to the branches in Germany, to help reorganize the League.

13. ECONOMICA. **Mar:** For M's lectures on polit eco, see ← :8.

APRIL

14. THE *NRZ-REVUE*. **Apr c.11:** The third issue of the *Revue* is pubd in Hamburg, dated Mar. Its contents consist of the third installment of M's *Class struggles* series (#M148) and of E's "German campaign [etc.]" (#E328). **Apr M:** For no. 4, M finishes an addendum to his *Class struggles*: an article on financial speculation under Bonaparte (#M489). M&E write an article on Kinkel (#ME69) for the same number. **Apr 16:** Lassalle writes M reporting on his activity in Düsseldorf in the interests of the *Revue*. **Apr 18:** M&E finish, and date, the "Review" of the period Apr-Mar (#ME135), for no. 4. **Apr CD:** M&E write a book review of Girardin's book on socialism and taxation (#ME140—perhaps written by M alone), for no. 4; also a brief ed note on one Heinrich Didier (#ME54C).

15. POLITICAL AFFAIRS. **Apr 5:** M&E participate in an international meeting organized by the Fraternal Democrats for Robespierre's birthday. E's speech recalls English revolutionary traditions, incl the Levelers. **Apr M:** M&E, with Willich, as representatives of the CL, meet with leaders of the London Blanquists (Société des Proscrits Démocrates Socialistes), Adam and Vidil, and with Harney for his Chartist left wing. They agree to establish a Société Universelle des Communistes Révolutionnaires on the basis of a six-point program mentioning the "dictator-ship of the proletarians" (#ME80) [→ :38]. **Apr c.M:** The CL/CC, under M, sends Dronke as emissary to Switzerland to reestablish the CL there (together with W. Wolff in Zurich) and to counteract the secret society of the reformist Democrats called Revolutionäre Zentralisation (Revol. Zent.). Dronke is to do likewise in Baden. **Apr 23:** In Elberfeld, 122 defendants go on trial for participation in the uprising of May 1849, incl E in absentia [← 49:25], on the basis of an indictment (cf *MECW* 10:602) which recounts E's doings [→ :19].

16. REFUGEE-AID COMM. **Apr 7:** About 30 refugees issue a joint statement supporting the S-D Refugee Aid Comm against attacks on it by its Democratic opponents (R. Schramm, Struve, etc.) and thanking M and the other comm members for its work (cf *MECW* 10:350). **Apr 8:** At a meeting of the refugee comm, minutes taken by E (#ME157B) show testimony on how little Schramm, Struve, et al are doing for refugees (cf *MECW* 10:612). **Apr 9 to May:** M&E write letters to Weydemeyer, T. Schuster, Lassalle (and prob others) requesting a fund collection for refugees in Germany; also requesting contributions to finance the *NRZ-Revue*. **Apr 20:** The refugee comm issues a statement, cosigned by M as chairman, refuting insinuations that the comm is partisan in distributing aid (#ME164). **Apr 23:** M (as chairman), E, and others sign the financial statement of the aid comm, which also appeals against the machinations of "Struve, Bobzin, Bauer, and others" who on Apr 22 set up a rival comm (#ME157C).

17. PERSONAL. **Apr:** Because of unpaid rent, the M household goods are seized by bailiffs. The family is forced to move, at first into the German Hotel at no. 1 & 2 Leicester Street, adjoining Leicester Square, where they live until May A [→ :21].

MAY

18. THE *NRZ-REVUE*. **May 5:** Naut (in Cologne) sends M 25 talers from sales. **May c.20:** The fourth issue of the magazine is pubd in Hamburg, dated Apr. Contents: a French poem by Louis Ménard on the June days of 1848, "Jambes"; E's article on the ten hours' bill (#E246); three book reviews (#ME139, 141, 140); the "Review" of Mar-Apr (#ME135), and a "Miscellany" comprising two minor articles (#M489, #ME69) and a piece about Karl Vogt by W. Wolff. **May 25:** M makes a draft of £15 on Naut without informing him; it is partially covered by Weydemeyer with 20 talers from *Revue* sales in Frankfurt.

19. POLITICAL AFFAIRS. **May c.1:** On behalf of the CL/CC, E writes W. Wolff (in Switzerland) to follow the activity of the Revol. Zent. group in Switzerland and Germany and to report regularly. **May 2:** Sazanov (in Geneva) writes M that he has become a communist and asks him to collaborate with a "communist" periodical planned in Paris with Herzen and Pyat. Since the latter two are anticommunists, M does not reply. **May 6:** M&E warn Pardigon, a leader of the French Blanquist group in London, against close relations with G. Struve's émigré group, otherwise the CL would break off relations. **May 7:** In Elberfeld, the trial of the 122 defendants [← :15] ends; most are found guilty and sentenced to various jail terms. **May 9:** W. Wolff sends in a report [← :19]. **May c.M:** On a GWEA outing, M makes the acquaintance of W. Liebknecht, who has come to London after his expulsion from Switzerland. (Liebknecht's memoirs date this "summer.") **May 28:** The *Times* pubs a letter from the "Democratic Socialist Comm for German Political Refugees" (signatures headed by M) repudiating Struve's activities (#ME179). **May c.D:** At the CL/CC, H. Bauer reports on his trip to Germany, just concluded. **c.May:** On behalf of the CL/CC, M&E establish relations with the left wing of the Hungarian emigration, incl Türr and Johann Bangya.

20. PRUSSIAN SPY CAMPAIGN. **May 22:** There is an assassination attempt against Friedrich Wilhelm IV in Berlin by an ex-soldier, Max Sefeloge, a royalist lunatic. **May 25:** The *Neue Preussische Ztg* links this attentat to an alleged trip by M to Berlin at the time. **May D:** The Prussian government presses the English to apply its Alien Act provisions against the refugees; M&E, as well as others, find themselves dogged on every side by spies and "tails," prob both English police spies and Prussian agents. **May 30:** M, E, and Willich, on behalf of the GWEA, write to the Prussian ambassador, Baron Bunsen, requesting the issues of the *Neue Preussische Ztg* with the allegations reported in the press (#ME89).

21. PERSONAL. **May 8:** The M family moves to 64 Dean Street, Soho. Around this time E starts living at 6 Macclesfield Street, which is a continuation of Dean Street.

JUNE

22. POLITICAL AFFAIRS. **June A** (if not already May D): M&E write a second circular ("Address to the CL") to the League membership, reporting on the work of the organizn (#ME3). **June M:** A CL member from Solingen, Karl Klein, visits M in London on behalf of the Cologne branch. Through him, M sends the "Address" to the Cologne members, also

his proposal to accept Lassalle into the League. **June 14:** M&E, usually also with Willich's signature, send letters to various papers denouncing the Prussian spy campaign against London refugees [← :20], also denouncing efforts to apply the English Alien Act to harass refugees. **June 15:** The *Sun* prints one of these letters (#ME122), likewise *NS*; the *Spectator* prints a longer one (#ME123); a letter to the *Globe* (#M909) goes unpubd. **June 18:** Röser writes, for the Cologne branch, that it opposes accepting Lassalle into CL membership because of his "autocratic principles." **June 25:** M&E write separate statements (#ME165) replying to the editor of the *NDZ*, Lüning, who has reviewed the *NRZ-Revue* and made critical remarks about M's *Class struggles in France* (#M148) [→ :29].

23. REFUGEE-AID COMM. **c.June:** M addresses himself to Savoye (in Paris) for financial support to the comm's work. **June 14:** The comm, in a statement signed i.a. by M&E, refutes the charge made by émigré political enemies that it is aiding only communists (#ME68). **June 30:** M sends his regrets (#M891) to a refugee public meeting in London that illness prevents him from attending; he refers to his defense of the June 1848 insurgents of Paris.

24. ECONOMICA. **June M:** M obtains an admission card to the British Museum Library. **c.June to Aug:** M resumes giving lectures on polit eco, partly at home, partly at the GWEA.

JULY

25. POLITICAL AFFAIRS. **July 2:** M&E send a letter, for publ in the German press, exposing the *Weser-Ztg*'s falsified quote from the *Spectator* on the Prussian spy campaign (#ME183); pubd July 10. **July 3:** Dronke sends reports to E and to the CL/CC reporting on his organizn work in Switzerland and on his dealings with the Revol. Zent. group [← :19], which is proposing unity. (The CL/CC will reject the proposal.) **July 18:** A. Goegg (in Paris) writes M asking for more detailed info on the works on socialism that M is planning to write. —Dronke sends E a second report on his organizing work in Switzerland, esp his dealings with d'Ester and Techow. **July D:** In the CL/CC controversy arises with Willich over his leaning toward closer relations with the émigré group of Democrats in London (*KMC* dating: c.Aug).

26. REFUGEE-AID COMM. **July:** A communal lodging and eating house for refugees is set up, also the beginnings of a common workshop for the jobless. **July 30:** A financial statement for May-July, which reports on this communal enterprise, is signed by M&E et al (#ME157D).

27. LETTERS TO MARX. **July 15:** Charles A. Dana of the *NYDT* [← 48:81] writes M assuring him of his friendship and asking him to forward an enclosed letter to Freiligrath. **July or Aug** (summer): Johannes Miquel writes his first letter to M, declaring he is a communist and referring to "dictatorship of the proletariat." (Erroneously dated by *KMC* and by Bernstein in *NZ*.)

28. ECONOMICA. **c.July:** M begins a systematic study of the economic history of the past decade, on the history of prices, the bank system, economic crises in England and Europe, incl the file of the London *Economist*. In the course, M comes to the conclusion that just as the 1847 economic crisis was behind the 1848 outbreak, so returning prosperity conditioned the later reaction. By July D he concludes that the economic crisis has definitely ended and revolution is no longer imminent. **July D to Oct:** M incorporates the foregoing view in his "Review / May to Oct" (#ME136), which will appear in *NRZ-Revue*, no. 5/6. This "Review" includes a section which will later become Part IV of his *Class struggles in France* (#M148). **July:** For M's lectures, see ← :24.

29. W&P. **July 4:** NDZ pubs the M&E statements (#ME165) [← :22]. **July to Oct-Nov:** During this period E works on his history of the *Peasant war in Germany* (#E579) for *NRZ-Revue*.

AUGUST

30. POLITICAL AFFAIRS. **Aug 21:** In a discussion with Techow (in a wineshop, E and K. Schramm present) M vainly tries to persuade him to quit the Revol. Zent. group [← :19] and join the CL. **Aug c.28:** At a meeting of the S-D Refugee Aid Comm, a sharp conflict [← :25] takes place between M plus the comm majority and Willich, who says he is leaving the comm. **Aug c.29:** At a GWEA meeting, Willich announces his resignation from the refugee comm; M&E criticize him sharply. Most GWEA members side with Willich; the basic issue is Willich's desire for adventurist policies looking to a quick revolution, hence reestablishment of the 1848 alliance with the Democrats, i.e., a fast replay of 1848. In contrast, M has concluded [← :28] that the 1848–49 revolutionary crisis is now over.

31. EMIGRATE TO AMERICA? **Aug c.D:** M considers plans to move to America with his family, E to follow in Nov. M asks Rothacker, who is going to America, to make contacts for this purpose and to survey the prospects for founding a paper.

32. ECONOMICA. **Aug:** For M's lectures, see ← :24.

33. W&P (E). **c.Aug** (or betw May D and Aug): E writes part of an article, intended for *NRZ-Revue*, on the reformist German writers, like Grün, who raise the slogan of abolishing the state and talk of "anarchy"; it remains, unfinished (#E566.5).

SEPTEMBER

34. SPLIT IN THE COMMUNIST LEAGUE. **Sep c.1:** At a CL/CC session there is a sharp controversy between M and Willich [← :30]. M spurns Willich's challenge to a duel, but K. Schramm accepts despite M's dissuasion. (For the membership list of the CL/CC, see #M474.5.) **Sep 10–15:** M&E, with H. Bauer and Pfänder, announce their resignation from the S-D Refugee Aid Comm. The GWEA supervisors check the comm's financial accounts and find all correct. **Sep 11:** The Willich–Schramm duel takes place in Ostend; Schramm receives a minor head wound from a pistol shot. **Sep 14:** Röser, for the Cologne branch, writes M urging that he republish the *Com Manifesto*, rewriting it in light of 1848–49, and that he finish his book on polit eco. **Sep 15:** At a session of the CL/CC, at which M speaks twice (#M836.5), the first stage of the split takes place after a sharp debate in which a majority of the CC supports M's view. M's organizational proposal is that the London membership form two branches and that the CC move to Cologne (cf *MECW* 10:625–30). However, the Willich–Schapper faction will in fact form its own CC, thereby consummating a split formally. **Sep 17:** M&E plus 10 supporters send in a statement of resignation (#ME163) from the GWEA, whose majority supports Willich–Schapper, and from the refugee comm. **Sep 18:** M&E, with H. Bauer and Pfänder, sign their last financial statement of the refugee comm, for the period Aug 1 to Sep 10 (#ME157E). **Sep c.20:** M sends the minutes of the Sep 15 split meeting to Cologne; Eccarius is assigned to send Cologne a complete report. **Sep 24:** Through H. W. Haupt as emissary, M sends Röser (in Cologne) a letter on the split. Haupt is also commissioned to organize a new branch in Hamburg. **Sep 25:** Röser sends M the provisional opinion of the Cologne branch Exec on the split, and requests documents and communications. **Sep D to Oct A:** M&E send letters on the split to CL friends in Germany—to W. Wolff (in Zurich), Weydemeyer (in Frankfurt), Dronke (in Geneva), et al.

35. POLITICAL ACTIVITY. **Sep 10:** E makes a much-applauded speech at a Fraternal Democrats meeting called to protest the

London visit of Austrian Field Marshal Haynau (cf *MECW* 10:624).

36. ECONOMICA. Sep to next Aug: For M's reading and study in this period, see → :50, 51; 51:60–69. This represents roughly the period between the suspension of the *NRZ-Revue* work and the outbreak of the Crimean War (cf ← :3).

37. W&P. Sep: During this time M is in the midst of working on his "Review" of May-Oct (#ME136) for the magazine (see also a fragment ascribed to Sep-Oct, #M563.5); and E is working on his *Peasant war in Germany* (#E579) [← :29].

OCTOBER

38. POLITICAL AFFAIRS. Oct 1: Haupt [← :34] sends M his first report on Cologne, the reconstitution of the CC there, and its first steps. **Oct 9:** M, E, and Harney send a letter (#ME171) to the French Blanquist group stating that they consider the SUCR [← :15] to be "long since" dissolved; the original agreement will be burned at E's house on Oct 13.

39. THE *NRZ-REVUE*. Oct: M helps Eccarius write his article on tailoring for the magazine. M&E write an ed note (#ME53) specially hailing this article by a worker in the trade. **Oct 26:** Harney writes M apologizing for failing to write a promised article for the magazine; he promises to do so for a future issue. **Oct 29:** M writes Weydemeyer (in Frankfurt) to redeem Mrs. M's pawned silverware [← 49:27, 28], then sell it, and remit the difference [→ :43]. **Oct c.D:** M asks Haupt (in Hamburg) to raise funds there, and assigns him to proofread no. 5/6 of the magazine. — M writes Daniels (in Cologne) to sell a part of the library M had left there.

NOVEMBER

40. POLITICAL AFFAIRS. Nov 1: Goegg (in Paris) writes M that the Société de la Ligue des Peuples invites him to collaborate on its paper. **Nov 2:** Röser again [← :34] writes M about reprinting the *Com Manifesto*. **Nov 9–30:** The first English trans of the *Manifesto*, by Helen Macfarlane, is pubd in Harney's *Red Republican*, with an ed note naming the authors (cf #ME33). **Nov 11:** The London CL, M participating, proposes to the Cologne CC that the Willich–Schapper group be formally expelled since they have set up a parallel organization (cf *MECW* 10:633). — King Friedrich Wilhelm IV of Prussia sends a secret memo to Prime Min Manteuffel on a plan to invent a "Communist plot" [→ 51:1].

41. THE *NRZ-REVUE*. Nov 1: M&E finish, and date, the "Review / May to Oct" (#ME136), which includes also what will later be Part IV of M's *Class struggles* (#M148). **Nov c.10:** M asks Haupt to take up with pub'r Schuberth the possibility of continuing publ of the *Revue* as a quarterly. **Nov 13:** Haupt sends M £2½ collected in Hamburg [← :39]. **Nov 29:** The last issue of the *NRZ-Revue*, double number 5/6, is pubd in Hamburg, dated "May to Oct." Contents: E's *Peasant war in Germany* (#E579); a reprint of Section III of the *Com Manifesto* (naming the authors—cf #ME54D); Eccarius's article on tailoring in London [← :39]; and the "Review / May to Oct" (#ME136). **Nov D to next Feb:** M makes efforts to continue the magazine as a quarterly, in discussions with CL members in Cologne and Hamburg as well as with publishers [→ :46].

42. ECONOMICA. Nov-Dec: For M's reading, with emphasis on money and banks, see → :51.

43. PERSONAL. Nov A: M receives a letter (Oct 14) from Rothacker (NY) with unfavorable news on the prospects for founding a paper there [← :31]. **Nov 10:** Weydemeyer (in Frankfurt) informs M that the sale of his silverware [← :39] will hardly exceed the cost of redemption [→ :48]. **Nov 19:** M's son Guido (Heinrich Guido) dies suddenly.

44. ENGELS: TO MANCHESTER. Nov M: E departs for Manchester to go to work in the firm of Ermen & Engels, mainly to support M while he works out his theory of polit eco. From this time on M&E carry on a regular correspondence, beginning with M's letter of Nov 19. E's first residence in Manchester is 70 Great Ducie Street, Strangeways [→ 52:38]. **Nov D:** In Manchester, E begins a study of military science.

DECEMBER

45. POLITICAL AFFAIRS. Dec 1: The new CL/CC in Cologne issues a circular ("Address") to the membership on the split in the League; text in ST/ME12 (CCT) 254. **Dec 3:** Haupt (in Hamburg) sends M a report on the League situation there and on differences with Nothjung, emissary of the Cologne CC. **Dec 18:** M receives the Cologne circular and a draft of the CC's new statutes (for which, see *MECW* 10:634, incl M's notes on the statutes); also a communication to the London CL on Bruhn's activity in Hamburg with a request to take a position on it; and info on the fantastic plans for revolution sent by Willich in letters to H. Becker. **Dec D:** M&E draft a statement for Pfänder and H. Bauer against a Willich–Schapper slander campaign (#ME52).

46. PUBL PLANS. Dec 2: Re his plan to publish *NRZ-Revue* as a quarterly beginning

Feb [← :41], M writes H. Becker (in Cologne) about undertaking the task. M also asks about the possibility of publishing a German trans of his *Poverty of philosophy* (#M681) and a "library" of socialist literature in a series of small pamphlets. —M urges E to write a critical essay on Mazzini for the quarterly *NRZ-Revue*. **Dec 13:** M writes H. Becker (in Cologne) about his plan to publish M's *Collected essays* (#M151), from 1842 and later; this letter (not extant) prob contained specifications of the contents [→ 51:6].

47. ECONOMICA. **Dec:** M makes notes on Ricardo's book *On the principles of polit eco* [etc.], esp on Ricardo's money theory (#M581). For M's reading during the last months of this year, see → :51.

48. PERSONAL. **Dec 1:** M and his wife attend a lecture by Ernest Jones on the history of the popes. **Dec 2:** The M family moves to 28 Dean Street, Soho, into two or three furnished rooms. **Dec 13:** Weydemeyer proposes to M that a lottery be held for the silverware [← :43]; M will not give his consent.

49. ENGELS. **Dec 9:** Harney invites E to translate his *Peasant war in Germany* (#E579)

for publ in *Friend of the People*. **Dec M:** E replies that he lacks time right now, and (Dec 16) Harney assures him there is no hurry. **Dec D:** E begins studying the Russian language. **Dec c.24–31:** E sojourns in London, staying with M. **Dec 30:** At a New Year's affair in London held by the Fraternal Democrats, attended also by M and his wife, E gives a talk on the causes of the failure of the revolution (cf *MECW* 10:637).

YEAR APPENDIX

50. *M's Reading in the Sep-Oct Period.* *MEW* mentions the following authors studied in this period: J. S. Mill, John Fullarton, R. Torrens, Th. Tooke; and the file of the *Economist*. *KMC* mentions the following: G. Garnier, J. Taylor, J. W. Gilbart, J. F. Reitemeier, N. W. Senior, W. Blake; also A. Alison, J. Graham, W. Jacob, R. Moore, A. Mundell, R. Ruding, F. W. Reden.

51. *In the Nov-Dec Period.* M studied works by Böckh, J. G. Büsch, W. Jacob. Also see ← :47 for M's study of Ricardo's work (cf #M581 for M's notes). Other notes on: E. Solly.

1851

CONSPECTUS

1. The Communist League led by M, much weakened by the recent split, holds its weekly London branch meetings with varying regularity. Those attending include Liebknecht, K. Schramm, Pieper, F. Wolff, Seiler, H. Bauer, Eccarius, Pfänder, Rings, Klose, Hain, occasionally Freiligrath; in Dec, also W. Hirsch and Gümpel. (W. Wolff is in Manchester, as is E.) Meanwhile, as reaction deepens, left-wing sentiment declines and the Communists are increasingly isolated; for example, Harney, trying to maintain harmony with all elements, aligns himself in practice with the right-wing émigrés. In Germany a wave of police arrests of Cologne Communists presages an anti-Communist witch-hunt (which will climax in 1852) [← 50:40]. M&E become increasingly alienated by the antics of all the émigré sects. Bonaparte's coup d'état in December augurs mounting reaction in France too.

2. M is left without a press organ of his own; efforts to found one prove fruitless. He collaborates with Ernest Jones's *Notes to the People*, begins contributing journalistic correspondence to the *New York Daily Tribune* (*NYDT*), then hears that Weydemeyer is founding a weekly in America; but he has no

reliable outlet for political writing. On the personal side, constant financial straits and material misery make for a great deal of unhappy pressure.

3. *Economica.* M works intensively on polit eco, regularly visits the British Museum Library, and fills about 14 notebooks with excerpts and notes. The work is interrupted in Dec by the Bonaparte coup d'état and his work on *The 18th Brumaire* (#M267). Still, he has no publisher for the work in sight. For the authors read, see → :61–71.

4. In Manchester, E is at work in the family business, but has few political co-thinkers at hand; he does little serious writing, until he starts writing M's articles for *NYDT*. His main intellectual outlets are his busy correspondence with M and his continued study of military science and languages.

JANUARY

5. POLITICAL AFFAIRS. **Jan 5:** The London CL, M participating, approves the new draft Rules proposed by the Cologne CC [← :45]. **Jan 10:** Miquel (in Göttingen) writes M reporting on his activity for the CL. **Jan 25:** W. Wolff (in Zurich) writes M about the tribulations of German refugees in Zurich; he has nothing to report on the CL. **Jan 27:** M draws up a statement replying to an attack by Ruge pubd in the Bremen press on Jan 17; signed by M&E (#ME162). (The Bremen paper will not print it.) —H. Becker (in Cologne) writes M with more info on Willich's letters containing plans for a "revolution" (putsch) under a dictatorship [→ :10]. **Jan c.28:** M meets with Landolphe and informs him on the split in the CL. **Jan 31 to Feb 14:** The *Deutsche Londoner Ztg* reprints the "Review / May to Oct" (#ME136) in part.

6. PUBL PLANS. Jan A: M corresponds with Schabelitz (in Bern) on publ of the *NRZ-Revue* as a quarterly in Switzerland. **Jan c.6:** M receives a letter (Dec 15) from Wilhelmi (in Cincinnati) proposing that M&E contribute to German-American papers he is going to found. (M will decline.) **Jan M:** M wants to force pub'r Schuberth by court action to continue publishing the *NRZ-Revue* as a quarterly, and Jan 17 he asks W. Haupt (in Hamburg) to get a lawyer [→ :11]. **Jan 27:** Becker informs M that the *Collected essays* project [← 50:46] is being held up by lack of book paper [→ :11].

7. ECONOMICA. Jan A: M is studying the question of ground rent. **Jan 7:** M writes E with a criticism of Ricardo's theory. **Jan 29:** E presses M to hurry and finish his book.

8. PERSONAL. Jan 6: M appeals to E for money: the landlady is pressing for two weeks' unpaid rent. **Jan 8:** E sends £1. **Jan c.19:** Social soiree at M's house brings Harney and his wife, Liebknecht, Eccarius, Pieper.

9. ENGELS IN MANCHESTER. Jan 5: E attends a Chartist meeting at which E. Jones defends the platform of the left Chartists. **Jan 8:** E informs M that he plans to organize a local club or regular meetings based on discussions of the *Com Manifesto* with Chartist left-wingers. **Jan D:** E intends to write a series of articles for Harney's *Friend of the People* on the émigré Central Comm of the European Democracy (Mazzini, Ruge, Ledru-Rollin, etc.) [→ :13].

FEBRUARY

10. POLITICAL AFFAIRS. Feb c.1: M asks H. Becker (in Cologne) to send him the Willich letters [← :5]. (He will not get them.) **Feb 7:** Dronke (in Geneva) informs M on the activity of A. Majer, emissary of the Willich–Schapper group in Switzerland, against M and his group; Dronke asks for info and suggestions. **Feb A:** Meeting Landolphe, M learns that he now supports Willich–Schapper and will participate with L. Blanc in a Willich–Schapper banquet on Feb 24, anniversary of the Feb Revolution. **Feb 11:**

Harney supports a meeting (held to honor Polish Gen. Bem) together with Willich–Schapper and L. Blanc; M denounces this (to E) as Harney's turn toward allying himself with the anti-M wing of the emigration. **Feb 21:** M urges E. Jones not to support the so-called Banquet of the Equals (celebration of the Feb Revolution anniversary on Feb 24) with the new émigré alliance of L. Blanc + Willich–Schapper + Harney. **Feb c.22:** The French Blanquist Tessier du Mothay informs M on the background of the Feb 24 banquet, involving a Byzantine tale of clique rivalry between L. Blanc and Ledru-Rollin in the French emigration, with Blanc now lining up Harney and Willich–Schapper on his side. **Feb 24:** Two of M's supporters, K. Schramm and Pieper, try to attend the banquet at the Highbury Barn Tavern, chaired by Willich. They are beaten up physically and thrown out, in a public act. Among others, Harney is present, sees this, and makes no protest. At midnight Pieper, clothes ripped, comes to M's house and tells him about it. **Feb 27:** *La Patrie* (Paris) reveals that Blanqui had, on request, sent (Feb 10) a "toast," or political message, to the Feb 24 banquet, but since Blanqui's toast had attacked L. Blanc and others, it had been suppressed by the banquet organizers [→ :14]. **Feb 28:** M sends an account of the Feb 24 affair to the Cologne CL and asks that the German workers be informed.

11. PUBL PLANS. Feb 3: H. Becker (in Cologne) sends M a file of the old *RZ*, to be used in editing the *Collected essays* project [← :6]; he had found the *RZ* file after much effort. **Feb 4:** Haupt (in Hamburg) informs M that the lawyer for the proposed court action against Schuberth [← :6] wants his expenses guaranteed; the matter is dropped. **Feb D:** M sends the *RZ* file back to Becker, marked to indicate what to condense out of which articles, for the proposed *Collected essays*.

12. ECONOMICA. Feb 3: M sends E his views on his developing theory of money, resulting from his study of polit eco and his criticism of Ricardo.

13. ENGELS IN MANCHESTER. Feb 12: E informs M that he has sent Harney three articles in the planned series [← :9] and speaks of six more (none extant); also that he has helped to found a Chartist branch locally. **Feb 13:** On hearing of Harney's turn toward a right-wing alliance [← :10], E resolves to write Harney withdrawing the articles he has sent. **Feb 26:** Together with M, E sends a letter to Harney sharply condemning him for his participation in the Feb 24 banquet and for his new political alliance. (This inaugurates a period of distant relations with Harney.)

MARCH

14. BLANQUI'S TOAST. **Mar c.3–4:** E visits M in London to discuss how to expose the scandal of the Feb 24 "Banquet of the Equals," the beating-up of Schramm and Pieper, and the suppression of Blanqui's toast [← :10], now disclosed. M&E translate Blanqui's toast into German and English. The German version, with a prefatory note by M&E (#ME81), is printed up in 30,000 copies for wide distribution. **Mar 5:** E sends an open letter to the *Times*, signed "Veritas," dealing with this affair and enclosing a copy of Blanqui's toast in English (#E827); it is not pubd. **Mar A:** L. Blanc, Willich and Schapper, and the other banquet organizers publicly deny all knowledge of Blanqui's toast, denying its suppression. (Not long after, a conscience-torn Vidil reveals that these people, as the organizing comm, formally voted, seven to six, to suppress the toast.) **Mar c.10:** M sends a report on the latest happenings to the Cologne CL/CC, with Blanqui's toast. **Mar 15:** Harney in his *Friend of the People* pubs an open letter by K. Schramm on the Feb 24 attack, with an ed note assuring Schramm of his confidence.

15. OTHER AFFAIRS. **Mar D:** Rothacker (in NYC) informs M that Weitling's *Republik der Arbeiter* and other German-American Democratic papers are printing attacks on M. **Mar c.D to Apr A:** M has two meetings with the Hungarian "baroness" Wilhelmine Beck, former Kossuth agent, to discuss the Hungarian emigration. **16.** PUBL PLANS. **Mar 1:** H. Becker (in Cologne) reports that the first three printer's sheets of M's *Collected essays* (#M151) have been typeset [← :11]; he also sends 50 talers. **Mar 20:** M sends Daniels (in Cologne) an extensive critique of a big work by Daniels that he has just read, *Mikrokosmos*, subtitled "Sketch of a physiological anthropology" (M's letter is not extant). **c.Mar:** To E. I. Koch, a German Catholic priest and contributor to *New Yorker Staatszeitung* who wrote Feb 26 with the request, M sends 20 copies of the *Com Manifesto* plus the English trans in *Red Republican*, and proposes that the trans be pubd as a brochure.

17. ECONOMICA. **Mar:** In Notebook VII, M writes up some "Reflections" on polit eco (#M728). **Mar D to Apr:** Continuing his study of Ricardo, M indexes Ricardo's book (#M582) and makes notes (#M583). Also see #M527, a still-unpubd ms. **18.** PERSONAL. **Mar:** In desperate financial circumstances, M draws a draft on his mother in Trier, thereby leading to a heated correspondence. **Mar 28:** M's daughter Franziska is born. **Mar 31:** M writes E of a

"mystère" (secret matter) which he promises to explain in his next letter and which involves E in some way [→ :23].

APRIL

19. POLITICAL AFFAIRS. **Apr 12:** Daniels (in Cologne) writes M that Lassalle is "isolated" and his efforts at "reconciliation" with the Communist group have been rejected; he warns that Lassalle may appeal to London. **Apr M:** M asks Weerth and Daniels to obtain money and a passport for W. Wolff, who has been expelled from Zurich and will go to London. In his letter to Daniels, M defends Lassalle against the Cologne branch. **Apr 24:** Daniels replies, expressing the Rhenish Communists' view that Lassalle is "a shallow *blagueur* and a pure-Democratic charlatan," that the hostility to Lassalle is not "personal" in origin, and that M is "deluded" in Lassalle's favor. **Apr-May:** After the falling-out with Harney [← :13] M's relations with E. Jones become close; by now (if not earlier) M begins working with Jones's *Notes to the People* (writing and general editing) and helping Jones with his articles about cooperativism.

20. PUBL PLANS. **Apr 2:** M proposes that E write a history of the Hungarian revolutionary war of 1848–49. **Apr 5:** H. Becker (in Cologne) writes M about his plan to publish a communist magazine *Neue Zeitschrift* with Bürgers, Daniels, Weydemeyer, et al; he requests M's collaboration. **Apr 8:** M asks Weerth (in Hamburg) to write an article against Kinkel for this projected organ. **Apr 9:** M promises Becker he will contribute as requested. **Apr 15:** Becker pubs a prospectus for the *Collected essays* (#M151). **Apr D:** The first fascicule of the *Collected essays* is pubd in Cologne. **Apr:** E drafts a memo (not for publ) discussing the prospects from a military standpoint of a revolutionary France faced in 1852 by counterrevolutionary invasion (#E177).

21. STUDIES. **Apr c.2:** In a letter to Daniels (in Cologne) M criticizes Feuerbach's philosophic views, and opines that Daniels has not fully freed himself of this influence [cf ← :16]; M also requests shipment of Feuerbach's works. **Apr 24:** Daniels sends M the seven volumes of Feuerbach's works.

22. ECONOMICA. **Apr 2:** M writes E: "In five weeks I will be finished with all the economic crap.... It is beginning to bore me." **Apr 3:** E replies: "I'm glad you're finally finished with the Economics. The thing has really dragged itself out for too long a time...." **Apr A:** M asks Freiligrath and Daniels to find a pub'r for his Economica. Freiligrath, via Ebner (in Frankfurt), tries

Cotta, who says no. **Apr-May:** Stimulated by an article in the 1845 *Economist,* M studies literature on the application of electricity to raising land productivity; he corresponds on this with E and Daniels. —M continues his study of Ricardo; he makes notes on Ricardo's system (#M580).

23. PERSONAL. **Apr 2:** Re the "mystère" [← :18], M writes E that he will have to visit E in Manchester to discuss it. —M's desperate financial situation [← :18] is eased a bit by receipt of money from E. **Apr c.15:** M receives £50 from Cologne friends via Daniels. **Apr c.16:** He receives £5 from Weerth. **Apr c.17–23:** M visits E in Manchester, where i.a. he discusses the "mystère" (which prob concerns Helene Demuth's pregnancy—see *Demuth, Frederick).

MAY

24. POLITICAL AFFAIRS. **May 2:** M sends the Cologne CL/CC a report on the whole episode of Blanqui's toast [← :14]. **May 4:** M attends a lecture by E. Jones on the cooperative movement [← :19]. **May 18:** M encounters Harney at a lecture by Robert Owen, for the first time since their falling-out [← :13]. **May c.18:** Freiligrath arrives in London from Cologne, and reports on the activity of the Cologne CL/CC, which is planning to hold a communist congress in a few weeks. **May 22:** Haupt (in Hamburg) writes M of the beginnings of the new police crackdown on the Communists in Germany: arrest of Nothjung on May 10 in Leipzig (after touring Germany as a field organizer), arrest of H. Becker and Röser in Cologne on May 19. **May 28:** Freiligrath informs M of the arrest of Bürgers on May 23 in Dresden. — Freiligrath and E. Jones visit M. **May D:** The outlines of the German police campaign become clear; those arrested are charged with treason. To maintain contact with Cologne, M begins correspondence with Bermbach, a CL member (*KMC* dates M's contact with Bermbach a month later). All this is the beginning of the process leading to the Cologne Communist trial of 1852.

25. W&P. **May c.3:** From Becker, M receives a single copy of his *Collected essays,* first fascicule (#M151), just off the press [← :20]. M sends Becker, as requested, a copy of *Poverty of philosophy* (#M681) for excerpting in Becker's planned magazine [← :20]. **May 19:** The arrest of Becker [← :24], added to financial difficulties and other police harassment, means the collapse of the *Collected essays* project and of Becker's proposed *Neue Zeitschrift* [← :20]. **May CD:** Most of the *Collected essays* edn is confiscated by the police at the Hartmann bindery; few copies, if any, go on sale. **May D:** M agrees to write a preface to Daniels's work on anthropology [← :16]; he will expound this thought: "The Communists have to show that only under communist conditions can the technological truths already attained be put into practice." —M begins work on an article for E. Jones's *Notes to the People,* which he is now supporting very actively [← :19; → :28].

26. ECONOMICA. **May 12:** Lassalle writes M that he is "voraciously hungry" for his opus on polit eco, which he asks about.

JUNE

27. GERMANY: ANTICOMMUNIST WITCH-HUNT. **June c.A:** M writes Miquel a letter dealing with the arrests of Rhineland Communists (SOURCE: *KMC*). **June c.4:** Mrs. Keene, wife of the London *Daily News* correspondent, brings M letters from Daniels (in Cologne) confirming that the arrest of Becker and Bürgers suspends the plans for *Neue Zeitschrift* and M's *Collected essays* [← :25]. **June c.5:** W. Wolff, expelled from Switzerland, arrives in London. **June 7–c.8:** E visits M in London, no doubt i.a. to discuss the CL crisis in Germany. **June 10:** Weydemeyer (in Frankfurt) informs M of other arrests in Germany. **June D:** As a result of police seizures of CL literature found in the homes of Communists arrested, a number of German papers publish the "Address to the CL" (#ME2) and other CL documents—first a Dresden paper on June 28, then others (into July).

28. W&P. **June 14:** Jones's *Notes to the People* pubs M's article on the French constitution of 1848 (#M180). **June c.M:** M asks Lassalle to find a pub'r to continue issuing the *Collected essays* (#M151) [← :25]. **June 26:** Lassalle reports his fruitless negotiations.

29. ECONOMICA. **June 27:** M explains to Weydemeyer that the subject ramifies so much that he cannot finish before another "six to eight weeks," but the work is "rapidly" ending.

30. PERSONAL. **June 23:** Helene Demuth [← :23] gives birth to a son; see *Demuth, Frederick.

JULY

31. POLITICAL AFFAIRS. **July A:** M and other CL leaders come into conflict with K. Schramm, who, just before leaving for Paris, wants to deposit the CL document files with Louis Bamberger rather than M. **July 8:** Writing to Freiligrath, M discusses his letter rejecting the invitation of the right-wing Democrats (Ruge, Fickler, Goegg, etc.) to help them found an émigré club; Freiligrath emphasizes his political solidarity with M. **July**

c.10: Miquel [← :27] writes M about the effect of the Communist arrests in Germany on intimidating the Democrats. —M writes Lassalle a letter with "descriptions of the German professors of revolution in London," i.e., the émigré Democrats. **July c.24:** M attends the funeral of Gustav Julius, a German "True Socialist" writer who, M felt, was evolving leftward.

32. W&P. July 9–22: Weerth, who has been living in the same house as M, is about to leave London, and M asks him to deal with the pub'r Campe (in Hamburg) about publishing a paper. **July 31:** M writes E about a project to supply the German-American press with articles through a lithographed correspondence service, aided by E and Wolff.

33. ECONOMICA. July c.20: M requests Reinhardt (in Paris) to send him Dureau de la Malle's *Economie politique des Romains* via Karl Weerth. (Reinhardt will send the volumes on July 23.) **July c.D:** Ebner (in Frankfurt), to whom M on Freiligrath's recommendation has sent the plan of his opus, promises M to find a publisher. (Ebner is actually an Austrian police agent.) **July 31:** M writes E reporting that Ebner has written that Cotta will prob publish the Economica.

34. PERSONAL. July: M's continuing financial situation is so bad that it interferes with his work.

AUGUST

35. POLITICAL AFFAIRS. Aug 2: M sends Weydemeyer (in Zurich), who is preparing to emigrate to America, a recommendatory letter by W. Wolff to Reichhelm, co-owner of the *New Yorker Staatszeitung*, and suggests he look up Dana of the NYDT. **Aug 18:** Bermbach [← :24] sends M a report on the Prussian government's investigation directed against the arrested Cologne Communists.

36. ÉMIGRÉ ANTICS. Aug 19: Since the London weekly *How do you do?* has slanderously linked M to the Prussian min of the interior, F. von Westphalen (M's brother-in-law), M visits the weekly's office accompanied by Freiligrath, W. Wolff, and Ziegenhainer, and demands redress from the pub'r L. Drucker and editor H. Beta. **Aug M:** The Basel pub'r Schabelitz visits M a few times and fills him in on the doings of the London German emigration, Kinkel's émigré club, Ruge's group, etc. **Aug 25:** M sends E a load of gossip about the London émigré world. Through Ulmer, Rumpf, and Liebknecht, M is in contact with a small opposition group in the ranks of the right-wing Democrats and the Willich–Schapper–controlled GWEA. **Aug 30:** In a German émigré flysheet pubd in London, E. Meyen writes that M is now

completely isolated politically whereas in the first period of the emigration he had a dominant position.

37. PROUDHON'S NEW BOOK. Aug A: M reads *Idée générale de la révolution au XIXe siècle*, sees it as a direct polemic against communism, and plans to publish a critical brochure against it. **Aug 8:** M writes E a long letter with a detailed summary of the contents of Proudhon's book. **Aug c.16–21:** E begins reading and annotating Proudhon's book (cf #E196) [→ :46]. **Aug 20:** M proposes to Hoffmann & Campe (Hamburg pub'r) to print his planned brochure against Proudhon's book. **Aug 26:** H&C reply with a refusal.

38. NYDT CONNECTION BEGINS. Aug c.7: M receives a proposal from Charles A. Dana that he (also Freiligrath) write articles for the *NY Daily Tribune* (KMC dates receipt of letter as Aug c.5). **Aug 8:** M informs E of Dana's proposal, and asks him to write an article on the German situation by the 15th. **Aug 14:** M suggests that E write a series of articles on "Germany from 1848 on." **Aug 21:** E begins work on the series later known as *Revolution and counterrevolution in Germany* (#E699) [→ :46].

39. W&P. Aug D: M learns from E. Jones's letter that M's 1848 article on the June revolution in Paris (#M425) has been translated in *Notes to the People*.

40. ECONOMICA. Aug AB: M gives a close reading to Dureau de la Malle's work [← :33].

41. ENGELS IN MANCHESTER. Aug c.2: E informs M that he is under constant surveillance by the Manchester police, and suggests that political documents be kept in a safe place.

SEPTEMBER

42. POLITICAL AFFAIRS. Sep A: Dronke (in Geneva) writes M on the politically ambiguous role of Sazanov and on Swiss political affairs; also, he and two Frenchmen have translated half the *Com Manifesto*, Sazanov the other half. **Sep 23:** M sends E a long criticism of an article by Techow, "Outlines of the approaching war [and revolution]." **Sep 26:** E returns an equally long analysis. **Sep 29:** M's friend Weydemeyer sails from Le Havre for America [→ :46]. **Sep:** M&E read in the press about the arrest of Paris members of the Willich–Schapper group and the start of the investigation into the so-called German-French plot (which will be featured in the Cologne Communist witch-hunt). Many German papers echo the Prussian government's fiction that M is responsible for Willich–Schapper documents. **Sep 30:** A Cologne correspondent of the Augsburg AZ pubs the tale that the police investigation was helped by an alleged indiscretion by M in connection with a Baroness Beck [→ :45].

43. ECONOMICA. Sep c.25: Freiligrath writes M that pub'r Löwenthal (in Frankfurt) has finally rejected the publ of M's opus.

44. PERSONAL. Sep 24: Mrs. M's cousin Werner von Veltheim (Ostrau) sends M £14, 15 shillings.

OCTOBER

45. POLITICAL AFFAIRS. Oct A: M receives a request from Ewerbeck (in Paris) for biographical material on M&E for Ewerbeck's French book on Germany. (M&E will agree, Oct M, to send him a few lines.) —Since on Oct 8 Pieper is going to Frankfurt as a private tutor in the Rothschild family, M commissions him to get info on the arrests of Communists when he passes through Cologne, by contacting Mrs. Daniels. —M writes a recommendatory letter to Dana for Weydemeyer, and gets Freiligrath to do the same. **Oct 4:** M writes a statement (#M849) denouncing the Baroness Beck tale [← :42]; it is pubd in Germany on Oct 9, 18. **Oct 6:** Karl Blind and his wife visit at M's house, along with Freiligrath, F. Wolff, Liebknecht, and Pieper. **Oct c.M:** M sends A. Cluss (Washington, D.C.) his views on the "German-American revolutionary loan" which Kinkel is collecting in the US; M suggests that Cluss participate in the Kinkel congress being held in Cincinnati. **Oct 22:** Bermbach sends M an extensive report on the Prussian government's investigation into the arrested Cologne Communists. **Oct 24:** Pieper (in Frankfurt) reports to M on his findings in Cologne. **Oct 27:** Dronke arrives in London.

46. W&P. Oct M: E resumes work on his critique of Proudhon's new book [← :37]. **Oct 16:** M proposes to Weydemeyer (in NYC) publ of the Macfarlane English trans of the *Com Manifesto* as a pamphlet. (This will not be done.) **Oct 22:** Bermbach reports to M on his failure to find a German pub'r for M's *Poverty of philosophy* (#M681). **Oct 25, 28:** E's first two articles in the *NYDT* series on Germany (#E699) are pubd under M's name. **Oct 31:** M proposes to Weydemeyer that he publish a "pocket library" of pamphlets reprinting major articles from *NRZ* (incl W. Wolff's "Silesian billion," Weerth's feuilletons, #E461, #M95, and so on), or else M&E's anti-Heinzen articles of 1847 (#M531, #E152), or even new articles, and also that he take orders for *NRZ-Revue* copies. (This will not be done.) **Oct D:** E sends M his ms notes on Proudhon.

47. ECONOMICA. Oct A: M commissions Pieper (see ← :45) to see Ebner (in Frankfurt) about finding a pub'r for the Economica or for

Poverty of philosophy (#M681). **Oct 13:** M writes E that Ebner has another pub'r prospect for the Economica, a Dessau bookdealer. (Nothing will come of this.) **Oct 24:** Pieper reports that Ebner has had no success with publishers. **Oct 30:** Ebner sends M a report on his (alleged) efforts to find a pub'r for the Economica, and requests M to write him on London émigré matters.

48. PERSONAL. Oct 21: Reinhardt, Heine's secy in Paris, writes M conveying Heine's best wishes. **Oct:** M works himself deeply into debt [→ :53].

49. ENGELS IN MANCHESTER. Oct into 1852: E continues his study of Russian and other Slavic languages, also Slavic history and literature. He reads Bowring's *Specimens of the Russian poets*, and he excerpts Lomonosov, Derzhavin, Sumarokov, Bogdanovich, Kheraskov, Karamzin, Zhukovsky, Krylov, and other Russian writers. He reads some classic works in the original, incl Pushkin and Griboyedov, and translates some of *Eugene Onegin* into prose.

NOVEMBER

50. POLITICAL AFFAIRS. Nov 7: Pieper writes M on his meeting with Miquel and on Miquel's proposals for new methods in presenting communist propaganda. **Nov M:** M asks Cluss (in the US) to help Weydemeyer, who has recently emigrated [← :42]. **Nov:** K. Schramm, who was arrested in Paris (Sep A) and then expelled, is once again working in close assoc with M.

51. W&P. Nov 6–28: *NYDT* pubs four more articles in E's series on the German revolution (#E699). **Nov 24:** M writes E that he has again gone through E's notes on Proudhon [← :46] and proposes to combine E's views with his own critique to make a brochure on Proudhon, to be pubd. Some days ago (M relates) he had read Proudhon's earlier *Gratuité du crédit* in the library, and found it worthless. **Nov D:** From Cluss's letters M learns that the first articles sent in have begun appearing in *NYDT* [← :46].

52. ECONOMICA. Nov c.5–15: See → :53 on M's visit to E. **Nov 17–18:** Pieper and Ebner (in Frankfurt) write M on various unsuccessful attempts to get a pub'r. **Nov 24, 27:** M&E exchange ideas on questions involved in M's opus, esp in re Proudhon vs Bastiat. E supports, and M rejects, a suggestion by pub'r Löwenthal that the opus begin with the history of polit eco—to be followed, adds E, by volumes on "the Socialists," the "critique of polit eco," and "the famous positive part—what you 'really' want." E urges that the main point is to appear in print "with a big book."

53. PERSONAL. **Nov c.5–15:** M visits E in Manchester, also meeting Weerth and W. Wolff; he discusses his *Economica* with E. **Nov 11:** Having been haled into court for his debt to one Göhringer, M is ordered to pay up. He is kept afloat by small sums sent by E and Weerth, and by £20 drummed up by Freiligrath. **Nov 24:** After returning from Manchester, M sends E his first letter addressed no longer to "Lieber Engels" but to "Lieber Frederic" [→ 56:10].

DECEMBER

54. POLITICAL AFFAIRS. **Dec 1:** To break the press "conspiracy of silence" about the arrests of the Cologne Communists, M sends letters to Paris for publ in the French press; W. Wolff is doing the same for America and England; M asks E to work up letters to the *Times* and the *Sun*. —M meets with some newly arrived German refugees who are in opposition to the Willich–Schapper leadership of the GWEA.

55. *THE 18TH BRUMAIRE.* **Dec 2:** Louis Bonaparte executes his coup d'état and declares himself emperor as Napoleon III. **Dec 3:** Writing to M, E comments on the coup as a parody of Napoleon's "18th Brumaire" (Nov 9, 1799). E thinks this event makes it advisable to postpone efforts to get press publicity on the Cologne Communists. **Dec 4, 6, 30:** Reinhardt (in Paris) sends M valuable letters reporting on the situation in France. **Dec 9:** In a letter to E, M admits he is "quite bewildered" by the French events, but makes some analytical remarks. **Dec c.19:** M begins work on his essay *The 18th Brumaire of Louis Bonaparte* (#M267).

56. WEYDEMEYER'S *DIE REVOLUTION.* **Dec 16:** E receives a letter (Dec 1) from Weydemeyer (in NY) asking for articles for his forthcoming weekly *Die Revolution;* E sends it on to M (rec'd Dec 17) suggesting that M write an article on Bonaparte's coup. **Dec c.19:** M&E discuss the writing of articles for Weydemeyer with W. Wolff, F. Wolff, Weerth, Freiligrath, Eccarius. M begins work on his essay (see Dec 16 above). **Dec 19:** M writes Weydemeyer about the articles he expects to send shortly, and asks him to announce a series of articles on Proudhon, a "critique by KM" [← :51]. **Dec 27:** M asks Freiligrath to write a New Year's poem for *Die Revolution.*

57. W&P. **Dec c.30:** M receives his first news from Dana on the appearance in *NYDT* of the articles sent in [← :51], for which he receives £1.

58. ECONOMICA. **Dec A:** M rejects Lassalle's plan to set up a joint-stock company in Germany to publish the opus.

59. PERSONAL. **Dec 2:** M, accompanied by Freiligrath, visits Marie Schmidt-Dähnhardt, wife of Max Stirner. **Dec c.20 to Jan c.3:** E visits M in London.

YEAR APPENDIX

60. M's notebooks of excerpts and notes are so marked that it is possible to assign the works to specific months.

61. January. M studies the circulation of money and currency, in writings by W. Jacob, S. Bailey, H. C. Carey, Lord Overstone (S. J. Loyd); also W. Clay, T. Joplin, W. H. Morrison, G. W. Norman, and D. Salomons; and the file of the *Economist.*

62. February. Economic writings of Hume and John Locke; works by John Gray, G. M. Bell, J. Francis; also R. Hamilton, J. G. Kinnear, T. Mortimer, P. J. Stirling.

63. March. Works by Ricardo, C. Bosanquet, J. W. Bosanquet, T. Tooke, Torrens, Raguet; also Adam Smith on money theory (edited by McCulloch); also A. Gallatin, J. G. Hubbard, W. Leatham, T. Twiss. He rereads Adam Smith's *Wealth of nations,* this time in English.

64. April. Works by A. Serra, Montanari, Torrens, W. C. Taylor, J. Steuart, J. Morton; and Ricardo's *Principles of polit eco,* this time in English; also W. M. Gouge, and the *Economist* for 1845.

65. May. Works by H. C. Carey, Malthus, Mackinnon, Tuckett, and De Quincey.

66. June. Works by Malthus, Torrens, Carey, Ravenstone, Hodgskin, R. Jones, G. Ramsay, J. Barton, W. Blake, D. Buchanan, T. Chalmers, J. R. McCulloch, Scrope, Tuckett.

67. July. Works by Hodgskin, Robert Owen, J. Fielden, T. Hopkins, Ricardo, P. Gaskell, S. Laing, N. W. Senior, J. C. Symons, J. Anderson, M. de Dombasle, R. Somers, Sir Edward West, J. Liebig; also statistics from the *Edinburgh Review* and (July D) a rereading of Malthus's essay on population.

68. August to November (*MEW summary*). M studies the history of landed property, the problem of colonial settlements, population density, credit, banking system, etc., and makes notes, with critical remarks, on works by Somers, Loudon, Wakefield, Prescott, Hodgskin, Quételet, S. P. Newman, Townsend, Malthus, Hume, Gray, Doubleday, W. P. Alison, A. Alison, Hardcastle, Price, Faucher, McCulloch, et al; also works on problems of agronomy and agricultural chemistry, e.g., by Liebig and Johnston.

69. August (*KMC summary*). Works by W. T. Thornton, A. Alison, Johnston; also many works on colonization and the slave trade, incl Prescott, Buxton, Howitt; works by Wakefield and Hodgskin; and Sempere on the Spanish monarchy. —(*Rubel list*) Works by

Doubleday, Malthus, Purves, R. Vaughan, Townsend, Brougham, Hodgskin, Heeren, Merivale, Wakefield, Sempere. **70. Ca. September.** Works by J. Dalrymple, John Gray, H. Hallam, K. D. Hüllmann, F. W. Newman. **71. October-November** (*KMC summary*). M again reads on money and banking, incl works by G. Julius and Hardcastle; also many works, mostly in German, on agronomy and the history of technology, incl works by Poppe, Beckmann, Ure, and Johnston. — (*Rubel list*) The Bastiat–Proudhon controversy on *Gratuité du crédit*, and works by T. Corbet, C. Coquelin, F. Vidal, A. Quételet. His notebook on technology incl notes on Poppe and Beckmann. —(*MEW summary*) M studies the history of technology, in connection with his inquiry into the influence of machine production on factory work. — (*Misc.*) Other notes in 1851 notebooks: E. Forcade, E. C. Tufnell.

1852

CONSPECTUS

1. Most of this year is dominated by the German police crackdown on, and then the trial of, the Cologne Communists, which effectually breaks the movement and brings about the dissolution of the Communist League. M is long occupied with defense work, relief work, and publicism on behalf of the victims. Politically, the year is dominated by the consolidation of Bonapartism in France. M's major work is his study of Bonapartism (short title, *The 18th Brumaire*, #M267). At the same time, his work for *NYDT* becomes regularized.

2. Except for the July-Aug period (for which, see → :56) M is unable to carry on much basic study and reading. E, in Manchester, continues his military studies, with special attention to the revolutionary warfare of 1848–49 in Hungary and Italy, since he plans to write its history. He reads works by Clausewitz, Jomini, Willisen, Hoffstetter, Kuentzel, Görgey, et al. This study will continue to Mar 1853.

JANUARY

3. POLITICAL AFFAIRS. **Jan M:** The group in GWEA opposing the Willich–Schapper leadership sets up a new German workers' society, with Stechan as chairman; M supports them and helps formulate their statutes. **Jan 15:** M attends the London CL branch meeting; a letter from Cologne reports on the government's continued delay in bringing the Cologne defendants [← 51:24] to trial. —E. Jones visits M, and they discuss support to Jones's *Notes to the People* as against Harney's *Friend of the People*, in which M's opponents are collaborating. **Jan 20:** The French émigré Madier visits M. **Jan 22–26:** M writes Freiligrath with critical comments on the latter's anti-Kinkel poem; Freiligrath revises the poem. **Jan 24–29:** On the basis of info received Jan 24 from Bermbach (in Cologne), M requests E to draft a letter to the *Times* on the treatment of the Cologne Communist prisoners. E sends his draft on Jan 28; M sends it to the *Times*, dated Jan 29, signed "A Prussian" (#ME180). E sends a similar letter to the *Daily News*. Neither is pubd; efforts to get protests into the English press on the Cologne witch-hunt are fruitless.

4. W&P. **Jan 1:** M sends Ch. 1 of *The 18th Brumaire* (#M267) to Weydemeyer for publ in his magazine. **Jan 6:** The first issue of Weydemeyer's *Die Revolution* appears in NYC. It reprints a part of the "Review / May to Oct" (#ME136) under M's name, and runs the announcement requested by M [← 51:56] for his planned critique of Proudhon. **Jan 9:** Mrs. M sends Ch. 2 of *The 18th Brumaire* to Weydemeyer, also M's request that Weydemeyer write up the case of the Cologne Communists, about which the German-American press under Kinkel's influence is silent. **Jan c.20:** M receives Weydemeyer's letter of Jan 5 and learns about the publ of his first number, and about other German-American papers in NYC, esp the Turn-Ztg, in which Weydemeyer has just pubd (Jan 1) an article titled "The dictatorship of the proletariat." (The Turn-Ztg begins publishing E's *Peasant war in Germany*, #E579, from Jan 1852 to Feb 1853.) **Jan 23, 30:** E writes two articles for *Die Revolution* on England (#E241); unpubd. **Jan 30:** M sends Ch. 3 of *The 18th Brumaire*, with other material for publ.

5. ECONOMICA. **Jan 30:** M inquires from Weydemeyer about a possible American publisher for his opus.

6. PERSONAL. **Jan 2–24:** M is ill in bed for two weeks, continuing his work on *The 18th Brumaire* (#M267) only with great difficulty. **Jan 7:** Freiligrath sends M £10 raised among his friends.

FEBRUARY

7. POLITICAL AFFAIRS. **Feb c.1–3:** Weerth, in London for a few days, visits M. **Feb c.2–3:**

M is visited by several French revolutionaries, incl Massol, Villières, Bianchi, Sabatier. **Feb 3:** M is visited for the first time by the Hungarian officer Bangya, who gives him info on the mutual relations of Kossuth, Mazzini, Kinkel, and the anti-Kossuth Hungarian émigrés. Bangya also offers the collaboration of Szemere and Perczel on Weydemeyer's *Die Revolution*. **Feb c.5:** M receives from Ewerbeck (in Paris) some copies of his book *L'Allemagne et les Allemands* [← 51:45], in which M is praised as a critical genius who has drawn the final revolutionary consequences from the Hegelian dialectic. **Feb c.6:** M receives from A. Cluss (in the US), dated Jan 20, a report and materials on A. Goegg's "Revolutionsbund" (League of Revolution) in America, and on Heinzen's attacks on M's communism in his paper *Janus*. **Feb 13:** M writes Weydemeyer with info on the case of the Cologne Communist prisoners and asks him to get material into the German-American press. **Feb 15:** Reinhardt (in Paris) sends M info on the situation in Paris, which M uses in part for his *18th Brumaire*. (M will send excerpts from Reinhardt's letter to Lassalle, Feb 23.) **Feb 18:** M receives a report from Weydemeyer on his activity in America, also requesting CL documents. **Feb c.19:** At the CL meeting, M moves to exclude W. Hirsch, who has been shown to be a Prussian police agent; the place and time of CL meetings are changed [→ :13]. **Feb 24:** M receives an invitation to a banquet for the fourth anniversary of the Feb Revolution held by the right-wing French emigration; he does not attend.

8. ECONOMICA. **Feb 23:** Writing to Lassalle, M refers to the "definitive rejection of my *Economics* by the bookdealers."

9. W&P (M). **Feb 6:** M sends Schabelitz (in Basel) Pfänder's anti-Willich statement for publ in *Schweizerische National-Ztg*. **Feb 13:** M sends Ch. 4 of *The 18th Brumaire* (#M267) to Weydemeyer. **Feb 18:** M receives from Weydemeyer (dated Feb 6/7, with addendum by Cluss) the news that *Die Revolution* has suspended publ. **Feb 20:** M suggests to Weydemeyer that *The 18th Brumaire* be pubd in separate fascicules. **Feb c.D:** M gets E. Jones to write a criticism of Heinzen for *Die Revolution* (in expectation of its resurrection). Jones sends the article on Mar 5. **Feb 27:** Mrs. M sends Weydemeyer Ch. 5 of *The 18th Brumaire*, also an article on Hungary by Bangya.

10. W&P (E). **Feb M:** E is overwhelmed by work in his firm, and has little time to write. **Feb 18:** M asks E to sharpen his criticism of the Frankfurt Assembly Left in his next *NYDT* article in the series on Germany (#E699). **Feb 21:** *Notes to the People* pubs the first part of E's article on the French workers' apathy in Bonaparte's coup (#E653).

Feb 27: In a letter to Weydemeyer, E discusses the political and economic situation in England; he promises another article on England. (This was either not written or was one of those that got lost—cf #E241.) —*NYDT* pubs one article this month in E's series on Germany (#E699).

11. PERSONAL. **Feb M:** M falls into esp deep financial straits, and is unable to write. **Feb D:** M has to pawn his overcoat and cannot go out to the library; the household cannot buy on credit from the butcher; M's eyes hurt from the strain of working at night.

MARCH

12. POLITICAL AFFAIRS. **Mar 5:** In a letter to Weydemeyer, M gives him advice for his political polemic against Heinzen, incl a notable statement about his (M's) special contributions on the class struggle and on the "dictatorship of the proletariat." **Mar M:** Sorge, stopping in London en route to NYC, visits M. **Mar c.15:** M receives from Cluss (Mar 1) a report on the right-wing emigration in America, Kossuth, Kinkel, Goegg, Heinzen, et al, and a request for advice on how to fight them. **Mar 24:** At a regular CL meeting, M reports on Cluss's and Weydemeyer's activity in America, esp against Heinzen and Kinkel; the meeting approves. **Mar 25:** M writes Weydemeyer on Jones's plan for a new Chartist paper; also about a deal in which *Die Revolution* would publish Szemere's pamphlet against Kossuth and add Bangya as an editor, thus Hungarian alliance to bring him $500 (from Szemere's wing of the Hungarian emigration). **Mar D:** Besides spending time with Bangya, M makes the acquaintance of the Hungarian, Col. Szerelmey.

13. THE COLOGNE COMMUNIST CASE. **Mar 2:** From an anonymous letter signed "A." (dated Feb 29), M learns that W. Hirsch [← :7] sent the Berlin police a spy report on the London CL meeting of Jan 15, thereby causing the house search of Mrs. Daniels in Cologne. **Mar 3:** M writes E that his letters are being opened by the police. **Mar 6:** *Kölnische Ztg* pubs M's statement (sent Mar 3) refuting a calumny in the Cologne Communist case (#M850).

14. ECONOMICA. **Mar 17:** M writes pub'r Wigand (in Leipzig) about publishing his opus. **Mar 20:** Wigand replies in the negative, referring to the "risks to be run from the state."

15. W&P. **Mar c.2:** M receives from *NYDT* payment (£9) for the first nine articles in the series on Germany (#E699). Four articles in this series are pubd this month. **Mar 5:** M sends Weydemeyer Ch. 6 of *The 18th Brumaire* (#M267), plus articles by others. **Mar c.A:** At Bangya's request, M writes some "pen sketches" of the right-wing leaders of the Democratic emigration; he gives them to Bangya for forwarding to Paris. **Mar 25:** M sends the concluding Ch. 7 of *The 18th Brumaire* to Weydemeyer. **Mar 27:** Jones's *Notes to the People* pubs the second part of E's study on worker apathy in the Bonaparte coup (#E653). **Mar D:** M is planning to write an article against Mazzini's attacks on socialism, for Weydemeyer's magazine.

16. PERSONAL. **Mar A:** M receives £3 from Lassalle. **Mar 18:** Writing to M, E mentions that his firm in Manchester may be liquidated and that he may move to Liverpool, where he will be burdened with less work; E also describes his progress in studying Russian.

APRIL

17. POLITICAL AFFAIRS. **Apr A:** Szemere (in Paris) sends M, via Bangya, the German ms of his pamphlet on Kossuth, Görgey, and Batthyány, for publ by Weydemeyer in America. **Apr 16:** M proposes to invite Bangya to a CL meeting; Bangya declines. **Apr 23, 30:** M writes Cluss (in the US) about the Harney–Jones conflict in the Chartist movement. **Apr 27:** Dronke arrives in London from Paris. **Apr 30:** M sends Weydemeyer material for his article in the NY *Turn-Ztg* on Kinkel and his "revolutionary loan" campaign, which held a congress in London yesterday; included is info on factional fights in the Kinkel camp.

18. W&P. **Apr:** *NYDT* pubs three articles in the series on Germany (#E699). **Apr 10:** Jones's *Notes to the People* pubs the final third part of E's study of worker apathy in Bonaparte's coup (#E653). **Apr 16:** M receives Weydemeyer's news (of Mar 30) that he has no money or pub'r to put out *The 18th Brumaire* (#M267) as a pamphlet or to continue publishing *Die Revolution*. M writes Weydemeyer to try to get Dana to publish *The 18th Brumaire* in English; failing this, to return the ms immediately, for publ in London in German or English. **Apr c.24:** M hears from Weydemeyer (Apr 9) that a German worker, a tailor from Frankfurt, has contributed his savings of $40 so that *The 18th Brumaire* can be pubd; work will begin immediately. **Apr c.28:** Bangya proposes that M write an anonymous pamphlet of "character portraits" of the German émigré leaders, for a German bookdealer with whom he claims contact. **Apr 30:** M writes E about Bangya's proposal, the pamphlet to be written by both of them, using excerpts from past letters and other materials. (This will become *The great men of the emigration*, #ME72.)

19. PERSONAL. **Apr c.13:** E spends several days with M in London (*KMC* dates this Apr 11–13, the Easter holiday). **Apr 14:** M's child Franziska dies of bronchitis. **Apr 16:** Franziska's funeral: M has to borrow money for this from a neighbor, a French émigré.

MAY

20. POLITICAL AFFAIRS. **May A:** M corrects the German trans of Szemere's pamphlet [← :17]. **May c.20:** M receives Bermbach's letter (May 3) from Cologne with the news that the Cologne Communist trial is scheduled to begin in June or July. **May D:** K. Schramm moves to America, bearing a "cautiously worded" recommendatory letter by M. **May D to June CD:** M helps E. Jones in his work on the new Chartist organ *The People's Paper*, on both business and editorial aspects and by supplying foreign news items; the subscription list grows.

21. ECONOMICA. **May 4:** E writes M on the latest report from Ebner about the possibility (indefinite) of lining up Löwenthal as pub'r of the opus.

22. W&P. **May AB:** M starts drafting a *NYDT* article on Gen. Klapka's program (#M346.5); not finished. **May c.4:** M receives Dana's proposal (Apr 20) that he write *NYDT* correspondence on current English politics. **May 6:** Bangya presses M to finish *The great men of the emigration* (#ME72). **May c.19:** Weydemeyer pubs *Die Revolution* in NYC as an irregular periodical, containing M's *18th Brumaire* (#M267) and Weydemeyer's reply to anti-M attacks by Tellering and Heinzen. **May:** M&E work at collecting material for *The great men of the emigration;* they solicit Dronke, W. Wolff, Cluss, Freiligrath, Weydemeyer, et al for biographical material on émigré leaders. **May D to June CD:** M visits E in Manchester, where they work on *The great men* (*KMC* dates this May c.26 to June c.26).

23. PERSONAL. **May 21:** E's personal situation is improved as a result of a new business agreement between the partners of Ermen & Engels; he can now increase his financial aid to M; he sends M £10 at once. **May D:** See ← :22 for M's visit to Manchester.

JUNE

24. THE *GREAT MEN* PAMPHLET. **June c.8:** M asks Bangya for an advance payment for the pamphlet, a payment which Bangya was supposed to have given Mrs. M. **June 12:** Bangya writes Mrs. M that he is not in a position to pay. **June c.25–28:** Returning to London from Manchester, M dictates (alternately to his wife and Dronke) a clean copy of the pamphlet (#ME72), to be sent to Bangya.

25. POLITICAL AFFAIRS. **June D:** M&E hear from Weydemeyer about the formation of a CL branch in NYC.

26. LIBRARY. **June 29:** Helped by Freiligrath, who vouches for him to Panizzi, director of the British Museum Library, M renews his library card, which he has not used since the end of 1851 [→ :30].

JULY

27. POLITICAL AFFAIRS. **July 1–3:** M devotes "a great deal of running around" to raising money for the funeral of the wife of CL member Klose. **July 22:** M receives a letter from Cluss (July 4) on the activity of Kossuth and Kinkel in America, incl news of Kinkel's public statement that "M&E are rascals who have been thrown out of the London pubs by the workers." M sends an inquiry about this invention to Kinkel, who is now in London. **July 24:** Kinkel refuses to respond except to challenge M to sue. M replies with a sharp denunciation of Kinkel's dishonesty. **July:** From Bangya M gets info bearing on the Prussian government's case against the Cologne Communists: on the role of the agent-provocateur Cherval-Krämer who as a police agent led a Willich–Schapper group in Paris and figured in the "German-French plot" with which the Prussian police are trying to link the Cologne defendants. **c.July:** M makes the acquaintance of Eduard Vehse, who comes from Paris with a letter from Reinhardt.

28. ECONOMICA. **July 19:** Ebner (in Frankfurt) writes E that his efforts to get a pub'r for M's opus are still fruitless.

29. W&P. **July A:** M gives Bangya the ms of *The great men of the emigration* (#ME72) for publ [← :24]. **July 27:** NYDT pubs one article this month in the series on Germany (#E699).

30. STUDIES. **July A to Aug:** E studies and makes notes on Görgey's book and other writings on the Hungarian revolution. **July to Aug:** M resumes work in the BM Library [← :26], studying general history, history of political institutions, culture, and the position of women. (For details, see → :56, 57.)

AUGUST

31. POLITICAL AFFAIRS. **Aug A:** M&E learn that the Cologne Communist trial, set for July 28, has now been postponed for three months. **Aug 5–7:** M receives from Cluss (July 22) a secret June 2 circular of Kossuth's urging German-Americans to campaign in the US presidential election for US armed intervention in Europe to provoke revolutionary changes; Cluss has had this printed in the *NY Herald*. To air this irresponsible proposal, M has Jones publish it in his *People's Paper* (Aug 7) with a critique. **Aug 17:** Weydemeyer writes E that his NYC branch of the CL has five members. **Aug 19:** M receives a letter (July 9) from Bermbach reporting on the situation of the Cologne defendants and on house searches by the Cologne police looking for letters from M. **Aug c.M:** M makes the acquaintance through Bangya of the Hungarian émigré Gustav Zerffi, recently arrived from Paris. Through Zerffi, M sends *The 18th Brumaire* (#M267) and a letter to Szemere (in Paris), whom he asks to write for Jones's *PP*. **Aug to Oct:** M&E follow the struggle going on inside the German emigration around the money collected by the German-American "loan" (fund) organized by Kinkel [← :17]. Their source of info is Imandt (a CL member since July), who is urged by M to send reports to the German-American press.

32. ECONOMICA. **Aug 19:** M offers Leipzig pub'r Brockhaus *Die Gegenwart*, a work (to be written) on "modern literature on polit eco in England 1830–1852," discussing the "general works" on the subject and "special works" on "population, colonies, the bank question, protective tariff and freedom of trade, etc."; also a work on "the present state of the parties [in England]." **Aug 27:** Brockhaus rejects these proposals.

33. W&P. **Aug 2:** M writes his first article for *NYDT*, about the English elections, and sends it to E for trans. **Aug AB:** E translates it and breaks it into two articles, dated Aug 6 and 10 (#M272, 138). **Aug c.16:** M writes another *NYDT* article on the English elections. Again E translates it and divides it into two, dated Aug 20 and 27 (#M189, 758) [→ :36]. **Aug 19:** *NYDT* pubs one article this month in the series on Germany (#E699). **Aug 21, 25:** M's first articles (#M272, 138) are pubd in *NYDT*. **Aug c.23:** M writes Bangya, pressing for publ of the *Great men* pamphlet (#ME72) [← :29]. **Aug D:** M has Pieper translate the first chapter of *The 18th Brumaire* (#M267) into English, believing he has a bookdealer lined up to publish it [→ :36]. **Aug M to Sep:** M inquires from Lassalle, Ebner, Streit, and Naut about the possibility of publishing *The 18th Brumaire* in Germany—in vain.

34. STUDIES. **Aug c.19:** M runs across literature on military affairs in the BM Library and sends E a list.

SEPTEMBER

35. POLITICAL AFFAIRS. **Sep A:** From Zerffi (in Paris) M receives a piece by L. Häfner on some leaders of the German emigration. **Sep 15, 21:** M mobilizes his supporters to back Jones at two Chartist meetings where Jones is attacked for the revolutionary policy of his *People's Paper*, by moderate Chartists (Holyoake et al) who want to concentrate on universal suffrage, dumping the rest of the Chartist program. Jones is upheld. **Sep c.20:** The Cologne Communist trial is finally set to begin on Oct 4. **Sep c.24–27:** Weerth, in London, stays with M. **Sep c.24:** Through Bangya's good offices, M talks with an Orleanist agent who travels between Paris and London, and gets info on Orleanist plans in France. **Sep 24:** Bermbach sends M the passages in the indictment of the Cologne Communists in which M's name figures. **Sep D:** M writes to Bermbach, using the address of the Cologne merchant Kothes, and urges him to send news on the trial.

36. W&P. Sep AB: At M's request, E revises Pieper's English trans of *The 18th Brumaire* [← :33]. But efforts to obtain English publ are vain. Also vain are efforts to get it pubd in Germany, after writing to Lassalle, Ebner, the bookdealer F. Streit (in Coburg), and Naut (in Cologne). Bookdealers turn the proposal down because of M's subversive reputation at a time when an anti-Communist witch-hunt is getting under way. **Sep 4, 11:** *NYDT* pubs M's articles on England (#M189, 758) [← :33]. **Sep 18:** *NYDT* pubs one article this month in the series on Germany (#E699). **Sep c.D:** M sends Zerffi one of his *NYDT* articles on England, for publ in France. Zerffi offers it to Girardin's *La Presse*, which rejects it.

37. ECONOMICA. Sep AB: The fear by bookdealers of publishing writings by M (see ← :36) equally militates against the possibility of getting M's opus on polit eco pubd, even if it were finished (cf → :53).

38. PERSONAL. Sep AB: The M household is in financial trouble: there is no money for a doctor or medicine for Mrs. M, daughter Jenny, and Helene Demuth, who are ill; they can afford to eat only bread and potatoes; M cannot write his *NYDT* articles because he cannot buy newspapers. **Sep 9:** M gets £4 from E. **Sep 13:** He gets £2 from Freiligrath. **Sep or Oct:** In Manchester, E moves from 70 Great Ducie Street, Strangeways [← 50:44] to no. 48 on the same street. (Note: Sometime between now and 1858, E moves to 34 Butler Street, Greenheys; see → 58:4.)

OCTOBER

39. COLOGNE COMMUNIST TRIAL. Oct 4: The Cologne CL members who were arrested in May 1851 are finally put on trial. From now until the end of the trial (Nov 12) M and his friends labor to help the defense expose the

> **NOTE**
> References here to the charges and issues at the Cologne trial can be fully understood only by reading a detailed account of it: for example, M's pamphlet on the trial (#M762) or the explanatory intro to ST/ME12 (CCT).

government's evidence, by sending documents and other materials to Cologne by various channels. **Oct 14:** M sends a critique of the government's indictment, for the use of chief defense counsel Karl Schneider, to Bermbach via the merchant Kothes. **Oct 17:** Kothes is arrested in Cologne and interrogated; he deposes that he passed M's letter to Bermbach. (He will be released Oct 20.) **Oct 18–21:** Bermbach is arrested and interrogated, his house searched, then he is released. **Oct c.20:** M sends (via Dronke) various materials on the prosecution witness Hentze to defense counsel Schneider. **Oct 21:** M sends the German press a statement charging Police Chief Stieber with perjury for his Oct 18 testimony about Cherval; M threatens to publicize Stieber's 1848 letter to *NRZ* [← 48:85] in which Stieber claimed Democratic views. M's statement (not extant) is not pubd by any German paper; the Prussian post office sends it to Stieber. **Oct 23:** Bermbach is again arrested, at Stieber's instigation. **Oct 24:** *Kölnische Ztg* pubs Stieber's testimony of Oct 23 on the (fake) minutes book of the CL/CC (called the "Original-Protokollbuch" by the police agent W. Hirsch). **Oct 25–26:** M, with the help of friends (E, Weerth, Steinthal, Freiligrath, Ebner, Dronke, Liebknecht, et al), draws up a detailed letter to defense counsel Schneider, giving info on Cherval, to refute Stieber's testimony; it also discusses the political differences between the Willich–Schapper league documents cited by the prosecution and the documents of Marx's CL. M sends several copies of this letter, plus supplementary documents, to Schneider by various routes, to ensure receipt. (This letter is not extant; its content is given in M's letter to E, Oct 28.) **Oct 25:** M is under police surveillance in London and the English government is opening his mail: so he writes to E. **Oct 26:** M sends Bürgers' defense counsel Hontheim, via Ebner, material for the defense, incl mss by W. Hirsch and Stieber's 1848 letter to NRZ. M receives from Schneider an urgent request to supply evidence to expose the fake "Protokollbuch." **Oct 27–28:** M has a London magistrate's court certify various documents disproving the "Protokollbuch" and sends them to counsel Schneider, along with other documents refuting Stieber's testimony, plus instructions to Schneider, addressing them by different routes. **Oct 28:** *Kölnische Ztg* reports the testimony of Oct 27 by a police inspector about a (forged) letter by M accompanying the "Red Catechism." **Oct 30:** Several London papers publish a statement on the Cologne trial (#ME31) signed by M, E, Freiligrath, W. Wolff. —M signs an affidavit at the Marlborough Street police court that he had nothing to do with the "Red Catechism" [→ :45].

40. PLANNING A DEFENSE PAMPHLET. Oct 25: M proposes to E the publ, after the trial ends, of a circular "for the info of the public" to expose the Prussian trial. He asks E to contact pub'r Campe (in Hamburg). **Oct 27:** M now proposes not a mere circular but a pamphlet, not for political discussion but to attack the Prussian witch-hunt; he asks E to raise money.

41. OTHER POLITICAL AFFAIRS. Oct 10: L. Häfner writes M defending himself against the rumor, said to be spread by the police, that he is a police spy. **Oct c.M:** Heine sends his regards to M, via Reinhardt. **Oct 20:** M is visited by the Hungarian, Col. Pleyel, who presents a recommendatory letter from Bangya; M gives him a similar letter to E.

42. BANGYA. Oct AB: Disturbed by the delay in publishing the *Great men* pamphlet (#ME72), M&E try to find out more about Bangya's claims. **Oct c.7:** M asks Weerth (in Bradford) to get info via Franz Duncker on the bookdealer Eisenmann (in Berlin) who was supposed to have ordered the pamphlet. **Oct 10:** E urges M to demand an accounting from Bangya. **Oct 26:** Weerth writes M that Duncker says that Bangya's "Eisenmann" does not exist. **Oct c.28–29:** As E urges, M makes remonstrances to Bangya. In a letter to E, Oct 29, Bangya says the brochure will either appear in Nov or he will return the ms [→ :49].

43. W&P. Oct 8: M writes Cluss (in the US) with suggestions for articles against Kinkel and Heinzen, and sends material. **Oct 19:** *NYDT* pubs M's article (#M533) on Bonaparte's relations with supporters of Kossuth, based on info from Bangya and Zerffi. (It will be reprinted in other US papers and evokes a storm of indignation from pro-Kossuth papers.) **Oct c.20:** M receives from Cluss 130 copies of the brochure edn of *The 18th Brumaire* (#M267) pubd in NYC by Weydemeyer. **Oct:** The *People's Paper* republishes M's four *NYDT* articles on the English elections (#M272, 138, 189, 758). —*NYDT* pubs the last two articles in the series on Germany (#E699); a final article written by E for the series is not pubd.

44. PERSONAL. Oct 25–27: M's landlord threatens the bailiff to collect the rent; to buy writing paper M has to pawn an overcoat.

Oct 27: M receives £2 from E. **Oct 28:** M receives about £15 from Dana in payment for *NYDT* articles.

NOVEMBER

45. COLOGNE COMMUNIST TRIAL. Nov 1 (rec'd 3): Defense counsel Schneider (in Cologne) acknowledges the safe receipt of the letters and documents sent by M from Oct 25 to Nov 1, partly in three copies. **Nov 2:** M's statement on the "Red Catechism" (#M943) [← :39] appears in the London press; M sends it to Schneider. **Nov 5–8:** M and friends make an investigation and prove that W. Hirsch fabricated the "Original-Protokoll-buch" [← :39] on orders from the spy Fleury acting for Police Lt. Greif, who was assigned by the Prussian embassy in London. **Nov 10:** M tells E that he thinks all the Cologne defendants will be acquitted. **Nov 12:** The Cologne trial ends with seven of the defendants given three to six years in jail, four acquitted. **Nov 14:** M learns this news from the German press of Nov 13.

46. DISSOLUTION OF THE COMMUNIST LEAGUE. Nov 17: M presents the London CL with the proposal to dissolve, since the League has ceased de facto to exist in Germany as a result of the police suppression; the proposal is adopted.

47. W&P AFTER THE TRIAL. Nov 16: M asks E to write an article on the trial for *NYDT* [→ :54]. **Nov CD to Dec 2:** M works on a pamphlet on the Cologne trial (#M762) [← :40], incl new material on the evidence. He contacts Schabelitz (in Basel) for publ [→ :50]. The Prussian police hear of the coming pamphlet, give advance orders for its seizure, and try to line up the Belgian and other police to do the same. **Nov 20, 29:** The *Morning Advertiser* pubs a statement on the trial (#ME58) signed by M, E, Freiligrath, W. Wolff. **Nov D:** M drafts an appeal for material support to the Cologne prisoners and their families, and forms an aid comm with Freiligrath as treasurer. The appeal is signed by 20 people, incl E. Jones [→ :50]. (For text, cf *MEW* 8:602.)

48. CONTACTS. Nov 3, c.9: M meets with Vehse [← :27], who leaves London on the ninth. **Nov M to Dec:** M has several meetings with K. Blind, who has moved from Belgium to London. **Nov 28, 30:** M meets with Weerth, who is going off to the West Indies.

49. W&P. Nov 1–29: *NYDT* pubs four articles written by M, on the looming economic crisis, English political affairs, etc. (#M645, 670, 62, 672). **Nov 15:** One of the articles on England that E wrote for Weydemeyer [← :4] is pubd in the NY *Turn-Ztg* (#E241). **Nov c.26:** Weerth writes M that another bookdealer named by Bangya, Collmann of Berlin, is not traceable [→ :51].

DECEMBER

50. DEFENSE PAMPHLET. **Dec 1:** The pub'r Schabelitz (in Basel) asks M to send him his pamphlet on the Cologne trial [← :47]. **Dec 2:** M finishes dictating a clean copy of his *Revelations concerning the Communist trial in Cologne* (#M762). **Dec 6:** M sends the ms to Schabelitz for publ. **Dec 7:** M sends a copy of the ms to Cluss (in the US), also a copy of the appeal for aid to the Cologne victims [← :47], now dated Dec 7 [→ 53:4]. **Dec 11:** Schabelitz writes M that the printing of the pamphlet has begun [→ 53:5].

51. BANGYA AFFAIR ENDS. **Dec 3:** M writes Bangya demanding an accounting on the delay in publishing the *Great men* pamphlet (#ME72) [← :42], and asking for info on the various (nonexistent) publishers named by Bangya. Bangya replies the same day, promising clarification; "trust me." **Dec 24:** M writes to Zerffi about the Bangya problem. **Dec 27:** Zerffi replies that Bangya has long had relations with the Prussian police and prob gave them the ms. **Dec 28:** M writes Zerffi that he prefers not to expose Bangya right now, before the publ of the Cologne defense pamphlet. **Dec 30:** Szemere, in his first letter to M, warns against both Bangya and Zerffi, who "at most are good only to get something *from* the enemy camp." Szemere praises *The 18th Brumaire* (#M267).

52. THE AFFAIR OF KOSSUTH'S "SECRETARY." **Dec 1:** *NYDT* pubs a letter to the editor by M (#M435) on the piece pubd Oct 19 (#M533) re relations with Bonaparte by Mazzini and Kossuth supporters. M denounces attacks by the "crypto-Royalists" and stresses he was not attacking Kossuth but warning him. **Dec A:** M receives from Cluss (in the US) an open letter by a self-styled secy to Kossuth, attacking M. **Dec AB:** M sends his original piece (#M533) to Kossuth (in London, via Bangya) and requests his stand on the "secretary." Kossuth replies he has no secy in America and thanks M for the warning. **Dec 14:** M sends a letter to *NYDT* (#M740) quoting Kossuth's reply; pubd Jan 4.

53. ECONOMICA. **Dec 7:** M writes (to Cluss) that the Cologne trial has totally eliminated the possibility of getting a publisher for his opus (cf ← :37).

54. W&P. **Dec 10, 28:** M writes an article for *NYDT* on English politics (#M635) and has it translated by Pieper; pubd Dec 28. **Dec 11, 18:** In two issues of his *People's Paper*, Jones promises publ of M's *18th Brumaire* (but it will not be pubd). **Dec 22:** E's article on the Cologne trial [← :47], sent Dec 1, is pubd in *NYDT* (#E423).

55. PERSONAL. **Dec M to Jan 10:** E visits M in London (*KMC* dates: Dec c.23 to Jan c.10). **Dec c.20:** M asks Lassalle to send money to Herwegh (in Zurich), who is in financial straits.

YEAR APPENDIX

56. In the July-Aug period [see ← :30] M does much reading esp on political and cultural history. *MEW* lists the following authors: Machiavelli, Hüllmann, Wachsmuth, Sismondi, Eichhorn, Bouterwek, G. Jung, Ségur, "and others." *KMC* adds: Hallam, Dalrymple, Meiners, Millars; also works by and about Giordano Bruno.

57. M's Notebook XVIII incl works by Forbonnais, Sismondi, Bouterwek, and G. Bruno; plus poetical works in various languages.

58. Notebook XIX, marked Aug, incl works by W. Alexander, W. Drumann, J. G. Eichhorn, G. Jung, Meiners, J. Millar, J. A. de Ségur, Thomas, Wachsmuth.

1853

CONSPECTUS

1. M fulfills two tasks in the aftermath of the Cologne Communist trial: organizn of material aid for the victims and their families, and the publ of a defense pamphlet exposing the Prussian government's travesty of justice, *Revelations concerning the Communist trial in Cologne* (#M762). M's writing is mainly devoted to the large issues of European and English politics in *NYDT* articles, esp as the Russo-Turkish conflict turns into the Crimean War, while E focuses on militaria, his spe-cialty. M's interest in digging into English diplomatic history and the role of Palmerston in foreign policy branches off from this, leading to cooperation with the cranky anti-Russian Urquhart. Another subject is the Far East, and Britain's relations with India and China. Parts of about a dozen articles deal with the signs of economic crisis in Europe. M&E's *NYDT* articles gain some prestige, but M grows increasingly dissatisfied with *NYDT*'s use of his articles and payment for them. In England, M's main journalistic connection is with Ernest Jones's *People's Paper;* besides writing for it, M lets it reprint some *NYDT* articles. In America (esp Apr to Dec) M's continuing contact is with ex-CL members Weydemeyer and Cluss. M approves their collaboration with *Die Reform*, the organ of the Amerikanischer Arbeiterbund (German-American workers' league), and he involves Eccarius, Pieper, Dronke, and other members of his London circle in producing contributions.

2. Research on all the abovementioned issues requires much study at the British Museum Library; for details, see → :49–55.

3. E's situation in Manchester undergoes no essential change, though he tries to find alternatives to his commercial work.

JANUARY

4. POLITICAL AFFAIRS. **Jan-Feb:** M corresponds with Cluss and Weydemeyer (in the US) about collecting a material-aid fund in America for the victims of the Cologne trial. **Jan 10:** Cluss sends out to the German-American press the appeal for aid to the Cologne victims which M has sent [← :50]. (It will be pubd in a couple of papers.) **Jan:** M makes the acquaintance of the Prussian ex-lieutenant Steffen, of Cologne, whom Freiligrath gave a recommendatory letter on Jan 2. (M will see Steffen often until July D; he performs various services for M. When Steffen moves to Chester in Aug, M will remain in correspondence with him for the following year.)

5. W&P. **Jan to Mar:** M corresponds with Cluss (in the US) on the possibility of an American edn of the Cologne defense pamphlet [→ :15]. **Jan 11:** Schabelitz (in Basel) completes the printing of the defense pamphlet (#M762). **Jan CD:** The pamphlet comes off the press in Basel. **Jan:** M's reply to Kossuth's "secretary" (#M740) [← 52:52] is pubd in *NYDT* on Jan 4. *NYDT* pubs two other articles on English politics this month (#M228, 868).

6. ECONOMICA AND OTHER STUDIES. **Jan to Mar:** M studies the theory of money and other questions of polit eco, also the history of culture, and history of the Slavs. (For details, see → :49–55.) For E's studies, see ← 52:2.

FEBRUARY

7. POLITICAL AFFAIRS. **Feb 12:** Through E. Jones, M gets an invitation from the Chartist exec to attend a public Chartist meeting on Feb 22. **Feb M:** M is visited a number of times by Zerffi, who tells of Bangya's activity as a spy [← 52:51].

8. *NYDT* ARTICLES. **Feb:** Five articles pubd this month, as follows. **Feb 2, 23:** Two articles on English politics and economic conditions (#M674, 230). **Feb 9:** Another, with an important section on "The Duchess of Sutherland and slavery" (#M271). **Feb 18:** Another ditto (#M135), the first article for *NYDT* written by M in English, on Jan 28. **Feb 25:** First article on the insurrection in Milan (#M423).

MARCH

9. POLITICAL AFFAIRS. **Mar to Apr A:** In view of the sharpening antagonisms between Russia and the Western powers over the Balkans and the Middle East (the "Eastern Question"), M&E exchange letters discussing their opinions. At M's request E writes articles which will appear in *NYDT* during Apr (#E654, 874).

10. URQUHART. **Mar 9:** E calls M's attention to a book by Urquhart he has just read, *Turkey and its resources* (1833). E gives a thumbnail sketch of the book's cranky ideas on Islam, etc., and calls Urquhart "this crazy M.P. who claims that Palmerston is paid by Russia" [→ :15].

11. W&P. **Mar 7:** Pub'r Schabelitz (in Basel) writes M that 2000 copies of an extra order for the Cologne "Revelations" pamphlet (#M762), printed for Germany, have been seized by police in a border village between Switzerland and Baden. **Mar 12:** *People's Paper* reprints M's article on Sutherland and slavery (part of #M271) [← :8]. **Mar 25:** M hears from Cluss (Mar 6) that the "Revelations" pamphlet (#M762) will be pubd in the Boston *Neu-England-Ztg* [→ :15]. **Mar:** *NYDT* pubs three articles on Continental affairs and English politics, incl two dealing with the Milan insurrection and the role of Kossuth (#M59, 641, 320).

12. PERSONAL (M). **Mar c.7–10:** M is ill with a bad liver inflammation. **Mar 10:** M writes E: "I came near to croaking. . . ."

13. PERSONAL (E). **Mar 9:** E writes M that he is financially "in a tight fix"; that he will move to cheaper lodgings in about a week, and reform his lifestyle to cut down expenses, at least until his father comes to Manchester.

APRIL

14. POLITICAL AFFAIRS. **Apr 8:** M hears from Cluss (Mar 24) that the police agent W. Hirsch will publish his "Confessions of a mouchard," claiming that M gave the ms of *The great men of the emigration* (#ME72) to the police, distorting M's relation to Bangya. **Apr 9:** M writes an exposé of Hirsch (#M374) and sends it to a NY German-American paper [→ :19]. **Apr 17:** Writing to Cluss (in the US), M approves his and Weydemeyer's connection with *Die Reform*, an "honest" workers' paper. (M will maintain this association for the rest of the year; some of his London circle will contribute to *Die*

Reform, which will reprint some of M&E's *NYDT* articles.) **Apr 26:** M is informed anonymously that Berlin Police Chief Stieber and a Prussian police official named Goldheim have met in London to hatch police conspiracies against leftists, still using W. Hirsch. M checks this info, and sends it to Cluss and Weydemeyer for publ in the US press. **Apr 26–29:** M writes the same info up for the beginning of an *NYDT* article (#ME145). **Apr 28:** Lassalle asks Mrs. M to give him the issue numbers of the *NYDT* with M's articles, so that he can obtain them.

15. W&P. **Apr:** M's "Revelations" pamphlet (#M762) is reprinted in installs in the Boston *Neu-England-Ztg* [← :11], and (Apr c.24) is pubd as a pamphlet in about 500 copies. **Apr c.9 to May:** M&E seek a publisher for the *Great men* pamphlet (#ME72) without success. **Apr:** The *PP* continues to republish M's *NYDT* articles (#M320); in addition it now pubs the first articles that M writes specially for it, on Gladstone and his budget (#M547, 438, 821.5). —*NYDT* pubs six articles by M: three mainly on Continental affairs (#M434, 479; #ME25), two on the alleged "Berlin conspiracy" (#M76, 77), and one on English politics (#M3); and it pubs three articles on the Turkish question by E (#E654, 874, 916). The article #E874 gives a sketch of Urquhart as a "romantic" reactionary with a bee in his bonnet, glorifying Turkey, but he is the Liberals' authority on the subject [← :10].

16. STUDIES. **Apr-May:** M reads on the newly interesting subject of the history and development of the Asian and other colonial countries; see → :53. **Apr:** E, still immersed in military studies, takes up the tactics of a revolutionary army in case of a war with Russia. He reads Herzen's *Du développement des idées révolutionnaires en Russie*; and he continues working on the Russian and South Slav languages.

17. PERSONAL. **Apr:** M is again in great financial distress, esp since *NYDT* is paying very irregularly. **Apr D:** E sends money to M after Mrs. M writes (Apr 27) that she has appealed to a number of people without avail. **Apr 30 to May 19:** M stays with E in Manchester.

MAY

18. STUDIES ON THE EAST. **May:** M's attention turns to the Far East esp under the impulsion of the forthcoming debate in Parliament over the extension of the East India Co. charter. He begins to study English rule in India, incl the main historical works on the subject, also Indian agrarian conditions, and British diplomatic relations bearing on India.

(For details, see → :53, 54.) **May D to June M:** M&E correspond on historical problems of the Asian East, esp the key fact that private property in land is not dominant. **May-June:** E studies the history of the Middle East; he works on the Persian language, and reads the works of Hafiz and Mirkhond in the original. He reads Ch. Forster and, on M's recommendation, Bernier's book on the Mogul Empire.

19. W&P. **May 5:** M's exposé of Hirsch (#M374) [← :14] is pubd in a German-American paper. **May:** *NYDT* pubs two articles by M on English and Continental affairs (#M312, 783) and two dealing with the Swiss insurrection (#ME145, #E798). To article #M783, on May 6, *NYDT* appends a laudatory ed note calling it a "masterly exposition" on Gladstone's budget. **May M:** Re *NYDT*, Mrs. M informs Cluss and Weydemeyer of M's dissatisfaction: *NYDT* appropriates his [often really E's] important articles for unsigned editorials (leading articles) while putting M's name on insignificant pieces; but M cannot afford to have this practice stopped by threats since he needs the *NYDT* payments to live. **May c.31:** E receives a bundle of 440 copies of the "Revelations" pamphlet (#M762) printed in Boston [← :15], and sends all but a few copies to M.

20. POLITICAL AFFAIRS. **May 20:** E sends M the funds collected in America in response to the appeal for the Cologne victims [← :4]. **May D to June A:** M receives from Weydemeyer (May 9) and from Cluss info and clippings on Willich's attacks on the "Revelations" pamphlet (#M762), pubd in the German-American press, and also their own rejoinders to Willich.

21. PERSONAL. **May 19–20:** M returns to London from Manchester [← :17].

JUNE

22. *NYDT* ARTICLES. **June AB:** M is beginning to hear that his *NYDT* articles are highly esteemed in America. For example, the US economist Carey sends his book *Slavery at home and abroad*, which cites M's article on Sutherland and slavery (#M271) [→ :26]. **June 2:** M's letter to E makes clear he is more disgruntled than ever at the way *NYDT* prints his articles [see ← :19]. M says he will complain to Dana. **June 14:** In a letter to E, M makes a jaundiced political comment on the *NYDT* editors' "socialistic pretences": "in the form of Sismondian-philanthropic-socialistic anti-industrialism, they represent the protectionist—i.e., industrial—bourgeoisie in America." **June:** *NYDT* pubs six articles. Besides one dealing with Continental affairs (#M501) and one on the Russo-Turkish conflict (#M952), they deal in whole or part with M's new studies on Asia: a major article on "Revolution in China and in Europe" (#M773), two articles dealing in part with the British East India Co. (#M12, 798), and a notable article on "The British rule in India" (#M115).

23. STUDIES. **June:** In the BM Library M collects material for his *NYDT* articles on India and the English colonial question; also on the history of Denmark. (For details, see → :54, 55.) **June 2:** M warmly recommends that E read Bernier's book on Mogul India. **June 14:** M sends E critical comments on Carey's new book on slavery [← :22] and other works by this author, and an important analysis of the Indian village community under Oriental despotism.

24. POLITICAL AFFAIRS. **June 2:** M receives the package of about 420 "Revelations" pamphlets (#M762) sent by E [← :19]. **June to Aug:** M corresponds with Lassalle (in Düsseldorf) on how these pamphlets can be illegally shipped into Germany and distributed. E proposes to send them in cotton yarn packages; but none of the plans proves feasible. **June c.14:** M sends Cluss and Weydemeyer (in the US) a letter of tactical advice, esp to continue collaboration with *Die Reform* in spite of its political defects. He also sends Cluss a critique of Carey's economics which Cluss will work up for an article in the Sep issue of *Die Reform*. **June c.20:** M gets the news from Cluss that a meeting of the CC of the Amerikanische Arbeiterbund to discuss the line of *Die Reform* was dominated by the viewpoint advocated by Weydemeyer in line with M's principles.

25. PERSONAL. **June 2–9:** M&E concern themselves about getting paying work for their friends W. Wolff and Pieper. **June D:** M is visited by his sister Louise and her husband J. C. Juta, who were married June 5 in Trier.

JULY

26. *NYDT* ARTICLES. **July:** *NYDT* pubs nine articles, five of which include sections on the question of India and British rule (#M294, 402, 954; #ME150; and esp #M257 on the history of the East India Co.); the other four are on English and Continental affairs (#M950, 801, 447, 978); for English economic conditions, cf #M294. **July c.15:** M receives a letter from Dana saying that M's articles are "highly valued" by the *NYDT* publishers and the public; M notes that Dana says nothing about limiting the number of articles. **July 18:** M, writing E about Dana's letter, also relates that about two weeks ago in Parliament, John Bright referred to his *NYDT* articles on Gladstone's budget.

27. POLITICAL AFFAIRS. **July 20:** Szemere (in Paris), in a letter to M, repeats his warning against Zerffi.

28. STUDIES. **c.July to Nov:** M studies

parliamentary reports, diplomatic documents, and other materials on 1807–50, esp re the history of English foreign policy. **July A or later:** E reads Herzen's proclamation against serfdom, addressed "To the Russian nobility," pubd by the Free Russian Printshop in London.

29. PERSONAL. **July A:** M is visited by Dr. Abraham Jacobi, one of the Cologne Communist victims, who has been released from jail. **July 8:** M gives Jacobi a recommendatory letter to E and to Borchardt in Manchester. **July 9:** Jacobi shows up on E's doorstep at 4 A.M. E will help him find lodgings in Manchester. **July D to Aug A:** E goes to London to meet his mother, who has come from Germany for a short stay.

AUGUST

30. *NYDT* ARTICLES. **Aug:** *NYDT* pubs six articles; two deal with India (#M984 and an important article on "The future results of British rule in India," #M340); four articles on English, Danish, Russian, and Irish affairs, and on the war question (#M314, 396, 9, 983).

31. POLITICAL AFFAIRS. **Aug M:** M is visited by Heise, newly emigrated to England. (They will maintain relations until Heise moves to Manchester.) **Aug 18:** Freiligrath forwards M a letter (dated July 31) he has received for M from Karl W. Klein, former CL member in the Rhineland, now in Philadelphia, who offers to help reestablish relations with Rhenish elements, and asks for articles for the German-American paper *Gradaus*. M replies "diplomatically" to Klein (he tells E on Sep 7) with advice stressing that factory workers should remain independent of petty-bourgeois philistine elements in the Rhineland (letter not extant).

32. THE F. MARX/BAKUNIN IMBROGLIO. **Aug 19:** The *Morning Advertiser* pubs an anonymous article by I. G. Golovin, a liberal friend of Bakunin, "Europe—A single man." **Aug 23:** The *Advertiser* pubs a piece titled "The Russian agent Bakunin," signed F.M. (an Englishman named Francis Marx, an Urquhartite), charging that Bakunin is linked with the Russian government. **Aug 24:** A letter by Golovin, Herzen, and a Polish émigré Worcell attacks F.M.'s article. **Aug 27:** F.M. replies in a statement linking the outbreak of European revolution to the work of czarist agents. **Aug 29:** Golovin and Herzen publish another letter, "Who is F.M.?" which insinuates that F.M. is really *Karl* Marx; they mention that already in 1848 a "German paper" (meaning the *NRZ*) had made the same charge [← 48:46]. **Aug 30:** M writes an open letter (#M510) detailing the facts of the 1848 case, how *NRZ* cleared Bakunin's name, M's subsequent friendly relations with Bakunin, etc., and attacks F.M.'s amalgam of Russian machinations with the revolution; pubd in the *Advertiser* on Sep 2. **Aug 31:** The *Advertiser* pubs a poison-pen letter by Ruge, who charges that *NRZ* knowingly pubd lies about Bakunin (to be cont'd; → :34).

33. PERSONAL. **Aug to Oct A:** M is in great financial distress; he has to pawn essential possessions to get some money.

SEPTEMBER

34. BAKUNIN IMBROGLIO (CONT'D). **Sep 2:** The *Morning Advertiser* pubs M's letter (#M510) [← :32]. **Sep 3:** The *Advertiser* pubs an unsigned attack on M, more vitriolic than the previous one, by Golovin (without Herzen this time). M sends his contemplated reply to E, and asks for help in dealing with this situation. **Sep 4:** M sends his reply to the *Advertiser*, which refuses to print it. **Sep 7:** M sends a letter to the *People's Paper*, quoting both Golovin's last piece and his own reply (#M913); pubd in *PP* on Sep 10.

35. *NYDT* ARTICLES. **Sep:** *NYDT* pubs six articles: on the Turkish question in England (#M951), and on Continental and English affairs (#M959, 10, 784, 963, 671); the last three articles begin to point to a threatening economic crisis.

36. ECONOMICA. **Sep:** Using passages from M's letters, Cluss writes an article on Carey for a New York German paper; see #M53.5 **Sep 15:** Writing to Cluss, M remarks that he has hoped to finish his opus by now but it doesn't look as if he will be able to do so. **Sep 29:** E sends M data on the position of certain branches of the economy in England.

37. STUDIES. **Sep:** As Europe moves toward the Crimean War, M abandons his intention of returning to his economic studies (broken off since c.Apr) and plans to investigate the prehistory of this war. From now until May 1854, M fills a number of research notebooks with the results of this study. **Sep D to Oct A:** M studies recent Danish history in order to write on that country for *NYDT*.

38. PERSONAL. **Sep 6:** There is a passing spat between M and W. Wolff over a lost book.

OCTOBER

39. PALMERSTON ARTICLES. **Oct 22 to Dec 24:** M pubs a series of eight articles on Lord Palmerston and English foreign policy in the *People's Paper* (#M474). M originally started these for *NYDT*, which however pubs them less completely; the first of the *NYDT* articles (#M626) appears this month.

40. *NYDT* ARTICLES. **Oct:** *NYDT* pubs six articles—four mostly on the approaching crisis, strikes, and economic affairs (#M990,

989, 631, 985); one on the Russo-Turkish war by E (#E716); and the Palmerston article (#M626) mentioned above (see ← :39). (The *NYDT* series on Palmerston will appear Oct 19 to Jan 11, in four articles.) **Oct 12:** In a letter to E, M analyzes the situation in France and suggests that E write an article for *NYDT* on the consequences of the threatening economic crisis on the Bonapartist regime.

41. URQUHART. **Oct 4:** In *NYDT* article #M990, M quotes Urquhart for his info and at the same time calls his interpretation "good for nothing." **Oct D:** M, having read with astonishment that Jones has called Urquhart an "ally of Russia," writes to Cluss, sending notes to guide him in writing up a piece on Urquhart in the American press [→ :45].

NOVEMBER

42. POLITICAL AFFAIRS. **Nov A:** M asks Dronke and W. Wolff to continue writing for *Die Reform*. **Nov 2:** In a letter to E, M announces his conclusion on Palmerston: it is the same as "that monomaniac Urquhart— that for some decades Palmerston has been sold to Russia." M thinks inquiry into diplomatic history (i.e., history of foreign policy) has been neglected. **Nov M:** M tells Cluss that he has become very thick with Urquhart, who has lent him several books.

43. POLEMIC WITH WILLICH. **Nov c.21:** M receives from Cluss the *Belletristische Journal und New-Yorker Criminal-Zeitung* (this is a single paper) carrying Willich's attack on M's "Revelations" pamphlet about the Cologne trial (#M762). **Nov 21–23:** M asks E, Steffen, and Dronke to send him statements on Willich, for a reply. Steffen complies on Nov 22, E on Nov c.22; Dronke delays answering. **Nov c.21–28:** M writes a polemical pamphlet in reply to Willich, *The knight of the noble consciousness* (#M429). **Nov 25:** A joint statement answering Willich, by Weydemeyer, Cluss, and Jacobi, using material sent by M, is pubd in *Belletristische Journal*. **Nov 29:** M sends Cluss the ms of the pamphlet for publ [→ 54:5].

44. W&P. **Nov:** *NYDT* pubs 11 articles: seven on English and European affairs by M (#M628, 54, 986, 651, 258, 440, 704—the last dealing with economic problems) and four by E on the war in Turkey (#E498, 356, 616, 711). **c.Nov:** M inquires from Dana if there is any possibility of publishing in America articles on the history of German philosophy [→ :47]. **Nov 5:** *PP* puts a special ed note on Article 3 of M's series on Palmerston (#M474) [← :39] pointing to the importance of this work in exposing ruling-class policy in England. **Nov 26:** The same Article 3 is reprinted in the *Glasgow Sentinel*.

DECEMBER

45. POLITICAL AFFAIRS. Dec A: M receives an Urquhart brochure in the mail, sent anonymously; however, M sends Urquhart a note of thanks. **Dec 9:** Urquhart, replying he was not the sender, expresses appreciation of M's article on Palmerston and asks for permission to reprint it through the pub'r Tucker. **Dec 19:** Cluss's short piece on Urquhart based on M's notes [← :41] is pubd in *Die Reform*. (For the text, see ed note, *MEW* 28:734 n.586 and #M212.5.) **Dec CD:** M is visited by G. Lewy (or Levy) of Düsseldorf, representing ex-CL members in the Rhineland. Lewy wants to persuade M that it is necessary to organize an uprising of factory workers in Iserlohn, Solingen, et al; M explains this is not on the order of the day, indeed useless given current German conditions.

46. NYDT ARTICLES. Dec: *NYDT* pubs seven articles: five by M on the Turkish war, Palmerston, and other English and European affairs (#M494, 720, 802, 630, 953—the last dealing with industrial crisis), and two by E on the progress of the war (#E627, 910). **Dec 14:** Writing to E, M comments wryly on how Dana appropriates E's militaria for editorials, which arouse much public attention, and how Dana did the same with M's Palmerston articles. **Dec 20:** M sends *NYDT* an article dealing with press comments on Palmerston's resignation, but it is not printed.

47. W&P. Dec c.14: M receives from his brother-in-law J. C. Juta an invitation to contribute to the Cape Town daily *De Zuid-Afrikaan* [→ 54:5]. **Dec c.16:** Article 3 of the Palmerston series (#M474) appears as a pamphlet titled *Palmerston and Russia* in the series Political Fly-Sheets, no. 1, London, E. Tucker pub'r (this edn will be sold out in a few weeks) [← :45]. **Dec 24:** The last article in the Palmerston series (#M474) is pubd in *PP*. **Dec D:** M receives Dana's reply (Dec 16) to his question [← :44] about publishing on German philosophy. Dana stipulates that such articles for American papers must not contain anything offensive to religious feelings.

48. ENGELS' HOPES. Dec M: To free himself from his commercial job, E makes efforts to become military correspondent for a Lon-don paper; then he could live in London near M and devote himself to writing the history of the Hungarian revolution of 1848–49. But his efforts are unsuccessful. **Dec D to Jan 1:** E visits M in London.

YEAR APPENDIX

49. M resumes his economic studies in Jan after a hiatus; but for various reasons he is soon sidetracked again and goes to other subjects.

50. January. M's reading includes works by G. Opdyke, F. W. Newman, Herbert Spencer, and Banfield.

51. January to March. M's reading covers the history of India. Under the theory of money, history of civilization, and history of the Slavs, his reading incl works by W. Wachsmuth, F. Galiani, R. Kaulfuss, and (about this time) L. von Stein.

52. March to Apr CD. *MEW* lists works by the English economists F. W. Newman, Opdyke, Spencer, Banfield; also the file of the *Economist*. M shows special interest in questions of money circulation, land ownership and rent of land, population theory, and the role of the state.

53. April to May. M reads works by McCulloch, Klemm, Bernier, Saltykov, and others on the history and economy of India and China. In connection with Parliament's discussion of the East India Co. charter, M studies the Parliamentary Blue Books and the history of the company.

54. May M to June. In connection with the East India Co. and with Indian agrarian conditions, M studies writings by Mun, Bernier, Campbell, and Raffles; also W. Wilks, Robert Patton, D. Urquhart, and British diplomatic documents on India, esp publications of the India Reform Assoc and Urquhart's *Portfolio*.

55. June. *MEW* lists works on India by Chapman, Dickinson, Mill, Campbell, and other writers. M excerpts questions about the English colonial system and Indian social and political conditions. In addition, he studies the history of Denmark (for *NYDT* articles): works by Droysen, Samwer, and Olshausen. *KMC* dates his reading on Denmark as Sep D to Oct A.

1854

CONSPECTUS

1. M's work as *NYDT* correspondent seems for a while to offer the prospect of a steady income; but affected by the economic crisis, *NYDT* retrenches and M's contribu-tions are curtailed. Besides, *NYDT*'s practice of using his best articles (best from its standpoint) as unsigned editorials prevents gaining a journalistic reputation and higher payment. M makes another connection: with the *Neue Oder-Zeitung* (*NOZ*) of Breslau (Wroclaw). In between he has tried a South African paper, also the Urquhartite press in England. The current focus of journalistic work is the ongoing war; later, the new insurrection in Spain; routinely, English and European political (sometimes economic) affairs. M's political ties are mainly still with Ernest Jones's wing of Chartism in England, and with the restricted Marx circle (what is left of it) elsewhere, incl Cluss and Weydemeyer in America, Lassalle and the Cologne people in Germany. His constant accompaniment is the pressure of poverty and ill health.

2. M's special studies during the year (noted in place) include English diplomatic history (with Lord Palmerston as the villain), and Spanish and Greek history; but he also continues his work on polit eco. Statistical and other economic data which he collects are utilized in *NYDT* articles. (For details, see → :55–57.)

3. E continues working in the field of military studies, and at M's request for *NYDT* articles, he makes a number of specific analyses as well as providing a running analysis of the war operations. From June to Nov he goes back to working on the history of the Hungarian Revolution of 1848–49, still planning a book which he will never write. He tries to find a way to leave Manchester by getting a job as military correspondent for a London paper (see → :10, 18, 23), but the scheme fails.

JANUARY

4. *NYDT* ARTICLES. **Jan:** *NYDT* pubs three articles: on England and Russia (#M277) and on the course of the war (#M873, #E628). **Jan 2:** M receives Dana's letter (Dec 16) saying that *NYDT* cannot sign M's name to leading articles. Dana reports that the military articles (actually by E) have made a sensation; the author is rumored to be Gen. Winfield Scott. **Jan 9:** M receives the text of an Urquhart speech, and quotes it for half of his *NYDT* article #M873; he prefaces it by repudiating Urquhart's views; the article is pubd Jan 28.

5. W&P. **Jan 10:** From pub'r Tucker, M receives a proposal to publish a second edn of the flysheet *Palmerston and Russia* [← 53:47], since the first edn is exhausted; M agrees [→ :9]. **Jan 14:** M writes an article for the *Zuid Afrikaan* (Cape Town) as proposed by brother-in-law Juta (#M979) [← 53:47; → :14]. **Jan M:** M's polemical pamphlet against Willich [← 53:43] titled *The knight of the noble consciousness* (#M429) is pubd by Weydemeyer and Cluss in NYC. **Jan CD:** M negotiates over the publ of a new pamphlet on Palmerston composed of his *NYDT* articles (#M626). **Jan 25:** M informs E he has

received via Dana a proposal to write a series of articles on Kant for a magazine; M wants E to collaborate. (Nothing will come of this proposal.)

6. PERSONAL. **Jan 1:** E returns to Manchester [← 53:48]. **Jan A:** M and his family are ill with the grippe.

FEBRUARY

7. *NYDT* ARTICLES. **Feb:** *NYDT* pubs eight articles, mostly concerned with the war and the policy of Russia and England (#M977, 211, 190, 86, 795; #ME60; #E252, 418). Article #M86 has a section on the convocation of the Labour Parliament; #ME60, on the English electoral system. Article #M795 reflects M's study (Feb A to 10) of documents on the Eastern question in the Blue Books.

8. POLITICAL AFFAIRS. **Feb 9:** M writes E about his meeting with Urquhart, just held; Urquhart seems to be an obsessed monomaniac and would-be savior. **Feb 10:** Lassalle sends M some confidential info about Bonaparte's war preparations and Prussia's policy on the looming Anglo-French war against Russia. **Feb c.17:** M hears from Lassalle that the Prussian government is planning mass arrests of Democratic leaders; he writes this news up for *NYDT* (#M221, pubd Mar 9).

9. W&P. **Feb A:** M's *Palmerston and Russia* appears in a second edn [← :5] titled *Palmerston and Poland*. Tucker also issues a pamphlet reprinting two articles from M's Palmerston series (#M474), Articles 4 and 5 titled *Palmerston and the treaty of Unkiar Skelessi* (so on the cover: the inside title page is *Palmerston, What has he done?*), Political Fly-Sheets, no. 2. **Feb 9:** M sends E some copies of the anti-Willich pamphlet (#M429) [← :5] and of *Palmerston and Russia*, with the request to send copies also to W. Wolff and Dronke.

10. ENGELS: MILITARY CORRESPONDENT. **Feb D:** E starts making plans to persuade the *Daily News* (London) to take him on as military correspondent; he begins working on an article "The fortress of Kronstadt" (#E287) as a specimen [→ :18].

11. PERSONAL. **Feb D to Mar:** Together with M, E helps Heise, ex-editor of *Die Hornisse*, establish himself in Manchester.

MARCH

12. *NYDT* ARTICLES. **Mar:** *NYDT* pubs 10 articles: on Prussian and French plans (#M221) [← :8], English politics (#M215), European affairs and the war (#M639, 512), Austria (#M68), the Greek insurrection (#M359), the Labour Parliament (#M619, 439), incl two on the war (#ME192,

(#E713). **Mar 28:** In a letter to Dana, M gives
vent to his protest against *NYDT's* use of his
articles as unsigned editorials [← :1]; he
forbids Dana to use anything except militaria
as unsigned editorials, or else to take his name
off all pieces printed (*MEW* dates this letter
Mar 27) [→ :40].
    13. THE LABOUR PARLIAMENT. Mar 6:
This workers' congress in Manchester votes
unanim at its first session to invite Dr. Marx as
an honorary delegate. **Mar 7:** M writes up
the congress for *NYDT* (#M619); pubd Mar
24. **Mar 9:** M replies to the invitation by
sending a message of greetings (#M468).
Mar 10: M's message is read to a session by E.
Jones (who tells E about it). —M writes
another article on the congress for *NYDT*
(#M439); pubd Mar 29. **Mar 18:** Jones's *PP*
pubs M's letter to the Labour Parliament
(#M468).
    **14. SOUTH AFRICAN CONNECTION. Mar
6:** M's article #M979 [← :5] is pubd in the
Zuid Afrikaan; but a second article, which M
had sent Feb 14, has not been pubd. **Mar 14:**
M sends a third article (not extant) to this
paper, but it too will not be pubd.
    15. PEOPLE'S PAPER. Mar 18: PP pubs
two pieces which M gave to Jones to help his
work: M's letter to the Labour Parliament
(#M468), and a fuller version (#E682) of an
NYDT article by E (#E713).
    **16. LASSALLE, RUSSIA, AND THE WAR.
Mar 7:** In a letter to M, Lassalle expounds his
differing views on Russian military and diplomatic policy and on Palmerston's role. **Mar
c.9:** M sends Lassalle's letter to E, for comment on the military aspect. **Mar c.11:** M
sends E a second letter received from
Lassalle. **Mar 23:** E writes M a critique of
Lassalle's views on the conduct of the war [→
:10].
    17. STUDIES. Mar D to Apr A: M reads J.
Hammer-Purgstall as part of his study of the
Eastern question.
    **18. ENGELS: MILITARY CORRESPONDENT.
Mar 30:** E sends a long letter (#E440) to the
Daily News editor to win a job as military
correspondent [← :10], enclosing his article
#E287 as specimen [→ :23].

APRIL

    19. *NYDT* ARTICLES. Apr: *NYDT* pubs
six articles, almost entirely revolving around
the Crimean War. Articles #M250 and 814 are
based on M's study of the Blue Books on the
secret correspondence of the English ambassador to Russia with the Foreign Office in 1853.
Article #M223—written Mar 28, date of the
Anglo-French declaration of war on Russia—
is based on M's study of official documents
and a book by C. Famin. Article #M974, on

Parliament's debates, deals with the secret
1844 negotiations between the czar and English diplomats on the partition of Turkey.
(See also #ME55.5.) Article #M793 deals
with the relation of Austria and Prussia to the
war. Article #E595 is E's military analysis of
the course of the war. For an additional article
on Britain, pubd only in the *Semi-Weekly
Tribune,* see #M111.5. **Apr 22:** M is waiting
for Dana to reply to his last protest [← :12];
meanwhile, he tells E, he is resolved to insist
on increasing his payment to at least £3 per
article.
    20. ABOUT PALMERSTON. Apr A: M reads
Washington Wilks's *Palmerston in three ep-
ochs* (1854). **Apr 6:** Replying to Lassalle's
discussion letter [← :16], M first deals with
the military questions, then strongly restates
his view of Palmerston as a conscious agent of
Russia [→ :29]. **Apr 20:** The *Morning Advertiser* pubs an article by an Urquhartite who
writes that "Mr. Marx" is still a supporter of
Urquhart's [see ← 53:32]. M wants to disavow
any support of Urquhart, but fears the *Advertiser* will reply it meant F. Marx. **Apr 22:** M
writes E he will wait for a good occasion to
disavow Urquhart publicly.
    21. POLITICAL AFFAIRS. Apr D: E helps
Heise [← :11] write an article for *Die Reform*
against the putschist ideas of A. Schimmel-
pfennig, who is connected with Willich in
America. (The article is not pubd since *Die
Reform* suspends publ.) **Apr c.D:** M meets
with Edgar Bauer to get info about a Dr. Wiss,
who has pubd attacks on M&E in Weitling's
Republik der Arbeiter; he sends this material
to Cluss for use in the German-American
press.
    22. STUDIES. Apr D to May: M studies
Spanish; he reads Cervantes' *Don Quixote* and
Calderón in the original.
    **23. ENGELS: MILITARY CORRESPONDENT.
Apr AB:** The *Daily News* is favorable to
accepting E as writer on military affairs [←
:18]; at its request E writes the opener
(#E710.5) of a series of articles on Russia's
armed forces. **Apr c.12:** E receives the proofs
of this article and a letter from editor H. J.
Lincoln asking E's terms. **Apr 20:** E informs
M that Lincoln has suddenly broken off the
arrangement, apparently after finding out
about E's political views; E speculates that
Pieper may have committed an indiscretion.
But E is thinking of finishing the articles
nonetheless and offering them to the *Times.*

MAY

    24. *NYDT* AND *PP*. May: *NYDT* pubs five
articles, all on European affairs (#M750, 358,
360, 89) except one attacking Gladstone's
financial quackery (#M111). Article #M750

argues that Europe needs a solution to the Eastern question, since it is an egotistic illusion that any people can win liberty at the cost of another people's independence. In addition an *NYDT* leading article "Prussian policy" (May 19) may be by M/E; see #M711 in the *Register*. **May 27:** PP pubs E's survey of military events in the war (#E258), which will appear in *NYDT* on June 9. This is the last article by M/E in *PP* until Apr 1856.

25. POLITICAL AFFAIRS. May c.10: M receives a letter from Cluss about a plan by German-American émigrés to launch an English paper in London; they want M on the editorial staff. (The plan will not be realized.) **May c.12:** M learns from Cluss that *Die Reform* ceased publ on Apr 26 for lack of money. **May D:** Since his correspondence is under police surveillance, M arranges to use two cover addresses in order to correspond with Germany.

26. Studies. May A: As a result of the Greek insurrection in Thessaly and Epirus, M studies the history of the Greek state in the late 1820s and early 1830s, and reads H. H. Parish. **May to June A:** M reads a collection of Italian documents of 1848–49 pubd in the *Archivio triennale delle cose d'Italia dall' avvenimento di Pio IX all' abbandono di Venezia*, and finds it the best thing he has seen on the "Italian revolutionary party" (M to E, May 3). **May to July:** M's notebooks show his reading on Spain, as that country moves toward revolution (see → :55.)

27. PERSONAL. c.May: Bertha (Levy) Markheim, sister of J. Rodenberg and a friend of Miquel, sojourns in London for a few weeks and becomes very friendly with the M family. **May c.8 to May D:** M is very ill, with a large facial carbuncle. He is unable to write; hence E does more than usual of the *NYDT* articles. The children have the measles.

JUNE

28. NYDT ARTICLES. June: *NYDT* pubs eight articles, half by E, because of M's illness [← :27]. E's articles deal with military aspects of the war (#E269, 742, and 258; re the last, see ← :24); one of E's articles (#E617) discusses the bad condition of the English army. An article by M concentrates on the military side (#M323), but two others take up important political issues. M shows (#M939) that the Austrian-Prussian treaty is a pact to maintain the prewar status quo against upsets. Article #M734 makes a political statement on the war: it is "a mistake to describe the war against Russia as a war between liberty and despotism," for the war aim is "the maintenance of the balance of power and the Vienna treaties—those very treaties which annul the

liberty and independence of nations." M also inserts a public repudiation of Urquhart's politics. The remaining article (#M60) is a denunciation of the English oligarchy's policy in clearing the estates in Scotland and Ireland. **June 6:** Under this date *MEW* lists an article sent by M to *NYDT* "which begins the exposure of a Bonapartist representative, the French commander-in-chief Saint-Arnaud" but remains unpubd. (Note that the abovementioned #M734, which was sent in June 9, deals with Saint-Arnaud.)

29. POLITICAL AFFAIRS. June 1: In a letter to Lassalle, M continues his argumentation about Palmerston's role [← :20], and also makes a strong statement of political rejection of the "romantic reactionary" Urquhart. **June 2:** M receives a visit from Dr. K. C. Otto, a Danish Democrat.

30. ENGELS: STUDIES. June: E resumes his work (till Nov) on the history of the Hungarian Revolution of 1848–49; he plans to write the book during the winter.

31. PERSONAL. June c.3 to c.21: Mrs. M falls very ill; M cannot pay Dr. Freund's medical bill of £26, until E helps out. **June 27 to July A:** Mrs. M, with the children and Helene Demuth, goes to Edmonton (S. Seiler's cottage) to convalesce [→ :36].

JULY

32. NYDT ARTICLES. July: *NYDT* pubs seven articles, all dealing in whole or part with the current politico-military state of the war (esp #ME160, 149; #E911; also #M975, which discusses foreign-policy conflicts in the British ruling class). Three also contain sections on the new insurrection in Madrid by Gens. O'Dónnell and Dulce (#M407, 305, with a preliminary comment in #M561). An editorial pubd July 11, refuting the czar's reputation as a great statesman, is a dubious case (#M797?).

33. POLITICAL AFFAIRS. July 20: E passes on to M some info from Dronke on ex-CL members Naut, Daniels, Becker, et al.

34. W&P. July 27: M informs E of pub'r Tucker's proposal to publish some of M's articles on Palmerston as separate pamphlets. M is also thinking of writing two other pamphlets: a general pamphlet on Palmerston, and a pamphlet (with E) on "the diplomacy and military action of the English" in this war.

35. STUDIES. July CD: M studies A. Thierry's *Essai sur l'histoire de la formation et des progrès du Tiers État* (1853); M has read previous works by him too. **July 27:** M sends E a critique of Thierry as "the father of the 'class struggle' in French historiography" who yet remains completely bourgeois in outlook.

36. PERSONAL. **July 8:** Mrs. M goes to Trier to visit her mother [→ :39]. **July to Sep:** M is in deep financial distress.

AUGUST

37. NYDT ARTICLES. **Aug:** NYDT pubs 10 articles. Article #M289 on "The English middle class" has been much altered by the editors. Two articles deal with the war debates in Parliament which M attended in person (#M976, 69). Others take up the new uprising in Spain, in whole (#ME169, #M297) or in part (#M962, 824, 302, 301). "Espartero" (#M297), based on M's studies, concludes that this leader cannot lead the popular liberation struggle. "That bore of a war" (#ME169) welcomes the return of barricade fighting in Spain as prelude to a mass revolutionary movement: a "new revolutionary era" is possible. E's article (#E47) is on the war.

38. STUDIES. **Aug to Dec A:** In connection with the Spanish events, M pursues his study of Spanish history in the BM Library, reading in English, French, and Spanish (for details, see → :57). M uses this material for beginning (Aug 25) to write his series on "Revolutionary Spain" (#M780) for NYDT [→ :40].

39. PERSONAL. **Aug 21:** Mrs. M leaves Trier [← :36]. **Aug 23:** She returns to London. **c.Aug:** Miquel writes M, from Paris, that he is coming to visit, but fails to do so on account of illness.

SEPTEMBER

40. NYDT AND SPAIN. **Sep:** NYDT pubs eight articles: a two-article series by E on the capture of Bomarsund (#E120, 121); four articles by M mainly on the new Spanish insurrection (#M259, 774, 727, 788—the last is largely on miscellaneous European affairs); and the first two articles in M's important new series on "Revolutionary Spain," pubd Sep 9 to Dec 2 (#M780). **Sep 2:** M writes E that his "principal study" right now is on Spain; he has covered 1808–14 and 1820–23, and has now come to 1834–43. **Sep 29:** M has received a reply from NYDT's publishers to his proposition [← :12], and tells E: they propose that M write only "editorial articles," i.e., unsigned; and they offer only half of the income he has received up to now, pleading the impact of the economic crisis; M is to send only one article a week.

41. POLITICAL AFFAIRS. **Sep 8, 13:** M receives two letters from Jones on the difficult situation of the People's Paper, asking M to help out as much as possible. **Sep 13:** M reports to E on the hard material situation of their friends Pieper and Steffen.

OCTOBER

42. NYDT ARTICLES. **Oct:** NYDT pubs 10 articles. Four are war analyses (#E46, 522, 70, 486—the last two arouse much attention in NY by their perspicacity). Three are articles in the "Revolutionary Spain" series (#M780, Articles 3–5); one is on miscellaneous European affairs (#M153). Two others (#ME151, 152) were sent in as a single article, and were separated in NY into an "I told you so" editorial on the "Sevastopol hoax" and a news dispatch of miscellaneous European news; the latter ends in a comment that Barbès has discredited himself as a revolutionary by supporting France against Russia in the war.

43. POLITICAL AFFAIRS. **Oct D** (after Oct 29): M is invited to participate in an anti-Bonaparte comm formed by the Chartists to protest the planned visit of Bonaparte to England. On Jones's proposal, M is elected an honorary member along with liberal leaders like Mazzini, Hugo, L. Blanc, et al. M declines; he tells Jones that this action should have a purely English character. Jones agrees and follows this line in the comm.

44. STUDIES. **Oct M:** M studies the history of the Seven Years' War in connection with his inquiry into English policy on the Crimean War. **Oct D:** M reads Chateaubriand, Congrès de Vérone (1838), in connection with his studies on Spain.

NOVEMBER

45. NYDT ARTICLES. **Nov:** As presaged by Dana [← :40], there is a sharp falling off in NYDT publ of articles sent in by M; four articles are pubd this month. Three are articles by E giving analyses of the war (#E740, 116, 907—the first arouses special attention in NY, like its Oct precedents). One is the sixth article in M's "Revolutionary Spain" series (#M780). **Nov 14, 21:** M sends in two articles for the "Revolutionary Spain" series which are not pubd; see #M780, Articles J and K, also #M823. **Nov 30:** Writing to E, M mentions that his income from NYDT has been reduced.

46. POLITICAL AFFAIRS. **Nov 22:** M writes E about the efforts by K. Blind and other right-wing émigré leaders in London to organize protest meetings against Russia and against the policy of the German princes in the Crimean War; they want to include all émigré factions, incl M. But M refuses to participate, since he does not share their position on the war. He plans, if necessary, to hold a counter-meeting with the English Chartists. (But the émigrés' meeting fails to come off.)

47. W&P. **Nov D:** M is asked by Tucker to write for a planned London periodical.

48. STUDIES. **Nov 28 to Dec 2:** M reads R. S. Ripley, *The war with Mexico* (1849), and A. de Solis, *Historia de la conquista de Méjico* (1844), and sends these books to E. M discusses Ripley's book in three letters (Nov 30; Dec 2, 15).

DECEMBER

49. NYDT ARTICLES. **Dec:** NYDT pubs only four articles (the fewest since Jan). Two by E are war analyses (#E67, 192); two are the last articles in M's "Revolutionary Spain" series (#M780). In addition M sends (Dec 8) an article for this series which is not pubd (see #M780, Article L).

50. *NEUE ODER-ZEITUNG.* **Dec c.2:** M receives a proposition from the NOZ via Lassalle, who had been asked to get M paying pen work: to act as London correspondent for this Breslau paper, which is owned by the liberal M. Friedländer (Lassalle's cousin) in partnership with Elsner and J. Stein, at the "miserable" rate of 20 (later 30) talers per month. **Dec 2:** M asks urgently for E's opinion (which is not extant). **Dec 15:** M writes E that he is starting "next week" to write for NOZ, at 30 talers a month; he says he has accepted mainly for the sake of his wife's peace of mind. **Dec 20:** M writes Elsner he will begin writing on the 23rd. **Dec 29:** M writes his first piece for the paper (#M761) [→ 55:3].

51. ECONOMICA. **Dec to Jan:** M reads through his notebooks on polit eco of past years, to review the material and "have it ready for revision." He finishes a short conspectus, headed "Money, credit, crises," cross-referring to the corresponding notebooks with excerpts from various writers (Gilbart, H. Thornton, Tooke, Hubbard, J. S. Mill, Fullarton, et al), giving the author's name, title of work, notebook page. He will use this material later for the *Grundrisse* and

for Vol. 3 of *Capital* (SOURCE: *MEW Daten.* Compare this reference to the conspectus with #M528.)

52. STUDIES. **Dec to Jan:** E studies books and other materials on the history of Russia and the Slavic peoples, in various languages, incl Russian. He reads Haxthausen, Herzen, Ranke, Safařik, Engel, et al. About this time (end of the year to early 1855) he drafts a pamphlet on *Germandom and Slavdom* (#E337.5); see → 55:1.

53. MISCELLANEOUS. **Dec A:** E corresponds with Dronke about delivering 65–70 copies of the last issue of the old NRZ, sent from Germany by Naut.

54. VISITS. **c.Dec:** In his Dec 20 letter to Elsner, M mentions that Edgar Bauer visits him "once a week" [→ 55:50]. **Dec 16:** K. Blind and his wife visit M. **Dec c.22 to Jan A:** E visits M in London.

YEAR APPENDIX

55. **May to July.** For this period, M's notebook lists the following writers on Spain, Greece, and other subjects: H. H. Parish, A. Thierry, T. M. Hughes, M. de Marliani, and M. A. Principe; also three anonymous works: *Una plumada sobre la indole y tendencia de la revolución en España* (1846), *Examen critique des révolutions d'Espagne de 1820 à 1823 et de 1836* (1837), *The crisis of Spain*, second edn (1823). Written above this list in the notebook are the names "Campomanes, Jovellanos," perhaps notations on reading to be done.

56. **June-July:** *MEW* lists the author Florez in addition to some others on the preceding list.

57. **Aug to Dec A:** M's reading in Spanish history includes the works of Toreno, Pradt, Jovellanos, Chateaubriand, and M. de Marliani.

1855

CONSPECTUS

1. The new task absorbing M's energies most of this year (Jan to Oct) is correspondence for the Breslau paper Neue Oder-Zeitung (NOZ), for which M&E write over 130 articles—until financial distress forces NOZ to suspend their contributions. In contrast NYDT pubs only 43 of their articles all year (not counting D&A cases); but finally M succeeds in getting a renegotiation of terms. In addition, Dana is instrumental in getting an order from *Putnam's Monthly* for E's long study "The armies of Europe" (#E32). — Early this year E finishes [← 54:52] a pam-

phlet on *Germandom and Slavdom* (#E337.5) which is an attack on Pan-Slavism; but no pub'r can be found [→ :21, 27].

2. Aside from this political journalism, which is largely concerned with the military and political events of the Crimean War and with current politics in England, M&E have little involvement with political affairs. On the personal side, the death of M's son Edgar has a staggering impact on his morale.

JANUARY

3. *NEUE ODER-ZEITUNG.* **Jan:** M begins writing for this paper [← 54:50]: he produces a stream of 12 articles, beginning with a two-article "Retrospective" of the past period #M761). E's *NYDT* article #E102 is revised or *NOZ* as #ME107. Three other articles deal with the war situation (#ME187, 77; #M324). The remaining seven deal mostly with English political affairs and the economic crisis #M689, 405, 716, 24, 618, 147, 636). Of these, #M405 is a four-part study of the advancing crisis (cf *NYDT* article #M159, → :4).

4. *NYDT* ARTICLES. **Jan:** *NYDT* pubs four articles: one on the economic crisis in Britain #M159) and three about the state of the war #ME118; #E485, 102).

5. ECONOMICA. **Jan-Feb:** M continues to work through his notebooks on polit eco [← 54:51], and prepares an index to them. These notebooks include excerpts on problems of ground rent and population theory from several years of the *Economist* and from D'Avenant, Alison, Petty, Boisguillebert, Locke, Steuart, et al. **Jan 23:** In a letter to Lassalle, M replies to a number of economic questions, esp the effect of the Corn Laws on prices and wages; he promises to send statistical info from his notebooks.

6. STUDIES. **c.Jan:** M studies Roman history up to Augustus, reading i.a. Niebuhr's *Römische Geschichte*, and concludes that its key is the struggle of small and large landed property with slavery as the conditioning factor and the debt problem as the consequence. (Note: M writes E, Mar 8, that he did this work "a while ago," but *MEW* dates it Feb D, and *KMC* Jan-Feb.) **Jan D:** M makes a conspectus of the record of the fallen Aberdeen coalition government, Dec 1852 to Dec 1854, and sends it to E (Jan 31) for use in #ME83; M uses this material for #M311, 955.

7. VISIT. **Jan c.D:** Spilthoorn, expelled from Belgium, visits M on his way to America; M gives him a recommendatory letter to Dana.

8. PERSONAL. **Jan 7:** Lassalle sends M 200 talers, for himself and Countess Hatzfeldt. **Jan 16:** M's daughter Eleanor is born. She is sickly at first, and it is feared she will die.

FEBRUARY

9. *NOZ* ARTICLES. **Feb:** *NOZ* pubs 15 articles. Four are M's rewrites of *NYDT* articles by E: #ME78 revises #E253; #ME111 revises #E787, plus a supplement on England; and #ME112 and 39 are M's versions of #E914 (pubd in *NYDT* in Mar). The other *NOZ* articles are on English political affairs: four on Aberdeen's fall (#M609.5, 311, 644, 955)—of which, however, one (#M644) is a more general analysis, discussing "The parties and cliques" of English politics. Two (#M634, 150) are on the sharpening of the

economic and political situation. One (#M488) is a two-part follow-up of M's previous pamphlet on Lord Palmerston (#M474). The four others on English politics are #M609.7, 369, 382, 394.

10. *NYDT* ARTICLES. **Feb:** *NYDT* pubs only five articles: three on the war (#E253, 192.5, 787), and two mainly on the fall of the Aberdeen cabinet (#M310, #ME83). The writing of these articles is also partly meshed with the articles pubd in *NOZ*.

11. POLITICAL AFFAIRS. **Feb 2** (or earlier): M receives a letter from Lassalle on the political situation inside Germany; M forwards the letter to E. **Feb 2:** Writing to E, M reports that on Feb 1 he attended (on Jones's invitation, and with Götz) a meeting of an International Comm of émigrés called to organize an anniversary affair for the Feb Revolution of 1848. M sits by as a silent spectator, and decides he wants to have nothing to do with these émigrés. **Feb 13:** M informs E that he has been invited to participate in the planned anniversary meeting, but he will decline, esp because Herzen is involved. (The meeting sponsored by the International Comm will take place Feb 27.)

12. PERSONAL. **Feb c.9 to Mar 3:** M suffers from an eye inflammation due to intensive work on his economic notebooks; this is followed by a bad cough. He is confined to bed for a few days, unable to write. His son Edgar and baby Eleanor are also ill. The doctor recommends moving to a more healthful district than Soho.

MARCH

13. *NOZ* ARTICLES. **Mar:** *NOZ* pubs 19 articles. Only two are mainly on the war (#E191, #ME108, which are similar resp to #E681 and #E65 pubd in *NYDT* in Apr). Nine deal with English political affairs, esp Palmerston and foreign policy (#M627, 446, 107, 293, 121, 21, 560, 504, 393), plus two on Palmerston and the Anglo-French alliance (#M607, 608). Article #M504 reports on the Mar 16 free-trader meeting in London at which Jones et al spoke strongly against the effort to drag the workers' movement into support of the bourgeois campaign. Two other articles write up the Commission of Inquiry into the British military system, which M analyzes (#M161, 162); one discusses the Irish M.P.s in Parliament (#M422). Three articles inaugurate a closer inquiry by M into the developing crisis of Bonapartism in France (#M118, 535; #ME43—the last is M's version of the *NYDT* article #E274 in Apr).

14. *NYDT* ARTICLES. **Mar:** *NYDT* pubs only two articles: #M198, which is another version of the *NOZ* article #M107 on the

British constitution (the class compromise of the ruling circles) and #E914, "The war that looms on Europe."

15. PERSONAL. **Mar 3:** M writes E that he plans to come to Manchester for a short time because of his bad health and need for a change. **Mar M to Apr 6:** M's son Edgar is critically ill with gastric fever; Mrs. M is shaken and falls ill too. M takes care of both and becomes exhausted by night watches. E as usual supports the family financially. **Mar 30:** M writes E that hope for Edgar's recovery has been given up by the doctor; Mrs. M is ill and overwrought; M's head is "burning"; he thanks E for his help [→ :18].

APRIL

16. NOZ ARTICLES. **Apr:** NOZ pubs five articles, only one by M (#M810, on a French scandal). Three articles by E deal with war analyses (#E566, 6, 197—the last is a critique of the French military). As for the fifth, on Apr 17 M sends both NOZ and NYDT a two-part article by E attacking Pan-Slavism (#E338); NOZ pubs it Apr 21, 24 (as for NYDT, see → :20). M tells Elsner, NOZ editor, that these articles are the "beginning of a polemic against Pan-Slavism."

17. NYDT ARTICLES. **Apr:** NYDT pubs nine articles, only two by M: one (#M99) on the report of the British inquiry into the condition of the army (also written up in Mar for NOZ), and a think-piece (#M702) on the role of the classes in the opposition to the war in France and England. E's seven articles are all on some aspect of the ongoing war, three of them denouncing esp the role of Bonaparte and his generals (#E274, 501, 500); the others are #E681, 65, 629, 741.

18. PERSONAL. **Apr 6:** M's son Edgar dies in his arms. M informs E that he and his wife plan to go to Manchester for a stay. **Apr 9:** The child's funeral takes place. **Apr 12:** M writes E that he feels "broken down"; since the funeral he has had violent headaches; he thanks E profusely once again. **Apr 18 to May c.6:** M and his wife stay in Manchester. Meanwhile, NOZ contributions are taken over by Dronke who, however, sends only one or two articles.

MAY

19. NOZ ARTICLES. **May:** NOZ pubs 13 articles. Two by E (#E302, 117) are versions of NYDT articles, on the state of the war (cf → :20). Article #ME118.5 is M's version of #E509 (which will appear in the June NYDT) plus a passage on Palmerston. Outside of #M656 (on Italy and Austria), the other articles are on aspects of English political

affairs: on the issue of electoral reform (#M605, 816, 612) and a related analysis of English parties (#M532), plus other matters (#M23, 315, 388, 643, 244).

20. NYDT ARTICLES. **May:** NYDT pubs two articles, on the state of the war: #E302 (which also appears in NOZ) and #E510 (which is a version of #E117 in NOZ). **May 5, 7:** The two-part article against Pan-Slavism (#E338) which M sent Dana [← :16] is not pubd in NYDT as written; they are printed rewritten and distorted by editorial changes (#E251, 57, both D&A cases). **May 18:** M writes E that NYDT must either come out against Pan-Slavism or else M may be forced to break with the paper. M calls E's attention to Herzen's announced periodical Polyarnaya Svezda.

21. W&P. **May AB:** M asks Elsner, an NOZ editor, for a German pub'r to put out a brochure on Pan-Slavism by E [← :1; → :27]. —Tucker's series Political Fly-Sheets pubs a collection of articles that includes some in M's "Lord Palmerston" series (#M474); Tucker's foreword expresses thanks to M.

22. PERSONAL. **May c.6:** M and his wife return to London [← :18]. **May M:** M informs Lassalle of the death of his son Edgar.

JUNE

23. NOZ ARTICLES. **June:** NOZ pubs 15 articles. Only one is by E (#E372), naturally on the course of the war. The war is also the main subject of three others (#ME44, 1; #M39—the last is a two-part article). Except for three miscellanies (#ME91; #M518.5, 516), the other articles are on English political affairs (#M392, 389, 58, 637, 356, 470, 690, 44; about the last, see → :25).

24. NYDT ARTICLES. **June:** NYDT pubs four articles, all by E, all on the course of the war (#E194, 305, 736, 509; about the last, cf #ME118.5 in NOZ, ← :19).

25. MASS DEMONSTRATION. **June 24–25:** M takes part, with Liebknecht, in a big demonstration in Hyde Park against a bill to tighten the Sunday laws; the demonstration impresses M with its revolutionary extraparliamentary aspect. The next day M writes an article about it for NOZ (#M44); pubd June 28 [→ :33].

26. "ARMIES OF EUROPE." **June 1:** Dana writes M proposing an article on the armies of the various European countries, for Putnam's Monthly. **June 15:** M forwards the request to E, who undertakes the job. **June 27 to July c.3:** M collects material for E's article in the BM Library, esp on the Spanish and Neapolitan armies. **June D to July A:** E writes the first part of "The armies of Europe" (#E32) [→ :37].

79

27. W&P. June c.20: Elsner [← :21] reports that bookdealers reject M's proposal for a brochure on Pan-Slavism because they are afraid of becoming known as revolutionary publishers.

28. ECONOMICA. June D (after June 19): Schily (in Paris) writes M that various people urge him to publish his opus on polit eco as soon as possible.

29. PERSONAL. June CD: M has a very bad toothache.

JULY

30. NOZ ARTICLES. July: NOZ pubs 14 articles. Two are by E on the war (#E553, 568.5); three deal partially with Crimea (#ME40, 147, 79). The rest are on English political affairs, with a concentration on Lord John Russell, the Whig leader (#ME147; #M790, and the first in a series on Russell, #M486); the others are #M517, 22, 395, 390, 391, 629, 85 (re #M22, see → :33).

31. NYDT ARTICLES. July: NYDT pubs five articles: four on the war by E (#E303, 422, 340, 502—the last is on Bonaparte), and one (#M260) on some background history about the war.

32. "ARMIES OF EUROPE." July A: E finishes the first installment of his long essay on "The armies of Europe" (#E32) [→ :41]. **July D:** He finishes the second installment.

33. POLITICAL AFFAIRS. July 1–2: M takes part in another Hyde Park demonstration against the Sunday closing bill [← :25], avoiding arrest only by accident; he writes an article on it the next day (#M22); pubd July 5. **July 17:** M sends E info on ex-CL members now in America and on other German revolutionary émigrés. —Ex-CL member W. Strohn visits M. **July 28:** Having received a letter from Lassalle on July 27 and learning he will visit Paris, M invites him to come to London. In this letter he confesses that his son's death [← :18] has left him shaken in heart and mind and left his wife broken down.

34. PERSONAL. July 17 to Sep 11: Since neither M nor his wife has recovered from the shock of their son's death [cf ← :33], they go away to stay in a cottage in Camberwell, near London, at 3 York Place, Denmark Road. The cottage belongs to ex-CL member Imandt, who will be away in Scotland. (SOURCE: MEW Daten; but the pamphlet London Landmarks dates this residence as Sep A to Nov D.)

AUGUST

35. NOZ ARTICLES. Aug: NOZ pubs 15 articles, incl five articles in the series on Lord John Russell (#M486) which began July 28. Two other articles (#M349, 155) are mainly

devoted to English political affairs, plus another on military affairs (#M452), and one describing a London meeting, held Aug 8, engineered by the government to steer pro-Polish sentiment into a Polish legion for the war (#M506). Four articles deal with aspects of the war (#M511, 387, 603; and #ME9—the last is a two-parter on the Anglo-French military effort). In addition M prepares three articles for NOZ based on sections of E's long essay "The armies of Europe" (#E32, see → :37); the second of these three articles takes up the class meaning of flogging in the British army, with M adding details to E's original material. (We list this second article independently as #ME59; pubd in NOZ, Aug 31.)

36. NYDT ARTICLES. Aug: NYDT pubs three articles: one on the war by E (#E912), two on English affairs (#M444, 487).

37. "ARMIES OF EUROPE." Aug: The first installment of E's "The armies of Europe" (#E32) is pubd in Putnam's Monthly, covering France, England, Austria.

38. PERSONAL. Aug: M and his wife are in Camberwell [← :34] all this month.

SEPTEMBER

39. NOZ ARTICLES. Sep: NOZ pubs six articles: three on the war by E (#E546, 546.5, 717); another on the war (#ME105); one on O'Connor's funeral (#M588); one on economic affairs (#M157). **Sep 4:** NOZ editor Elsner writes M about the financial difficulties of the paper. **Sep 11:** M replies that if NOZ cannot pay him but continues to publish, he is willing to forgo payment, since the paper is doing a useful job under difficult conditions [→ :47].

40. NYDT ARTICLES. Sep: NYDT pubs five articles: four on the war (#E899, 71, 267; #M66), and one on English military affairs (#M42).

41. W&P. Sep: The second installment of E's "Armies of Europe" (#E32) is pubd in Putnam's Monthly, covering Prussia, Russia, and the small German states. E finishes writing the third installment [→ :49]. **Sep 1:** M informs E that Putnam's Monthly, via Dana, is asking for a piece on "The improvements in modern warfare." **Sep 6:** After the death of Roland Daniels (in Cologne) on Aug 29, M writes a note of condolence to his widow, and tells her (also E, in a letter the same day) that he will write an obituary article on Daniels for NYDT; also a notice signed by M, E, Freiligrath, and W. Wolff should appear in the German-American press. M asks Steffen, via Freiligrath, to supply biographical info. **Sep AB** (after Sep 8): E makes a chronology of the main events in the Crimean War (#E141), as an aid in writing articles.

42. PERSONAL. Sep c.4: Dr. Freund sues M for nonpayment of his medical bills. **Sep 12:** From Camberwell [← :34] M goes to Manchester and stays at E's (until Dec A)—because of Dr. Freund's suit (SOURCE: MEW Daten; see ← :34). **c.Sep:** Mrs. M receives about £100 in a legacy from her uncle, Heinrich Georg von Westphalen, who died at the end of last winter.

OCTOBER

43. NOZ ARTICLES. Oct: NOZ pubs six articles: two on the war (#E568, #ME131), three on English problems (#M589, 240.5, 160.5), and one on French military and economic affairs (#M331). **Oct 3, 7:** NOZ editor Elsner writes M asking him to send no more articles since the paper has to close down soon [← :39]. M receives the letters after a little delay, since he is in Manchester [← :42].
44. NYDT ARTICLES. Oct: NYDT pubs three articles, all by E, on the war (#E193, 341, 773).
45. PERSONAL. Oct A to Nov A: M has a very bad toothache, which i.a. makes writing impossible.

NOVEMBER

46. NYDT ARTICLES. Nov: NYDT pubs three articles, by E, on the war (#E630, 42.5, 710). **Nov A:** In a letter to Dana (not extant) M says he wants new terms for his NYDT contributions. **Nov 20:** Dana writes promising that NYDT will take each week two articles sent in by M, at the rate of $10 per article [→ :49].
47. W&P. Nov 8: M writes NOZ editor Elsner that he has suspended all writing for that paper, as requested [← :43]; he praises NOZ for doing as much as can be done under present German conditions. **Nov 13:** M sends NOZ his last (known) article for that paper; pubd Nov 16 (#M83.5). **Nov 17:** Urquhart's Sheffield Free Press reprints Arti-

cle 3 of M's "Lord Palmerston" series (#M474); it is also issued as a pamphlet in the series Free Press Serials, no. 4A.
48. PERSONAL. Nov A: M meets his old friend G. Weerth, who has been on an adventurous tour of South and Central America and the American West; Weerth returned July D from the West Indies and is off to the tropics in a week. **Nov:** M stays at E's in Manchester all month [← :42]; Mrs. M remains in London.

DECEMBER

49. W&P. Dec 11: Having received Dana's new terms for NYDT articles [← :46], M sends Dana's letter to E, remarking "You see that our maneuver succeeded." **Dec 29:** Urquhart's Free Press (London) begins publ of M's entire series on Palmerston (#M474), complete for the first time since its original publ in 1853; the series is also pubd as a pamphlet in the series Free Press Serials, no. 5, now titled The life of Lord Palmerston. **Dec:** M starts his special researches on Anglo-Russian diplomatic relations in the 18th century, which will lead to his writing of #M764; he writes (Dec 28) his first article on this subject (#M936), for which, see → 56:2. — The third and last installment of E's essay "The armies of Europe" (#E32) is pubd in Putnam's Monthly.
50. VISITORS. Dec c.A: Lina Schöler, a family friend, is on a visit to the M family; she gives M more info about the Cologne Communist trial. **Dec 12:** Edgar Bauer [← 54:54] pays M an unexpected visit, this time accompanied by his brother Bruno Bauer, who has been in London for two weeks and will stay for a while. **Dec 14:** M sends E a lively pen sketch of Bruno Bauer's reactions to England.
51. ENGELS. Dec A: M returns to London from his stay with E (KMC dates this Dec c.4). **Dec 12:** E sends M an account of the textile workers' strike in Manchester. **Dec c.24 to Jan A:** E is staying with relatives in London, and sees M constantly during this time.

1856

CONSPECTUS

1. With publication in NYDT reduced to a trickle (less than two articles per month), M&E try to establish themselves in Putnam's Monthly, without success. They publish a number of articles in the People's Paper again, but that outlet comes to an end. M's uneasy collaboration with the Urquhartite press continues; these journals are in fact in the midst of the long publ of M's Revela-

tions on the diplomatic history of the 18th century (#M764)—a research work which forms M's main preoccupation for months during this year. Other studies from time to time capture his attention; but he does not return to polit eco until the end of the year, as an economic crisis looms. In this connection he also writes a half dozen articles for NYDT on the signs of European economic crisis, pubd during the last quarter of the year.

JANUARY

2. NYDT ARTICLES. Jan: NYDT pubs only two articles: #E902 on the war and #M936 on "Traditional English policy," pubd Jan 12. The latter article is the first written by M as a result of his new researches (started at least by Dec 1855) on the diplomatic relations between England and Russia in the late 17th and early 18th centuries, which will lead to his *Revelations of the diplomatic history* [etc.] (#M764) [→ :8]. **Jan AB:** M sends NYDT articles on the Danubian principalities (Moldavia, Wallachia) and on Sweden; they are not pubd (not extant).

3. PAN-SLAVISM. Jan to Apr: E works on a series of articles, 15 in all, against Pan-Slavism [← 55:21, 27] for NYDT. He studies the history, literature, and culture of the Slavs. The articles are sent to NY by M, but are rejected by NYDT (not extant) [→ :34].

4. URQUHARTITES. Jan 5: Urquhart's *Sheffield Free Press* reprints Article 6 of M's "Lord Palmerston" series (#M474). Meanwhile the *Free Press* of London is still reprinting the complete series [← :49], ending Feb 16. **Jan 18:** M sends E the Jan 19 issue of the *Free Press* with Urquhart's article "The Chartist correspondence," which shows Urquhart to be a virulent enemy of the left.

5. PERSONAL. Jan 18: M mentions (to E) that he has seen Bruno Bauer a few times [← :50] and relates some of Bauer's backward-looking views [→ :10]. **Jan to Feb M:** M, suffering from hemorrhoids, is in a depressed state of mind.

FEBRUARY

6. POLITICAL AFFAIRS. Feb c.25–28: M is visited—for the second time [← 53:45]—by Gustav Lewy of Düsseldorf, who has come to London as representative of Rhenish communists (ex-CL) to talk to M on two subjects. Lewy tells of the growing revolutionary temper of workers in Solingen, Iserlohn, Elberfeld, etc.; they want an open offensive. M warns against adventurism and an uprising that would be premature under present conditions, unless and until Paris gives the signal. Lewy also presents an effective case against Lassalle, whose politics and personal life have made Düsseldorf workers hostile to him. M, whose relations with Lassalle have been good, finds Lewy's case very impressive, but advises against any public break with Lassalle at this time. **Feb 7:** In a letter to M, E describes the internal political climate in France as more and more anti-Bonapartist; Bonaparte is declining rapidly among all classes. E also sends M the second article in his series on Pan-Slavism [← :3], intended for NYDT.

7. NYDT ARTICLES. Feb: NYDT pubs only two articles: #E254 on the war, and #M28 (see next item). **Feb 8:** M uses E's letter of Feb 7 (see ← :6) to write part of an article for NYDT on the situation in France (#M28).

8. STUDIES. Feb 12: M sends E a detailed account of the documents he has discovered at the BM [← :2], "concerning the struggle between Peter I and Charles XII, and the decisive role that England played," with the Whigs "sold" to Russia and the Tories to France. M appends a list of, and excerpts from, some of these documents. He wants to write this history up, and thinks of *Putnam's*. **Feb D to Mar AB:** To aid E's series on Pan-Slavism [← :3], M carries on studies at the BM on the history of the Slavic peoples. Writing on Feb 29, M gives E an account of the literature he has gone through, esp by Dobrovsky and Heffter, and supplies some French bibliography [→ :13].

9. W&P. Feb 16: The *Free Press* (London) ends its reprint of M's Palmerston series (#M474) [← 55:49].

10. PERSONAL. Feb 12: M tells E he has seen Bruno Bauer one or two times more [← :5]. Pieper has tried to introduce M to Wagner's music, but M finds it "frightful." **Feb 13:** For the first time, M addresses E, in a letter, as "Dear Fred" [← 51:53; → 57:18].

MARCH

11. POLITICAL AFFAIRS. Mar 5–7: M&E exchange letters on the questions raised by G. Lewy's visit [← :6]. **Mar 24:** Schily (in Paris), after a hiatus of about two years, writes M with an account of Heine's funeral (Feb 20, after his death on Feb 17) and about their common acquaintances in Paris: Reinhardt, Sazanov, Hess.

12. W&P. Mar c.25 to Apr D: M studies the diplomatic and military history of the fall of Kars (Nov 28, 1855), and writes on it for NYDT and PP—all pubd in Apr. He shows the responsibility of the English government for the defeat of Turkey. **Mar c.D:** Pub't Trübner (in London) evinces interest in publishing a brochure on this material [→ :19]. **Mar D:** M shows the ms of his NYDT article on Kars to Jones, who is impressed. **Mar 29:** Jones's PP announces it will publish M's article-series on the subject.

13. STUDIES. Mar 5: M supplements his letter of Feb 29 [← :8] to E with another letter on his bibliographic efforts in the BM on the history of the Slavic peoples; he writes about works by Eichhoff, Götze, Kapper, et al. **Mar c.25:** Re studies on the fall of Kars, see ← :12.

APRIL

14. POLITICAL AFFAIRS. Apr 10 or before: From Lewy of Düsseldorf [← :6] M receives a letter on his meeting with Miquel and the latter's views on the bourgeois Democrats. Lewy, who rejects Miquel's readiness to compromise, asks M's opinion. **Apr 16:** In a letter to E, in reaction to Lewy's letter i.a., M explains a point of worriment: in the future revolution Rhenish communists may leave themselves open to accusations of "treason to the fatherland." The solution in Germany involves underpinning the proletarian revolution with a peasants' revolt. In this letter M also reports that he has "again" had several meetings with Schapper, who has been in retirement for two years and is now a "very repentant sinner" about his political course. **Apr 26:** M sends E a letter received from Miquel, asking for M's views on the relation of the workers' party to the bourgeoisie in a coming revolution; Miquel opines that the proletariat must avoid measures that scare the bourgeoisie. **Apr 25:** A. Hamacher (in Cologne) sends M a letter with greetings from Cologne, Elberfeld, and Solingen workers, expressing a desire for contact with M; he asks M to send a representative with whom the Cologne and Düsseldorf groups can discuss questions about the Rhenish movement.

15. NYDT ARTICLES. Apr: NYDT pubs two articles: one on the fall of Kars (#M309) [← :12] and a survey of Bonaparte's France (#M90).

16. PP ARTICLES. Apr 5: For the first time since May 1854 PP pubs articles contributed by M: a survey of Bonaparte's France (#M325.5), and a more detailed study of the fall of Kars (#M308) [← :12] running in four installs (Apr 5–26). **Apr 14:** M takes part in celebrating the fourth anniversary of PP, the only émigré invited. He is the first speaker, on the historical role of the proletariat. **Apr 19:** PP pubs part of M's speech (#M827). **Apr 26:** PP pubs another article by M, on the House of Lords (#M380). **Apr:** Around this time M is again active in helping E. Jones editorially.

17. W&P. Apr D: M prepares a summary of his PP series on Kars [← :16] for the Urquhartite press, and sends it in (#M426) (see → :21).

18. STUDIES. Apr CD: M continues his studies, already begun [← :8], on Anglo-Russian diplomatic history. From now until Mar 1857 he researches and synopsizes diplomatic documents and historical literature in English, French, and German, esp from works by Motley, P. P. de Ségur, et al. The material will be embodied in parts of M's brochure #M764, *Revelations* [etc.].

MAY

19. THE "DIPLOMATIC HISTORY." May 27: M has an interview with pub'r Trübner about publishing his planned brochure [← :18]. **May 29:** Trübner's decision is postponed. (He will say no, May D or June AB.)

20. POLITICAL AFFAIRS. May 5–15: M sends material on Kossuth to Imandt (in Dundee), who uses it for an article in the local press. **May 23:** On returning from Ireland (see → :22), E writes M a report on what he found there; he calls Ireland the "first English colony."

21. W&P. May: NYDT pubs two articles: #M708 on Prussia, and #M808 on Sardinia and Piedmont. PP pubs one article: #M807 (which is a bit different from #M808 on Sardinia). **May 3:** The Urquhartite press (*Sheffield Free Press* and *Free Press* of London) pubs a summary of M's Kars series (#M426) [← :17] under the title "Kars papers curiosities." **May 6:** Cyples, secy of the Urquhartite foreign affairs comm, sends M a letter of thanks for his writings.

22. PERSONAL. May M: E and Mary Burns take a trip through Ireland, visiting Dublin, Galway, Limerick, Tralee, et al, returning home by May 23. **May c.M:** Mrs. M receives 192 talers as the remainder of her legacy from her uncle [← 55:42]. **May c.18 to June 3:** M is very ill, with rheumatism in the back; he cannot work for a while; the doctor advises leaving London. **May 22:** Mrs. M and the daughters go to Trier, where Mrs. M's mother is very ill [→ :29]. **May:** During this month, M studies Grimm's history of the German language.

JUNE

23. THE "DIPLOMATIC HISTORY." June AB: After Trübner's rejection of the brochure [← :19], M decides to publish the work (#M764) in the Urquhartite press. **June 14:** Ironside, editor of the *Sheffield Free Press*, writes M with his proposal for publishing this material; M agrees. **June 21:** M sends the first article in the series to Ironside. **June 28:** The series begins publ in the *Sheffield Free Press* [→ :26].

24. W&P. June: M writes an important study of the French Crédit Mobilier, in three articles for NYDT (#M332); two are pubd this month. PP pubs the first article in advance. —E reads the new book by the French pro-Bonapartist military writer Bazancourt, *L'expédition de Crimée jusqu'à la prise de Sébastopole*, and makes notes and excerpts (until Sep), headed "Saint-Arnaud." When M arrives in Manchester (see → :25), they discuss plans for a critical essay on the book by E [→ :36].

25. PERSONAL. **June c.7 to July** M: M travels with Pieper to Hull; then to Manchester, where they visit E.

JULY

26. THE "DIPLOMATIC HISTORY." **July 5, 12:** The *Sheffield Free Press* [← :23] pubs the second and third installs of M's *Revelations* [etc.] (#M764) with editorial cuts which deform the content. (One more install will appear, on Aug 2.) **July 17:** On M's behalf, Pieper writes Cyples (secy of the Urquhartite comm) in protest. Meanwhile, around this time Ironside, editor of the *Sheffield Free Press*, has written Cyples urging that M's series be killed immediately so as not to "entomb" the journal. **July 19:** Cyples replies to M with the hope he will continue to write his series. **July 22:** M cites Ironside's letter and declines. **July 31:** M is visited by Urquhart's "bulldog," Collet, sent by Urquhart himself to effect a compromise, which M refuses, though mollified by Collet's repudiation of Ironside. Collet informs M that Urquhart is going to launch a magazine, the *Diplomatic Review*. M is noncommittal, till the character of the new organ is clear.

27. POLITICAL AFFAIRS. **July c.A:** In response to a letter by Miquel [← :14] previously discussed with E, M analyzes the character of and forces in the German revolution (letter not extant). *MEW* summarizes: "M declares that the sole ally of the proletariat in a future revolution is the peasantry, and insists on the need for a merciless struggle against the bourgeoisie." Miquel shows M's letter to friends and cothinkers. **July 28:** M receives a letter from Miquel: he will come to London in 8–10 days. (This visit will not take place, because of illness.)

28. NYDT ARTICLES. **July 11:** NYDT pubs the third article on the French Crédit Mobilier (#M332). **July 25:** In response to the outbreak of revolution in Madrid, M writes the first of two articles on the event (#M775) [→ :32].

29. PERSONAL. **July 23:** Mrs. M and her daughters are in Trier [← :22] when her mother dies on this date [→ :33].

AUGUST

30. THE "DIPLOMATIC HISTORY." **Aug 11:** M writes Collet [← :26] that his proposition is accepted. The Urquhartite press will now publish the whole of M's series without editorial changes. **Aug 16:** The first installment of M's *Revelations* [etc.] (#M764) appears in the two Urquhart papers. (It will go on for 13 installs, until Apr 1857.)

31. POLITICAL AFFAIRS. **Aug 4:** E reports to M that he has just met his brother-in-law Emil Blank and rejected the suggestion that he ask the Prussian authorities for amnesty. **Aug 15:** Miquel replies to M's letter [← :27]. In *KMC's* summary, Miquel says "that without unleashing the forces of the proletariat to the utmost, an energetic centralizing revolution is not possible," but "for the moment" he holds it necessary "to hide the social question behind 'political radicalism.' " Miquel also describes the "dizzying" prosperity in Germany.

32. NYDT ARTICLES. **Aug:** NYDT pubs both of M's articles on the July revolution in Spain (#M775, 776) [← :28].

33. PERSONAL. **Aug:** Mrs. M and her daughters go from Trier [← :29] to Paris, where they stay with Reinhardt; they meet Schily [→ :35]. **Aug CD:** E sojourns in London, where his mother is visiting for a while. **Aug 28:** W. Wolff writes M of the death of their friend G. Weerth, in Havana on July 30, of a tropical fever [← 55:48].

SEPTEMBER

34. W&P. **Sep M:** M receives back from Dana the 15 articles on Pan-Slavism by E and three of his own on the Danubian principalities [← :3], rejected by NYDT because of disagreement with the content. **Sep 22:** M meets with Olmsted, of the American publishing firm of Putnam's (with Freiligrath present). They discuss contributions to *Putnam's Monthly*: an article on the Crimean War in connection with Bazancourt's recent book [← :24]; also an article on Heinrich Heine, who died earlier this year; and an article on "Ships against fortresses," and other militaria. M learns from Olmsted about the influence exercised by the Pan-Slavist, A. Gurowski, over the NYDT editors, thereby explaining NYDT's rejection of the articles on Pan-Slavism. **Sep D to Oct:** E writes an article for *Putnam's Monthly* on Saint-Arnaud, as a critique of Bazancourt's book (#E720) [← :24; → :36]. **Sep D** (after Sep 27): E tells M he plans to write an obituary article on G. Weerth [← :33] for a Berlin paper. E also discusses the coming economic crisis, which he thinks is due in 1857.

35. PERSONAL. **Sep c.10:** Mrs. M and the daughters return to London [← :33] (SOURCE of date: KMC). **Sep 19:** Strohn visits M. **Sep:** Mrs. M is to receive about £120 as a legacy from her mother, but meantime (M to E, Sep 22) M has to borrow from E for the expenses of moving to a new house, near Hampstead Road (9 Grafton Terrace, Maitland Park, Haverstock Hill), at a rental of £36; M tells E the move will take place Sep 29 (MEW dates it Oct A).

Besides, Mrs. M has fallen ill; household affairs are disjointed; M has little time to write. (*MEW*'s dating: Sep c.8 to Dec.) Note: Re the new address, the pamphlet *London Landmarks* gives it as 9 Grafton Terrace, Fitzroy Road, Kentish .Town; subseqly the entire street was renamed Grafton Terrace, and no. 9 was renumbered no. 46 [→ :39].

OCTOBER

36. W&P. **Oct 3:** Reinhardt (in Paris) sends M the annual report of the Crédit Mobilier, which M uses for articles. **Oct 9–27:** NYDT pubs three articles on the financial crisis in Europe (#M686, 524, 136). **Oct 23:** While the Urquhartite press is running his *Revelations* [etc.] (#M764) [← :30], M writes Collet (as he sends new mss) that he wants to renegotiate the terms of publ. **Oct 30:** M receives Collet's reply: Collet agrees, but is silent about the financial terms; M will have to press. **Oct c.30:** E finishes his article "Saint-Arnaud" on Bazancourt's book (#E720) [← :34]; M praises it highly [→ :41].

37. ECONOMICA. **Oct:** Spurred by the approaching economic crisis, M resumes his study of polit eco, esp the silver question. (Under date Sep to Dec, *KMC* adds that M puts together a collection of cited passages on the basis of his past notebooks of excerpts.)

38. STUDIES. **Oct CD:** M begins a study of the history of Poland, esp of the 18th- to 19th-century revolutions, reading works by Mieroslawski and Lelewel. (This will continue until Mar 1857.)

39. PERSONAL. **Oct A:** The M family

moves to the new house in Grafton Terrace [← :35; → 64:12].

NOVEMBER

40. POLITICAL AFFAIRS. **Nov 17:** Writing to M, E discusses facts pointing to a sharpening of the European financial crisis and a crisis looming in France, with Bonaparte's adventurism leading to revolutionary ferment; he also discusses revolutionary strategy in the coming upheaval. **Nov c.D:** M is visited by Valdenaire (of Trier).

41. W&P. **Nov:** NYDT pubs two articles: on the financial crisis (#M525) and on the Crédit Mobilier (#M263). —M writes two articles on Austria's maritime commerce (#M497, 498) which will be long delayed in getting pubd in NYDT. **Nov A:** E's essay "Saint-Arnaud" (#E720) [← :36] is sent off by M to *Putnam's Monthly* (not pubd; not extant). **Nov CD:** E works on an article for *Putnam's Monthly*, "Ships against fortresses" [← :34], reading related naval-war literature, esp W. James.

DECEMBER

42. W&P. **Dec:** NYDT pubs one article, on the European crisis (#M200). —Apropos of the Prussian-Swiss conflict over Neufchâtel, M studies the history of Prussia. **Dec 2:** M writes E with some remarks on Prussian history. Around this time he writes an article "The divine right of the Hohenzollerns" (#M247); it is pubd in PP on Dec 13—the last article by M/E in this paper. The article will be pubd in NYDT in Jan.

1857

CONSPECTUS

1. M gets a new source of journalistic income: contributions to the *New American Cyclopaedia* from July to next March, on a more or less steady basis. NYDT continues to publish the articles he sends in at a rate of a little over four per month; besides previous themes, the revolt in India and the impact of the economic crisis dominate the latter part of the year. *Broad Date:* The Urquhartite press finally completes publ of his *Revelations of the diplomatic history of the 18th century* (#M764), which it had begun last Aug.

2. With an economic crisis close at hand, M is spurred to intensify his work in polit eco in order to publish quickly. By July he commences the series of notebook drafts known as the *Grundrisse* (#M361). By Dec he

is working so hard that his health is undermined. In this month he pubs two articles in NYDT on the European economic crisis, and will continue on the subject in 1858.

3. E is ill during a good part of this year, and cannot help write NYDT and NAC articles at his previous pace.

JANUARY

4. NYDT: PROBLEMS. **Jan:** NYDT pubs five articles: on the Anglo-Persian war (#M36), Anglo-Chinese conflict (#M32), the Hohenzollerns (#M247—see ← 56:42 for the PP article), and Austrian commerce (#M497—written ← 56:41); and an article on mountain warfare by E (#E496). **Jan CD:** E writes a second article on mountain warfare for NYDT; M writes on financial questions; but these will not be pubd (not extant). **Jan 20:** M sums up his complaints against NYDT in a letter to E. For three weeks the copies of the paper, sent by Dana, show it has printed nothing M sent n, with a small exception. (M has not yet received the Jan issues.) In addition NYDT's point of view, due to Pan-Slavist influence, is antithetical. His income from NYDT is less than it was five years ago. He wonders what to do about it. **Jan 22:** E suggests he has to establish links with another NY paper. **Jan 23:** M agrees it is advisable to try the NY Times. He will write Dana, and stop contributing meanwhile, without an open break as yet. He laments: it is disgusting to be dependent on "such a rag" (NYDT), which turns political work into workhouse labor.

5. ECONOMICA. Jan 10: M writes E that he has begun reading De la réforme des banques [1856] by the Proudhonist A. Darimon and Proudhon's new book Manuel du speculateur à la Bourse. (M's critique of Darimon will begin the Grundrisse mss, now dated at Aug and after; cf #M361; but KMC dates start of work on them at Jan-Feb, continued Feb-Apr.)

6. STUDIES. Jan A: Edgar Bauer sends M a copy of Bruno Bauer's Russland und England (1854), among other Russophile pamphlets pubd by Bruno Bauer around the Crimean War. **Jan-Feb:** M drafts a brochure directed against B. Bauer's; it remains unfinished (ms extant but never pubd). In this period M studies Russian affairs and makes a table of Russian history, 973–1676. His reading includes Lallerstedt re relations with Russia, and Regnault.

7. W&P. Jan to Mar: E is overwhelmed with work at his office, and has little time to write NYDT articles. **Jan to Apr:** M's Revelations [etc.] (#M764) continues its slow publ in the Urquhartite press (cf ← :1).

FEBRUARY

8. NYDT: PROBLEMS. Feb: NYDT pubs two articles, both on the Anglo-Persian war (#M973, #E635). **Feb 6:** Having still received no NYDT issue with an article of his [← :4], M writes Dana, implying a threat to write for another NY paper, and presenting an "ultimatum." **Feb 16:** Writing to E, M cites more evidence to show that Dana is under the influence of the Pan-Slavist Gurowski [← :56:34], hence M's difficulties.

9. W&P: OFFER. Feb 5: M receives a letter from Miquel with an offer for him to write for Das Jahrhundert (Hamburg); M rejects this forthwith, since its pages are overrun with articles by such politicos as Ruge, Hess, Meyen, etc.

10. ECONOMICA. Feb M to July A: M continues [← :5] his study of economic literature; he reads and excerpts the new Vol. 5–6

of Tooke's History of prices, and Macleod's Theory and practice of banking.

MARCH

11. NYDT: PROBLEMS. Mar: NYDT pubs four articles: on the Anglo-Chinese conflict (#M640) and English political and economic affairs (#M546, 229, 154). **Mar 21:** M finally receives a reply from Dana, in an amicable tone, (Mar 5) [← :8], asking M to continue writing. NYDT will pay for one article per week whether pubd or no, plus any others pubd. Dana enumerates the articles lately pubd, and complains of their length. **Mar 24:** Reporting Dana's letter to E, M points out that his NYDT income is in effect being halved, but he has to accept because of his financial straits.

12. URQUHARTITE PRESS. Mar 25: M sends Collet the ms for Ch. 5 of the Revelations [etc.] (#M764) and duns him for payment; he also says he has an article for the Free Press, which he gives Collet some days later (before the 31st); it is #M937, on Bangya.

13. PERSONAL. Mar to July: Because of Mrs. M's worsening health (she has been ill for some time) and his difficult financial situation, M cannot pay the rent, and can hardly work at all [→ :18].

APRIL

14. NAC: BEGINNING. Apr 6: Dana writes M inviting him to contribute to the projected New American Cyclopaedia, which he and Ripley will edit; M is to write military articles mainly but not exclusively. **Apr 21:** M sends Dana's letter to E, asking his opinion. **Apr 22:** E exuberantly proposes forming a consortium ("bureau") to do virtually the whole encyclopedia; he raises many questions about which articles to do. **Apr 23:** M replies that the "bureau" idea is not feasible; he himself would like to do economists; he will propose subjects to Dana [→ :19].

15. NYDT ARTICLES. Apr: NYDT pubs eight articles: three on English politics (#M285, 227, 757), three on Europeans in China (#M803, 282; #E508), two on the British factory system (#M169, 286).

16. URQUHARTITE PRESS. Apr 1: The last installment of M's Revelations [etc.] (#M764) is pubd in the Free Press, having been dragged out since Aug 16, 1856. **Apr 9:** Writing to E, M says the chapters pubd constitute only an "introduction" to the question, in his mind. The Urquhartite editors are dragging their feet on payment, and M may have to break off relations. He recommends that E read Parish's Diplomatic history of Greece, Urquhart's Central Asia, and Thiersch on Greece.

17. POLITICAL AFFAIRS. Apr 26: After a

hiatus of nearly one and a half years, Lassalle (in Düsseldorf) writes M with an account of his travels, writing, and other activities. After consulting E and W. Wolff, M leaves the letter unanswered.

18. PERSONAL. **Apr:** Besides other family and financial difficulties [← :13], M himself falls ill. **Apr 22:** In a letter, E addresses M as "Dear Mohr" for the first time [← 56:10; → 63:11]. **Apr D to Oct:** E is very sick for several months; it is difficult for him to do NYDT or NAC articles.

MAY

19. NAC WORK. **May 8:** M tells E he has written to Dana about E's proposals [← :14]. —Dana sends M a letter with a list of military articles wanted for Vol. 1 under "A"; he also suggests an article on Aesthetics in one page, and queries the possibility of articles on European economists. **May 23:** M sends Dana's letter to E; he wonders how the "Yankee" expects to get the articles by July A; he thinks philosophic subjects are hard to do in English, and are too ill-paid. **May 28:** E agrees that Aesthetics cannot be done in one page. He discusses what he can do, and appends a list of 23 military articles to be done under "A" (of which only seven will actually be written). **May D to June:** M works on an article on Aesthetics, studying works by F. T. Vischer, E. Müller, et al; he leaves it unfinished (not extant).

20. NYDT ARTICLES. **May:** NYDT pubs three articles: on the Russian army (#E511), the English economy (#M116), and the Crédit Mobilier (#M194, first of two articles). — This month, preliminary to writing on the Crédit Mobilier for NYDT, M devotes some study to the topic.

21. POLITICAL AFFAIRS. **May M** (rec'd 22): Miquel writes M reporting on his activities in Göttingen and offering some views on polit eco (for which, cf M's letter to E of May 23).

22. STUDIES. **May:** M studies Swedish and Danish.

23. PERSONAL. **May to July:** M is in great financial distress, unable to pay rent or taxes. In May, because of a liver ailment, he cannot work, writing NYDT articles only with great effort.

JUNE

24. NAC WORK. **June 11** (rec'd c.27): Dana writes M promising to send the "B" list, and hoping to receive M's articles soon. He also returns the rejected article "Saint-Arnaud" (#E720) [← 56:41]. **June 29:** M sends Dana's letter to E, wondering how to stall Dana in view of E's inability to work.

25. NYDT ARTICLES. **June:** NYDT pubs

five articles: the second article on Crédit Mobilier (#M195), the French Bank Act (#M548), Spain (#M410), the Anglo-Persian treaty (#M652), and the Anglo-Chinese situation (#E583). **June 19:** M writes an article for NYDT on "British hypocrisy"; not pubd. **June 30:** M begins writing on the uprising in India [→ :29]. (M will cover the Indian liberation movement up to 1859.)

26. STUDIES. **June to next Feb:** Besides his studies on polit eco, M works hard at the BM on material for NAC articles, esp because of E's illness. M studies the history of military science in antiquity (Egypt, Assyria, Greece, Rome) and excerpts the works of Wilkinson, Clausewitz, Schlosser, Müffling, et al.

27. PERSONAL. **June AB:** E sojourns in London (KMC date: May c.30 to June c.10).

JULY

28. NAC WORK. **July:** See → :31. **July 6:** M writes E that he is in a quandary, since Dana is pressing for articles and E is ill. **July 11–24:** E writes his first NAC articles. **July 11 to Aug 10:** This date of composition is ascribed by MEW to the following NAC articles: #E5, 9, 10, 14, 38, 43, 45. **July 16:** M sends E his research notes for "Army." **July 24–28:** M collects excerpted material on the Spanish Armada and sends it to E, for NAC article #ME12.

29. NYDT ARTICLES. **July:** NYDT pubs two articles: on the European situation (#M819), and M's first article on the Indian uprising (#M772).

30. ECONOMICA. **July:** M drafts the ms "Bastiat and Carey" (#M362), the earliest ms of the Grundrisse proper; he leaves it unfinished.

31. STUDIES. **July AB:** M studies the history of warfare in antiquity, and excerpts the subject literature for E, for the NAC article "Army" (#E36). **July to next Mar:** In connection with military articles for NAC, E studies and excerpts works by Rüstow, Kaye, Jomini, Clausewitz, et al.

32. PERSONAL. **July 8:** Mrs. M gives birth to a child which dies immediately. **July 14:** M is worried about E's state of health, and writes him counseling abstention from all work. **July 28 to Nov 6:** E goes for a long rest cure to the seashore at Waterloo (near Liverpool), at Ryde (Isle of Wight), and on Jersey. During this time he can do even less writing for M than before. **July c.D:** Edgar Bauer visits M.

AUGUST

33. NAC WORK. **Aug:** E begins writing the long NAC article "Army" (#E36) [→ :38]. By Aug c.10 he has finished seven "A" articles [← :28], and around this date he writes two more (#E1, 7—the latter is a longish one on Afghanistan). **Aug 26:** M sends E the list of "B" articles sent in by Dana a while ago. Since they are mostly militaria and E cannot do much work, the situation is "not very good." M encloses a new letter from Dana received Aug 17.

34. NYDT ARTICLES. **Aug:** NYDT pubs six articles, plus a seventh sent in long ago (#M498). Of the six, all but one (#M621) are on the Indian revolt (#M766, 401, 557, 846, 400).

35. ECONOMICA. **Aug D to Sep M:** M drafts an intro to his planned work on polit eco (#M365, now called Intro to the Grundrisse).

36. STUDIES. **Aug AB:** M studies the latest medical literature in French, English, and German on the subject of E's illness.

37. VISITORS. **Aug c.10–c.15:** Imandt, visiting from Dundee, stays with the M family. **Aug M:** K. Schramm visits M on returning from America.

SEPTEMBER

38. NAC WORK. **Sep:** Twenty-two articles are finished and sent off. The longest of these, "Army" (#E36), had been started in Aug. Ten of these have been written or completed by M, all being biographies, of which only one (#M87, Blum) is nonmilitary and one (#M97, Bourrienne) is semimilitary; the rest are on French generals (#M82, 83, 117; #ME24), Russian generals (#ME18, 20), and one Pole (#ME19). E is represented by 10 short pieces on military terms (#E19, 61–64, 72, 82, 84, 92, 98), plus "Algeria" (#E12). In addition, three others have been started (#ME17, 23; #M81), to be finished in Oct. **Sep 11/12 to 22:** M&E exchange four letters discussing the career of Bernadotte for the NAC article. The M–E correspondence at this time contains several discussions of other figures, incl Blücher at some length. **Sep 18:** E's letter indicates he is going to do some articles (e.g., on French generals), but he can work only two hours at a time. **Sep 21:** M tells E of the devices he has used to stall Dana's demand for speed. On Sep 18 he received a curt letter from Dana about this. **Sep 22:** E promises to do some "B" articles. **Sep 23:** M is depending on payment for NAC articles to get him out of financial straits. **Sep 25:** M evaluates encyclopedias used in the course of the NAC work. Acknowledging receipt of E's "Army" (#E36), and praising it, M discusses the social role of armies in history.

39. NYDT ARTICLES. **Sep:** NYDT pubs six articles: four on the Indian revolt (#M767,

403, 421, 113), one on the Crédit Mobilier (#M333), and one on the political situation in Europe (#M676).

40. ECONOMICA. **Sep M:** M finishes [← :35] the draft now called Intro to the Grundrisse (#M365).

OCTOBER

41. NAC WORK. **Oct 6:** E sends M a list of suggested "C" articles. **Oct AB:** E writes seven short militaria (#E86–91, 97) and starts a long piece on "Artillery" (#E41) [→ :46]. **Oct CD:** The article on "Armada, Spanish" is finished (#ME12). Three other articles, started in Sep, are finished (#ME17, 23; #M81—the last two are long articles on Blücher and Bernadotte on which M&E had corresponded). **Oct 29:** E asks M to send him Dana's "D" list.

42. NYDT ARTICLES. **Oct:** NYDT pubs three articles, all on the Indian revolt (#M768–70). **Oct 13** (rec'd 26): Dana writes M that because of the economic crisis the NYDT has dismissed all its European correspondents save M and Bayard Taylor; he asks M to write only one article per week, at present mainly on India and the "financial crisis." **c.Oct:** Around this time M sends NYDT five articles on Bonaparte's financial policies which were not pubd (according to M's later letter of Apr 2, 1858).

43. STUDIES. **Oct to next Feb D:** M works intensively on the development of the economic crisis, and collects copious material on its course in Europe and America. He excerpts and annotates periodicals, and fills notebooks on the main processes and phenomena of the crisis in various countries. He also discusses it in correspondence with E, who sends him data relating to Manchester [→ :49].

44. ECONOMICA. **Oct:** M begins drafting a "Chapter on money" for his planned opus; this is the first chapter of the so-called Grundrisse (#M361) in Notebook I of this series.

45. CONTACTS. **Oct A:** M goes to visit E in Saint Helier (Jersey). He visits K. Schramm, who is ill with tuberculosis and is in great financial need. M gets Schramm work as correspondent for the US press. **Oct 6–29:** In letters E informs M about Harney's life on Jersey, and on the health of Schramm, whom he often sees during his stay in Saint Helier.

NOVEMBER

46. NAC WORK. **Nov 13, 16:** M presses E to finish "Artillery" [← :41]; but E is not yet capable of full-scale work. **Nov c.26:** E sends the finished article (#E41) to M. **Nov 27:** M does another biographical article, on Bugeaud de la Piconnerie (#M120).

47. NYDT ARTICLES. **Nov:** NYDT pubs

three articles: one on India (#M771), two on the financial crisis (#M73, 114).

48. POLITICAL AFFAIRS. Nov 15: E writes M a long letter on the economic crisis and its revolutionizing impact; his military studies, he feels, now take on a greater political interest. **Nov 24:** M, who has not seen E. Jones for a long time, now finds himself shocked by Jones's new turn to the right (unity with middle-class politicians). M writes E that Jones is behaving very stupidly; M is thinking of paying him a visit [→ :53]. **Nov D** (after Nov 24): M hears from Imandt that the Cologne Communist victims Becker and Reiff are now out of prison, but Bürgers, Nothjung, and Röser still have another year.

49. ECONOMICA. c.Nov: M finishes the "Chapter on money" [← :44], and begins the "Chapter on capital," in Notebook II of the *Grundrisse* notebooks (#M361); here he jots down a general plan for his economic opus. **Nov M:** M plans to publish next spring a German-language pamphlet on the economic crisis; he drafts a chapter on France [→ :52]. (Note: This dating is *KMC*'s; but cf → :52 [Dec 18].) **Nov 29:** M begins Notebook III of the *Grundrisse* notebooks.

50. PERSONAL. Nov 6: E returns to Manchester after a long stay away for his health [← :32].

DECEMBER

51. *NYDT* AND *NAC*. Dec: *NYDT* pubs three articles: two on the economic crisis (#M160, 300), one on the fighting in India (#E122). **Dec 7:** E still cannot work much or continuously, he writes M. **Dec 31:** Vol. 1 of the *NAC*, dated 1858, is pubd in NY, preface dated Dec 1, 1857.

52. ECONOMICA. Dec 8: M writes E that he is "working nights like crazy," often until 4 A.M., in order to finish the basic lines [*Grund-*

risse] of his Economica "before the deluge" (economic crash). Mrs. M writes K. Schramm along the same lines. **Dec M:** M finishes Notebook III of the *Grundrisse* notebooks, still on the "Chapter on capital," and starts Notebook IV (#M361). **Dec 18:** M writes E that they should write a pamphlet about the economic crisis for publ around springtime. He reports he is doing an enormous amount of work with a double aim: to work out the main features [*Grundzüge*] of his Economica, and to study the current economic crisis. **Dec 21:** M writes Lassalle along the same lines; he explains that because of his gainful work (*NYDT, NAC*) he can work on the Economica only at night, thus damaging his health. **Dec 25:** M sends E a long exposition of his views on the economic crisis in France after reviewing his notebooks of excerpts and notes on "French commerce, industry, and crises."

53. POLITICAL AFFAIRS. Dec A: M receives 100 talers from Miquel. **Dec 17:** After a considerable hiatus, Lassalle writes M, i.a., about his new book on Heraclitus; he complains that M did not answer his previous letter [← :17]. Lassalle encloses a letter from Max Friedländer inviting M to contribute to the liberal Vienna paper *Die Presse*. **Dec 21:** M writes Lassalle requesting to see copies of *Die Presse* to ascertain its political tendency. M is not inclined to accept, i.a. because Friedländer stipulates there are to be no attacks on Palmerston [→ 59:21]. **Dec 22:** Writing to E, M notes that Jones [← :48], who is under attack in the movement for preaching unity with middle-class politicians, "seems to be avoiding me"; but M is still thinking of surprising him with a visit. **Dec D:** Pieper pays M a visit.

54. PERSONAL. Dec M: M is in bad financial straits because tax payments are due; E helps him out. **Dec D:** M's doctor tells him he has to cut out night work to save his health.

1858

CONSPECTUS

1. M concentrates on making drafts for his planned opus on polit eco. He leaves off writing the *Grundrisse* notebooks (#M361) by May-June, and having acquired a publisher in Mar, sets out (by Aug, after several delays) to write the final text for publ. This will be pubd in 1859 as *Contribution to the critique of polit eco* (#M181). The delays have been due to renewed troubles: illness, domestic difficulties, lack of money. In early 1858 he writes a few articles for *NYDT* on the economic crisis in Europe.

2. The work of writing articles for the *New American Cyclopaedia* (*NAC*) peters out by Mar, for the most part. Contributions to *NYDT* continue; it pubs a little over five articles per month on the average.

3. M&E's political involvement reaches a low point. But besides M's work on polit eco, he is also immersed in other studies as the year opens; see ← 57:43.

4. *Engels' address in Manchester:* Sometime in 1858 E moves from 34 Butler Street, Greenheys, to 6 Thorncliffe Grove, Oxford Road. (The date he moved to Butler Street is not known; cf ← 52:38; → 60:6.)

JANUARY

5. *NAC WORK.* **Jan:** E writes eight short articles on military terms, mostly in "C" (#E78, 114, 119, 123, 124, 126, 128, 129), plus two on "B" battles (#E83, 95); he begins an article on "Coehorn" (#E147). M writes a significant article on Bolívar (#M88), criticizing the "Liberator" as a Bonapartist type. **Jan 5:** M raises the question with E of giving up NAC work in order to ease the strain on E, whose health is still precarious. **Jan 6:** E refuses to give up; he will start on the Cs this evening (in fact he sends a batch of Cs the next day). **Jan 23:** M sends E Dana's letter asking for new "B" articles, incl one on "Bengal Rebellion." M must comply since he has overdrawn on Dana's funds. But he does not think the Bengal article (Indian revolt) can be done fast (E agrees, Jan 25). **Jan D:** M gathers material in the BM for E's use in NAC articles such as "Camp," "Catapult," etc. **Jan-Feb:** See ← 57:26.

6. NYDT ARTICLES. **Jan:** NYDT pubs three articles: two on the economic crisis (#M201, 334), one on the fighting in India (#E739).

7. ECONOMICA. **Jan 11:** Writing to E, M remarks that he has made so many errors in calculation during his work on polit eco that he has turned in despair to reviewing algebra in order to improve his arithmetic. **Jan c.16:** Reporting to E on his progress, incl rejection of all current views about the nature of profit, M mentions that he has been helped by leafing through Hegel's *Logic* "by mere chance" (since Freiligrath sent him some Hegel volumes that formerly belonged to Bakunin). If he ever has time, he would like someday to "make available to the ordinary human understanding, in 2 or 3 printer's sheets, what is *rational* in the method Hegel discovered." **Jan 22:** M fills Notebook IV of the *Grundrisse* notebooks (#M361), and starts Notebook V, still on the "Chapter on capital," §2. **Jan 29:** M asks E for some "practical elucidation" on the circulation of capital and its effect on profit and price, since he is at the point in his work where he needs this material.

8. POLITICAL AFFAIRS. **Jan 14:** In France, F. Orsini makes an attempt to assassinate Bonaparte. (This will be frequently referred to in M's articles.) **Jan c.16:** M writes E that E. Jones is worse than ever in his rightward course [← 57:53]; Reynolds and O'Brien are attacking him from the left. (This is prob a comment on Jones's meeting of Jan 13.) **Jan 28:** M receives from Lassalle the latter's new book on Heraclitus [← 57:53; → :13].

9. PERSONAL. **Jan 15:** K. Schramm dies, of tuberculosis. (M, informed by Harney and R. Schramm, sends the news to E, Jan 25; but E

was notified by Harney on Jan 16. **Jan:** M is ailing because of too much night work; he is also in financial distress.

FEBRUARY

10. NAC WORK. **Feb:** E writes five minor articles (#E80, 96, 107, 113, 130), finishes "Coehorn" (#E147), and starts "Burmah" (#E111). **Feb 1:** M sends E a list of the "B" articles they have worked on. (This letter also gives a vignette of M's working day at the BM.) **Feb 14:** M reports that Dana has questioned his article on Bolívar as "partisan," and M agrees he portrayed Bolívar in a very unfavorable light [← :5]. **Feb 18:** E joins in complaining of the low rate of payment for "in very many cases independent works instead of the lousy compilations he [Dana] otherwise gets." **Feb 22:** M explains that he cannot threaten Dana about stopping writing because of his overdrafts on Dana's funds. **Feb 24:** E advises caution before breaking with the NAC and Dana over the low rates, since then they (M&E) would need to find an outlet for articles on the Continent.

11. NYDT ARTICLES. **Feb:** NYDT pubs five articles: on England's economy (#M101), on the attentat against Bonaparte (#M63), and three on India (#M53, #E665, 215).

12. ECONOMICA. **Feb:** M finishes (Feb A) Notebook V of the *Grundrisse* notebooks (#M361), fills all of Notebook VI, and (Feb D) starts on Notebook VII, all still on the "Chapter on capital," §2. **Feb 10:** Lassalle offers to seek a Berlin pub'r for the opus. **Feb 22:** M accepts Lassalle's offer; he says he plans to publish the opus in fascicules (serial parts), since he cannot finish the whole work at once, and besides it will be easier to find a pub'r this way; during the last few months M has been doing the "final working-out," though slowly. M then describes his overall plan for the work, an arrangement in six books. —Writing to E the same day, M mentions the point about fascicule publ.

13. POLITICAL AFFAIRS. **Feb 1:** M has been reading Lassalle's book on Heraclitus [← :8] and gives E a mordant opinion of it as an "old-Hegelian" and "rubbishy concoction" (M also evaluates the book in a letter to Freiligrath, Feb A; not extant) [→ :25]. **Feb 10:** M receives via Freiligrath a letter (Dec 19) from Friedrich Kamm (in NYC) reporting that a German "communist club" has been founded in NYC with 30 members, Oct D; its by-laws are enclosed. Kamm asks for documents, literature, and info on communist groups in Europe, esp Germany. M postpones answering till he gets info on Kamm from E, W. Wolff, Freiligrath, and Imandt. —Lassalle writes M with an account of the "jubilation" and hopes of the Prussian bourgeoisie, who expect a new liberal course from the marriage of the crown prince to Princess Victoria of England. **Feb 22:** Writing to Lassalle, M agrees to write a weekly article on European and US economic affairs for *Die Presse* of Vienna [← 57:53].

14. PERSONAL. **Feb 22:** In a letter to E, M remarks of his own "troubled life" that "there is nothing so stupid for people with universal aspirations than to get married at all and thus make themselves prey to the petty miseries of domestic and private life."

MARCH

15. NAC WORK. **Mar:** E finishes "Burmah" (#E111), writes #E85, and begins the long article on "Cavalry" (#E131) [→ :27]. M&E begin "Beresford" (#ME21). **Mar 11:** E says he suspects Dana has shortened the articles M sent in, hence M's payment calculations are off. (This indicates that M&E have not yet seen the pubd Vol. 1.)

16. NYDT ARTICLES. **Mar:** NYDT pubs four articles: except for one on English politics (#M234), they are on the crisis of Bonaparte's regime (#M262, 785, 678); increasingly M sees the development of a revolutionary situation in France, with Bonaparte's power seen as "The rule of the pretorians" (title of #M785).

17. ECONOMICA. **Mar 2, 4:** M asks, and E answers, questions about wear-and-tear and replacement of machinery in industrial practice, as M studies this subject, re research on the cycle of industrial reproduction. M reads esp Babbage, *On the economy of machinery and manufactures.* (There is more discussion in M's letter of Mar 5.) **Mar 11:** In response to Lassalle's last letter (Mar 3), M gives a detailed discussion of terms to be negotiated with a publisher; also, info on the planned content of the first fascicule of the opus. **Mar 26:** Lassalle writes M that Duncker (in Berlin) has agreed to publish the opus, under certain conditions; the first fascicule must be ready by May D. **Mar 29:** M receives this letter, and reports it to E, favorably. **Mar:** M continues working in Notebook VII of the *Grundrisse* notebooks (#M361), and finishes §2 of the "Chapter on capital" or thereabouts.

18. PERSONAL. **Mar 2:** M mentions to E that their correspondence is under police surveillance; the Urquhartites say the post office has an extensive "black cabinet" for the purpose. **Mar CD to Apr:** M is again plagued by a liver ailment; he cannot pursue his work on polit eco.

APRIL

19. NYDT AND NAC. **Apr:** NYDT pubs five articles: four by M on aspects of the

crisis of French Bonapartism (#M92, 649, 337, 317), and one by E on the fighting in India (#E782). —M&E finish "Beresford" (#ME21) for NAC.

20. ECONOMICA. **Apr 2:** M presents E with a detailed plan of his proposed opus, arranged in six books (cf ← :12). **Apr 9:** E makes a brief comment on M's outline, esp on its present abstract-dialectical character, along with discussion of the industrial situation in Manchester. **Apr:** M does not work this month on the *Grundrisse* notebooks (#M361) because of illness.

21. POLITICAL AFFAIRS. **Apr 29:** Writing to E, M stresses the significance of the movement for the emancipation of the serfs developing in Russia.

22. PERSONAL. **Apr:** M is almost completely unable to work as his gall bladder and liver ailments worsen. **Apr 9:** Mrs. M writes E that in connection with the contract for the Economica with Duncker [← :17] M's agitation and worry are increasing daily since it is impossible for him to complete the work on time.

MAY

23. NYDT AND NAC. **May:** NYDT pubs six articles: three on English political and economic affairs (#M519, 281, 384), one on Bonaparte and Mazzini (#M500), two on India (#M37, #E220). —E begins "Fortification" (#E286) for NAC [→ :27].

24. ECONOMICA. **May 6–c.24:** While staying at E's in Manchester (see → :26), M works out with E his analysis of "Capital in general"—"in detail," as he later says (letter to E, Jan 13–15, 1859). **May D to June A:** M works on the last pages of Notebook VII, leaving the ms unfinished, as he turns to preparing a ms for publ. **May 31:** Writing to E, M says he is going to begin revising the ms for printing; he has to prepare an index to his notes [→ :29]. —Writing to Lassalle, M tells of his illness and asks Lassalle to inform pub'r Duncker he will be in default on sending the first fascicule, which he will now work on "with zeal."

25. POLITICAL AFFAIRS. **May 31:** M's letter to Lassalle offers some critical comments on Lassalle's new book on Heraclitus [← :13]. **May D:** After a long hiatus, M receives a letter from Weydemeyer (in Milwaukee), dated Feb 28 (the reason for this long delay is unexplained). Weydemeyer recommends one Albrecht Komp [→ :31] to M, and reports on the American workers' movement and its difficulties. (For M's reply, see → 59:13.)

26. PERSONAL. **May 6–c.24:** M stays at E's in Manchester; he takes up horse riding for his health. **May c.8:** Cluss, visiting London for a short while, wants to see M but finds only Mrs. M at home.

JUNE

27. *NYDT* AND *NAC*. **June:** *NYDT* pubs seven articles: three on India (#M483; #E697, 100), two mainly on English affairs (#M839, 673), one on Bonaparte (#M91), one on Bangya (#M209). —For *NAC*, E finishes "Fortification" (#E286) [← :23] and "Cavalry" (#E131) [← :15].

28. POLITICAL AFFAIRS. **June 4, 10:** Lassalle writes M of his dueling affair with one Fabrice and asks his opinion. After consulting E and W. Wolff, M offers their joint opinion, with a discussion of duels in different cases. **June 6:** Schapper visits M. **June c.D:** M meets with the Hungarian revolutionist Klapka, at Freiligrath's.

29. ECONOMICA. **June A:** See ← :24. **June AB:** M makes an index to his seven *Grundrisse* notebooks (#M364). **June-July:** See → :30.

30. PERSONAL. **June:** M is in great financial distress, esp since his daughter Eleanor is ill and Mrs. M is in an ill and nervous state due to continuing household troubles. This situation will continue through July [→ :34], and as a result M does not start work on drafting the opus on polit eco (which is overdue) until Aug.

JULY

31. POLITICAL AFFAIRS. **July c.2:** M receives a letter from Komp (introduced by Weydemeyer; ← :25), who reports on a German-American communist club he has formed with F. Kamm [← :13], and asks for M's *Poverty of philosophy* (#M681), *NRZ* issues, and regular correspondence by M [→ 59:14, re Weydemeyer].

32. W&P. **July:** *NYDT* pubs four articles: three on India (#M876, 399; #E376), one on England and the slave trade (#M112). **July 17:** The London émigré paper *Neue Zeit* pubs a squib by M (inserted into the paper through Liebknecht) ridiculing an advertisement by Kinkel (#M911). (It kicks up a scandal and brings denials from Kinkel.)

33. STUDIES. **July 14:** In a letter to M, E writes of his studies in natural sciences, and discusses how the latest discoveries confirm Hegel's dialectic method in the study of nature.

34. PERSONAL. **July 15:** Because of his financial straits [← :30] M lays before E an account of his finances, expenditure, income, etc., and asks what to do about this financial "quagmire" [→ :37].

AUGUST

35. *NYDT* ARTICLES. **Aug:** *NYDT* pubs four articles, all on current English affairs (#M385, 398, 283, 158). —During this month M sends *NYDT* three articles which it does not print: on China (written Aug c.15), on the slave trade in Cuba (written Aug 17), and on the Anglo-Chinese peace treaty (sent Aug 27).

36. ECONOMICA. **Aug 8:** In a letter to E, M remarks that he has been almost entirely unable to write for the past two months and his obligation to send the ms to Duncker is "becoming urgent." **Aug A:** M begins writing the *Contribution to the critique of polit eco* (#M181) on the basis of his *Grundrisse* notebooks (#M361); that is, he drafts a new version of the "Chapter on money." (For part of an early draft, see #M182, written Aug A to Nov M.) During this work, M will read the new book by Maclaren, *Sketch of the history of the currency.*

37. PERSONAL. **Aug A:** M works out a temporary solution to his financial distress [← :34]: on the basis of E's warranty, Freiligrath arranges for M a loan of £40 at 20% interest. The money is immediately used to send Mrs. M to Ramsgate for her health, in accordance with doctor's orders.

SEPTEMBER

38. *NYDT* ARTICLES. **Sep:** *NYDT* pubs three articles: two on the history of the opium trade (#M376, 377), one on Bangya (#M25). The latter is based on material received through Collet and stemming from Constantinople.

39. ECONOMICA. **Sep 21:** M writes E that in two weeks he will send the first two fascicules to pub'r Duncker.

40. POLITICAL AFFAIRS. **Sep 21:** Writing to E, M remarks that E. Jones has "decidedly" gone over to the side of the bourgeois reformers [← :8].

OCTOBER

41. POLITICAL AFFAIRS. **Oct 7:** Writing to M about E. Jones [← :40], E reports on Jones's line in a Manchester meeting, and goes on to generalize about the bourgeoisification of the English proletariat and its roots in the position of England as exploiter of the world. **Oct 8, 21:** M&E exchange letters on the prospects of the proletarian movement in Europe. **Oct 22:** Lassalle writes M about his own planned work on economics, which will be finished in about two years.

42. *NYDT* ARTICLES. **Oct:** *NYDT* pubs 10 articles: on England and China (#M33, 34), the English economy (#M106), Mazzini (#M503), France (#M548.5), serf emancipation in Russia (#M721), the Prussian king's insanity (#M427, 428, 713), and the fighting in India (#E698).

43. ECONOMICA. Oct 7, 21: E repeatedly queries M about sending his ms to the pub'r. **Oct 22:** M confesses that the ms will not be sent for "weeks."
44. PERSONAL. Oct c.31: M visits Pieper, who is ill in hospital.

NOVEMBER

45. NYDT ARTICLES. **Nov:** NYDT pubs eight articles: on Prussian political affairs (#M13, 14), English politics (#M550, 551, 424), Russia in Asia (#E709, 718), Montalembert's opposition in France (#E634). For an unfinished draft, possibly for NYDT, see #M872.2.
46. ECONOMICA. **Nov M:** M starts a new chapter on "The commodity," which will in fact precede the chapter on money in the finished book (#M181). **Nov 12:** Writing to Lassalle, M generalizes that this work is "the result of fifteen years of research, hence of the best period of my life"; hence "economics as a science in the German sense is still to be done...." He expects to finish in about four weeks, "since I have really only just begun the [final] writing." **Nov 29:** M writes E that his wife is making a clear copy of the ms, but it will not be sent off by the end of the month, because of ill health, domestic troubles, and the expansion of the ms beyond his original intentions. **Nov to Jan:** For the final drafting of the Contribu-

tion to the critique of polit eco (#M181), see → 59:10.
47. POLITICAL AFFAIRS. **Nov 22:** K. Blind and his wife visit M, for the first time in over a year.
48. PERSONAL. **Nov 2–10:** M is suffering from toothache and a mouth abscess.

DECEMBER

49. NYDT ARTICLES. **Dec:** NYDT pubs five articles: on Prussian political affairs (#M15, 16, 821), France's economy (#M699), and a review of Europe in 1858 (#E250). — Two articles sent in by M are not printed: on the Anglo-Chinese peace treaty (written Dec 14) and on US Pres. Buchanan's open letter (written Dec 21).
50. ECONOMICA. **Dec:** M continues to work on preparing the ms for printing. In letters to E, he mentions (Dec 11) that his wife is still making a clear copy; he claims (Dec 16) that the ms will go out to the pub'r soon; and (Dec 22) that it has to be sent to Duncker before the end of the year.
51. POLITICAL AFFAIRS. **Dec 6:** Freiligrath's letter to M encloses a poem he has just written on the death of Kinkel's wife, in which (M thinks) he glorifies Kinkel himself and reflects his (Freiligrath's) own pro-bourgeois trend. **Dec 11:** Freiligrath's poem is printed in the London Neue Zeit; M writes E on what it shows about Freiligrath.

1859

CONSPECTUS

1. In Jan, M finally finishes, ready for publ, the first two chapters of his long-awaited opus on polit eco; as the first fascicule of the long work still to be written, it is pubd in June under the title Contribution to the critique of polit eco (#M181). M is intensely disappointed by the "conspiracy of silence" that greets it in the German press, though there is much notice of the book in the German-American papers. M makes plans for continuing the work. For his readings and studies, see→ :76–78.
2. Among the reasons for M's inability to concentrate on polit eco is an increasingly time-consuming foofaraw in the émigré world launched by Karl Vogt, which turns into a vendetta against M for semiaccidental reasons. It will eventually—in 1860—compel M to publish a whole book, Herr Vogt (#M372). Since like all émigré vendettas the story is complicated, yet occupies much space in the following pages, a background summary (→

:6) is added to this Conspectus to guide the reader.
3. Journalism. M&E's articles in NYDT this year average slightly over five per month. The work for NAC has petered out: E writes two long articles for the encyclopedia, "Fortification" (#E286) and "Infantry" (#E378). Vols. 4, 5, and 7 of the NAC are pubd this year, containing 16 articles written by M/E. M gains a new outlet: the London organ of the German-English GWEA, Das Volk. M starts working to save it, and then builds it up as an émigré voice, but it collapses financially before the end of the year. However, M&E publish some articles in it.
4. During this year M's political ties with two supporters are fraying. One is Freiligrath, who is visibly slipping over to the other side, little by little if not demonstratively. In the case of Lassalle, too, there is no break, but there is a great deal of political tension, esp over political line on the Italian war (Austria vs France and Piedmont). In this connection, while Lassalle publishes a pamphlet looking

(M feels) to Prussian aggrandizement, E publishes *Po and Rhine* (#E587), which attacks both Prussianism and Bonapartism, in favor of Italian unification.

5. M's mathematical mss (#M499) are dated "prob from the late 1850s to the end of M's life"; perhaps this is the place to mention them. M pursues these studies particularly in connection with his work on polit eco; cf ← 58:7.

6. *Background: The Vogt-Blind Affair.* Karl Vogt is a natural scientist of some repute, a philosopher known for his mechanical-materialist views, and also a political figure among liberals. In the emigration he has become a virulent enemy of revolution and a sympathizer with Bonapartism. (It will be revealed in 1871 that he has even accepted money for his propaganda activities from Bonaparte's secret funds.)

7. In April of this year Vogt issues a programmatic statement, in which M detects a pro-Bonapartist leaning; Vogt publishes a book on European politics [→ :35] which further convinces M that he is an agent of Bonapartist propaganda in international politics.

8. In May, Karl Blind, a well-known Democratic journalist, informs M that Vogt is actually being paid by Bonaparte and is suborning other émigrés for Bonapartist propaganda; Blind claims to have proof. M passes this info on to two friends: E. Biskamp, editor of *Das Volk* (with which M is now collaborating), and Wilhelm Liebknecht, who is now a London correspondent for the prestigious Augsburg *Allgemeine Ztg.* Biskamp publishes an article in *Das Volk;* M himself writes nothing on Vogt. Vogt in his Swiss exile assumes that the *Das Volk* article by Biskamp emanates from M, and replies with an article filled with personal slanders against M of a rather bizarre character—pure inventions. M's only response is to have Vogt's diatribe reprinted in *Das Volk,* with some comments (prob by Biskamp). However, the fur flies when Blind—unbeknown to M or (prob) to Biskamp—writes a flysheet attacking Vogt as a Bonapartist agent, and prints it up in Hollinger's printshop (where *Das Volk* is also printed). It is this anonymously issued flysheet that provokes the subsequent imbroglio, for Vogt assumes that it must be M's. The anti-Vogt flysheet is then reprinted by Biskamp in *Das Volk,* and—worse still—sent by Liebknecht to the *AZ,* which publishes it.

9. Two developments precipitate the series of events which can be followed in the *Chronicle:* (1) Vogt institutes a lawsuit against the *AZ,* which he selects as target because of the paper's importance and because it is in Germany. (2) Karl Blind, the main instigator of

the brouhaha, now gets cold feet and starts running for cover: first he refuses to furnish his promised proof, and then he advances to loud lies that he had never had anything to do with the flysheet. But because Vogt's scurrilous attacks are directed against M, and because they are echoed by Vogt's friends and M's enemies, M becomes inextricably involved in this teapot tempest, which begins turning into a massive campaign to discredit M personally. As such, it is no longer an émigré curiosity: M's future is at stake, since Vogt goes all-out to destroy his reputation. (To be continued; see → 60:1.)

JANUARY

10. ECONOMICA. **Jan betw 13–15:** M writes E that he expects to send the completed ms to Duncker on Jan 19. "Don't keel over but despite its title 'Capital in general' these fascicules contain *nothing* on capital, but only the two chapters. . . ." The missing subject will constitute the third chapter, which will follow "quickly." (Actually it followed in eight years, as *Capital.*) **Jan 21:** M finishes the ms, which is now titled *Zur Kritik* [etc.] with subtitles (see #M181) showing it is only the first section of a larger work. Instead of the planned five to six printer's sheets, it is now 12, and consists of only two chapters. M writes E asking for £2 since he has no money for postage—or for insurance of the package, since he retains no copy. **Jan 25:** After getting the postage from E, M sends the ms to Duncker (in Berlin), late today. **Jan 26:** M informs E that he has sent the ms; also informs Lassalle (whom he asks to send reports on "Prussian affairs"). **Jan 31:** M receives from Berlin the postal receipt confirming the ms's arrival.

11. *NYDT* ARTICLES. **Jan:** *NYDT* pubs five articles: on the Ionian Islands (#M724), Ireland (#M304), the Russian emancipation (#M274), Italy (#M723), and the war prospect (#M980). **Jan 25:** M writes an economic review for *NYDT;* not pubd (not extant). **Jan 28:** M asks E to write on the situation of the Manchester cotton industry. (E writes it, but is not received by M, who thinks it was intercepted in the mails.)

12. POLITICAL AFFAIRS; FREILIGRATH. **Jan 6:** M, anxious to halt Freiligrath's apparent trend [← 58:51] toward collaboration with Kinkel, who is founding a new weekly *Hermann* in London, suggests to E that he write Freiligrath; and (Jan c.6) M writes Freiligrath himself. **Jan 7:** Freiligrath replies that he has nothing to do with *Hermann* and anyway will not adopt Kinkel's politics. **Jan 23:** Imandt (in Dundee) writes M about the editorial relations in the GWEA weekly *Die*

Neue Zeit, which since Nov has been edited de facto by Edgar Bauer. **Jan 25:** E writes Freiligrath urging him not to support Kinkel.

FEBRUARY

13. ECONOMICA. **Feb 1:** Writing to Weydemeyer after a long hiatus (see → :14), M gives him an outline of his planned opus in six books, and tells him of the coming publ of the first two chapters by Duncker—it will be a "scientific victory"—but a contract for further publ depends on sales. **Feb 2:** M receives a letter from Lassalle (Jan 31) mentioning that Duncker has not yet received the ms. M is afraid the Prussian government is holding it up (he tells E), and writes Lassalle. **Feb 8:** M has not yet heard that Duncker has the ms. **Feb 9:** M receives Duncker's letter (Feb 7): the ms came Feb 1. **Feb M:** M inquires from Dana about an American pub'r for an English trans (to be done by E&M together, M writes on Feb 21) [→ :18]. **Feb 23:** M sends the preface to Duncker. Although it is dated Jan 1859, it must have been finished only now. (M originally intended to use #M365, and wrote this preface as an afterthought.) **c.Feb:** M draws up a table of contents of his Grundrisse notebooks ("Review of my own notebooks") (#M366) for use in writing the follow-up. **c.Feb-Mar:** M writes a draft outline of the planned opus as a whole (#M363). **Feb 28 to Dec:** M works on the continuation of the volume just pubd, to take up "Capital in general." (For his reading, see → :76–78.)

14. POLITICAL AFFAIRS. **Feb 1:** After a long interval M finally answers Weydemeyer's letter [← 58:25]: he explains the delay; gives news of various friends; reports that he has broken with E. Jones ("a ruined man") who has reconciled himself with the "bourgeois radicals"; also reports on the doings of Kinkel and Freiligrath; and finally (see ← :10, 13) writes in detail about the coming publ of his economic opus. —M also finally replies to Komp [← 58:31] (letter not extant). According to M's summary in his letter to Weydemeyer, M explains he has given up all organizational liaisons because émigré machinations make him retire to his studies: "My time was too precious to me to be wasted on futile efforts and petty quarrels." **Feb 2:** Lassalle's letter of Jan 31 (← :13) reports on the enthusiasm of the Prussian bourgeoisie and pseudo-Democracy for the "new era" in Prussia; M replies with thanks for the report. **Feb 4:** In a long letter to Lassalle, M discusses the looming war in Italy (France–Piedmont vs Austria). **Feb 12:** To provide "some comforts" for Eccarius, who is very ill, M pawns his wife's last frock. **Feb D:** M has

Imandt (in Dundee) write a note against K. Blind for the Triersche Ztg (SOURCE: KMC).

15. NYDT ARTICLES. **Feb:** NYDT pubs four articles: on Prussian political affairs (#M17), the European crisis (#ME97), Bonaparte (#M492), and the French army (#E294). **Feb 1:** M works on articles for NYDT which will, however, remain unpubd (not extant). **Feb 8:** M writes an article on Bonaparte's speech from the throne and his anonymous pamphlet; not pubd (not extant).

16. PERSONAL. **Feb 16–22:** M is visited by brother-in-law J. C. Juta, who next (Feb 6) goes to Manchester, bearing M's recommendatory letter to E.

17. PO AND RHINE (E). **Feb c.24:** E informs M that he intends to write a pamphlet titled Po and Rhine, viewing the coming war (Austria vs France–Piedmont) and its meaning for national unification in Germany and Italy. **Feb 25:** M is fired with enthusiasm for E's plan, sends Lassalle a letter asking him to find a pub'r, and sends E two letters the same evening urging him to finish quickly. He suggests anonymity: the pamphlet will be ascribed to a prominent general till the author is triumphantly disclosed in a second edn. **Feb D to Mar 9:** E works on the pamphlet (#E587).

MARCH

18. ECONOMICA. **Mar 7:** M receives from Berlin the first galley proofs of his book, after long delay; then no more. **May 10:** M asks E to inquire from Lassalle about Duncker's delay in typesetting. **Mar 14:** E brings up the matter in his letter to Lassalle. **Mar 15:** M receives another batch of galleys from Duncker, but chafes at the slow pace of typesetting. **Mar 17:** M returns the corrected proofs. **Mar 25:** M grumbles to E: only three galleys received in eight weeks. **Mar 28:** M complains to Lassalle about Duncker's delay. **Mar D:** M receives Dana's letter (Mar 15) about getting an American pub'r [← :13]: no American pub'r will issue a book on polit eco; even Carey has to publish at his own expense.

19. NYDT ARTICLES. **Mar:** NYDT pubs 11 articles: on British manufactures (#M840, 841); the English reform bill (#M540); the war prospect in Prussia and France (#M981, 982); other articles on French affairs (#M375, and an article which NYDT divides into #M648 and 818); and three by E on military aspects of the European war scene (#E53, 334, 133). M writes another article on the English reform bill, but it is not printed (not extant).

20. NAC WORK. **Mar 15:** Dana writes M asking for articles on "Fortification" and "Infantry" [→ :39, 57].

21. *DIE PRESSE.* **Mar 27:** M receives, via Lassalle, another proposal [← 57:53] from Friedländer to write for *Die Presse* (Vienna), this time with no conditions imposed. **Mar 28:** M writes Lassalle he now accepts the proposition [→ :28].

22. *PO AND RHINE* (E). **Mar 3:** M suggests to E that he give this pamphlet a touch of anti-Bonaparte slanting, in favor of Italian emancipation. **Mar 9:** E finishes the pamphlet (#E587) and sends the ms to M. **Mar 10:** M acknowledges receipt and praises the work; the same day he sends it on to pub'r Duncker in Berlin.

23. LASSALLE'S "SICKINGEN." **Mar 6** (rec'd 28): Lassalle sends M his newly pubd verse drama *Franz von Sickingen*, asking for critical comments.

24. PERSONAL. **Mar D:** M asks his mother for a loan. (She refuses.)

APRIL

25. ECONOMICA. **Apr 8** (rec'd 11): Lassalle informs M that the book will not be off the press till May M. **Apr c.20:** M asks Freiligrath to translate a passage from the Greek poet Antipater, which M will later use in *Capital*, Vol. 1, Ch. 15 (English edn), section 3b. (Freiligrath sends Stolberg's trans, Apr 22.)

26. *NYDT* ARTICLES. **Apr:** *NYDT* pubs four articles: on the Indian economy (#M357), the proposed peace congress (#M700, #E633), and war prospects (#E377). M writes still another [← :19] article on the English reform bill which is not pubd (not extant).

27. NAC WORK. **Apr 9:** M writes E about Dana's requests [← :20]. —Writing to Dana, M asks for a higher pay rate.

28. *DIE PRESSE.* **Apr 12:** Friedländer [← :21] sends M info on payments and conditions. **Apr 15:** M sends his definite acceptance [→ :40].

29. LASSALLE'S "SICKINGEN." **Apr 19:** In response to Lassalle's request [← :23] M sends him a longish critique of the drama, with remarks on general problems of literature.

30. *PO AND RHINE* (E). **Apr 5:** The pamphlet (#E587) is pubd in Berlin in an edn of 1000. **Apr 8** (rec'd 11): Lassalle so informs M.

31. *HERR VOGT.* **Apr c.20:** M visits Freiligrath and there reads the political program sent out by Vogt to a select number, giving his views on the coming Italian war. **Apr 22:** M tells E that Vogt's program shows a "certain leaning toward Bonaparte" [→ :35].

32. OTHER POLITICAL AFFAIRS. **Apr 22:** In a long letter to E, M discusses the alignment of European powers looking to the coming war and the parliamentary debate on it.

33. PERSONAL. **Apr 4:** M asks Lassalle to advance him a loan on the payment due from Duncker. **Apr 8:** Lassalle sends £14.

MAY

34. *DAS VOLK.* **May c.2:** M holds a meeting of his émigré circle concerned with the situation in the London GWEA (incl Pfänder, Lochner, Liebknecht, et al). M criticizes the GWEA paper *Neue Zeit*, which has just been suspended for lack of money, and urges no revival. (It is perhaps at this gathering that M declares—as he writes E on May 18—that "our designation as representatives of the proletarian tendency comes from nobody but ourselves. . . ." **May 7:** The first issue of a new weekly, *Das Volk*, is pubd under GWEA auspices, run by E. Biskamp. **May 9:** M attends an Urquhart-organized public meeting on the Italian war, sitting on the platform as a special guest. He is accosted by Julius Faucher, who urges him to write for Biskamp's *Das Volk*, which will break Kinkel's hold on the London German press. **May 11:** Biskamp visits M to gain his support. M declines to join the ed board but agrees to recruit contributions and subscriptions and permit reprinting of his *NYDT* articles, provided the paper opposes the pro-Prussian and pro-Bonapartist émigrés; he also approves Liebknecht's liaison with Biskamp (KMC dating: May 10). **May 14:** *Das Volk*, no. 2, carries, at M's proposal, a notice of E's *Po and Rhine* (#E587), quoting from it and identifying the author as a noted representative of the "proletarian party." **May 18:** M tells E that people in Manchester (W. Wolff, Gumpert, etc.) should subscribe to and disseminate *Das Volk*, as an anti-Kinkel measure and as a possible channel for their views. M also writes Imandt along the same lines. **May 20:** Imandt replies that the paper is too bad now; M&E should write for it first. **May 24:** To improve *Das Volk*, M asks E to write a military-analysis article for it on the Italian campaign; E immediately does so. **May 28:** E's article (#E115) is pubd in *Das Volk*. **May D:** M asks Schapper (via Pfänder) to join GWEA and strengthen its leadership.

35. *HERR VOGT.* **May c.A:** M reads Vogt's new book *Studien zur gegenwärtigen Lage Europas* (pubd Apr), which convinces him of Vogt's collaboration with Bonapartist propaganda; it supports Bonaparte's foreign policy. **May 9:** At the Urquhartite public meeting (see ← :34) M is accosted by Karl Blind, who says Vogt has received money from Paris for pro-Bonapartist propaganda, that Vogt has tried to suborn German publicists, that he is connected with Prince Napoleon ("Plon-Plon"); Blind claims to have evidence of these "treasonous intrigues." **May 11:** When Biskamp and Liebknecht visit M about *Das Volk* (see ← :34), M tells them about Vogt's program [← :31] and Blind's info. **May 14:** *Das Volk*, no. 2, carries an unsigned article by Biskamp titled "Der Reichsregent," attacking Vogt as treasonous, written without M's knowledge. **May 18:** Writing to E, M notes that Meyen has pubd a eulogy of Vogt's new book in *Freischütz* (Hamburg).

36. ECONOMICA. **May c.18:** M hears from Weydemeyer (Mar 27) and Komp (Apr 24) about 100 American subscriptions to the forthcoming book. **May 21:** M sends this news to pub'r Duncker. **May D:** In letters to E (May 24, 25, 27) M fumes over Duncker's delay of his book in order to get Lassalle's Italian-war pamphlet out. **May 28:** M writes a sharp letter to Duncker protesting the delay and his lack of response to letters. **May 31:** Duncker replies that the delay was due to the pamphlets of both E (#E587) and Lassalle.

37. LASSALLE'S "SICKINGEN." **May 18:** E sends Lassalle a critique of his drama [← :29] from a literary and historical standpoint. **May 27** (rec'd June 10): Lassalle sends M a lengthy reply to his and E's letters on the drama.

38. LASSALLE ON THE WAR. **May c.14:** Lassalle writes M of the forthcoming publ of his pamphlet *The Italian war and the tasks of Prussia*. **May 18:** As a result, M writes E proposing to issue a "party manifesto" setting forth their position on the Italian war and criticizing Lassalle's, which is an "enormous blunder." **May 25:** M receives a copy of Lassalle's pamphlet; to pay the two shillings postage on it, he has to pawn his last serviceable overcoat.

39. NYDT AND NAC. **May:** NYDT pubs seven articles: one on the financial panic (#M316), the rest on aspects of the war situation (#ME191; #M307, 67; #E636, 898, 908). —For the NAC, E begins work on a long piece on "Fortification" (#E286).

40. *DIE PRESSE.* **May 5:** Disquieted by Friedländer's lack of response [← :28], M inquires from Lassalle. **May c.14:** Lassalle replies that his own correspondence with Friedländer has been broken off. **May 16:** M writes directly to Friedländer. (He gets no immediate reply.)

41. MAZZINI. **May 27:** M writes E that he is favorably impressed by Mazzini's anti-Bonapartist position on the Italian war as pubd in *Pensiero ed Azione* on May 16. **May D:** M says as much in NYDT article #M502 (pubd June 17). He drops the idea of sending Mazzini a copy of E's pamphlet (#E587) when he sees Mazzini's whole text, with its antisocialist diatribes (as he tells E June 1).

42. PERSONAL. **May 27:** M receives £5 from E.

JUNE

43. ECONOMICA. **June 4:** At M's suggestion, *Das Volk* pubs most of the preface to the new book (#M181). From here it will be reprinted in a number of German-American papers. **June A:** E, who has now read the galleys, writes M of his high opinion. **June 7:** M replies that "your judgment is the only one important to me." **June 11:** The book *Contribution to the critique of polit eco* (#M181) is pubd in Berlin in an edition of 1000. **June 22:** M, still unaware of publ, writes another stiff letter to Duncker about the delay, threatening to issue a "public statement."

44. *HERR VOGT.* **June 2:** Vogt, reacting to the *Das Volk* article by Biskamp [← :35], which Vogt ascribes to M, pubs in the *Schweizer Handels-Courier* an article on M filled with bizarre personal slanders, titled "Zur Warnung." **June c.6:** M proposes to Biskamp to reprint Vogt's article in *Das Volk*. **June 7:** M writes E about Vogt's article: he will have it reprinted in *Das Volk*. M also informs E that Blind has resigned from Kinkel's *Hermann* and broken with Kinkel himself because Kinkel took Vogt's Bonapartist money, thus likewise becoming a "traitor." **June 11:** As proposed by M, *Das Volk* reprints Vogt's attack of June 2, with an editorial comment. **June M:** An anonymous flysheet is pubd, denouncing Vogt as a Bonapartist agent, titled "Warnung zur gefälligen Verbreutung." (It is later shown that this flysheet was written by K. Blind, and printed in Hollinger's printshop where *Das Volk* is also printed; cf → :49.) **June 18:** *Das Volk* reprints the anonymous anti-Vogt flysheet; M is away from London at this time (see → :48). **June 22:** The prestigious *Allgemeine Ztg* of Augsburg reprints the anti-Vogt flysheet, sent in to it by Liebknecht who is its London correspondent, under the title "Vogt und die deutsche Emigration in London."

45. NYDT AND NAC. **June:** NYDT pubs eight articles, all on some aspect of the war situation: on Mazzini [cf ← :41] (#M502), on Austria (#M373), on Prussia (#M714), and reportage by E (#E279, 68, 783, 631, 51). **June c.9:** E finishes "Fortification" (#E131) for NAC; it is in M's hands on June 10.

46. *DAS VOLK.* **June 10:** M discusses *Das Volk* with editor Biskamp, and declares that he and E are now willing to support the paper publicly and to obtain support by their friends (KMC dating: June 6–10). **June 11:** *Das Volk* carries an ed statement on the enlargement of the paper's circle of contributors by adding M&E, Freiligrath, W. Wolff, and H. Heise (cf *MECW* 16:624). **June c.12 to July c.2:** While M is on a visit to E in Manchester (see → :48), they discuss *Das Volk* and questions about its publ. They take up its material support with various friends, and collect about £25 for the paper from E, W. Wolff, Dr. Gumpert, Dr. Borchardt, Dr. Heckscher. M also talks about it to Imandt and Heise in Dundee. **June**; *Das Volk* pubs three articles by E on the course of the war (#E257, 134, 56). M contributes "Spree and Mincio" (#M837), and also, with Biskamp, the first two in a series spoofing Kinkel's *Hermann* (#M342).

47. LASSALLE. June 10: M writes Lassalle, postponing a reply on "Sickingen" [← :37]. Re Lassalle's pamphlet on the war, M notes curtly that his London communist circle disagree with it and will prob express their views in print.

48. VISIT. June c.12 to July c.2: M visits E in Manchester. M also takes a trip to Dundee (Scotland)—see ← :46 re *Das Volk*. M returns to Manchester before going home.

JULY

49. HERR VOGT. July c.4: M learns from Freiligrath that K. Blind is denying authorship of the anti-Vogt flysheet [← :44]. **July c.M:** M has a conversation with Blind, with Liebknecht and Hollinger present. Liebknecht attests that in June M (KMC: June betw 14–22) he saw the proofs of the anti-Vogt flysheet in Hollinger's shop with Blind's handwritten corrections. But while Blind admits telling M the contents of the flysheet on May 9, he denies he is the author of the flysheet, in fact swears so on his word of honor. M is convinced that Blind is lying in order not to come out against Vogt openly and publicly. **July:** Vogt institutes a libel lawsuit against the Augsburg *AZ* [← :44]; it will be tried in Oct [→ :60]. **July 22:** M reports to E on another matter relating to Blind: while M was in Manchester [← :48] Blind made an unsuccessful attempt to take over control of *Das Volk* on condition that M and the Communists were ousted from the paper. Blind denies to M that this ever happened.

50. DAS VOLK. July A: On returning from Manchester [← :48] M undertakes the de facto management and editorship of the weekly, since it is in financial collapse and its continuation is doubtful; he installs Lessner as expediting clerk, and while the paper lasts [→ :54] he is very busy with all administrative affairs of the paper. **July:** During this month M&E publish 11 pieces in *Das Volk*, as follows. July 2 issue: A military article by E (#E66). July 9 issue: Another military article by E (#E69); an article by M on "Erfurterei" (#M296) ("The Reaction executes the program of the Revolution . . ."); and more of the pieces spoofing *Hermann* (#M342) [← :46].

July 16 issue: The last of the spoofs (#M342); also a note on E. Jones (#M590.5). July 23 issue: First of a series surveying the Italian war (#E397; cf also #E397.5), and a documentary "Russian memoir" reprinted by M from the *Free Press* (see #M321) but not written by M. July 30 issue: The second part of the war survey (#E397), an article on the French invasion threat (#M419), and the first in a series "Quid pro quo" on Prussian diplomacy (#M725). **July c.27:** Since in the July 23 issue Biskamp reprinted a patrioteering poem by Freiligrath without M's knowledge, M has Biskamp insert a sharply critical note on it in the July 30 issue (cf *MECW* 16:635).

51. ECONOMICA. July 19, 22: M proposes to E to write a review article on the book for *Das Volk*, and makes some suggestions for it [→ :54]. **July c.25:** E urges pub'r Duncker that M's book should be advertised in the press.

52. NYDT ARTICLES. July: NYDT pubs five articles: on the peace (#M991, 646) and on the war (#E134, 523, 351).

AUGUST

53. HERR VOGT. Aug A: The Augsburg *AZ*, sued by Vogt [← :49], calls on Liebknecht to supply proof of the charges against Vogt. Liebknecht appeals to M to help. **Aug M:** M feels it is proper to help *AZ* against Vogt in this situation, despite the paper's own reactionary character. He tries to help Liebknecht find Blind, who is, however, out of town [→ :56].

54. DAS VOLK. Aug: M&E supply several articles before the paper ceases publ: the last three of the "Quid pro quo" series (#M725) [← :50]; the last article in E's survey of the war (#E397); and E's review-article on M's book on polit eco (#E687), of which two installs are pubd, remaining unfinished; perhaps also a political review (cf #M675?). **Aug 20:** The paper ceases publ, after publishing three issues this month, for lack of money to pay bills. **Aug D:** M spends much time winding up the affairs of *Das Volk*; he has to pay the printer a part of the printing bill from his own pocket. (For the rest of the year M will be in esp bad financial straits.)

55. NYDT AND NAC. Aug: NYDT pubs five articles: four on the outcome of the war, esp in Bonaparte's France (#M940, 949, 335, 490), one on British commerce (#M102). In addition M supplies the documentary "Russian memoir" (see #M321) reprinted from the *Free Press* (cf ← :50). **Aug c.13:** M gets a proposal from Dana to write the article on Hegel for NAC. M decides to refuse because Dana's stipulation is: "With absolute impartiality," i.e., no criticism.

SEPTEMBER

56. HERR VOGT. Sep 8: K. Blind writes Liebknecht a flat denial that he had anything to do with the anti-Vogt flysheet, and even asserts now, about his May 9 disclosures to M, that M is giving a false interpretation of this private conversation. Liebknecht sends Blind's letter to M. **Sep c.10:** After seeing Blind's letter, M takes Liebknecht to see Collet of the London FP; for M has remembered that the May 27 issue carried an unsigned article which referred to the Vogt story without naming Vogt. Collet attests that this article came from Blind, who asked that the authorship be kept secret. **Sep 17:** M obtains a sworn affidavit by A. Vögele, typographer in Hollinger's printshop, saying that the anti-Vogt flysheet was set in that shop, that the ms was in Blind's writing, and that Hollinger had cited Blind as the author. M writes a letter to Liebknecht summarizing the case to refute Blind's claims, and listing the proofs that show Blind at the least played the initiatory role in issuing the flysheet.

57. NYDT AND NAC. Sep: NYDT pubs four articles: on "Population, crime and pauperism" (#M677), British economic affairs (#M495), Kossuth and Bonaparte (#M433— see → :58), and the first of a series on "The new Chinese war" (#M542). **Sep D:** E begins work on the article "Infantry" for NAC, with M urging he make it long rather than deep; but he is slowed by an eye inflammation [→ :61].

58. POLITICAL AFFAIRS. Sep 1: The Hungarian émigré Szemere visits M and informs him about Kossuth's dealings with Bonaparte at the beginning of the Italian war, his repudiation of republicanism, etc. **Sep 5:** M writes an article for NYDT on Kossuth's relation to Bonaparte (#M433), pubd Sep 24; also pubd, shortened, in the FP and elsewhere. **Sep CD:** For M's letter to the London Free Press, see #M802.5.

59. PERSONAL. Sep 5: The printer Hollinger sues M for £12 on the debt left by Das Volk [→ :64]. **Sep 8–20:** E undertakes a trip through Scotland with his parents, who have come from Germany on a visit. **Sep 21:** M is again in financial crisis [← :54]; he is threatened with having his gas, water, etc., turned off because of nonpayment of bills; he turns to E for help as usual.

OCTOBER

60. HERR VOGT. Oct 1: At M's suggestion, Liebknecht writes K. Blind about the new testimony by Collet and Vögele [← :56]. **Oct 5:** M's letter to E includes a summary of the Vogt–Blind affair to date. **Oct 9:** Collet visits M, and on Blind's behalf, asks M not to use his (Collet's) info about the May 27 FP article [←

:56]. M indicates that he cannot bind himself. **Oct 19:** At the request of the AZ editor H. Orges for evidence of Blind's responsibility for the anti-Vogt flysheet, M sends the statement by the typesetter Vögele [← :56], along with a covering letter (#M461), to be used in the trial of Vogt's lawsuit. **Oct 24:** Vogt's libel lawsuit against AZ is tried. (It is dismissed on a technicality.) **Oct 27:** AZ pubs the Vögele testimony with M's letter (#M461).

61. NYDT AND NAC. Oct: NYDT pubs three articles, all by M in his series "The new Chinese war" (#M543–45). **Oct 10:** M receives E's finished article on "Infantry" for NAC (#E378) and sends it off.

62. ECONOMICA. Oct 2: Responding to a prod from Lassalle re the promised second part, M replies that he plans to rewrite his ms for it, but will not finish before Dec D, the firm deadline; he is working on an English trans of the first part (i.e., #M181); because of the lack of response in Germany, he is thinking of doing the rest in English, so that it will get more attention. **Oct-Nov** (autumn): M gives lectures on polit eco, based on #M181, "privately" to a "selected circle" of 20–30 workers, incl ex-CL members; cf #M600.5. **Oct to Dec:** M resumes some reading in polit eco in spite of distractions, though he tells E (Nov 3) that "my work is going ahead poorly." (For his reading, see → :77.)

63. POLITICAL AFFAIRS. Oct D to Nov A: Differences arise between M and Freiligrath over the latter's role in the London Schiller festival which Kinkel dominates.

64. PERSONAL. Oct c.20: M settles Hollinger's suit [← :59] for £12.

NOVEMBER

65. HERR VOGT. Nov 3: M brings E up to date with the following info. AZ wrote Blind that it had documentary proofs and urged him to speak up. Blind went to see Hollinger, who asked why he (Blind) didn't assume responsibility for his flysheet. Blind then claimed that, while he had written the ms of the flysheet, the author was a friend of his (unnamed). M adds: the truth is that Blind's friend Goegg had furnished the weightiest of the anti-Vogt charges. But Goegg must keep his anti-Vogt indignation secret since he poses as Vogt's friend and has financial ties with Vogt's camp. —Meyen's Freischütz pubs an editorial article on Vogt's lawsuit attacking M, asserting that Blind had not authored the flysheet and accusing M of defaming Blind. **Nov 6:** M writes a reply to Meyen (#M592) and sends it to AZ and Die Reform, with a copy to Lassalle. —In his letter to Lassalle, M gives a summary account of the

Vogt–Blind affair. He mentions that Vogt is saying publicly and privately that M is the originator of the denunciation (which was actually by Blind). **Nov 9:** In *AZ*, Blind publicly denies authorship of the anti-Vogt flysheet, and pubs statements by Hollinger and Wiehe calling the affidavit by typographer Vögele a "malicious invention." **Nov 14:** In a letter to Lassalle, M explains why Vogt wants to use this affair to discredit M and his friends. **Nov 15:** M writes to Lassalle to try to get the reply to Meyen (#M592) pubd in the *Volks-Ztg*. (It will not be pubd.) —In response to Blind's public denial of Nov 9, M writes a statement for publ in *AZ* refuting it (#M851). **Nov 19:** M's reply to Meyen (#M592) is pubd in *Die Reform*, with the dateline Nov 7. (The *AZ* does not publish it.) **Nov 21:** M's statement on Blind's denial (#M851) is pubd in *AZ*.

66. POLITICAL AFFAIRS. **Nov 22:** In response to Lassalle's repeated inquiries about M's views on the Italian war, M writes him a letter criticizing his position in terms of the reactionary meaning of the war and the role of Bonaparte and Russia in it. M also suggests that Lassalle should have discussed the question with his comrades in Britain (i.e., the M circle) before publishing his pamphlet. **Nov D:** Relations with Freiligrath become tense over two matters: an article by H. Beta in *Gartenlaube* attacking M for ruining Freiligrath's creativity, to which Freiligrath makes no response; and a public statement in *AZ* on Nov 15 in which Freiligrath adopts a "neutral" stance on the Vogt affair.

67. NYDT ARTICLES. **Nov:** *NYDT* pubs two articles: on English political corruption (#M273), and on the peace treaty (#M726). **Nov 17:** M sends *NYDT* an article on the Suez question; not pubd (not extant).

68. ECONOMICA. **Nov 6:** M's letter to Lassalle expresses disappointment over the German press's silence on his book (#M181). While it has gotten much notice in the German-American press, M fears it may be too theoretical for the working-class public in America.

69. PERSONAL. **Nov:** To add to M's financial troubles, he is sued for unpaid bills by the milkman and other tradesmen.

70. ENGELS. **Nov:** E continues his study of the Gothic languages and plans to improve his Old Norse and Anglo-Saxon. —E participates in the local celebration by the German community of the Schiller centenary, attends the anniversary affair (Nov 10), helps the younger people put on a performance of *Wallenstein*, taking part in writing a special intro for it. (However, E does not at this time join the Schiller Institute formed in Manchester as a result.)

DECEMBER

71. *HERR VOGT.* **Dec 11:** In *AZ*, a statement by Blind again claims he did not write the anti-Vogt flysheet, and Freiligrath's statement again disclaims any connection with the Vogt affair. This gives rise to the rumor that "Freiligrath has broken with M." **Dec:** Vogt's book *Mein Prozess gegen die Allgemeine Ztg* [My lawsuit against the *AZ*] is pubd in Geneva; large parts of it are devoted to fabricated slanderous tales invented against M and his fellow communists.

72. POLITICAL AFFAIRS. **Dec 13:** In a letter to E, M sees the movement toward revolution in Russia advancing more rapidly than elsewhere in Europe. **Dec c.15:** M meets with Juch, editor of *Hermann* since July. The meeting has been initiated by London bookdealer A. Petsch with a note to M on Dec 11, because W. Eichhoff is being prosecuted in Berlin by Stieber for articles which he pubd against Stieber in *Hermann*. M gives Juch his booklet on the Cologne Communist trial (#M762) as material for the defense, and advises calling W. Hirsch (who is in jail) as a defense witness. (Hirsch *will* be called as witness; but in May 1860 Eichhoff will be sentenced to 14 months in prison by the Berlin court.)

73. ECONOMICA. **Dec 23 or 24:** Writing to E, Mrs. M admits that the household faces a sad Christmas despite E's help, and that their "secret hopes" invested in the success of M's book (#M181) have been destroyed by the "conspiracy of silence" in the German press.

74. STUDIES (E). **Dec 11 or 12:** E writes M that he is in the process of reading Darwin's new book *Origin of species* (pubd Nov 24): it is "excellent," demolishes teleology in its last recourse, and proves that there is historical development in nature.

75. NYDT ARTICLES. **Dec:** *NYDT* pubs three articles: on Germany (#M948), China (#M935), and England and Bonaparte (#M420).

YEAR APPENDIX

76. See ← :13 (Feb 28 to Dec): Continuing his studies in the BM Library, M reads the English, French, Italian, and other economists, esp Wayland, Petty, Malthus, J. S. Mill, Molinari, Galiani, and makes many excerpts.

77. **October to December.** Among the authors excerpted in M's notebooks are R. Jones, Malthus, Vanderlint, Hopkins, Bailey; also some authors in the Custodi set of volumes on polit eco, incl Verri, Beccaria, Ortes.

78. **The Notebooks of 1859–62.** M's notes on the following authors are assigned to this period; there is a possibility of duplication

1860

CONSPECTUS

1. This year is dominated by M's work of self-defense against the fantastic slanders trumpeted in a book by Karl Vogt, then a noted scientific and political figure. (For the events leading up to this, see ← 59:6.) M's work is concentrated first on preparing documentation for a lawsuit against a German periodical (the Berlin *National-Ztg*) which reprints Vogt's slanders) and then, esp after this suit is quashed by the Prussian courts, in preparing a book *Herr Vogt* (#M372) which is pubd Dec 1. Note that in the following pages there are allusions (e.g., "Cherval") which are not worth explaining here in the space necessary; they are explained in M's book.

2. M does get some work done on his major economic opus, but not much. At this point M is still planning to write a continuation (Ch. 3) of his published book #M181, this chapter to take up "Capital in general" and constitute the end of Book I in the projected six books making up the total opus.

3. E makes a new connection as outlet for his military-science writings, the *Volunteer Journal*, for which he writes a number of pieces, esp on the "Volunteer movement" (see *Volunteer Corps). E also contributes to a military periodical in Germany, the *Allgemeine Militär-Ztg* of Darmstadt.

4. Other journalistic work has fallen off substantially. NYDT pubs an average of under three and a half articles per month. E writes only one article for NAC ("Navy," #E504); the previously written article "Infantry" (#E378) is pubd this year in Vol. 9 of the encyclopedia.

5. *Marx's Studies.* In connection with the preparation of *Herr Vogt*, M studies associated political history—see → :28; also the reference to miscellaneous reading (incl mathematics and Darwin), for which see → :59, 62. Polit eco is, as before, listed under "Economica"; for some readings, see → :65, 66.

6. *Engels Address in Manchester.* Sometime during this year E moves from 6 Thorncliffe Grove, Oxford Road [← 58:4] to 252 Hyde Road [→ 62:4].

JANUARY

7. *HERR VOGT.* **Jan 22, 25:** In two articles by F. Zabel, the Berlin *National-Ztg* reproduces the material in Vogt's book [← 59:71]

containing Vogt's slanderous fabrications against M and his tendency, and gloats over discrediting M. **Jan 25:** M writes E that he heard of the N-Ztg articles the day before. **Jan 27:** M gets info on the contents of Vogt's book from Julius Faucher, and orders a copy. **Jan c.27** (rec'd 30): Lassalle writes M, emphasizing the importance of answering Vogt, but expressing disbelief that Vogt is paid by the Bonaparte government. **Jan 29–30:** M obtains the N-Ztg's Jan 25 article, with its fantastic charges about forgery and other criminal activity. He writes E. Fischel, a Berlin lawyer (Urquhartite), about the feasibility of instituting a libel lawsuit against the N-Ztg. **Jan D:** Besides deciding on a lawsuit, M begins to collect materials for a brochure replying to Vogt's book (#M372). (At this point M wants E to collaborate.) However, even Vogt's correspondents in London have not yet received a copy. M learns from Juch that *Hermann* received, but did not print, many articles by Vogt directed against the M tendency. **Jan 31:** See → :9.

8. POLITICAL AFFAIRS. **Jan c.12:** Writing to E, M opines that the most important happenings in the world are the movement for the abolition of slavery in the US inaugurated by John Brown and the movement for the emancipation of the serfs in Russia. He is heartened by an *NYDT* report of a slave revolt in Missouri. (E agrees—letter of Jan 26.) **Jan 28** (rec'd 31): Imandt writes M that Heise died Jan 25.

9. ECONOMICA. **Jan to Feb A:** M begins to read and study for the next part of the opus; he spends much time at the BM. (For details, see → :65.) **Jan M:** Writing to E, M notes that the factory inspector Leonard Horner has resigned his post (last Nov), and he wonders if the Manchester mill owners forced him out. **Jan 31:** Writing to M, E agrees on the necessity of answering Vogt, but proposes that the reply be less painstaking than M is likely to make it, because the major task is the work of theory undertaken in the book on polit eco, and this has to be continued, as the main way available to M&E to gain influence [→ :16].

10. *NYDT.* **Jan:** NYDT pubs only one article: on the Moorish war (#E624).

11. STUDIES (E). **Jan-Feb:** E works on theoretical and practical problems of military science; he studies the history of various types of weapons.

FEBRUARY

12. *HERR VOGT.* **Feb A:** M works intensively on gathering materials—incl letters and newspapers from 1848–49—for his lawsuit and the projected anti-Vogt brochure (#M372). He begins writing to many people—"at least fifty letters"—asking for material to expose Vogt: to Schapper, W. Wolff, Lelewel, Borkheim, Imandt, Schily, Rheinländer, et al; and he receives replies with material and also with expressions of indignation at Vogt's slanders. **Feb 2:** Schapper sends info on Cherval. **Feb 3** (rec'd prob c.5): Fischel (in Berlin) [← :7] writes that in his opinion a libel suit against the *N-Ztg* could be successful. **Feb 3:** At M's request, E looks through all the written material in his possession from 1850–52. **Feb 4:** M pubs a flysheet or circular (#M701) addressed, with Urquhart's agreement, to *FP* editor Collet, showing that Blind is lying about the anti-Vogt flysheet. **Feb 6:** M writes a public "Statement" (#M617) announcing his lawsuit against the *N-Ztg* (pubd Feb 10 in several German papers, Feb 17 in the Augsburg *AZ*). —The London *Daily Telegraph* pubs a long article of over two columns on "The journalistic auxiliaries of Austria" repeating Vogt's slanders. M sends a letter to the editor (#M904) demanding a correction and threatening a libel suit. (The letter is not pubd, and the paper answers evasively.) —At an anniversary celebration of the London GWEA, which M attends (see → :15), a unanim resolution is adopted condemning Vogt's slanders. **Feb 8:** With the help of Juch and esp Schapper, M gets an affidavit from the typesetter J. F. Wiehe, retracting his previous statement (pubd by Blind in *AZ*, Nov 9) and testifying that Blind and Hollinger had gotten it from him by various promises. **Feb 11:** M visits E. Jones for legal info on the case and a possible libel suit against the *Daily Telegraph*. Jones opines that on the basis of Wiehe's affidavit he can get an arrest order against Blind. Jones writes a letter (pubd by M in *Herr Vogt*) testifying to the falsity of Vogt's slanders against M. **Feb 12:** M gets an affidavit signed by the typesetter Vögele repeating his testimony [← 59:56] on Blind's authorship of the anti-Vogt flysheet. **Feb 12–13:** M sends copies of the Wiehe and Vögele affidavits to several émigrés who know Blind, incl Pyat and L. Blanc; to the latter M remarks that he wouldn't like to institute a criminal action against Blind, for his family's sake.

13. PREPARING THE LAWSUIT. **Feb 13:** To Counselor Weber, whom Fischel has recommended as M's Berlin lawyer, M begins to send material collected for the suit against the *N-Ztg*. M finally obtains a copy of Vogt's

book. —M visits Borkheim (who was not personally known to him before) for info on Vogt's tale of a "Schwefelbande." Borkheim gives him a detailed account of the background of Vogt's story. **Feb 13 to Mar 25:** M stays with E in Manchester, working on the case. Together with W. Wolff they plan what to publish in the press against Vogt. M reads E's materials (letters, etc.) on his tendency 1849–53, and continues his correspondence to gather more material. They send Siebel to Geneva to get help from J. P. Becker and G. Lommel about Vogt's relations with Bonaparte. **Feb 15:** The *Daily Telegraph* pubs an open letter by K. Schaible, a family friend of Blind's, stating that he, Schaible, was the author of the anti-Vogt flysheet, not M or Blind. **Feb 21:** M sends a letter to *AZ* (not for publ) protesting its refusal to print M's communications about the case (#M923). **Feb 21–24:** M writes a long letter to his lawyer, Weber, with informational material for use on the case against the *N-Ztg*, dated and sent Feb 24 (cf *MEW* 30:465). **Feb 23 to Mar A:** Correspondence between M and Lassalle on the Vogt affair becomes tense because of Lassalle's equivocal attitude. **Feb 27:** Nothjung (in Breslau) writes M about an article by Julius Stein in the *Breslauer Ztg*, attacking M. **Feb 28:** M writes a short reply (#M863) to another attack by Meyen in *Der Freischütz* of Feb 9–18 in five installs [→ :20].

14. CASE OF FREILIGRATH. **Feb:** M's relations with Freiligrath worsen as the latter drifts closer to M's enemies. **Feb 8, 12:** M sends Freiligrath Wiehe's and Vögele's affidavits; Freiligrath does not respond. **Feb 23:** M writes Freiligrath a long letter stressing the importance of this case to the "historical vindication of the party" and to its potentialities in Germany. **Feb 28:** Freiligrath's reply refuses to support M against his enemies in this conflict; he wishes to stand aside from the "party" out of "purity." **Feb 29:** Replying, M makes clear he is speaking of "party" as a political tendency, not a formal organizn; and he defends its "purity." Note: This episode marks Freiligrath's effective political break with M's communism, but formally they will remain increasingly distant friends.

15. POLITICAL AFFAIRS. **Feb 6:** M, having received (Jan 28) a special invitation to attend the 20th anniversary celebration of the London GWEA—"in recognition of his services to the development of communist principles"—participates in the affair. (See ← :12 for anti-Vogt resolution.) **Feb 27:** Nothjung's letter to M (see ← :13) describes Nothjung's own straitened circumstances in Breslau. (M enlists E to write Lassalle to help him; → :21.)

16. ECONOMICA. **Feb 3:** In response to E's plea [← :9], M writes that besides activity on the Vogt case, "I am working out my *Capital.*" (This title here means the planned chapter on "Capital in general.") M adds: "If I sit down to it with determination, it will be finished in six weeks. . . ."

17. PERSONAL. **Feb 13 to Mar 25:** M stays at E's in Manchester. E leaves Mar 22 (see → :21).

18. ENGELS. **Feb 4–20:** E works on a sequel to his *Po and Rhine* (#E587), viz., a pamphlet *Savoy, Nice and the Rhine* (#E725), on national unification in Italy and Germany [→ 25].

19. NYDT ARTICLES. **Feb:** NYDT pubs seven articles: on English and French affairs (#M11, 291, 555, 284), the Moorish war (#E493), military reform in Germany (#E487), and Savoy and Nice (#E724).

MARCH

20. HERR VOGT. **Mar 3:** M sends Counselor Weber [← :13] another long letter with material for the case, incl an appended "Supplementary information" (#M454) summarizing his own career. **Mar 6:** Schily (in Paris) sends M a full account of the activity of Vogt and his friends in Switzerland. **Mar 7:** M's reply to Meyen (#M863) [← :13] is pubd in *Die Reform*, not in *Der Freischütz*. **Mar 8** (rec'd Mar c.D): Dana sends M a testimonial letter for the case, as requested; he carefully makes clear that M is a "patriotic German." **Mar 23:** M receives through Rheinländer a letter from J. P. Becker (in Paris) with info on the "Schwefelbande" tale and Cherval's activity in Switzerland. **Mar 25:** M leaves E's home in Manchester [← :17] and returns to London. **Mar 27:** M sends Counselor Weber the letters by Dana and J. P. Becker. **Mar D to Apr M:** M looks through the NRZ file for material on Vogt.

21. ENGELS. **Mar 15:** E writes Lassalle asking him to find a job for Nothjung [← :15]. **Mar M:** E receives news that his father is seriously ill. His family is trying to get Prussian permission for a fortnight's visit by E. **Mar 20:** Engels Sr dies in Barmen, before the government grants the permit. **Mar 23:** E arrives in Barmen for his father's funeral [→ :25].

22. NYDT. **Mar:** NYDT pubs one article: on the Moorish war (#E494).

APRIL

23. HERR VOGT. **Apr c.A:** Siebel, having returned from Switzerland [← 13], gives M a report on his mission in Geneva. **Apr 9:** M asks Lassalle to furnish biographical material on Zabel, editor of the N-Ztg (which M is suing). **Apr 16:** Lassalle sends some info on

Zabel. **Apr 18:** The Prussian courts throw out M's libel suit against the N-Ztg and Zabel: at this point the Berlin public prosecutor (later the municipal court, followed by the Appeals Court and the High Court) [→ :34]. **Apr 24:** M learns of the first action from Counselor Weber; the authorities have rejected the suit because no "public interest" is involved. M now realizes that Weber has blundered in instituting a criminal case, not a civil suit, since it naturally lies in the "public interest" of the government to have revolutionists discredited by slander [→ :34, 37, 51]. **Apr c.D:** Lommel (in Geneva) sends M new material on Vogt's activity as a Bonapartist agent.

24. POLITICAL AFFAIRS. **Apr A:** M receives Weydemeyer's Mar 17 letter requesting European correspondents for *Stimme des Volkes* pubd by the Chicago Workers Society. **Apr 9 to July 24:** M sends a number of letters to friends in England, France, Switzerland, and Germany, asking correspondence for Weydemeyer: to Lassalle, J. P. Becker, G. Lommel, Liebknecht, Eccarius, Borkheim, Siebel; he also corresponds with Weydemeyer about *Stimme des Volkes.* **Apr M:** M receives and reads the new book by the Hungarian Szemere, *La question hongroise (1848–1860)*, sent by the author, but he delays answering because the book flatters Bonaparte and Palmerston [→ :35].

25. ENGELS. **Apr A:** E remains in Barmen [← :21] until Apr 6. His brothers propose, and he accepts, a deal whereby E gives up his interest in the firm in Engelskirchen in exchange for a share of £10,000 in the Manchester firm of Ermen & Engels as of 1864. — E's brochure *Savoy, Nice and the Rhine* (#E725) [← :18] is pubd unsigned in Berlin.

26. NYDT ARTICLES. **Apr:** NYDT pubs three articles: one on German political affairs (#M717), and the first two articles in E's series on rifled cannon (#E541).

27. PERSONAL. **Apr 12:** M receives £100 from E, with "great joy in the whole house."

MAY

28. HERR VOGT. **May to Nov:** M continues work on his anti-Vogt book (#M372). In the course, he studies the political and diplomatic history of the 19th century, and excerpts books, papers, and parliamentary reports on Bonaparte's foreign policy. **May 10** (rec'd May M): The Russian writer N. I. Sazanov (in Paris) sends M a complimentary letter repudiating the Vogt slanders.

29. POLITICAL AFFAIRS. **May:** M continues efforts to get European correspondence for *Stimme des Volkes* [← :24], and (May 8) sends editorial suggestions to Weydemeyer. **May**

2: In a letter to Lassalle (not extant), M gives him much info on the Cologne Communist trial, esp Stieber's false testimony, to be forwarded to W. Eichhoff's lawyer for use in Eichhoff's court case against Stieber [← 59:72]. **May c.M:** M meets with Fischel, who has come to London.

30. ECONOMICA. May 10: Sazanov's letter (see ← :28) stresses the importance of M's book (#M181) for the development of economic science, and reports that the book's content was presented in a special lecture by a Moscow Univ. professor.

31. NYDT ARTICLES. May: NYDT pubs three articles: on Sicily (#M817), Bonaparte's war (#M684), and E's third article on rifled cannon (#E541).

32. PERSONAL. May to Sep: M's liver ailment flares up, considerably hindering his work.

33. ENGELS. May 10: E informs M about the new conditions, following his father's death, for his work in the Manchester firm [← :25]. **May 12 to c.25:** E goes to Barmen because his mother is ill, and stays there until she recovers. **May c.25–26:** Returning from Barmen, E stays for a short time with M in London.

JUNE

34. HERR VOGT. June 8: The Berlin municipal court (Stadtgericht) quashes M's libel suit against the N-Ztg and Zabel [← :23] on the ground that the N-Ztg's statements were "not beyond the bounds of permissible criticism." **June 26:** M receives this news from Counselor Weber. **June c.29:** E presses M to finish his anti-Vogt book quickly.

35. POLITICAL AFFAIRS. June 2: After some delay [← :24] M finally writes Szemere on the latter's new book, expressing agreement with some criticisms. **June c.2:** In a letter to Lassalle, M explains his relations with Urquhart and his tendency, evaluates Urquhart's position on foreign policy, and generalizes on the problem of the relation of communists to temporary allies on given issues. **June 14:** M gives Weydemeyer further suggestions for Stimme des Volkes [← :29]. **June c.19:** M visits Borkheim and persuades him to write a reply to the book just pubd (June 15) by the Bonapartist Edmond About, Napoléon III et la Prusse. (In the following months M will give Borkheim a number of suggestions, and read the proofs of his book Napoleon III und Preussen.) **June:** In connection with his work on Herr Vogt re Bonaparte's foreign policy, M makes annotated extracts from Szabó's recent book on European diplomatic history (#M305.5).

36. NYDT ARTICLES. June: NYDT pubs

three articles: on Prussian political affairs (#M18, 408), and Garibaldi in Sicily (#E321).

JULY

37. HERR VOGT. July: M continues work on his anti-Vogt exposé, which is now turning into a good-sized book (#M372). **July 11:** The Berlin Appeals Court (Kammergericht) rejects M's appeal [← :34; → :41]. **July 29:** M receives this news from Weber. **July D to Aug AB:** M continues to receive material from Lommel, Schily, and J. P. Becker (cf Ch. 10 of M's Herr Vogt).

38. POLITICAL AFFAIRS. July 19: M sends Weydemeyer more suggestions on Stimme des Volkes [← :35]. **July c.24:** M receives Weydemeyer's July 5 letter with the news that this paper must retreat from daily to weekly publ [→ :42]. **July CD:** M gives aid to Eccarius, who is ill and in bad financial straits.

39. ECONOMICA. July to Dec (second half of year): While working on his anti-Vogt book, M pursues studies on polit eco. (For details, see → :65, 66.)

40. NYDT ARTICLES. July: NYDT pubs two articles: on British commerce (#M103), and the British Volunteer corps (#E103).

AUGUST

41. HERR VOGT. Aug 1: E sends M £5 to defray the cost of the legal proceedings; he again presses for speed on the anti-Vogt book. (He repeats this Aug 15.) **Aug 2:** M tells Counselor Weber to appeal the case from the Appeals Court [← :37] to the High Court [Obertribunal].

42. POLITICAL AFFAIRS. Aug c.27: M receives Weydemeyer's Aug 11 letter reporting that he has resigned as editor of Stimme des Volkes [← :38].

43. NYDT ARTICLES. Aug: NYDT pubs 10 articles: on the British economy (#M842, 843), the British military (#E101), the Franco-Russian alliance (#M804), Garibaldi's operations (#M409, #E322), the question of a French invasion of England (#E188), and miscellanies (#M246, 632, 554).

44. ENGELS AND THE VOLUNTEERS. Aug 11: E attends the military review of the Volunteers (riflemen) in Newton, and gets an invitation to write for the English military weekly, The Volunteer Journal, for Lancashire and Cheshire (VJ). **Aug 24:** E sends his first article on the Volunteer movement (#E685), dealing with the Newton review, to the Allgemeine Militär-Ztg of Darmstadt, with a letter (#E442) [→ :50].

SEPTEMBER

45. HERR VOGT. Sep 7: M's letter to Lassalle shows that he has decided (after efforts in

June-July to line up Meissner of Hamburg as pub'r) to have his anti-Vogt book (#M372) pubd in London. **Sep 15:** M's letter to E says he is planning to have it pubd by the London bookdealer Petsch, printed at Hirschfeld's shop. E's crossing letter argues that publ in London would be a big mistake. **Sep CD:** M makes an agreement with Petsch, who takes on part of the printing costs and also distribution. **Sep 25:** Writing to E, M proposes the title *Dâ-Dâ Vogt*, as better than the suggested *Karl Vogt* [→ :51]. **Sep c.27:** Work on the book begins, slowly, at Hirschfeld's printshop. (This does not mean the ms is in final shape.)

46. POLITICAL AFFAIRS. Sep 11: In a letter to M, Lassalle returns to the dispute over the Italian war, to justify his position. In the same letter he reports that Bürgers has joined the liberal Nationalverein and come out for Prussian hegemony in Germany. **Sep 15:** M replies so as to cool past differences, and proposes that Lassalle draft a new programmatic statement for the "party." Apropos of Bürgers, M informs Lassalle that Miquel too has joined the pro-Prussian liberals. **Sep 17:** Lassalle replies that M&E should draft the programmatic statement, with W. Wolff.

47. ECONOMICA. Sep 15: Writing to Lassalle, M thinks the work will be pubd next Easter, and will be more popular than the last volume (#M181) "to some degree"; he reports that this volume (#M181) has caused a stir in Russia (cf ← :30).

48. NYDT ARTICLES. Sep: NYDT pubs six articles: on European and English economic problems (#M208, 355, 104), Austria (#E738), and Garibaldi (#E323, 320).

49. NAC WORK. Sep 8 (rec'd 24): Dana urgently asks M for an article on "Navy," even though M had previously declined this. **Sep 25:** M urges E to do the article somehow, since he is again on overdrafts of NYDT funds [→ :56].

50. ENGELS AND THE VOLUNTEERS. Sep 8, 14: E's first article on the Volunteer movement (#E685) is pubd in Germany, then in the VJ [← :44]. **Sep M:** E writes the first of a series of three articles on the French light infantry (#E297); pubd in VJ on Sep 27.

OCTOBER

51. HERR VOGT. Oct 1: E objects to M's suggested title [← :45] and proposes *Herr Vogt* (#M372). **Oct 2:** M tells Lassalle (repeated to E, Oct 25) that he will later publish a pamphlet in English titled (On) *Prussian Justice*. **Oct 5:** The Prussian High Court hands down the final rejection of M's appeal [← :41]. —E writes M stressing his (also W. Wolff's) objection to the title *Dâ-Dâ Vogt*. **Oct 23:** M receives news of the High Court's action from Weber; he revises

Ch. 11 of his book. **Oct-Nov:** M goes over the galley proofs of his anti-Vogt book, and makes revisions, with various additions and supplementations.

52. NYDT ARTICLES. Oct: NYDT pubs two articles: on Russia and Austria (#M794), and Prussian affairs (#M19).

53. ENGELS AND THE VOLUNTEERS. Oct 5, 20: E's remaining two articles on the French light infantry (#E297) are pubd in the *Volunteer Journal*. **Oct 13:** The VJ pubs E's article "Volunteer artillery" (#E890), his first of a series on various branches of the Volunteer movement. **Oct c.15:** E gets a proposal from the *Allgemeine Militär-Ztg* (Darmstadt) [← :44] to write articles regularly.

NOVEMBER

54. HERR VOGT. Nov: M receives contributions to pay the printing costs of the anti-Vogt book: £12 from Lassalle and Hatzfeldt (Nov 3), £12 from Borkheim (Nov c.M), and £5 from E (Nov 14). **Nov 5:** M tells Counselor Weber to send the letters and documents of his N-Ztg lawsuit to Lassalle for safekeeping. **Nov 8:** M concludes his work on the book (#M372). **Nov 12:** M adopts the title *Herr Vogt* as advocated by E [← :51] rather than *Dâ-Dâ Vogt* as urged by Mrs. M. **Nov 17:** M writes the preface. —He pays the printer Hirschfeld £25 as part of the printing costs. **Nov 24:** M sends out a statement (#M852) to three German papers announcing his book against Vogt [→ :61].

55. NYDT ARTICLES. Nov: NYDT pubs two articles: on Prussian affairs (#M685), and European financial problems (#M526).

56. NAC WORK. Nov c.22: E finishes the long article "Navy" (#E504); M receives it Nov 23.

57. ENGELS AND THE VOLUNTEERS. Nov 3, 17: VJ pubs the first two parts of E's "History of the rifle" (#E355). **Nov 24:** VJ pubs E's "Volunteer engineers" (#E891).

58. POLITICAL AFFAIRS. Nov c.20: Szemere visits M, from Paris.

59. STUDIES. Nov 23: Writing to E, M mentions—re his wife's illness—that the only occupation by which he can maintain the necessary "quietness of mind" is mathematics. **Nov D to Dec 19:** M studies the natural sciences (SOURCE: MEW Daten). **Nov 19 to Dec 19:** See → :62.

60. PERSONAL. Nov 19 to Dec: Mrs. M is very ill with smallpox; while M cares for her, the children live with Liebknecht.

DECEMBER

61. HERR VOGT. Dec 1: M's book *Herr Vogt* (#M372) is pubd in London (KMC

dating: Nov 30). —The Augsburg *AZ* pubs M's statement announcing the book (#M852) [← :54]; other papers do not. **Dec M:** M inaugurates activity to promote the book, sending notices, review copies, etc.
62. STUDIES. Dec 19: Writing to E, M mentions that for the last four weeks, during his wife's illness [← :60] he has been reading "all sorts of things," and specif mentions two: Darwin's *Origin of species* ("this is the book that contains the basis in natural history for our conception") and Bastian's *Der Mensch in der Geschichte* ("confused").
63. PERSONAL. Dec 16–23: As a result of the strain of his wife's illness [← :60] M too is ailing, taking medicine and bed rest. **Dec D:** With the help of Siebel, M recovers the rest of the library he left behind in 1849 in Cologne.
64. ENGELS AND THE *VJ*. Dec 8, 15, 29: The *VJ* pubs three more articles in E's series "History of the rifle" (#E355). **Dec 20:** E is informed that the *VJ* plans to publish his articles separately under the title *Essays addressed to volunteers* (#E249).

YEAR APPENDIX

65. Early in the year [← :9] M spends much time at the BM studying factory inspectors' reports for 1855–59, also the works of Adam Smith, Quesnay, Turgot, Malthus, and others, besides rereading E's *Condition of the working class in England* (#E171). *KMC* lists Jan c.D for his excerpting of a number of classics in politics, incl Montesquieu's *Esprit des lois*, Locke, Hobbes, Aristotle's *Politics*, Plato's *Republic*.
66. For the second half of the year [← 39], according to *KMC*, M excerpts i.a. the following: Sismondi, J. Tucker, and J. Bellers; and studies of the Physiocrats in the collected edn by Eugène Daire.

1861

CONSPECTUS

1. M's journalistic activities are severely affected by the outbreak of the US Civil War: NYDT sharply curtails foreign correspondence, so that all year it pubs only 10 articles sent in by M (none at all between Feb and Oct). In Oct the Vienna daily *Die Presse* finally starts publishing M's contributions, which are mainly concerned with the American war. E continues publishing his militaria in the *Volunteer Journal*. Another press outlet looms: Lassalle plans to found an organ in Germany; but M&E, after consideration, decline to come in as editors without editorial power, and in any case Lassalle's project does not take form. M&E's writing for *NAC* had come to an end in 1860; this year E's long article "Navy" (#E504) is pubd in Vol. 12.
2. M's work on his economics opus—still conceived as a Ch. 3 continuing his 1859 book (#M181)—takes on new life in August. From here until July 1863, M works more or less steadily, if often slowly, on researches, excerpting, notes, and drafts, which will add up to a big ms of 23 notebooks bearing the same title as his 1859 book. For some specific subjects included in these "notebooks of 1861–63," see → :42, 45.

JANUARY

3. HERR VOGT. Jan 3: M sends copies of the book (#M372) to Siebel to forward to papers in western Germany. **Jan 19:** Lassalle writes M thanking him for the copy of *Herr Vogt* and admitting that he is now convinced Vogt is a Bonaparte agent.
4. PRUSSIAN AMNESTY. Jan 12: The new Prussian king, Wilhelm I, issues an amnesty for political émigrés. **Jan 15:** Borkheim proposes to M the organizn of a meeting of German émigrés in London on the amnesty; M does not take the proposal up. **Jan 18:** M proposes that E write an English critique of the royal amnesty as the worst offered in any country, not applying to the actual refugees of the 1848–49 revolution; M will get it into the *Times* and other papers. (E does write this piece, but it is not extant.) **Jan 22:** M sends E's critique of the amnesty (which he calls a "statement") to the *Times* and the *Standard*. **Jan 29:** Since E's statement has been rejected by the *Times* and the *Standard*, M plans to send it to the *Manchester Guardian* and to German émigré organs. (It will not be pubd.)
5. POLITICAL AFFAIRS. Jan 7: With the first secessions in the American South, E writes M that the South's game is "risky" and its slave system is doomed. **Jan c.22:** M receives Lassalle's letter of Jan 19 in which Lassalle writes of his plan to found a "party" organ in Germany and asks who of the former NRZ editors would return to Germany to work on it.
6. NYDT ARTICLE. Jan: NYDT pubs one article: on Austria (#E625). **Jan c.28:** M receives a letter from Dana informing him that NYDT will suspend publ of his articles for six weeks; Dana also declines to pay for several articles sent in by M but not pubd (see → :9).

7. ENGELS AND THE VJ. Jan 5, 12, 19: The VJ concludes publ of E's eight-part series on "History of the rifle" (#E355). Jan D: E revises an article on "French armaments" (#E293) which was originally written for NYDT, and submits it to the VJ [→ :12].

8. STUDIES. Jan 16: M again [← 60:62] writes admiringly of Darwin's *Origin of species*, in a letter to Lassalle.

9. PERSONAL. Jan-Feb: M is in deep financial trouble, worsened by the cessation of income from NYDT (see ← :6). He is unable to pay taxes, rent, school fees. Dana has protested his making a draft on NYDT for £30. M himself, under doctor's care since Jan M, is completely unable to work. Jan 3: M is visited by his sister Louise and her husband J. C. Juta of Cape Town.

FEBRUARY

10. POLITICAL AFFAIRS. Feb 6, 14: M&E exchange letters on Lassalle's proposal for an organ in Germany [← :5].

11. NYDT AND NAC. Feb: NYDT pubs one article, on German affairs (#E333)—the last article pubd until Oct. Feb 15: M writes Lassalle that the NAC has been suspended (repeated Mar 28). It is not clear how M got this false impression.

12. ENGELS AND THE VJ. Feb 2: The VJ pubs "French armaments" (#E293) [← :7]. Feb A: E reads Marshal Bugeaud's book *Aperçus sur quelques détails de la guerre* (third edn, 1846), and excerpts the section on physical and moral factors in infantry fighting; he translates excerpts for publ in the VJ with his introductory remarks. It is pubd in three parts, beginning Feb 9, 16 (#E563).

13. STUDIES. Feb CD: For evening relaxation M reads Appian's Greek history of the Roman civil wars, with great admiration for Spartacus and contempt for the Roman generals (as he tells E Feb 27). (MEW combines this reading with Thucydides [→ :23] under "studying the history of antiquity.")

14. PERSONAL. Feb 19: Schapper writes M about his vain efforts to raise money for him. Feb M: M decides to go visit his uncle Lion Philips in Zaltbommel, Neth., to get financial help. The cost of the trip is covered by a £20 draft on Lassalle and £30 from E. M's passport is in the name of K. J. Bühring. He also plans to go on to Berlin. Feb 28: M leaves for Zaltbommel [→ :15].

MARCH

15. MARX'S TRIP. Mar AB: M is in Zaltbommel, Neth. [← :14] at the home of his uncle Lion Philips, from whom he gets £160 as an advance on his share in his mother's estate. He remains here until Mar c.16. Mar 7: M writes Lassalle that he will come to Berlin, esp to discuss the project to publish a paper [← :10]; he writes E with more discussion of the project. Mar 17 to Apr 12: M arrives in Berlin and stays as Lassalle's guest. The main business discussed is Lassalle's plan to publish an organ in Germany; no conclusion is reached. The main problem is whether editorial control will lie with M&E or Lassalle (see also → :17). Mar 18: As a result of a discussion with Countess Hatzfeldt, M writes a letter to the French Blanquist Dr. Watteau (in Brussels), saying that he has taken steps to start a support action for Blanqui, who has been imprisoned again. —Because of the recent amnesty [← :4], M discusses with Lassalle the possibility of getting his Prussian citizenship restored. Lassalle drafts a renaturalization application addressed to the Prussian police chief von Zedlitz-Neukirch (#M52). Mar 19: Lassalle personally presents the application to von Zedlitz. —In the evening M goes with Lassalle and Hatzfeldt to see the comedy *Die Journalisten* by G. Freytag ("disgusting"). Mar 20: The three attend a ballet performance in the Berlin Opera House ("deadly dull"). Mar 21: Lassalle gives a dinner in M's honor, attended by some high-ranking notables of the Prussian opposition, incl Gen. Pfuel, the painter G. Bleibtreu, the historian F. C. Förster, et al; M also meets the writer Ludmilla Assing, whom he describes cuttingly. Mar 25: M submits a statement (#M860) supporting his renaturalization application to von Zedlitz. Mar 30 (rec'd Apr 5): The police office sends M a rejection of his application. Mar 30: M meets his old friend Köppen, who presents his book *Die Religion des Buddha und ihre Entstehung* (1857–59), and tells how Zabel gained control of the *National-Ztg.* (M will see Köppen again Apr c.10. Cf M's letter to E, May 10.)

16. ENGELS AND THE VJ. Mar 9: E writes a short preface for the collection *Essays addressed to volunteers* (#E249) [← 60:64]. Mar c.16: This collection (#E249) is pubd as a brochure, by the VJ. Mar 16: The VJ pubs another article in E's series on the Volunteer movement, "Volunteer generals" (#E892).

APRIL

17. MARX'S TRIP: BERLIN. Apr 1–12: M is still in Berlin [← :15]. Apr 2: Writing to Siebel (in Barmen), M mentions that he intends to get Brockhaus (instead of Duncker) as pub'r of his economics opus, through Lassalle's contact with Brockhaus. He is remaining in Berlin only for his renaturalization effort [→ :30]. Apr 5: M receives notice of the police's rejection of his renaturalization application [← :15]. **Apr 6:** M submits a statement to von Zedlitz replying to this rejection (#M862). **Apr c.A:** M attends a session of the Second Chamber of the Prussian Landtag (Diet), in the press section. (For his impression, cf his letter to E of May 10.) —M meets the assessor Julius Friedländer (brother of Max) and tells him he is ready to contribute to the Vienna *Presse* [← 59:40]. **Apr c.10:** M meets with Köppen again [← :15]. **Apr 10:** M submits an application (#M50) for naturalization and a residence permit in Berlin, to the local police (Berlin District 33). —Police Chief von Zedlitz's office replies negatively to M's statement of Apr 6 (#M862); M receives the reply the same evening. **Apr 11:** M sends a letter to von Zedlitz (#M457) in response to this last document, notifying him of his local application, also notifying him that he empowers Lassalle to act for him in this matter after he leaves Berlin. **Apr 12:** Departing from Berlin, M signs a legal statement empowering Lassalle. —On leaving, M borrows a number of economic works from Lassalle, incl Rodbertus, *Soziale Briefe an von Kirchmann, Dritter Brief*, and Roscher, *System der Volkswirtschaft*.

18. MARX'S TRIP: RETURN ROUTE. **Apr c.14:** M stops to visit Siebel in Elberfeld, and meets various people in Barmen. (Date: Perhaps he arrives Apr 13 and leaves 15.) **Apr c.16–19:** M stops in Cologne, meeting the attorney Karl Schneider II (defense attorney in the Cologne Communist trial of 1852); also visits J. J. Klein (ex-defendant) and Roland Daniels's widow. **Apr c.19–20:** M stops in Trier, staying at his mother's for two days. She cancels some of M's old IOUs. **Apr 21–29:** M returns via Aachen, Zaltbommel, Rotterdam, Amsterdam, arriving in London Apr 29 (cf → :20).

19. ENGELS AND THE *VJ*. **Apr 6, 20:** The *VJ* pubs "Brighton and Wimbledon" (#E99), "Company drill" (#E153), both on the Volunteer movement.

MAY

20. VISIT. **May A:** M's cousin Jacques Philips (who had told M in Rotterdam that he was leaving for London on May 5) comes to visit M. Hence M is unable to carry out his plan of going from Rotterdam via Hull to Manchester, to see E before returning to London.

21. POLITICAL AFFAIRS. **May A:** According to a report from Paris in the Augsburg *AZ*, Herr Vogt is banned in France. **May 7, 10:** M&E exchange letters on Lassalle's plan for a German organ [← :15]; they agree to reject it, since Lassalle's conditions are unacceptable, esp his own editorial control. **May 8:** M,

having made inquiries on Blanqui's maltreatment in Mazas (Paris) prison—where he was jailed in Mar—reports his findings in a letter to Lassalle (cf M's discussion with Hatzfeldt, ← :15) who is to get info into the German press. **May 11:** M meets with Simon François Bernard and E. Jones to discuss organizing a protest demonstration in London against the prison abuse of Blanqui, and to get material on it into the London press. **May M:** M, as promised, reports on his activity on Blanqui's behalf in a letter to Hatzfeldt (sent via Lassalle), giving details on "Bonaparte's infamies against Blanqui" and on the "whole case" in general, to help her work for his release [→ :26].

22. ECONOMICA. **May 7:** M reports to E that he has made arrangements through Lassalle for Brockhaus to publish the next part of the work [← :17].

23. STUDIES. **May D:** M rereads Thucydides' history of the Peloponnesian War, with great appreciation (cf letter to Lassalle, May 29) [← :13].

24. ENGELS. **May c.3:** E sends a letter of protest to the Schiller Institute, Manchester, in which he is active, against the bureaucratic practices of the Institute library (#E438). **May 4, 11:** The *VJ* pubs two articles by E (#E11, 704). **May c.20–23:** E visits M in London, and gets his detailed account of his trip to Germany.

JUNE

25. *DIE PRESSE.* **June 10:** From Max Friedländer—in a letter of June 7 sent by J. Friedländer—M receives a definite offer to write two trial articles for the paper, one on the US Civil War and one on England, with good terms for subseq articles [← :17]. M asks E to do the military part of the American article [→ :26].

26. POLITICAL AFFAIRS. **June 12:** In response to M's request (see ← 25), E sends M a letter with a long survey of the situation in the American war, with an optimistic view of the North's power. This is the first (since ← :5) of a long series of exchanges in M&E's correspondence dealing with the Civil War, going on for the next several years. (An overview is available in Part III of ST/ME10.) **June 14** (rec'd c.18): Hatzfeldt [← :21] writes M that articles about the prison maltreatment of Blanqui have been gotten into German and Italian papers (incl the Augsburg *AZ*), with the help of Ludmilla Assing and the *NOZ*'s ex-editor Julius Stein. Hatzfeldt also reports that M's application for renaturalization [← :17] has been rejected by the Berlin police. **June 19:** M tells E he has received a letter from Dr. Watteau (pseudonym: Denonville), who is organizing international protest against Blanqui's treatment in prison; Watteau wrote about financial help for publishing a protest pamphlet; through him, Blanqui has warmly thanked M and the "German proletarian party" for their aid. M writes that it is very good "we again have direct contact with the staunchly revolutionary party in France." **June D:** W. Wolff visits M from Manchester.

27. ECONOMICA. **June 10:** M writes E that "a week ago" he set to work on the opus "seriously."

28. READING AND STUDY. **June A to July 28:** M reads Lassalle's new book *System der erworbenen Rechte* (System of acquired rights), sent by the author.

29. ENGELS AND THE *VJ*. **June 8:** The *VJ* pubs another article by E on the Volunteers (#E909). **June 22:** The *VJ* starts publishing E's four-part article dealing with Gen. Waldersee's views (#E896); its publ will be ended Nov 8.

JULY

30. POLITICAL AFFAIRS. **July 1, 3, 5:** M&E exchange letters on the social roots and military course of the US Civil War, esp the South's secession. **July 1:** Lassalle writes M with an account of his vain efforts for the restoration of M's Prussian citizenship with various government departments [← 26]. **July M:** M writes Dr. Watteau [← :26] on the steps he has taken on Blanqui's behalf. **July c.18:** M receives (July 3) via Schily a letter by J. P. Becker (sent Jan 15) from Naples, requesting advice on his (Becker's) activity in Italy to form a German legion. **July c.27:** Lassalle writes M that he and Hatzfeldt are taking a trip to Italy, and asks M to send recommendatory letters to "Garibaldi, Mazzini, Garibaldists, Mazzinists, etc." in various Italian cities. **July 28:** Dr. Watteau sends M more info on Blanqui's prison treatment; he reports that Blanqui received a copy of M's first letter to Watteau, and asks support for the press campaign to stop Blanqui's deportation to Cayenne. Watteau also encloses a letter by Blanqui to be forwarded to Lacambre.

31. ECONOMICA. **July 1:** Lassalle's letter (see ← :30) reports on negotiations with Brockhaus for publ of M's opus [← :17]; Brockhaus will decide after seeing the completed ms. **July 20:** M reports this to E, adding: unfortunately this means Brockhaus will rely on its literary advisers, who are asses; besides, the ms is not finished, and is going too slowly. **July 22:** M replies to Lassalle that he will take up publ by Brockhaus when the ms is finished.

32. *DIE PRESSE*. **July A:** M holds up sending articles to the paper [← :25] for the time being, because of its support to the Schmer-

ling government's pseudoconstitutionalism [→ :39].

33. PERSONAL. **July 2–22:** M is suffering from an eye inflammation, which hinders working.

AUGUST

34. ECONOMICA. **Aug:** M makes a definite start at drafting the chapter on "Capital in general," and will continue at it until July 1863 (cf ← :2).

35. POLITICAL AFFAIRS. **Aug c.15:** W. Wolff writes M about his impressions of Germany on visiting there after a 12-year absence.

36. VISIT TO ENGELS. **Aug D to Sep AB:** M stays at E's in Manchester; for activities, see → :38.

37. ENGELS AND THE *VJ*. **Aug 10:** The *VJ* pubs E's article on the Newton review (#E483).

SEPTEMBER

38. VISIT TO ENGELS. **Sep AB:** While in Manchester [← :36] M attends a session of the economics-statistics section of the Assoc for the Advancement of Science (whose conference is held Sep 4–11).

39. *DIE PRESSE*. **Sep AB:** From Manchester, M writes the editor inquiring about its political viewpoint on the government crisis in Austria. **Sep 27:** M sees in the *Times* that *Die Presse* has changed its pro-Schmerling attitude; this will facilitate his writing for the paper.

40. *NYDT* ARTICLES. **Sep 18, 21:** Resuming work for *NYDT*, M sends two articles (#M29, 108), for the first time since Jan D (pubd Oct).

41. POLITICAL AFFAIRS. **Sep A:** M sends Lassalle [← :30] a recommendatory letter to J. P. Becker (in Naples). **Sep c.23:** M is visited by Ernst Oswald, ex-Prussian and Garibaldian officer, who gives him info on the Italian movement. M helps him emigrate to America, and gives him a recommendatory letter to Dana. **Sep 27:** Dr. Watteau [← :30] writes requesting the forwarding of an enclosed communication to Lacambre; he again asks about financial aid to a press campaign on Blanqui's behalf. **c.Sep to Nov:** W. Eichhoff is a frequent visitor at M's.

42. ECONOMICA. **Sep:** In the course of his restarted work [← :34] M investigates the problem of the transformation of money into capital (SOURCE: KMC).

OCTOBER

43. *DIE PRESSE*: BEGINNING WORK. **Oct c.7:** M receives Friedländer's letter agreeing to his sending articles. **Oct D:** M sends two articles on the US Civil War (#M563, 146) which he began earlier [← :25, 32] and now nishes. **Oct 29:** M receives a letter from Friedländer giving him his credentials as London correspondent, and informing him that one article (#M563) has already been pubd (Oct 25); Friedländer replies satisfactorily on the political query [← :39], and beginning Nov, will pay £1 per article and a half pound per correspondence dispatch.

44. NYDT ARTICLES. **Oct:** NYDT pubs three articles, dealing mainly with British affairs, incl the cotton trade (#M29, 108, 80) [← :40]; these are the first pubd since Feb.

45. ECONOMICA. **Oct:** M is investigating the production of absolute surplus value. **Oct c.25 to Dec 1:** M begins study of relative surplus value (SOURCE for both items: KMC).

46. POLITICAL AFFAIRS. **Oct D:** M learns that, in the Gotha monthly Stimmen der Zeit, a certain Abt has pubd a virulent attack on him, regurgitating Vogt's slanders [→ :49].

47. PERSONAL. **Oct 30:** Cheered by his new work for Die Presse and the resumption of work for NYDT, M writes E an optimistic letter about ending his financial difficulties → :53].

48. ENGELS IN GERMANY. **Oct 3 to Oct D:** E is on holiday visiting his relatives in Germany, esp Barmen.

NOVEMBER

49. POLITICAL AFFAIRS. **Nov 5:** Schily (in Paris) writes M about Abt's attack [← :46], which was also directed against Schily and Imandt for reviewing M's Herr Vogt (#M372) in the press. **Nov 7–8:** M reacts to the threat of intervention in Mexico by England and Spain alongside France (decided on at the Convention of London, Oct 13) by writing two articles against the "monstrous" enterprise, one for Die Presse (#M413), one for NYDT (#M414); pubd resp Nov 12, 23. **Nov 8:** The Trent affair is precipitated when a US Federal warship forcibly takes two Confederate commissioners off the British steamer Trent, leading to a tense danger of war with Britain. From Nov D to Jan, M will write a number of articles on the British-American conflict for Die Presse and NYDT. **Nov 10:** M remits to Dr. Watteau [← :41] a first installment on moneys collected by the London GWEA, to finance a pamphlet on the trial and imprisonment of Blanqui. In his letter M calls Blanqui "the head and heart of the proletarian party in France." **Nov 11:** The Prussian min of the interior Schwerin notifies Lassalle that M's renaturalization application is definitively rejected. (Lassalle informs M on Nov 22, rec'd c.26.) **Nov 21:** Schily proposes that M write a reply to Abt [→ :57].

50. DIE PRESSE. **Nov:** The Vienna paper pubs seven articles by M: on American,

English, and French affairs (#M199, 146, 264, 413, 529, 326, 242); cf ← :43, 49. KMC notes that while M writes and sends in 15 articles for Die Presse during this month, only seven get printed (during Nov-Dec). The eight unpubd articles are not extant, and these do not enter into our Register tabulation. This should be kept in mind regarding similar notes in subseq months.

51. NYDT ARTICLES. **Nov:** NYDT pubs three articles (#M481, 105, 414); see ← :49 (Nov 7–8); #M105 discusses British commerce.

52. ENGELS AND THE VJ. **Nov 22:** The VJ pubs E's "Volunteer officers" (#E893).

53. PERSONAL. **Nov-Dec:** Despite M's optimism [← :47], he is thrown into bad financial straits by having to finish paying the printing costs of Herr Vogt (#M372) [← 60:54]; he seeks help from his mother and other relatives, also Siebel. Mrs. M is very ill because of the accumulated strains.

DECEMBER

54. DIE PRESSE. **Dec:** The Vienna paper pubs nine articles by M: four on the Trent affair (#M941, 31, 691, 183), four others on the US Civil War (#M202, 26, 988, 620), and a vignette of an English libel trial (#M942). Of about 15 articles written by M for the paper this month, nine are not printed (not extant); cf similar note for Nov. **Dec 27:** Writing to E, M complains that Die Presse "is printing scarcely half of my articles." **Dec D:** Eichhoff reports to M on the attacks by the Kölnische Ztg against Die Presse for printing M's articles on the US Civil War.

55. NYDT ARTICLES. **Dec:** NYDT pubs two articles, on aspects of the US Civil War in England (#M815, 697).

56. ECONOMICA. **Dec 9:** M tells E that his work is going slowly, but the coming volume will be more popularly written, the method being more concealed than before. **Dec 10:** J. V. Weber, a GWEA member, asks M for a critical evaluation of the views of the German economist Wirth and his paper Der Arbeitgeber, as basis for a discussion with Wirth in the German press.

57. POLITICAL AFFAIRS. **Dec 4:** Imandt, consulted by M about a reply to Abt [← :49], advises against tangling with this "bagatelle." **Dec 19:** M writes E discussing the US–British conflict over the Trent affair; cf also M's articles for Die Presse (see ← :54).

58. ENGELS AND THE VJ. **Dec 6:** The VJ pubs E's military view of the US Civil War (#E431).

59. PERSONAL. **Dec:** See ← :53 re M's financial straits. **Dec 12:** Dronke visits M. **Dec c.24:** Dronke gives M £50 for a debt owed to E; M uses it to pay part of his debts.

1862

CONSPECTUS

1. The beginning of the year sees the end of M's long period of contributions to the *New York Daily Tribune*. And by Dec he suspends all contributions to *Die Presse* (Vienna), which has been failing to print many of the articles he sends in. This leaves him without a regular journalistic outlet. E still occasionally contributes militaria to the *Volunteer Journal* and a Darmstadt magazine.

2. Much of M's journalistic output has latterly been on the US Civil War and its impact on Europe; both M&E are following American events closely, as is evidenced in their correspondence. No doubt many of the articles not pubd by *Die Presse* were on the Civil War too, among them articles dealing with the colonial expedition to Mexico.

3. This is a critical year for M's relations with Lassalle. On the one hand Lassalle's visit to London [→ :34] brings home to M the extent of Lassalle's tendency toward reformistic state socialism and dictatorial aspirations; on the other, by the end of the year Lassalle is on the way to launching himself into Prussian politics—first, by appealing to the bourgeois liberal movement (unsuccessfully). This development will unfold next year.

4. *Engels' Address in Manchester*. Sometime this year E moves from 252 Hyde Road [← 60:6] to Tennant Street, number unknown (one source gives this location as: Tenent Street, Ardwick) [→ 64:4].

5. *Economica: The Transition to the Title "Capital."* M makes much progress this year on his economics opus, and at the end of the year he will adopt the title *Capital* for it. Up to now he has conceived it as a direct continuation of his 1859 book (#M181) [← 60:2]. He fills 14 thick notebooks (numbered V to XVIII) under the old title.

6. Our entries in the following pages mainly follow *MEW*, which refers the start of his work on *Theories of surplus value* to Jan. *KMC*'s chronology is a little different. Until Mar it has M working mainly on the theory of relative surplus value [← 61:45]; in Apr he begins on the historical material (*Theories of surplus value*), taking up mercantilism, the Physiocrats, the classical economists, the socialist economists, and the vulgar-economists—finishing about Nov. In the course, about May to Aug, he works out his theory of ground rent. At the end of the year he writes on capital and profit, surplus value and profit, rate of profit, merchant capital, and money capital. So goes the *KMC* view.

7. In any case, whether M starts work on *Theory of surplus value* in Jan or Apr, he certainly continues it for more than a year until July 1863.

JANUARY

8. ECONOMICA. **Jan:** M begins working on the history of polit eco since the middle of the 17th century, writing the notebooks which will later be pubd as *Theories of surplus value* (#M877). Under Jan-Feb, *MEW* lists M's work on questions of capitalist reproduction, a critical analysis of Adam Smith's "dogma," and the formulation of his own basic theory on reproduction, which will later figure in Vol. 2 of *Capital*.

9. *DIE PRESSE*. **Jan:** The Vienna paper pubs five articles: two related to the US Civil War (#M693, 606), one on French economy (#M336), English politics (#M192), and the railway system (#M865). During this month M also writes some articles for *Die Presse* that it does not print. **Jan 7:** The editor, Friedländer, writes M that some of his articles have not been printed because they are unsuitable for the paper's readership; Friedländer suggests keeping in mind an "Austrian bourgeois public." He sends £15 in payment.

FEBRUARY

10. *DIE PRESSE*. **Feb:** The Vienna paper pubs five articles: on the US Civil War and England (#M482, 45), and on English political and economic affairs (#M600, 280, 214). During this month M also writes some articles that *Die Presse* does not print, incl (Feb D) one on Russia's policy of conquest in the Far East. **Feb 25:** M complains to E that of every four articles written, perhaps one is printed "and often none"; during the last two months the paper has printed so few that little has been added to his income.

11. *NYDT* ARTICLES. **Feb 1:** *NYDT* pubs one article this month, on the US Civil War in English opinion (#M295). **Feb 15:** M writes what will be his last article for *NYDT*, "The Mexican imbroglio" (#M509) [→ :41].

12. POLITICAL AFFAIRS. **Feb 13** (rec'd c.26): J. P. Becker (in Geneva) writes M for help in publishing his brochure *Wie und wann?* on the issue of German unification. Becker also asks permission to translate *Herr Vogt* (#M372) into French, esp parts of special interest to the Swiss and the French, to educate young revolutionists. (M replies Feb 26 that he will do what he can about the first request, and gives permission for the second.) **Feb 24:** A letter from W. Eichhoff (in Liverpool) to M inaugurates a correspondence (lasting to June D) in which M helps

Eichhoff carry on a polemic against Kinkel in *Hermann*, and via Eichhoff, helps Wilhelm Weber (in Neustadt) put out a pamphlet directed against Kinkel and the Kinkel cult in Germany [→ :18].

13. PERSONAL. Feb 25: M writes (to E, apropos of his financial troubles) that daughter Jenny has been under a doctor's care for the last two months: Jenny is now old enough (M explains) to see and understand the family's difficulties, "and this, I believe, is a principal cause of her physical ailment."

MARCH

14. NYDT: THE END. Mar 10: M's last article, on "The Mexican imbroglio" (#M509) [← :11], is pubd. **Mar 15:** M tells E that he feels the NYDT is on the point of sacking all its European correspondents. **Mar 28** (rec'd Apr c.13): Dana writes M that the NYDT's space is taken up by the war and M should suspend contributions. Dana adds that he himself is planning to quit the paper.

15. DIE PRESSE. Mar: The Vienna paper pubs three articles, on aspects of the US Civil War (#M27, 812; #ME8—the last in two parts). During this month M writes a number of articles that are not printed.

16. ENGELS AND THE VJ. Mar 14: The VJ pubs another military analysis of the Civil War by E (#E901).

17. ECONOMICA. Mar 15: M reports to E that his writing is not going as it should; the work is suspended for weeks at a time because of household difficulties (money troubles and illness).

18. MARX VISITS ENGELS. Mar 30 to Apr c.25: M goes to Manchester on a visit to E. Eichhoff comes in from Liverpool to discuss his campaign against Kinkel [← :12]. E gives M a note for £50, discounted by Borkheim.

APRIL

19. MARX IN MANCHESTER. Apr: Most of this month [← :18] M is at E's in Manchester.

20. POLITICAL AFFAIRS. Apr 15: Schily (in Paris) sends M greetings from his old Paris acquaintance Abarbanel, who has now become well-to-do. **Apr 20:** J. P. Becker (in Geneva) sends M galley proofs of his pamphlet *Wie und wann?* [← :12] and requests his opinion. **Apr 28:** M tells Lassalle he is wrong in his poor opinion of J. P. Becker, who is "one of the noblest German revolutionaries since 1830."

21. OPINIONS. Apr 28: M sends Lassalle a favorable word about his new book *System der erworbenen Rechte* [← 61:28] but strongly urges him to read Vico's *La science nouvelle* (1844 French edn). M also reports he has read Varnhagen's *Tagebücher* (1861) with interest, but finds it shallow.

22. ECONOMICA. Apr 28: M's letter to Lassalle says that the new volume will not be finished for two months. M proposes that Lassalle write a review of the 1859 volume (#M181) for the Brockhaus magazine *Unsere Zeit*.

23. DIE PRESSE. Apr 22: Friedländer, the editor, proposes that M write special reports on the Industrial Exhibition opening in London May 1. **Apr c.28:** M declines to do this on the ground that visits to the Exhibition would be too expensive; but he will continue sending one article per week. **Apr 28:** M asks E to send an article for *Die Presse* on the American battle of Corinth, also to comment regularly on future Civil War developments.

24. PERSONAL. Apr D: M is again (or still) in extreme financial difficulties; he owes £20 for rent, and has no money to redeem the children's and Helene Demuth's pawned clothing.

MAY

25. DIE PRESSE. May: The Vienna paper pubs four articles, on aspects of the US Civil War and its European impact (#M411, 292, 938; #ME156). **May c.A:** At Schily's request, M has *Die Presse* publish an anti-Kossuth article by Hungarian refugees in Paris.

26. ENGELS ON THE CIVIL WAR. May 5: In correspondence with M, as requested [← :23], E sends a description of the battle of Corinth and the fighting in Virginia. **May 12:** In correspondence, E raises the question of the North's lack of "revolutionary energy" and leans to a pessimistic view of its chances for victory. **May 23, 27:** More letters by E describe the important events of the American war, providing material for M's articles in *Die Presse*. **May 29:** E informs M about Anneke's and Willich's military posts in the northern army.

27. POLITICAL AFFAIRS. May A: M receives back from Koller the remainder of 330 copies of *Herr Vogt*. **May 19** (rec'd June c.6): Steffen (in Boston) writes M about Heinzen's attack on revolutionists in *Der Pionier*, and asks info on Heinzen's political past, so as to reply. **May 21:** Schily asks M for info on the competence of English civil courts for lawsuits against military personnel (for an article in the *Deutsche Gerichts-Zeitung*).

28. ECONOMICA. May 27: M tells E he is working hard on his draft of economic history [← :8].

29. STUDIES. May 5: E, studying the organzn of the Indian native army, asks M to supply the relevant parliamentary reports and materials from the English War Ministry.

May 8: Writing to Lassalle, from whom he had borrowed Rodbertus's *Soziale Briefe* [← 61:17], M gives a brief opinion on the book [→ :30].

JUNE

30. ECONOMICA. June 16: Writing to Lassalle, M gives a longer critique [← 29] of Rodbertus, also of Ricardo's theory of ground rent. **June 18:** Writing to E, M reports that in spite of terrible conditions at home, he is working hard and well at the opus; he is finished with working out the theory of ground rent, and has found out what is wrong with Ricardo's theory. Moreover, since Apr he has "discovered some nice and surprising things" which will go into the forthcoming volume. (Note: Under June to Aug, MEW states that "In the course of working on *Theories of surplus value* M develops his theory of the average rate of profit and price of production, as well as the theory of capitalist ground rent . . .") [→ :40]. —Also in this letter, M asks E for an explanation of Italian bookkeeping, in order to illuminate Quesnay's *Tableau Economique*.

31. READING AND STUDY. June c.A: M receives, via Bucher, Lassalle's new book *Herr Julian Schmidt der Literarhistoriker*, also copies for E and W. Wolff. **June M:** M rereads Darwin's *Origin of species*. **June 18:** In a letter to E, M criticizes Darwin's application of Malthusianism to plants and animals, among which Darwin thinks he recognizes "his English society." While Hegel described civil society as a "spiritual animal kingdom," Darwin sees the animal kingdom as civil society.

32. DIE PRESSE. June: The Vienna paper pubs one article, on the US Civil War in Europe (#M288). During this month M writes three other articles for the paper that are not printed.

33. PERSONAL. June: M is in a desperate financial plight as *Die Presse* fails to publish enough of his articles. Mrs. M tries in vain to raise money by selling part of M's books.

JULY

34. LASSALLE VISIT. July 9 to Aug 4: Coming to London for the Industrial Exhibition, Lassalle meets frequently with M. In a series of conversations M learns of Lassalle's plan to launch a movement among German workers based on the demands for universal suffrage and producers' cooperatives with state aid (by the Prussian state). M reaches the opinion that Lassalle's state-socialistic views are essentially reformist and reactionary. To Lassalle's proposal that M be English correspondent for his planned organ, M replies he would be willing "for good pay" but without political responsibility for the paper, since he and Lassalle "agree politically on nothing" save certain distant objectives. In addition, M forms a low opinion of Lassalle's personal character, and bristles with hostility.

35. POLITICAL AFFAIRS. July c.5: On the recommendation of Lassalle and Hatzfeldt, M visits Schweigert, a former Austrian army captain who had fought in Italy under Garibaldi, and hears of the "liberation plans" of the German officer Rüstow for Germany—plans which M criticizes as adventurist (KMC dating: July 2). **July 20:** Reinhardt, from Paris, visits M. **July 28:** Through Lassalle, M has his first and only meeting with Bucher, who participates in a M family outing with Lassalle. **c.July:** Liebknecht leaves London and moves to Berlin.

36. DIE PRESSE. July: The Vienna paper pubs four articles: on the Taiping rebellion (#M140), English affairs (#M809), the US Civil War and England (#M871), and navies in the Civil War (#E15), the last being the only article by E sent to *Die Presse*. During this month, M sends one article that is not pubd.

37. US CIVIL WAR: DISCUSSION. July 30: In a letter to M, E increases his pessimism [← :26] about victory by the North, which is not waging war "in a revolutionary way," while the South fights in earnest [→ :41].

38. ECONOMICA. July 11: M tells E he is "working like a horse on the book."

39. PERSONAL. July: M's financial plight [← :33] continues; E's help lets him wipe out a part of his debt.

AUGUST

40. ECONOMICA. Aug 2: M writes a long letter to E explaining the analyses he has worked out, in criticism of Ricardo's theory, esp stressing the importance of the organic composition of capital. **Aug 9:** In a follow-up letter M presents three points on the theory of absolute ground rent, for E's consideration. **Aug 20:** M urges E to come to London for a few days to discuss his conclusions in polit eco: "I have overturned so many old things [ideas] that I would like to consult with you on some of the points." M also poses a question (about machinery) to E as a "practitioner in the field."

41. US CIVIL WAR. Aug 7: In response to E's pessimism [← :37] M disagrees: the North must turn to revolutionary war methods even though so far it has been trying to wage the war "constitutionally" [→ :48]. **Aug 9:** Writing an article for *Die Presse* (#M386) M emphasizes the political side of the Civil War, and incorporates the view just expressed to E.

42. DIE PRESSE. Aug: The Vienna paper

pubs three articles: on aspects of the Civil War [#M386, 791, 1]. One article written by M this month is not printed. **Aug 19, 27:** As correspondent for *Die Presse*, M applies for, and receives, a permanent pass to the Industrial Exhibition (open May to Nov).

43. PUBL PLANS. **Aug 2:** E attends a Volunteer review in Heaton Park, near Manchester. (He writes an article on it for the *VJ* and, in German, for the *Allgemeine Militär-Ztg*, pubd Sep or Nov—cf #E686.) **Aug 2 to Aug M:** M makes plans to write to the NY *Evening Post*, a pro-abolitionist daily, offering to contribute.

44. PERSONAL. **Aug A:** Imandt visits M. **Aug 3:** Before Lassalle leaves London [← :34], M reveals his financial plight under questioning; Lassalle agrees to arrange for a loan of £15 plus possible future drafts provided E guarantees repayment. **Aug c.12, 20:** E arranges a draft of £60 (400 talers) on Lassalle through Borkheim, in an emergency measure to avoid M's financial collapse. Then Lassalle sends M an acceptance of the draft on the condition of E's written guarantee of repayment (rec'd by M Sep 9). **Aug 19 to Sep A:** Mrs. M and the children go to Ramsgate for her health.

45. MARX'S TRIP. **Aug 28:** M travels to Zaltbommel, Neth., again [← 61:15] to see his uncle Lion Philips for financial help, but Philips is away on a trip. M goes on to Trier [→ :46].

SEPTEMBER

46. MARX'S TRIP. **Sep A:** From Zaltbommel [← :45] M goes to Trier to see his mother. On the way he stops in Cologne, meeting Kapp, ex-NRZ writer recently returned from America, who tells him about Willich's and Steffen's military posts with the North, also about other German émigrés' roles in the war. In Trier, M's financial business with his mother is unsuccessful. **Sep c.7:** M arrives back in London.

47. POLITICAL AFFAIRS. **Sep 11:** Eichhoff asks E to help distribute in England a brochure banned in Germany, W. Weber's *Meine Ausstossung aus dem Turnverein zu Neustadt a.H.*, which criticizes the liberals' position on German unification. **Sep D:** At W. Wolff's request, and through Siebel, M gets the *Elberfelder Ztg* and some other west German papers to print the Breslau government's reply to Wolff's application for restoration of citizenship.

48. US CIVIL WAR. **Sep 10:** In correspondence with E [← :41] M flatly predicts the North will win in the end despite its present weaknesses. He opines that E lets himself be swayed too much by military considerations, as against political, in estimating the outcome.

49. *DIE PRESSE*. **Sep:** The Vienna paper pubs two articles: on Garibaldi in London (#M505), and on English poverty (#M993).

50. ECONOMICA. **Sep:** Investigating Ricardo's theory of accumulation, M, in his notebooks on *Theories of surplus value*, develops his theory of capitalist accumulation and economic crisis (SOURCE: *MEW Daten*).

51. PERSONAL. **Sep A:** M takes steps to get a job in an English railway office, with the help of his cousin August Philips. (He will fail to get the job because of his illegible handwriting.) **Sep 12–29:** E takes a vacation trip to Germany, via Belgium and Luxemburg. After traveling along the Moselle and the Rhine and through Thuringia, he visits relatives in Barmen and Engelskirchen. **Sep 25:** This is the date on a new legal agreement signed by E with G. Ermen, on E's participation in the firm of Ermen & Engels (the date may have been affixed by the lawyers involved, signed by E in advance) [→ 64:19.5].

OCTOBER

52. POLITICAL AFFAIRS. **Oct AB:** M&E begin to get more or less regular correspondence from Liebknecht, who has returned to activity in Germany [← :35], on the situation and problems of the workers' movement; in turn they try to influence his policies and activities (*MEW* lists this under "Oct AB to Sep 1864"). **Oct 12:** Bertha Markheim writes M that Miquel considers his joining the Nationalverein (pro-Prussian liberals) as a "means to an end" [→ :57]. **Oct CD:** Schily visits M, from Paris.

53. US CIVIL WAR. **Oct 7:** Writing an article for *Die Presse* (#M602), M paints Lincoln as a man without exceptional ability who nevertheless performed the task of a "hero" because of the sociopolitical organizn of the North's society. **Oct 29:** Writing to E, M remarks similarly that all Lincoln's acts appear meanly pettifogging, but this does not change their historic content, whereas the French decorate even unimportant points in "drapery."

54. *DIE PRESSE*. **Oct:** The Vienna paper pubs three articles: on Garibaldi in England (#M341), the Civil War (#M602), English bread (#M98). He writes two other articles which are not pubd.

55. PERSONAL. **Oct A:** M receives £20 from his cousin August Philips.

NOVEMBER

56. US CIVIL WAR. **Nov 5:** E is still unconvinced [← :41] that the North is capable of following a serious revolutionary policy in waging the war à la France in 1792–93. **Nov**

15: E expresses further disappointment with the North, esp as a result of the growing strength of the Democratic party, whose vote comes from northern fear of "inundation by the Negroes." **Nov 17:** M again [← :48] reproves E for looking at the Civil War one-sidedly; he cites his own reading of the US press.

57. POLITICAL AFFAIRS. Nov 6: Lassalle writes M requesting immediate repayment of his £60 [← :44]; E raises the money for M. **Nov 7:** M writes Lassalle that the money is being sent (via Freiligrath); his letter is written in a mollifying tone, stressing his troubles: "this state of mind in which I would like most to put a bullet through my head. . . ." **Nov c.10–13:** M organizes a collection among close friends to pay the funeral costs for Eccarius's three children, dead of scarlet fever. **Nov 18:** Bertha Markheim again [← :52] writes M about Miquel and his going over to the Nationalverein: in her opinion he remains true to his past views and speaks of M with the greatest respect. She also writes of Pieper and Dr. Kugelmann, who are concerned with M's interests and collect his writings.

58. W&P. Nov: Die Presse pubs four articles, all on the US and the Civil War (#M615, 872, 270, 243). M's last article for the paper, on the same subject (#M290), is written Nov 29 [→ :60]. **Nov 1, 8:** E's article on the Heaton Park Volunteer review [← :43] is pubd in the Allgemeine Militär-Ztg (#E686). **Nov c.18:** The Allgemeine Militär-Ztg makes E an offer for more articles, to be pubd as a regular column "Militärische Briefe aus England" [Military letters from England]; E is also to report on English achievements in the military-technical field.

59. PERSONAL. Nov AB: M is again in a bad financial plight, unable to pay for coal or groceries. **Nov 14:** He asks E for immediate help; E sends money the next day.

DECEMBER

60. DIE PRESSE: THE END. **Dec 4:** M's last article (#M290) [← :58] is pubd. Around this time M suspends further contributions to the paper, mainly because it is failing to print so many of the articles he sends in.

61. POLITICAL AFFAIRS. Dec 3: Freiligrath writes M transmitting inquiries by Dr. Kugelmann of Hanover about M's economics opus (sent by Kugelmann on Nov 21) [→ :62]. **Dec 17–23:** Mrs. M in Paris (see → :62) reports to M that the French socialists still look to Blanqui as their leader. **Dec 28:** M writes to Dr. Kugelmann in answer to his queries [see → :62], thus inaugurating a long correspondence with him; he asks Kugelmann to keep him informed on the political situation in Germany, where a revolution is approaching. **Dec c.D:** Lassalle sends M a copy of his speech to the Berlin progressives, Was nun? Zweiter Vortrag über Verfassungswesen [→ 63:6].

62. ECONOMICA—CAPITAL. Dec 17–23: Mrs. M in Paris seeks to arrange for a French trans of M's forthcoming opus through Schily and Abarbanel; she meets with M. A. Massol and Elie Reclus, who want to undertake the trans. **Dec 28:** Writing to Kugelmann (see ← :61), M summarizes the state of the opus, and for the first time in writing, mentions that "the second part" [considering #M181 as the first part] will appear under the title Das Kapital (plus the subtitle), as an independent work rather than as a continuation of the 1859 volume (#M181). (Very likely M had discussed this with E in Manchester; see → :63.) M explains something of the contents of the forthcoming book, the reasons for its delay, possible publisher, French trans prospects, the "conspiracy of silence," the question of scientific presentation vs popularization, etc. He states that the volume is finished except for the making of a clear copy. (This, of course, will turn out to be premature.) **Dec:** M writes the first draft of the section on capital and profit corresponding to the first three parts of Vol. 3 (SOURCE: MEW Daten).

63. MARX IN MANCHESTER AND LIVERPOOL. Dec c.5–13: M spends a few days with E, then visits Eichhoff in Liverpool.

1863

CONSPECTUS

1. During the first part of this year M thinks he is finishing the drafting of the forthcoming volume of Capital (so entitled now: see ← 62:62); but in Aug, instead of merely doing a clear ms copy as planned, he finds himself launched on a new draft version of the material, in a more "popular" way. In fact this redrafting will continue until the end of 1865, and will produce a large ms (notebooks of 1863–65) from which all the volumes of Capital will eventually be quarried. Before this Aug turning point, M has been working, in particular, on the material later pubd as Theories of surplus value (#M877) [← 62:8].

In addition, we should note that around mid-year [→ :27] M starts on a ms called "Results of the immediate process of production" (#M759), which he works on until (perhaps) the end of 1866, leaving it unfinished. —Beginning with this year our rubric "Economica" is replaced by M's title *Capital*.

2. This year, M's connections with the movement in Germany have improved, esp through correspondence with Liebknecht, now active in Germany, and with Dr. Kugelmann in Hanover. However, the organizational initiative in the country has been taken by Lassalle: he allies himself (Feb) with a Leipzig workers' committee which wants to found an independent working-class movement and offers the leadership to Lassalle *faute de mieux*. Simultaneously Lassalle inaugurates secret meetings with Bismarck, in an unsuccessful attempt to make a political deal with the monarchy. On May 23 (after holding his first meeting with Bismarck) Lassalle presides over the founding of the German General Workers Assoc (GGWA: *Allgemeine Deutscher Arbeiterverein* or *ADAV*) in Leipzig. For the next 15 months (i.e., until his death) Lassalle will conduct agitation on behalf of his organizn.

3. *MEW* has a broad-dated item, Apr A (1863) to Sep AB (1864), which it summarizes as follows: "In letters to Liebknecht, M advocates the policies of proletarian revolution and presents his views on Lassalle's activity. Since M&E ascribe a positive role to Lassalle's agitation to free the German workers from the influence of the bourgeois progressive party, they decide provisionally not to come out publicly against Lassalle. They urge their supporters in Germany, in the first place Liebknecht, to win influence in Lassalle's GGWA in order to promote a revolutionary current in it."

4. *Indefinite Date:* Sometime this year, in Manchester, E makes the acquaintance of the noted chemist Carl Schorlemmer, already a communist in politics, who will become one of his closest friends and companions.

JANUARY

5. *CAPITAL.* **Jan:** M finishes drafting the main body (but not all) of his *Theories of surplus value* (#M877), which he regards as a concluding historical-critical part of the total work. He draws up a plan for the first and third parts (subseqly, vols.) of *Capital*. In Part 1 M plans to take up the process of production of capital, in Part 3 the problems of capital and profit. **Jan 24, 28:** Working on a section about machinery, M goes back to the notebooks he had previously written with excerpts on the history of technology. Writing to E, he

poses practical questions about automatic machinery in cotton spinning. He attends a class on technology for workers given at the Geological Institute by Prof. Robert Willis.

6. LASSALLE. **Jan 2:** Writing to E, M gives a cutting summary of Lassalle's pamphlet *Was nun?* [← 62:61]. **Jan 28:** Having just read Lassalle's new pamphlet *Science and the worker* (his defense speech of Jan 16 before the Berlin Criminal Court, on trial for the publ of his *Workers' program*), M summarizes it for E as a bad vulgarization of the *Com Manifesto*.

7. POLITICAL AFFAIRS. **Jan 24:** Collet asks M for info on the connection between the Russian ambassador in Washington and the Southern states.

8. DEATH OF MARY BURNS. **Jan 6:** E's companion, Mary Burns, dies in bed around midnight, suddenly, of a heart condition. Her death is not known until morning. **Jan 7:** E writes M of her death. **Jan 8:** M's return letter seems to treat the news with indifference, mainly concerned with M's own domestic woes. **Jan 13:** E's letter shows how much he is nettled by M's. **Jan 24:** M apologizes for his letter of Jan 8, and explains his state of mind with contrition. **Jan 26:** E expresses gratification at M's apology. (This ends the first and last episode of coolness between the two.)

9. PERSONAL. **Jan:** The M family is in a trough of material distress, esp because of the cessation of M's work for *Die Presse*. The household is in dire need, lacking food and coal; the children have no clothes or shoes to wear, and cannot go to school. **Jan 26:** E sends M a £100 bill of exchange to alleviate the situation.

FEBRUARY

10. POLAND. **Feb 13:** The outbreak of insurrection in (Russian) Poland on Jan 22 is reflected in M's letter to E: "the era of revolution is now again fairly opened in Europe," and hopefully the "lava" will flow east to west. **Feb 17:** In view of Prussia's intervention, M feels that it is imperative to "speak out," i.e., publish; he proposes an immediate manifesto by the London GWEA, E to write the military part, M the foreign-policy ("diplomatic") section. —E writes that he looks forward to guerrilla warfare, for which Polish émigrés have prepared. **Feb 19:** E, who has been thinking of a pamphlet for two weeks, agrees to M's proposal. **Feb 20:** M suggests that they do a pamphlet in addition to a short manifesto, with the same division of labor. **Feb c.21:** E outlines the planned pamphlet, to be titled *Deutschland und Polen. Politisch-militärische Betrachtungen bei polnischen Aufstands von 1863* [Germany and

Poland: Politico-military considerations with respect to the Polish uprising of 1863]. **Feb CD to Mar:** M&E collect material for the pamphlet on Poland, making excerpts from the English, German, and French press and from books on the history of Poland, Prussia, and Russia, and on Prussian-Polish relations. (See→ :12 for continuation.)

11. PERSONAL. **Feb c.1–13:** Because of continual overstrain, M suffers an eye inflammation; he is temporarily forbidden to read, write, or smoke. **Feb 13:** M writes E that he is better now but had feared going blind or mad. (In this letter, M signs himself "Mohr" for the first time [← 57:18].)

MARCH

12. POLAND. **Mar (or Feb CD to Mar):** Besides collecting material for the pamphlet [← :10] M writes two drafts of sections, on Prussia's and Russia's policy of conquest vis-à-vis Poland, and on the history of the rise of the Hohenzollern dynasty. M's ms of over 60 pages is headed "Poland, Prussia and Russia" (#M666); for ms notes on Prussia, see also #M715. By Mar, M has read and excerpted: K. G. J. von Griesheim, *Über den Krieg mit Russland* (1848); C. Rössler, *Sendschreiben an den "Politiker der Zukunft . . ."* 1858); G. F. Cölln, *Vertraute Briefe über die inneren Verhältnisse am preussischen Hofe* (1807). **Mar to May:** M fails to finish the pamphlet because of continual illness (recurrence of his liver ailment) [→ :21].

13. POLITICAL AFFAIRS. **Mar 18:** Dr. Kugelmann writes his first letter to M (see → :14). **Mar 26:** M attends a TU meeting in St. James's Hall held by the London TU Council to show solidarity with the North in the US Civil War, chaired by John Bright. M helped to organize this meeting, through Eccarius. **c.Mar:** M receives his first letter from Liebknecht since the latter returned to Germany [← 62:35]; Liebknecht reports on his activity in Berlin, esp his relations with the *Norddeutsche Allgemeine Ztg.*

14. CAPITAL. **Mar 18:** Kugelmann writes to offer his services in promoting the forthcoming opus in Germany; he reports on the reception of the 1859 book (#M181). **Mar to July:** M carries on studies at the BM for longish periods at a time. In connection with the part of *Capital* already written, he makes supplementary excerpts from books on the history of polit eco, encompassing eight notebooks. Using this material, he writes individual historical-critical sketches and remarks, which are supplements to the main text of *Theories of surplus value*, esp a sketch on Petty. (SOURCE: *MEW Daten*.)

15. PERSONAL. **Mar to May:** M suffers from a continuing liver ailment. **Mar D to Apr:** Mrs. M is ill in bed, suffering from an attack of deafness; daughter Jenny has diphtheria (cf M to E, Apr 9). **Mar c.D to July 6:** E, through Dronke, sends the sum of £250 to M, part of it by Mar 24, most of it on July 6.

APRIL

16. POLITICAL AFFAIRS. **Apr 7, 9:** M receives from Lassalle his new pamphlet *Offnen Antwortschreiben . . .* [Open letter of reply . . .], pubd Mar 1 in response to an invitation by a Leipzig workers' comm (see ← :2). M criticizes the pamphlet in a letter to E: it reveals Lassalle's aspirations to be the "future labor dictator" as the representative of "science" and on the basis of state socialism. **Apr 10:** The *Berliner Reform* pubs a distorted story about M's stay in Berlin in 1861 [← 61:15, 17] and about M's discussions with Lassalle for publ of an organ. **Apr 13:** M sends in a denial (#M924); pubd Apr 17. **Apr A to Sep 1864:** See ← :2 for M's relations with Liebknecht and Lassalle.

17. READING AND STUDY. **Apr 8:** E reports to M that he has read the new books by Sir Charles Lyell, *Geological evidences of the antiquity of man*, and T. H. Huxley, *Evidence as to man's place in nature*; they are "very good." **Apr 9:** M reports to E that he has reread E's *Condition of the working class* (#E171) with nostalgic pleasure.

18. POLAND. **Apr-May:** M continues to read more works on Poland for his pamphlet project [← :14], esp on diplomatic history.

MAY

19. POLITICAL AFFAIRS. **May 1:** Liebknecht sends M a report on his collaboration with August Brass's *Norddeutsche Allgemeine Ztg.*

20. CAPITAL. **May to July A:** M carries on new studies in the BM: he makes notes on the history of theories of surplus value, and writes on the transformation of surplus value into capital, original accumulation, colonial systems, and the reproduction process of capital (SOURCE: *MEW Daten*).

21. POLAND. **May 29:** M informs E that he is giving up the pamphlet project [← :10, 12], since he has been unable to finish it because of his liver ailment and the pressure of other plans.

22. READING AND STUDY. **May:** E again takes up study of the Serbian language, and reads Vuk Karadžić's collection of folk songs.

23. PERSONAL. **May D to June D:** Daughter Jenny is beset by a cough again [← :15].

JUNE

24. LASSALLE. **June 8:** In course of secret talks with Bismarck, Lassalle sends him the statutes of the newly founded GGWA and, crowing over the dictatorial powers he enjoys as its pres, proposes a deal for a "social monarchy" which is to impose an antibourgeois "social dictatorship" based on the support of a Lassalle-led proletariat (through universal suffrage). **June c.A:** M receives from Lassalle a copy of the latter's new pamphlet on taxation. **June 12:** In a letter to E, M makes a mordant critique of this pamphlet's content and style; but right now, he says, he does not want to get into a public dispute with Lassalle.

25. ENGELS: MILITARIA. **June:** E reads the first two vols., just pubd, of Kinglake's *Invasion of the Crimea*, and works on a review of it for the *Allgemeine Militär-Ztg* (#E407); it remains unfinished.

26. CAPITAL. **June 22:** M writes E that as soon as his household situation improves, he will make a clear copy of his ms, then go to Germany himself to "peddle" it to a pub'r, and later take up the matter of translations.

JULY

27. CAPITAL. **July 6:** In a letter to E, M presents a graphic table (alternative to Quesnay's Tableau Economique) summarizing his view of the process of reproduction of capital, with an outline of three "categories" in the process. **c.July:** Prob around this time (or c.June), M starts work on the ms called "Results of the immediate process of production" (#M759) [→ 64:2; 66:3].

28. READING AND STUDY. **July A:** M occupies himself a good deal with mathematics, esp calculus.

29. PERSONAL. **July 6:** M gets the bulk of the £250 made available [← :15] by E.

AUGUST

30. CAPITAL. **Aug:** M, having decided on a systematic presentation of the theoretical part of his opus, begins drafting a new version, which will provide the basic ms for the three vols. of *Capital*. This drafting will go on to about the end of 1865. (*KMC* dates this beginning at July M.) **Aug 15:** M writes E that the new ms is taking on a "passably *popular* form," 100% more comprehensible than the 1859 book (#M181).

31. POLAND. **Aug 21:** M meets the Polish colonel Lapinski and other officers who want to form a Polish committee in London and a German legion to support the fighting Poles. M helps Lapinski's efforts to collect money among the German émigrés, and asks E's aid

in Manchester. Lapinski also gives M an account of his and Bakunin's unsuccessful expedition from Sweden to Poland.

32. PERSONAL. **Aug 7 to Sep c.2:** Mrs. M and the family sojourn in Hastings, their departure delayed because Helene Demuth has to go to Germany for two weeks on family affairs (*KMC* dating: Aug 12 to Sep 2).

SEPTEMBER

33. POLITICAL AFFAIRS. **Sep 12:** M passes on to E various pieces of info he has gotten from Lapinski [← :31].

34. POLAND. **Sep:** M gets the London GWEA involved in activity in support of the Polish uprising [← :31].

35. ENGELS: MILITARIA. **Sep D:** E visits Liverpool harbor. He writes an article for the *Allgemeine Militär-Ztg* on the development of ironclad ships and artillery in the US Civil War; not pubd.

OCTOBER

36. POLITICAL AFFAIRS. **Oct 16:** Liebknecht (in Berlin) sends M an account of his break with August Brass [← :19], and of the activity of Lassalle and Schulze-Delitzsch [→ :39].

37. POLAND. **Oct D:** In connection with support work for the Polish uprising [← :34], M writes a "proclamation" for issuance by the London GWEA (#M695)—signed by 11 names (the GWEA's Refugee Aid Comm, not incl M) and pubd as a flysheet. Its theme is that an independent and unified Germany depends on an independent Poland.

38. ENGELS' TRIP. **Oct M:** E makes a holiday trip to visit his mother in Germany.

NOVEMBER

39. POLITICAL AFFAIRS. **Nov:** At the request of Vahlteich (GGWA secy), 50 copies of the GWEA "Proclamation" (#M695) [← :37] are sent to Liebknecht (in Berlin) to be distributed to GGWA members. **Nov c.A:** M writes Liebknecht [← :36] warning against having too close relations with Lassalle and against public alignment with him. **Nov 13:** Liebknecht sends M an account of his relations with Lassalle and of Lassalle's propaganda work in Germany, also a report on his own activity in the Berlin workers' assoc.

40. PERSONAL. **Nov:** M falls dangerously ill with an outbreak of carbuncles. **Nov 30:** M's mother dies, in Trier [→ :41].

DECEMBER

41. MARX'S TRIP. **Dec 2:** M receives a telegram announcing his mother's death [← :40]; he writes E asking for money to make the trip to Trier. **Dec 7–c.18:** M is in Trier; he is concerned i.a. with settling his mother's estate and his own inheritance. **Dec c.19:** M spends a day with relatives in Frankfurt, his aunts Esther Kosel and Babette Blum; but he is unsuccessful in seeing any publisher. **Dec 21:** M arrives in Zaltbommel, Neth., at his uncle Lion Philips', who is M's mother's executor. **Dec 21 to Feb M:** M, having again

fallen ill with carbuncles, stays in Zaltbommel; he is cared for by his uncle, cousin Antoinette ("Nannette"), and Dr. van Anrooy [→ 64:5].

42. PUBL PLANS (E). **Dec 3:** E informs M that he intends to write a brochure on the Schleswig-Holstein question, and asks M to find a pub'r in Germany. (E will not carry this intention out.)

1864

CONSPECTUS

1. The year begins in the doldrums, but two events in Sep give M's work a sudden turn: the International is founded in London; and M learns of Lassalle's death in a duel on Aug 31, which will set the new Lassallean movement in Germany adrift. The International will dominate all aspects of M's activity for the next several years.

2. Still, all year—with interruptions due to illness or sudden tasks—M continues work on *Capital*. (*MEW* makes a special point of noting this for the second half of the year; but in the last quarter M's time is esp commandeered by the growing pains of the International.) M is working on redrafting all of *Capital*, and this work will go on until the end of 1865 (see ← 63:1). During this period M also works on the unfinished ms #M759, prob irregularly.

3. Esp during the doldrum days, M spends time reading up on natural sciences, such as physiology and anatomy, (For details, see → :48.)

4. *Engels' Address in Manchester.* Sometime this year E moves from Tennant Street [← 62:4] to 86 Mornington Street, Stockport Road, Ardwick—his last residence in Manchester before removal to London in Sep 1870.

JANUARY

5. MARX'S TRIP (CONT'D). **Jan c.A:** In Zaltbommel [← 63:41], M, still laid up with illness at his uncle's house, is treated by Dr. van Anrooy. M reads Renan's life of Jesus.

6. W&P (E). **c.Jan:** E writes an article on the English army (#E244) for the *Allgemeine Militär-Ztg*, but leaves it unfinished.

FEBRUARY

7. MARX'S TRIP (CONT'D). **Feb c.14 or 15:** M leaves Zaltbommel [← :5] for Amsterdam. **Feb c.15–18:** M makes a stopover in Amsterdam, seeing cousin August Philips, and in Rotterdam (two days), seeing cousin Jacques

Philips; both cousins are lawyers. **Feb 19:** M arrives back in London.

8. POLITICAL AFFAIRS. **Feb 11:** Kertbény (in Brussels) writes M asking for biographical info on Bangya, for use in a work on the Hungarian movement. **Feb 21:** M sends Kertbény some material in reply. **Feb c.25:** Pieper visits M, from Bremen.

9. W&P (E). **Feb 16:** The *Manchester Guardian* pubs a letter by E on "The strength of the armies in Schleswig" (#E784).

10. PERSONAL. **Feb CD to Apr A:** M is ill with carbuncles, unable to work.

MARCH

11. POLITICAL AFFAIRS. **Mar 29:** M writes uncle Lion Philips (in Zaltbommel) a chatty letter about world politics and its stupidities; he condemns Prussia's policy in Schleswig-Holstein, sees "serious conflicts" ahead, and hopes for continued peace since war would postpone revolution in France.

12. PERSONAL. **Mar 12:** M goes to Manchester to visit E, to tell him about his trip to Germany and Holland. (*MEW* says "for a few days"; *KMC* dating is Mar 12–c.25.) **Mar:** M receives his share of his mother's estate, a small legacy. —During this month the M family moves into a new house: 1 Modena Villas, Maitland Park, Haverstock Hill, in northwest London (which in 1868 will be renamed 1 Maitland Park Road) [→ 75:15].

APRIL

13. POLITICAL AFFAIRS. **Apr M:** The London GWEA asks M to draft an address to Garibaldi (who is visiting England this month) and to take part in a deputation; M declines. **Apr 21:** M visits editor Collet and discusses the Schleswig-Holstein question, on which Collet is preparing an article for his *Free Press*. **c.Apr:** M reads Lassalle's new book on economics, *Herr Bastiat-Schulze von Delitzsch* [→ :17].

14. PERSONAL. **Apr 14:** M writes uncle Lion Philips another chatty letter [← :11]

about ancient arithmetical methods and Epicurus; the M daughters are learning Dutch. **Apr D:** W. Wolff (in Manchester) falls seriously ill; E spends much time at his bedside [→ :15].

MAY

15. W. WOLFF'S DEATH. **May 3:** Since W. Wolff is very ill [← :14], M goes to Manchester. M&E meet with Eichhoff, Strohn, and Dronke. **May 9:** Wolff dies. (His will, made Dec D 1863, leaves M £800 and his books.) **May 13:** Wolff's funeral: M gives a short funeral speech, but has to stop several times. **May 16:** M&E visit E. Jones and renew their friendship with him. **May 19:** M&E return to London together. **May 22:** E returns to Manchester. **May D to June:** M plans to write a biographical account of Wolff, and starts putting together the materials, data, etc. He requests info on Wolff's early life from Elsner, editor of the *Breslauer Morgen-Ztg*. M does not carry this through; but cf #E918.

16. *CAPITAL*. **May D to Dec:** M continues his work on drafting the new ms, with interruptions due to ill health.

JUNE

17. GERMAN MOVEMENT; LASSALLE. **June 1–c.16:** Two worker émigrés from Solingen, Fritz Moll and J. Melchior, who plan to go to America, visit M in London, and inform him on the state of the workers' movement in the Rhineland, incl Klings's activity, and on the activity of the GGWA, incl Lassalle. M helps organize the collection of a fund to expedite their departure to America, and gives them a recommendatory letter to Abraham Jacobi (in NY). **June 3:** M writes E a criticism of Lassalle's new book on economics [← :13] as a plagiarism on his own work *Wage-labor and capital* (#M968), which he (M) happens to have looked over just days before. **June 6:** M receives a letter (June 3) from Liebknecht reporting his activity in the Berlin workers' assoc and his relations with Lassalle. M answers with general approval, but advises that Liebknecht should not identify himself politically with Lassalle while not coming out openly against him. **June c.10:** M sends Liebknecht some financial aid. **June 12:** Liebknecht writes M of a talk given by Lassalle which reveals his orientation toward an alliance with the Bismarckian monarchy. **18.** POLITICAL AFFAIRS. **June 7, 16:** M's letters to E discuss the problems of the Schleswig-Holstein war, as the London Conference (to settle the war) miscarries [→ :20]. **June D to July A:** M writes an article on Russia's relation to this war, for Collet's *Free* *Press*; it is not pubd (not extant) (*KMC* dating: Aug). **June 27:** E writes an article (#E243) comparing England's military strength with Germany's, for *Allgemeine Militär-Ztg* [→ :20].

19. READING AND STUDY. **June D to Aug AB:** M is ill, under a doctor's care, unable to work. During his illness he studies physiology and anatomy, and reads a number of works, as well as attending lectures. (For details, see → :48.)

19.5. PERSONAL. **June 30:** E and G. Ermen sign new "Articles of Agreement" regulating E's participation in the firm of Ermen & Engels [← 62:51].

JULY

20. POLITICAL AFFAIRS. **July 6:** E's article on English and German military strength (#E243) [← :18] is pubd in *Allgemeine Militär-Ztg*—E's last article in that periodical. **July 25:** In correspondence with E, M continues [← :18] to discuss the Schleswig-Holstein war.

21. PERSONAL. **July 7:** E is elected a member of the Board of Directors of the Schiller Institute in Manchester, the cultural society of the German community. **July c.20 to Aug 10:** M is in Ramsgate for his health.

AUGUST

22. DEATH OF LASSALLE. **Aug 28:** Lassalle fights a duel with Yanko von Rakowitza, and is fatally wounded. **Aug 31:** Lassalle dies [→ :27].

23. POLITICAL AFFAIRS. **Aug 31:** Writing to E in continued discussion of the Schleswig-Holstein war [← :20], M admits he is not clear about the events and needs more facts to clarify his views.

24. READING AND STUDY. **Aug:** Continuing his reading in the sciences [← :19], M reads W. R. Grove's *Correlation of physical forces* with great appreciation of its philosophical approach, esp because it shows the interrelation of natural forces and abolishes metaphysical spooks like "latent heat," electrical "fluid," etc.

25. PERSONAL. **Aug 16:** M receives word from his uncle Lion Philips (in Zaltbommel) that a maid in his household has come down with smallpox; M's plan to visit there with his daughters is therefore called off. **Aug 17:** M writes his uncle urging him to send all family members away, citing his own experience with smallpox. In a chatty letter he writes of the "frightful railway accidents" in England and the "homicidal neglect" by profit-hungry directors. **Aug 30:** Mrs. M, ailing for a week with cholerine, goes to Brighton by herself.

SEPTEMBER

26. FOUNDING OF THE INTERNATIONAL (IWMA). **Sep 3:** *Bee-Hive* announces that a public meeting will be held Sep 28 in which a deputation elected by Paris workers will reply to an Address issued by English workers and propose a plan for uniting all peoples. "Several distinguished exiles and friends of the people have already been invited. . . ." **Sep 17:** *Bee-Hive* runs an advertisement for the public meeting at St. Martin's Hall, Long Acre (London). **Sep AB or M:** Le Lubez, a French émigré involved with trade unionists Odger and Cremer in organizing the meeting, comes to ask M to take part on behalf of the German workers, and to "supply a German worker to speak at the meeting." M supplies Eccarius. **Sep 26:** Eccarius, after seeing Odger on Sep 25, sends M an urgent note asking for help on what to say at the meeting. **Sep 28:** Hours before the scheduled meeting, Cremer sends M a letter to admit him to the "committee room" of the hall, where he is to meet the organizing comm "at half 7" (the meeting being scheduled to begin at 8 P.M.). As the meeting goes on, with Prof. E. S. Beesly in the chair, M sits on the platform with the organizing comm, silent; Eccarius gives his speech. After the speeches, a motion to establish an international assoc (unnamed) is passed, and a comm to draw up by-laws is elected, comprising 34; M and Eccarius are the two Germans on it.

27. AFTER LASSALLE. **Sep 1:** Freiligrath sends M the news, received from Klapka (in Geneva), that Lassalle has been wounded in a duel; M visits Freiligrath the same evening. **Sep 2:** M writes the news to E and to Mrs. M (in Brighton). **Sep 2 or 3:** M learns from Freiligrath of Lassalle's death [← :22]. He sends a telegram to E (rec'd Sep 3). **Sep c.12:** M receives a letter from Liebknecht (which KMC dates Sep 2) reporting that Schweitzer and other GGWA leaders and workers have proposed that M come to Germany and assume leadership of the organizn as president succeeding Lassalle. —M replies that he is willing to accept under certain conditions. **Sep 12:** M writes a letter of condolence to the Countess von Hatzfeldt on Lassalle's death. **Sep D:** Liebknecht writes M that Bernhard Becker is willing to forgo the GGWA presidency in favor of M. **Sep 28:** Klings (in Solingen) writes M asking whether he prefers B. Becker or M. Hess for the GGWA presidency [→ :32].

28. CAPITAL. Sep M to Dec: M works hard on the opus.

29. ENGELS' TRIP. Sep 8–9: E spends a couple of days with M in London. **Sep 10 to Oct AB:** E first joins his mother, who is on holiday in Ramsgate, and then takes a trip through Schleswig-Holstein (where the fighting has ended), getting acquainted with the political situation and the state of the Austrian and Prussian armies.

30. THE INTERNATIONAL: NAMES AND ABBREVIATIONS. In this *Chronicle*, to avoid confusion, we use a uniform nomenclature for the offices and official bodies of the International, even though there was a certain variation. For further info, see *IWMA.

The Organization. The full English name was usually International Working Men's Association, in four words (*abbrev.*: IWMA).

The Leading Committee. Its most common name eventually became General Council (*abbrev.* GC). Here we use this exclusively. In point of fact it started as a Provisional Comm, named itself Central Council in the first month, and settled on General Council only toward the end of 1866.

Officers. Besides a president (whose office was abolished in Sep 1867), the GC was run by a general secretary (*abbrev.* gen secy) and served by members appointed to act as liaison with given countries or nationalities. A liaison officer was called a corresponding secretary (*abbrev.* corr secy) for the given country. Marx was the corr secy for Germany.

Executive Committee. This function was performed by a comm of officers and corresponding secretaries called the Sub-Committee, sometimes the Standing Committee. Here we use the first only (*abbrev.* Sub-Comm).

Note: In reporting motions, proposals, nominations, etc., we assume they are carried, unless otherwise specified or qualified.

OCTOBER

31. IWMA: FIRST DAYS. Oct 5: The Prov Comm elected at the St. Martin's Hall meeting [← :26] holds its first session at 18 Greek Street, Soho. M proposes Cremer as secy, and states that the corr secy for Germany will be named by the GWEA (which will name M). A Sub-Comm of nine is elected to draft a programmatic statement; M is included, though by this time he has left the meeting with Eccarius. **Oct 8, 11:** Ill with carbuncles, M misses the first session of the Sub-Comm and the second session of the GC, at which program drafts and by-laws (Rules) are presented by Weston, an old Owenite, and Maj. Luigi Wolff, a Mazzini follower (later revealed to be a Bonapartist agent). **Oct 12:** Eccarius informs M about the two meetings and of the drafts submitted. **Oct 13:** Cremer notifies M of the Sub-Comm session of Oct 15; M does not attend it. **Oct 18:** At GC: M is "frightened" by Le Lubez's programmatic statement and L. Wolff's proposed Mazzinist-type Rules for "a sort of central government" of the working classes. Le Lubez's "sentiments" are adopted, but M and Eccarius succeed in having the text referred back to the Sub-Comm. **Oct 20:** The Sub-Comm session at M's house discusses the drafts, and decides to meet again on Oct 27, leaving the drafts with M. **Oct 21–27:** M casts his new programmatic draft in the form of an "address to the working classes" (the Inaugural Address, #M397), and also recasts the Rules (#M707). **Oct 27:** The Sub-Comm adopts M's drafts with slight change [→ :35].

32. GGWA AFTER LASSALLE. Oct 1: Countess Hatzfeldt writes M asking him to compose a memoir in appreciation of Lassalle. **Oct 4:** M replies to Klings [← :27] that both B. Becker and Hess are too weak for the GGWA presidency; that he (M) has already written declining the post [perhaps to Liebknecht]; but he suggests that the congress might go ahead and elect him, as a "party demonstration" against the government and bourgeoisie, thereby giving him an occasion to make a political statement in declining. **Oct c.9:** Liebknecht writes M proposing that he should decline the presidency, if it is offered, in favor of B. Becker. Schweitzer et al are planning a weekly organ. **Oct 16:** M replies to Hatzfeldt [← :32] without accepting her proposal.

33. *CAPITAL*. Oct 4: M writes Klings that hopefully the opus will be finished in a couple of months.

34. STUDIES (E). Oct CD: After returning to Manchester, E continues his studies on German philology and history.

NOVEMBER

35. IWMA: INAUGURAL ADDRESS. Nov 1: At GC: M reads his draft of the Inaugural Address (#M707) and Provisional Rules (#M707) [← :31]; they are adopted unanim, except that the word "profitmongers" is struck out by a vote of 11–10. **Nov 5:** The Address and Rules are pubd in *Bee-Hive*. **Nov c.24:** They are pubd as a pamphlet. **Nov 29:** M sends six copies of the pamphlet to Kugelmann, for forwarding also to Bertha Markheim and Miquel. **Nov D to Dec A:** M sends out copies of the pamphlet to

various countries: to Bakunin (in Italy), also for forwarding to Garibaldi; to Schily (in Paris), for i.a. Tolain, Elie Reclus; to Weydemeyer, et al. M also informs his friends about the founding of the IWMA. In his letter to Bakunin, M suggests an Italian trans of the Inaugural Address.

36. IWMA: ORGANIZATION. Nov 1: At GC: New members are co-opted; M proposes Pfänder and Lessner. **Nov 4:** M writes E his first detailed letter recounting the founding of the IWMA. **Nov 7:** E responds with dubiety about the IWMA's prospects, but he is glad M is in contact with working-class representatives. **Nov 8:** At GC: M proposes that GC reports be communicated to the press. Under co-optations, M proposes Lochner, Kaub. He moves that no one can be a GC member who is unable to attend meetings. **Nov 15:** At GC: M attends. **Nov 22:** At GC: M proposes that workers' organizations be invited to join as a body, with a representative on the GC. With M seconding, Eccarius is elected one of two vice-presidents. **Nov 29:** At GC: M proposes that only paid-up members can be elected to the GC.

37. IWMA: THE ADDRESS TO LINCOLN. Nov 22: At GC: A. Dick proposes an address congratulating Lincoln on reelection, to be drafted by the Sub-Comm. **Nov 22–29:** M works on drafting the address (#M884). **Nov 29:** At GC: M's draft, presented by the Sub-Comm, is unanim adopted. In the ensuing argument on whether the address should be presented by an M.P., it is decided that "working men should rely on themselves and not seek for extraneous aid."

38. GERMANY: GGWA AFFAIRS. Nov 4: Liebknecht writes M requesting that M&E write for the *Social-Demokrat* which Schweitzer is founding in Berlin Dec 1, and reporting that B. Becker is assured of the GGWA presidency since Lassalle's testament nominates him to that post. **Nov 11:** Schweitzer sends M an invitation to write for his forthcoming paper, enclosing a prospectus. **Nov M:** M&E exchange letters on the Schweitzer proposal, on the list of other contributors, the bad title ("Social-democrat" instead of a class title like "Proletarian," they say), etc. **Nov c.17:** M writes Liebknecht agreeing to collaborate, i.a. on the ground that the paper's prospectus shows no overt Lassallean thesis or glorification of Lassalle. M also sends the Inaugural Address (#M397) for publ. **Nov 19:** Schweitzer again presses M to accept, and asks for comments on the prospectus. **Nov 28:** Schweitzer writes M greeting M&E's acceptance.

39. KARL BLIND. Nov c.20: M receives from Weydemeyer (letter to E of Oct) info on Blind's attacks on Lassalle in the German-

American press. **Nov 21:** Countess Hatzfeldt writes M asking him to reply to an attack on Lassalle by Blind, pubd Nov 17 in the Stuttgart *Beobachter*, in which Blind also boasts of his influence in America. **Nov 28:** M writes a reply to Blind (#M900) and sends it to the *Beobachter* with a covering letter (#M462); M mentions Lassalle only in his last paragraph, since the problem is complicated by the fact that Blind attacked Lassalle's pro-Bismarckism, though only for his own purposes [→ :47].

40. POLITICAL AFFAIRS. **Nov 3:** Informed of Bakunin's presence in London, M pays him a visit (their first meeting in 16 years); they discuss the Polish uprising of 1863–64 and the IWMA; Bakunin promises to work for the IWMA in Italy, where he is going tomorrow. **Nov 9:** E sends M a *Manchester Guardian* clipping of Nov 8 showing how the work projects set up for relief of the unemployed are used by the bourgeoisie as means of saving money on local taxes; E stresses that this is worse even than the French "National Workshops" of 1848. **Nov 24:** In a letter to Weydemeyer, E analyzes the military advantages of the South over the North, and predicts that with the end of slavery the US will see a boom assuring it a new place in history.

41. *CAPITAL.* **Nov 18:** For the opus, M asks E for pubd material on the crisis in the cotton industry and its effect on the workers. **Nov 29:** M tells Kugelmann the opus will be ready for printing "next year."

42. PERSONAL. **Nov AB:** M is suffering from carbuncles, unable to work.

43. ENGELS. **Nov 2:** E's letter to M describes his impressions of Schleswig on his trip [← :29]. **Nov 7:** E attends a meeting of the Board of Directors of the Schiller Institute in Manchester [← :21].

DECEMBER

44. IWMA: POLISH QUESTION. **Dec 6:** The Sub-Comm takes up the Address to the Polish people proposed by Peter Fox and the British GC members (referred by the GC on Nov 29). M criticizes Fox's view of France's record on Poland, and other points; M stresses "the constant betrayal of Poland by the French from Louis XV to Bonaparte III." The Sub-Comm decides that the draft is to be altered in

accord with M's proposals. **Dec 13:** At GC: Fox's view of France's foreign policy is debated, with M and others critical; debate to be continued. **Dec 20:** At GC: Fox defends his position again. The Minutes record no other discussion; debate to be continued. **Dec 29:** At GC: With M absent, Fox proposes deferral again. **Dec:** M draws up extensive notes on France's relation to the Polish struggle for liberation (#M665), for use in the next GC discussion [→ 65:5].

45. IWMA: PROBLEMS AND PUBL. **Dec 2:** M asks E to buy shares in *Bee-Hive* since the GC is trying to get control away from Potter [→ 65:32]. **Dec 10:** M sends E a report on IWMA developments, incl the Polish question (see ← :44). L. Blanc would like to become an honorary member but M has seen to it that this category does not exist. **Dec 23, 25:** The Address to Lincoln (#M884) [← :37] is pubd in the British press. **Dec:** The Inaugural Address (#M397) is pubd in Schweitzer's *Social-Demokrat*, in M's German trans.

46. GERMANY: GGWA AFFAIRS. **Dec c.18:** In a letter to Liebknecht, M criticizes the Lassalle cult of the *Social-Demokrat*, calls on Liebknecht to win German organizations and trade unions for the IWMA, and protests against the *Social-Demokrat*'s publ of his private letter on Lassalle to Hatzfeldt. **Dec 22:** Writing to Siebel (in Elberfeld), M suggests that Klings should propose unity with the IWMA to the forthcoming GGWA congress in Düsseldorf, Dec 27. —Writing to Hatzfeldt, M rejects the idea of reprinting his *18th Brumaire* (#M267). **Dec 30:** Schweitzer replies to M's criticisms [← :46] only with the request that he have patience (i.e., shut up).

47. KARL BLIND. **Dec 3:** M's reply to Blind (#M900) [← :39] is not pubd by the Stuttgart *Beobachter*, only his covering letter (#M462). **Dec 10:** M's reply (#M900) is pubd in another German paper through Hatzfeldt's good offices.

YEAR APPENDIX

48. Under date June D to Aug AB, M reads a number of works on physiology and anatomy, by the following authors i.a.: W. B. Carpenter, P. B. Lord, A. Kölliker, J. G. Spurzheim, T. Schwann, and M. J. Schleiden.

1865

CONSPECTUS

1. This is the busiest year for M since 1849 or 1850. In the first place it is the first full year of his activity in the General

Council (GC) of the International (IWMA). He attends 30 (out of 47) GC sessions, meetings of the so-called Sub-Committee (the GC's exec comm), and other IWMA business bodies. He becomes the de facto leader of the organization, because of his intellectual domination of the leading people and the confidence reposed in him by the block of British trade-unionists as well as most of the Continental members of the GC. He holds no executive post, only member of the Sub-Comm and corr secy for Germany (occasionally corr secy for some other country).

2. As a consequence of IWMA activity M also becomes involved in other arenas: the Reform League—a propaganda group for electoral reform, a wider franchise, founded at a Feb 23 mass meeting, dominated by IWMA people but always in danger of going over to control by its bourgeois-liberal wing; the Land and Labour League; the newspaper *Workman's Advocate*. M's relation to the movement in Germany—at this point dominated by Lassalle's group, the GGWA—is also intertwined with the prospects for the IWMA in that country, esp after M&E break with the Lassallean leader J. B. von Schweitzer in Feb. After Feb, M's connections are with the anti-Lassallean opposition, esp Liebknecht. (He scarcely knows Bebel as yet.)

3. Yet throughout the year—with interruptions due to illness, trips, etc.—M keeps working on *Capital*, and by the end of the year succeeds in finishing what he considers to be the ms of the first three books (vols.) of his economics opus. While the final draft of Vol. 1 still lies ahead, this is the main ms—taken together with the notebooks of 1861–63— from which the rest of the work will later be quarried by E. But as before, M is still dogged by financial difficulties, and shored up by E's generosity. KMC gives a figure: for the second half of this year, E's donations to M amount to £95. —*Indefinite Date:* All "Confessions" game forms occur in this year; see #M170, #E178, and → :18.

4. Let us repeat two things to be kept in mind for the life of the IWMA. (1) In reports of GC and other meetings, all proposals, motions, etc. are assumed to be carried unless otherwise qualified. (2) Rubrics are not exclusory: those that do not mention IWMA affairs may still include IWMA affairs; the rubric "IWMA: GC sessions" is not the only one where GC sessions may be mentioned; the rubric "Political Affairs" usually means "*Other* Political Affairs," since IWMA affairs are prob covered under other headings; and so on.

JANUARY

5. IWMA: GC SESSIONS. **Jan:** M attends Jan 3, 24, 31; absent Jan 10, 17. **Jan 3:** At GC: As discussion resumes on Fox's address on Poland [← :44], M gives a historical talk on France's policy re Polish liberation, based on his notes (#M665); the GC votes to amend the

address accordingly. **Jan 24:** At GC: M reports that the GGWA expresses its agreement with the IWMA but cannot affiliate for legal reasons (see his draft report, #M251.5). —M proposes a procedure for electing (co-opting) new GC members. **Jan 31:** At GC: Regarding the forthcoming founding of the Reform League, M proposes two conditions of support: programmatic advocacy of universal manhood suffrage, and IWMA representatives on the leading comm.

6. MARX IN MANCHESTER. **Jan c.7–14:** M stays with E in Manchester, discussing IWMA and GGWA affairs. **Jan 13:** They meet with E. Jones.

7. GERMANY: GGWA. **Jan A:** As the Prussian government confiscates the first regular numbers of the new *Social-Demokrat*, M writes Schweitzer urging him to break with the regime. **Jan 13:** *Social-Demokrat* pubs a Paris article by Hess attacking the Paris members of the IWMA, esp Tolain, as Bonapartists. (Schweitzer had pubd a previous attack on the IWMA, Dec 30, in a "Message" by the GGWA pres. B. Becker.) **Jan 14, 16:** M writes to Schily (in Paris) for info on Hess's article (SOURCE: *KMC; GCFI* gives date as Jan 16). **Jan 16:** M writes Schweitzer a stiff letter protesting the two attacks on the IWMA, asking if this is a declaration of war. **Jan 19:** Schily informs M that the slanderous charges against Tolain (above) emanate from the co-op organ *L'Association*, whose ed board includes Lefort. **Jan c.20:** Liebknecht informs M, on the basis of info from Hatzfeldt, about Lassalle's proposal to Bismarck: GGWA support of Prussia's policy of conquest in Schleswig-Holstein in exchange for universal suffrage. Liebknecht asks M to support B. Becker against Hatzfeldt, and to write in this sense to Klings and J. P. Becker. **Jan c.22 to c.25:** M communicates Liebknecht's view to Klings via Siebel and to J. P. Becker via Schily. **Jan CD:** From replies by Schily and Schweitzer to his letters of Jan 14 and 16, M concludes that publ of the Hess articles was not Schweitzer's fault but due to the "pure and simple asininity" of Liebknecht (who works with Schweitzer on the *Social-Demokrat*) and the asininity-cum-malice of Hess. **Jan 24:** Acceding to Schweitzer's request of Jan 23, in order to make up for his letter of Jan 16, M writes an essay on Proudhon (who died on Jan 19) in the form of a letter to the editor (#M593). In M's mind the criticisms partly apply to Lassalle too [→ :17]. **Jan c.25:** M writes Schweitzer insisting that he must come out against Bismarck and avoid even the semblance of a flirtation between the workers' party and "Pissmarck" (as M reports to E, Feb 3). **Jan 27:** In the *Social-Demokrat* Schweitzer pubs the first of a number of

articles (going on till Mar 1) which establish his pro-Bismarck orientation.

8. ENGELS AND THE GGWA. Jan 25: In a letter to E reporting on IWMA and GGWA affairs, M suggests that since the *Social-Demokrat* wants E to contribute, a good subject might be the current question of Prussian military reform, which might permit a critique of both the liberal Progressives and the Lassalleans and their relation to the Prussian regime. Jan D: E agrees, and begins work on an essay, which will indeed turn into a pamphlet (#E644) [→ :16]. Jan c.27: E revises his 1862 trans of an old Danish song "Herr Tidmann," directed against the feudal aristocracy (#E349), and sends it to the *Social-Demokrat* for publ, with a commentary implicitly baiting the pro-Bismarck line of the paper [→ :17]. Jan 27: Re Liebknecht's info about Lassalle and Bismarck [← :7], E writes M that this was objectively a betrayal of the German workers' movement to the Prussian regime regardless of Lassalle's subjective motivation; he raises the question of making this info about Lassalle public.

9. IWMA: FRENCH SECTION. Jan 24: On the basis of the rumors spread by Hess's article [← :7] and charges of Bonapartism rife about Tolain and the Paris section, the GC discusses the situation. On M's proposal it is agreed to hold up sending membership cards to Paris till the truth is investigated and Schily sends further reports [→ :13].

10. POLITICAL AFFAIRS. Jan c.A: M writes Bakunin (in Florence) [← 64:40] for news of what he is doing (SOURCE: *KMC*). Jan 25: M, in a letter to E, asks Lizzie Burns to become an individual member of the IWMA, stressing that membership is open to women.

11. *CAPITAL*. Jan 30: Strohn informs M that the Hamburg pub'r Meissner says he will be glad to publish the opus, terms to be settled [→ :20].

FEBRUARY

12. IWMA: GC SESSIONS. Feb: M attends all four—Feb 7, 14, 21, 28. Feb 14: M reports on the formation of a Manchester branch and on steps in Switzerland to form a section.

13. IWMA: THE FRENCH CONFLICT BEGINS. Feb 5: Schily (in Paris) sends M another report which leads M to believe that the conflict in the French section is settled [← :9]. Feb 7: GC session hears a letter from Fribourg to Le Lubez saying that Tolain is willing to resign if necessary in view of the GC's Jan 24 action. But the GC decides not to accept the resignation on the ground that it does not believe the rumors about the Bonapartist links of the Paris section leaders. M then proposes that Lefort be appointed the IWMA's "literary defense"

(press representative and defender) in Paris. Feb 21: GC hears there is a sharp conflict in Paris between the Proudhonist tendency led by Tolain and Fribourg and the republican tendency which supports Lefort. It decides to send Le Lubez to Paris to settle the differences, and (on M's proposal) appoints Schily to cooperate with Le Lubez. Feb c.22: M writes Schily personally about his appointment and makes suggestions on how to smooth over the conflict, above all to make sure the Paris section stays in the IWMA. Feb 24: The Paris section (Proudhonist-dominated) votes to protest the GC's appointment of Lefort on the ground that only workers should hold leading positions; this resolution, signed by 32 members, is directed to the GC. Feb 25 (rec'd 28): Schily informs M about Paris's opposition to the GC appointment of Lefort, also Le Lubez's opposition. Feb 28: GC session, with Tolain and Fribourg present representing the resolution of the 32, hears a long discussion on their report (M participating), and finally refers further inquiry to the Sub-Comm.

14. TENSION WITH SCHWEITZER AND THE GGWA. Feb 1: Schweitzer's *Social-Demokrat* pubs another article by Hess retailing current slanderous rumors about the French IWMA's ties with Bonaparte [← :7]. Feb 2: M writes a "furious letter" to Liebknecht [cf ← :7] with a "very last warning" of a break with the *Social-Demokrat* if its policy does not change. Feb 3: M writes E consulting on next steps, with the aim of making a "declaration of war" against the "knaves or fools" who look to a working-class alliance with Bismarck (i.e., Schweitzer). Feb 4: Schweitzer writes M asking him to keep in mind "how difficult our position is" in Germany; the main thing is to "grow strong." Feb 5: Schweitzer pubs the second article in his series on the Bismarck ministry, clearly showing his "flirtation with Bismarck" (E to M, Feb 7). Feb 6: M sends E a draft statement to be sent to Schweitzer attacking the Hess articles and laying the basis for a possible break. Feb c.8: M sends this joint statement to Schweitzer (#ME182). Feb 11: Schweitzer writes M to mollify him with retractions in the paper: Hess is to retract, and the editor is to state that his own investigation shows the Hess charges are untrue; however, Schweitzer's letter ignores the M–E statement's thrusts at Bonapartist pro-Bismarckism. Feb 12: The *Social-Demokrat* pubs Hess's retraction. —Liebknecht writes M on the situation in the GGWA, and advises that M's break should be pitched on political grounds under the circumstances.

15. BREAK WITH SCHWEITZER AND THE GGWA. Feb 13: M decides not to press for publ of the statement (#ME182) because of the retraction and because a break should be motivated by the *Social-Demokrat*'s pro-Bismarckism. To E, M advises they should write no more for the paper. To Schweitzer, M writes a longish letter summarizing their political relations and criticizing the Lassallean policy on Bismarck, the Lassalle personal cult, anti–trade-unionism, the democratic struggle against Prussianism, etc. **Feb 15:** Replying to M's letter of Feb 13, Schweitzer says he is willing to learn from M on "theoretical questions" but not on "practical questions of current tactics," i.e., M cannot judge his policy of alliance with Bismarckian Prussianism. —The same day Schweitzer pubs another article in his pro-Bismarck series implicitly arguing for a favorable attitude toward the regime. **Feb 17:** In still another article Schweitzer extols the regime for its program to solve the "workers' question," and urges Bismarck to go forward "if necessary with blood and iron." —Liebknecht gives Schweitzer a warning against these *Social-Demokrat* articles, and writes M to this effect. **Feb 18:** M is in receipt of Schweitzer's letter of Feb 15, his pro-Bismarck articles in the paper of Feb 15 and 17, and Liebknecht's letter of Feb 17—all adding up to a breaking point. M drafts a statement breaking off further relations with the *Social-Demokrat*, and characterizing Lassalleanism as "royal Prussian government-socialism." He sends the draft to E, saying that Schweitzer is "hopeless—prob in a secret understanding with Bismarck." **Feb 22:** E sends the statement back with his approval. **Feb 23:** M sends the statement (#ME166) to Schweitzer, via Liebknecht, for publ in the paper. M sends two copies to Siebel, for publ in the German press. —In a letter to Kugelmann, M gives an extensive summary presentation of his views on Lassalleanism, Schweitzer's course, and the value of the IWMA. **Feb 28:** At the GC session M announces his break with Schweitzer's *Social-Demokrat*.

16. ENGELS' PAMPHLET. **Feb 9:** E finishes the draft of a pamphlet on *The Prussian military question and the German workers' party* (#E644), which he had begun [← :8] as an article for the *Social-Demokrat* but now plans to publish separately; he sends it to M. **Feb 10, 11:** M sends E a number of suggestions and emendations on the ms. **Feb 12–13:** E revises his ms accordingly. **Feb 27:** E writes an announcement (#E21) for the forthcoming pamphlet and sends it to friends in Germany for publ in the press (pubd in Mar).

17. W&P. **Feb 1–5:** M's essay-letter on Proudhon (#M593) [← :7] is pubd in the *Social-Demokrat*. **Feb 5:** E's trans of "Herr

Tidmann" (#E349) [← :8] is pubd in *Social-Demokrat*.

18. ECCARIUS INCIDENT. **Feb c.7:** M gives a talk at the 25th anniversary celebration of the London GWEA; he criticizes the Lassallean view on state aid to producers' cooperatives. **Feb 15:** The *Social-Demokrat* pubs a report on the meeting, written by Eccarius, in which M's view is badly distorted. **Feb 22–25:** Eccarius, questioned, admits that Schweitzer had not altered his report; the distortion was his own. M writes Liebknecht about this, and in a letter to E, relates his astonishment over Eccarius's "blunder," which he ascribes to illness.

19. POLITICAL AFFAIRS. **Feb 7:** Bakunin (in Italy) writes M [← :10] a letter excusing his silence and inactivity for the IWMA. **Feb c.9–10:** M takes part in a comm to organize on Mar 1 a meeting celebrating the Polish uprising of 1863 (Feb D, on behalf of the GC, he will oppose efforts by liberals to postpone the meeting as inopportune) [→ :25]. **Feb M:** M makes the acquaintance of Paul Lafargue, who visits him with a recommendatory letter from Tolain. **Feb c.20:** M is proposed as editor of the reorganized *Bee-Hive*, and (Feb 25) he so informs E. (M will decline.) **Feb 23:** The Reform League [← :2] is founded, with M's enthusiastic support behind the scenes in the IWMA. **Feb 25:** M boasts to E that the IWMA effectively controls the new Reform League through the trade-unionists in its leadership. (In this period M meets with, and corresponds with, E. Jones on the League's work and policies.)

20. *CAPITAL.* **Feb 5:** E writes M in approval of a deal with Meissner for publ [← :11], urging M (as usual) to make haste. **Feb 9** (rec'd c.12): Strohn sends M a draft of a contract with Meissner for publ of *Capital.* **Feb to Mar M:** Despite his involvement in IWMA and other affairs, M works intensively on the opus, often at night.

21. PERSONAL. **Feb 6:** E attends a meeting of the Board of Directors of the Schiller Institute. **Feb M to Mar M:** M suffers from carbuncles and furuncles. **Feb c.27 to Mar 7:** M is visited by his brother-in-law J. C. Juta of Cape Town and his niece Caroline Schmalhausen of Maastricht.

MARCH

22. IWMA: GC SESSIONS. **Mar:** M attends Mar 7, 14; absent Mar 21, 28, because of his trip.

23. IWMA: FRENCH CONFLICT. **Mar 4, 6:** The Sub-Comm, commissioned by the GC [← :13], meets twice on the dispute, with Tolain and Fribourg present. In preparation for the first meeting M has jotted down notes based on Schily's letters (#M576.5), and has drafted motions (#M621.5) which are adopted by the Sub-Comm. They confirm the present French leadership; withdraw Lefort's appointment [← :13] while urging his collaboration in the movement, because the GC cannot impose an officer on a section; and appoint Schily as GC delegate to the Paris exec. **Mar 7:** GC adopts four resolutions drafted by M on behalf of the Sub-Comm (with some modification), also special instructions to Schily on Lefort's right to form a parallel branch in Paris. GC stresses it does not accept the French principle limiting official posts to workers. (Note: For the resolutions, see GC Minutes, in *GCFI* 1:76. *MEW* 16:82 gives, in German trans, the text of the resolutions as drafted in M's notebook. These are not in the *Register*.) **Mar 11:** Cremer and Fox visit M to discuss the Paris conflict. **Mar 12:** Jung asks help from M in drawing up a summary of the Paris conflict for French members. (M agrees the next day.) **Mar 14:** At GC: In response to protest against appointment of a non-Frenchman (Schily), M says that Schily, who does not want the job, would resign if there were opposition to him in France. (On Mar 20, Schily writes M refusing to accept the appointment.) **Mar 16–18:** M draws up a memorandum for Jung's guidance on the issues in the French conflict (#M508), and (Mar 18) goes over it with Jung.

24. GERMANY: GGWA. **Mar 1:** M&E's statement breaking with the *Social-Demokrat* (#ME166) is pubd in eight German papers. **Mar 3:** It is pubd in the *Social-Demokrat* itself, and elsewhere. **Mar c.7:** E's pamphlet *The Prussian military question* [etc.] (#E644) is pubd by Meissner (Hamburg). **Mar 8:** In response, Schweitzer pubs an article giving a distorted account of M&E's action, even citing Karl Blind's attack on M. **Mar c.13:** M writes a review notice (#M765) of E's pamphlet, and sends it to *Hermann* for publ. **Mar 15:** M writes a reply to Schweitzer, describing the events leading up to the break (#M861); pubd in *Berliner Reform* Mar 19, and in other papers Mar 20–25. **Mar 18:** M's review notice (#M765) of E's pamphlet is pubd in *Hermann*. It highlights the difference in the pamphlet's attitude toward bourgeois progressivism and feudal reaction resp. **Mar 26:** The *Social-Demokrat* pubs a virulent speech made Mar 22 by GGWA pres B. Becker, against M, Liebknecht and the IWMA. Around this time, also, Schweitzer pubs another attack on M. **Mar 28:** M writes a rejoinder to the latest attack by Schweitzer, decrying the need to polemize against Lassalle "sycophants" (#M925); pubd Apr 1. **Mar 29:** Liebknecht writes M on the situation in the GGWA, the Berlin organizn's

proposal to depose B. Becker, and his (Liebknecht's) speech of Mar 27 against Becker's attack on M. (Liebknecht mails this letter on Apr 1.)

25. POLITICAL AFFAIRS. **Mar 1:** M attends the meeting on the Polish anniversary, in St. Martin's Hall, which he helped organize [← :19]. The meeting adopts a resolution in the name of the IWMA [→ :29]. **Mar 2:** F. A. Lange (in Duisburg) writes E asking M&E to support a planned periodical. M suggests, Mar 7, that E decline politely. **Mar 10:** Writing to Weydemeyer, E surveys the course of the military operations in the US Civil War. **Mar 11, Mar M:** In connection with a Mar 11 joint conference of John Bright's group of bourgeois radicals who are for "household suffrage" only, M is burdened with frequent consultation with IWMA people active in the Reform League, who are concerned about the forthcoming electoral-reform bill [→ :34]. **Mar M:** Klings, on his way to America, stops off in London and visits M. **Mar 16:** E. Jones (in Manchester) writes M, re the coming Reform Conference, that he will support the IWMA position (universal manhood suffrage) against the liberal proposal (household suffrage). **Mar 18:** M, on the eve of leaving for Zaltbommel (see → :27), sends Jung a note on Jones's letter, for a report to the next GC meeting (#M566.5). **Mar 29:** E replies to Lange, incl a critique of Lange's book on the "labor question."

26. CAPITAL. **Mar 21:** Pub'r Meissner sends M a contract for *Capital*, stipulating that the whole ms must be in by the end of May at the latest. (The letter arrives Mar c.23, while M is away.)

27. PERSONAL; MARX'S TRIP. **Mar 6:** E attends a Board of Directors meeting of the Schiller Institute. **Mar 13:** Writing to E, M complains he is "hellishly harassed" by his great workload and long night hours resulting from working on *Capital* along with his work for the IWMA, "since I am in fact the head of the thing." **Mar 19 to Apr 8:** M travels to Zaltbommel, Neth., to visit his relatives, the Philips family.

APRIL

28. MARX IN ZALTBOMMEL. **Apr 1:** Staying with the Philips family [← :27] M fills out a "Confessions" game form (#M170Z). **Apr 8:** M leaves Zaltbommel for home.

29. IWMA. **Apr:** GC sessions: M attends Apr 11, 25; absent Apr 4 (on trip). **Apr 11:** M attends the GC for the first time since Mar 14. He is named corr secy for Belgium, replacing the resigned Le Lubez (and will retain this post till Jan 16, 1866); he proposes Dupont as corr secy for France; he reports on the arrest of

Charles Longuet (in Paris) for publishing an antigovernment pamphlet; and supports a motion to tighten up conditions for membership in the GC. **Apr 13:** M asks H. Jung, corr secy for Switzerland, to send *Der Weisse Adler* (Zurich) a correction to its report on the Mar 1 Polish meeting in London (#M185); pubd Apr 22. **Apr 15:** As corr secy for Belgium M writes Fontaine (in Brussels) asking for a report on the IWMA in the country. —Liebknecht sends M a letter from the Berlin compositors' union (of which Liebknecht is a leader) asking for help to the Leipzig printers, on strike since Mar D. **Apr c.20:** M writes Schily (in Paris) about help for the Leipzig printers. **Apr 25:** At GC: M reports on the German printers' strike and their request, and is named to a delegation to the London compositors' union. —M nominates Schapper as GC member. (Schapper is elected on May 2.)

30. GERMANY: GGWA. **Apr 8:** M writes a rejoinder to B. Becker's attack [← :24], entitled "The 'President of Humanity'" (#M688); pubd Apr 13. **Apr 12:** M attacks the opportunism of the GGWA leadership in a talk to the London GWEA. **Apr c.26:** M asks Liebknecht to recruit individual members of GGWA to IWMA; this points to the perspective of forming IWMA branches in Germany parallel to GGWA.

31. *CAPITAL.* **Apr 12:** In response to M's request, E sends him info on the development of the cotton crisis in England and worldwide.

MAY

32. IWMA AFFAIRS. **May:** GC sessions: M attends all six—May 2, 9, 16, 20, 23, 30. **May 2:** At GC: M reports that the French section is reorganizing (based on Schily's letter of Apr 27). Cremer proposes an address to Americans on the assassination of Lincoln. **May 2–9:** M drafts an address to Pres. Andrew Johnson on the Lincoln assassination (#M5). **May 9:** At GC: M's draft address (#M5) is adopted unanim. (Signed by GC and dated May 13; pubd May 20 and after.) —M writes E again [← 64:45] asking him to buy *Bee-Hive* shares to help the GC gain control. **May 16:** At GC: M reports on sending *NYDT* a copy of the address to Johnson, and on a great International meeting on the Lincoln assassination held in Geneva and addressed by J. P. Becker. **May 30:** As the GC discusses the English government's plan to hold an International Exhibition, M recommends concentrating on the IWMA's own congress to be held in Belgium.

33. IWMA: DEBATE WITH WESTON. **May 2:** Weston begins reading to the GC his paper

on his anti-TU viewpoint (which he first raised in M's absence on Apr 4). **May 20:** GC holds a special meeting (no minutes extant) at which Weston completes his presentation of his view that TU struggles for higher wages are useless and even harmful, theses which he has been writing about in *Bee-Hive*. —M sends E a short report on Weston's views. **May 23:** At GC, Weston "resumed the adjourned debate on his proposition regarding wages" (GC Minutes). M gives an extempore criticism in opposition; further debate is deferred [→ :38].

34. POLITICAL AFFAIRS. **May 1, 13:** M reports to E with great enthusiasm on the work of the Reform League [← :25] under IWMA leadership.

35. *CAPITAL.* **May 9:** M writes E that he expects *Capital* will be finished by Sep 1, despite interruptions. **May to July D:** M works intensively on the opus [→ :43]. **May to July:** In debating with Weston in the GC (see ← :33), M is making advance use of ideas of polit eco which he has worked out for *Capital* and which he has not otherwise written up.

36. PERSONAL. **May 1:** A social gathering at M's house for daughter Jenny's birthday is attended by E. Jones, Odger, Cremer, Fox, Jung. **May M to c.Oct:** Edgar von Westphalen returns from Texas and lives with the M family. **May to July:** M suffers continually from carbuncles and bilious attacks. **May 20:** M remarks to E that, when he lacks the patience to read or write because of carbuncles, he spends time studying the differential calculus.

JUNE

37. IWMA AFFAIRS. **June:** GC sessions: M attends June 6, 20, 27; absent June 13. **June 6:** At GC: M takes part in discussing the need for a newspaper as organ of the British workers, on the basis of a proposal by an American, Leon Lewis (with suspicious motives, M thinks). **June 24:** M reports to E he has convinced the GC members to postpone holding a regular congress in favor of a limited conference in London [→ :41].

38. IWMA: DEBATE WITH WESTON. **June 6:** At GC, M announces that when Weston's views come up again, he will read a paper in reply and propose counterresolutions. **June 20:** At GC, M reads the first part of his anti-Weston paper, followed by brief discussion. **June 27:** At GC, M presents the rest of his paper. (See #M971 for its later publ as *Wages* [or *Value*], *price and profit*; see #M972 for M's notes.) Debate is postponed to the next session. There is sentiment to print the papers by both Weston and M, but money is lacking. M himself is not eager to see publ because Weston is not a worthy opponent and the publ would anticipate part of the content of *Capital*.

39. READING AND STUDY. **June 24:** M tells E he has read Regnault's *La question européenne* (1863), and expresses interest in the theory of Prof. Duchinski that the Great Russians are not Slavs.

40. PERSONAL. **June-July:** M is in financial need, since setting up the household and paying debts has cost him about £500.

JULY

41. IWMA. **July:** GC sessions: M attends only July 4; absent July 11, 18, 25. (See → :44.) **July 4:** At GC: Discussion begins on the Weston–M debate, by Eccarius and others; M is present but not recorded as speaking. (Discussion will continue at the July 18 and Aug 15 sessions, without M.) **July 25:** At GC (M absent): The Sub-Comm presents the position prepared by M [← :37] proposing that a preliminary conference be held in London in Sep in lieu of a regular congress, together with a proposed agenda. —M writes Fontaine (in Brussels) making clear that IWMA sections have the right to elect their own representatives to the GC; he also reports the decision to hold a conference.

42. GERMAN AFFAIRS. **July c.4:** Liebknecht informs M that he has been expelled from Berlin (and Prussia) by the government.

43. *CAPITAL.* **July D:** M tries to reserve time to work on his opus, in face of the demands of IWMA affairs (cf → :44). **July 31:** Writing to E, M says he still has three chapters to write to finish the first three books (i.e., Vols. 1–3), before going on to the fourth (*Theories of surplus value*) which will be the easiest; but he cannot bring himself to send any part off until the whole work is done, since it constitutes an "artistic whole" and has a dialectical structure; Fox is sure of getting a pub'r for an English trans, which will also pay the best.

44. PERSONAL. **July 29:** M tells the Sub-Comm he will be out of town on a trip for the next two weeks, as a subterfuge to remain undisturbed by IWMA business while he works on *Capital* (in fact he will withdraw for over three weeks) [→ :45]. **July 31:** Writing to E, M apologetically laments his humiliating financial dependence on E, and explains he is mainly concerned about ensuring his daughters' future, now that they are growing up. "The sole thought that sustains me is that the two of us are carrying on a company enterprise in which I am devoting my time to the theoretical and party side of the business."

AUGUST

45. PERSONAL. **Aug AB and M:** While M is temporarily withdrawn from IWMA work [← :44], illness makes it difficult for him to work on *Capital*. He occupies himself with reading on astronomy, esp the astronomical theories of Daniel Kirkwood; he makes inquiries about Kirkwood to W. N. Molesworth and exchanges letters with E about him. (*KMC* dating: July D to Aug c.20; *MEW* dating: Aug.)

46. IWMA. **Aug:** GC sessions: M attends Aug 28; absent Aug 1, 8, 15, and prob 22. **Aug 22:** After skipping the first three GC meetings of the month, M returns to work by attending a meeting of the Sub-Comm. (So according to his letter to E of this date; while there is also a GC meeting this evening, its minutes do not mention M.) Following the GC session there is a meeting of shareholders to transform *The Miner and Workman's Advocate* into *The Workman's Advocate*, under the control of IWMA people; M does attend this meeting. In fact, either this evening or around Aug D, M is elected to the Board of Directors (along with other IWMA leaders) of the new organ which in Sep will become the IWMA's official organ. **Aug 28** (possibly **Aug 29**): M attends this GC session, for the first time since July 4. He sponsors a resolution criticizing *Bee-Hive* for misappropriating a contribution by a Welsh IWMA member, who had complained to the GC.

47. GERMAN AFFAIRS. **Aug 5, 7:** M&E exchange letters lamenting Liebknecht's propensity for blunders, his intellectual laziness, and general incompetence, all of which often leads by reflection to embarrassment for M himself. While Liebknecht writes rosy letters, M complains, he has not organized six people into an IWMA branch. E agrees, but at the moment "he is the only reliable connection we have in Germany." (Note: From here on, M&E's correspondence will be peppered with such expressions of opinion on Liebknecht—whom, by the way, both men like personally.)

48. *CAPITAL.* **Aug c.4–5:** In a letter to M (not extant), E misunderstands M's remarks about an "artistic whole" [← :43]. M explains again that he has to finish the whole ms before printing can begin, but he will do so as fast as possible.

49. ENGELS' TRIP. **Aug D to Sep M:** E goes on a tour of Germany, Switzerland, and Italy (incl a stop in Como).

SEPTEMBER

50. IWMA AFFAIRS. **Sep:** GC sessions: M attends Sep 12, 19; absent Sep 5; the main business is preparing for the London

Conference. **Sep 11:** M writes Liebknecht asking him to attend the conference or send a report on the German movement. **Sep 12:** At GC: M proposes Dell as treasurer. Discussion of the forthcoming conference takes place, M participating (to be continued next meeting). **Sep M:** M invites E. Jones to speak at the anniversary soirée during the conference on Sep 28. (That same day Jones will send M a note pleading inability to attend.) **Sep 19:** M proposes Bobczynski as GC member. He announces he will read a report (Liebknecht's) from Germany, but no German delegates will attend; he also announces his invitation to Jones. M is re-elected to the reorganized nine-member Sub-Comm (at this point called Standing Comm), which proposes that the first regular congress be held in 1866.

51. IWMA: LONDON CONFERENCE. **Sep 25–29:** M attends all sessions, also many comm meetings. **Sep 25** (session): M participates in the discussion of finances and membership dues, and of the *Workman's Advocate* as IWMA organ. He is made a member of a commission to conduct a foreign-correspondence department in the paper. **Sep 26** (session): M proposes for the GC that next year's congress be held in Geneva, in Sep or Oct; he accepts May as a result of the French delegates' arguments. M and Fribourg propose a number of questions to add to the agenda. **Sep 27** (session): M reads the report on the Sub-Comm's meeting with Continental delegates. (He will participate in a similar meeting on Sep 29.) **Sep 28:** A soirée is held in St. Martin's Hall to celebrate the IWMA's founding; M is not scheduled as a speaker; J. P. Becker represents the German-speaking movement.

52. ENGELS' TRIP. **Sep AB to Sep M:** See ← :49.

OCTOBER

53. IWMA. **Oct:** GC sessions: M attends Oct 10, 17; absent Oct 3, 31. **Oct 3:** At GC: M (absent) is commissioned to do the report of the London Conference (later reversed, → :56). **Oct 10:** At GC: M and Bobczynski propose Louis Oborski as GC member. **Oct 17:** At GC: M supports the proposal to cooperate in the Nov 29 anniversary celebration of the Polish uprising of 1830, and has the work assigned to the Sub-Comm. **54.** POLITICAL AFFAIRS. **Oct 8:** Lothar Bucher (ex-Lassallean collaborator with Bismarck) sends M, on Bismarck's behalf, an offer to write a monthly article on economics for the *Preussische Staats-Anzeiger*, i.e., an offer to buy him up. (M sends a sharp refusal, prob Oct c.D.) **Oct 16:** An Urquhartite group,

the Saint Pancras (London) Foreign Affairs Comm, asks M for info about Russia's expansionist aspirations. **55.** PERSONAL. **Oct 1:** De Paepe, Jung, J. P. Becker, and Kaub gather at M's for a (frugal) Sunday dinner. **Oct 20 to Nov c.2:** M stays at E's in Manchester.

NOVEMBER

56. IWMA. **Nov:** GC sessions: M attends Nov 21, 28; absent Nov 14. **Nov 19:** M visits Jung, who is ill, to discuss IWMA affairs. **Nov 21:** At GC: On M's proposal, the provision for a GC report on the first year of the IWMA is rescinded because the French have issued one. M reports on IWMA progress in Germany, based on letters from Liebknecht (Nov 16) and others (Nov 13). M proposes Coullery (in Switzerland) as a GC correspondent. **Nov 28:** At GC: M reports on J. P. Becker's proclamation on behalf of the IWMA in German Switzerland. **57.** GERMANY: GGWA. **Nov 13:** Three active workers in the Berlin movement, Metzner, S. Meyer, and A. Vogt, write M asking him to come to Germany to take over the leadership, or at least to support it with his advice. They describe the bad state of the movement and urge that M's personal presence would contribute to unifying the best forces. (M replies Nov c.D; letter not extant.) **58.** POLITICAL AFFAIRS. **Nov 30:** M receives a membership card in the Land and Labour League. **59.** CAPITAL. **Nov 20:** M asks E to send data on the condition of the workers in Manchester's cotton industry, needed for *Capital*. **60.** PERSONAL. **Nov 3:** J. Conradi writes M that M's aunt Esther Kosel has died in Frankfurt.

DECEMBER

61. CAPITAL. **Dec D:** M finishes his rough draft of all three books (vols.) of *Capital*—so he later (Feb 13, 1866) informs E. For his start on Vol. 1, see → 66:3. **Dec:** For the treatment of ground rent, M's studies in the BM cover the literature on agricultural economics, esp on agrochemistry; he reads Liebig and Schönbein. **62.** IWMA. **Dec:** GC sessions: M attends all—Dec 19, 26. **Dec 18:** J. P. Becker informs M of his plan to publish *Vorbote* as the German-Swiss organ of the IWMA, beginning Jan, and urges M&E to contribute. **Dec 19:** At GC: M reports on the affiliation of new groups in Basel, Zurich, and Geneva. **Dec 26:** At GC: M responds to unsigned attacks on the GC pubd by Vésinier in *L'Echo de Verviers* (Belgium) on Dec 16, 18, as the opening volley by the right-wing Vésinier–Le Lubez faction in the London French emigration.

63. POLITICAL AFFAIRS. **Dec 5:** M participates in a shareholders' meeting of the *Workman's Advocate*, supporting the fight to prevent a takeover by a wing led by a Liberal M.P. **Dec 12:** M attends a mass meeting held

in St. Martin's Hall by the Reform League, an "enormous triumph" by an IWMA-sponsored movement (M to E, Dec 26).

64. GERMANY. GGWA. **Dec 4:** Metzner [← :57] writes M from Berlin on the state of the GGWA. (M's reply of Jan 15 is not extant.)

65. PERSONAL. **Dec:** M is in great financial distress (M to E, Dec 26).

1866

CONSPECTUS

1. M's activity in the IWMA continues to dominate all of his work; see remarks ← 65:1–2. Alongside IWMA affairs are ancillary activities and issues that interpermeate, even where here treated under separate rubrics. For example, there is the Reform League, which M and the IWMA helped to establish as a movement promoting universal suffrage [← 65:2].

2. *Reform League.* In the early part of the year M is still chortling over its successful Dec 12 meeting (M to Kugelmann, Jan 15), but even as he does so (M to J. P. Becker, Jan c.13) he adds that "On the other hand, this movement is taking up too much of our best working-class forces." He will continue to be proud of IWMA influence in the League (cf M to Nannette Philips, Mar 18), but in the course of this year, bourgeois elements in its leadership win a majority for their proposed Reform Bill which is far from universal manhood suffrage (passed 1867). Subseqly (cf Nov 18, 1868) M's correspondence will refer to the "false policies of the Reform League."

3. *Capital.* In Jan or Feb (see → :8, 12) M begins making a "clear copy" for the printer of what will be Vol. 1; this draft steadily takes shape during the year, despite the inevitable interruptions due to money troubles and illness. And in fact in Nov, M actually sends the first batch of ms pages to the publisher. He tells E in retrospect that during this summer and autumn it was not questions of theory that caused most delay, but rather the treatment of "physical and bourgeois conditions" of the economy. (Sometime during this year M also quits further work on his unfinished ms "Results of the immediate process of production," #M759.)

4. *Engels.* His most ambitious political work this year is the essay "What have the working classes to do with Poland?" (#E915), the writing of which extends over three months, Mar to May, though it remains unfinished.

JANUARY

5. IWMA. **Jan:** GC sessions: M attends Jan 9, 16, 23; absent Jan 2, 30. **Jan 9:** At GC: Since at the Jan 2 session Le Lubez again brought up Vésinier's attacks on the GC [← 65:62], M counterattacks; he defends the Paris IWMA from Vésinier's slanders, condemns Vésinier's anonymity as sneaky, and proposes that Vésinier be called on to present evidence for his charges or face expulsion; an amendment by Le Lubez fails to get a second. **Jan 13:** M reports (in a letter to J. P. Becker) that the Vésinier–Le Lubez faction is losing support even among the French, esp Ch. Longuet. **Jan 16:** At GC: M proposes that Longuet be named corr secy for Belgium (instead of M). —From now on the GC is meeting at 18 Bouverie Street, instead of Greek Street [← 64:31]. **Jan 23:** At GC: M agrees with a proposal to discuss principles for the forthcoming congress but proposes this be prepared by defining "the general purposes and ruling principles" of the Inaugural Address and Rules. M presents Liebknecht's letter (see → :7) reporting on the IWMA in Leipzig, and De Paepe's letter of Jan 14 on Belgium. **Jan 27–30:** M meets with Jung and edits the latter's reply to Vésinier's attacks. **Jan 30:** At GC: With M absent, Jung presents the draft; it is referred to the Sub-Comm. (It will be pubd in *L'Echo de Verviers* on Feb 20; the text is in *GCFI* 1:317, 357.)

6. POLITICAL AFFAIRS. **Jan 5, 15:** In an effort to get articles for J. P. Becker's *Vorbote* [← 65:62], M asks E, Kugelmann, and Liebknecht to write for the paper. **Jan 22:** At the St. Martin's Hall meeting celebrating the Polish uprising of 1863, chaired by Oborski, M represents the IWMA in supporting the resolution of sympathy with the Polish liberation struggle.

7. GERMAN MOVEMENT. **Jan 18:** Liebknecht's letter to M recounts his activity for the IWMA in Leipzig. He reports that von Hofstetten, copublisher of the *Social-Demokrat*, has asked if M&E might resume writing for this paper; that he (Liebknecht) offered no hope of this, but he wonders if M&E might not in fact use the paper to propagandize for the IWMA's aims [→ :14].

8. *CAPITAL.* **Jan 1:** M begins making a clear copy for the printer (see ← :3), while revising stylistically, etc.; he works at it intensively—working at the BM by day, writing by night. **Jan 15:** M writes Kugelmann and Liebknecht that he is working at it 12 hours a day, and intends to personally bring the ms to the Hamburg pub'r in Mar. **Jan c.30:** The work comes to a temporary halt as M falls very ill as a result of overwork (see → :11).

9. W&P; PUBL PLANS. **Jan:** S. Meyer (in Berlin) writes M of his plan to publish a new edn of the *Com Manifesto* for distribution to workers [→ :16]. —A. Hilberg (in Vienna) invites M to write for his proposed *Internationale Revue* (Jan 2); M agrees (Jan 15); Hilberg suggests quarterly reports on the English economy (Jan 18) [→ :16]. **Jan 5:** M asks E to write a piece explaining why workers should support Polish independence, since the issue is the crux of the right-wing opposition faction organized around the new London French branch (Le Lubez) and the "Proudhonist gang in Brussels" (Vésinier). **Jan 26:** E asks M for material on how the emancipation of the serfs was carried out in Russia and the situation of the Russian peasantry. **Jan D to Apr 6:** E works on the article "What have the working classes to do with Poland?" (#E915) [→ :19]. **Jan 29:** Mrs. M writes a reportorial letter to Becker for publ in *Vorbote*, describing with enthusiasm the Sunday evening lectures on science for workers given by Huxley, Lyell, et al ("Sunday Evenings for the People"). Mrs. M's piece is sharply anticlerical in content, pubd in Feb issue (cf *MEW* 16:510).

10. STUDIES (E). **Jan 4:** E, who has been continuing his reading in natural science, recommends Tyndall's *Heat considered as a mode of motion* as a pioneering effort at giving the subject a rational form.

11. PERSONAL. **Jan D to Mar A:** M falls very ill, with carbuncles. After some improvement, though still confined to bed, he continues working on *Capital;* when unable to work, he reads Walter Scott.

FEBRUARY

12. *CAPITAL.* **Feb:** Instead of merely making a clear copy for the printer [← :8], M enters upon a rewriting of the entire ms of Vol. 1; this will produce the final draft of this first vol. by Aug 1867. (Perhaps this course already began in Jan.) **Feb 13:** In a letter to E, M, still bed-ridden [← :11], gives a detailed description of the state of his work. He has gone through much new material, incl develop-

ments in agrochemistry, for the scientists Liebig and Schönbein "are more important in this matter than all the economists put together." He will bring the first vol. to Meissner as soon as it is ready.

13. IWMA. **Feb:** GC: M is ill and absent from all sessions (Feb 6, 13, 20, 27). **Feb A:** Corresponding with the GC from his sickbed, M succeeds in getting Eccarius appointed editor of *Commonwealth* (new name of *Workman's Advocate*), plus an ed board of mostly GC members (incl M).

14. GERMAN MOVEMENT. **Feb c.10:** M sends Liebknecht a sharp reproof of his weakness in thinking of making an accommodation with the Lassalleans [← :7].

15. PERSONAL. **Feb:** During this month E donates about £60 to M. **Feb 14–18:** E spends a few days with M in London.

16. PUBL PLANS. **Feb A:** Mrs. M replies to S. Meyer [← :9] on behalf of the ailing M, telling him that the *Com Manifesto* is not to be changed in republication, since it is now a historic document [→ :19]. **Feb AB:** Re the *Internationale Revue* [← :9], M writes Hilberg that he does not know if he can send anything for the first issue.

MARCH

17. IWMA. **Mar:** GC sessions: M attends Mar 13; absent Mar 6, 20, 27. **Mar 6:** At GC: with M still absent, the Mazzinist Luigi Wolff, though no longer a GC member, comes to attack Jung's reply to Vésinier [← :5], boost Mazzini, and denigrate socialism. Under his influence, some of the British members (incl Odger, Howell, Cremer) support a resolution withdrawing some "offensive expressions" about Mazzini and Wolff in Jung's reply; only a few non-British members are present. **Mar 10:** M holds a "council of war" at his house, attended by the corr secretaries for the Continent, to mobilize their forces against the Mazzinist influence of L. Wolff (who is allied with the right-wing Vésinier–Le Lubez faction). The "council of war" decides that on Mar 13, M is to combat the new resolution in their names. **Mar 12:** At a meeting of *Commonwealth* shareholders [← :13] M succeeds in getting Eccarius retained as editor, against Cremer's urging. **Mar 13:** At GC: In the name of the corr secretaries, M protests the validity of the Mar 6 resolution, refutes the claims made by L. Wolff and Mazzini, and defends socialism. The GC invalidates the resolution. In M's view the outcome is esp good because now the British members realize that M is supported by all the Continental secretaries, that it is not a question of "German influence." **Mar 24:** M's letter to E summarizes the background of conflicts going on in and

around the GC, esp involving three deleterious influences: the more conservative TU
leaders on the GC (e.g., Odger, Cremer); the
right-wing London French faction (e.g., Le
Lubez); the Mazzinist faction (e.g., L. Wolff).
    18. POLITICAL AFFAIRS. **Mar 13:** The Ital-
ian émigré Cesare Orsini is brought by French
members to the GC session (where he speaks
against L. Wolff); M meets Orsini. **Mar 15:** M
gives Orsini a recommendatory letter to E.
(*KMC* dating: Mar 13.)
    19. W&P. **Mar or Apr:** S. Meyer's new
edn of the *Com Manifesto* (#ME33) [← :16] is
pubd in Berlin, in a small printing, paid for by
Meyer; this is its first republication inside
Germany. **Mar 19:** E, as chairman of the
Schiller Institute (Manchester), issues an Institute circular (#E142). **Mar 24, 31:** *Commonwealth* pubs the first two parts (out of
three) of E's essay on the working classes and
the Polish question (#E915) [← :9; → :24].
    20. MARX AND ENGELS ON HOLIDAY. **Mar
15 to Apr c.10:** M is at Margate, ailing with
rheumatism and insomnia. **Mar D to Apr 1:**
E vacations in Wales.

APRIL

21. IWMA. **Apr:** GC sessions: M attends
Apr 10, 17; absent Apr 3, 24. **Apr 6:** In a
letter to E, M laments the harm done by his
absence from IWMA affairs: in England the
trade-unionist GC members have become cool
to IWMA work, which has also been hurt by
Reform League competition; a congress is
scheduled for May but seems doomed for lack
of preparation. M wonders if he should go to
Paris to convince the French to postpone the
congress. **Apr 10:** M attends his first GC
session since Mar 13 (and before that, since
Jan 23). GC discusses the date of the next
congress, Jung proposing June 4. **Apr 17:** At
GC: The Mazzinist L. Wolff attends and
renews his attack as on Mar 6; after a long
discussion (M included), M proposes that a
French trans of the Mar 6 resolution be
forwarded to *L'Echo de Verviers* for publ (the
Minutes do not explain why). **Apr 23:** In a
report to E, M sees some improvement in the
situation since his return; the IWMA's help to
the London tailors' strike has been a "sensation"; M has decided not to attend the coming
congress in Geneva.
    22. POLITICAL AFFAIRS. **Apr 9:** Bismarck
presents the Bundestag with his plan for a
German parliament elected on the basis of
universal suffrage (as part of his buildup for
war with Austria). **Apr 13:** E comments (to
M): "So Bismarck has made his universal-suf-
frage coup, even if without his Lassalle."
Apr 22: Lafargue (prob after consultation with
M) sends a letter to Blanqui via Watteau,

about the progress and character of the IWMA,
urging the support of the Blanquist tendency
in France. (Watteau will forward it to Blanqui
with the comment that it was clearly inspired
by M himself.)

MAY

23. IWMA. **May:** GC sessions: M attends
May 1, 8, 15; absent May 22, 29. **May 1:** At
GC: After discussing the Paris section's insis-
tence on a congress in May, the GC decides on
postponement to Sep 3 (M supporting). —
Lessner, pres of the German Tailors' Comm in
London, reports on the importation of German
strikebreakers against the Edinburgh tailors'
strike (which had begun Mar 26). M volunteers to warn the German press against the
British effort to recruit scabs in Germany.
May 3: M gets the strike material from the
German Tailors' Comm, and (May 4) writes up
a circular "Warning" (#M987), and sends it to
Liebknecht. (It will be pubd May 15 in at least
three German papers; at the May 15 GC, M
will read clippings from the Leipzig press
echoing the warning.) **May 8:** At GC: M
proposes Bobczynski as corr secy for Poland. —M participates in discussions on
finances and on congress preparations. —
Fox serves notice that at the next meeting he
will discuss a passage in E's last installment
on Poland (see → :24). **May 15:** At GC: Fox
criticizes E's article for ascribing the division
of Poland to the corruption of its aristocracy;
and M replies briefly. (This exchange is not in
the GC Minutes.)
    24. ENGELS' ARTICLE ON POLAND. **May 5:**
The third installment of E's "What have the
working classes to do with Poland?" (#E915)
[← :19] is pubd in *Commonwealth*. **May 17:**
After the May 15 GC discussion (see ← :23), M
urges E to continue with further installs; the
Polish émigrés are eager for them. (But in fact
E will not write any more.)
    25. *CAPITAL.* **May c.14:** After a long in-
terruption due to illness, M resumes work on
the ms, despite continued weakness and
financial distress, which slow the work.
May 25: In response to M's request, E supplies
info on the development of the economic
crisis in the Manchester–Liverpool textile
industry.

JUNE

26. IWMA. **June:** GC sessions: M attends
June 12, 19, 26; absent June 5. **June 12:** Jung
and M propose Pierre Leroux as GC member.
(No further action recorded.) —M reports
IWMA progress in Saxony, based on Liebknecht's report. —Discussion on the outbreak of the Austro-Prussian War ("Seven

Weeks' War") is scheduled for next session. **June 19:** At GC: Eccarius opens the discussion on the war before an extra-large meeting; seven others participate, incl "M, who made a highly interesting speech" (Minutes). The subject focuses on the "question of nationality in general" rather than the war itself, since the French want to "negate" nationality differences altogether. M's speech ridicules the claim that nationality is only a "reactionary superstition," and shows the French chauvinist assumptions behind this "Proudhonized Stirnerism" (anarchoid verbiage) (cf M to E, June 20). **June 26:** At GC: Continuing the war discussion, Jung (in a speech supported by M, who does not himself take the floor) stresses the connection between the war and the prospect of revolution. Bobczynski and Carter offer a resolution advocating that workers be "neutral" in this war between "tyrants," and use their organized strength "in striking a final blow at all the tyrants of Europe and proclaiming their own liberty" [→ :30].

27. POLITICAL AFFAIRS. **June 9:** M hands in his resignation from the Board of Directors of *Commonwealth* at a meeting of the board, since the paper is now controlled by a manufacturer and dependent on bourgeois support.

28. AUSTRO-PRUSSIAN WAR (E). **June 20 to July 6:** E pubs a five-part series "Notes on the war" ("from a strictly military point of view") in the *Manchester Guardian* (#E532). **June:** See ← :26 for IWMA discussion of the war.

29. PERSONAL. **June to Aug:** M is suffering from a liver ailment and carbuncles. The household is in great financial distress; everything possible has been pawned; M even lacks writing paper [→ :35].

JULY

30. AUSTRO-PRUSSIAN WAR: CONSEQUENCES. **July 3:** The battle of Sadowa (Königgrätz) ends the fighting with a smashing defeat of Austria by Prussia. (The preliminary treaty of Nikolsburg on July 26 will be followed by the Treaty of Prague on Aug 23, formally closing the war.) **July AB:** M&E receive letters from Paul Stumpf (in Mainz) (June 30 and July 10 to M, July 16 to E) reporting Liebknecht's pro-Austrian tendency and asking for M&E's attitude toward the war. **July 7, 9, 12:** M&E exchange letters on the outcome of the war, mainly trying to judge the international consequences on the various European powers and the prospects for revolution. **July 17:** At GC, the discussion on the war [← :26] is ended, with M again giving a talk on his views. An amended form of the Bobczynski–Carter resolution [←

:26] is voted unanim, advising workers to be "neutral" as to the contending governments, and to use their organized strength "in working out their social and political emancipation." **July 21:** M contemptuously notes (to E) how Bismarck's success has brought adulation: "Our Englishmen worship success, as usual"—likewise Ruge and Kinkel. **July 25, 27:** In an exchange of letters, M&E agree on the historical meaning of the Prussian victory: the unification of Germany will unfortunately proceed under Prussian hegemony, but the new situation must be used to work for the national unification of the proletariat.

31. IWMA. **July:** GC sessions: M attends July 10, 17, 24, 31; absent July 3. **July 10:** At GC: Lessner and M nominate W. Massman as GC member. —M raises the question of *Commonwealth*'s failure to print GC proceedings [← :27]. **July 17:** At GC: See ← :30 for discussion on the war. **July 24:** At GC: Discussing the forthcoming Geneva Congress agenda, M seconds the proposal to retain London as the GC seat. He discusses organizational dues by affiliates; with Lafargue, nominates F. Le Maître as GC member; and proposes measures to foster Italian representation at the congress. **July 31:** At GC: Reporting for the Sub-Comm, M makes proposals about the Geneva Congress agenda; proposes that the gen secy report on membership and finances, that the congress initiate a statistical inquiry into workers' conditions, and that affiliated societies pay certain annual dues.

32. GERMAN MOVEMENT. **July 27:** Carl Klein (in Solingen) informs M on local IWMA activity.

33. *CAPITAL*. **July 7:** Writing to E, M says he has been keeping his nose to the grindstone for the last two weeks, and hopes to be finished with Vol. 1 by Aug D. Apropos of advances in rifle design, he says that war (the "manslaughter industry") confirms "our theory about the determination of the *organization of labor by the means of production*." **July D:** M studies the latest official reports on child labor in English industry and on the living conditions of the English proletariat.

34. STUDIES. **July AB:** Impelled by contact with British and French Positivists (Comtists), M studies Comte, and finds him far inferior to Hegel (M to E, July 7).

35. PERSONAL. **July:** M's financial plight [← :29] is alleviated by money from E.

AUGUST

36. IWMA. **Aug:** GC sessions: M attends Aug 7, 14, 28; absent Aug 21. —All month M devotes much time to preparatory work for the Geneva Congress. He draws up the "Instructions for the [GC] Delegates" (#M406)—draft resolutions on nine subjects. But he has decided not to attend the congress, since finishing *Capital* is more important (M to Kugelmann, Aug 23). **Aug 14:** At GC: M reports for the Sub-Comm on the mode of electing and paying the gen secy. **Aug 28:** The GC elects its delegates to the congress. **Aug 31:** In a letter to J. P. Becker (in Geneva), M makes a number of suggestions for the congress's work, esp the advisability of electing Jung to the chair; he warns Becker about Cremer's and Odger's politics.

37. GERMAN MOVEMENT. Aug 10: Liebknecht informs M that he has come into control of the Leipzig *Mitteldeutsche Volkszeitung* (which has been going bankrupt), and asks for subscriptions and contributors. **Aug 13:** M tells E that the sample copies sent by Liebknecht show the paper to be worthless. **Aug D:** The paper is suppressed, and Liebknecht is unable to revive it.

38. POLITICAL CONTACTS. Aug 20: Weydemeyer dies in St. Louis.

39. *CAPITAL.* **Aug 23:** M writes E and Kugelmann that new carbuncle outbreaks force him to limit his work on the ms to a "very few hours a day." He tells Kugelmann that Vol. 1 will not be finished before Oct.

40. STUDIES. Aug A: M reads Trémaux's *Origine et transformation de l'homme et des autres bêtes* with great interest; he writes about it to E (Aug 7, 13, Oct 3) and to Kugelmann (Oct 9).

41. PERSONAL: FINANCES. Aug: M gets 80 talers as a legacy from his aunt Esther Kosel [← 65:60]. **Aug to Nov A:** M suffers continued financial distress, in part due to extra expenses stemming from Laura's engagement to Lafargue. His letters to his Dutch relatives (Philips family) asking for money remain unanswered. E helps as much as he can. **Aug 10:** E, sending £10, remarks that he wishes he could provide M with more than £200 a year; if the cotton business were going better, he could increase this to £250. **Aug 23:** Writing to Kugelmann, M mentions that if he emigrated to America, he could earn more from writing for the press, "but I consider that my vocation is to remain in Europe and complete my years-long work."

42. PERSONAL: OTHER. Aug 6: M's daughter Laura becomes "half engaged" to Paul Lafargue (M to E, Aug 7); it is understood that Lafargue must take his M.D. examinations in London and Paris before they can get married. **Aug D to Sep M:** Mrs. M vacations at a seaside resort. **Aug 24:** E goes on a trip to Germany, incl a visit to Engelskirchen to attend a niece's wedding. (He will be back in Manchester by Sep D, perhaps sooner.)

SEPTEMBER

43. IWMA. Sep 3–8: The first regular congress of the IWMA takes place in Geneva. M does not attend [← :36]; but his "Instructions" (#M406) (draft resolutions) are presented on Sep 4, and permeate most of the congress's work. The Rules (which M will work over, following the congress; → :47) are taken up on Sep 5. M's name comes up esp at the Sep 8 session, in the discussion on the Proudhonists' proposal to exclude nonworkers as delegates, when British TU delegates laud M's contributions to the movement. M is elected to the new GC. **Sep 18:** At GC: After the congress delegates report, M moves a vote of thanks. M reports on publicity gained in the German press to stop importation of strikebreakers in the Manchester tailors' strike. **Sep 25:** At GC: M is reelected corr secy for Germany along with most other secretaries. —Lawrence and Carter propose M for GC president, as a demonstration against the Proudhonist view (cf Sep 8, above); but M declines and nominates Odger; three votes are nevertheless cast for M. —M is glad when Fox is elected gen secy over Cremer, but he moves a testimonial to Cremer for past services. —M moves to reconstitute the Sub-Comm.

44. POLITICAL AFFAIRS. Sep CD: M reads the report of the Baltimore founding congress of the National Labor Union (Aug 20–25), the results of which he will praise (M to Kugelmann, Oct 9), esp the eight-hour-day demand, which the IWMA raises also. **Sep c.24:** Collet visits M for info on the Prussian electoral system.

45. ENGELS' TRIP. Sep D (or earlier): E returns from his trip to Germany [← :42].

OCTOBER

46. IWMA AFFAIRS. Oct: GC sessions: M attends Oct 2, 9, 23; absent Oct 16, 30. **Oct 2:** At GC: M discusses conditions for TU affiliation and dues; and takes part in discussing the Belgian section's complaints against Corr Secy Longuet. **Oct 9:** At GC: On M's motion, the GC protests the French government's seizure of congress documents from J. Gottraux as he returned from Geneva. —M protests the French section's plan to publish the congress minutes in its own report of the congress since only the GC has this task. — M participates in discussing the prevention of French scabbing against the English hairdressers' association. —M reports for the Sub-Comm on dues by affiliated organizations. **Oct 9:** In a letter to Kugelmann, M evaluates the Geneva Congress, its impact on Europe, and the negative role of the Proudhonist tendency. **Oct 20:** M is prob present at a meeting of the Sub-Comm. **Oct 23:** At GC: M participates in discussing the Sub-Comm's report on the decision of the Geneva Congress (Sep 8) to exclude Le Lubez from the GC.

47. IWMA: PUBL OF THE RULES. **Oct M:** M and Lafargue begin work on preparing a revised edn, in French, of the 1864 Rules (#M707), based on decisions of the Geneva Congress (which, however, are still unavailable because of the seizure of documents [← :46; → :50]).

48. *CAPITAL.* **Oct 13:** In a letter to Kugelmann, M describes the overall plan of the opus in four books comprised in three vols. (Vol. 1 to contain Books 1–2); Vol. 1 will be issued separately. He will bring the first printer's sheets of ms to Meissner personally next month, he expects.

49. PERSONAL. **Oct 2:** M gets £45 from E. **Oct 13:** M asks Kugelmann if he knows anyone who can make him a loan of about 1000 talers for at least two years.

NOVEMBER

50. IWMA. **Nov:** GC sessions: M attends Nov 20, 27; absent Nov 6, 13. **Nov 20:** At GC: M proposes a Jan 22 commemoration of the Polish uprising of 1863. —He is named a member of the GC delegation to the London Trades Council on Dec 12. **Nov 27:** At GC: M attacks the fake-liberal Bonaparte government for its continuing seizure of IWMA mail. Jung reports that the Prussian government too has seized newspapers mailed, from Geneva through Prussia, to himself and M, i.a. —It is announced that M and others have been invited to attend a dinner sponsored by the Polish emigration to commemorate the Polish uprising of 1830. M says he will attend (but illness will prevent him from doing so). **Nov D:** The new French edn of the Rules, revised by M and Lafargue [← :47] is pubd (#M786).

51. ECCARIUS ON MILL. **Nov:** M begins helping and "coaching" Eccarius who is writing a series of articles on polit eco titled "A working man's refutation of . . . John Stuart Mill," for *Commonwealth* (pubd Nov 3 to next Mar 23) [→ 67:3].

52. *CAPITAL.* **Nov M:** M sends the first batch of ms to pub'r Meissner in Hamburg.

DECEMBER

53. IWMA. **Dec:** GC sessions: M attends Dec 18; absent Dec 4, 11. **Dec 18:** At GC: M reports on articles in French and British magazines which treat the IWMA as one of the leading phenomena of the century. —Organizn of the Jan 22 Polish affair [← :50] is referred to the Sub-Comm. **Dec:** M and Lafargue continue working on preparing a new English and French edn of the Rules (#M786) [← :50].

54. *CAPITAL.* **Dec 20:** Meissner proposes that M not bother with galley-proof corrections, making only necessary alterations and revisions. **Dec D:** M agrees.

55. PERSONAL. **Dec:** M receives word of the death of his Dutch uncle, Lion Philips.

1867

CONSPECTUS

1. M's activity in the IWMA goes busily forward only in the second half of this year—he skips all but three GC meetings up until July 9—since he is intensively involved with finishing Vol. 1 of *Capital* for publ. Then there is the next period of correcting galley proofs and prodding the publisher. And when it is finally pubd in Sep, M&E set about breaking through the silence of the German press. Even before publ, they try to get notices into the press (see → :12). Under date Apr CD to June, *MEW* has a generalized item: "M&E take steps to publicize the coming publ of *Capital* in the press. They try to arrange for English and French translations."

2. M continues to keep in touch with the German movement, esp through Liebknecht and (for info) Kugelmann; but in addition they start paying new attention to the Irish question, dramatized by the struggle of the Fenians against the English government.

3. *Continuing Item:* From Nov 1866 until Mar M, 1867, M spends time helping Eccarius write his series of articles on J. S. Mill's economics [← 66:51]. On June 27, M tells E that the work has much impressed the Comtists, "Mr. [Frederic] Harrison & Co."

JANUARY

4. IWMA. **Jan:** GC sessions: M is absent from all (Jan 1, 8, 15, 29). **Jan 22:** At the anniversary celebration of the Polish uprising of 1863, M gives a talk as IWMA representative (#M828). He is assigned to propose the second of four resolutions: "That liberty cannot be established in Europe without the independence of Poland."

5. *CAPITAL.* **Jan AB:** M is working esp on finishing the chapter on the general law of capitalist accumulation; in this connection he reads T. Rogers's *History of agriculture and prices in England*, sent him by E. **Jan 29:** E sends M new data on the Manchester cotton industry and its labor conditions.

6. PERSONAL. Jan-Feb: M, still suffering from carbuncles and insomnia, is threatened with eviction and the seizure of his household goods; he owes £20 to the baker alone. E helps out. Jan 19: In a letter to E, M speaks of making a trip to the Continent to put his affairs in order.

FEBRUARY

7. IWMA. Feb: GC sessions: M attends Feb 26 for the first time this year; but no participation is recorded in the Minutes. He is absent Feb 5; the sessions of Feb 12 and 19 are called off.

8. POLITICAL AFFAIRS. Feb 18: M sends a Hanover paper a denial of its report that he is planning a trip to the Continent to agitate for a Polish uprising (#M186); the paper pubs (Feb 21) a short note on the denial. Feb 28: M gives a speech at the 27th anniversary celebration of the London GWEA; he discusses capital's exploitation of wage-slaves, and suggests that the German revolution may be the first to overthrow capitalism (report pubd by Lessner on Mar 3, #M826).

9. READING AND STUDY. Feb 25: M enthusiastically recommends that E read two "little masterpieces" by Balzac, "Le chef d'oeuvre inconnu" and "Melmoth réconcilié."

MARCH

10. IWMA. Mar: GC sessions: M attends Mar 5, 12; absent Mar 19, 26. Mar 5: At GC: M is one of the members who is to solicit London TUs for financial aid to the striking bronze workers of Paris. Mar 12: At GC: no participation by M is recorded.

APRIL

11. CAPITAL: MS FINISHED. Apr 2: M informs E that he has finished rewriting Vol. 1 and wants to bring the ms to Meissner in Hamburg personally. Apr 4: E replies how glad he is, and sends £35 for the trip to Germany.

12. MARX'S TRIP. Apr 10: M sails at 8 A.M. for Hamburg, in heavy weather the very first evening; most passengers are seasick, not M. Apr 12–c.16: M arrives in Hamburg at noon and spends the first evening with Meissner; they hit it off, as they discuss arrangements for printing Capital. Meissner wants to publish the opus in three vols. but does not want to leave the historical part for last, since he counts on it for sales of the whole; M agrees. He gives Meissner the ms he has brought. Apr 16: Meissner sends the ms

to Wigand's printshop in Leipzig. Apr c.17 to May 15: M stays in Hanover as guest of Dr. Kugelmann, with whom he has only corresponded up to now. Apr 17: M writes J. P. Becker that printing has started on the opus ("surely the most fearsome missile ever hurled at the heads of the bourgeoisie") and asks him to get notices into the Swiss press about its forthcoming appearance. (In the next months Becker will put various notices into his *Vorbote*.) Apr 23: M asks Liebknecht to get such notices into the German press. —In Hanover, M gets a visit from a "satrap of Bismarck's," the lawyer E. Warnebold, member of the Nationalverein, who says he wants to "utilize M's great talents in the interests of the German people" (i.e., buy him up). M thinks he was sent by Bismarck. Apr c.23: M is also visited by the head of the local statistics bureau, who admires M's exposition of the economics of money. M is invited to the "society of the Europeans" (the anti-Prussian, North German people of the Nationalverein) and to dinner by a railway magnate. In fact he finds he has unexpected influence among "the 'cultivated' officialdom." Apr 25: M. von Bennigsen comes to Kugelmann's to visit M. Apr 29: Wigand's printshop in Leipzig begins the printing of Capital. Apr 30: M writes S. Meyer (in NYC) that Vol. 1 is coming out soon and he hopes Vols. 2 and 3 will appear before a year is up. Apr D: M asks Bürgers to get a notice on Capital into the Rheinische Ztg (Düsseldorf) which he edits.

13. IWMA. Apr: GC sessions: M is absent from all (Apr 2, 9, 16, 23, 30), partly because of his trip. Apr 16: At GC: Lafargue "on behalf of M" asks the GC to censure Odger for moving a resolution congratulating Bismarck, at a Reform League meeting on Apr 3. Apr 23: The GC adopts a Lessner–Lafargue resolution to "repudiate any solidarity" with Odger's action. Apr 27: A newly edited version of the Rules (#M787) is pubd in French in the Courrier International; in English it will be pubd May 1. Apr 30: M writes S. Meyer (in NYC) asking him to establish sections of the IWMA in America, since it "has become a power" in European countries.

MAY

14. MARX'S TRIP. May 1: M (still staying with the Kugelmanns in Hanover) writes Ludwig Büchner (in Darmstadt) for info about a pub'r for a French edn of Capital. May 5: M receives from the printer the first galley proofs of Capital—"on my birthday." May c.6–10: Kugelmann persuades M of the need for "a supplementary, more didactic explanation of the form of value." (As to how, see →

:17. In the second edn, M will do this by revising Ch. 1, sec. 3.) **May 7:** Writing to E from Hanover, M comments bitterly on the Mar 9 speech in the North German Reichstag by the ex-communist Miquel, now turned a pro-Bismarck National Liberal, in which Miquel said that "even freedom" must be temporarily sacrificed in order to establish Bismarck's united Germany. **May 16–17:** On the return trip from Hanover to London, M stops in Hamburg, where he has more business with Meissner, and makes the acquaintance of Wilhelm Marr. (*KMC* dates this Hamburg stay at May c.14–18.) **May 19:** M arrives in London. (On the train into London, he accidentally meets Bismarck's niece, Elizabeth von Puttkamer.)

15. MARX IN MANCHESTER. **May c.21 to June c.2:** M goes to Manchester to visit E (accompanied by Hermann Meyer, a friend of Weydemeyer who has come from St. Louis to London to see M&E). In Manchester, M works on proofreading and correcting *Capital;* discusses with E the problem of getting an English trans, and Kugelmann's proposal (see ← :14) for a revision of the exposition on the form of value.

16. IWMA. **May:** GC sessions: M is absent from all (May 7, 14, 21, 28). **May CD:** A Brussels IWMA member, A. Vandenhouten, writes M on the causes of miners' unrest in the Charleroi coalfields.

JUNE

17. *CAPITAL.* **June 3:** M sends E five printer's sheets of galleys to look over, and asks his advice on how to write the Supplement giving a popular explanation of the form of value [← :14]. (This Supplement will be printed as an appendix to the first edn; it will be integrated into subseq edns.) **June 10:** M sends the printer back his corrections of the 14th set of *Capital* galleys. **June 16:** E makes his suggestions for the Supplement, and writes his opinion on the first galleys of *Capital* he has looked through. **June 17–22:** M drafts the Supplement on value. (On June 27, M sends E a detailed outline of the Supplement.) **June 22:** M writes E that "your satisfaction [with *Capital*] is more important to me than anything the rest of the world may say of it. At any rate I hope the bourgeoisie will remember my carbuncles as long as they live." M explains he has written the Supplement on value in such a way as "to be dialectical in this respect too," so that the " 'nondialectical' reader" can understand the basic theory. He points to the passage where he explicitly refers to Hegel's law of the transformation of quantity into quality "as holding good alike in history [i.e., society] and

natural science." **June 24:** E recommends Samuel Moore as English translator of Vol. 1, and promises to supervise the trans. **June 27:** M asks Meissner to speed up the printing. **June D:** M gets the 20th set of galley proofs from Meissner.

18. IRISH QUESTION: FENIANS. **June 27:** Having read the English commissioners' report on the treatment of political prisoners, esp Fenians, M sends the book on to E, and writes that "the report on the [treatment of the] Fenians sickens me. . . ." He notes pridefully that Mrs O'Donovan Rossa has written a "very flattering letter" to the IWMA.

19. IWMA. **June:** GC sessions: M is absent from all (June 4, 18, 25). **June 4:** At GC: M is elected to the commission on drafting the call for the next congress (but he will not function on it; cf → :22).

20. PERSONAL. **June c.30:** M receives £100 from E, shortly before E goes off to the Continent [→ :26].

21. ENGELS. **June AB:** E, who is following the latest developments in chemistry, reads Hofmann. **June 28:** As chairman of the Schiller Institute in Manchester, E signs a circular to subscribers to the building fund (#E143).

JULY

22. IWMA. **July:** GC sessions: M attends July 9, 16, 23, 30; absent July 2. His attendance on July 9 is his first since Mar 12. **July 9:** At GC: M proposes the first point for the agenda of the Lausanne Congress, formulated "On the practical means" to enable the IWMA to be "a common center of action for the working classes, female and male," in the struggle for emancipation. —At this session, Eccarius is elected gen secy. **July M:** Although on July 9 the GC had adopted an English-language call to the Lausanne Congress and commissioned Lafargue to do the French version, M helps Lafargue write a draft which is considerably different. It is pubd as a flysheet in London, also July 30 in France, in Aug elsewhere. **July 16:** At GC: M is elected to the GC delegation to the London Trades Council. (He will not attend, being occupied with finishing the preface to *Capital.*) **July c.23:** M receives a letter (July 10) from F. A. Sorge about his founding an IWMA branch in Hoboken, N.J. Sorge, who writes on behalf of the German Communist Club of NY, asks for the Inaugural Address and Rules, etc. **July 23:** At GC: M speaks about a Parliamentary Blue Book whose statistical data refute the recent outcry in the press about the pernicious effect of the TUs in driving the iron trade out of the country. (The Minutes with an account of his talk are pubd in the press on July 27.) —M moves to enjoin the French from publishing an agenda for the Lausanne Congress other than the GC's. **July 30:** At GC: M announces that the peace program for the Lausanne Congress will be taken up Aug 6. (It will actually be Aug 13.)

23. *CAPITAL.* **July c.10:** M sends the Supplement on value (to be included in Vol. 1 as an appendix [← :17]) to the printer. **July 25:** M finishes the preface to Vol. 1, and sends it to pub'r Meissner.

24. POLITICAL AFFAIRS. **July:** M receives a letter from Köttgen, whose son has visited him. **July D:** Contretemps with Freiligrath: a new book, *Zwölf Streiter der Revolution* by G. Struve and G. Rasch, contains Rasch's biographical sketch of Freiligrath with attacks on M&E and W. Wolff, attacks which Freiligrath apparently tolerates. M writes Freiligrath (July 20) for an explanation, but he replies evasively.

25. PERSONAL. **July D to Aug M:** M is in new financial distress due to the expense of his three daughters' trip to the Lafargue family in Bordeaux; E sends £15.

26. ENGELS ON TOUR. **July 5 to Aug A:** E takes a trip through Sweden, Denmark, and Germany, keeping a travel diary of brief impressions; in Hanover he visits Kugelmann.

AUGUST

27. *CAPITAL:* VOL. 1 IS FINISHED. **Aug 14:** M receives from the printer the 48th (penultimate) set of galley proofs. **Aug 15–16:** M finishes his correction of the last (49th) set of galley proofs at 2 A.M., and writes a letter to E thanking him for his devoted help which alone made the task possible—"I embrace you, full of thanks!" **Aug 24:** M writes E that he is working on Vol. 2; he takes up the question of the circulation of capital. **Aug 26–27:** E sends, as requested, data on the economics of replacement funds for the amortization of machinery. **Aug 27:** M sends an excerpt from the preface to Vol. 1 to S. Meyer (in NYC) for publ in the American press.

28. IWMA. **Aug:** GC sessions: M attends Aug 13, 27; absent Aug 6, 20, 29. **Aug 6:** At GC: M (absent) is nominated as a GC delegate to the Lausanne Congress. **Aug 13:** At GC: M declines the nomination as congress delegate. —M opposes official IWMA representation at the congress called in Geneva by the liberal League of Peace and Freedom, since the international union of the working classes is "in itself a peace congress"; but he favors IWMA people attending "in their individual capacity." This position is adopted unanim. (The Minutes with M's talk are pubd Aug 17.) **Aug 27:** At GC: In a general discussion

on the first point of the Lausanne Congress agenda [← :22], M says he is against turning the IWMA into a "debating club" but is for "discussing great questions" (so say the Minutes). **Aug D:** M goes over the GC's report to the Lausanne Congress, and signs it (SOURCE: KMC).

29. POLITICAL AFFAIRS. **Aug 27:** M writes Vermorel, editor of *Courrier Français*, a private letter criticizing his publ of "Russian lies" about the Greek-Turkish conflict on Crete and his treatment of Pres. Johnson's role. (M will tell E, Sep 4, that in consequence the paper changed its policy.) **Aug c.29:** In response to Borkheim's request of Aug 27, M sends him suggestions for his speech against Russian policy at the Geneva Peace Congress [→ :37].

30. ENGELS' TOUR. **Aug A:** E returns to Manchester [← :26].

SEPTEMBER

31. *CAPITAL:* PUBLICATION. **Sep 4–7:** Even before publ, M&E's publicity work gets excerpts pubd in some periodicals (*Zukunft*, Stuttgart *Beobachter*, *Bee-Hive*). **Sep 11–12:** M&E exchange letters on how to get notices of *Capital* into the bourgeois press by pretending to attack the book. **Sep 14:** Publ day: Vol. 1 comes off the press in Hamburg, in an edn of 1000 copies. **Sep CD:** M sends copies to friends: Beesly, Fox, Kaub, Kugelmann, Schily, the London GWEA, also to Freiligrath (but without inscription) and to Bakunin [→ :37] (see also → :34).

32. IWMA. **Sep:** GC sessions (following the congress): M attends Sep 17, 24. **Sep 2–8:** The second congress of the IWMA takes place in Lausanne; M does not attend. At the ninth session (Sep 6) M is reelected to the GC. **Sep 7–12:** Lessner and Eccarius send M reports on the congress from Lausanne, and following it, on the Peace Congress in Geneva. **Sep 11:** In a letter to E, M sums up the progress made by the IWMA with great satisfaction, and concludes that "in the next revolution, which is perhaps nearer than it seems to be, we will have this powerful engine in our hands." **Sep 17:** At GC: M attends; no participation recorded. **Sep 24:** At GC: M is reappointed corr secy for Germany. Odger is not reelected pres; instead the post is abolished—on M's proposal (M to E, Oct 4) though the Minutes ascribe the motion to Hales. —Since Fox announces he is going to attack Eccarius for his congress reports in the *Times*, M counterattacks by referring to Fox's secret letter to J. P. Becker about moving the GC out of London.

33. POLITICAL AFFAIRS. **Sep c.4:** M sends a note to the *Courrier Français* citing data on mass poverty in Prussia given by the director of the Central Statistical Archives of Prussia, Otto Hübner (#M498.5); the piece is pubd Sep 6 with some garbling. **Sep D:** When M learns Sep c.20 that Liebknecht has been elected to the North German Reichstag from a Saxon district (in the Aug 31 election), he sends suggestions for Liebknecht's maiden parliamentary speech (which is given Sep 30, attacking the government's passport bill; M will express his approval to E, Oct 4).

34. MARX IN MANCHESTER. Sep 13–c.16: M goes to Manchester with Paul Lafargue, to stay at E's. M&E discuss how to get press notices of *Capital* pubd.

OCTOBER

35. IWMA. Oct: GC sessions: M attends all four—Oct 1, 8, 22, 29. **Oct 1:** At GC: Fox postpones his attack on Eccarius, and M accordingly postpones his counterattack [← :32]. **Oct 8:** At GC: Fox finally makes his attack on Eccarius, attacking M as well; after the discussion, on M's proposal no action is taken against Eccarius; but M is privately glad that Eccarius has been hauled over the coals for his *Times* articles. —M reports on Liebknecht's election and his maiden speech [← :33]. **Oct 22:** At GC: M reads excerpts from Liebknecht's Oct 17 speech at the North German Reichstag attacking the standing army and Bismarck's policy in the "Luxemburg affair." (Liebknecht's speech is pubd in *Bee-Hive* on Oct 26 along with the GC Minutes.) **Oct 29:** At GC: M attends; no participation recorded.

36. GERMAN MOVEMENT. Oct c.8: Liebknecht asks M for info on the powers of English parliamentary commissions, since he plans to propose a commission of inquiry into workers' conditions in Germany. **Oct 19:** Requested by M, Collet sends materials on this subject. **Oct CD:** M sends Liebknecht info in answer to his request, plus some English parliamentary acts.

37. POLITICAL AFFAIRS. Oct 3: Since Bakunin does not acknowledge receipt of *Capital* [← :31], Mrs. M writes J. P. Becker for his address. **Oct c.5:** To supply *Vorbote* with an article, M being ill, Mrs. M writes a reportorial letter to the editor, J. P. Becker, on the Lausanne Congress, the Geneva Peace Congress, and the publ of *Capital;* it is pubd in the Oct issue. **Oct A:** At Borkheim's request, M arranges (Oct 4) to have Lafargue revise the language of Borkheim's speech at the Geneva Peace Congress (which has just been pubd as a pamphlet, *Ma perle devant le Congrès de Genève*); but soon M explains (in a letter to Kugelmann, Oct 11) the danger, already visible, that the silly pamphlet will be ascribed to

him (M) by malicious enemies; Vogt has already done so. (Bakunin will soon do worse.) **Oct 8:** Juch sends M an article by Beta (Bettziech) which attacks Juch and also M, and asks help in answering it. M writes Juch only a few lines (cf M to E, Oct 14). **Oct 17:** Hermann Meyer, returning to America, visits M. **Oct 24:** The German tanner Joseph Dietzgen, now working in St. Petersburg, sends M a long letter expressing admiration for M's writing and setting forth his own materialist views in philosophy [→ :42]. **Oct 27–28:** M is urged by Maughan, an old Owenite, to be active in the Free Thought movement and combat Bradlaugh's influence; M politely declines.

38. *CAPITAL*. Oct 10–12: M&E correspond with each other, and both with Kugelmann, on how to break through the silent treatment of *Capital* in the press and get notices into papers. **Oct 12:** E writes two reviews for publ, one for *Zukunft* (#E696), pubd Oct 30 in shortened and distorted form, and one for the *Rheinische Ztg* (#E695), which is not pubd. **Oct 22:** E writes a review for *Elberfelder Ztg* (#E691); pubd Nov 2.

39. PERSONAL. Oct-Nov: M, beset by financial troubles, tries to raise money in order to be able to work on Vol. 2 of *Capital*. Borkheim says he is willing to furnish £150 on the basis of E's warranty, but sends only £40.

NOVEMBER

40. IWMA AFFAIRS. Nov: GC sessions: M attends Nov 5, 19, 20, 26; absent Nov 12. **Nov 5:** At GC: M supports the right of Fox, who is corr secy for America, to write paid articles for *Bee-Hive* on American affairs.

41. IWMA AND THE FENIANS. Nov: Summary of the Background: There is at this point a wide protest movement to stop the execution of five Fenians (Irish nationalists) who were condemned to death in Sep for (unproved) participation in an action to free Fenian prisoners of the police. Some GC members join the protest, along with M, but others hang back. M has been giving much thought to the Irish question—national independence (cf M to E, Nov 2, 30; E to Kugelmann, Nov 8). M favors support of the Fenians, though with serious criticisms of their ideas and policies. Given the split in GC members' views, M brings about a GC discussion of the issues, open to the public and with the Irish and British press invited. **Nov 19:** At GC: Several pro-Fenian speeches are made by GC members, only Lucraft demurring, but all approve sending a protest against the executions. The discussion is to continue Nov 26. **Nov 20:** A special GC session adopts M's draft of a "memorial" to the government for commutation of the Fenians' sentences (#M313) [→ :45]; pubd in French on Nov 24. **Nov 26:** At GC: M has prepared notes for a speech (#M577) which, however, remains undelivered since he yields the floor to Fox, because the three Fenians have now been executed. Fox also introduces a resolution, which is referred to the Sub-Comm [→ :46].

42. POLITICAL AFFAIRS. Nov 8: Carl Klein writes M asking help for the Solingen producers' cooperative. **Nov 14, 26:** M&E exchange letters about Dietzgen's letter to M [← :37]. **Nov 15:** Borkheim (in Geneva) writes M inviting him to write for the Peace and Freedom League organ *Les Etats-Unis d'Europe*. The idea of his writing for this sheet is "pure nonsense," writes M to E (Nov 29).

43. CAPITAL. Nov 2: E's review (#E691) [← :38] is pubd in *Elberfelder Ztg*. **Nov 3–8:** E writes a review for *Düsseldorfer Ztg* (#E690); pubd Nov 17.

44. PERSONAL. Nov: M is almost entirely unable to work because of furuncles and insomnia.

DECEMBER

45. IWMA. Dec: GC sessions: M attends Dec 3, 17; absent Dec 31. **Dec 3:** At GC: M reports on the coming publ of Liebknecht's new weekly in Leipzig, *Demokratisches*

Wochenblatt. **Dec 17:** At GC: To ensure the pamphlet publ of the new edn of the Rules (#M787), M offers to advance the money. — The GC confirms the "memorial" on the Fenian prisoners (#M313) [← :41]. **Dec D:** The Rules pamphlet (#M787) is pubd.

46. IRISH QUESTION. Dec 16: M gives a lecture at the London GWEA on the Irish question, taking up the history of Ireland's subjection and explaining the IWMA's views (#M743, 625).

47. GERMAN MOVEMENT. Dec 6: M writes, and sends to Guido Weiss for *Die Zukunft*, an article, "Plagiarism" (#M657), showing that the GGWA Lassalleans have used passages from *Capital* verbatim (some garbled) without mentioning the source, in *Social-Demokrat* articles. M's article is pubd Dec 12. **Dec 11:** In a letter to M, Liebknecht defends his pro-Austrian sympathies, which spur his anti-Prussianism. **Dec 16, 17:** M&E exchange letters on how to carefully tackle Liebknecht on this issue.

48. CAPITAL. Dec 12–13: E writes two more reviews, and (through Kugelmann's good offices) both are pubd on Dec 27, one in the Stuttgart *Beobachter* (#E688), the other in the business organ *Gewerbeblatt aus Württemberg* (#E693). For the first E follows the tactic outlined in M's letter of Dec 7. **Dec CD:** In spite of continuing bad health (carbuncles), M continues his work on Vol. 2 [→ 68:3].

1868

CONSPECTUS

1. M is absent from all GC meetings for the first four months, resuming IWMA work only in May. In Nov, Bakunin—who has only recently begun to adopt anarchism as his ideology—begins to make his power-play in a bid to nucleate the IWMA with his parallel bore-from-within operation, the "Alliance of the Socialist Democracy." This inaugurates the conflict which we will follow in the next four years.

2. Though E writes more reviews to leaven the press, *Capital* is still getting the silent treatment in the bourgeois German press; but both wings of the German workers' movement give it considerable publicity. The conflict between these wings comes to a boil in Sep: on one side the Lassallean group (GGWA) led by Schweitzer; on the other the Bebel–Liebknecht group, which finally forms a loose federation of workers' associations. (See the summary → :50.)

3. M continues to do sporadic work on *Capital*. For the period Jan to Mar (or Apr) he

studies the literature on ground rent and agriculture (see → :72). He gets info from Schorlemmer about the latest books on agrochemistry, fertilizers, etc. In the second half of the year M occupies himself now and then with certain problems of Vols. 2 and 3, i.a., reading reports on Irish agrarian conditions, esp tenancy.

4. M's inactivity in the IWMA for the first four months and also his spotty work on *Capital* are both due in part to his continuing health problems and financial difficulties. More than once he raises the idea of moving to Geneva in order to live more cheaply. During this year he receives about £400 from E. His illnesses are largely bad headaches and carbuncles.

JANUARY

5. CAPITAL. Jan to Mar/Apr: See ← :3 for a summary. **Jan AB:** E writes another review, for the *Neue Badische Landeszeitung* (#E694); pubd Jan 21. **Jan 7:** Having read the just-pubd review of *Capital* by Prof. Dühring, E takes a dim view of it, in a letter to M. **Jan 8:** M, however, thinks Dühring has been "very decent," though full of errors. In a notable statement, M describes the three elements of *Capital* that are "fundamentally new" [→ :13]. **Jan 10:** J. Card (in Geneva) asks M for authorization to make a French trans. **Jan 22:** Schweitzer, in the *Social-Demokrat*, begins a series of articles (until Apr 24) on *Capital*, quoting many passages. **Jan 26:** Hermann Meyer (in the US) writes E of the interest that *Capital* has elicited in America. The NY pub'r Schmidt (whose name figures on the title page) told Meyer that *Capital* would have sold better if copies had been sent out for review. Dana's *Sun* has today pubd excerpts, while dissociating itself.

6. IRISH QUESTION. **Jan 6:** The German workers' singing society Freundschaft (London) asks M to give a lecture on Ireland.

7. IWMA. **Jan:** GC sessions: M is absent from all (Jan 21, 28).

8. AUTOBIOGRAPHY. **Jan 17:** K. M. Kertbény asks M for an autobiographical sketch for use in the Leipzig *Illustrirte Ztg.* **Jan 30:** M sends such a sketch or outline (#M70), via Kugelmann.

9. ENGELS. **Jan D to Mar:** E, as chairman of the Schiller Institute, devotes much time to its building program.

FEBRUARY

10. *CAPITAL.* **Feb 4, 11:** M&E exchange letters about two of Dühring's books on polit eco, *Die Verkleinerer Carey's* [etc.] (1867), which Kugelmann has sent M, and *Capital und Arbeit*, which M has read (Feb 4) in the BM. **Feb 20:** M asks E to write a review of *Capital* for Liebknecht's *Demokratisches Wochenblatt* [→ :13].

11. POLITICAL AFFAIRS. **Feb 2, 5:** Carl Coppel, a young Hanover banker recommended by Kugelmann, visits M.

12. IWMA. **Feb:** GC sessions: M is absent from all (Feb 4, 11, 18, 26).

MARCH

13. *CAPITAL.* **Mar 2–13:** E writes a review (#E689) for the *Demo Wochenblatt* [← :10]; pubd Mar 21–28. **Mar 6:** Writing to Kugelmann, M analyzes Dühring's economic writings [← :5, 10]; he states his view on Hegel's idealist dialectics and his own materialism. **Mar c.21:** M informs Schweitzer, via Eichhoff, that he has no objection to the *Social-Demokrat's* continuing its series [← :5] though pub'r Meissner has objected.

14. IWMA. **Mar:** GC sessions: M is absent from all (Mar 3, 10, 17, 24, 31).

15. JOURNALISTIC OFFER. **Mar 11:** The

Vienna editor W. Angerstein asks M to write regularly for the Vienna *Telegraph* and the new *Allgemeine Volkszeitung,* organ of the workers' assocs.

16. GERMAN MOVEMENT. **Mar c.13:** E gives Liebknecht suggestions for a Reichstag speech against the new trade regulations.

17. READING AND STUDY. **Mar:** M reads G. L. von Maurer's *Einleitung zur Geschichte der Mark* [etc.] ... *Verfassung* (1854) with great interest, and finds "new proof" of his thesis that the Asian-type village community everywhere forms the starting point in Europe (cf M to E, Mar 14, 25).

18. PERSONAL. **Mar 6, 17:** Writing to Kugelmann, M discloses that he has often discussed moving to Geneva, where living is cheaper; but the BM is necessary for finishing *Capital* and the IWMA would "fall into very bad hands and go wrong." **Mar 24:** At the BM, M is suddenly stricken by illness and has to go home.

APRIL

19. *CAPITAL.* **Apr 22:** M reports to E that he has resumed work on *Capital,* though for only three hours a day because of headaches; and that he has worked out the solution to a problem on the relation of the value of money to the rate of profit. **Apr 30:** In response to a problem posed by E (Apr 26), M writes a lengthy explanation of the rate of profit and surplus value, material for Vol. 3. **Apr:** E makes a synopsis of Vol. 1, but leaves it unfinished (#E799).

20. POLITICAL AFFAIRS. **Apr A:** Coppel [← :11] comes to visit M again but does not see him because M is ill. **Apr 3:** Freiligrath thanks M for sending *Capital,* saying that "many young Rhineland merchants and factory owners" will be enthusiastic about the book, and this is its "proper purpose"; this is his last letter to M (cf M to Kugelmann, Apr 6.) **Apr 11, 20:** M&E exchange letters on the events of the Geneva building workers' lockout.

21. IWMA. **Apr:** GC sessions: M is absent from all (Apr 7, 14, 21, 28).

22. GERMAN MOVEMENT. **Apr 6:** Writing to Kugelmann, M vents irritation at the political weakness of Liebknecht's *Demo Wochenblatt* in adapting to the South German People party's anti-Prussianism: Liebknecht "does not have enough dialectics to strike at both sides at the same time" [cf → :35].

23. AUTOBIOGRAPHY. **Apr 26:** Schily sends M the request by Elisée Reclus for biographical data about him, to be used in an article about M. **Apr c.28:** M satisfies this request (but whatever he sent is not extant).

24. PERSONAL. **Apr 2:** M's daughter

Laura and Paul Lafargue are married at the Registry Office in London, and leave for France on their honeymoon. **Apr AB:** M suffers from carbuncles, unable to work; he takes an arsenic treatment on E's advice; after Apr 22 he is again able to work a few hours a day. **Apr 30:** M sends E a jocular thought for his 50th birthday, due May 5: "If that Prussian lieutenant told you, 'Twenty years in the service and still a lieutenant,' I can say: A half century on my shoulders and still a pauper! How right my mother was: 'If only Karell had made capital instead of etc.!' "

25. ENGELS. **Apr 1–5:** E stays in London with M, to attend Laura's wedding [← :24]. He fills out a "Confessions" game sheet for daughter Jenny's album (#E178).

MAY

26. IWMA. **May:** GC sessions: M attends May 5, 12, 26; absent May 19. **May 5:** M attends the GC session for the first time this year; no participation recorded. **May 12:** At GC: M proposes that the IWMA issue an "official denunciation" of the Belgian government's shooting down of the Charleroi coal strikers. **May 19:** M is absent from the GC because he is again ill with carbuncles. **May 26:** At GC: M favors moving the coming congress away from Brussels because of the Belgian antiforeigner law and harassment of the IWMA. He has been (May 25–29) drafting a resolution on this [→ :31] —M is named to a comm of three to draw up an "address of denunciation" against French and Belgian strikebreaking and harassment of the IWMA. (This material will later be incorporated into the GC report to the congress, #M325).

27. *CAPITAL.* **May 20:** M gives a lecture on wages at the London GWEA. **May 22:** E, who has been corresponding with M since Jan about a review for the Comtist *Fortnightly Review*, begins work on it around this time; he writes M that it is hard to "make the dialectical method clear to the Englishmen reading the magazine. . . ." **May 23:** In response, M gives E some pointers on how to write the review [→ :33, 40]. **May-June:** M takes up some problems of Vol. 2, esp questions relating to Part II on the turnover of capital; on this, he rereads i.a. Smith, Turgot, Tooke.

28. GERMAN MOVEMENT. **May 7:** In reply to Schweitzer's request of Apr 29, M sends him advice on how socialist deputies should handle the question of lowering the German tariff on pig iron.

29. DIALECTICS. **May 9:** In a letter to Dietzgen, M writes that after finishing *Capital*, "I will write a [book on] 'Dialectics.' The real laws of dialectics are already contained in Hegel—to be sure, in mystical form. It is a

question of stripping this form off" (cf ← :13 27).

30. PERSONAL. **May CD:** M is again ailing with carbuncles. **May 29 to June c.15:** M stays with E in Manchester, accompanied by daughter Eleanor.

JUNE

31. IWMA AFFAIRS. **June:** GC sessions: M attends June 16, 23, 30; absent June 2, 9. **June 2:** At GC: M being absent, his resolution on the congress site [← :26] is moved by Jung, who proposes London; GC postpones action. **June 9:** Jung proposes to postpone the site question and ask the Belgians' opinion. **June c.15:** M returns to London from Manchester. **June 16:** At GC: M withdraws the resolution after the Belgian section is heard from (cf M to E, June 20). **June 23:** At GC: M reports on Germany. —M prevails on R. Shaw to remain GC treasurer. —M moves that the Labor Reform Assoc in America be invited to send congress delegates. —M proposes that an address to British and Irish TUs, in re the coming congress, be drawn up by Hales and Lafargue. **June 30:** At GC: M is present but no participation is recorded.

32. IWMA: EICHHOFF PAMPHLET. **June 6:** W. Eichhoff (in Berlin) writes M for help in drafting a propaganda article on the history of the IWMA. M begins gathering materials. **June 26:** M writes (or finishes writing) notes and suggestions for Eichhoff. **June 27:** M sends off to him a large package of documents, clippings, publications, etc. [→ :38].

33. *CAPITAL.* **June 28:** E finishes work on his review for *Fortnightly Review* (#E692) [← :27], and goes over it with Samuel Moore, who is supposed to sign it [→ :40].

34. POLITICAL AFFAIRS. **June A:** M receives a request from S. Meyer (in NYC; letter of May 20) to send the addresses of Anglo-American socialists in Chicago and NYC, for use by Sorge.

35. GERMAN MOVEMENT. **June 24:** In a letter to Kugelmann, M repeats [← :22] his low opinion of Liebknecht's political work in *Demo Wochenblatt*, also repeating his remark on dialectics. **June 28:** Schweitzer extends M an honorary invitation to the GGWA congress in Hamburg, and asks if he will accept [→ :39].

36. PERSONAL. **June c.18 to July c.10:** M is in great financial distress. Daughters Jenny and Eleanor are ill with scarlet fever. M is afflicted with insomnia. E sends £45.

JULY

37. IWMA AFFAIRS. **July:** GC sessions: M attends all four—July 7, 14, 21, 28. **July 4:** M sends (via S. Meyer) credentials to Sorge as American representative of the IWMA. **July 7:** At GC: M proposes a public statement repudiating the French émigré F. Pyat who, though not an IWMA member, has made a provocatory speech under the auspices of the London French branch, calling for Bonaparte's assassination. M's one-sentence motion (see GCFI 2:224) is pubd in Belgium, July 12–26. (Cf M to E, July 7.) **July 14:** At GC: M reports on the GGWA, the Prussian ban on its Berlin organizn, and its congress in Hamburg coming Aug M. —M proposes a statement denouncing the English government for suppressing the word *Polish* in a document in line with the Russian decree suppressing the name Poland (text in the Minutes; pubd July 18). **July 21:** At GC: M reports on the organizn of TUs by socialists (Bebel and associates) in southern and eastern Germany. — M proposes that the next meeting discuss congress issues, esp the problem of machinery. —M takes part in a discussion of the poor response to the GC's statistical questionnaire. **July 28:** At GC: M reports on invitations he has declined, one from Germany (see → :39) and one from Vienna (to which the GC assigns Fox). —M opens the GC's discussion of congress issues with a long talk on "the influence of machinery in the hands of the capitalists" (#M599), based on *Capital*; pubd in *Bee-Hive* on Aug 1.

38. IWMA: EICHHOFF PAMPHLET. **July:** Eichhoff's planned article turns into a pamphlet as he works on it [← :32]. Besides supplying materials, it is possible that M also furnishes answers to questions by Eichhoff, and perhaps even draft passages. **July 18 to D:** M checks proofs of Eichhoff's pamphlet. **July 29:** Eichhoff finishes the pamphlet. (It will be pubd in Aug, in Berlin, titled *Die Internationale Arbeiterassociation—ihre Gründung, Organisation, politisch-sociale Thätigkeit und Ausbreitung.*)

39. GERMAN MOVEMENT. **July c.2:** In reply to Schweitzer's invitation [← :35], M writes that he has no objection to accepting but he is uncertain about going to the congress; he calls on Schweitzer to work to unify GGWA and IWMA and to send delegates to the Brussels Congress. **July 8:** Schweitzer requests M to recommend a *Social-Demokrat* correspondent in London. **July 17–23:** Liebknecht (July 17, 22) and Bebel (July 23) write M about their limited alliance with Schweitzer's GGWA, and urge M to go to the GGWA congress as GC delegate. **July 28:** At the GC session M proposes that a delegate be sent to the GGWA congress, funds permitting. (M arranges for Eccarius to be the delegate; → :42.)

40. *CAPITAL.* **July 1:** E sends M his *Fort-*

nightly Review piece (#E692) [← :33; → :44]. **July 4:** M asks S. Meyer to send American newspapers on US land ownership and agricultural conditions, also criticisms of Carey, for use in Vol. 2 about ground rent. **July c.11:** M writes a short piece (#M534) replying to the claim made in some press notices of *Capital* that he plagiarized Bastiat. (No info on whether or where M sends this piece for publ.) **July 11:** To Kugelmann, M sends a concise refutation of a review of *Capital* in a Leipzig paper (sent by Kugelmann, July 9); this is in effect a short essay on the concept of value. **July:** M begins dealing with a number of problems for Vols. 2 and 3; see ← :3 for a note on July-Dec (second half of the year).

41. PUBL PLANS. **July 26:** Kugelmann tells E that Keil, editor of *Gartenlaube*, wants to run a biographical article on M—so according to Kertbény. **July 29:** E writes a hasty short biographical sketch and sends it to M. The same day M returns it with marginal changes indicated, also changing the title from "A German political economist" to "A German socialist," disliking both [→ :57]. **July 31:** E sends the piece (cf #E405) off to Kugelmann.

AUGUST

42. IWMA. **Aug:** GC sessions: M attends all four—Aug 4, 11, 18, 25. **Aug 4:** At GC: M reports on two German strikes, partly after a Kugelmann letter. —As the GC resumes discussion of "The influence of machinery" [← :37], M sums up briefly and offers to present a resolution (reported in *Bee-Hive* on Aug 8). —Writing to E, M suggests that perhaps the GC should be transferred for the next year to Geneva, in order to expose the mudslinging of the London French branch about the present GC's concern for its "nice dictatorship." **Aug 6:** E argues against this idea. **Aug 11:** At GC: M proposes a congress resolution on "The influence of machinery" as discussed July 28, Aug 4; the resolution is pubd Aug 22. —In the GC discussion on the reduction of the workday (opened by Eccarius), M participates with a substantial talk (#M614). —M sends Lessner his revised version of the "Call to the German workers of London" (call to the congress) drafted by Lessner (pubd Aug 15 in *Hermann* in the name of the London GWEA). **Aug 18:** At GC: M reports on affairs in America; on police repression in Vienna; on the publ of the Eichhoff pamphlet [← :38]; and on the invitation to himself to attend the GGWA congress [← :39]. —In the election of three GC delegates to the Brussels Congress, M proposes Dupont and Mrs. Harriet Law; Dupont is elected, Mrs. Law loses by one vote. **Aug 25:** At GC: M presents his congress resolution on reduction of the workday (pubd in *Bee-Hive* on Aug 29). —M supports a motion to permit the Geneva Society of Free Thinkers to have a delegate to the congress. —M signs Eccarius's credentials as GC delegate to the GGWA congress in Hamburg. (Eccarius leaves London on Aug 29.) **Aug c.25 to Sep 1:** M writes the GC Report to the Brussels Congress (#M325) [→ :47].

43. GERMAN MOVEMENT. **Aug 13** (rec'd 15): Schweitzer sends M a ceremonial invitation to attend the GGWA congress, signed by 24 regional representatives of the GGWA Exec (dated July 6), together with a letter (by Schweitzer) inviting him as a guest of honor. **Aug 18:** M replies he is "too busy" preparing the IWMA congress to accept, but he welcomes the appearance in the GGWA platform of demands for political freedom, shortened workday, and international working-class cooperation. His communication (#M929) is read to the GGWA assembly Aug 24, and pubd in the press Aug 28–29. **Aug 25:** At the GGWA congress Bracke gives a lecture on *Capital*.

44. *CAPITAL.* **Aug 1 to Sep 25:** Dietzgen's review of *Capital*, written at M's suggestion, is pubd in *Demo Wochenblatt* in four installs. **Aug 10:** M informs E that Morley, editor of *Fortnightly Rev*, has rejected E's review of *Capital* (#E692) [← :40], finding it "not to his taste." **Aug 25:** See ← :43.

45. PERSONAL. **Aug 5–20:** Mrs. M and the children, who are convalescing from scarlet fever, go to Ramsgate for their health. Mrs. M returns Aug 20, leaving the children until M's arrival. **Aug 21–c.24:** M, who is suffering from a bilious disorder, stays at Ramsgate with the children.

46. ENGELS. **Aug 29:** E attends a workers' meeting organized in Manchester by E. Jones.

SEPTEMBER

47. IWMA: BEFORE THE CONGRESS. **Sep 1:** Last GC session before the congress: M presents his draft of the GC report (#M325).

48. IWMA: BRUSSELS CONGRESS. **Sep 6:** The Third Congress opens in Brussels (until Sep 13); M is not present. **Sep 7:** The GC report (#M325) is read to the evening session by Dupont, to "prolonged applause." **Sep 8:** From Brussels, Lessner sends M a long letter reporting on the congress so far. **Sep 9:** The subject "Influence of machinery" is discussed at the evening session, on the basis of M's draft resolution [← :42]; in the course, Lessner presents excerpts from *Capital*. **Sep 10:** The congress adopts the draft resolution as preamble and adds a Proudhonist conclu-

sion. —In London, M sends Eccarius and Lessner advice on policy at the congress on the war question and on mutual credit (the Proudhonist nostrum), also remarks on the congress's unrepresentative nature. M also clips the *Times'* leading article on the IWMA and sends it to Schweitzer (who will publish a note on it in *Social-Demokrat* on Sep 16). **Sep 11:** At the business ("administrative") session in the morning, the German delegates introduce a resolution recommending to workers the reading and trans of M's *Capital*; it is reported here that the GGWA congress in Hamburg has adopted a similar resolution, also the Bebel-Liebknecht group in its Nuremberg gathering. —At the evening session on mutual credit, M. Hess openly attacks Proudhonism and refers the delegates to M's *Poverty of philosophy* (#M681). **Sep 12:** Evening session: the reduction of the workday is discussed [← :42]. **Sep 13:** Last session: The names of the new GC (incl M) are announced.

49. IWMA: AFTER THE CONGRESS. **Sep 14:** Since S. Meyer and A. Vogt (in the US) have written M (July 31, Aug 4) about their dissatisfaction with the naming of Sorge as IWMA representative [← :37], M asks Meyer if he is willing to take the job. **Sep 22:** First session of the new GC: Eccarius, supplemented by M, reports on the founding congress in Nuremberg (Sep 5–7) of the Union of German Workers Assocs (*Verband Deutscher Arbeitervereine*) of which Bebel and Liebknecht are leaders; it has voted to join the IWMA and has set up an exec comm of IWMA for Germany. —M gives other reports on German and American activities. —In the GC's discussion of the Brussels Congress, M defends the behavior of the French (Proudhonist) delegates against British strictures. **Sep 29:** At GC: The corr secretaries are all reelected, incl M for Germany. —M proposes Stepney as GC treasurer, and S. Meyer and Pelletier (in NYC) as US correspondents. —M reports on a German strike.

50. GERMAN MOVEMENT. **Sep:** *Background:* The conflict in the German movement between the Lassallean GGWA, led by Schweitzer, and the loose federation of workers' assocs led by Bebel (see ← :49) comes to a head; and each side seeks to line up M to attack the other. M's view is a divided one, since while the GGWA is socialist and carries on some good propaganda work, it functions as a sect, a dictatorial one; while the Union of German Workers Assocs (formed Sep 5–7) is politically tied up with bourgeois liberals (the South German People's party) and does not take a clear class line. In short, as M sees it, the Bebel–Liebknecht group is pursuing an opportunist course, and Schweitzer a sectarian one. **Sep 5–7:** The UGWA is founded in Nuremberg, out of the workers' assocs influenced by Bebel and Liebknecht (see ← :49). **Sep 15:** Schweitzer sends M a flattering letter intended to woo his support. **Sep 16:** The Prussian government cracks down on the GGWA, closing down its Berlin branch; a police decree dissolves the organizn in Leipzig (its HQ). Liebknecht urges M to use this moment to strike for "unity" by attacking Schweitzer. **Sep 23:** M tells Liebknecht he will not intervene against Schweitzer. **Sep 26:** Writing to E, M comments on the positive side of the crackdown: the German workers will have to learn to organize without state permission: "A people that has been trained up in this bureaucratic way must go through a complete course in 'self-help.' " **Sep 30:** E leans to advising an attitude of neutrality. **Sep D:** E writes an article for Liebknecht's *Demo Wochenblatt* "On the dissolution of the Lassallean workers' assoc" (#E552A) [→ :56].

51. POLITICAL AFFAIRS. **Sep D:** With the outbreak (Sep 18 naval uprising) of the Spanish revolution of 1868–74, M&E start following its events (*MEW* dating: Sep D to Nov A).

52. *CAPITAL.* **Sep 16:** E suggests that there is urgent need of "a short popular presentation of the content of [*Capital*] for workers"; M agrees, and proposes that E do it. **Sep 30:** Danielson (via Lyubavin) sends M a letter saying that the pub'r Polyakov plans to publish a Russian trans of *Capital* (KMC dates Danielson's letter Sep 18) [→ :59].

53. ENGELS. **Sep A:** E spends a few days in Ostend with his mother, who is visiting there from Germany. In the course of this trip E meets with M in London. **Sep 16:** E resigns from the Board of Directors of the Schiller Institute (Manchester) over the board's invitation to Karl Vogt to lecture (#E815).

OCTOBER

54. IWMA AFFAIRS. **Oct:** GC sessions: M attends all three—Oct 6, 13, 20. **Oct 4:** In reply to assertions by Max Hirsch and E. Biskamp in German papers that the IWMA has no connections with English workers' organizations, M writes a refutation, reciting the facts (#M177) (pubd in *Demo Wochenblatt* on Oct 17). **Oct 6:** At GC: As Eccarius is hauled over the coals for his self-serving *Times* reports on the Brussels Congress, M refrains from either taking part or defending Eccarius, since Eccarius has deserved it. —M favors GC support to Odger's parliamentary candidacy, and is named to draft a statement ("address") (cf M to E, Oct 10). **Oct 13:** At GC: M's statement of GC support to Odger's candidacy (not extant) is adopted after Odger

denies the report he supports the Liberal party. —M reports on the formation of TUs in Germany. —M is elected a GC delegate to a meeting (Oct 14) of TU representatives to discuss a new bill on the legal status of unions. **Oct 14:** M attends this meeting with Jung. **Oct 20:** At GC: see → :55.

55. IWMA: THE LONDON FRENCH BRANCH. **Oct 19:** After the so-called London French branch (Le Lubez, Besson, Pyat, etc.) sends an abusive letter to Jung against the Brussels Congress decision to provisionally expel Vésinier as a slanderer, Jung raises the problem to M, who suggests scaring the "cowards" with threat of a libel suit, in order to avoid a public scandal. **Oct 20:** The London French branch holds a meeting purporting to decide whether the IWMA "should become a political assoc," under posters glorifying Pyat. Meeting the same evening, the GC hears a report from a French émigré about criminal elements in the London French branch. The matter is referred to the Sub-Comm, which meets Oct 24 to take it up [→ :61].

56. GERMAN MOVEMENT. **Oct 3, 10:** E's article on the dissolution of the Lassalleans [← :50], followed by a supplementary piece, is pubd in *Demo Wochenblatt* (#E552). **Oct 8:** Schweitzer overtly bids M attack the Bebel group (UGWA). **Oct 10:** M writes E weighing the merits of the two sides, and decides to bluntly tell Schweitzer he must choose between real class organization or his present sect type of organizn. —In Berlin, the dissolved GGWA is reestablished with new statutes. **Oct 13:** M writes a letter to Schweitzer with an important political statement; it is along the lines decided, and analyzes Lassalle and Lassalleanism on politics and organizn. **Oct 27:** The masons' union in Leipzig writes M asking for copies of the by-laws of the English TUs.

57. CURIOSA. **Oct 15:** Kugelmann writes M that Prof. Hanssen of Berlin has stated he is willing to offer M a professorship. **Oct 26:** In a letter to Kugelmann, M discusses his attitude toward magazine puffery of literary figures, specif with reference to the Kugelmann–Engels effort to get a biographical article about M into *Die Gartenlaube* [← :41]. M asks Kugelmann to drop it, as "beneath the character of a scientific man." He mentions that "a long time ago" he ignored a request for a biographical entry in *Meyers Konversations-lexikon* (encyclopedia).

58. DIETZGEN. **Oct c.A:** M receives from Dietzgen the ms of his work *Das Wesen der menschlichen Kopfarbeit,* sent from St. Petersburg in Sep. **Oct 4:** After reading it, M sends it on to E (who does not read it immediately). **Oct 28:** In a letter to friends,

M includes a very complimentary reference to Dietzgen as "one of the most gifted workers I know."

59. CAPITAL. **Oct 4:** M receives Danielson's letter [← :52] about a Russian trans. **Oct 7:** M writes Danielson about the state of his work on Vol. 2 (which will "perhaps" appear in six months), explains why it is delayed, and adds that "Vol. 1 constitutes an independent whole." He includes a brief autobiographical summary and a photograph. **Oct 12:** Writing to Kugelmann, M comments on the "irony of fate" that the Russians should be first to translate *Capital:* due to pure intellectual "gourmandise." **Oct D to Nov A:** While studying the literature on ground rent and agricultural relations, M devotes special attention to the village-community institution, its place in the socioeconomic systems of peoples, incl the Slavic peoples, esp in Russia, through the various eras. Borkheim helps him with translations of the Russian sources.

60. ENGELS. **Oct 2:** The secy of the Schiller Institute, A. Davisson, asks E to reconsider his resignation [← :53], but E refuses. **Oct M:** E reads the first vol. of Darwin's *Variation of animals and plants under domestication*, and finds it has nothing new and important as compared with Darwin's previous work (cf E to M, Oct 22).

NOVEMBER

61. IWMA AFFAIRS. **Nov:** GC sessions: M attends Nov 3, 17, 24; absent Nov 10. **Nov 3:** At GC: M reports on the formation of a Berlin branch of the Bebel group (UGWA). —M supports steps to publicize confirmation of Vésinier's expulsion by the Brussels Congress comm of investigation [← :55]. —M is assigned to write a GC address to the Spanish Cortes about the revolutionary developments in Spain. —M is assigned to help in the final preparation for publ of the report on the Brussels Congress (resolutions, etc.) begun by Eccarius. **Nov 17:** At GC: Discussing Odger's defeat in the election [← :54], GC members admit that M's predictions concerning it had been correct, as well as his criticism of "the false policy of the Reform League" (cf M to E, Nov 18). **Nov 24:** At GC: M reports on a letter from Saxon miners wishing to join the IWMA. —M participates in a discussion of the American ambassador in London and of Mazzini's death. **Nov-Dec:** M, as assigned (above, Nov 3), helps to produce a collation of the 1866 and 1868 congress resolutions, which is first pubd in *Bee-Hive* (Nov 21, Dec 12), later as a pamphlet [→ 69:10].

62. IWMA: BAKUNIN AND GENEVA. **Nov 29:** Bakunin's front organizn, the Alliance (or

International Alliance) of the Socialist Democracy, via a letter by J. P. Becker, asks the GC for acceptance into the IWMA as a parallel international organizn. **Nov 20:** Serno-Solovyevich, a Russian in the Geneva section, writes M reporting on the Swiss scene and requesting him to write theoretical articles for *L'Egalité* (which is going to start Jan 1) [→ :69].

63. DIETZGEN. **Nov 6:** E, having now read Dietzgen's ms [← :58], sends M his mixed evaluation. **Nov 7:** M agrees, and adds that it is unfortunate that Dietzgen has not studied Hegel [→ :71].

64. POLITICAL AFFAIRS. **Nov:** M has dinner (Nov 1) at Collet's, whom he has not seen for a long time. He writes Collet half-jocular letters (Nov 2–c.20) about how Peel's Bank Act of 1844 can be used by the Russian government against the Bank of England (one of the letters will be pubd Dec 2, #M381; cf M to E, Nov 23). **Nov 6:** The London GWEA asks M to give a speech at its celebration of Robert Blum's anniversary. **Nov c.12:** M receives from L. Büchner a copy of his book *Sechs Vorlesungen über die Darwinsche Theorie.* M discusses the book, M to E, Nov 14. **Nov 21:** E. Jones asks M to support his parliamentary candidacy in Greenwich; M declines (cf M to E, Nov 23). **Nov 23:** Learning from its secy C. Speyer that the London GWEA has adopted a communication to German workers which amounts to an endorsement of the GGWA-Schweitzer-Lassallean policy as against the Bebel UGWA, M sends his resignation from the GWEA to Speyer (#M864). **Nov D:** Speyer has M make changes in the GWEA communication so that it no longer appears to take Schweitzer's side; M withdraws his resignation (cf *MEW* 32:753, n. 258). (GWEA will issue its revised statement on Dec 9; pubd Dec 24.)

65. CAPITAL. **Nov 14:** M asks E to send him data on the role of the banks in commerce, for *Capital*, Vol. 2.

66. PERSONAL. **Nov:** M is again ailing with carbuncles. —Daughter Jenny, unbeknown to M, takes a job as tutor in an English family, to begin Jan; M reluctantly agrees. **Nov 29:** See → :67.

67. ENGELS. **Nov 29:** In a letter to M, E recounts that he is negotiating with partner Ermen: when E's contract with the firm ends next June 30, Ermen will buy him out. E offers to settle M's financial situation by paying up his current debts and giving him £350 a year for all expenses [→ 69:16].

DECEMBER

68. IWMA AFFAIRS. **Dec:** GC sessions: M attends Dec 1, 15, 22; absent Dec 8. **Dec 1:** At

GC: M moves that the IWMA oppose any favorable reception to the US ambassador R. Johnson, who does not represent the American workers. —M reports on Liebknecht's letter about model by-laws for German TUs. —M supports R. Shaw as corr secy for America. —M is appointed "keeper of archives" for the IWMA. **Dec 15:** M takes part in a discussion on dues from affiliated societies. —M promises to have the draft address to the Spanish Cortes [← :61] in time. —M offers to make a requested résumé of the GC's work since the last congress. — Re Bakunin's Alliance, see → :69. **Dec 22:** M proposes a discussion on the Greek-Turkish conflict at the next meeting. —M proposes that Jung write an official reply to attacks on the IWMA in the Swiss bourgeois press. — Bakunin's Alliance: see → :69.

69. IWMA: BAKUNIN'S ALLIANCE. Dec A: Declining regular collaboration on *L'Egalité* for lack of time [← :62], M writes Serno-Solovyevich his opinion of the position of Bakunin and his group at the Bern Congress of the Peace and Freedom League, and criticizes the Bakunin program plank about "equalization of classes" rather than abolition of class differences. He asks about Bakunin himself. **Dec 15:** At GC: M argues for rejecting the affiliation of Bakunin's front organization [← :62] since the IWMA cannot admit a parallel international organizn; he is assigned to write the GC's reply. —M makes marginal comments on a copy of the program of Bakunin's Alliance (#M733), and sends it to E for his opinion. **Dec 18:** In reply, E criticizes the Bakunin program and opposes accepting it into the IWMA. **Dec 22:** At GC: M's draft reply rejecting the Bakunin Alliance's affiliation (#M412) is read by Jung, and adopted (with an addition by Dupont) to be sent to the

membership. —From Switzerland, Bakunin writes M a wooing, flattering letter, claiming to be M's "disciple," interested only in the workers' movement, and falsely asserting he has broken with Herzen. (Bakunin will later explain to Herzen that this letter is a hypocritical stratagem.) **Dec 28:** M receives Bakunin's letter, and writes Jung to send the GC decision to De Paepe (in Brussels), whom Bakunin is getting set to win over.

70. GERMAN MOVEMENT. Dec 2: Schweitzer writes M that he is willing to accept M's personal mediation between his Lassallean group and the Bebel group (UGWA). **Dec 5:** Writing to Kugelmann, M comments that Schweitzer is correct on one point: Liebknecht's incapacity as an editor and incompetence in political understanding. M also inquires whether Mrs. Kugelmann is active in "the great German campaign for women's emancipation." **Dec 12:** Following up the last query in another letter to Kugelmann, M boasts that the GC has elected a woman member, Mrs. Harriet Law, and points to the historical lesson that "great social changes are impossible without the feminine ferment" and that social progress is measured by the social position of women.

71. READING. Dec 5, 12: Writing to Kugelmann for Dietzgen's current address, M gives his evaluation of Dietzgen's work [← :63]. **Dec 14, 16:** M&E exchange letters on Ténot's book *Paris en décembre 1851*, which has just been a sensation in France.

YEAR APPENDIX

72. In the period Jan to Mar/Apr, among the authors on agriculture and agronomy excerpted by M are K. Fraas, J. H. von Thünen, and J. C. Morton.

1869

CONSPECTUS

1. The IWMA is steadily advancing in influence, at the same time becoming more clearly socialist in politics with the adoption of a land-collectivization resolution, which represents the defeat of Proudhonism in the movement. The coming disruption by the Bakunin operation is still only a cloud on the horizon. M is very busy and at the heart of all IWMA activities, personally involved also with the constant calls for help to strikes, etc., in a dozen countries. With the GC, he esp gets involved in the Irish question (its immediate aspect being the struggle to free the Fenian

prisoners) and in the founding of the Land and Labour League (for land nationalization).

2. For about half the year M is still trying to maintain a public attitude of neutrality in the conflict between the two wings in Germany, the Lassalleans under Schweitzer and the loose federation led by Bebel (UGWA). But in Aug an opposition group within the Lassallean movement joins with the UGWA to form a new workers' party, usually called the "Eisenachers" (SDWP); and M will increasingly adopt the latter as "his" movement, while lamenting its mistakes and inadequacies (esp Liebknecht's incompetence).

3. Neither M nor E does much writing

without immediate connection with all this activity. M works at *Capital* from time to time—see esp the period Feb c.13 to Aug. On the personal side, E is liberated from business by a deal with his partner, and settles an annuity on M, which will help to alleviate the latter's chronic financial problems.

JANUARY

4. IWMA AFFAIRS. **Jan:** GC sessions: M attends Jan 5, 12; absent Jan 19, 26. **Jan 2:** At a Sub-Comm meeting discussing the request by Emile Aubry (Rouen section) for help to locked-out workers, M is commissioned to bring the matter before the GC. **Jan 5:** At GC: M reports for the Sub-Comm on the Rouen lockout and makes proposals to help. —M reports on an important strike in Basel and proposes to censure the Swiss IWMA comm for not keeping the GC informed. **Jan 12:** M suggests that the leading comm of a national section be called federal comm, not central or general comm.

5. IWMA: BAKUNIN OPERATION. **Jan 22:** Liebknecht writes M that J. P. Becker (in Geneva) has unfortunately become tied up with Bakunin, and asks M to do something about it.

6. POLITICAL AFFAIRS. **Jan 25:** Ruge, having read *Capital*, sends a friend an enthusiastic appraisal of the work as "epoch-making." (A friend of the recipient will send the letter to M on Feb 4, and M will inform his own friends during Feb.) **Jan 26:** E informs M that E. Jones died today.

7. *CAPITAL.* **Jan-Feb:** M looks through the *Money Market Review* and the *Economist* of 1868 and on, and makes numerous excerpts.

8. W&P. **Jan D:** M prepares a second edn of his *18th Brumaire* (#M267); he sends the corrected and revised text to publ Meissner (Hamburg) [→ :21].

9. PERSONAL. **Jan 1:** M's first grandchild is born in Paris, to Laura: Charles Etienne Lafargue (nicknamed Schnaps). **Jan:** M has a bad case of the grippe for almost four weeks.

FEBRUARY

10. IWMA AFFAIRS. **Feb:** GC sessions: M attends all four—Feb 2, 9, 16, 23. **Feb 2:** At GC: M proposes to raise aid from the English TUs for the Basel ribbon weavers and silk dyers locked out last Dec for belonging to the IWMA. —M reports on E. Jones's funeral of Jan 30. **Feb 9:** At GC: M is present, but no participation is recorded. **Feb 16:** At GC: M reports on the Lugau (Saxony) miners, and discusses the attempt by Zurich manufactur-

ers to stop IWMA organizn of workers. —M proposes that the GC announce three agenda points for the coming Basel Congress (education, credit, the land question) and invite others. **Feb 23:** At GC: M presents E's long report on the conditions of the Saxon miners (#E673), for which see → :11. —M supports Boon for GC membership. **Feb:** The resolutions of the 1866 and 1868 congresses, which M had helped prepare for publ [← 68:61], are pubd as a pamphlet. (For text, see *GCFI* 3:284.)

11. IWMA: ENGELS. **Feb 13:** M involves E in IWMA work for the first time by asking him to draft a report for the GC on the Saxon miners' conditions. **Feb 17–21:** E writes the report (#E673) and sends it to M. **Feb 23:** M presents it to the GC (see ← :10), which resolves to get it pubd in the press. **Feb 27:** *Bee-Hive* pubs a short account. (M's German trans will be pubd in three German papers during Mar.)

12. IWMA: BAKUNIN OPERATION. **Feb 27:** Bakunin's Alliance, in response to the GC's action [← 68:69] claims that it is conforming to the GC's conditions of admission, esp by dissolving its branches and abandoning its "international" structure, and demands the GC's opinion of its program [→ :18].

13. *CAPITAL.* **Feb 11:** Writing to Kugelmann, M mentions a German univ. lecturer in polit eco who has written M that *Capital* wholly convinced him but his position forces him to be silent "like other colleagues." This "cowardice of the mandarins of the profession" plus the press "conspiracy of silence" has harmed the book's sales. Meissner is still 200 talers short of his production costs. **Feb c.13 to Aug:** After the interruption due to illness, M resumes work on *Capital*; he studies questions of credit and bank circulation, also commercial mathematics, in books by J. L. Foster, F. E. Feller, and C. G. Odermann, making many excerpts. **Feb D:** M reads J. L. Foster's *Essay on the principle of commercial exchanges* (1804) between Feb 27 and Mar 1, when he praises it to E.

14. POLITICAL AFFAIRS. **Feb D:** Lafargue (in Paris) writes M that Blanqui lends M's *Poverty of philosophy* (#M681) to all his friends and has "the greatest esteem" for M, whereas he has only contempt for Proudhon.

15. W&P. **Feb 16:** De Paepe (in Brussels) writes M that he has failed to find a publisher for a French edn of M's *18th Brumaire* (#M267). **Feb CD:** M vainly pursues the effort himself.

16. PERSONAL. **Feb c.4–7:** E stays in London with M; they visit Beesly. **Feb 25:** E pays the first quarterly installment (for Jan-Mar) of M's new annuity [← 68:67] (cf E to M, Feb 25).

MARCH

17. IWMA AFFAIRS. **Mar:** GC sessions: M attends Mar 2, 9, 23; absent Mar 30. **Mar 2:** At GC: M reports on anti-TU police actions in Nuremberg. —M calls the GC's attention to a pamphlet pubd on the condition of life insurance companies. —M nominates GC speakers for the Sunday League meeting of Mar 16. **Mar 9:** At GC: M reports on the German bookbinders' union. —In connection with the Sunday League's drive for Sunday observance, M argues that the best guarantee against Sunday labor is factory legislation, not religious observance. —For action on the Bakunin Alliance, see → :18. **Mar 21:** S. Meyer (in NYC) sends M his first report on the German-American movement. **Mar 23:** At GC: M proposes rescinding the GC resolution for an address to the Spanish Cortes [← 68:61, 68] because of events in Spain.

18. IWMA: BAKUNIN OPERATION. **Mar 4:** Eccarius receives the Feb 27 communication from Bakunin's Alliance and informs M. **Mar 5:** M drafts a reply (#M344) for submission to the GC, and sends it to E, who approves it Mar 7. **Mar 9:** At GC: M presents his draft reply; it is adopted and ordered sent out to sections as before. The decision accepts the dissolved Alliance into IWMA sections, and states that sections may shape their own theoretical programs as long as these do not run counter to the IWMA's [→ :40].

19. GERMAN MOVEMENT. **Mar 27:** Bebel warns M, on the eve of the GGWA congress at Barmen-Elberfeld, not to be taken in by Schweitzer's maneuvers. **Mar 28–30:** At the GGWA congress, where Liebknecht has been invited to present the Bebel view, a large number of delegates abstain in the vote of confidence in Schweitzer: a moral defeat for the latter.

20. POLITICAL AFFAIRS. **Mar M:** M declines an invitation to be a speaker at a memorial meeting for E. Jones.

21. W&P. **Mar 4:** Hearing of Liebknecht's plan to publish E's *Peasant war in Germany* (#E579) in his paper, E writes M that he would prefer it be pubd as a separate brochure; he proposes that the paper run his *Prussian military question* (#E644) instead. **Mar 8:** Meissner writes M that commercial considerations require postponing publ of The *18th Brumaire* (#M267) [← :8]. **Mar 15:** E suggests publishing a larger book containing both The *18th Brumaire* and the three articles comprising M's *Class struggles in France* in the *NRZ-Revue* (#M148). **Mar 20:** M thinks this suggestion undesirable for various reasons.

22. READING AND STUDY. **Mar M:** M reads Castille's *Les massacres de juin 1848,*

and Vermorel's *Les hommes de 1848;* he sends Beesly his annotated copy of the Vermorel.

23. PERSONAL. **Mar A:** M plans to visit Laura, who is ill in Paris, but he has to put off the trip since the French police learn of his intention. **Mar 27:** Daughters Jenny and Eleanor go to Paris to visit the Lafargues [→ :35]. **Mar to Apr:** In spite of bad health M continues his IWMA activity and work on *Capital.*

24. ENGELS. **Mar D to Apr A:** E takes up the study of the Dutch-Frisian language.

APRIL

25. IWMA. **Apr:** GC sessions: M attends Apr 13, 20, 27; absent Apr 6. **Apr 13:** At GC: M reports on the first socialist speeches made in a parliament: made in the North German Reichstag by Schweitzer and Fritzsche (GGWA) and by Bebel (who speaks as an IWMA member as well as for the UGWA). — M criticizes the IWMA's Geneva comm for getting involved in "every little strike" without effective preparation. —M brings up, and the GC discusses, the problem of the London French branch, which is again compromising the movement. —M proposes that the inheritance question be put on the agenda of the coming congress, as requested by Geneva. **Apr 20:** After a report from Hins (in Belgium) on the massacre of strikers in Seraing, M is assigned to write an address on "The Belgian massacres." **Apr 27:** M reports that since "fresh outrages" have occurred in Belgium, the GC address should be taken up next week to get new info; other measures should be taken in the English movement [→ :30]. —M reports on Gen. Cluseret's reply to Bonapartist slanders.

26. GERMAN MOVEMENT. **Apr 5, 6:** On the basis of Liebknecht's report (Apr 3) on the GGWA congress [← :19], M&E discuss Schweitzer's setback with satisfaction. **Apr 6:** F. W. Moll sends M a report on the anti-Schweitzer tendency inside the GGWA and on the Solingen section of the IWMA. **Apr 12:** E. Werner writes M for the German bookbinders' union (Leipzig) asking info on bookbinders' unions and publications in other countries. **Apr 15:** H. Hillmann writes M for the Elberfeld socialists in opposition to a compromise between Bebel's UGWA and Schweitzer's GGWA.

27. POLITICAL AFFAIRS. **Apr 10:** In response to J. M. Ludlow's article on Lassalle in the *Fortnightly Rev,* M sends *Capital* to Ludlow, points to its preface's passage on Lassalle, stresses that he rejects Lassalle's politics and that he (M) showed the "historical necessity" of TUs when all economists and socialists were still condemning them.

28. READING AND STUDY. **Apr M:** M rereads Diderot's *Le neveu de Rameau*, one of his favorite books, a "unique masterpiece" (cf M to E, Apr 15).

29. PERSONAL. **Apr c.12 to May A:** M suffers from a liver ailment and is unable to work.

MAY

30. IWMA. **May:** GC sessions: M attends May 4, 11, 18; absent May 25. **May 4:** At GC: M presents his address on "The Belgian massacres" (#M75) [← :25], and discusses the issues. The GC decides to publish it as a flysheet and circulate it widely in Continental languages; it is pubd through May in English, French, and German. —M reads the GC an appeal issued by the Working Men's Union of NY on behalf of the striking horse-car conductors. **May 11:** At GC: Referring to Eccarius' *Bee-Hive* report on the GC address on the Belgian massacres, Lessner criticizes Eccarius for suppressing M's name and putting himself forward instead; M takes part in the discussion. —M presents his draft of an address to the National Labor Union of the US (#M7), calling on the workers to stop the threat of an Anglo-American conflict; pubd May 15–22 in English and German. **May 18:** At GC: M reports on the police background of the leader of a Brussels "Revolutionary Committee" (with a name similar to the IWMA's) which advocates killing, etc. (This group had been disavowed by the GC on May 11.) —M discusses the warmongering tendency in the US government. —M reports on a debate in Antwerp between a capitalist and an IWMA workman.

31. GERMAN MOVEMENT. **May 16:** E. Gogarten (in Radevormwald) writes M asking for help in establishing a philanthropic-social weekly. **May 24:** Moll, for the Solingen socialists, asks M to get shareholders for the Solingen producers' cooperative and to raise financial support for it. **May 28 to June A:** E. Werner [← :26] asks M to establish a link between the Leipzig bookbinders and the English union; he also reports on the founding of a Leipzig section of the IWMA, consisting of members of the GGWA, the local workers' assoc, and the TUs. In response, M sends him info from Manchester about the English unions.

32. POLITICAL AFFAIRS. **May A:** M gets a visit from Eichhoff. —M receives a letter from S. Meyer (in NYC) with much info on the US workers' movement; also a letter from Harney (who has moved to America) asking for a copy of *Capital*. **May D:** M gets the Urquhartite *Diplomatic Rev* to publish a series of articles on Russian policy by Borkheim.

33. *CAPITAL.* **May A:** M reads the official British reports on child labor in agriculture. —Harney's letter from America (see ← :32) says he wants to find a translator and a NY pub'r for an American edn of *Capital.*

34. W&P. **May c.14 to June 23:** M reads the galley proofs of the second edn of his *18th Brumaire* (#M267) [→ :38].

35. PERSONAL. **May 4–19:** Mrs. M goes to visit the Lafargues in Paris; she returns with daughter Eleanor [← :23]. **May 10:** E sends money to M for the families of the victims of the Belgian massacres. **May c.14:** M hears from Vienna that Peter Fox has died there after a short illness. He writes Fox's rich mother to make sure she gives financial support to Fox's widow and children. **May 25 to June 14:** M stays with E in Manchester, accompanied by daughter Eleanor; they make a three-day excursion to the Yorkshire village of Bolton Abbey, where M meets the geologist John Dakyns, who has applied to join the IWMA and who agrees with M's hostility to Comtism.

JUNE

36. IWMA. **June:** GC sessions: M attends June 15, 22; absent June 1, 8, 29. **June 9:** Looking to the coming IWMA congress, De Paepe (in Brussels) writes M asking him to draft a resolution on the collectivization of landed property, as against the position of the Proudhonists [→ :40]. **June 15:** At GC: M attends, but no participation is recorded. **June 22:** At GC: M reads out a letter from Solingen criticizing the "so-called free religious communities" of the Friends of Light movement. —M reports on Werner's requests for the Leipzig bookbinders [← :31].

37. POLITICAL AFFAIRS. **June 23:** M attends a TU mass meeting in Exeter Hall, in support of the bill to extend TU rights, where Beesly makes an "excellent speech" recalling the June 1848 days in France.

38. W&P. **June 23:** M writes, and dates, the preface (#M268) to the second edn of The *18th Brumaire* (#M267) [→ :43].

39. PERSONAL. **June AB:** M stays in Manchester [← :35], until June 14.

JULY

40. IWMA. **July:** GC sessions: M attends all four—July 6, 13, 20, 27. **July A:** In response to De Paepe's request [← :36], M sends him a longish letter (not extant) criticizing the Proudhonist doctrine on landed property. **July 6:** At GC: M reports on IWMA progress in Holland, esp Amsterdam. —GC resumes precongress discussion of the land question (begun June 29). M takes part, with two talks on the issue, esp criticizing the Proudhonist view (#M598). **July 13:** At GC: M reports on the German cigarmakers' strike, on the basis of letters from Fritzsche (July 11) and Liebknecht (July 7). **July 20:** At GC: M opens the GC's precongress discussion on the right of inheritance: he refutes Bakunin's line (abolition of inheritance as a basic programmatic plank), and agrees to present a resolution at the next meeting. **July 27:** At GC: M reports that Bakunin's Alliance has accepted the GC's conditions [← :18], and proposes it be admitted.

41. GERMAN MOVEMENT. **July c.2:** M declines Liebknecht's invitation to attend the Eisenach congress of workers' assocs called by the Bebel UGWA [→ :48]. He urges Liebknecht to drop his past policy of alliance with the bourgeois-liberal People's party, which should be opposed as he opposes the Lassallean sect; and he presses for carrying out the Nuremberg resolution [← 68:49] on integration with the IWMA (cf M to E, July 3). **July c.14** (rec'd c.17): Liebknecht asks M to draft a sociopolitical program for the coming Eisenach congress of the new party, and also to issue a statement against Schweitzer. **July c.20:** M protests, in a letter to Liebknecht, against the assertion in *Demo Wochenblatt* that the GC has sided with its tendency against Schweitzer. **July 27:** In a letter to Bebel, M criticizes J. P. Becker's proposal to structure the IWMA according to language rather than nationality, and warns against affiliating the new Eisenacher party to Becker's "German-language group of the IWMA" in Geneva instead of directly to the GC.

42. POLITICAL AFFAIRS. **July 27:** Elisée Reclus visits M and gets a copy of the *18th Brumaire* (#M267) autographed. **c.July-Aug:** The letters between M&E come under police surveillance—first some, then all are read by the police (SOURCE: *MEW Daten*).

43. W&P. **July c.20:** The new (second) edn of M's *18th Brumaire* (#M267) is pubd in Hamburg. (This is KMC dating; cf E to M, July 25.) **July c.28:** E revises his unpubd draft [← 68:41] of a biographical article on M (#E405) [→ :50]. **c.July-Aug** (summer): E begins work researching for a history of Ireland (cf #E352, 353).

44. READING AND STUDY. **July D:** M reads with great interest the book by G. Klemm, *Die Werkzeuge und Waffen* (1858).

45. ENGELS: LIBERATION. **July 1:** With the June 30 end of his contract with Ermen & Engels, E ceases to work in the Manchester firm: "Hurrah! . . . I am a free man!" He celebrates, with his guest Eleanor (M's daughter), by taking a long walk in the fields.

46. PERSONAL. **July 7–12:** M stays with the Lafargues in Paris, under the name A.

Williams. He makes no political visits, but does much city walking, observing Paris's "Haussmannization" and its decline in female pulchritude. (M's letter to E, July 14, says he arrived in Paris "Tuesday [July 6] evening"—even though he was present at the GC that evening.) **July 18–30:** M suffers from a painful abscess which interferes with his working.

AUGUST

47. IWMA. **Aug:** GC sessions: M attends Aug 3, 10, 17, 24; absent Aug 31. **Aug 3:** At GC: M reports on the coming Eisenach congress (see → :48) which will establish a new party; also on his rejection of J. P. Becker's scheme for IWMA language groups [← :41]. —M makes proposals for the agenda of the coming Basel Congress, to stress the "education question" over the "credit question." —M reads his draft of the GC report to the Basel Congress on the inheritance question (#M744); adopted. **Aug 4:** Writing to E, M comments on the Aug 3 GC session: he would gladly see the GC transferred to another city if there were capable people there; "the thing is getting boring." **Aug 10:** At GC: Discussing the education point on the congress agenda, M argues that free compulsory education need not be "governmental," i.e., run by the state, even if state-superintended (cf #M590). —M reads the GC an "amusing article" by a French government organ slandering the IWMA as wanting "la dictature universelle." —M proposes that the woman pres of the Lyons silk workers, Philomène Rozan, be given special credentials to the coming congress so that she can attend. —M reports a telegram announcing formation of the new Eisenacher party in Germany (see → :48). —M makes proposals on the presentation of the GC financial report to the congress. **Aug 13:** M urges Jung to attend the meeting of the carpenters' union, where delegates to the Basel Congress will be discussed. **Aug 17:** At GC: In the continued discussion on the education question, M reaffirms the IWMA position in favor of combining education with labor and technological training, but not in the form distorted by the bourgeoisie; he argues for excluding religion from the public schools (cf #M590). —Discussing the existing English and Continental peace societies, M declares he is "against having anything to do with peace societies"; they are "against the working man." —M is assigned to send membership cards to Vienna. **Aug 24:** At GC: M is assigned to draft the GC's annual report to the congress. **Aug 31:** At GC: Lafargue explains that M is absent because of illness, and that he has not yet finished the GC report [→ :53].

48. GERMAN MOVEMENT. Aug 7–9: In Eisenach, the Bebel tendency (UGWA) unites with a group of oppositionists splitting from the Lassallean GGWA and with groups of independent trade-unionists, to form a new party, the Social-Democratic Workers party (SDWP). This party will be commonly known as the "Eisenacher party." **Aug 9:** M is informed of the founding of the SDWP by a telegram from Liebknecht. **Aug c.15:** E. Werner writes M of the intention of the Leipzig section of the IWMA to join the new party, and asks his advice. **Aug 19:** M is informed by letter of the Eisenach congress's decision to affiliate with the IWMA.

49. POLITICAL AFFAIRS. Aug 17: Elisée Reclus visits M, and accompanies him to that evening's GC session. **Aug 18:** Writing to E, M reports that Polish building workers in Posen have won a strike through help by Berlin unions, and sees the class struggle as a force doing away with national prejudices. —M expresses special regret over the sudden death (July 27) of W. Sylvis, pres of the National Labor Union (US). (The GC session of Aug 17 had decided to send an "address of sympathy" to the NLU.)

50. PUBL PLANS. Aug 9: Max Friedländer writes M asking him to write for the Vienna *Neue Freie Presse.* **Aug 11, 21:** E's biographical sketch of M (#E405) [← :43] is pubd in German papers.

51. PERSONAL. Aug 3: E sends M £100 to cancel old debts due to mishandling of funds by Mrs. M.

52. ENGELS. Aug c.19 to Sep A: E goes on a trip to Germany, where he spends a few days with relatives in Engelskirchen.

SEPTEMBER

53. IWMA: BEFORE THE CONGRESS. Sep 1: GC session: M's draft of the GC report to the congress (#M747) is taken up and adopted. **Sep 4, 6:** M sends to Basel his GC report and the draft resolutions on education and on inheritance.

54. IWMA: BASEL CONGRESS. Sep 5: The Fourth Congress opens in Basel (until Sep 12); M does not attend. **Sep 7:** The congress hears the GC report (#M747), read in French by F. Robert. **Sep c.8–9:** Lessner sends M reports from Basel on the course of the congress. (*KMC* lists his letters of Sep 7, 8, 9, 11.) **Sep 11:** The new GC is elected, incl M. —M's draft on the inheritance question (cf #M744) is read to the congress and the question is discussed, but Bakunin's position (abolition of inheritance) gets a plurality vote, though no resolution is carried.

55. IWMA: AFTER THE CONGRESS. Sep 14, 28: GC sessions: M is absent (on a trip—see

→ :56). **Sep 14:** GC session: All corr secretaries are reelected, incl M for Germany. M is named to a comm on cooperation with the National Labor Union (US), as proposed by A. C. Cameron to this session. (Lafargue sends M a report of this session, Sep c.20.)

56. MARX'S TRIP TO GERMANY. Sep c.10–17: M travels, accompanied by daughter Jenny, to visit Kugelmann (in Hanover). On the way they stop at Bruges and Liège; spend a day at Aachen, with M's cousin Karl Philips; travel up the Rhine to Cologne; visit Dietzgen in Siegburg; go to Bonn; spend a day with Paul Stumpf in Mainz; and then head for Wiesbaden, from which they travel to Hanover, arriving on Sep c.17. **Sep c.18 to Oct 17:** M and Jenny stay with the Kugelmanns in Hanover [→ :59]. **Sep 30:** In Hanover, M meets with a delegation of metal workers' union men, led by union treasurer J. Hamann, discussing problems of TU/party relations [→ :66].

57. W&P. Sep c.D: E prepares a second edn of his *Peasant war in Germany* (#E579) [→ 70:57]. —Prob around this time: a Russian trans of the *Com Manifesto* (#ME33) is pubd in Geneva as a pamphlet, without an imprint, prob done by Nechayev (not Bakunin); the trans is garbled and distorted [→ 70:29].

58. ENGELS' TRIP TO IRELAND. Sep 6–23: E, accompanied by Lizzie Burns and Eleanor M, takes a trip through Ireland, visiting Dublin, Killarney, Cork. E takes special note of the soldiery, decimation of the population, general distress, and the consequences of English colonial rule. **Sep 27:** E writes M (in Hanover) describing his impressions of his Irish tour; he asks M to negotiate with Meissner for publ of a book on the history of Ireland, on which he has begun work (cf #E352).

OCTOBER

59. MARX'S TRIP: RETURN. Oct 3: In Hanover [← :56] M is visited by members of the Brunswick Exec Comm of the SDWP (Eisenacher party), Bracke, Bonhorst, and Spier. **Oct 8–9:** M is in Hamburg, where he meets with pub'r Meissner. **Oct 11:** M arrives back in London. **Oct 12:** E, in London, visits M (*KMC* dating for E's visit: Oct 12–c.18). **Oct D:** M has a bad case of the grippe.

60. IWMA. Oct: GC sessions: M attends Oct 19, 26; absent Oct 5, 12. **Oct 19:** At GC: M is present for the first time since the congress. Toward the session's end Lucraft asks M to "say something on anything he pleased." M reports briefly on progress in Germany, TU organizn in Vienna, and the admission of women as members of the bookbinders' union in Leipzig (organized by the Eisenachers). **Oct 26:** At GC: M takes part in the discussion evoked by the great pro-Fenian demonstration in London (Oct 24); he is optimistic about the possibilities of action and the trend against anti-Irish prejudice; he is named to a comm to draft a resolution for the release of the Fenians. —M reports on the Dutch workers' congress in Arnhem on Oct 19, and reads a letter from the Leipzig bookbinders (E. Werner).

61. IRISH QUESTION. Oct M to Dec: M devotes time to studying the Irish question (for his reading, see → :75). During this period M is active in the GC in mobilizing support for the Irish national struggle. **Oct 24:** M, together with his wife and daughters Jenny and Eleanor, attends the great demonstration in Hyde Park in defense of the Fenians. **Oct 26:** At GC: See ← :60. **Oct to Dec:** E works on his planned history of Ireland (#E352) [← :58], researching the historical literature and original sources in Gaelic.

62. GERMAN MOVEMENT. Oct 25: Bonhorst, of the Brunswick Exec of the SDWP (Eisenachers), writes M for advice on activity among the German peasants. **Oct 30:** In a letter to E, M criticizes Liebknecht's weakness and incompetence in the face of the German press campaign against the Basel Congress's decision in favor of land collectivization.

63. CAPITAL. Oct 18: M examines the ms, received from Paris, of a French trans of Ch. 2 by Charles Keller; he writes his comments on it, and returns the ms to Paris via Lafargue. **Oct 23:** Lafargue informs M that Keller has reached Ch. 3.

64. STUDY OF RUSSIAN. Oct c.20: From Danielson (in St. Peterburg) M receives Flerovsky's work *Polosheniye rabochevo klassa v Rossii,* on the condition of the working class in Russia. **Oct D to Jan:** M begins to learn Russian, in order to read Flerovsky's book and also the economic works of Chernyshevsky. M also uses Herzen's *Tyurma i ssylka* as a learning text, from Nov to Jan 9 (cf Mrs. M to E, Jan c.17, 1870).

NOVEMBER

65. IWMA. Nov: GC sessions: M attends Nov 2, 16, 23, 30; absent Nov 9. **Nov 2:** At GC: M inquires about steps to establish a British section of the IWMA. —M questions the inactivity of the corr secy for Belgium, M. Bernard. **Nov 9:** At GC: A letter from M (who is absent) is read, proposing discussion of the Irish question and volunteering to open it. **Nov 16:** At GC: M opens a discussion on the Irish question, specif the attitude of the British government, with a long talk, esp

attacking Gladstone; he proposes a resolution in favor of amnesty to the Fenian prisoners (speech and resolution, #M834). —M reads the GC a letter from De Paepe (Nov 13) proposing to remove the inactive corr secy for Belgium, Bernard; Jung and Dupont are to see Bernard. **Nov 23:** At GC: Discussion on the Irish question continues; Odger and Mottershead attack M's view from a pro-Gladstone stance; M sums up, in favor of "speaking out boldly"; he challenges Odger to submit amendments, for action at the next meeting (cf #M610). —M reports on the metal workers' strike in Lüneburg, on the basis of letters from Hamann and Bomm (see → :66). **Nov 30:** At GC: M's resolution on the Irish question is adopted unanim, though Odger's objections (to soften criticism of Gladstone) lead to discussion by M et al. (Resolution, #M834, is pubd Nov 21, 28, in English press, later on the Continent.) —M reports on an economists' congress at which a Belgian businessman approved the massacre of strikers at Seraing; also on the election of an IWMA worker to the Geneva cantonal council. —M announces he will bring up the case of *Bee-Hive* before the GC.

66. GERMAN MOVEMENT. Nov 1: Re Bonhorst's request [← :62], E points out to M that the Basel Congress resolution for land collectivization is having a good effect; the movement must differentiate small peasants from big landowners; it does not demand the former's collectivization. **Nov 5:** Hamann [← :56] writes M that the metal workers' union has broken with the Lassalleans and invites him to attend the new union's congress in Brunswick. **Nov 13:** Liebknecht urges M to write on theoretical subjects for the *Volksstaat* (organ of the Eisenachers). **Nov 16:** Bomm, the metal workers' secy, writes M about getting aid for the Lüneburg strikers (see ← :65). **Nov 27:** Hamann's report of his conversation with M [← :56], somewhat garbled, is pubd in *Volksstaat* (reprinted from the October number of the union paper). (See ST/14, 2:580.)

67. LAND AND LABOUR LEAGUE. Nov c.14: The Address of the Land and Labour League (founded Oct 27, for land nationalization) is drafted by Eccarius and edited by M, before publ as a pamphlet. **Nov 30:** M gets a membership card in the new league, so dated (prob at the GC meeting).

68. CAPITAL. Nov: M works on the section about ground rent and differential rent. He reads Carey's *Principles of social science,* Johnston's *Notes on North America,* and other works; and corresponds on these problems with E, who also reads Carey.

69. PERSONAL. Nov c.8–26: M is ailing with carbuncles.

DECEMBER

70. IWMA. Dec: GC sessions: M attends Dec 14; absent Dec 7. **Dec 4:** M sends the GC resolution on the Fenians (#M834) [← :65] to Isaac Butt, head of the Irish Home Rule movement. **Dec 14:** At GC: The GC takes up the stream of attacks on it made by the pro-Bakuninist organ *L'Egalité* (Geneva) and *Le Progrès* (Le Locle); M and others refute the points raised [→ 70:4]. —Re the conflict in Germany of Lassalleans vs Eisenachers, M points out that Liebknecht, but not Schweitzer, is an IWMA member and accepts the GC as arbiter. —M stresses the crucial importance of the Irish question "as the solution of the English [question], and the English as the solution of the European." **Dec c.17:** M sends a detailed letter to De Paepe, for the Belgian federation, on the disorganizing work of the Bakuninist Alliance in the IWMA. **Dec 30:** M and Jung visit R. Shaw, a founder of the IWMA, the day before his death [→ 70:3].

71. POLITICAL AFFAIRS. Dec 3: M writes an eight-page memorandum (not extant) on the reasons for the land-collectivization decision of the Basel Congress, for use by Applegarth, who asked for it (GC, Nov 30) to justify the position before certain parliamentary figures. **Dec 15:** The London GWEA, via

Speyer, invites M to its Christmas social affair. **Dec 16:** M gets a visit from Strohn. **Dec 19:** Juch invites M to write an article for the first number of the *Londoner Deutsche Post.*

72. GERMAN MOVEMENT. Dec AB: M strives to raise money for the Solingen producers' cooperative, through Menke (in Hamburg). **Dec 17:** Gutsmann (in Breslau) writes M asking the GC to issue appeals for funds for the striking miners of Waldenburg.

73. CAPITAL. Dec 10: M informs E that Keller [← :63] is interrupting his French trans of *Capital* to start translating *The 18th Brumaire* (#M267). (Keller will not accomplish this task.)

74. ENGELS' TRIP TO GERMANY. Dec D to Jan 6: E goes to Germany, on the way visiting M in London; he stays with family people in Barmen.

YEAR APPENDIX

75. For the period Oct M to Dec, M's reading in Irish history includes works by the following authors: J. P. Curran, Edw. Davies, Giraldus Cambrensis, J. P. Prendergast, Edw. Wakefield, and Arthur Young; also Cobbett's *Political Register,* and pamphlets by Geo. Ensor and A. O'Connor.

1870

CONSPECTUS

1. During the first half of the year the IWMA is progressing much as in 1869, with M active in several fields, including the Irish question (Fenians), still. In Germany his connection is now with the new "Eisenacher party" (SDWP), led by Bebel. The Bakunin operation in the Swiss IWMA is becoming more troublesome but does not yet look lethal to the movement. Then the Franco-Prussian War breaks out in July, followed quickly by Prussian victories and an upheaval in France which brings about the final downfall of Bonaparte and the accession of the Third Republic. The French sections of the IWMA are in turmoil; the German government arrests the leaders of the movement; in England the IWMA swings into a campaign for recognition of the French Republic.

2. In Sep, Engels, having last year ended his connection with his Manchester firm, is finally able to move to London, near M. On the one hand this will mean their closest cooperation, but on the other we will now be able to record less of their activity, for the previously voluminous M–E correspondence

now drops to a trickle. This massively affects the sources for any biographical record, including this *Chronicle.*

JANUARY

3. IWMA. Jan: GC sessions: M attends Jan 1, 4; absent Jan 11, 18, 25. **Jan 1:** At GC: special meeting on the Bakunin problem; see → :4. **Jan 4:** At GC: M proposes R. W. Hume as a US correspondent, Serraillier as corr secy for Belgium, Pfänder as a GC member. —M moves to adjourn the GC's Irish discussion; he announces the death in prison of the Fenian, Richard Burke. —M is named to a GC delegation to attend the funeral of R. Shaw [← 69:70] and proposes a letter of condolence. —M defends the demand for reduction of the workday, against Bakuninist criticism; and announces that the Sub-Comm has replied to the charges of *L'Egalité* (see → :4). —M reports on a letter from Bracke, for the Eisenachers' Brunswick Exec, requesting loans to aid the striking miners of Waldenburg, Silesia [← 69:72]. **Jan 5:** M attends Shaw's funeral with the GC delegation. **Jan c.8:** M writes an obituary for Shaw (#M587);

pubd Jan 15. **Jan 8:** M meets with Cowell Stepney in the Reform Club. **Jan 23:** The Sub-Comm meets at M's house. **Jan 25:** At GC: In M's absence, Jung reports that M has received a letter (dated Jan 12) from the Hanover metal workers' Exec about contact with English unions.

4. IWMA: BAKUNIN OPERATION. **Jan c.1:** M drafts the GC's reply (#M345) to the recent stream of attacks on it by the Bakuninist center in Switzerland [← 69:70]. **Jan 1:** A special meeting of the GC takes up this document and adopts it, for circulation to IWMA sections. **Jan c.8:** M puts some finishing touches on the piece, for Jung to send it out. M himself sends it to the Brussels section, along with a letter to De Paepe on the problem, esp written for the Belgians (not extant), which also deals in detail with the work of the IWMA. **Jan 16:** The reply (#M345) is signed by the GC members and sent out to the IWMA sections as a "confidential communication" headed "The GC to the Federal Council of Romance Switzerland." **Jan 24:** In another letter to De Paepe, M summarizes the facts about the destructive work of the Bakuninists and transmits testimony from Geneva on their authoritarian character.

5. *CAPITAL.* **Jan 24:** In his letter to De Paepe (see ← :4), M asks for info on books dealing with landownership and the agricultural economy in Belgium.

6. READING AND STUDY. **Jan 9:** M finishes reading Herzen's *Tyurma i ssylka* in the course of his learning Russian [← 69:64].

7. PERSONAL. **Jan c.1:** Another grandchild for M: daughter Laura (Lafargue) gives birth to a baby girl (who, however, will die soon) [→ :16]. **Jan M to Mar A:** M is ill, with carbuncles and a cold.

8. ENGELS. **Jan 6:** E returns to Manchester from his German trip [← 69:74]. **Jan to Apr:** E continues work on his history of Ireland (#E352); he studies Old Irish laws, and reads books by Wakefield, Prendergast, Murphy, and others.

FEBRUARY

9. IWMA AFFAIRS. **Feb:** GC sessions: M is absent from all (Feb 1, 8, 15, 22).

10. IWMA: BAKUNIN OPERATION. **Feb 19:** The Sub-Comm takes up the appeal of A. Richard, a Bakuninist who has been expelled in a conflict in the Lyons section. Writing to E today, M says this case has been produced by the anti-Bakunin fight in Lyons, but although Richard is a Bakuninist, there is no case against him "and I will see to it that no injustice takes place" [→ :18].

11. IRISH QUESTION. **Feb 21:** M sends De

Paepe a letter full of material on the atrocities of the English government's treatment of Irish (Fenian) political prisoners, to be used for an article. **Feb 27, Mar 6:** De Paepe prints M's account as-is, in two parts (#M287), in *L'Internationale* (Brussels). **Feb 27 to Apr 19:** With M's help, daughter Jenny (using the pseudonym J. Williams) writes a series of eight articles on the Irish question for *La Marseillaise* (Paris), attacking the cruel treatment of Fenian prisoners (pubd Mar 1 to Apr 24 [→ :20]; the text is in ST/ME28 [IIQ] 379, in English).

12. POLITICAL AFFAIRS. **Feb 6, 13:** M is visited by Dakyns. **Feb 12:** Neumayer (in Vienna) asks M to send material on the land question which he needs for his defense in court. **Feb 18:** After a hiatus of some years, Imandt writes to M, on personal matters.

13. GERMAN MOVEMENT. **Feb 8:** E sends money to the Solingen workers who have formed a producers' cooperative [← 69:72].

14. W&P (E). **Feb 11:** E, having received (Jan 28) Liebknecht's request of Dec 20 for permission to republish the *Peasant war in Germany* (#E579) and his request for a new introduction, writes a new preface (#E580) by this date, and sends it for comment to M, who heartily approves (Feb 12) [→ :29].

15. READING AND STUDY. **Feb 10, 12:** M, having read to page 150 of Flerovsky's book [← 69:64], writes E about it with great admiration.

16. PERSONAL. **Feb D:** Laura's baby [← :7] dies at about two months of age.

MARCH

17. IWMA AFFAIRS. **Mar:** GC sessions: M attends Mar 15; absent Mar 1, 8, 22, 29. **Mar 15:** At GC: M attends for the first time since Jan 4. In response to the application for affiliation by a Paris group of "proletarian Positivists" (Comtists)—an application already accepted by the GC on Feb 8—M and others establish that the group cannot belong as a Positivist branch of the IWMA but only as individual members constituting a section (cf M to E, Mar 19). **Mar 22:** GC approves the affiliation of a Russian section in Geneva, which has asked (Mar 12) that M represent it in the GC. **Mar 24:** M sends a communication (#M343) to the Russian section in Geneva informing it of the GC action and agreeing to represent it; he refers admiringly to the writings of Chernyshevsky and Flerovsky and to the issue of Polish liberation (pubd Apr 15). —Having received a request for membership from the pub'r of *Het Volk* (Rotterdam), Phillipp von Roesgen von Floss, M sends a query about him to Coenen (in Antwerp). **Mar 29:** In M's absence, the GC votes to send him its sympathy on his illness.

18. IWMA: BAKUNIN OPERATION. **Mar 5:** The Sub-Comm meets for the second time [← :10] on the case of Richard (in Lyons), and although Richard is a Bakuninist, votes to clear him completely of the charges and to reverse his expulsion by the Lyons section. **Mar 8:** At GC: The report of the Sub-Comm is unanim adopted; pubd Mar 27 in *L'Internationale*. **Mar 28:** M warns Germany against the Bakuninists: as corr secy he sends the Eisenacher party Exec a "Confidential communication" (#M172), via Kugelmann, containing the Jan 1 circular (#M345) [← :4] plus a summary of the Bakuninist problem. **Mar D:** M warns France: he writes Lafargue (in Paris) about the problem and asks him to keep an eye on Bakunin's supporters in Paris.

19. GERMAN MOVEMENT. **Mar 16:** M writes Liebknecht protesting against the publ in *Volksstaat* of Nechayev's reply (edited by Bakunin) to Borkheim's anti-Bakunin article in *Zukunft*; he also criticizes evidences of the "Lassalle cult" in *Volksstaat*. **Mar 23:** M sends 3000 IWMA membership cards to the Eisenachers' Brunswick Exec. **Mar 24:** M requests the Brunswick Exec to send its quarterly report on the movement in Germany, in accord with IWMA Rules. **Mar 28:** M's "Confidential communication" (#M172) to Germany: see ← :18.

20. IRISH QUESTION. **Mar 1–29:** The first five articles in daughter Jenny's pro-Fenian series [← :11] are pubd (the third article is a collaboration with her father). **Mar 5:** Writing to the Lafargues, M states his basic view on the importance of the Irish question as a key to the English revolution, which in turn is a key to world revolution. **Mar 5, 19:** M sends E an account of the background of Jenny's articles and their reception. **Mar 7:** E reports that in his work on the history of Ireland, he is now dealing with the 19th century. **Mar 19:** M gives his views on the Irish question to Pigott, editor of the *Irishman*. **Mar to June:** E follows the debates in Parliament on the Irish question, specif the bill for police measures in Ireland and Gladstone's Land Bill for Ireland (SOURCE: *MEW Daten*).

21. W&P. **Mar 16:** M's preface (#M268) to the second edn of *The 18th Brumaire* (#M267) is pubd in *Volksstaat*.

22. *CAPITAL.* **Mar c.10–23:** M resumes work on the opus; he finishes his first revision of the ms for Vol. 2. (SOURCE: *KMC*; but *KMC*'s references do not seem to justify the date).

23. PERSONAL. **Mar c.1:** M receives the news of the death of Laura's baby [← :16]. **Mar 22 to Apr c.10:** M suffers from a cough and carbuncles.

APRIL

24. IWMA AFFAIRS. **Apr:** GC sessions: M attends Apr 12, 19, 26; absent Apr 5. **Apr 12:** At GC: With this session M resumes more or less regular attendance. —M and Dupont are named to draft an address denouncing the French government's arrests of striking Le Creusot miners [→ :31]. —M, on Lafargue's recommendation, proposes IWMA credentials for Henri Verlet, editor of *La Libre Pensée* (Paris). —M announces he will raise the question of *Bee-Hive*. —M sends Sorge (in the US) 15 copies of the report of the Basel Congress. **Apr 18:** As M sends Verlet's credentials to Lafargue, he warns against establishing any branch with "sectarian labels," either communistic labels or (as in Verlet's case) "freethinker." **Apr 19:** At GC: M opposes the proposal sent (Mar 26) by Hume (in the US) requiring the naming of different French, German, etc., representatives for American workers. **Apr 26:** At GC: M proposes that the GC break with the now bourgeoisified *Bee-Hive*; he is named to draft a resolution [→ :31]. —M reports on the joint congress of the Dutch and Flemish sections of the IWMA at Antwerp. —M proposes postponing the address on the Le Creusot strikers.

25. IWMA: BAKUNIN OPERATION. **Apr c.M:** Lafargue sends M an extensive report on the activity of the Bakuninists and Proudhonists in Paris, esp Paul Robin [← :18]. **Apr 19:** In a long educational letter to the Lafargues, M summarizes Bakunin's ideas and his operations in the IWMA.

26. IRISH QUESTION. **Apr 9:** In a letter to Meyer and Vogt (in the US), M makes a statement on the key political importance of the Irish question for a revolutionary perspective [cf ← :20] and on propaganda about the issue in America. **Apr 14–15:** M&E exchange letters on the lessons of the Poor Law Inspectors' reports for 1870, esp on tenancy.

27. POLITICAL AFFAIRS. **Apr c.19, 27:** M twice visits the dying Karl Schapper (Schapper dies Apr 28) [→ :32]. **Apr:** M is visited a number of times by Flourens, with whom he discusses the machinations of the Democratic émigrés and the London French branch.

28. GERMAN MOVEMENT. **Apr 28:** In a letter to Bracke (of the Eisenachers' Brunswick Exec), E writes about the importance of getting workers' representatives into the Reichstag. (An excerpt will be pubd May 14 in *Volksstaat*.)

29. W&P. **Apr 2, 6:** E's new preface (#E580) [← :14] to the *Peasant war in Germany* (#E579) is pubd in *Volksstaat*, which also begins serial publ of the work itself (five chapters, until June 25). **Apr 29:** M receives from Geneva six copies he has ordered of the Russian trans of the *Com Manifesto* [← 69:57]; he sends one to E.

30. ENGELS. **Apr:** E again accepts election to the Board of Directors of the Schiller Institute (Manchester) [← 68:60], but he is no longer active in its work.

MAY

31. IWMA. **May:** GC sessions: M attends May 3, 17; absent May 10, 24, 31. **May 3:** At GC: M reports on the French government's persecution of the IWMA to promote its Bonapartist plebiscite; wholesale arrests Apr D. He proposes a declaration denouncing the charge of conspiracy, which is impossible for a real working-class organization. The declaration (#M222) is pubd May 4 and after. — M presents a resolution (#M751) on breaking with *Bee-Hive* [← :24]; it is pubd in the press during the month. *NB:* The GC Minutes erroneously include this item under May 17. **May 7:** Liebknecht writes M that the Eisenacher party invites the IWMA to hold its 1870 congress in Germany. **May 9:** Bracke sends the official invitation for the party Exec. **May 10–15:** M&E exchange letters on the place for the next congress. **May 10:** At GC: In M's absence, Jung proposes M's draft resolution (#M752.5) publicly disavowing the so-called London French branch (now calling itself the French Federal Branch), which had been expelled two years before but is still using the IWMA's name. **May 17:** At GC: M presents the invitation from the Eisenacher party to hold the next congress in Germany; he proposes Mainz. —See under May 3 for an erroneous entry. **May 24:** At GC: M is absent. As a result of a to-do in the English and French press over the GC's decision to hold the next congress in Germany, for the first time a GC member, Harris, echoes the charge made by IWMA enemies that the English GC members are only a "tool" of M and the German members.

32. POLITICAL AFFAIRS. **May 5:** M visits Borkheim, who is ill. **May 7:** M asks E for material for an obituary on Schapper [← :27]. **May 19:** In a letter to M on France after the plebiscite, E derides Bonaparte as an ass without historical perspective, while the French workers are showing that action (not theory) is their element. **May c.23:** M receives from Sorge newspapers and statistical publications on the situation of American workers (sent May 10).

33. GERMAN MOVEMENT—BAKUNIN. **May c.4:** In a letter to Liebknecht, M bids him take a stand in *Volksstaat* against Bakunin and his supporters.

34. PERSONAL. **May 23 to June c.22/23:**

M and daughter Eleanor stay with E in Manchester.

35. ENGELS. **May to July M:** E works on drafting his history of Ireland (#E352) on the basis of his researched material (#E353); he leaves the work unfinished before ending the second chapter.

JUNE

36. IWMA. **June:** GC sessions: M attends June 28; absent June 7, 14, 21. **June 11–12:** Liebknecht and the German party write M and the GC proposing to postpone the coming congress in Mainz to Oct 5 because of the Reichstag elections in Sep. **June 14:** M&E write to the Brunswick Exec of the German party asking for energetic preparations for the congress, and warning against Lassallean attempts to disturb its work (#ME184); this letter is pubd in *Volksstaat* on June 26. **June 21:** At GC: M, though absent, is assigned to draft an address in support of locked-out building-trades workers in Geneva. **June 27:** M writes the German party Exec his strong opposition to postponing the congress. **June 28:** At GC: M reports that Mainz has offered its Marble Hall for the IWMA congress. —M is instructed to write NY that the GC cannot afford to send a delegate to the congress of the National Labor Union (Cincinnati, in Aug). —Since the Federal Council of Romance Switzerland (Geneva) has asked the GC to take a position on the Bakuninist split at the Apr 4–6 congress in La Chaux-de-Fonds, M proposes that the GC recognize both committees, one as the Federal Council, the other (Bakuninist) as a local council only. The resolution (#M752), dated June 29, will be pubd July 23–24. —M proposes that the GC seat be transferred from London to Brussels.

37. PERSONAL. **June c.23:** M and daughter Eleanor return to London from Manchester [← :34].

38. OPINIONS. **June 27:** In a letter to Kugelmann, M discusses some recent notices of his writings in Germany, esp Lange's dim view of Hegel and the dialectical method.

JULY

39. IWMA. **July:** GC sessions: M attends all four—July 5, 12, 19, 26. **July 5:** At GC: M takes part in discussing the situation in France, where the government's crackdown on the IWMA has put its leaders on trial (June 22 to July 5). —M reports on the organizational problems of the American section. — After some discussion of the transfer of the GC seat out of London [← :36], M agrees to continue the discussion, even though the proposal has been passed. —An appeal drafted by M on behalf of the locked-out Geneva building-trades workers [← :36] is adopted (#M478). **July 9:** Sub-Comm meeting: M participates in working up the agenda of the coming congress. **July 12:** At GC: The Sub-Comm's points for the congress agenda are discussed, and elucidated by M. A point is added: a declaration against war. M explains that the "representation of labor question" has been dropped because the political question of working-class parliamentary representation is presently applicable only to England. —M summarizes the question of moving the GC's seat away from London [← :39]; there is an ensuing discussion with Hales. —M defends the GC action on the London French branch [← :31] against F. Le Maître, and proposes to ask the Paris section's opinion. **July 14:** In accord with the GC decision on moving the GC seat, M sends a communication (#M173) to the sections asking their opinion. —M sends Jung a revised version of the agenda for the coming congress, esp intended for Swiss and Belgian papers (#M696). **July 19, 26:** GC sessions: see → :40.

40. FRANCO-PRUSSIAN WAR. July 18: Eugen Oswald writes M inviting him to sign a statement against the war that is being got up by a group of French and German émigrés [→ see below, July 26]. **July 19:** France declares war on Prussia. —The GC assigns M to write an address on the war. M insists on a GC discussion first, since the address must be focused internationally; a discussion ensues. —M reports on France (from a letter by Lafargue), esp re the absence of war feeling and the French section's antiwar manifesto. **July 19–23:** M writes the First Address on the war (#M318). **July 20:** M gets an offer from N. L. Thieblen of the *Pall Mall Gazette* to go to Prussia as its war correspondent or do other writing on the war. —Writing to E, M expresses his first thoughts on the war, which he calls a "farce": the "French need a thrashing," and Prussian victory would be useful for the advancement of the German workers' movement (but cf → below, July 28). **July 22:** In a letter to M, E predicts Bonaparte will be defeated in the war. **July 23:** Sub-Comm meeting: M presents his draft of the address on the war (#M318), which is adopted. **July 26:** At GC: M's address on the war (#M318) read and approved; pubd July 28 in *PMG*. — M reports the refusal to vote war credits in the North German Reichstag by Bebel and Liebknecht, and their antiwar declaration. —M reports on the police persecution of the IWMA in France, and the arrest of Tolain. —Writing to Oswald [← see above, July 18], M replies that he has already signed the IWMA's address on the war and that only the working class can be a real antiwar force, but he does

not close the door to signing [→ :45]. **July 28:** In a letter to the Lafargues, M gives his second thoughts on the war: "I should like that both, Prussian and French, thrashed each other alternately . . ." but that Prussia win only ultimately, since Bonaparte's defeat is likely to provoke revolution in France. He notes that "On both sides it is a disgusting exhibition." Reporting that English workers are saying a plague on both their houses, he adds: "For my own part, I do everything in my power, through the means of the International, to stimulate this 'neutrality' spirit. . . ." In a letter to E, M remarks that "fortunately" war feeling in Germany stems only from the middle class, not the working class, except for the Lassalleans. **July 29:** M sends Liebknecht the First Address on the war (#M318) for publ in *Volksstaat*, and informs him of the GC's approval of his and Bebel's antiwar protest in the Reichstag.

41. ENGELS. July c.5: At the request of M's daughter Jenny, E writes a note (#E528) for a preface to a collection of Irish songs by J. Rissé of Hanover (who, however, will not use it). Jenny sends it off via Kugelmann, July 17. **July 20:** M informs E of Thieblen's offer [← :40 (July 20)] and suggests that E might use this opportunity to write for *PMG*. **July c.27:** After making arrangements with *PMG*, E begins writing his long series of articles "Notes on the war" (#E531), on military aspects of the fighting, which he will continue until Feb M, 1871. The first article appears in *PMG* on July 29. (See the *Register* for the table of articles.)

42. POLITICAL AFFAIRS. July 3–4: M is twice visited by Lopatin (recommended to him by Lafargue); they discuss the Russian revolutionary movement, esp Chernyshevsky's banishment, and problems of the Russian trans of *Capital*, which Lopatin is working on.

43. PERSONAL. July: M has continuing attacks of his old liver ailment.

AUGUST

44. IWMA. Aug: GC sessions: M attends Aug 2; absent Aug 9, 16, 23, 30. **Aug 2:** At GC: M reports on antiwar statements in Germany, and has the Sub-Comm take up the case of a jailed antiwar protester in Paris. —As against a Belgian proposal to shift the 1870 congress of the IWMA to Amsterdam, M proposes to consult the organizn on holding a conference instead of a congress, postponing the latter because of the war. —The GC decides to print another 1000 copies of the address on the war (#M318); few copies are left. —In a communication to the Brunswick Exec of the German party (#M928), M explains why the congress must be postponed and asks for support. He sends the same request to J. P. Becker (in Switzerland), and answers an inquiry about Bakunin's past political course, esp in 1848–49. **Aug 6:** M suggests to Jung that he send the GC resolutions on the Bakunin Alliance to the Swiss federal comm in Geneva (Perret) for publ. **Aug 12:** M receives okays on the congress postponement from the German party and J. P. Becker's comm in Switzerland, and gives them to Jung for the GC. **Aug to c.Dec:** Since a number of corr secretaries have gone to France, M is burdened with almost all of the GC's international correspondence.

45. FRANCO-PRUSSIAN WAR. Aug 3: M finally agrees to sign Oswald's antiwar statement [← :40], reluctantly, and with two provisos. E's name is added on the same terms (Aug 5–7). **Aug 7:** The IWMA address on the war (#M318) is pubd in *Volksstaat*, with passages on Prussia and Bismarck omitted to avoid suppression. **Aug 10:** Writing to M, E expresses his conviction that Bonaparte's fall is looming, and sends reports on the latest fighting. **Aug 12:** M revises Liebknecht's German trans of the address (#M318), and Eccarius sends it for publ in the Aug issue of Becker's *Vorbote* (Geneva). **Aug c.12:** From the Brunswick Exec of the German party, M receives a request for a statement of policy on the war in view of the dispute between the Exec and Liebknecht–Bebel over the defensive element in the war. **Aug 15, 17, 20:** M&E exchange letters on war policy and the situation created by Prussia's victories over the French armies. **Aug 22–30:** While M is visiting in Manchester M&E write a letter to the Brunswick Exec on war policy in answer to their request (#ME88) [→ :48]. **Aug 28:** M collects clippings from the French press in his notebook (cf #M573). **Aug 31:** The Oswald antiwar statement [← :45] is pubd in *Volksstaat*. **Aug:** In his *PMG* series [← :41] E pubs 15 "Notes on the war" (nos. II to XIV, plus two articles with separate titles) (#E531). In article no. XII, pubd Aug 26, E analyzes the French retreat and predicts the disaster of Sedan.

46. MARX'S TRAVELS. Aug 4: M gets £40 from E for a trip to Ramsgate, for his health. **Aug 9:** M and daughter Jenny go to Ramsgate. **Aug 11:** Mrs. M and Eleanor come to Ramsgate too. M is suffering from severe rheumatic pains and insomnia. **Aug 20–22:** M stays in London to consult a physician. **Aug 22–30:** M visits with E in Manchester. **Aug 31:** M returns to London.

47. W&P. Aug 22–30: While in Manchester, M works with E on an article on Karl Blind (#ME106), an exposé on his politics, mostly drafted by E; it remains unfinished.

SEPTEMBER

48. WAR AND REVOLUTION IN FRANCE. Sep 1: Writing to Sorge, M predicts that the present Prussian victory over France will lead inevitably to a war between Germany and Russia which will be "the midwife to the inevitable social revolution in Russia." **Sep 4:** E writes M on the new situation in France created by the military defeat: he expects a "government of the left." **Sep 5:** In Germany the Brunswick Exec of the Eisenachers issues a flysheet with the party's position on the war; it quotes an excerpt from M's letter (#ME88) [← :45] (reprinted in *Volksstaat* on Sep 11). —At four in the morning M receives a telegram from Longuet (in Paris) on the fall of the Bonaparte Empire and the proclamation of the Third Republic.

49. DEFENSE OF THE FRENCH REPUBLIC. Sep 5–10: M is active in pushing the GC into the lead of the developing movement in England for the defense of the new French republic, esp for its diplomatic recognition by England. **Sep c.6 to c.12:** M receives several telegrams from the Paris Federal Comm urging the GC to do everything possible to force England to recognize the Third Republic. **Sep 12:** M writes Prof. Beesly asking for aid to Serraillier's destitute family and for support of the movement to recognize the French republic. **Sep 13:** GC session: M reports on Serraillier's going to Paris, where he has joined the National Guard; his wife should be granted a £1 stipend. M also reports on the requests from Paris for pressure on the English government. —The GC session ends when, summoned by a telegram, its members hasten to a TU meeting to swing the vote for a resolution supporting the French republic. **Sep 14:** M sends IWMA campaign directives in defense of the French republic to Belgium, Switzerland, and the US. **Sep 16:** M writes to Prof. Beesly again, urging him to break through the silent treatment of the IWMA, its manifestos and its activity, in the English press, and to write an article on the IWMA for the *Fortnightly Rev.* (Beesly's article is pubd Nov 1.) **Sep D:** M gives Applegarth ideas for a delegation to Gladstone to press for recognition of the French republic.

50. POLICY ON THE WAR. Sep 6: GC session: M reports on the German party's request for advice on war policy [← :45] and his reply; on the Paris section's address "To the German people" issued Sep 4–5; and on the organizn of antigovernment meetings by the German workers. After a discussion in which M attacks German annexationism in Alsace-Lorraine, M is named to a commission to draft an address to the German workers. (For his writing of the Second Address on the war,

#M813, see → :52.) —M meets with Serrail-
lier (who is leaving for Paris the next day as
the GC's representative) and discusses how to
help the Paris sections. **Sep 7:** E discusses
the French situation with Dupont (who is
preparing to go to France). Writing to M, E
criticizes the chauvinistic aspects of the Paris
address "To the German people," also criticizes the weak bourgeois leadership of the
Third Republic, which will capitulate to the
Germans; a guerrilla war by the French is
unfortunately not likely. **Sep 9:** In Germany,
the members of the Brunswick Exec of the
Eisenacher party are arrested by the government and imprisoned, for issuing the party's
manifesto on the war [→ 71:17]. **Sep 12:** In a
letter to M, E stresses that the French workers
must not allow themselves to be used as the
French bourgeoisie's tools to fight the Prussians; their chance comes after peace is
signed. **Sep 13–14:** M&E exchange letters on
the news of the German government's arrest of
the Eisenachers' Exec. **Sep 14:** M sends a
communication (#M597) to English periodicals, protesting this German arrest (pubd in
PMG on Sep 15). **Sep 16:** M writes E to have
Dupont reply to the chauvinistic manifesto
sent out by the Marseilles section of the
IWMA. (This is the last letter in the M–E
correspondence before E moves to London.)
Sep 16–22: M collects clippings from the
French press in his notebook (cf #M573).
Sep 17: E's article "How to fight the Prussians" is pubd in PMG, as part of the series
#E531; seven other articles in this series are
pubd this month. **Sep 20:** GC session: M
reports on the German arrest of the Eisenacher
party leaders and on police suppression of
other antiwar activities in Germany. **Sep 27:**
GC session: M reports on government repression of the workers' movement in Germany
and the advance of reaction in France. —In a
discussion of English foreign policy, M attacks the English adherence to the 1856 Treaty
of Paris, which limits England's naval power
and strengthens Russia.
 51. IWMA AFFAIRS. **Sep:** For most
IWMA work, see ← :50. —GC sessions: M
attends all five—Sep 6, 9, 13, 20, 27. —
During this period, esp Sep AB, because of the
absence of other corr secretaries in France, M
often works as late as 3 A.M. busy with IWMA
work. **Sep 6:** At GC: M criticizes the NY
activity of Hume, the GC-appointed representative; the GC is to inquire into this. —M
seconds the nomination of the Russian Lopatin as GC member. **Sep 20:** M proposes E
(who has moved to London—see → :53) as GC
member. —M takes part in further discussion of how to improve Hume's work in
America.
 52. THE SECOND ADDRESS ON THE WAR.

Sep 6: At the GC session, after discussion (see
← :50) M is named to a commission to draft an
address to the German workers. —M writes E
of his plan to write a Second Address on the
war, esp directed against German annexationism, and asks E for comments on the military
side of the question, for inclusion. —M
receives a letter from the Paris comm of the
IWMA urgently requesting a new GC manifesto on the war situation; M replies with a
discussion of what the French might do. **Sep
6–9:** M works on drafting the Second Address
on the war (#M813), using E's material on
Alsace-Lorraine. **Sep 9:** A special GC session
adopts M's Second Address (#M813); pubd as
a leaflet Sep 11–13. **Sep 14:** M sends the text
of the Second Address on the war to correspondents in various countries. **Sep c.14:** M
translates the Second Address into German,
for publ in the IWMA German press. **Sep 20:**
At the GC session, M proposes that the First
and Second Addresses (#M318 plus 813) be
pubd together in a single pamphlet (this is
done Sep D). At this point the IWMA, shortly
to become world-famous as a mighty red
octopus swallowing up the world, has only £5
in its treasury. **Sep 21:** M's German trans of
the Second Address (#M813) is pubd in
Volksstaat.
 53. ENGELS MOVES TO LONDON. **Sep 20:**
Having finally settled all affairs connected
with the termination of his work in the firm of
Ermen & Engels, E moves from Manchester to
London, into M's neighborhood, at 122 Regent's Park Road, N.W. (KMC dates the move
Sep c.18).
 54. JOURNALISTIC OFFER. c.Sep/Oct: V.
A. Sleptsov (in St. Petersburg) invites M to
write on polit eco for the Russian journal
Znaniye, appearing Oct 1, which he edits
(KMC dating: c.Sep; MEW dates receipt Oct).

OCTOBER

 55. IWMA. **Oct:** GC sessions: M attends
all four—Oct 4, 11, 18, 25. E attends from Oct
11 on. **Oct 4:** At GC: E is elected as GC
member. —M discusses the campaign for
recognition of the French republic by the
English government, Gladstone's evasions,
and "the Prussianism of the [English] middle
class and their government." **Oct 11:** At GC:
E attends for the first time. —M reports on
continued antiwar meetings and government
arrests in Germany, and on the Lyons rising of
Sep 4 and the farcical Bakunin putsch of Sep
28, which the Rouen IWMA has protested.
Oct 18: At GC: M reports on news from
Serraillier (in Paris). —M criticizes the Belgian section's suppression of the Second
Address (#M813) by failing to publish it in its
press. **Oct 25:** At GC: M reports on Brussels

(which has now partially pubd the Second Address), on Bordeaux (Lafargue's work), on NY, and on Schweitzer's slandering of the IWMA. —M proposes that GC sessions discussing internal matters be closed to non-members of the IWMA. —M proposes P. Robin (a Bakunin follower) as GC member; he supports E for financial secy, but E declines the job.

56. POLITICAL AFFAIRS. **Oct 19:** M continues his correspondence with Prof. Beesly [← :49] with a letter about Bakunin's Sep 28 putsch in Lyons and his farcical "abolition of the state."

57. W&P. **Oct:** E's *Peasant war in Germany* (#E579) is pubd as a brochure by the *Volksstaat* press, with a new preface (#E580) [← :29]. —In his *PMG* series of "Notes on the war" (#E531), E pubs 11 articles.

58. READING AND STUDY. **Oct CD:** E begins studying the work of the German historian G. H. Pertz, *Das Leben des Feldmarschalls Grafen Neithardt von Gneisenau,* for his series "Notes on the war" (#E531). He will use this material in the article "Prussian franc-tireurs" on guerrilla warfare, pubd Dec 9.

NOVEMBER

59. IWMA. **Nov:** GC sessions: M&E attend Nov 1, 8, 15, 29; both absent Nov 22. **Nov 1:** At GC: M reports on letters from the US, esp Bolte's (Oct 12) on the American movement, and reads part of an address on the war adopted by a joint meeting of the French and German branches in America. He also reports on Lafargue's letter (Oct 28) about the movement in Bordeaux. —For the US, M opposes the formation of a CC over the "Yankee element" (native-born) as long as the IWMA there is mainly French and German. **Nov 8:** At GC: M&E attend, but no participation is recorded. **Nov 15:** At GC: M reports on NY agitation in favor of the French republic (letter from Sorge, Oct 30). —M points to Russia's repudiation of limitations in the 1856 Treaty of Paris and suggests a GC discussion on the treaty [← :50]. —E reports on the movement in Vienna. **Nov 29:** At GC: M reports on Germany: more government persecution of the imprisoned SDWP leaders and more antiwar demonstrations in the country. —M proposes Dupont as IWMA representative in Manchester, for better ties with the local Trades Council.

60. GERMAN MOVEMENT. **Nov 17:** In connection with the charge of treason against the imprisoned SDWP leaders in Germany, M at Bracke's request makes a notarized deposition at the London Lord Mayor's office that the SDWP never requested to be a branch or section of the IWMA though many members

were admitted as individuals—this for use by defense counsel in the German court trial. **Nov 29:** For M's report on Germany at GC, see ← :59.

61. W&P (E). **Nov:** E pubs 11 articles in the *PMG* series "Notes on the war" (#E531), incl "The fighting in France" (pubd Nov 11) denouncing the barbarous conduct of the Prussian army against the French irregulars.

DECEMBER

62. IWMA. **Dec:** GC sessions: M&E attend all three sessions—Dec 6, 13, 20. **Dec 6:** At GC: M&E move to ignore Collet's request that the GC help to get aid to Garibaldi from liberals "by putting socialism in the background." —M&E propose a checkup on GC members' recent attendance. **Dec 13:** At GC: M reports the founding of a new section at the Hague. —M takes part in the discussion of how to help strikers of the Elastic Web-Weavers Union. —M&E propose keeping a record of GC members' absence without cause. **Dec M:** M asks IWMA members in Netherlands and Flanders to send the GC local IWMA papers (notice pubd Dec 18 in *L'Internationale*). **Dec 20:** At GC: M reports on the formation of a CC for US sections (letter from Bolte, Dec 6). —M cautions against pressing Belgian and other sections for dues payments at this time. —On M's proposal, a comm (incl M&E) is set up to take any necessary action on the case of the imprisoned German party leaders, before the next meeting on Jan 3. —The GC attendance record for the four months Sep-Dec shows that, save Eccarius, M&E have the best record (one absence). —E is assigned to write the GC address to the sixth congress of the Belgian federation (Dec 25–26); he sends it (#E864) on Dec 23 (pubd Jan 1). **Dec:** M sends Sorge (in the US) various GC publications.

63. *CAPITAL.* **Dec D:** M hears from Lopatin (in St. Petersburg) who i.a. reports on the seizure of a Russian paper for an article quoting from *Capital,* and on the state of the publ of the Russian edn of *Capital.*

64. POLITICAL AFFAIRS. **Dec 13:** Writing to Kugelmann, M discusses the consequences of the German war victory: self-exposure of the German bourgeois republicans and "our professors"; the turning of English public opinion against Germany. But the war "has given the French proletariat practice in arms, and that is the best guarantee of the future." **Dec CD:** M and his family make the acquaintance of the Russian revolutionary Elizaveta L. Tomanovskaya (pseud.: Dmitrieyeva), who comes to London on behalf of the IWMA Russian section in Geneva to discuss the work of the section. M also discusses with her questions about the development of the Russian village community. (She will become friendly with the family, and see M frequently, until Mar M, 1871, when she will become one of the leading women militants in the Paris Commune.)

65. GERMAN MOVEMENT. Dec 19: Sending money collected in England for the families of the imprisoned German party leaders, E writes to Mrs. Natalie Liebknecht with praise for the victims—Bebel, Liebknecht, Hepner—who have just been arrested (Dec 17) in Leipzig for their antiwar activities.

66. W&P (E). Dec: E pubs 10 articles in the *PMG* series "Notes on the war" (#E531).

67. READING AND STUDY. Dec D to Jan A: M reads Chernyshevsky's writings on common property in land in Russia.

1871

CONSPECTUS

1. This year is dominated by France. Even before the outbreak of the Paris Commune, one of the GC's main tasks is organizing an international campaign in defense of the new French Third Republic, in particular a campaign for English recognition of the republic. During the 72 days of the Commune (Mar 18 to May 28) M is closely involved both politically and emotionally. With the defeat of the Commune, and during the entire second half of the year (and beyond) the GC and M face the big problem of Communard refugees needing money, jobs, papers, etc. There are political lessons to be discussed. There is a veritable flood of lies and calumnies engulfing the IWMA (along with the Commune) in the world press. On the other hand there is new interest in the movement, and many letters of inquiry to be followed up. In England, after the establishment of a separate British Federation with its own Federal Council, there develops a clique of English trade-unionists, headed by John Hales, hostile to the GC and to M. On the Continent the Bakunin operation, which is nucleating IWMA sections, esp in Switzerland, Italy, and Spain, starts going into high gear.

JANUARY

2. FRANCE AND THE WAR. **Jan 3:** GC session: M discusses the Dec 30 statement issued by a group of Comtists plus some GC members, on the French situation, mostly favorably; he remarks that Beesly and his Comtist (Positivist) friends are the only (bourgeois) elements who support the campaign for recognition of the French republic; but he criticizes the concluding call for England to declare war on Prussia in aid of France. **Jan 17:** GC session: M proposes to query the IWMA status of the German Swiss paper *Felleisen* which is supporting the annexation of Alsace-Lorraine; i.e., he implies a threat of expulsion. —M gives a talk on Jules Favre's political record, to counteract Odger's support of Favre at mass meetings on Jan 6, 10. **Jan 21:** Writing to Meyer (in the US), M reports on the English workers' movement for recognition of the French republic—which, however, unfortunately "thinks it can conduct a revolutionary war without a revolution." **Jan 24:** GC session: E proposes that the GC discuss the attitude of the English workers on the present phase of the war. M&E discuss the advisability of publishing the material in M's Jan 17 talk on Favre (see above). **Jan 31:** E gives a long talk (cf #E545) initiating GC discussion of the topic raised Jan 24, on IWMA policy in the present phase of the war situation: he favors the campaign to defend the French republic in England (a campaign for recognition) but opposes the drive by the Comtist group to bring about an English declaration of war against Prussia; he discusses English foreign policy in this period. Boon states his disagreement with E's flat opposition to military intervention by England, for it may be feasible for the workers to "compel the government to make war for liberty abroad." While debate is adjourned, E presents some tentative resolutions (which are pubd Feb 4). **Jan:** M obtains confidential info on the difficulties of the German army in France (through J. Miquel) and sends it (via E) to Lafargue (in Bordeaux) since it may be useful for organizing popular resistance to the German invasion.

3. IWMA. **Jan:** GC sessions: M&E attend all four—Jan 3, 17, 24, 31. See ← :2 for some business. **Jan 1:** E's GC address to the Belgian sections (#E864) [← 70:62] is pubd in Brussels. **Jan 3:** At GC: M&E participate in a discussion on Hales's expulsion from his union. —They propose an appeal for financial aid to the families of the imprisoned German socialist leaders, Bebel et al. —E reports on the slack state of the Spanish IWMA (letter from F. Mora, Dec 14). —E is appointed corr secy for Belgium. **Jan 17:** At GC: M reports sending money for the German political prisoners. **Jan 20:** Eccarius informs M that the *Eastern Post* is willing to publish IWMA material (GC reports, etc.). **Jan 21:**

Writing to Meyer (in the US), M makes proposals for the activity of the CC of the American sections, and reports on the IWMA's situation in various countries. — Writing to Harney, M deplores the fact that most of the TU leaders in the GC look on it "only as a means of furthering their own petty personal aims," esp to get into Parliament. **Jan 24:** At GC: M discusses the formation in the American IWMA of a CC of foreign-language sections. —Again urging aid to the German prisoners, M reports a letter (Jan 18) from Mrs. Natalie Liebknecht on prison conditions. **Jan 31:** At GC: M reports on the paper *Revolución Social* in Palma, and criticizes its Bakuninist leaning; the GC decides to send it its documents on Bakunin's Alliance. —E is appointed temporary corr secy for Spain.

4. *CAPITAL.* **Jan 21:** M asks Harney (in the US) to get him some documents on the disposal of public lands in the US, from Washington, for Vol. 2. (Harney will reply in Feb that these documents are out of print.)

5. GERMAN MOVEMENT. **Jan AB:** M&E are active in organizing the GC's financial aid to the families of the imprisoned German socialists (see ← :3). **Jan 13:** M sends £5 in the name of the GC to the wives of Bebel and Liebknecht, and warns against printing articles by Nechayev in *Volksstaat*. **Jan 16:** M sends a communication to the liberal *Daily News* (#M330) on Bismarck's police-state regime in Germany and the persecution of the German socialists; pubd Jan 19.

6. POLITICAL AFFAIRS. **Jan 1:** Reinhardt (from Paris) visits M; M has him send money to the families of Bebel and Liebknecht. (In the ensuing months M meets with Reinhardt a number of times.) **Jan 7:** M receives a letter from E. Tomanovskaya (Dmitriyeva) with data on czarist agricultural policies, also a copy of *Narodnoye Delo* (pubd by the Russian section of Geneva) with an article on agrarian reform and common property in land in Russia. **Jan 21:** Writing to Meyer (in the US), M reports on his progress in studying Russian and praises the works of Chernyshevsky and Flerovsky.

7. W&P. **Jan:** E pubs seven articles in the *PMG* series "Notes on the war" (#E531).

8. PERSONAL. **Jan to May:** M suffers severely from a chronic cough.

FEBRUARY

9. FRANCE AND THE WAR. **Feb 4:** In long letters to Lafargue and Kugelmann, M gives a condemnatory analysis of the French "Government of National Defense" which is preparing to capitulate to the Prussians instead of carrying on a revolutionary war against them. **Feb 7:** GC session: Debate continues [← :2] on E's statement about war policy;

some GC members, incl Eccarius, frankly come out in favor of war, as against E. (M&E do not take the floor at this session.) **Feb c.12:** M hears from Lafargue (letter of Feb 9) on the results of the elections to the French National Assembly. **Feb 14:** GC session: M reports on Serraillier's speech in Paris. — Debate resumes on war policy: M gives a long talk in support of E's position. **Feb 19:** M is visited by Serraillier (returned from Paris today), who reports on the situation in France. **Feb 21:** GC session: M states that the account of his Feb 14 talk at the GC given in the Minutes and in the *Eastern Post* is so error-filled as to be impossible to correct; he gives some examples. **Feb 28:** GC session: Further debate on war policy, with M&E participating, takes place. E reports on developments in France. Serraillier (who has been in France since last Sep 7) gives a long report on his experiences. M comments on Odger's support to Favre and the French government.

10. IWMA. **Feb:** GC sessions: M&E attend all four—Feb 7, 14, 21, 28. See ← :9 for some business. **Feb 13:** On behalf of the GC, E writes a communication "To the Spanish Federal Council" (#E866) in reply to the council's letter of Dec 14. **Feb 14:** At GC: M reports on developments in Vienna and in Prussia. **Feb 28:** At GC: Near the conclusion of the GC discussion on war policy, E suggests another such discussion on another topic: the program of the bourgeois-liberal Land Tenure Reform Assoc.

11. GERMAN MOVEMENT. **Feb 4:** At the request of Morley, editor of the *Fortnightly Rev*, M invites Johann Jacoby to write an article on German affairs for the magazine. (Jacoby declines, Feb 12.)

12. PERSONAL. **Feb A:** M has a new grandson: a third child is born to daughter, Laura Lafargue [→ :38].

13. W&P (E). **Feb:** E pubs three articles in the *PMG* series "Notes on the war" (#E531).

MARCH

14. FRANCE AND THE WAR: ON THE EVE. **Mar 7:** GC session: M reports on France, incl Tolain's move to the right. —On war policy: M returns to the question of the 1856 Treaty of Paris [← :2], discusses British naval and foreign policy, and opines that pacifism acts "always in favor of the greatest military power." **Mar 14:** GC session: M tells of press reports that the French IWMA has expelled all Germans except M, Liebknecht, and Jacoby; the GC will write for info. M reports on other canards about the IWMA in the Paris press. —The adjourned debate on war policy [← :9] resumes, with M discussing the London Black Sea Conference just taking place (Jan to Mar). E gives a summing-up talk. The only proposition acted on is one urging England to renounce the Treaty of Paris.

15. PARIS COMMUNE: BEGINNING. Mar 18: Revolution breaks out in Paris, after a confrontation on the butte Montmartre; the CC of the National Guard is installed in City Hall. (The news reaches England on Mar 19.) **Mar 19 to May D:** M immediately begins to follow the French and English press on the events in Paris, filling notebooks with excerpts and notes from the papers. One set of notebooks covers newspapers of Mar 18 to Apr 30 (#M572) [→ :20]. **Mar 21:** GC session: Serraillier reports that letters make clear that the so-called Montmartre affair of Mar 18 was not a mere mob action. E gives a long "description of the state of things in Paris" based on letters and the press; Serraillier supplements. —M proposes a GC delegation go to tomorrow's "republican meeting" (founding of the Central Republican Assoc) to have the audience express sympathy with the "Paris movement." —M presents a statement denouncing the press reports about anti-German expulsions in the Paris IWMA (#M859); pubd Mar 23 et seq. —Serraillier reports that the *Paris-Journal* has pubd a forged "Marx" letter. **Mar 21:** M sends letters to the *Times* and to German papers (signed by M&E, drafted by E) denouncing the forged "Marx" letter being spread from Paris to the European press (#ME181); pubd Mar 22 in the *Times*. **Mar 23:** M sends a communication to *Volksstaat* (#M920) denouncing the forged letter and citing the Mar 21 statement (#M859); pubd Mar 29. **Mar 27:** H. Scheu (in Vienna) writes M urgently requesting reliable info on the Paris events and the IWMA's position. **Mar c.27–28:** M has a talk with Serraillier before the latter returns to Paris. **Mar 28:** GC session: M proposes that the GC issue an address to the people of Paris; M is assigned to write it. (This will be #M143.) —M announces that Serraillier has gone back to Paris. **Mar 29:** Jung reports to M the content of a brief letter he has just received from E. Tomanovskaya (Dmitriyeva) from Paris. **Mar 30:** Leo Frankel, the Commune's commissioner for labor and commerce, writes to M asking his views on what social measures the Commune should take [→ :20]. **Mar 31:** In response to a request from P. Coenen of *De Werker* (Antwerp), M sends this paper a denunciation of the forged "Marx" letter (#M922); pubd Apr 8. **Mar c.31:** M sees reports from Serraillier on the situation in Paris: these are his letters to his wife of Mar 29, 30. **Mar D:** M begins sending out letters to various IWMA sections urging aid to the Commune—"several hundred" such letters by May.

16. IWMA. Mar: GC sessions: M&E attend all four—Mar 7, 14, 21, 28. See ← :15 for most of the business. **Mar 7:** At GC: M reports on the request of the NY comm to be considered the CC for the whole US; M favors only a CC of the foreign sections (to prevent domination of native branches by foreign-language sections) [← :3]. —E reports on the demise of the Palma paper [← :3]. **Mar 14:** At GC: M reports on the IWMA in NY and its new Irish section; and on the German elections: Bebel is the only socialist elected to the first Reichstag of the new German Empire. —M&E oppose calling a London Conference at present because of IWMA disorganization on the Continent. —M supports making the next GC debate treat the Irish question. **Mar 21:** At GC: M reports on the imprisoned German socialists, Bebel et al. **Mar 28:** At GC: M reports on government repression of the IWMA in Prussia and Vienna. —In a discussion of the new English republican movement, E argues that IWMA people in it should ensure its working-class character if it is not to become a mere clique; M says a serious republican movement must have a social program; the present "wire-pullers" have no such aim. —The GC attendance record for Jan-Mar shows that M&E and two others have a perfect record. **Mar c.31:** Coenen, editor of *De Werker* (Antwerp), writes M asking IWMA support for striking cigar workers.

17. GERMAN MOVEMENT. Mar 2: M sends Mrs. Natalie Liebknecht some info of use to the defense of the imprisoned socialists. **Mar 10:** Writing to two IWMA members in Solingen, K. Klein and F. Moll, E praises the "model conduct" of the German workers' movement in the war period. **Mar 30:** The German government releases Bebel, Liebknecht, and Hepner [← 70:50] pending their trial [→ 72:16].

18. POLITICAL AFFAIRS. Mar 29: Charles van Rodenback writes M from the Hague asking for British support to his paper *De Vrijheid*.

19. W&P (E). Mar 16: E pubs his last article on the war in the *PMG* series (#E531); see #E42).

APRIL

20. PARIS COMMUNE. Apr to May: M continues to send a stream of letters out to IWMA sections for aid to the Commune [← :15]. He maintains some communication with Commune leaders in Paris through a "German merchant" (prob N. Eilau) who travels between Paris and London all year round, often with oral messages rather than written; and thus provides some info to his Commune contacts (supplied to M by J. Miquel) on questions such as how to sell certain securities on the London Exchange (to finance the government), or the secret Bismarck–Favre agreement [→ :23]. **Apr 1 to May D:** M continues [← :15] to fill notebooks with excerpts and notes from the press on the Paris events. Besides a notebook covering Mar 18 to Apr 30 (#M572), M fills a notebook (#M573) with French press excerpts covering Apr 1 to May 2. **Apr c.2:** M receives Frankel's letter of Mar 30. (His reply is not extant.) **Apr 3:** M writes a letter to the *Times* refuting the Paris press slanders about IWMA fomenting the Commune (#M916); pubd Apr 4, 6. **Apr 4:** GC session: E tells the GC that in M's opinion, an address on the Commune would now be "out of place," because of the Apr 3 defeat of the Commune forces. **Apr 6:** Writing to Liebknecht, M briefly discusses the main mistake being made by the Commune leadership, failure to take the revolutionary offensive against Versailles. **Apr 12:** Writing to Kugelmann, M again discusses the mistakes of the Commune, along with enthusiasm over its revolutionary heroism. He underlines the political lesson that in a revolution it is necessary to smash the bureaucratic-military machinery of the state. **Apr M:** M gets reports on the situation in Paris from Serraillier's letters to his wife of Apr 12, 15. **Apr CD:** M begins writing the first draft of his address on "The civil war in France" (#M144) [→ 23]. **Apr 17:** In another letter to Kugelmann, M argues that if the Paris workers had not fought in this situation, their demoralization would be a greater misfortune than the consequences of defeat; and he stresses that with the Commune the proletarian struggle "has entered upon a new phase." **Apr 18:** GC session: M reports that Serraillier has been elected to the Paris Commune. As the question of writing an address is raised again, M opines that an address on "the general tendency of the struggle" is possible, perhaps preceded by issuance of a general resolution. —In response to the Paris IWMA's expulsion of Tolain (who has sided with Versailles) M&E say it should be confirmed by the GC if the facts are verified. **Apr 25:** GC session: M gives a long talk on the Commune, along the lines of the address he is preparing; he promises the draft for the next meeting. —M reports the election of both Serraillier and Dupont to the Commune and the right-wing attack on them. —Tolain's expulsion in Paris having been verified, E offers a resolution confirming the expulsion (#E678); pubd Apr 29. —Leo Frankel [← :15] sends M an inquiry about the Commune's selling French securities on the London Exchange. **Apr c.26:** M replies to Frankel's inquiry, also

writes about the attacks on Serraillier in Paris, the coming GC address on the Commune, and the utilization of M's emissary (the "German merchant") for messages [→ :23]. **Apr 29:** Schily (in Paris) writes M that if he wants to do research on French agriculture he can now work in the Paris libraries since the Commune is in control. (Schily is not joking.) **Apr-May:** M gets frequent visits from Fox Bourne, editor of the London *Examiner*, to discuss the Paris events; and these conversations positively affect the paper's treatment of the Commune.

21. IWMA. Apr: GC sessions: M&E attend Apr 4, 18, 25; E attends also Apr 11, but M is absent (for the first time since last Nov 22). —For most of the GC's business, see ← :20. **Apr 4:** At GC: E reports on the lockout of the Antwerp cigarmakers, who need help (letter of Coenen to M, Mar 29); E proposes measures. —E reports on the release of Bebel, Liebknecht, et al, from their German prison, awaiting trial (letter of Liebknecht to M, Apr 1). **Apr 5:** E sends a communication (#E569) to *Volksstaat* calling for German support to the Antwerp strikers; in a letter to Coenen, he reports on GC steps to support the strike, and asks Coenen to send *De Werker* regularly. **Apr 11:** At GC: E reports on events in Spain, and on the current press canard that M had once been Bismarck's private secy. **Apr 18:** At GC: E reports on Madrid's appeal for strike aid, and on pro-Commune mass meetings in several German cities. —M reports that the Prussian police had been prepared to arrest him if he came to Germany (info supplied by Miquel, via Kugelmann's letter of Apr 15). **Apr 19:** E sends Eccarius info on the textile strike in Barcelona, urging GC help among the Manchester workers. **Apr c.25:** E studies the letters and press reports received from Spain on the Barcelona strike. **Apr 25:** At GC: E reports on economic conditions in Spain. —M communicates Sorge's report of Apr 2 on the IWMA sections in NYC.

22. German Movement. Apr 5–8: *Volksstaat* reprints E's 1868 review of *Capital* (#E689). **Apr 6:** Writing to Liebknecht, M asks that Bebel send regularly the stenographic reports of Reichstag proceedings; he gives a biting portrait of Karl Blind in his present German-chauvinist phase. **Apr A:** Liebknecht proposes to M writing a new preface for a republ of the *Com Manifesto*. **Apr c.10, 12:** In letters to Liebknecht and Kugelmann, M reports that the Commune has pubd official documents confirming that Karl Vogt had been paid from the secret funds of the Bonaparte regime in 1859—just as had been charged at that time. (Liebknecht pubs this info in *Volksstaat* on Apr 15.) **Apr 13:** M advises Liebknecht that he and E will see about a new preface to the *Manifesto*, but cautions against reprinting from the NRZ-Revue (e.g., #M148) without new prefaces. He urges Liebknecht to reprint excerpts from *Capital*, esp on primitive accumulation.

MAY

23. PARIS COMMUNE. May: For M's letters in aid of the Commune and for his notebooks of press excerpts, see ← :20. **May 1:** M&E reject a proposal by E. Oswald and J. K. Kern to take part in a discussion of how to mediate between Paris and Versailles. — Reinhardt writes M from Paris. —Tomanovskaya's letter of Apr 24 from Paris arrives in Jung's hands and is shown to M. **May 2–22:** M is ill and cannot attend GC meetings. **May 2:** GC session: E explains, in M's absence, that M has not yet finished the address on the Commune. Eccarius proposes to suspend the rule requiring the signing of all GC names to official documents in the case of this address; E and others object. **May A:** M meets with the Russian Peter Lavrov, who has come from Paris on behalf of the Commune to establish direct relations with the GC. **May 9:** GC session: E explains that M is seriously ill, but the address on the Commune will be ready in four days, for action by the Sub-Comm. E gives a report on the events in Paris. **May c.10–c.M:** M works on the second draft of the address on the civil war in France (#M145). **May 11–13:** M again meets with the "German merchant" [← :20] who is his go-between with the Commune, and gets info on the situation in Paris (KMC dating: May c.9–13). **May 12:** Mrs. M writes a moving letter to Kugelmann on M's and the family's suffering over the plight of Paris; she fears Paris is on the eve of a massacre. **May 13:** M sends a letter, via his emissary, to Leo Frankel and L. E. Varlin of the Commune, with info and advice. **May c.M:** M begins drafting the final version of the address "The civil war in France" (#M143). **May 16:** GC session: E reports that M is still ill, the address still unfinished. **May 23:** GC session: M attends, and says he hopes to have the address by the next meeting; he discusses the meaning of the Commune at this point when it appears to be succumbing. M&E take part in a discussion of the looming refugee problem and the future persecution of the IWMA and the Communards. **May 30:** GC session: M presents his draft of the address "The civil war in France" (#M143); it is adopted unanim without further discussion.

24. IWMA. May: GC sessions: E attends all five—May 2, 9, 16, 23, 30; M is absent May 2, 9, 16. For most of its business, see ← :23. **May 9:** At GC: E reports on strikes in Spain and Belgium, and on a letter from New

Zealand. —E supports sending a GC representative to an Owen centenary meeting, with a glowing tribute to Owen; he defends Owen's contribution against Mottershead. **May 16:** At GC: M is provisionally named corr secy for Holland. —E participates in discussing nominees for gen secy, to replace Eccarius, who has resigned.

25. GERMAN MOVEMENT. May 4: M sends Liebknecht a summary of the evidence on Karl Vogt's subsidization by the Bonaparte regime [← :22] and replies to Vogt's denial. **May 5:** E writes an article for *Volksstaat* on the Vogt exposé (#E571) and sends it to Liebknecht; pubd May 10. E also asks the German movement to help the Antwerp and Brussels strikers.

26. CAPITAL. May 11: Danielson writes M asking him what changes he wants to make in the Russian trans of *Capital*.

27. PERSONAL. May 1: Daughters Jenny and Eleanor arrive at the Lafargues' (in Bordeaux) for a month-long visit [→ :32].

JUNE

28. IWMA AFTER THE COMMUNE. June: M&E begin the task, for the rest of the year and more, of organizing relief work for the Communard refugees and their families who have fled to London (and elsewhere). This involves a great deal of activity, noted below only partially. Until Sep, M will be an active member of the GC's refugee-aid comm, helping to get funds, provide jobs, and obtain passports and other papers for Communards still hiding in France. —GC sessions: M&E attend all four—June 6, 13, 20, 27. **June 6:** At GC: M gives a talk replying to enemies of the IWMA and the Commune, i.a., the International Democratic Assoc and the English press reporting on the Commune, incl an article by Mazzini etc. **June A:** M receives Sorge's letter of May 25 asking for a letter to the NY sections discussing the Commune and the June days of 1848. **June 11:** At a Sub-Comm meeting at E's house, with M also present, E presents a draft of a GC reply to Favre's charges against the IWMA (#ME85). **June c.13:** *The civil war in France* (#M143) is pubd—see → :29. **June 13:** At GC: E reports on the Sub-Comm meeting of June 11 and the reply to Favre (#ME85). M proposes a special campaign of exposure against Favre, as a duty to the Commune. —E reports on correspondence from Barcelona. **June 20:** At GC: This meeting sees the first blowup in the council over the Commune, in response to the outside press witch-hunt against the IWMA and the Communards. As E proposes a GC reply to Holyoake's attack on *The civil war in France*, Odger and Lucraft call GC members "satellites of Dr. Marx" and "tools," and walk out, resigning from the GC. The GC adopts the reply to Holyoake (#E776), which for the first time names M as the author of the address on the Commune. —M proposes a letter to the press denouncing Paris police forgeries of IWMA documents [→ :30]. —M&E propose J. P. McDonnell as GC member. **June 20:** Danielson (in St. Petersburg) writes M asking for all IWMA publications. **June 27:** At GC: E proposes that the Sub-Comm take care of Communard refugee relief. —E proposes a reply to a new attack on the GC by Lucraft and Holyoake (#E777); cf → :29. M opines that Odger has acted in a cowardly fashion. —M hands in "another £4" collected, for the new refugee-aid fund established at this session. **June 28:** T. Allsop, the old Chartist, writes M with info on Thiers's past. (In the ensuing period, to Sep A, M corresponds with and meets Allsop, esp on refugee-aid work.) **June 30:** E writes an article on *Volksstaat* (#E4) on the sensation stirred in England by the publ of *The civil war in France* (pubd July 5). — Robert Reid, the *Daily Telegraph*'s Paris correspondent during the Commune, writes M offering help to counteract the press campaign against the Commune [→ :33]. **June CD:** Writing to E on June 12 and 28, Carlo Cafiero of the Naples IWMA inaugurates a correspondence with E [→ :37].

29. *THE CIVIL WAR IN FRANCE*: **June c.13:** The GC address [← :23] is pubd as a pamphlet (#M143) in an edition of 1000. **June M to July M:** E translates the address into German, and sends it to Liebknecht for publ in *Volksstaat* and for forwarding to J. P. Becker for *Vorbote*. **June 28 to July 29:** *Volksstaat* pubs the address serially. **June c.D:** A second English edn is pubd, corrected and augmented (with the appended Notes now added), in 2000 copies.

30. OPERATION CANUTE. **June-July:** In response to the flood of fabrications, lies, rumors, and invective disseminated against the IWMA and the Commune, in the English and the world press, for a while M&E work at sending out replies, denials, etc. **June 8:** M sends the *PMG* a denial of its June 7 report that he has been arrested in Holland (#M465); pubd June 9. **June 12:** M&E send the *Times* a letter (#ME85) replying to Jules Favre's circular against the IWMA, signed by Hales as gen secy (pubd in the *Times* on June 13, and then, June D, incorporated into the second edn of *The civil war in France* as Note II). **June c.20:** M writes, on behalf of the GC, a letter to the *Times* (#M931) refuting Paris press fabrications that have appeared in that paper; not pubd. **June 20:** In reply to misstatements in the *Standard* of June 19, M writes a letter of rectification (#M915); not pubd. —E writes

a statement for the GC, replying to Holyoake's June 20 letter in the *Daily News* (#E776); signed by Hales as gen secy, dated June 21; pubd June 23–24. **June c.21:** As decided by the GC on June 20, E writes a letter on the fake IWMA documents filling the press, to be sent to the *Spectator* or *Examiner* (#E826); not pubd. **June 26:** M writes a letter (#M902) to the *Daily News* in reply to its attacks on *The civil war in France* and the IWMA; he takes responsibility for its charges against Favre as author of the address (partially pubd June 27; fully pubd July 1). **June 27:** E writes a statement for the GC replying to letters by Holyoake and Lucraft in the *Daily News* of June 26 (#E777); signed by Hales as gen secy; pubd June 29. **June 30:** M writes a sharp letter (#M466) to the editor of the *PMG*, Frederick Greenwood, on its charge that M slandered Favre; Greenwood does not print it (pubd July 8 in *Eastern Post*). —M sends a letter (#M926) to editor Max Friedländer of the *Neue Freie Presse* exposing a fabricated story about M and Herzen that had appeared in the Vienna *Presse*; pubd July 4.

31. CAPITAL. **June A:** M receives from Danielson (sent May 23) books and articles in Russian, incl writings by Chernyshevsky, and a letter informing him of the state of work on the Russian trans of *Capital*, also offering money toward the publ of Vol. 2. **June 13:** Replying to Danielson, M tells him that Vol. 2 is not finished, and that he cannot at present do his planned revision of Ch. 1 of Vol. 1 (he will do it for the second German edn).

32. PERSONAL. **June-July:** From Bordeaux [← :27] M's three daughters, with the Lafargue family, go on holiday to Bagnères-de-Luchon in the French Pyrenees, where Jenny will convalesce from a pleurisy attack [→ :43]. **June 13:** M writes warning them to move across the border into Spain, but Laura's baby is very ill [→ :38].

JULY

33. AFTER THE COMMUNE. **July:** For M's continued collection of press materials on the Commune, see the reference to a May-Aug notebook in ST/M76 (Notebook on the P.C.) 109 (cf #M574). M's work in collecting material is dated "June-July" in *MEW*, "June to Sep" in *KMC*. **July c.1:** Robert Reid [← :28] visits M and gives info esp on the conduct of the US ambassador, E. B. Washburne, in Paris during the Commune period. **July 4:** GC session: M reports on Reid's plan to make a lecture tour on the Commune and to sell copies of *The civil war in France*. **July 7:** Sub-Comm meeting approves M's draft of a GC address on US ambassador Washburne (#M521). **July 8:** M attends a meeting called by the Club International Socialiste of French émigrés to discuss a protest action against the sentences passed on the Communards. **July 10:** T. Dombrowski writes M to bring before the GC the case of the widow of J. Dombrowski, the Commune general; she needs help. **July 11:** GC session: M's address on Ambassador Washburne (#M521) is adopted (pubd as a leaflet July c.13). —M reports that a Mainz workers' meeting has adopted *The civil war in France* as its own. **July M:** M tries to get T. Dombrowski a position as correspondent for the *NY Herald.* **July 16:** *L'Internationale* (Brussels) begins publ (till Sep 3) of a French version (prob by M) of *The civil war in France.* —Lavrov and some Communard refugees visit M's house. **July 18:** M, accompanied by E, Serraillier, and Robin, visits Prof. Beesly to discuss measures to aid the Communard refugees. —GC session: E reports on translations of *The civil war in France,* and takes part in a discussion of ways and means of raising refugee aid funds. M reports on the case of Gen. Dombrowski's widow. **July 25:** GC session: M reports that the second edn of *The civil war in France* is exhausted, and suggests another printing. **July c.26:** M advises Robert Reid to reply to the *Daily Telegraph*'s assertion that Reid is not connected with the paper as claimed. (Reid writes M, July 27, 29; see → :39.) **July 30:** Lepelletier, Hubert, E. Glaser de Willebrord, et al meet at M's house to discuss publ of the proceedings of the French military court on the Communards [→ :41].

34. OPERATION CANUTE (CONT'D). July 4: M's letter to the *Neue Freie Presse* (#M926) is pubd [← :30]. —GC session: M recounts the attacks on the Commune by the Mazzinist Luigi Wolff, and introduces the refugee P. Tibaldi, who reports that Wolff got payments both from the French police and the Prussian government. —M reports his sharp letter to the *PMG* (#M466) [← :30]; E says he has severed his connection with the *PMG* (which pubd his "Notes on the war"). **July 8:** M's letter to the *PMG* (#M466) is pubd in *Eastern Post.* **July 11:** GC session: M reports the publ of a forged "Marx" letter in the *Morning Advertiser;* he will write. (He sends a letter, #M910, to the paper the same day; it is pubd July 13.) Since present at the GC session is the lawyer's agent for the Communard A. A. Assi, who is on trial in Paris—the lawyer wants to find out about certain forged "Marx" letters— the GC endorses exposé statements by M and Serraillier, which will help Assi's defense. **July 13:** M sends a letter (#M914) to the *Standard* exposing a forged "Marx" letter; pubd July 17. **July 25:** GC session: M reports that the pope has attacked the IWMA as the "incarnation of evil." —E reports Mazzini's

July 13 article attacking the IWMA, esp M and defending God, country, and property against it. (E's report is given in more detail in *Eastern Post,* July 29.) **July 28:** E writes an article replying to Mazzini (#E475) [→ :41].

35. IWMA AFFAIRS. July: GC sessions M&E attend all four—July 4, 11, 18, 25. For most of the business, see ← :33, 34. **July 4:** At GC: M proposes J. P. McDonnell as GC member, praising his career. —M presents Sorge's report of June 20 on the CC of the IWMA in America. —E reports on Cafiero's letter attacking Mazzini. **July 11:** At GC: M reports that the Home Ministry has written him, July 7, for copies of all IWMA documents. (These will be sent July 12.) —M proposes the Communard, C. Rochat, and Lochner as GC members. —E announces he will raise the question of holding an IWMA conference this year, preparatory to a congress. **July 18:** At GC: M&E take part in discussing proposed new GC members. —M takes up Odger's latest fabrications about the IWMA, i.a. his claim to be the author of the Inaugural Address. **July 25:** At GC: E proposes that the IWMA hold a closed conference in London in Sep, since a congress is now impossible. The Sub-Comm is assigned to propose the agenda. —In response to questions by P. Robin, M&E suggest that the Bakuninist Alliance has "forfeited its membership" because of nonpayment of dues and violation of its conditions of admission. **July 26:** M informs C. Caron of New Orleans that the GC has accepted his club as a section. **July 27:** M writes to N. Utin (in Geneva) of the GC decisions of July 25 on the coming London Conference and on the Bakuninist Alliance. He also sends info about the coming conference to the CC of the IWMA in NYC and to Liebknecht (via Kugelmann).

36. FRUITS OF NOTORIETY. July 3: M gives an interview to a *New York World* correspondent, R. Landor, mainly on the IWMA; Landor's account (#M417) is pubd July 18. **July 5:** Rutson, the Home Secretary's private secy, requests (via Prof. Beesly) the publications of the IWMA; M sends the material July 12 (cf M's report to GC, ← :35). **July 6:** C. A. Dana, now editor of the *NY Sun,* asks M to write articles on the IWMA. **July 20:** M is interviewed on the IWMA, the Commune, etc., by a correspondent of the *NY Herald* [→ :42].

37. POLITICAL AFFAIRS. July 1–3, 16, 28: In letters to Carlo Cafiero [← :28], E expounds the IWMA program and criticizes Bakuninism and Mazzini. **July 9:** Hins (in Brussels) writes M asking him to recommend correspondents for *La Liberté.* **July CD:** M studies materials on the trial of Nechayev pubd in the Russian paper *Pravitelstvenni Vestnik.*

38. PERSONAL. **July 26:** While the La-argues and the M daughters are in Bagnères-de-Luchon [← :32], Laura's baby boy ← :12] dies, at the age of six months.

AUGUST

39. IWMA AFFAIRS. **Aug:** GC sessions: Of the five sessions Aug 1, 8, 15, 22, 29, M is absent Aug 22, E is absent Aug 1 (ill). **Aug 1:** At GC: M reports on the case of R. Reid [← :33]. —M takes up some administrative problems (HQ, dues payments) and recom-mends filling some corr secy vacancies: E for Italy, and Alfred Herman to replace E for Belgium. **Aug 8:** At GC: In a discussion of helping the Newcastle engineers' strike, M makes a point about trade unions that come to the IWMA only when in trouble. —M pro-poses Longuet, Vaillant, and Theisz as GC members. —E proposes that GC meetings discussing the conference agenda be closed to visitors. **Aug 15:** At GC: M reports on devel-opments in America, i.a. Wendell Phillips has joined. —M proposes that the coming con-ference be confined to questions of organiza-tion and policy, esp the former, rather than theoretical issues. —E reports on Italy and Spain. He proposes Boon as auditor, and moves to extend Hales's term as gen secy. **Aug 22:** At GC: E reports on Spain, incl Lafargue's arrest (see → :43), based on a report just received from Mora of the Spanish Fed-ral Council. **Aug c.23:** The editor of the London Public Opinion asks M to write an article on the IWMA (see → :40). **Aug 25:** M writes an article about the IWMA for Dana's NY Sun (#M467); it also features the adven-ure of his three daughters in the Pyrenees (see 43); pubd Sep 9. **Aug 29:** At GC: M proposes to enforce exclusion of visitors since reports are somehow getting to the French police.

40. THE DRIVE AGAINST THE IWMA. **Aug :** GC session: M reports on the Catholic Working Men's International Assoc, set up in Malines (Belgium) to counteract the IWMA. —M gives a longish talk on the latest attacks on the GC by Odger and others. **Aug 19:** In a letter to Public Opinion (#M899) M refutes the slander which is current against himself (that he is "living on workers' contributions"), and shows it has been copied from the Bismarckian National-Ztg. The letter is sent by E; it is pubd Aug 26 with an apology by the editor. **Aug 30:** In a letter to La Verité, M exposes fake IWMA manifestos being circu-lated in the Paris press (#M896); pubd else-where Sep 3.

41. AFTER THE COMMUNE. **Aug:** A third (revised) edn of The civil war in France (#M143) is pubd. **Aug 1:** GC session: M reports on more forged IWMA documents

pubd in Paris. —M supports establishment of a commission to collect Commune docu-mentation and data. **Aug A:** M&E make vain efforts to raise funds to publish the Commu-nard court proceedings [← :33]. **Aug 7:** E writes a letter to the Times (#E828), signed Justitia, on the plight of the Communards in French prisons; M sends it to the Times with his covering letter (#M919); it is not pubd. **Aug 8:** GC session: E criticizes the response to the appeal for Communard refu-gee aid, and proposes a stepped-up drive among workers. **Aug 9:** E writes to Lavrov (in Paris) for a subscription to the Gazette des Tribunaux, which reports the Communard trials, and for a map of the Paris area (to study the military operations during the Commune). **Aug 10, c.16:** In letters to A. Hubert, French émigré in London, M sends facts and docu-ments needed by the defense in the Paris trials of Communards. **Aug 17:** M sends a letter to the London organ of the French government, L'International, refuting a slander against the GC (living off the workers, etc.) (#M898); not pubd; later (Aug 28) pubd in Volksstaat. **Aug 22:** GC session: E opposes the Bee-Hive scheme to colonize Communard refugees in French Canada. —An appeal for Commu-nard refugee aid to American workers (pro-posed by Bolte to M, Aug 7) is referred to M [→ :46]. **Aug 25, 29:** In letters to Bolte (in NYC) and M. D. Conway (an American in London), M requests the establishment of a fund to collect Communard refugee aid and help provide jobs. **Aug 29:** GC session: E takes part in a discussion of the refugee-aid fund. **Aug 31:** E's article against Mazzini (#E475) [← :34] is pubd in Italy.

42. NY HERALD INTERVIEW. **Aug 3:** The NY Herald pubs an unsigned interview with M (#M416?) [← :36]. **Aug 17:** On seeing the pubd interview, M sends a repudiation of it as garbled and distorted to the Herald and also to the Gaulois (Paris) which had pubd excerpts. (See #M897 for both texts.) **Aug 25:** M warns Bolte (in NYC) that the pubd interview is "altogether falsified." **Aug 27:** The Gaulois pubs M's communication (#M897); the Her-ald does not.

43. THE THREE SISTERS, OR PERIL IN THE PYRENEES. **Aug 1 or 2:** While M's three daughters and the Lafargue family are so-journing in Bagnères-de-Luchon, Lafargue learns he is to be arrested by the French police (as M had warned [← :32]); they cross the border to Bosost (Spain); Jenny and Eleanor return. **Aug 6:** On the French side of the border, Jenny and Eleanor are arrested by the French police, searched, harried, interrogated until the wee hours of the night, and held under house arrest for two days. **Aug 8:** At 11 P.M. they are taken to the gendarmerie barracks and held overnight there. **Aug 9:** They are released, but their English passports are not returned for another 10 days. **Aug M:** Finally obtaining their passports and checking that Lafargue is not in jail, they leave for England. —E writes Liebknecht what he has heard about the episode so far. **Aug 25:** In the course of a letter to NY Sun editor Dana, M tells the tale (#M467); pubd in the Sun, Sep 9.

44. W&P. Aug 28: Liebknecht writes M&E urging them to write a preface for a new edn of the Com Manifesto [← :22].

45. PERSONAL. Aug c.16: On the doctor's advice, M goes to Brighton to restore his health after overwork; Jung visits, Aug 20– 21. **Aug c.29:** M returns to London. (KMC dates the holiday Aug 17–26.)

SEPTEMBER

46. IWMA: BEFORE THE CONFERENCE. Sep: M&E attend all GC sessions—Sep 5, 12, 16. **Sep 4:** M sends a letter to the Evening Standard (#M908) replying to current slanders being spread about him from the German to the London press; pubd Sep 6. **Sep 5:** At GC: M&E present proposals on the organizn of the conference, attendance by GC members, election of French delegates (#ME120); they take part in discussing some financial problems. Both resign from the refugee-aid comm in order to devote their time to preparing the conference. Because of the press of business, M proposes a five-minute limit on speakers. —M sends Sorge an appeal for a US drive to aid the Communard refugees [← :41]. **Sep 8:** M is visited by the Communards Avrial and La Cécilia with Jung. **Sep 9, 11:** At Sub-Comm meetings, M&E present a proposal (#ME119) on a number of points dealing with the organizn of the conference, incl publ of the Rules in various languages; M is assigned to draw up the GC Report to the Conference. He proposes the formation of workingwomen's sections of the IWMA. **Sep 12:** At GC: E reports the organizational proposals of the Sub-Comm (which are adopted with some changes), and checks preparations for a financial report. **Sep M:** M is visited by Eugène Vermersch with other Communard refugees; the discussion touches on the "working-class dictatorship." **Sep 16:** At GC: The council takes up the last steps in conference preparations, and changes in French representation. E proposes that a corr secy represent a country not sending delegates. On E's motion, the GC elects six delegates (with M&E not running). —M proposes that the question of a British Federal Council be referred to the conference. **Sep c.16:** M meets and discusses with Anselmo Lorenzo of the Spanish section,

who has just arrived in London for the conference (during which time he stays with E). **Sep AB:** M&E compile a set of excerpts from the GC Minutes of 1869–71, as preparatory material (#ME56).

47. IWMA: LONDON CONFERENCE. Sep 17–23 (summary): M&E are present at every session and participate throughout, even on organizational details. In general, GC proposals are adopted: esp a new emphasis on political action and the formation of workers' parties in each country, and a repudiation of the Bakuninist operation in the IWMA, the Alliance. **Sep 17:** M explains the status of the conference to the delegates. He proposes a Comm of Inquiry on the "Swiss dispute" (i.e. the conflict over the Bakuninist Alliance), and is elected a member of this comm. **Sep 18:** On behalf of the GC, M presents its proposals (cf #ME133) on organizational problems: no. 1, on the name of Federal Councils (no "sectarian names"), and no. 2, on official translations of the Rules (esp to correct the garbled French trans on political action). Evening: The Comm of Inquiry meets at M's house; M gives a report on the Alliance (#M596). **Sep 19:** M presents GC proposal no. 3 (workingwomen's sections), no. 4 (enforcing statistics gathering), no. 5 (GC representatives to Federal Councils), no. 6 (enforcing dues payments). **Sep 19–21:** E prepares the GC financial report. **Sep 20:** Afternoon: M&E give talks on attitude toward trade unionism, in the discussion of a resolution by Delahaye on "International Federations" and decentralized "communes of the future." Evening: M speaks at length on labor political action, in the discussion of Vaillant's resolution, against abstention from politics. **Sep 21:** E gives a talk on political action (#E565) in the conclusion of that agenda point; M takes part again too. —M reports for the Comm of Inquiry on the Swiss affair (Bakuninist problem); he relates how the Bakuninist spokesman, P. Robin, fled the comm's discussion, and presents a three-point condemnation of the Alliance as a conspiratorial faction (cf #M754). **Sep 22:** M&E discuss various problems: financial affairs, composition of the GC, the necessity of IWMA activity among peasants in rural areas. M presents some GC proposals on "general organizn," incl setting up a British Federation, and discusses problems of illegal and secret organizn in countries where legal organizn is impossible, esp France; but no IWMA sections are to be organized as secret societies. E discusses Italy and Spain; M discusses America and Russia, and in the evening session, Germany and Ireland. M recommends that the new GC decide what conference decisions to make public.

48. IWMA: AFTER THE CONFERENCE. Sep

24/25: At a banquet celebrating the seventh anniversary of the IWMA, M gives a talk on the IWMA and the Commune (#M829) [→ :53]. **Sep 26:** GC session: M is present, E absent. M reports on letters from Copenhagen (from the board of *Socialisten*, Sep 18), and from Berlin (G. Kwasniewski, to whom M replies on Sep 29). —M proposes rejection of a Paris proposal to sponsor a utopian colony in New Caledonia financed by capitalists. — M proposes Hales for reelection as gen secy, Theisz as treasurer, Frankel as corr secy for Austria and Hungary. M is reelected corr secy for Germany, E for Italy; E is also a member of the Finance Comm. M takes part in the discussion raised by P. Robin about his (Robin's) behavior at the conference. **Sep D to Oct:** M again starts work on a revision of the Rules pamphlet on the basis of the conference decisions (#M347) [→ :52]. **Sep D to Nov M:** In letters to Germany (Berlin section, Liebknecht in Leipzig), M sends the conference decisions, and criticizes the inactivity of the Germans on the IWMA.

49. PERSONAL. Sep 5: The Bonapartist organ *L'Avenir Libéral* (Paris) prints a report of M's death, which is picked up by the press in other countries. **Sep 9:** The NY *Sun* prints M's account of the three sisters' adventure in the Pyrenees (#M467) [← :43], introducing it with a five-inch bank of headings beginning "The International's founder." **Sep 20:** In NYC, a Cosmopolitan Conference responds to the exaggerated news of M's death by adopting a eulogistic memorial resolution, reported in *Woodhull & Claflin's Weekly*, Sep 23. **Sep 23:** M sends to *Woodhull & Claflin's Weekly* his daughter Jenny's account of the Pyrenees episode [← :43], with a covering letter by M (#M921) [→ :53].

50. HOLIDAYS. Sep c.13–15: E goes to Ramsgate for a few days. **Sep 28 to Oct 3:** M and his wife plus E are on holiday in Ramsgate.

OCTOBER

51. IWMA AFFAIRS. Oct: GC sessions: E attends all seven—Oct 2, 7, 10, 16, 17, 24, 31; M is absent Oct 31, for the first time since May 16. For other business, see also → :52. **Oct 2:** At GC: E is named corr secy for Spain; M, corr secy for Russia. M proposes McDonnell as corr secy for Ireland, Zabicki for Poland, Jung for Switzerland. **Oct 7:** At GC: E proposes the public expulsion of G. Durand as a French police spy. **Oct 10:** E writes Cafiero (in Naples) on the results of the London Conference. —M is visited by the Communards Cournet, Maujean, Guinard. —At GC: M proposes a Comm of Inquiry to find out who has given the report of the London Conference to

the press [→ :56]. **Oct 17:** M reports for the comm reviewing the by-laws of the new "French Section of 1871" in London; his resolution (#M753) is adopted. —E reports on the IWMA in Italy and Spain. —M tells of a report from a "Slavonic Section" in Zurich (which will turn out to be a Bakuninist split group). **Oct 24:** M proposes Jung as treasurer instead of Theisz. **Oct 31:** E presents his draft of a GC reply (#E775) to A. Cochrane-Baillie's attack on the IWMA in the *Times* [→ :57].

52. IWMA: IMPLEMENTING THE CONFERENCE. Oct 7: At GC: As postconference committees are set up to carry out its decisions, M is named to the comm to prepare a new edn of the Rules (#ME133), and a statement on Nechayev (#M224); E, to the comm on the political-action resolution. —M&E begin the work of collecting and preparing publ of the resolutions [→ :57]. **Oct 10:** M insists on a special meeting (Oct 16) for hearing a report on the conference. **Oct 14:** M writes a resolution for the GC repudiating any connection with Nechayev (#M224). **Oct 16** (erroneously dated Oct 14 in *MEW*): M summarizes the various tasks assigned to the GC. —M presents his resolution on Nechayev (#M224); publ in IWMA press, Oct 18 to Nov. —E proposes to implement the decision on a British Federal Council. —E and Johannard are assigned to draw up an address to the workers of Italy. (Nothing more on this will be heard.) —M is named to prepare the circular to the sections containing the conference resolutions [→ :57]. —E reports the comm's draft of the political-action resolution, which is accepted. **Oct 20:** E writes a covering letter (#E836) to send the resolution on Nechayev (#M224) to *Gazzettino Rosa* (Milan), which pubs both on Nov 3. **Oct 24:** At GC: M—who, with E, has finished the work [← :48] of revising and preparing the Rules for a new edn, incorporating all changes since 1866—reports the result to the GC, and proposes a printing of 5000 (#M347) [→ :57].

53. W&P. Oct 15: A news account of the IWMA banquet [← :48] and M's speech there is pubd in the NY *World* under the heading "The reds in session . . ." (#M829). **Oct 21:** Jenny's story of the Pyrenees and M's covering letter (#M921) [← :49] are pubd in *Woodhull & Claflin's Weekly*.

54. CAPITAL. Oct 17: Danielson writes M that the Russian trans of *Capital* has gone to press.

55. PERSONAL. Oct D to Nov D: M is ill for a month and cannot attend GC meetings.

NOVEMBER

56. IWMA AFFAIRS. Nov: GC sessions: E attends all four regular sessions—Nov 7, 14,

21, 28; M attends only Nov 28. Attendance at the special Nov 5 session is not known, but M can be assumed absent. For other business, see → :57–59. **Nov 5:** At a special session, the GC adopts a resolution (submitted by a Sub-Comm meeting in which M participated) regulating the US organizn; it approves the authority of the CC in NYC as against Section 12 (text: *GCFI* 5:338). **Nov 7:** At GC: E reports on info from Italy, esp Garibaldi's break with Mazzini in Oct (cf #E749) [→ :57 (Nov c.8–9)]; also on news from Berlin (letter of Jozewicz to M, Nov 6), and from Holland. —The GC adopts M's resolution (presented by Serraillier) on what is wrong with the so-called French Section of 1871 and its Rules (#M604) [← :51]. **Nov 12:** In Sonvilier (Switzerland) the Jura Federation holds a congress run by the Bakuninists, which issues a circular declaring war on the GC. From this point the process leading to the destruction of the IWMA speeds up. **Nov 13:** M&E, at M's house, meet with Garibaldi's son Ricciotti. **Nov 14:** At GC: E reports on the Rome congress of the Mazzinist workers' societies, Nov 1–6. —Eccarius, having been bearded by M, confesses that it was he who gave the London Conference proceedings to a paper [← :51]. **Nov 16:** M writes Jung about linking Paris and London goldsmith workers in a fight for a shorter workday. **Nov 21:** At GC: E supports the election of three Blanquist Communards as GC members. **Nov 28:** At GC: M objects to a GC member (Barry) voting in the GC under the instructions of the British Federal Council. —M reports his denial about Dilke (#M858) (see → :57). —E is authorized to reply to Mazzini's attack [→ :63]. **Nov D:** A "Count Albert Potocki," posing as a Polish émigré, writes M offering his services to distribute IWMA material in Poland and Russia; he is actually a London agent of the Russian secret police, J. Bałaszewicz-Potocki. **Nov 23:** M sends Potocki IWMA pamphlets and refers him to the corr secy for Poland, Wróblewski. **Nov 29:** M sends Potocki a note (apparently in response to his letter of Nov 27) inviting him to visit that evening. **Nov c.30:** M asks Borkheim for material on Bakunin, esp Bakunin's activity at the Peace Congress in Geneva in 1868.

57. IWMA: PUBLICATIONS. Nov c.6: The Resolutions of the London Conference, compiled by M&E [← :52] (#ME133), are pubd in English and French edns. **Nov 6:** M sends these publications to IWMA people in the US and Germany. **Nov 7:** At GC: E moves to grant printer Truelove's request to put an advertisement for the Owen centenary on the back of the IWMA Rules. **Nov c.8:** The revised edn of the Rules (⚹M347) is pubd as a pamphlet in English. (The French edn will come out in Dec, the German in Feb

1872.) **Nov c.8–9:** E expands his report on the situation in Italy [← :56] for publ in the *Eastern Post* (#E749); pubd Nov 11. **Nov 11:** E's statement against Cochrane-Baillie (#E775) [← :51] is pubd. **Nov 15:** The Resolutions of the conference (#ME133) in German are pubd in *Volksstaat*. (In Nov-Dec they are pubd in various Continental papers and in a German pamphlet edn.) **Nov 24:** M sends the *Frankfurter Ztg* a denial (#M858) of its report that Sir Charles Dilke has been made an honorary IWMA member; pubd Nov 28.

58. GERMAN MOVEMENT AND IWMA. Nov 17: M writes Liebknecht demanding he take a position in *Volksstaat* on the struggle against the Bakuninists in the IWMA. —At Bracke's request, for use in court, M sends an affidavit that the German party has never been an IWMA section though many members are individually affiliated. **Nov 28:** GC session: M reports, in accord with a telegram received today, that the trial of the Brunswick Exec of the SDWP has resulted in various prison terms for the defendants.

59. IWMA: INTERNATIONAL CORRESPONDENCE. Nov A: Through a letter by the Communard refugee R. Wilmart, M tries to influence the IWMA members in France to an understanding of the GC's trouble with the London French section and also of the attacks on Lafargue in Bordeaux (SOURCE: *KMC*). **Nov 9:** M replies to Sorge's queries of Oct 10 by giving his views on organizational problems faced by the IWMA in the US; M also tells Sorge of the GC's conflict with the London "French Section of 1871." **Nov 10:** M cautions Speyer (in the US) that only letters with an official IWMA character can be supervised by the GC, not personal correspondence. He urges: "You must try to win over the trade unions at all costs." **Nov 13:** Responding to a Nov 1 letter from Th. Cuno, M inaugurates contact with this German socialist who is building an IWMA section in Milan; E sends the London Conference documents, and explains various questions. (He will correspond with Cuno until Feb M next.) **Nov 23:** In a letter to Bolte (in the US), M summarizes his organizational principles: the International is the "real organizn of the working class for struggle" counterposed to all the socialist sects, which become reactionary. M reviews the struggle to supersede Proudhonism, Lassalleanism, now Bakuninism, in order to build a class political movement. —In a letter to C. Palladino (in Naples), E explains why the London Conference replaced a regular congress. **Nov 25:** In a letter to the Spanish Federal Council in Madrid, where the Bakuninists are operating, E asks that GC letters be answered, otherwise action will have to be taken (#E847). **Nov 29:** E writes a GC statement to the *Proletario Italiano* replying to its Nov 23 pro-Bakuninist distortion of the political-action plank of the IWMA (#E831); not pubd.

60. CAPITAL. Nov 9: M sends Danielson a list of changes and proof corrections for the Russian edn of *Capital*, and repeats he has no time to undertake his promised revision of Ch. 1. **Nov 28:** Meissner informs M that the edition of Vol. 1 is nearly exhausted. **Nov D:** M begins negotiations for a second edn.

61. W&P (E). Nov 4: E writes an article for *Volksstaat* on the spate of business swindles in England (#E539); pubd Nov 11.

DECEMBER

62. IWMA AFFAIRS. Dec: GC sessions: M&E attend Dec 5, 19; both are absent Dec 12. **Dec 2:** Barry informs E of the machinations by Hales and his friends to use the British Federation against the GC. **Dec 5:** At GC: After Barry speaks on the factionalism of the British Federal Council, M&E support the proposal that Hales not remain both the gen secy of the GC and the secy of the British council. —M&E propose Regis as GC member. —E reports on the Danish IWMA and the agrarian question (cf → :63). **Dec 8:** M is visited by a delegation from the refugee-aid comm to discuss its problems. **Dec 17:** At a meeting of the refugee-aid comm, M supports the proposal to accept the money collected for refugees at a Dec 11 meeting where Bradlaugh had attacked the Commune and M; he opposes the view that this money is tainted by Bradlaugh. **Dec 19:** At GC: M talks about Bradlaugh's lecture of Dec 11 attacking the Paris Commune, in which that reformer-liberal "proved" that M was a Bonapartist by quoting a half-sentence from *The civil war in France*; also about further attacks by Bradlaugh in the *Eastern Post* on Dec 16 (cf → :63). —M reports that the English government has made a deal with the French to prosecute Communard refugees (letter from the journalist N. L. Thieblin, Dec 16). —M reports on info from Berlin (letter of Jozewicz, Dec 6–7) about new Lassallean attacks on the IWMA; on disputes in the American IWMA, esp the split in the CC led by Section 12; on the Dec 2 conference of Geneva IWMA sections, where the Bakuninists were overwhelmingly defeated (report from Utin). —E reports that *La Emancipación* (Spanish

IWMA) has accepted the political-action resolution of the London Conference; and that the Lancashire cotton manufacturers were for reducing the workday to nine hours; he explains why, in their own interests. —E is named to a delegation to see the US embassy about helping the refugees to emigrate.

63. IWMA: PUBLICATIONS. Dec A: The new French edn of the IWMA Rules (#M347) [← :57] is pubd. **Dec 5–6:** E writes a reply (#E829) for the GC to Mazzini's attacks on the IWMA of Nov 16, 23, and (Dec 6) sends it to *La Roma del Popolo* with a covering letter; pubd Dec 12, 21. **Dec 5–10:** E writes a note on the state of the IWMA in various countries (#E567), prob part of a letter to Bignami, for publ in *La Plebe*; pubd Dec 12. **Dec c.6–7:** E writes up his report on the position of the Danish IWMA on the agrarian question (#E596); pubd Dec 9. **Dec 20:** M writes a letter (#M905) to the *Eastern Post* refuting Bradlaugh [← :62] as a slanderer; pubd Dec 23.

64. IWMA: INTERNATIONAL CORRESPONDENCE. Dec: M corresponds with G. Luciani (who has moved from London to Rome) on the state of the IWMA in Italy. **Dec 6–7:** F. Jozewicz, secy of the Berlin IWMA section, sends M a report on section activity in the light of M's organizational advice [→ 72:9]. **Dec 22:** Daughter Jenny sends the Kugelmanns a year-end letter in which she portrays the misery of the Communard refugees in London, tells of M's activities, and writes of the machinations of the Bakuninists in the IWMA, etc. **Dec D:** M learns (letter from Mancini, Dec 22) that he has been elected an honorary member of the Associazione Democratica in Macerata (Italy), along with Mazzini and Garibaldi. —Wróblewski informs M of IWMA progress in Cracow [→ 72:3]. **Dec 30:** Writing to Lafargue (in Madrid), E asks him to enlighten the Spanish IWMA on the GC's criticisms of the circular issued by the Bakuninists at Sonvilier [← :56].

65. CAPITAL. Dec: M begins revising Vol. 1, esp the first chapter, for the second German edn. **Dec 12:** Daughter Laura writes M, and Paul Lafargue writes E, that the Paris pub'r Lachâtre has agreed to publish a French edn of *Capital*.

66. W&P. Dec 30: The *Com Manifesto* is pubd in *Woodhull and Claflin's Weekly* (NY), in the 1850 English trans by Macfarlane.

1872

CONSPECTUS

1. The IWMA is now shaken apart by internecine conflicts: above all, the conspira-

torial-factional work of the Bakuninist operation under the name of the Alliance of the Socialist Democracy. At the Hague Congress the International effectively collapses, as

Marx decides that the organization is no longer viable. Other centrifugal tendencies add to the picture: the reformist trade-union-ist wing in Britain comes out into the open under John Hales; in America a group of faddist cranks (the notorious Section 12) splits away from the workers' branches; the Blanquist Communards in emigration are pulling in still another direction. One of the results is a flood of IWMA documents.

2. Three important new edns of *Capital* are prepared this year, beginning with the first trans of the work: the Russian edn. Two other edns involve M in a great deal of labor: the second German edn of Vol. 1, for which he makes important revisions (esp of Ch. 1), and the French trans. The latter turns into a massive task for M, as he undertakes to revise, indeed rewrite, the trans prepared by J. Roy.

JANUARY

3. IWMA AFFAIRS. **Jan:** GC sessions: M&E attend all five—Jan 2, 9, 16, 23, 30. **Jan 2:** At GC: M&E take part in discussing the powers of the provisional comm of the British Federation and its relation to the GC, the problem being Hales's machinations [← 71:62]. —M reports that the Belgian IWMA congress has indirectly turned down some London Conference decisions. —M reports that Wróblewski has news from Cracow of the adhesion to the IWMA of the Socialist-Democrats. **Jan 9:** At GC: M reports on the Rules of the Polish section and of the British Federal Council. He points out that two members of the latter are also officers of the rival, hostile Universal Republican League; they should choose. —E's questioning brings out Hales's double-dealing with different sets of British Federation rules. **Jan 16:** At GC: M reports for the Sub-Comm on its investigation of the Rules of the British Federal Council and its composition. —E reports on the strike movement in Rome. **Jan 18:** E writes Liebknecht on the situation in the IWMA esp in Belgium, also in Spain and Italy, and makes suggestions for *Volksstaat*. **Jan 19:** E writes Lafargue (in Madrid) about the situation esp in the British IWMA, also in other countries. **Jan 23:** At GC: M reports on the Chemnitz congress of the Saxon Social-Democrats (Jan 6–7), which has supported the GC against the Bakuninists (letter of Lieb-knecht to E, Jan 10). —M reports receiving a Dutch version of the Rules. —E reports on gains in Turin, and on anti-IWMA canards in Italy. —M&E participate in a discussion raised by a Hales–Mottershead quarrel. **Jan 30:** At GC: M&E report approval of section rules in Holland, Zurich, Milan. —E reports

on the IWMA in Spain, esp its persecution by the government. —M reports that an interna-tional manufacturers' agency is being planned in Berlin to spy on and combat the IWMA. —M&E take part in a discussion on Eccarius' outside activities (articles on the London Conference) [← 71:56]. E proposes disap-proval of Eccarius on one point.

4. IWMA: DEFENSE AGAINST BAKUNINISM. **Jan 2:** As M&E inaugurate preparations for the next congress, E writes Liebknecht about ensuring a good delegation from the German movement. **Jan c.3:** E writes an article for *Volksstaat* on the Bakuninist Sonvilier con-gress [← 71:56] (#E179); pubd Jan 10. **Jan 14:** Writing to a Turin workers' assoc, E criticizes Bakuninist anårchism. **Jan M:** begins work on a GC reply to the Sonvilier circular of the Bakuninists; he collects mate-rial on the Bakunin operation in the IWMA (this will be pubd as the pamphlet #ME5) [→ :15]. **Jan 24:** E's letter to Cuno presents a critique of the Bakuninist theory of the state and of their actions in the IWMA.

5. POLITICAL AFFAIRS. **Jan 16, c.27:** M responds to new attacks pubd by Bradlaugh in his *National Reformer*, Jan 7; he demands that Bradlaugh present proof, in two letters to the *Eastern Post* (#M906, 907), pubd Jan 20, 28. **Jan 28:** M is asked by Lissagaray to join the Cercle d'Etudes Sociales of Communard refugees, just founded, Jan 20 [→ :11].

6. W&P. **Jan 10:** Liebknecht writes E urg-ing a new edn of M's *Poverty of philosophy* (#M681). **Jan 18:** E replies that it is more important for M to work on a French edn of *Capital*.

7. CAPITAL. **Jan c.15 to Feb c.15:** Through Longuet (letter of Jan 13) M deals with Joseph Roy for a French trans of *Capital*, and concludes a publishing agreement with Lachâtre (Paris). **Jan c.20:** M asks his cousin August Philips (in Amsterdam) to help fi-nance the French edn of *Capital*. **Jan 26:** Philips declines, saying he is willing to help M personally but not to promote his revolu-tionary ideas. **Jan:** M continues revising *Capital* for the second German edn, esp revising Ch. 1. By Jan c.20 he sends 24 printer's sheets to Meissner.

FEBRUARY

8. IWMA AFFAIRS. **Feb:** GC sessions: Of the three GC sessions this month, M attends Feb 6, both attend Feb 13, and E attends Feb 20. **Feb 6:** At GC: M reports that the Baku-ninists A. Richard and G. Blanc have pubd a pro-Bonapartist pamphlet. —M moves for an absolute ban on strangers at GC sessions. — M reports on a letter from T. Devy (in the US) about Bradlaugh and Prince Napoleon. —M takes part in a discussion of refugee-aid problems. —M remains silent as Eccarius protests the GC's censure vote [← :3]. **Feb 9, 10:** M&E receive letters from W. H. Riley inviting them to contribute to his new paper *International Herald*, to appear Mar 1. **Feb 10:** A German edn of the Rules (#M347) [← 71:57] is pubd in *Volksstaat*; also around this time, a German pamphlet edn. **Feb 13:** At GC: E is assigned to look into Riley's new *International Herald* (see above), which offers space to the GC. —M reports on the German IWMA (letter from Jozewicz, Feb 10). —M reports Swiss police harassment and house search of Utin (in Geneva), at Russia's behest. —M proposes an inquiry into the Belgian IWMA in view of *La Liberté*'s favoring Swiss Bakuninist news. —M supports setting up a Judicial Comm to discuss personal disputes (specif, between British GC members) in order to spare the GC. —E reports on Spanish IWMA affairs. **Feb 20:** At GC: E reports on Spanish developments, on Riley's *International Herald*, and on the protest against the police harassment of Utin (#ME48). —E takes part in a discussion of how to deal with Boon's charges against Hales. **Feb 20 to Mar A:** M prepares to talk in the GC on the conflict in the US sections between the CC led by Sorge and the "humbugs" of Section 12 led by Victoria Woodhull [→ :13]. **Feb c.D to May D:** M gathers notes and materials, which he heads "American split" (#M30), for future reports and discussions of the subject. **Feb 27:** The regular GC meeting is not held because the streets are blocked by the public procession celebrating the Prince of Wales's recovery from illness ("the row in the streets," says M). **Feb 29:** M&E work with Jung on the refugee-aid accounts of the GC, as the refugee-aid comm is reorganized into a mutual-aid assoc.

9. IWMA: INTERNATIONAL CORRESPONDENCE. **Feb 1:** M sends Jozewicz, Berlin IWMA secy, dues stamps and info on IWMA publications, and announces the forthcoming pamphlet against Bakuninism (#ME5). **Feb 20:** M&E send off a GC statement protesting the Geneva police outrage against Utin (#ME48) [← :8]; pubd Feb 24. **Feb 24:** M writes Jozewicz about various organizational criticisms, and criticizes the party Exec in Hamburg for lack of IWMA work.

10. IWMA AGAINST BAKUNINISM. **Feb 7:** E writes a reply (#E810) to recent attacks on the IWMA by editor Stefanoni of *Libero Pensiero* (Florence). He sends this to *Gazzettino Rosa* (Milan) with a covering letter (#E821); pubd Feb 20. **Feb 15:** E writes Liebknecht about Stefanoni's attack and other Bakuninist machinations in Italy, and proposes that Liebknecht publicly break his

present relations with Stefanoni. **Feb 16:** In a letter to J. P. Becker (in Switzerland), E recounts the struggle against Bakuninism in Spain. **Feb c.18:** E sends official credentials to the Italian GC member Regis (in Geneva) for his trip to Italy on behalf of the IWMA.

11. POLITICAL AFFAIRS. **Feb 3:** Agreeing to Lissagaray's request [← :5], M attends a meeting of the Cercle d'Etudes Sociales. **Feb 12:** M informs Adolphe Hubert that the French politician Crémieux is in London for negotiations with the Bonapartists; M writes likewise to Pelletier.

12. CAPITAL. **Feb 2:** Roy writes M that he is setting to work on the French trans. **Feb 9:** M sends Lachâtre the contract for the French edn, for signing. **Feb 15:** According to E's letter to Liebknecht, "M has signed the contract for a French trans of *Capital*."

MARCH

13. IWMA AFFAIRS. **Mar:** GC sessions: M&E attend Mar 5, 12, 19. On Mar 26, E attends, M is absent. For other business, see → :14, 15. **Mar 5:** At GC: M presents resolutions (#M756) on the split in the American IWMA between the CC and Section 12, incl temporary suspension of Section 12 and the requirement for a two-thirds proletarian composition. The first articles are adopted at this meeting, the rest held over for the next. —M reports on the English government's postponement of action against the refugees [← 71: 62]. **Mar 12:** GC: M presents the rest of his resolutions (#M756) on the American split; the two-thirds requirement is opposed by Eccarius and two others, but all articles are adopted. —M is named as a speaker at the first anniversary celebration of the Paris Commune on Mar 18 (inaugurated by the GC, Feb 20). —M reads a letter reporting from and on New Zealand (from James M'Pherson, Nov 23, 1871). —E calls attention to the GC rule that all members' names are appended to official GC documents. —He complains that Hales rewrites his (E's) reports for the *Eastern Post*; and he supplements last week's report on Italy, also reports on Spain. **Mar 13:** M begins drafting resolutions (#M755) for the Mar 18 Commune meeting. **Mar 18:** At the Commune anniversary meeting (which has to change halls when an upholder of law and order named Wilkinson refuses his premises at the last moment), M is one of the "English speakers," and his resolutions (#M755) are adopted. **Mar 19:** At GC: E reports on the Spanish movement (letter of J. Mesa, Mar 11), on the work of the Portuguese section, esp of its new organ *O Pensamento Social* (letter of Nobre-França and Tedeschi, Mar 10), and on the Ferrara (Italy) section. —E questions

Barry's relations with the Gladstone government. **Mar 26:** At GC: E presents a report from the Spanish IWMA by Mora (Mar 15); E is to send a GC message to its Saragossa Congress of Apr 7 [→ :21].

14. IWMA: INTERNATIONAL CORRESPONDENCE. **Mar 10–19:** E as corr secy for Portugal establishes relations with the Portuguese IWMA. **Mar 12:** M writes a letter (#M893) to *La Liberté* (Brussels) on the anti-GC falsehoods in the book by the Communard G. Lefrançais, *Etude sur le mouvement communaliste à Paris, en 1871;* the letter is pubd on Mar 17. **Mar 15:** M sends Sorge the GC resolutions on the American split. **Mar 20:** Victoria Woodhull writes M from NYC that she will come to London this year. (M does not reply.) **Mar 27:** E writes a letter of greetings to the Spanish Federal Council (#E846) on behalf of the GC. **Mar CD to May A:** The corr secy for Ireland, McDonnell, informs E of new IWMA sections in Dublin, Cork, Bradford, etc., and on the strike movement in Cork; E meets with McDonnell and discusses problems of the Irish section.

15. IWMA AGAINST BAKUNINISM. **Mar 5:** M&E finish work on the GC circular *Les prétendues scissions dans l'Internationale* [The alleged divisions in the International] (#ME5). —At GC: M reports on the content of this circular as a blow against Bakunin's Alliance; E gives further explanations; the GC authorizes publ [→ :27]. —E communicates Regis's report from Italy [← :10] of Mar 1, on the Bakuninists' lack of influence there. **Mar 7:** In a letter to Pio (Danish IWMA), E explains the GC's fight against the Bakuninists, and asks the Danish Federation to approve the London Conference decisions. **Mar to Aug:** M&E's work now is dominated by preparations for the coming congress of the IWMA and the fight against the Bakunin operation. E is esp involved with the movement in Spain, in contact with Lafargue in Madrid.

16. GERMAN MOVEMENT. **Mar 5:** At GC: M reports on the Leipzig police harassment of the sales of IWMA publications. **Mar 11:** The treason trial of Bebel and Liebknecht opens in Leipzig. **Mar 13:** Bruno Geiser (in Breslau) writes M reporting on the movement in his city. **Mar 18:** Paul Lindau, editor of the Berlin *Gegenwart,* asks M to write for his periodical. (M will refuse, despite letters from Lindau's sister, Anna Vivanti, of Mar 21, 27; and recommends that Lindau get an article by Tibaldi on Mazzini.) **Mar 19:** At GC: M reports on Geiser's letter from Breslau, and on the continuing trial of Bebel and Liebknecht. **Mar 20:** M sends Geiser suggestions for work. **Mar 26:** The Leipzig treason trial ends: Bebel and Liebknecht are sentenced to

two years in prison. **Mar 28:** Liebknecht writes M&E of the outcome of the trial.

17. POLITICAL AFFAIRS. **Mar-Apr:** In response to a request from Dupont (in Manchester), M sets down his views on land nationalization, as a memorandum (#M537) for use by Dupont in a local discussion [→ :28].

18. *CAPITAL.* **Mar 18:** M writes a letter (#M131) to the French pub'r Lachâtre, which will be pubd (in facsimile) as a preface to the French edn, appearing in the first fascicule [→ :54]. **Mar 19:** Meissner informs M that he has begun printing the second German edn of *Capital* in fascicules, in 3000 copies [→ :32]. **Mar 27:** The first Russian edn of *Capital* is pubd in St. Petersburg, in 3000 copies. Danielson sends a copy to M [→ :22]. **Mar to May:** M works at correcting the proofs of the second German edn, and also works on his revision of the French trans [→ :32].

19. W&P. **Mar 17:** Writing to Sorge, E asks for copies of the recent publ of the *Com Manifesto* in *Woodhull & Claflin's Weekly* [← 71:66] and in French in *Le Socialiste;* he thinks the trans may be useful despite their defective quality.

APRIL

20. IWMA AFFAIRS. **Apr:** GC sessions: M&E attend Apr 16, 23, 30; M attends Apr 2, E attends Apr 9. **Apr 2:** At GC: M censures Hales for derogating Irish IWMA branches in England and refusing Rules pamphlets to McDonnell, corr secy for Ireland. After McDonnell reports on persecution of the IWMA in Ireland, M proposes a commission to write a manifesto against Irish police terrorism; M is named to the commission. — M reports on the treason trial of Bebel and Liebknecht in Leipzig [← :16]. **Apr 9:** At GC: In M's absence, E supports McDonnell's draft of a manifesto against Irish police terrorism, written with M's help. (It will be pubd as a handbill and in IWMA papers.) —E reports on the Danish movement (letter from Pio, Mar 24); he has advised North Schleswig workers to vote for the working-class candidate whether Danish or German. —E reports a letter (Liebknecht to M, Apr 2) on the Leipzig treason trial, to be pubd in the *Eastern Post.* —E proposes acceptance of Rozwadowski as GC member for the London Poles. **Apr 13:** The Sub-Comm asks E to give the GC financial report to the coming congress; E begins to prepare it (cf #E790). **Apr 13–16:** M writes a declaration for the GC (#M856) on the anti-IWMA speech made in the House Apr 12 by A. Cochrane-Baillie. **Apr M:** M is informed that his letters are subjected to censorship in France and

England. **Apr 16:** At GC: M presents his declaration on Cochrane-Baillie (#M856); it is pubd Apr CD (dated Apr 17). —E introduces a declaration, unidentified in the Minutes, which is postponed after some discussion; it may be on the "Universal Federalist Council," and perhaps the same as #M857 (for which, see → :24). —E joins in stressing that the GC is not a body of delegates from affiliates. **Apr 22–23:** E writes a statement for the GC on the police harassment of Cuno in Italy (Milan) and his expulsion to Bavaria (#E564), on the basis of Cuno's letter of Apr 17. **Apr 23:** At GC: M criticizes Eccarius' sabotage of GC decisions on the US situation. —M takes part in discussing Dr. Sexton's nomination as GC member. —E reports on the harassment of Cuno; his statement (#E564) is adopted; pubd Apr 27. —E announces that he and M have had 1000 copies of the declaration on Cochrane-Baillie (#M856) printed at their own expense. —M&E move to accept Harris's resignation from the GC. **Apr 30:** At GC: M supports the demand that Weston retract his signature to the "Universal Federalist Council" attack on the IWMA. —E reports on the "arson plot" charge against the IWMA in Milan (letter from Cuno, Apr 25). —E proposes added GC sessions because of the press of business.

21. IWMA: INTERNATIONAL CORRESPONDENCE. **Apr c.A:** M gives Rochat, an IWMA member moving to Brussels, info and advice on activity in Belgium for the GC. (Rochat will send M his first report on May 1.) **Apr A:** E makes an Italian trans of a letter by Liebknecht directed against Stefanoni [← :10] and sends it to Cafiero for publ; pubd in *Gazzettino Rosa*, Apr 20. **Apr 3:** E writes greetings on behalf of the GC to the Saragossa Congress of the Spanish IWMA (#E820) [← :13]; pubd Apr 13. **Apr 6:** E sends a telegram of greetings to the Saragossa Congress (#E863); pubd Apr 13. **Apr 16:** E's letter to the Ferrara workers' assoc affiliating to the IWMA (#E869) [← :13] explains IWMA organizational principles, in response to the Ferrara communication of Mar 3. **Apr 23:** Writing to Liebknecht, E congratulates him and Bebel on their behavior before the court in the Leipzig treason trial. **Apr D:** In a letter to Pio (in Denmark), E stresses the importance of drawing small peasants into the workers' movement. **Apr CD to Aug:** E gathers the materials on the secret activity of the Bakuninist Alliance in Spain sent him by Lafargue and J. Mesa.

22. *CAPITAL.* **Apr A:** M receives from Danielson [← :18] a copy of the Russian edn just off the press, plus a letter on Chernyshevsky and Lopatin (whose fate has been worrying M). —M sends Meissner 42 printer's sheets of ms for the second German edn (*KMC*

dating: Apr c.10). **Apr 9:** The Russian edn of *Capital* goes on sale. **Apr c.10:** M sends Meissner a draft of a prospectus for *Capital* (not extant), as requested by him on Apr 8. **Apr-May:** M continues work on the German and French edns (cf ← :18).

23. W&P. **Apr:** After the GC decides (Apr 9) to publish a French edn of *The civil war in France* (#M143), M revises an extant trans, and corresponds (Apr 26, 30) with E. Glaser de Willebrord (in Brussels) on printing arrangements [→ :30]. **Apr 13:** *La Emancipación* (Spanish IWMA) pubs an excerpt from M's *Poverty of philosophy* (#M681) titled "The theory of the class struggle." **Apr 20:** Liebknecht informs E that *Volksstaat* intends to republish the *Com Manifesto* soon, and asks for the promised new preface [→ :34]. —E writes an article on the strike of English farm workers, which will be pubd as the first "Letter from London" in *La Plebe*, Apr 24, inaugurating E's collaboration with Bignami's paper (#E448). **Apr 23:** Replying to Liebknecht's letter of Apr 20, E says it will take time to bring Part III of the *Manifesto* up-to-date for a new introduction, but he promises to send a "short foreword" soon.

MAY

24. IWMA AFFAIRS. **May:** GC sessions: E attends all seven—May 4, 7, 11, 14, 18, 21, 28; M attends May 11, 21, 28. **May 4:** At GC: E reports on the new section in Ferrara (Italy). **May 7:** At GC: E reports on the Saragossa Congress of the Spanish IWMA (cf #E722); on Italy (Milan; Ferrara's Rules); and on the arrest of the IWMA leaders in Copenhagen. —E proposes Cournet as corr secy for Denmark, and Le Moussu as French corr secy for the Western Hemisphere. —E moves a second letter [← :20] to Weston, who has not responded to the charges. **May 11:** At GC: see → :25. **May 14:** At GC: E reports on the Spanish IWMA. —E upholds the Irish sections in England against Hales's attack, and denounces Hales's aim of subordinating Irish sections to the British Federal Council (cf #E664). **May 18:** At GC: E is present, but no participation is recorded. **May 20:** M writes a declaration (#M857) for the GC exposing the so-called Universal Federalist Council of the IWMA as a fake organized by old opponents of the IWMA; the declaration is dated May 20, perhaps indicating it was adopted this day by the Sub-Comm. **May 21:** At GC: M presents this declaration (#M857) for adoption; pubd May 26. **May 22:** E writes Liebknecht urging clarification of the German party's relations to the IWMA and asking for assurance that the SDWP will be represented at the coming congress. **May 27:** M sends Liebknecht the

GC declaration against the "Universal Federalist Council" (#M857) for publ in *Volksstaat*. **May 28:** At GC: M reports on the May 19–20 congress of the Belgian IWMA in Brussels, where the abolition of the GC (a Bakuninist plank) was proposed. M suggests that the next GC session take up the coming IWMA congress. —M proposes Cournet as corr secy for Holland. **May 28:** M writes Danielson that he will withdraw from IWMA work after the coming congress, in order to finish *Capital*; he writes De Paepe (in Brussels) that after the congress he will accept no administrative function—he will be "again a free man" [→ :31]. **May c.D:** In correspondence with the Dutch Federation, M discusses holding the coming congress in Holland.

25. ECCARIUS BREAKS RELATIONS. **May 2:** In a curt note to M, Eccarius makes a personal break with him, culminating a period in which he has moved into the anti-M opposition on the GC. **May 3:** M sends Eccarius a chiding but friendly letter asking him to reconsider. (Eccarius does not reply.) **May 7:** GC session: E proposes not to accept Eccarius' resignation as corr secy for America until the GC takes up the whole situation incl charges against Eccarius' conduct; but the GC votes to accept the resignation. **May 11:** GC session: M presents charges against Eccarius' conduct as corr secy for America and his sabotage of GC decisions on the American conflict; E supports M; the GC agrees to ask for documents from America. **May 20:** Eccarius writes Liebknecht that he has broken with M. Liebknecht queries Mrs. M, who, however, asks E to reply in her stead. **May 27–28:** E sends Liebknecht a detailed account of Eccarius' recent factional activity in the GC.

26. THE AMERICAN IWMA SPLIT. **May 4, 8:** The GC resolutions on the American split (#M756) [← :13] are publ in the US and Germany. **May 7, 11:** GC session: see ← :25 re Eccarius. **May c.15:** M receives an extensive report by Sorge (letter of May 2) on the American IWMA, on the negligence of Eccarius as corr secy for America and his support of Section 12; also on the attacks on M made by Heinzen's *Pionier*. **May 21:** GC session: M presents a thorough review of the American internal conflict to date, and debates the situation with Eccarius. **May 28:** GC session: In response to queries from America, M&E move that the GC endorse only the Council led by Sorge, not the parallel organizn set up by Section 12; this motion is carried, against Hales and Eccarius. M reports on the American convention nominating Woodhull for president and calls it all "humbug" (based on letter from Sorge, May 7). **May D:** This is the end point of the notes (#M30) made by M under the heading "American split" [← :8].

27. IWMA AGAINST BAKUNINISM. **May 7:** E sends Liebknecht, for publ in *Volksstaat*, an article by Lafargue on the Bakuninist secret operation in Spain, pubd in *La Emancipación*; he also urges publ of Lafargue's report on the Saragossa congress of the Spanish IWMA which has appeared in *La Liberté*. **May 7–8:** In a letter to Cuno (Seraing, Belgium), E reports on the Bakuninist operation in Spain and Italy, and urges him to fight it in Belgium. **May 23:** M writes a reply (#M616) to renewed attacks on the GC and on M by Stefanoni in *Libero Pensiero* of Mar 28; pubd May 28 in *Gazzettino Rosa*. **May 28:** Writing to Danielson on other matters, M asks him for info on the connection between Bakunin and Nechayev. (Danielson replies on June 4.) **May D:** The GC circular, *The alleged divisions in the International* (#ME5), an exposé of the Bakuninist operation, is pubd as a pamphlet in Geneva in 2000 copies, and sent out to IWMA sections (*KMC* dating: June A).

28. POLITICAL AFFAIRS. **May 8:** M's memorandum on the nationalization of the land (#M537) [← :17], somewhat revised by Dupont, is read by Dupont to a Manchester section meeting [→ :33]. **May 17, 20:** M is again invited to attend the Cercle d'Etudes Sociales of the French Communards, of which he is a member [← :5].

29. *CAPITAL.* **May A:** M sends the first two sets of galley proofs of the French trans to pub'r Lachâtre (Paris). **May 15:** By this date 900 copies of the Russian edn [← :22] have been sold, a good record (Danielson so informs M in letter of June 4). **May 28:** M thanks Danielson for the copy of the Russian edn which he sent; the trans is "masterly," he says.

30. W&P. **May 7:** E promises Liebknecht an article in reply to the "absurd Proudhonist stuff" on the housing question which has appeared in *Volksstaat* in Feb-Mar. Around this time E rereads Proudhon's *Idée générale de la révolution*, in preparation. **May 8:** Paul Lindau again [← :16] asks M to write an article on the IWMA for his paper *Die Gegenwart*. (M declines.) **May c.22:** E writes Part I of his reply on "The housing question" (#E358), for *Volksstaat* [→ :33]. **May 23:** M writes a reply (#M737), for publ in *Volksstaat*, to an anonymous article (by Lujo Brentano) pubd in *Concordia* accusing M of falsifying a citation from Gladstone (this inaugurates a controversy which will go on for two decades) [→ :33]. **May 27:** M sends Glaser de Willebrord (in Brussels) the last galley proofs of his French version of *The civil war in France* (#M143) for pamphlet publ [→ :33]. **May D:** For publ of *The alleged divisions* (#ME5), see ← :27.

JUNE

31. IWMA AFFAIRS. June: GC sessions: M&E attend all four—June 4, 11, 18, 25. Most GC business, directly or indirectly, concerns the forthcoming congress and the fight against Bakuninism. —During this month M and Lafargue begin work on revising the Rules in conformity with the new proposals being made by the GC (#M348), for adoption by the congress. **June 4:** At GC: M argues that the Belgian Federal Council, which repudiates the London Conference resolution on political action, need not be consulted in recognizing a new French section in Brussels which does support the GC. **June 11:** At GC: M proposes to hold the coming congress in Holland, Sep 2. He discusses the Bakuninist campaign to abolish the GC, which makes the "question of organizn" the main point before the congress. He proposes that the next GC be composed of the corr secretaries, each elected by the nation represented, one each. The ensuing discussion is adjourned. —E announces the arrival of the new pamphlets *The alleged divisions* (#ME5) [← :27] from the Geneva printer. — M proposes not to accept the dues of an illegally constituted Bakuninist section in Geneva. E protests selective editing of the GC Minutes by the gen secy, Hales. **June 14:** E sends a communication to a Turin group (#E839) in defense of the GC against the Bakuninists. **June 18:** At GC: E supports the proposal from Holland to hold the coming congress at the Hague. —M&E propose that the GC devote the whole of the next meeting to the congress, leaving other matters to the Sub-Comm. —E is named to a comm to draft a statement of reasons for choosing the congress site. (This statement, #E679, written by E today, is pubd in the IWMA press, June 29 et seq.) —E reports a letter from the Spanish IWMA (A. Lorenzo, June 15) asking that the congress take up the "question of organizn." —M&E criticize the British Federal Council's (Hales's) neglect of dues stamps. —E again discusses the GC Minutes [see June 11, above] and Hales's resignation. **June 21:** M writes Sorge that the congress will open Sep 2; he stresses its significance for the IWMA's fate, and asks that the American organizn be sure to send two or three delegates. **June 25:** At GC: E proposes a precongress discussion on the IWMA Rules; and M&E take part in the ensuing discussion, esp on GC powers and functioning. —E proposes that the Sub-Comm be empowered to act on breaking off with the *Eastern Post*. **June 27:** Writing to the Kugelmanns, daughter Jenny echoes her father [← :24] in saying that he is convinced he cannot finish *Capital* if he continues his GC work; he will give up his GC post after the congress [→ :36]. **June 28:** Sub-Comm meeting: E is to write the British Federation (C. Keen) about breaking with the *Eastern Post*.

32. CAPITAL. June: Meissner begins printing the second German edn of Vol. 1 in nine serial parts [→ :38]. M is still working on revising the French trans. **June c.D:** M sends the last corrected galley proofs of the second German edn to Meissner. **June 27:** See ← :31.

33. W&P. June: For new edns of the *Com Manifesto*, see → :34. **June 1:** M's reply to Brentano (#M737) [← :30] is pubd in *Volksstaat* [→ :47]. **June 15:** The *International Herald* pubs the report on land nationalization made by Dupont on May 8 in Manchester, based on M's memo (#M537), but without mentioning M's name [← :28]. **June M:** The French pamphlet edn of *The civil war in France* (#M143) is pubd in Brussels in an edn of 9000 copies. **June 26:** In connection with the Leipzig treason trial, *Volksstaat* pubs an 1870 letter by M&E [← 70:36] addressed to the German party Exec (cf #ME184). **June 26 to July 3:** *Volksstaat* pubs Part I of E's essay on "The housing question" (#E358), in three installs [→ :57].

34. How THE "MANIFESTO OF THE COMMUNIST PARTY" BECOMES THE *COMMUNIST MANIFESTO*. At the Leipzig treason trial of Bebel and Liebknecht (Mar 11–26) the prosecution reads the *Manifesto* into the official court record on Mar 13. As part of that court record, the text now becomes legally publishable, for the first time in Germany. The party immediately sets about producing a book edn of the trial record (see ST/43), which begins appearing in serial fascicules on Apr 17. Liebknecht writes E that he will publish the *Manifesto* and asks for a new preface; E promises at least a short foreword [← :23]. It is the third fascicule of the book about the trial which contains the text of the *Manifesto* (from the court record); and Liebknecht sends the galley proofs of this fascicule to E, for his corrections. **June 5–6:** E writes Liebknecht that he is correcting the proofs as fast as possible and hopes to do a "short preface" by tomorrow. **June c.15:** The third fascicule of the book comes off the press, containing the text of the *Manifesto*, but of course no preface. **June 24:** M&E finish, and date, the new preface (#ME36); E sends it to Liebknecht, for the offprint publ of the *Manifesto*. **June D:** The *Volksstaat* press publishes an offprint edition of the *Manifesto* (offprinting from the third fascicule); it contains the new preface by M&E. *It is this offprint which for the first time bears the title Das kommunistische Manifest.*

Note: There is no record that Liebknecht discussed the title change with M or E, or informed them in advance; but in any case, whether or not he did, M&E made no objection. For Liebknecht, we may conjecture, the title change was motivated by legal considerations, keeping in mind that publication of the *Manifesto* had heretofore been illegal. By changing the title, the obvious direct link to the old illegal pamphlet was obscured from the eyes of the police, and the reference to an obviously illegal organization ("Communist party") was dropped.

Nevertheless the *Volksstaat* press, that is, Liebknecht, did *not* produce a real edn of the offprint pamphlet edn for circulation in Germany. Inside Germany it was the third fascicule that was distributed, in some thousands of copies—sans title, sans preface. The offprint edition—which is historically labeled the 1872 edition—was actually produced in only a few copies plus a batch of a hundred sent to E himself, who apparently remained unaware of this detail. E sent copies of this edn around Europe, in response to requests, as a model for foreign edns and reprints, etc. Thus this ghost-edition became the progenitor of many real ones (cf ST/2).

JULY

35. IWMA AFFAIRS. July: GC sessions: M&E attend July 2, 16, 23, 30; E attends July 9 (M absent). —During this month, M, with Lafargue, continues working on the Rules (#M348), as in June. **July 2:** At GC: In a discussion on GC powers, E proposes that the GC's suspension powers be balanced by new safeguards; M agrees, so that the GC "never could constitute itself a power in opposition to the Assoc"; the GC thus puts a limit to its present powers. **July 5:** See → :36 for the Sub-Comm meeting on the Bakuninists. **July 9:** At GC: E supports dropping the statute on statistics gathering since the sections have never complied. —E opposes Hales's motion permitting any member to speak at will at any other section. —E opposes Barry's motion to weaken the class character of the Preamble to the Rules (#M347–348). **July 16:** At GC: M objects to deleting "working men's" from the designation of the congress; in the wording of

the Rules, E and others maintain that "men" should be understood as a generic term including both sexes. —E proposes emergency power for the GC to change the convocation of the congress. —M supports Vaillant's motion on future GC composition: three (or fewer) representing each nationality, with power to fill vacancies but not co-opt (cf ← :31). **July 18:** As corr secy for Italy, E responds to the application for affiliation of the Comm for the Emancipation of the Working Classes in Parma (June 7) and sends a copy of the Rules (#E822). E also sends the Rules to a section in Florence, and (via Bignami) confirms the affiliation of four workers in Imola. **July 19:** Sub-Comm meeting: M&E take part in the discussion of the Hague as the congress site. M is named to draft the main GC report to the congress, E to do the general financial report. **July 21:** M writes an article "To the striking miners in the Ruhr Valley" (#M930) on IWMA help and encouragement to the strike (which began June 13); pubd in *Volksstaat*, July 27. **July 23:** At GC: M&E support Vaillant's motion to insert the political-action resolution of the London Conference into the Rules. —M proposes that the two-thirds rule on proletarian composition which was adopted for America [← :13] be added to the General Rules. **July 27:** Sub-Comm meeting: M&E take part in solving various practical problems in the preparations for the congress; also in accepting the Rules of the German-Swiss section and the Ferré section (Paris).

36. IWMA AGAINST BAKUNINISM. July 5: Sub-Comm meeting: E translates Bakunin's attack on the GC circular (#ME5). The Sub-Comm decides not to reply since Bakunin offers no facts but only "coarse language" (this refers esp to the anti-Semitic vituperation in Bakunin's piece). The Sub-Comm requests the GC to propose expulsion of Bakunin and his Alliance at the congress; M&E are assigned to compile the case; E is to ask the Spanish Federal Council about its relation to the Alliance. —E reports on anti-Bakuninist sentiment at the Belgian congress (letter of A. Herman, June 18). —E reports on letters from Turin (July 1) and from the Portuguese Federal Council (Nobre-França, June 24), expressing agreement with the GC. **July 24:** As decided on July 5, E drafts a letter to the Spanish Federal Council (#E865) challenging its hidden ties to the Bakuninist Alliance and demanding an explanation. **July 27:** Sub-Comm meeting: E submits his draft letter to the Spanish Federal Council (#E865) [→ :42]. —M discusses a protest from the Bakuninist Jura Federation against holding the congress in the Hague. Jung is assigned to write the reply (which is erroneously ascribed to M in ST/27—cf #M346). **July 29:** Writing to Kugelmann, M stresses the "life and death" importance of getting German delegates to the coming Hague Congress, to protect the organizn "before I retire." **July 28:** NY Section 1 votes to give its mandate to M [→ :41].

37. HALES AND THE BRITISH FEDERATION. **July 10:** E is elected a delegate of the London GWEA to the British Federation congress in Nottingham. **July 19:** Sub-Comm meeting: M reviews Hales's factional war against the GC inside the organizn, and proposes that Hales be removed as gen secy; Hales's immediate suspension from the post is to go to the GC. M&E take part in discussing measures to counteract Hales's deleterious influence in the British Federation. **July 21–22:** Dupont, who on E's proposal of July 10 was named GC representative to the Nottingham congress of the British Federation, gives E a report on the congress proceedings. **July 23:** At GC: The Sub-Comm proposal to suspend Hales as gen secy is adopted; M proposes Milner for some of this work. **July 30:** At GC: As Hales's factional campaign at the British Federation congress is discussed, Hales attacks M&E and says he will refuse to give up the books. M says that this deserves expulsion; Hales withdraws his threat; his conduct is referred to the Judicial Comm. **July D to Aug AB:** M&E help Dupont organize a foreign section (of émigrés) in Manchester, affiliated to the British Federation.

38. *CAPITAL.* **July:** M continues the work of revising the French trans and correcting the first fascicule's galley proofs. **July 15:** Meissner sends M the first fascicule (five printer's sheets) of the second German edn, just off the press [← :32; → 73:29]. **July-Aug:** M corresponds with Nobre-França, Portuguese IWMA secy, about a Portuguese edn, and sends him (via E) the first vol.; he also requests him to collect material on land ownership in Portugal.

39. W&P. **July 3:** *Volksstaat* pubs the GC resolution (#E679) on the convocation of the Hague Congress, here signed by M as corr secy for Germany. **July c.9:** E writes an article on "The International in America" (#E382) for *Volksstaat,* using M's notes on "American split" (#M30) [← :8] and letters from US members; pubd July 17. **July 28:** M replies to a second anonymous article by Brentano, in *Concordia,* on the same allegation [← :30, 33], with a second article in *Volksstaat* (#M738); pubd Aug 7. **July:** Bignami asks E to write an article for his *Almanacco Repubblicano* [→ :56].

40. PERSONAL. **July A:** M's beloved grandson, the Lafargues' only surviving child, Charles Etienne (called "Schnaps"), dies in Spain after an illness (described as cholera and dysentery) lingering on since last Aug. **July 9–15:** M&E go to Ramsgate for a rest.

AUGUST

41. IWMA AFFAIRS. **Aug:** GC sessions: M&E attend all six—Aug 6, 13, 23, 27, 29/30, 30/31. —During this month M, with Lafargue, completes the revision of the Rules (#M348) started in June. **Aug 4:** Sub-Comm meeting: M reports on Holland, Italy, and the US. —M&E propose steps to expose a Bonapartist agent named Scholl. —For other business, see → :42. **Aug 6:** At GC: See → :42. **Aug M:** M receives a letter (July 30) from Speyer giving him a delegate's mandate to the congress (dated July 28) from NY Section 1; he also receives a letter (Aug c.15) from Hepner (addressed to E) with his delegate's mandate from the Leipzig section. **Aug 15:** M sends a letter to the *Times* exposing a forged "Marx" letter in today's *Times* (#M917); pubd Aug 16. **Aug 20:** M&E, with other GC members, meet with Sorge, who has arrived in London on his way to the Hague, and inform him of the situation in the IWMA. **Aug c.22:** E receives from O. Gnocchi-Viani, Rome section secy, a report on the movement in Rome and addresses for correspondence. **Aug CD:** E receives delegate's mandates to the congress from the Breslau section and NY Section 6 (the latter dated Aug 8). **Aug D:** As assigned [← :35], M drafts the GC Report to the Hague Congress (#M745; for his outline, see #M746). Sometime after Aug 27, M makes a list of extracts from the Minutes of the last two and a half years as part of his preparations for the congress; see #M306. —E, on behalf of the Sub-Comm, prepares the GC financial report [→ :49]. **Aug 27:** At GC: In a discussion of dues from affiliated societies, M remarks that the English TUs are "praised too much. . . ." —M moves that the GC propose a raise in members' dues to the congress; this is voted down 6–10; the GC votes, with M&E abstaining, to fix dues at one penny per month. **Aug 28:** Sub-Comm meeting: M smoothes out a murky squabble over Serraillier; and discusses the assignment of congress mandates. He proposes that charges between GC members should be taken up at the congress only when the new GC is elected. **Aug 29/30** (date uncertain): The GC elects its six delegates to the congress, incl M. **Aug 30/31:** M presents his draft of the GC report (#M745). —M&E oppose Jung's motion to hold the next congress on the Continent.

42. IWMA AGAINST BAKUNINISM. **Aug 4:** Sub-Comm meeting: E presents a letter from J. Mesa (July 28) which encloses the July 22 circular of the New Madrid Federation (pubd in *La Emancipación* on July 27) exposing the splitting activity of the Alliance, esp a secret letter by Bakunin to his supporters; E is assigned to translate the circular into three languages. —E presents a letter (July 26) from Cuno (in Liège) about an expulsion by the Belgian Federal Council under pro-Bakuninist influence. **Aug 6:** At GC: On behalf of the Sub-Comm, E presents his draft (done Aug 4–6) of a GC declaration denouncing the machinations of the Bakuninist Alliance and calling for its expulsion by the congress (#E324). **Aug 8:** Sub-Comm meeting: Since the Spanish Federal Council has given no substantive response to E's letter (#E865) [←:36], M submits another communication (#ME173) which cites the whole of #E865, for circulation to the Spanish membership. **Aug 15:** E writes to the New Madrid Federation recognizing it as a loyal branch opposed to the Bakuninists (#E325); pubd Aug 24. **Aug 15:** M writes Danielson asking him to obtain a copy of the threatening letter sent by Nechayev (Mar 3, 1870) to Lyubavin with the aim of releasing Bakunin from his paid undertaking to translate M's *Capital*; M wants the letter as evidence for the Hague Congress. **Aug 20** (rec'd c.28): Lyubavin sends M a copy of the Nechayev letter, along with his account of the episode. **Aug 23:** E writes a GC circular to the Italian sections (#E809) concerning the action of the Bakuninist-led Rimini Conference of the Italian Federation (held Aug 4–6) in openly breaking with the GC and calling for a rival congress; it is sent to sections in Turin, Milan, Rome, and Ferrara; pubd Aug 28 (incomplete) and Sep 29. **Aug 24:** In a letter to Liebknecht, E informs him of the strategy being planned by the Bakuninists for their operations at the Hague Congress. **Aug D:** E, on behalf of the Sub-Comm, drafts a report for the GC on the Bakuninist Alliance, for presentation to the congress (#E672). **Aug D to Sep A:** M receives from Utin (in Geneva) a report on the Nechayev trial and Nechayev's activity in Russia, and hands over this material to the congress commission of inquiry on the Alliance.

43. HALES AND THE BRITISH FEDERATION. **Aug 13:** At GC: E, appointed to give the financial report to the congress [←:35], asks Hales to turn over the books [cf ←:37]; Hales insultingly insists the books be audited first to forestall tampering (by E, presumably). **Aug 23:** At GC: M&E again demand that Hales turn over the gen secy's books. **Aug 27:** At GC: The GC reiterates M&E's demand for Hales's books. Later in the evening Hales finally accedes.

44. GERMAN MOVEMENT. **Aug 18:** Liebknecht writes E inquiring whether he is willing to be put forward as a Reichstag candidate in a safe Saxon district; M would be a snap to get elected if only he were a citizen. **Aug 24:** E replies that he must decline if only because he too has lost German citizenship by prolonged expatriation.

45. CAPITAL. **Aug 15:** M writes Danielson that he expects the first six fascicules of the French edn to appear "in a few days." He stresses that one should use both the French edn and the new second German edn, because of the changes and supplements embodied in them. **Aug c.15:** M receives from Danielson book reviews of *Capital* that have appeared in the Russian press. M sends Danielson part of the second German edn (the fascicules so far pubd). **Aug D to Oct A:** M corresponds with La Cécilia, who plans to translate *Capital* into Italian. (The plan will not be consummated because the intended publisher refuses to come to an agreement.)

46. READING AND STUDY. **Aug c.15:** M receives from Danielson the ms of Chernyshevsky's *Pisma bes adressa*. **Aug 15 to Dec 12:** M reads this work, translates the first letter into German, and makes a conspectus of the rest, with many excerpts; he also makes efforts to get the ms pubd.

47. W&P. **Aug 7:** *Volksstaat* pubs M's second reply to Brentano (#M738) [←:39].

SEPTEMBER

48. HAGUE CONGRESS. **Sep 1:** M&E, with Mrs. M and Eleanor, arrive in the Hague. Although the Congress officially opens tomorrow, a "preparatory assembly" takes place at 7 P.M., closed to nonmembers (on M's proposal). **Sep 2–7:** The Fifth Congress of the IWMA takes place. M&E are present and active at all working sessions except when busy with congress committees and other administrative business; they are much involved in the routine affairs of the congress, not necessarily noted below. Their main concerns here are: the struggle against the Bakuninist faction; adoption of the new political-action resolution; and (unexpectedly) the transfer of the GC seat to NY. During this stay in the Hague, M&E get better acquainted with Sorge and Cuno, with whom they have corresponded, and renew relations with Dietzgen, J. P. Becker, Kugelmann, Hepner, et al. (On Sep 4, R. Schramm, who is in the city, asks to talk with M, but is refused.)

49. THE CONGRESS SESSIONS. **Sep 2:** E moves that no reporter can report closed sessions. (Congress decides to exclude reporters from the hall.) —E moves a Credentials Comm of seven; M is elected; he meets with it from 3 to 8:30 P.M. when it reports back with a list of credentialed delegates and a list of challenges. **Sep 3:** M opposes recognizing the credentials of Sauva (US Sections 29 and 42), who is nevertheless accepted, 30–20. —In a discussion of Spanish credentials, as the Bakuninists attack Lafargue's mandate, E denounces the Alliance delegates as a secret clique out to rule or ruin. —M moves to expel the Alliance, and proposes a Comm of Inquiry. —Evening session: Re the credentials of a Bakuninist section in Geneva, M discusses how the Alliance conceals its secret character and how it got admitted into the IWMA: "I speak not against secret societies per se" but those that damage the IWMA. E charges that the Spanish Bakuninist delegates still belong to the Alliance. —In connection with a challenge to M. Barry's credentials by Hales and Mottershead, M attacks the English TU leadership as "more or less sold out to the bourgeoisie and the government." (Only two or three vote against Barry.) —M&E take part in a debate to void the mandate of US Section 2. —M reports on greetings received from the Porto Maurizio (Liguria) section, appointing M as its representative to the congress. **Sep 4:** For the Credentials Comm, M argues the case for voiding the mandate of W. West for US Section 12; it is voided 49–0. —E speaks against the Spaniards' motion that delegates cast votes weighted by the number of members represented; this motion is overwhelmingly defeated. **Sep 5:** In accord with the proposal by M and others, a Comm of Inquiry into the Bakuninist Alliance is elected (five). —The GC Report to the Congress, drafted by M (#M745), is read in four languages (by M in German); adopted unanim. —The main debate is on the Bakuninist proposal to abolish the GC altogether; neither M nor E takes the floor. —The Comm of Inquiry hears E present the GC's case against the Alliance (#E672), with presentation of documents. **Sep 6:** In the debate on the powers of the GC, M gives a talk on the issues (cf #ME96C). —M&E plus nine others present a surprise resolution (cf #ME96A) to move the GC seat to NYC, introduced by E, who also speaks for it. It is adopted 31–15, with 11 abstentions. —Afternoon: At the Comm of Inquiry on the Alliance, M&E argue the case to prove the continued secret existence of the Alliance, its abuse of the IWMA, and the episode of Nechayev's threatening letter to Lyubavin on behalf of Bakunin [← :42] (see #ME7AB, #ME96B). —Evening session: Debate on the Vaillant motion to confirm the political-action plank in the Rules does not see M&E taking the floor (cf #ME96D). **Sep 7:** Election of the new GC (to sit in NYC): M describes the three types of IWMA members in America. —E gives the GC financial report (cf #E789, 790). —The congress votes on the political-action resolu-

tion, 27 for, 4 against, 9 abstentions. —M&E are named to a comm to edit the congress minutes and documents. —Cuno reports for the Comm of Inquiry on the Alliance, which has heard many (incl M&E) testify before it. The comm proposes to expel Bakunin, Guillaume, and Schwitzguébel. In a separate statement, the Bakuninist member of the comm, Splingard, admits that Bakunin tried to establish a secret society inside the IWMA; the question is whether it still operates. M supports the comm's proposals in a speech from the floor. (The congress expels Bakunin and Guillaume by big votes, but Schwitzguébel is saved by 15–16.) The congress adjourns.

50. AMSTERDAM MEETING. Sep 8: M&E, with most of the delegates, take part in a public meeting in Amsterdam organized by the local IWMA section. M's speech discusses the results of the congress, esp the significance of the political-action decision, and includes a passage about the possibility of a peaceful or forcible accession to political power in different countries (#M835). E also speaks very briefly, content unreported. (A summary report of M's talk is included as part of an overall report in a local paper on Sep 10, and in *La Liberté* on Sep 15.) [→ :52]

51. MARX IN HOLLAND. Sep c.9 to c.16: M, Mrs. M, and Eleanor sojourn in Scheveningen, under the close surveillance of the Dutch police; E is with them until Sep c.11. **Sep c.10:** M meets with Cuno, who is going to America; they discuss the formation of new US sections. **Sep c.12:** E returns to London, and meets with Sorge before the latter departs for America. **Sep 12:** M, having read in *Le Figaro* of Sep 11 a fake report of an interview with him by a correspondent of *Le Soir*, sends a letter of denial (#M901) to *Le Corsaire*; pubd Sep 15. **Sep 14:** Liebknecht asks M&E to write a short report on the congress for *Volksstaat* in order to counteract the bad impression made by press reports. **Sep c.16–17:** M returns to London.

52. POST-CONGRESS PUBLICATIONS. Sep 17: M writes a letter to the *Daily News* (#M903) denying its Sep 12 report that he and E are planning to move to NYC; pubd Sep 18. **Sep 17–25:** E writes an article (#E555) on the Hague Congress in *Volksstaat*—part of a series, the others being by Hepner; pubd in two installs, Sep 28, Oct 9. **Sep 18:** M's GC Report to the Congress (#M745) is pubd in Germany in *Volksstaat*. **Sep 26:** Hepner asks M for notes on his Sep 8 speech in Amsterdam (#M835) about the use of force, for use in *Volksstaat*, since quoting the text pubd in *La Liberté* of Sep 15 would subject *Volksstaat* to prosecution [→ :56]. **Sep 29:** M's GC Report to the Congress (#M745) is pubd in French in *La Liberté*. **Sep D:** M&E begin preparing for publ the congress resolutions and documents (#ME132) [→ :56]. For M's miscellaneous notes, see #M518.

53. IWMA AFTER THE CONGRESS. **Sep CD to Dec:** In letters to IWMA members in various countries, M&E explain the significance of the Hague decision on independent working-class political action. **Sep 21:** E sends Sorge texts of the Hague decisions and also the address list of organizations of the IWMA. **Sep 26:** Terzaghi (in Turin) writes M asking for articles for *L'Emancipazione del Proletario.* **Sep D to Oct M:** E proposes, to the British Federal Council and a number of English TUs, immediate action against the export of English strikebreakers to Lisbon, in view of info received from the Portuguese Federation on the strikes in Lisbon [→ :55]. **Sep to Dec:** Hales carries on a campaign against M in the British Federation and various English branches, utilizing M's statement at the congress [← :49] that English TU leaders have sold out. **Sep:** The London French periodical *La Fédération* carries a series of articles by Vésinier attacking "M. Karl Marx." (Although KMC dating is Sep, it cites the issues of the paper for Aug 24 to Sep 14.)

54. *CAPITAL.* **Sep 17:** The first part (first five fascicules) of the French edn is pubd. On the first day 234 copies are sold. **Sep D to Oct:** M sends this first part to a number of friends and correspondents, incl Allsop, Beesly, Collet, Danielson, Dietzgen, Imandt, Keller, La Cécilia, Mongin (or Mougin), Rochat, Thieblin, Urquhart, Vaillant, van der Willigen.

OCTOBER

55. IWMA AFFAIRS. **Oct 5:** E meets with McDonnell and De Morgan to discuss the state of the Irish section. —E sends a report on the Hague Congress to the NY Section 6, which had mandated him. **Oct 12:** Sorge, now GC secy in NYC, writes M asking him to send advice, explanations, etc. (This inaugurates a long period of correspondence between M&E and Sorge, to whom they supply info on European developments, ideas, and other aid.) **Oct 16:** E sends a communication (#E817) to the British Federal Council calling its attention again [← :53] to the need for aid to the Lisbon strikers. **Oct CD:** E receives from Cuno a copy of the Hague Congress minutes and a letter. **Oct 31:** E writes a report to the GC (in NYC) on the IWMA in Spain (#E671) [→ :60]. **Oct-Nov:** E is active in the affairs of the British Federal Council and the Manchester section in fighting against the reformist leadership policies, which are opposed to the Hague Congress decisions, esp on political action.

56. POST-CONGRESS PUBLICATIONS: MORE. **Oct 1:** E writes an article for Bignami's *La Plebe* on the Hague Congress (#E381); pubd **Oct 5.** **Oct 2:** *Volksstaat* pubs a somewhat bowdlerized version [cf ← :52] of M's Sep 8 speech in Amsterdam (#M835) about the use of force in revolution (bowdlerized from the report in *La Liberté*) in order to avoid prosecution in Germany. **Oct 5:** E writes another article for *La Plebe*, "Once again on the Hague Congress" (Letters from London, II), against the Bakuninists (#E449); pubd Oct 8. **Oct A:** E writes an article attacking the conduct of the Alliance factionalists at the Hague Congress and their use of "imperative mandates" (#E369); pubd in Spain, Oct 13. **Oct 9:** *Volksstaat* pubs the second installment of E's article on the Hague Congress (#E555) [← :52]. **Oct 20:** In a letter to *Volksstaat* (#M927), M corrects some errors in its Oct 19 report of the congress, esp on the case of Schwitzguébel; pubd Oct 26. **Oct 21:** M&E are finished [← :52] with preparation of the Hague Congress resolutions and documents for publ (#ME132). **Oct CD:** These resolutions and documents (#ME132) are pubd as a pamphlet in a French edn [→ :67]. **Oct:** M's GC Report to the Hague Congress (#M745) [← :52] is pubd in England, Belgium, Spain, etc. —In response to Bignami's request [← :39], E writes an article "On authority" (#E538) against the basic theory of anarchism, and sends it off. (But see → :61.)

57. OTHER W&P. **Oct:** E writes Part III of his essay on "The housing question" (#E358) [← :33; → :67].

58. *CAPITAL.* **Oct 26:** *La Emancipación* pubs a Spanish version of M's preface to the first German edn and of M's letter to Lachâtre (#M131) in the French edn, under the title "Marx's Capital," and also carries news of the publ of the next serial fascicule of the French edn. **Oct D:** M writes to Anna V. Korvin-Krukovskaya about the French trans of *Capital* she was supposed to have made. (This will turn out to be a false report.) **Oct 10, 23:** Bignami writes M asking for authorization to issue an Italian trans. (The putative translator is apparently La Cécilia, but this plan is going to fall through.)

59. PERSONAL. **Oct 10:** M's daughter Jenny is married to Charles Longuet.

NOVEMBER

60. IWMA AFFAIRS. **Nov 2:** E informs Sorge (NY GC) of the formation of new Italian sections in Lodi and Aquila, sends him contact addresses for Spain, Italy, and Portugal, and encloses his Oct 31 report on Spain (#E671). **Nov 3, 17:** E receives the request from the Manchester Foreign Section to represent it in the British Federal Council [← :55]. **Nov 7, 13:** E writes to the new Lodi and Aquila sections welcoming them into the IWMA. His letter to Lodi (#E813) is pubd in *La Plebe* on Nov 17. **Nov 16:** In a letter to Sorge, E reports on the Blanquist pamphlet *Internationale et révolution*, on the Spanish IWMA, on the British Federal Council, etc. For M and himself, he urges the GC to declare that the Bakuninist Jura Federation, by the resolutions of its St. Imier congress, has excluded itself from the IWMA.

61. W&P. **Nov 3:** Bignami writes E acknowledging receipt of E's article "On authority" (#E538) [← :56]. (But Bignami is going to lose this ms when he gets jailed Dec AB [see → 73:19].) **Nov 12:** Bignami writes E again asking for articles for his planned *Almanacco Repubblicano* [← :39]; he asks for articles from M too [→ :67]. **Nov 14:** E writes an article on the Nov 3 Hyde Park demonstration organized by the Irish IWMA members for the release of the Fenian prisoners (#E450); pubd in *La Plebe* as "Letters from London, III," Nov 17. **Nov:** *La Emancipación* pubs the first Spanish trans of the *Com Manifesto*, translated by J. Mesa with some help from E, preceded by the 1872 preface (#ME36); pubd in six installs, Nov 2 to Dec 7.

62. GERMAN MOVEMENT. **Nov-Dec:** M&E criticize *Volksstaat* for taking too accommodating an attitude toward the Lassalleans (SOURCE: KMC, referring to letters to E from Liebknecht).

63. RUSSIAN CONTACTS. **Nov 25:** M asks Danielson (in St. Petersburg) to send a reliable address for further correspondence.

64. *CAPITAL.* **Nov 15–18:** M stays with the newly wed Longuets [see ← :59] in Oxford, in part to go over the French trans of *Capital* with Longuet.

DECEMBER

65. IWMA AFFAIRS. **Dec 3:** Liebers (in The Hague) sends M a report on the congress of the Dutch sections, which has rejected support to the Bakuninists. **Dec 7:** E sends Sorge a letter reporting on the situation of the IWMA in Holland, Spain, France, and England. **Dec 14:** E sends Sorge the English version of the Hague Congress resolution (#ME132), in the *International Herald*, and reports on Bignami's arrest in Italy (Dec AB), following the Nov 21 confiscation of *La Plebe* for publishing a GC address. **Dec 27:** Danielson (in St. Petersburg) informs M that Lyubavin [← :42] is willing to have the Nechayev letter made public. **Dec 30:** The GC (in NYC) names M as the curator of the archives of the old GC, incl the GC Minutes.

66. HALES AND THE BRITISH FEDERATION. **Dec:** A split in the British Federal Council develops as a wing, led by Hales, rejects the decisions of the Hague Congress, esp on independent political action (for these labor leaders are moving to get into bourgeois reform politics). **Dec 1:** A letter by Hales, virulently attacking the previous GC and M (dated Nov 6), is pubd in the organ of the Bakuninist Jura Federation. **Dec 7:** On M's advice, Riley makes his *International Herald* independent of the British Federal Council, as of this date. M&E plan to do a weekly supplement for the paper on international affairs. **Dec 10:** The Hales group pubs a secessionist circular rejecting the Hague Congress. The Manchester Foreign Section urges M&E to write a reply (esp in a letter by Wegmann to E, Dec 16). **Dec 20:** M&E write a reply (#ME177) to Hales's attack of Nov 6 (see Dec 1, above); pubd in *International Herald*, Dec 21. **Dec 21:** E writes a circular (#E465) for the Manchester Foreign Section in reply to the Hales group's secessionist circular of Dec 10; it is pubd Dec 23, signed by three members of the section. **Dec 23:** M writes an address to the membership (#M6) on behalf of the loyal Federal Council, explaining the politics and splitting tactics of the Hales group and its connection with the Bakuninist operation; pubd as a flysheet, Dec 31.

67. W&P. **Dec 11:** E writes an article for *La Plebe*, as a fourth "Letter from London" (#E451), on continued demonstrations in Hyde Park, policemen's strikes in England, and a survey of the European movement after the Hague Congress; pubd Dec 14. **Dec 14:** The Resolutions of the Hague Congress (#ME132) are pubd in English in the *International Herald*. **Dec 25 to Jan 8:** Part II of E's "The housing question" (#E358) is pubd in *Volksstaat*, in four installs. **Dec:** In response to Bignami's request [← :61] M works on a polemical article against anarchist antipolitics (#M404) [→ 73:9].

68. RUSSIAN CONTACTS. **Dec 12:** M writes Danielson on several matters, incl the Hague Congress and the role of the Lyubavin letter. Having received news of Lopatin's attempted flight from exile (in Danielson's letter of Dec 3), M indicates he has a plan to help Lopatin escape. M also asks for Russian reviews of *Capital*, and for data on Chernyshevsky, on whose behalf he wants to "arouse sympathy in the West"; also for N. I. Ziber's book on Ricardo's theory. M says he will study the forms of Russian landed property for Vol. 2 of *Capital*.

69. PERSONAL. **Dec AB:** M's two sons-in-law, Longuet and Lafargue, stay at M's house in London.

1873

CONSPECTUS

1. With the removal of the GC to NYC, and as the IWMA fades out of the picture, there is a sharp drop in the pressure of tasks on M&E; little is now happening. What is listed below under "IWMA Affairs" is a mop-up operation, the most important aspect being the publ of anti-Bakuninist material, esp an overall analysis of Bakunin's Alliance and his ideas, in a French-language pamphlet titled *The Alliance of the Socialist Democracy and the IWMA* (#ME6). It is mostly written by E and Lafargue, with M&E writing the short "Conclusion." In Germany, the Social-Democratic Workers party (Eisenachers) is threatened, in M&E's opinion, by a spirit of accommodation with the declining movement of the Lassalleans and with other nonrevolutionary currents.

2. The second German edn of *Capital* is completed and pubd this year; but the fascicule (serial) publ of the French edn goes on and on (until 1875, in fact), with M still burdened by his self-imposed task of virtually rewriting Roy's trans. During this year the first abridgment of *Capital* (Vol. 1) is pubd, done by J. Most (see ST/M51).

3. The new rubric seen below, "Russian Studies," signalizes M's turn toward studying the social and economic development of Russian society, in the original language. Besides Russian, M also studies the old Frisian language (so his notebooks reveal this year).

4. *Other Broad-dated Entries.* There are a number of continuing projects on Engels' part. Toward the end of this year [see → :49] E begins making notes for a work on German history, which, however, he never will put together; see #E530. E's historical synopsis of G. von Gülich's work on German history (#E181) is assigned by *MEW Daten* to the period c.Oct 1873 to Feb 1874. But it is given a much later date by ST/ME67 (Über Dt.) 522, namely, "prob the end of the 1880s or beginning of the 1890s." —About May of this year E begins working on another long-term project, a book on *Dialectics of nature* (#E221). This will go on for several years. For a list of notebook passages on this subject dated to 1873, see ST/E14 (DN) 446, or *MEW* 20:691. —For the beginning of an episode involving M's business venture with Le Moussu, see → 74:4.

5. *Indefinite Date.* This year marks a change in the handwriting used by M in his mss. "Since 1873," noted E in Apr 1883, M always wrote his manuscripts in Latin handwriting, whereas previously he used German (Gothic) letters.

JANUARY

6. IWMA AFFAIRS. **Jan 2:** M writes a letter to the *Times* (#M918) against a fabrication in the press about M and the IWMA; pubd Jan 3. **Jan 5:** Sorge, for the NY GC, sends E credentials as plenipotentiary representative of the IWMA for Italy, subject to final decision by the GC. (The credentials are pubd in *La Plebe*, May 10.) **Jan:** M reads the stenographic report of Nechayev's trial in *Pravitelstvennii Vestnik* in anticipation of his and E's work on the brochure (#ME6) directed against the Bakuninist Alliance [→ :23]. **Jan to Feb M:** E organizes an aid fund for the families of the editors of *La Plebe* arrested in Lodi; in this connection he corresponds with IWMA people in Spain and Austria, the German party Exec, the NY GC; and he forwards money from England. —E writes a series of reports on the activities of the IWMA on the Continent, for publ in the *International Herald* (#E675); the first of these is pubd Jan 11 [→ :14]. Perhaps in connection with these reports, cf E's notes #E529. —E continues in correspondence with Mesa (Spain), sends him GC documents, and gives financial aid to *La Emancipación*.

7. BRITISH FEDERAL COUNCIL. **Jan:** The imbroglio around the British Federation of the IWMA [← :66] continues. (*MEW* dates it Jan to May.) E in particular is involved in helping members of the British Federal Council fight the Hales group. **Jan 4:** E sends Sorge (NY GC) an account of the split in the British Federal Council, with documents, etc. — The *International Herald* pubs Hales's reply to M&E's letter of Dec 21 (#ME177). **Jan 11:** The *International Herald* pubs a rejoinder to Hales by Lessner, written after discussion with M&E. **Jan M:** M writes a reply (#M110) to a new circular by the Hales group of secessionists, esp discussing the decisions of the Hague Congress; pubd in the *International Herald*, Jan 25. **Jan c.22–23:** E writes to the British Federal Council requesting help for the striking clockmakers of Geneva; it is read at the Council on Jan 23. **Jan 26:** At the London congress of the secessionist (Hales's) British Federation, Jung gives a long speech against M.

8. GERMAN MOVEMENT. **Jan c.22:** E receives news of Bebel's victory in the supplementary Reichstag election, even though he is under fortress imprisonment; also news of the increase in *Volksstaat* subscriptions.

9. W&P. **Jan A:** E writes an article, "The 'crisis' in Prussia" (#E195), on revolutionary possibilities in Germany and the societal incompetence of the bourgeoisie; pubd in *Volksstaat*, Jan 15. **Jan 8:** *Volksstaat* ends the publ of Part II of E's "The housing question" (#E358) [← 72:67]. During Jan, E writes Part III [→ :14]. **Jan 11:** For #E675, see ← :6, Jan to Feb M. **Jan 22:** Bolte (in NY) asks M&E to write articles for the NY *Arbeiter-Ztg* and for a projected English-language paper [→ :11]. **Jan:** M sends Bignami his article on "Indifference to politics" (#M404) [← 72:67], to be pubd in *Almanacco Repubblicano* → :58]. **Jan-Feb:** M negotiates with Meissner for publ of a collected edn of his writings. (E mentions this to Liebknecht, Feb 12.)

10. *CAPITAL.* **Jan 24:** M finishes the Afterword to the second German edn (#M130), and sends it to Meissner.

FEBRUARY

11. IWMA AFFAIRS. **Feb 8:** E sends a memorandum (#E480) to Sorge, for the GC, with a number of informational items and queries on the international movement. **Feb 12:** M writes Bolte (in NY) explaining why it was a mistake to suspend the Jura Bakuninists instead of merely recognizing their exclusion [← 72:60]; he also reports on the congress of the secessionist British Federation [← :7]; and he agrees to write for the papers Bolte has proposed [← :9]. **Feb M:** M&E help Lessner and Vickery write a rejoinder to the report of the Jan 26 congress of the secessionist British Federation.

12. GERMAN MOVEMENT. **Feb 12:** Writing to Liebknecht, E sharply challenges signs that *Volksstaat*, Liebknecht, and some other party leaders wish to soft-pedal any opposition to Lassallean influence and even to Bakuninism. (*KMC* refers E's letters to Feb-Mar. *MEW Daten* refers to letters to Liebknecht and Hepner over the period Feb to June.)

13. POLITICAL AFFAIRS. **Feb 23–25:** In a letter to Mesa (not extant), E discusses the nature of the revolution going on in Spain and proletarian policy in it, and stresses the task of forming an independent political party of the working class (SOURCE: *MEW Daten*).

14. W&P. **Feb 1–15:** The last three articles in E's series on IWMA activities (#E675) [← :6] are pubd in *International Herald*. **Feb 8–22:** *Volksstaat* pubs Part III of E's "The housing question" (#E358) [← :9] in four installs. **Feb 12:** Re M's collected writings, see ← :9. **Feb AB:** At De Morgan's request, E translates a letter from Garibaldi to De Morgan on the republicans' struggle against clericalism and the monarchy, for publ in *International Herald*, Feb 15.

15. *CAPITAL.* **Feb 12:** M mentions (in a letter to Bolte) that up to this point Meissner has pubd the first eight (out of nine) fascicules of the second German edn [← 72:32; → :29].

16. RUSSIAN STUDIES. **Feb:** M reads a couple of satires by Saltykov-Shchedrin, sent him by Danielson. **c.Feb to Mar:** M reads books, received from Danielson, by A. A. Golovachov (on "ten years of Reform," 1861–71) and Ziber (on Ricardo), and begins studying the five-vol. work by A. Skrebitzky on the peasant question under Alexander II.

MARCH

17. IWMA AFFAIRS. **Mar 20:** E sends Sorge (NY GC) an informational report on the IWMA in England and on the Continent; he urges that the GC resolution on the self-exclusion of sections not recognizing the Hague decisions be implemented in Spain, the Jura, etc. **Mar 24:** M&E take part in the second anniversary commemoration of the Paris Commune, held by the British Federal Council and Communard refugees, which adopts a statement made up of passages from *The civil war in France* (#M143).

18. GERMAN MOVEMENT. **Mar 11:** In a letter to Mrs. Natalie Liebknecht, E inquires about the prison conditions of Liebknecht and Bebel and the possibility of improving their personal circumstances.

19. W&P. **Mar:** E finishes a second version of his article "On authority" (#E538) [← 72:61], and sends it to Bignami [→ :58].

20. *CAPITAL.* **Mar-Apr:** M corresponds with Bignami on the publ of an Italian edn. (This will not be accomplished, because of the government's harassment of Bignami.) **Mar 1, 22, Apr 12:** *La Emancipación* pubs a Spanish trans of the section of Vol. 1 on the transformation of money into capital. **Mar D:** M, still working on the French trans, consults Lafargue on some trans problems.

21. RUSSIAN STUDIES. **Mar 22:** Writing to Danielson, M asks for info on Chicherin's views on the historical development of common property in land in Russia, and on the dispute between Chicherin and the historian I. D. Belyayev.

22. PERSONAL. **Mar 20:** M and daughter Eleanor are on holiday in Brighton "for a few days" around this time: so writes E on this date.

APRIL

23. IWMA AFFAIRS. **Apr to July:** In accord with decisions of the Hague Congress, E and Lafargue work on a pamphlet (#ME6) to be pubd by the GC exposing the roots and operation of the Bakuninist Alliance, esp inside the IWMA; M collaborates with them; M&E write the "Conclusion." But note: even before Apr, M&E collected materials and documentation used here (cf #ME7, 96; #M518) [→ :36]. **Apr 7:** M asks J. P. Becker to start preparing for a Swiss delegation to the next IWMA congress, in Geneva, to protect the organizn against the Bakuninists. **Apr 15:** E sends an informational report to the NY GC, mainly on IWMA periodicals and publications (#E850). **Apr CD:** E collaborates with Vickery, British Federal Council secy, on preparations for the second congress of the British Federation in Manchester. —E works on editorial preparation of the minutes of the Hague Congress for publ in French; the project remains unfinished. **Apr D:** E writes a letter to Hepner refuting the distorted article on the IWMA pubd Apr 27 by the Lassallean paper *Neue Social-Demokrat.* Though it was not written by Hepner, part of the letter appears in *Volksstaat,* May 7 (#E543).

24. W&P. Apr-May: At Riley's request, E sends the *International Herald* notes on the workers' movement in various countries; on these notes by E (not extant), Riley bases items for the paper's column on TU news, pubd Apr 12, 26, May 3, 24 (SOURCE: *MEW Daten*).

25. CAPITAL. Apr 5: M sends the last corrected proof sheets of the second German edn to Meissner.

26. RUSSIAN STUDIES. Apr A: Danielson, as requested, sends M brief biographical data on Chernyshevsky. **Apr:** M studies agricultural conditions in Russia; reads articles on the question in the journal *Sovremennik,* incl an article by Chernyshevsky and a review of Chicherin by A. Severtsev.

MAY

27. IWMA AFFAIRS. May 2: E writes an article for *Volksstaat* (#E380) replying to the Apr 27 attack on the IWMA in the Lassallean *Neue Social-Demokrat;* pubd May 10. E's letter to Hepner (#E543) [← :23], on the same subject, appears in *Volksstaat* May 7. **May A:** M discusses the agenda of the second congress of the British Federation (Manchester, June 1–2) with Dupont and Serraillier, who are on the Federal Council. **May:** E's mandate as GC plenipotentiary for Italy [← :6] is pubd in *La Plebe.*

28. POLITICAL AFFAIRS. May 26, 31: M&E exchange correspondence on the strengthening of reaction in France, as MacMahon succeeds Thiers (May 24).

29. CAPITAL. May: Meissner pubs the last fascicule of the second German edn, thus completing publ in serial parts [← :15] (for book publ, see → :35). **May-June:** Despite deteriorating health, M continues working on

his revision of Roy's French trans; a part of the text, he finds, he has to translate afresh.

30. RUSSIAN STUDIES. May 22: Danielson, as requested, sends M a collection of materials on Russian landed property, esp on the *obshchina* (village community) and on bibliography.

31. EXPLORATIONS IN THEORY. May 30: "In bed this morning, the following dialectical ideas on the natural sciences came into my head": thus begins E's letter to M. This more or less inaugurates the period of several years during which E will work on notes on the "dialectics of nature" (cf #E221). M shows E's letter to the chemist Schorlemmer, who annotates his agreement with a number of points. **May D:** In discussions with Samuel Moore in Manchester, M maintains that it is (theoretically) possible to determine the "main laws of crises" by mathematical analysis of economic movements and their zigzags (tables of prices, discount rates, etc.); in fact M has at various times in the past tried to calculate these "ups and downs" as irregular curves (so he tells E, May 31).

32. PERSONAL. May 22 to June c.3: Since M's health is bad ("cerebral congestion," insomnia, cough, headaches), esp because of overwork on the French trans of *Capital,* E convinces him to go to Manchester to consult Dr. Gumpert. But when M arrives in Manchester, Gumpert is away in Germany. M awaits his return on June 2, meanwhile spending time with his friends Sam Moore (see ← :31) and Schorlemmer, and visits Dronke in Southport. **May 31:** M travels with Moore to Buxton, returning to Manchester on June 2, when he sees Dr. Gumpert. Gumpert puts M on a strict regimen incl a four-hour working limit [→ :38].

JUNE

33. IWMA AFFAIRS. June c.10: M receives a report from Wilmart (Buenos Aires, May 27) on his activity for the IWMA. **June 10–14:** On behalf of the GC, E translates its May 23 statement against the Bakuninists into English and French, and sends copies to the Federal Councils in Britain, Spain, and Portugal, and to *La Plebe* in Italy. **June 14:** E writes a short report to the NY GC on miscellaneous items of IWMA business (#E851). **June 19–20:** E writes an article reporting IWMA developments in various countries, for *Volksstaat* (#E307); pubd July 2. **June 29:** Bolte sends M info on the state of the IWMA in America.

34. GERMAN MOVEMENT. June 20: In an important letter to Bebel, E stresses political principles: the party should face toward the masses outside the movement, not toward recruiting from rival groups; one should not be fooled by cries for "unity" raised by splitters and sectarians; principles should not be sacrificed for short-range successes; etc.

35. *CAPITAL.* **June A:** The second German edn is pubd in book form [← :29] in Hamburg, with the imprint date 1872. **June-July:** M is still working at revising the French trans.

JULY

36. IWMA AFFAIRS. **July 2:** E's article-report on the IWMA (#E307) [← :33] is pubd in *Volksstaat.* **July 21:** M&E finish, and date, the "Conclusion" of the anti-Bakunin pamphlet (#ME6) [→ :44]. **July D:** M asks Perret (in Geneva) to find a bookdealer to handle the sale of this forthcoming pamphlet. **July 25:** E telegraphs Sorge (NY GC) that Serraillier has agreed to attend the coming IWMA congress in Geneva as the GC representative. **July 26:** E sends Sorge an informational report on IWMA affairs in various countries. **July:** E helps Larroque, a French IWMA émigré in Spain, establish ties with the Spanish IWMA, and from him E receives info on the movement in Spain and Bordeaux.

37. RUSSIAN STUDIES. **July to Oct:** Studying the history of common property in land in Russia, M reads works by V. I. Sergeyevich, F. Skaldin, K. A. Nevolin, N. Kalachov, et al.

38. PERSONAL. **July 1:** In a letter to Kugelmann, who has written (June 29) in great perturbation about reports that M is dangerously ill or even dead, E recounts M's health problems [← :32] and says he has improved. Kugelmann sends *Volksstaat* a note denying the pubd reports; pubd July 13. However, despite Dr. Gumpert's injunctions, M continues to work long hours at the BM.

AUGUST

39. IWMA AFFAIRS. **Aug 17:** NY Section 1 sends M a mandate as its delegate to the IWMA congress in Geneva. **Aug 29, 30:** M&E (the latter in Ramsgate) exchange letters on the question of going to the Geneva Congress; they decide not to attend; Serraillier [← :36] and Hepner should likewise not go [→ :43].

40. *CAPITAL.* **Aug 12:** M sends Danielson the last pubd fascicule of the second German edn [← :29].

41. RUSSIAN STUDIES. **Aug D:** M receives a letter from Danielson regretting he cannot send full biographical info on Chernyshevsky; he cautions that it would be premature for M to align himself with Chernyshevsky in the press.

42. PERSONAL (E). **Aug A to Sep A:** E takes the waters in Ramsgate, but goes to London for a day to organize the distribution of the anti-Bakunin pamphlet (#ME6).

SEPTEMBER

43. IWMA AFFAIRS. **Sep 3:** E drafts the text of a letter, for Serraillier's signature, addressed to the IWMA Geneva Congress, explaining why he is not attending (#E819) [← :39]. **Sep 27:** In a letter to Sorge (NY GC), M summarizes why the Geneva Congress was a fiasco; it is necessary to "let the formal organizn of the International recede into the background for the time being"; events will ensure "the resurrection of the International in improved form."

44. ANTI-BAKUNIN PUBLICATIONS. **Sep A:** The Engels–Lafargue–Marx pamphlet exposing the Bakuninist Alliance (#ME6) is pubd in French. **Sep AB:** E draws up a short presentation of this pamphlet for *Volksstaat* (#E111.5); it is pubd in four installs, titled "Cagliostro Bakunin." **Sep-Oct:** E writes a study "The Bakuninists at work" on the Spanish uprising of the past summer (#E59), for *Volksstaat* [→ :49].

45. *CAPITAL.* **Sep 25, 30:** M sends copies of the second German edn to Darwin and Herbert Spencer [→ :48].

46. PERSONAL. **Sep 2:** A first child is born to the Longuets (M's daughter Jenny), Charles Félicien, in London—at this point, M's only surviving grandchild [→ 74:27]. **Sep:** M is still ailing and is still under doctor's orders to limit his working hours.

OCTOBER

47. POLITICAL AFFAIRS. **c.Oct:** M makes the acquaintance of Edward Aveling. **Oct 31:** Eugen Jaeger, author of *Moderne Sozialismus,* writes M asking for full biographical info, for use in his second edn.

48. *CAPITAL.* **Oct 1, 21:** Darwin and Spencer, resp, send M polite acknowledgments of *Capital* [← :45]. **Oct 8:** Meissner sends M 1000 talers as payment for the second German edn.

49. W&P. **Oct 31:** E's "Bakuninists at work" (#E59) begins publ in *Volksstaat* [← :44; → :51]. **c.Oct to next Feb:** E makes notes for a projected historical work on Germany. For miscellaneous mss from this period, see #E530. According to *MEW Daten,* E's synopsis of a history by G. von Gülich (#E181) was also done in this period; likewise notes on C. E. Langethal. Re the dating of the Gülich synopsis, see ← :4.

50. PERSONAL (E). **Oct c.28 to Nov 20:** E sojourns in Engelskirchen because of his mother's death.

NOVEMBER

51. ANTI-BAKUNIN. **Nov 2, 5:** *Volksstaat* finishes publ of E's "Bakuninists at work" (#E59) [← :49]. (The pamphlet edn will appear either later this month or Dec D; see *Register.*) **Nov D:** E works at revising S. Kokosky's poor German trans of the anti-Bakunin brochure #ME6, for pamphlet publ by the *Volksstaat* press (which will take place in 1874) under the title, in German, *A plot against the IWMA.* **Nov:** M (also E after his return from Germany) meets several times with Utin, who is visiting London and gives new info on Bakunin's activities.

52. POLITICAL AFFAIRS. **Nov 8:** M and Utin (see ← :51) visit Beesly. **Nov c.M:** M is visited by the journalist Thieblen. **Nov 25–28:** Lopatin, who has come from Paris to London to see M (who is out of town—see → :55), meets with E, then returns to Paris on Nov 28. **Nov 29:** E informs M by letter of Lopatin's visit and his previous adventures.

53. CAPITAL. **Nov c.15:** M gives the BM Library some of the serial parts (fascicules) of the French edn of *Capital* (SOURCE: MEW *Daten*). **Nov D to Dec A:** E reads the ms of the French trans of *Capital* (SOURCE: MEW *Daten*).

54. OPINIONS. **Nov 30:** In a letter to E, M, having just read Sainte-Beuve's *Chateaubriand et son groupe littéraire sous l'Empire* (1861), sets down an analysis of why he detests Chateaubriand and his style.

55. PERSONAL. **Nov 20:** E returns from Germany [← :50] to London. **Nov 24 to Dec 15:** M and daughter Eleanor, both ill, go to Harrogate to take the waters. **Nov 28:** M makes a day's trip to Manchester to consult

Dr. Gumpert, who forbids him to work for the time being [→ :60].

DECEMBER

56. POLITICAL AFFAIRS. **Dec 28:** Kugelmann informs M that Miquel, on being asked, told him that M can return to Germany, prob without police harassment, if he refrains from behaving demonstratively.

57. CAPITAL. **Dec 7:** In a letter to E, M comments on the table of contents of a book by De Paepe (as announced in *L'Internationale*, Nov 23, 30, but in fact never pubd) in which De Paepe, purporting to expound M's polit eco, shows he does not understand it. **Dec c.24:** M informs pub'r Lachâtre that he intends to speed up the work on the French trans. **Dec 28:** Kugelmann's letter (see ← :56) reports a review of *Capital* by someone named Baron, in the journal *Im neuen Reich*.

58. W&P. **Dec:** Bignami's *Almanacco Repubblicano* for 1874 appears, with articles by M (#M404) and E (#E538) directed against anarchism.

59. SHAKESPEARE. **Dec 10:** E, writing to M, makes biting comments on a new book by R. Benedix which denounces "Shakespearomania"—yet "there is more life and reality in the first act of the *Merry Wives* than in all of German literature." Really! **Dec 11:** M naturally agrees: if people like Benedix understood Shakespeare, how would they get the nerve to put their own stuff on the boards?

60. PERSONAL. **Dec 15–17:** M, returning from Harrogate [← :55], goes to Manchester for another medical visit to Dr. Gumpert; on the 17th he returns to London. **Dec CD to Jan D:** M suffers from carbuncles.

1874

CONSPECTUS

1. We are now entering a period when M&E's activities become more and more limited to their writing, their scientific studies, and their correspondence with movement leaders.

2. *Broad-dated Entries.* All during this year M continues working on the French trans of *Capital*, correcting galley proofs as pub'r Lachâtre issues the serial fascicules [→ 75:41]. —Oct to Dec: *Volksstaat* reprints M's 1852 pamphlet on the Cologne Communist trial (#M762) [→ :37]. —M reads Bakunin's new book *Statism and anarchy* (in Russian) and makes a conspectus of its contents (#M178); this goes on through 1874 to early 1875. (KMC's erroneous dating is "c.Jan"

1874.) —E continues work on two long-term projects noted before [← 73:4]. Re E's plans for a history of Germany, see also → :7. Re E's studies on the *Dialectics of nature* (#E221): this year he does over 50 sketches, incl whole sections of the projected book; for a list of passages dated to 1874, see ST/E14 (DN) 446 or MEW 20:691.

3. Aside from writing projects, let us note two items. —For the period 1874 through c.Sep 1875, KMC says that M&E give help and advice to Leo Frankel in connection with his work inside the London GWEA against the Lassalleans. —For the period 1874 to about 1877, according to KMC, Lissagaray spends a good deal of time with the M family, as Eleanor's fiancé.

4. *Indefinite Entries.* A German-language pamphlet edn of the Engels–Lafargue–Marx exposé of Bakunin's Alliance (#ME6) is pubd under the title *A plot against the IWMA* (in German); the trans by S. Kokosky has been revised by E [← 73:51]. —In the first quarter of this year an unfortunate business venture in which M is involved comes to a head. In 1873 Lafargue entered into a business partnership with Le Moussu, a French Communard refugee, and George Moore, an English engraver, to exploit a patent of Le Moussu's for a photoengraving apparatus. Lafargue and Le Moussu split by Aug 1873; and somehow M enters into the enterprise in Lafargue's stead, financed by E (cf E to M, Dec 5, 1873). There is a falling-out in early 1874, and Frederic Harrison, the well-known Comtist, is called on to act as arbitrator; he decides in Le Moussu's favor. This takes place by or before Mar 1874. Extant also are two letters by M to Moore, dated Mar 26 and 28, dealing with some murky continuation of the imbroglio. (KMC erroneously dates the whole business Apr-May 1874.)

JANUARY

5. GERMANY: ELECTION VICTORY. **Jan 10:** In the Reichstag elections the SDWP (Eisenachers) elects nine deputies. **Jan M:** M gives Barry help and advice toward writing an article on the German election for the London *Examiner*. **Jan 19:** M's comment on the election, in a letter to Kugelmann, is that it "serves Mr. Bismarck and his middle-class tail right." **Jan 27:** E comments (to Liebknecht) that this victory "puts the German proletariat at the head of the European workers' movement...." **Jan D:** E contributes money to the election fund of the German party, collected by the London GWEA.

6. *CAPITAL.* **Jan-Apr:** M collects and studies material bearing on Vols. 2 and 3; he investigates the problems of land ownership, comparing ancient authors with the latest researches. (SOURCE: *MEW Daten*; cf M to Kugelmann, May 18.)

7. PUBL PLANS. **Jan 27:** Writing to Liebknecht, E mentions his work on the history of Germany [← :2], and says he has in mind articles for *Volksstaat*, perhaps a booklet, perhaps even a book, so deeply is he involved in "economic and statistical studies" for it.

FEBRUARY

8. GERMAN MOVEMENT. **Feb 27:** Bernhard Becker writes M about party electoral work in Germany, esp in Brunswick, and about his forthcoming book *Die Arbeiteragitation Ferdinand Lassalles* [→ :29]. **Feb D to Mar A:** E writes an article for *Volksstaat* on

the militarism of the Bismarck government (#E371) [→ :13].

9. POLITICAL AFFAIRS. **Feb 21–22:** E writes an article (#E245) for *Volksstaat* on the English parliamentary election just held, welcoming the election of two mine-union secretaries, and criticizing the running of workers' candidates as mere tails to the Liberal party instead of through an independent working-class party; pubd Mar 4.

10. OTHER W&P. **Feb 2, 18, Mar 5:** Liebknecht repeatedly proposes to M&E that the *Volksstaat* press be permitted to publish the *Poverty of philosophy* (#M681) and the *Holy family* (#ME76); M agrees [→ :38].

11. *CAPITAL.* **Feb to Mar A:** M continues his study of plant physiology and land fertilization, as part of his investigation of agricultural economics, and reads J. Au's book on *J. v. Liebig's Lehre* [etc.], as well as other works on agrochemistry.

12. PERSONAL. **Feb to Apr M:** M's health worsens again, with headaches and insomnia; he is unable to work part of the time.

MARCH

13. GERMAN MOVEMENT. **Mar 8, 11:** E's article on the militarism of the Bismarck government (#E371) [← :8] is pubd in *Volksstaat*. **Mar 13:** E writes an article for *Volksstaat* on Moltke and German military policy (#E744); pubd Mar 25. **Mar CD:** M&E are apprised of the dangerous influence of Prof. Dühring in the movement, by an article in *Volksstaat* (Mar 13, 20), "Ein neuer 'Communist,' " by Bebel (unsigned).

14. RUSSIAN CONTACTS. **Mar:** M is visited by Lavrov, editor of *Vperyod*, who has recently arrived from Zurich in order to continue publ of the periodical in London. **Mar-Apr:** M&E meet regularly with Lopatin, who shows them an article on M's economic theory by Ziber pubd in *Znaniye*, no. 1, 1874. M&E give Lopatin a recommendatory letter to J. Mesa (Spain).

15. W&P. **Mar 4:** *Volksstaat* pubs E's article on the English election (#E245) [← :9].

16. *CAPITAL.* **Mar M:** M begins to study the last several years of the English Blue Books, on English economy and economic policy; he has bought them from a wastepaper dealer.

17. PERSONAL. **Mar:** M's business dispute with Le Moussu [see ← :4] may have come to a head this month.

APRIL

18. PERSONAL. **Apr M to May 5:** M, unable to work because of headaches and insomnia, goes to Ramsgate to take the waters. Dr. Gumpert advises him (via E) to stop working altogether and go to Carlsbad for mineral-water treatments [→ :31].

MAY

19. RUSSIA AND POLAND. **May 3:** In response to the Russian CZAR's visit to England, the Polish revolutionary emigration (Wróblewski, Jan Krynski) issue an "Address of the Polish refugees to the English people." Wróblewski has E read it May 4–5. **May-June:** E writes an article (#E592)—the first of a series on "Refugee literature" in the *Volksstaat* (#E660)—on the Polish address, stressing the theme that support of Polish freedom is necessary to free Germany from Russian influence and to prepare revolution in Russia: "A people which oppresses another cannot emancipate itself" (pubd June 17).

20. *CAPITAL.* **May A:** After the long interruption due to illness, M resumes work (May betw 5–12) on the French trans. **May 12:** M sends Lachâtre the galley proofs he has finished, up to the three last fascicules. **May CD to July M:** M works on the three last fascicules.

21. OPINION. **May 18:** Writing to Kugelmann, M remarks that in the US, "the greatest obstacle is the professional politicians, who immediately try to distort every new movement and turn it into another 'business proposition.' "

JUNE

22. GERMAN MOVEMENT. **June A:** M&E write to Bracke in order to get him to raise the question in *Volksstaat* of changing the party program, in accord with a commission elected at the 1873 party congress, on program revision. (Bracke will raise the question July 1.) **June c.15:** E hears from Liebknecht on the persecution of the *Volksstaat* editors by the government. **June-July:** In letters to Liebknecht, W. Blos, and Hepner, M&E warn against Prof. Dühring's influence in the party and criticize his book *Kritische Geschichte der National-Ökonomie und des Socialismus.*

23. POLITICAL AFFAIRS. **June A:** M is visited by Georg Weber, of Kiel. **June 24:** E answers a letter from A. Wegmann (in Rio de Janeiro), and informs him of the state of the IWMA.

24. W&P. **June 17:** E's first article (#E592) in the series "Refugee literature" [← :11] is pubd in *Volksstaat*. **June:** E writes the second article in this series (#E621), analyzing the program pubd by the émigré group of Blanquist Communards; it makes a fundamental criticism of the Blanquist-type sect and its conception of revolutionary dictatorship (pubd in *Volksstaat*, June 26).

JULY

25. GERMAN MOVEMENT. **July c.28:** E hears from Liebknecht on the successful work of the party congress in Coburg, July 18–21; Liebknecht stresses that unification with the Lassalleans is out of the question, except for "tactical unity." (*KMC*'s erroneous dating is Aug 28.) **26.** W&P. **July 1:** Preparing a "third printing" of his *Peasant war in Germany* (#E579) for publ, E writes a supplement (#E581) to the preface of the 1870 second edn. (This will be pubd in 1875.) **July D to Sep:** E writes the third article (#E661) in the series "Refugee literature" for *Volksstaat*; it criticizes Lavrov's conciliatory attitude toward Bakunin [→ :37].

27. PERSONAL. **July CD:** M is convalescing in Ryde; his daughter Laura, on a visit to England, stays in Ryde July 11–13. M&E exchange letters (July 15, 21), chatting about European political affairs. **July 20:** M's grandson, Jenny Longuet's 11-month-old child Charles [← 73:46], dies of cholerine. M is very hard-hit.

AUGUST

28. POLITICAL AFFAIRS. **Aug 4:** In a letter to Sorge surveying the international scene, M comments on the decline of the IWMA in England, the TUs in France, the impotence of the anarchist "super-socialism" in Spain, Italy, and Belgium, and the role of Bismarck in Germany; he sees a "general European war" lying ahead. **Aug 12:** Sorge resigns as gen secy of the GC in NY. **Aug 14:** Sorge writes about this step to E (who receives it Aug D) [→ :33].

29. GERMAN MOVEMENT. **Aug 4:** In his letter to Sorge (see ← :28), M complains that *Volksstaat* is peppered with fanciful articles about the future socialist society by half-educated philistines and academics; he comments that B. Becker's booklet about Lassalle [← :8] is useful for finishing off the Lassallean sect. **Aug c.15–20:** E approves a proposal by Blos to publish a Cologne daily called *Neue Rheinische Ztg.* (But the plan is not carried out.)

30. PERSONAL. **Aug 1:** M applies for British citizenship. **Aug A:** M is unable to continue working on the French trans of *Capital* because of his persistent liver ailment. **Aug 6–9:** M accompanies his daughter Jenny to E, who is staying in Ramsgate. Jenny then stays on with E and his family (Lizzie Burns, and her niece Mary Ellen). **Aug CD:** E and Jenny go on a trip to Jersey [→ :34]. **Aug 29:** The Home Ministry rejects M's application for citizenship, on the (confidential) ground that "The man had not been loyal to his King" [of Prussia]. . . ."

31. MARX'S TRIP TO GERMANY. **Aug 15:**

On Dr. Gumpert's orders, M, accompanied by his daughter Eleanor, travels to Carlsbad to take the waters. **Aug 19 to Sep 21:** M and Eleanor sojourn in Carlsbad, at the Hotel Germania on the Schlossberg, together with the Kugelmann family. M spends time also with Max Oppenheim (Mrs. Kugelmann's brother), Simon Deutsch (a bibliographer), Otto Knille (a painter), and a number of physicians incl Dr. Gans Jr and Dr. Kraus.

SEPTEMBER

32. MARX'S TRIP (CONT'D). Sep: M and Eleanor remain in Carlsbad for the first three weeks of the month. M's personal relations with Dr. Kugelmann are drastically cooled by M's and Eleanor's revulsion at the way Kugelmann treats his wife; there is an open falling-out on Sep 6, which does not go so far as breaking off relations. **Sep 21:** M and Eleanor leave Carlsbad. **Sep c.22–23:** They stay in Dresden. **Sep c.23–25:** In Leipzig, M meets with Liebknecht, Blos (who has just been released from prison), and others of the Leipzig party. **Sep c.25–28:** In Berlin, M and Eleanor visit Edgar von Westphalen. **Sep c.29 to Oct c.1:** In Hamburg, M visits Meissner and meets with Geib and Auer on party affairs [→ :35].

33. POLITICAL AFFAIRS. Sep 12–17: E writes a long letter to Sorge, approving his decision to resign as GC gen secy [← :28]; the IWMA, E says, became unviable by becoming successful enough to be fought over; the next International will be directly communist and based on M's principles.

34. PERSONAL (E). Sep 5: E returns with his family and Jenny [← :30] from Jersey, arriving in London at 2 A.M.

OCTOBER

35. MARX'S TRIP (END). Oct c.3: M and Eleanor return to London.

36. GERMAN MOVEMENT. Oct 10: The Lassallean group makes a unity proposal to the SDWP (Eisenachers), in a note by Tölcke to Liebknecht. **Oct 26:** Liebknecht informs M&E of the unity proposal, remarking that it should be considered with great reserve. (M is also informed by H. Ramm, a *Volksstaat* editor.)

37. W&P. Oct 6, 8: *Volksstaat* pubs the third article (#E661) [← :26] in the series "Refugee literature," a criticism of Lavrov. **Oct c.20:** At the request of Lopatin (in Paris), E sends him this article (#E661), which Lopatin immediately forwards to his friends in St. Petersburg. **Oct 28 to Dec 18:** *Volksstaat* reprints M's 1852 pamphlet *Revelations concerning the Com trial in Cologne* (#M762), naming the author; it runs in 13 installs [→ 75:8].

NOVEMBER

38. GERMAN MOVEMENT. Nov 8: Geib (in Hamburg) reports to M on progress in the unity negotiations between the SDWP (Eisenachers) and the Lassalleans (GGWA), and on the forthcoming congress. **Nov 18:** Liebknecht again [← :10] urges M&E to permit republication of the *Poverty of philosophy* (#M681) and the *Holy family* (#ME76).

DECEMBER

39. GERMAN MOVEMENT. Dec c.13: M sees the official announcement of the planned unification of the Eisenachers and Lassalleans (SDWP and GGWA) in the Dec 11 issue of *Volksstaat.*

40. RUSSIAN STUDIES. Dec: M reads Chernyshevsky's work *Cavaignac* and again studies his *Pisma bes adressa*, pubd in Zurich during 1874. (*MEW Daten* dates this: end of 1874.)

1875

CONSPECTUS

1. In general, as stated for 1874, M&E's activities now tend to be limited to their writing, their scientific studies, and their correspondence. This will also be largely true for the next two decades.

2. Special attention this year focuses on the events leading to the unification of the two socialist organizations in Germany: the so-called Eisenacher party (SDWP) and the Lassalleans (GGWA), which merge at a Gotha congress. M writes his famous *Critique of the Gotha program* (#M207) to express his view that the Eisenachers could attain unification with the declining Lassallean movement without making any inadmissible concessions in principle.

3. Let us note the rubric "Russian Studies for *Capital*," which tends to become merely "Russian Studies." M is beginning to get involved in a study of Russian agrarian relations, using original sources, with the idea of treating this subject in Vols. 2 and 3 of *Capital.* There will be some evidence, as this work continues, that M's study of the Russian sources tends to become an end in itself; in any case, we here list it separately.

4. *Broad-dated Entries (Continuing).* M's work on the French edn of *Capital* finally ends in Nov with the publ of the last fascicule. —E's sporadic work on the *Dialectics of nature* (#E221) continues, from Mar on: the "Introduction" belongs to the period 1875–76, along with many other passages and fragments. For a list of passages dated to 1875, see ST/E14 (DN) 448 or *MEW* 20:693. —M's annotation of Bakunin's *Statism and anarchy* (#M178) [← 74:2] goes on to early 1875; he does not actually use his notes to write a reply. —For other 1874 entries which are continuing this year, see the references [← 74:3] to Lissagaray and Leo Frankel.

5. *Broad-dated Entries (This Year).* Two such are noted in *MEW Daten*. —Under June to Sep: "M&E receive info from socialists in France, Belgium, Denmark, Portugal, and the US on the situation of the workers' movements in these countries." —Under June to Dec: "M has frequent meetings with Lavrov and exchanges letters with him."

6. *Indefinite Entry.* Sometime this year a new edn of E's *Peasant war in Germany* (#E579) is pubd, for which E has written a supplement to the 1870 preface (#E581). It is pubd sometime before Nov A.

JANUARY

7. POLITICAL AFFAIRS. Jan 23: M&E speak at a meeting in the White Horse Tavern celebrating the 12th anniversary of the Polish uprising of 1863, chaired by Wróblewski, along with many ex-IWMA and Communard speakers (Frankel, Lissagaray, etc.).

8. W&P. **Jan 8:** M writes an Afterword (#M763) to his *Revelations* pamphlet on the Cologne trial (#M762), which *Volksstaat* has been reprinting [← 74:37]; the Afterword is pubd in *Volksstaat* Jan 27. (Prob shortly thereafter, the whole work appears as a pamphlet pubd by the *Volksstaat* press.)

9. *CAPITAL.* **Jan 30:** M, finishing work on the last three serial parts of the French trans, sends them to pub'r Lachâtre.

FEBRUARY

10. GERMAN MOVEMENT. **Feb 1:** Liebknecht writes E urging him to take up Prof. Dühring's writings in *Volksstaat*, since Dühring's influence in party circles is increasing [→ :16]; Liebknecht also urges a reply to Tkachov (see → :11). **Feb 23:** Bebel writes M&E asking their opinion on the "unity business" being discussed by the two parties [→ :12]. **Feb:** E notes the worsening of Franco-German relations and the aggressively militaristic course of the Bismarck government, on which he will publish an article in Apr [→ :17].

11. RUSSIAN AFFAIRS. **Feb 11:** M, having read a batch of Russian émigré publications sent him by Lavrov, writes him about the interesting material in it, esp the correspondence columns of *Vperyod*, most esp a report (by Lopatin) on a Siberian group, Ne Nashi, which opposes all existing social institutions. **Feb:** M reads Tkachov's reply to E's third article on "Refugee literature" (#E661) [← 74:37], and in a note on the pamphlet's title page, M advises E to "go after him [Tkachov]" lustily (*KMC* dating: c.Dec 1874; *MEW* dating: Feb or Mar). **Feb to Mar A:** E writes, as his fourth article in the "Refugee literature" series (#E662), a reply to Tkachov and a critique of Russian Populist ideology [→ :14].

MARCH

12. GERMAN MOVEMENT. **Mar 7:** *Volksstaat* and *Neue Social-Demokrat* publish a draft program for unification of the Lassalleans and Eisenachers (the "Gotha program"). **Mar c.10–11:** M&E see this draft program, but they have received no other info about it from Germany. **Mar 18:** After discussion with M, and writing as "we," E responds to Bebel's inquiry [← :10] with a sharp criticism of the draft program and the process of unification; he also charges that Liebknecht has deliberately kept M&E uninformed. E temporarily holds up mailing this letter since Bebel is still in prison (till Apr 1). **Mar 25:** Bracke writes to E along the same lines as Bebel. **Mar 28:** On the receipt of Bracke's letter, E sends Bracke the letter he has written to Bebel. (It is usually labeled letter of Mar 18–28.)

13. POLITICAL AFFAIRS. **Mar 3:** Dilke and Morley ask M to write a reply to the article by McDonnell, "KM and German socialism" (*Fortnightly Rev*, Mar 1), which calls M's economic analysis "rather childish" and his views "pessimistic" (SOURCE: *KMC*, which refers to a Mar 5 letter by Dilke). **Mar D to Apr:** M gets several requests from Glaser de Willebrord to write for his planned Belgian weekly *La Réforme Sociale*, which is to represent the now divided non-Proudhonist socialist tendencies. M approves, but adopts a wait-and-see attitude. **Mar-Apr:** M gives Barry advice and material for the latter's articles in the *Standard*, the *Hour*, etc.

14. W&P. **Mar 24:** *Volksstaat* pubs an article by E (#E283) on the Jan 23 Polish meeting, reporting the speeches made there by both M&E. **Mar A:** E finishes writing his fourth article in the "Refugee literature" series (#E662) [← :11], this one against Tkachov.

Perhaps he also begins work on his fifth article in the series (#E754), a continuation of the polemic against Tkachov's populism, for which, see → :17. **Mar 28, Apr 2:** Volksstaat pubs the fourth article (#E662).

15. PERSONAL. **Mar:** The M family moves [← 64:12] to 41 Maitland Park Road—M's last residence.

APRIL

16. GERMAN MOVEMENT. **Apr to May A:** M works on his critique of the draft unity program ("Gotha program") [→ :20]. **Apr 21:** Liebknecht again [← :10] urges E to write a critique of Prof. Dühring [→ 76:28]. **Apr 21, 23:** Liebknecht writes letters to E attempting to justify his course on the unity proceedings and on the draft program, in response to E's criticism.

17. W&P. **Apr 2:** Volksstaat completes publ [← :14] of E's fourth article in the "Refugee literature" series (#E662). E writes his fifth article (#E754) this month if he did not already begin it in Mar. **Apr 14:** Hepner (in Breslau) invites M to have M&E's "lesser writings" reprinted in a collected edn, through his press. **Apr 16–21:** Volksstaat pubs E's fifth article in the "Refugee literature" series (#E754), continuing the polemic against Tkachov's populism [→ :24]. **Apr 23:** Volksstaat pubs E's article (#E730) [← :10] on Bismarck's aggressive militarism; prob written this month.

18. POLITICAL AFFAIRS. **c.Apr:** M&E visit Pfänder, who is ill.

19. CAPITAL. **Apr 28:** M writes an Afterword (#M132) called "Avis au lecteur" to the French edn, pub in the last fascicule [→ :41]; it stresses that this edn possesses independent scientific value apart from the German edn.

MAY

20. GERMAN MOVEMENT. **May 5:** M sends his "critique of the Gotha program" (#M207) [← :16] to Bracke, with a covering letter, for the German party leadership, incl Auer, Geib, etc., besides Bebel and Liebknecht. **May 22–27:** At the Gotha unity congress, the new united party is established as the Social-Democratic (S-D) party of Germany; the program is adopted May 25 (pubd May 28); M's criticism are almost entirely ignored, and are even kept from Bebel's knowledge by Liebknecht's machinations.

21. POLITICAL AFFAIRS. **May 8:** M informs Lavrov of a "safe address" in Berlin (C. A. Schramm) through which they can correspond. **May 29:** M is visited by Max Oppenheim. **May 29–30:** Dupont sends M&E letters on his activity in America, and asks for IWMA material.

22. RUSSIAN STUDIES FOR CAPITAL. **May:** M reads Haxthausen, Die ländliche Verfassung Russlands.

23. CAPITAL. **May 20 to Aug:** M carries out a large number of calculations illustrating the difference between the rate of surplus value and the rate of profit (later used for Ch. 3 of Vol. 3).

24. W&P. **c.May:** E's fifth article in the "Refugee literature" series (#E754) [← :17] is pubd as a pamphlet titled "Social questions in Russia," with a new preface by E (#E755).

JUNE

25. POLITICAL AFFAIRS. **June 21:** E, who since the Hague Congress has remained in contact with the NY GC, receives from it copies of a confidential circular on the calling of a conference in Philadelphia for the purpose of spreading IWMA sections in Europe [→ :28].

26. READING AND STUDY. **June 18:** A letter by M to Lavrov shows the importance M ascribes to recently pubd experiments by the chemist M. Traube on the laboratory creation of an artificial cell. **June 27:** Hermann Schumacher, biographer of J. H. von Thünen, is moved by reading Capital to send M a copy of Thünen's book Der isolirte Staat; he asks M's opinion of his own preface to that work. (The book arrives while M is traveling, and his answer is delayed; see → :33.)

JULY

27. ON IWMA HISTORY. **July 14:** M addresses a letter to the anonymous author (actually Matilda Betham-Edwards) of an article on the IWMA in Fraser's Magazine (three installs, July-Sep), correcting a number of factual misstatements; M also warns that the announced condensation of Capital in English would violate his copyright, and comments pessimistically on the accuracy of translators.

AUGUST

28. POLITICAL AFFAIRS. **Aug 13:** E reports to the GC on the steps he has taken to distribute the circular on the Philadelphia conference [← :25], and describes the situation in the European IWMA sections (#E445).

29. CAPITAL. **Aug A:** At Liebknecht's request, M (helped by E) does some partial revision of a condensation of Capital pubd in a booklet by J. Most in 1873 (see ST/51); but M stipulates that his name is not to be used [→ 76:12].

30. PERSONAL (E). **Aug c.M to Sep c.22:** E is on holiday in Ramsgate.

31. MARX'S TRIP TO GERMANY. **Aug c.12:**

M leaves London for Carlsbad, to take the waters. **Aug c.13–14:** On the way, between Cologne and Frankfurt, M gets into a conversation with a Catholic priest about Bismarck's *Kulturkampf*. M stops in Frankfurt, visits the *Frankfurter Ztg* editorial office and has a long discussion with the editor L. Sonnemann; he also meets Guido Weiss. **Aug 15 to Sep 11:** In Carlsbad, M stays at the same hotel as before [← 74:31]. (For this stay, see → :32).

SEPTEMBER

32. MARX'S TRIP (CONCLUSION). **Sep:** In Carlsbad M sees much of the Russian historian M. M. Kovalevsky. He comes under the surveillance of the Austrian secret police. **Sep 11:** M leaves Carlsbad. **Sep 12–13:** M stops in Prague, where he visits Max Oppenheim. **Sep 20:** M returns to London.

33. READING AND STUDY. **Sep 21:** Responding to Schumacher's letter [← :26], M asks him to send his 1868 biography of Thünen; M points out the difference in their concepts of wages.

34. RUSSIAN STUDIES FOR *CAPITAL*. **Sep D to Oct:** M again intensively takes up polit eco, esp the study of Russian agrarian relations. He reads and excerpts some books pubd in 1875 in Berlin by Russian liberals, Y. F. Samarin, A. I. Koshelyev, K. D. Kavelin.

35. POLITICAL AFFAIRS. **Sep 25:** Imandt (in Dundee) sends M that day's issue of the *Dundee Advertiser*, which contains an unsigned article replying, on behalf of the IWMA, to the *Fraser Magazine* piece [← :27]. **Sep 27:** M replies that he suspects the author is Barry. **Sep c.27:** Carl Hirsch and Kaub (from Paris) visit M. **Sep 20:** Lavrov writes E about the publ of a pamphlet by "Nechayev's supporters" replying to the IWMA anti-Bakunin pamphlet by Engels–Lafargue–Marx (#ME6), a reply titled *Quelques mots d'un groupe socialiste révolutionnaire russe* [etc.] [→ :38].

OCTOBER

36. GERMAN MOVEMENT. **Oct 11, 12:** In similar letters to Bracke and Bebel, E analyzes what is wrong with the program adopted at the Gotha congress [← :20], stresses that this unity contains the germ of a future split, but assures that he and M will not come out against the program publicly because the public construes the program in a communist sense. **Oct 15:** Writing to Bebel, E conveys M's criticism of a recent boner in *Volksstaat*; in this connection E explains the sectarian anti-TU viewpoint of all socialist groups before M.

37. RUSSIAN AFFAIRS. **Oct 15:** In his letter to Bebel (see ← :36), E discusses the trend to revolution in Russia, indeed the next revolution may start there. **c.Oct-Nov:** M reads Slavophile brochures by Samarin and Dmitriev, and by Koshelyev.

38. POLITICAL AFFAIRS. **Oct A:** M&E read the pamphlet *Quelques mots* [etc.] [← :35], sent to E by Lavrov Sep D or Oct A. **Oct 8:** M writes Lavrov that in his opinion "this schoolboy piece" does not deserve a reply.

39. W&P. **Oct 5:** Bignami writes E proposing that M&E publish a volume of their writings in his Biblioteca Socialista series.

40. ENGELS' TRIP. **Oct CD to Nov 6:** E and his companion, Lizzie Burns, travel to Heidelberg in order to place her niece, Mary Ellen Burns, in a boarding school there. E interrupts the trip in Rheinau, where he meets an acquaintance, the chemist Pauli. On the return trip, he stops in Bingen and Cologne, and returns to London via Ostend. (The niece will stay in Heidelberg till Mar 1877.)

NOVEMBER

41. *CAPITAL*. **Nov D:** The last fascicule of the French edn comes off the press, the first having appeared as long ago as Sep 17, 1872. It contains M's Afterword (#M132) [← :19]. For M's mail-out of copies, see → :48. This edn is pubd in 10,000–11,000 copies, printed in Louis Lahure's Paris printshop. The selling price is 5 francs complete (6 francs bound).

42. RUSSIAN STUDIES FOR *CAPITAL*. **Nov 16:** Danielson sends M 10 vols. of Russian material on the work of the Tax Commission [→ :45]. **Nov-Dec:** Pursuing the subject of Russian agrarian conditions for Vol. 2 of *Capital*, M studies and excerpts works on agrochemistry (e.g., A. N. Engelhardt) and on physics and polit eco esp as related to agrarian problems. He reads I. I. Patlayevsky's book *Deneshnyi rynok v Rossii ot 1700 do 1762g*, an article by Engelhardt on questions of Russian agriculture, and a collection of military statistics pubd by the Russian general staff, fourth edn of 1871, on which he makes extensive notes.

43. AGAINST SOCIAL DARWINISM. **Nov 12** (sent Nov 17): Having read Lavrov's article of Sep 15 on "Socialism and the struggle for existence," E writes him, at his request, a longish letter on his views; E argues against the one-sided conception of seeing all society and history in terms of the "struggle for existence" rather than also cooperation.

43.5. MRS. MARX AS THEATER CRITIC. **Nov:** She writes her first article on the London theater, "From London's theater world," for the *Frankfurter Ztg und Handelsblatt*; pubd Nov 21 [→ 76:7].

DECEMBER

44. POLITICAL AFFAIRS. **Dec 3:** M writes Lavrov explaining that because of an attack of furuncles he cannot speak at the Dec 4 anniversary meeting celebrating the Polish uprising of 1830. **Dec 4:** E writes Wróblewski that he cannot attend the anniversary meeting because of a very bad cold. The letters of both M&E stress their belief that Polish liberation is a keystone to the emancipation of the European proletariat. The letters are read at the meeting and reported in Vperyod of Dec 31.

45. RUSSIAN STUDIES FOR *CAPITAL*. **Dec to Feb:** M studies the 10 vols. on the Tax Commission [← :42], and a collection of material from the Russian government bureaus for peasant affairs, sent him by Danielson. M considers this material very important for the study of land ownership, ground rent, and agrarian relations in general, in connection with his plans for Vol. 3.

46. *CAPITAL*. **Dec 17:** M informs Lavrov that because of the great length of the French edn, the subject index to this edn which had been prepared by Lavrov could not be used.

47. DIALECTICS. **Dec c.M:** In a letter to Dietzgen, M expresses his intention of writing a book on dialectics after he has finished *Capital*.

YEAR APPENDIX

48. On publ of the last fascicule of the French edn of *Capital*, Nov D, M sends out copies of the last 14 fascicules, or of the complete set of fascicules, to a large number of friends and correspondents (KMC's erroneous dating is May M). KMC gives part of this long list (followed by "et al") taken from M's address book of the 1870s. The following list of names, in alphabetical order, suggests a (partial) list of persons with whom M was on certain terms: Th. Allsop, Dr. Elizabeth Garrett Anderson, A. Bebel, J. P. Becker, Prof. E. S. Beesly, E. Bignami, W. Bracke, C. D. Collet, A. B. Combault, N. F. Danielson, C. De Paepe, Simon Deutsch, J. Dietzgen, Dr. F. Fleckles, Forcade (London), E. Glaser de Willebrord, Dr. E. Gumpert, A. Hepner, P. Imandt, M. M. Kovalevsky, La Cécilia, P. L. Lavrov, Lefèvre (London), W. Liebknecht, G. A. Lopatin, Mayall, O. Meissner, J. Mesa, E. Oswald, L. A. F. Pio, Regnaud (London), Robinson (London), C. Schorlemmer, F. A. Sorge, Herbert Spencer, A. F. J. Theisz, Guido Weiss, Mme Wollmann, and W. Wróblewski.

1876

CONSPECTUS

1. *Broad-dated Entries.* This year E is finally persuaded to undertake a thorough critique of Prof. Dühring, as he had been urged to do [← 75:10, 16]. After additional pressure in May, E agrees, and starts studying Dühring's books—first his writings on philosophy, which E contemns in letters to M, July 25 to Aug 25. E works on the first part of his *Anti-Dühring* (#E23) from Sep to next Jan A. —E's work on *Anti-Dühring* means dropping his previous work on *Dialectics of nature* (#E221), begun in 1873. For the short list of passages dated to 1876 (up to c.Mar), see ST/E14 (DN) 449 or MEW 20:693. For E's partial resumption of work on *Dialectics of nature*, see → 78:28. —For E's series on the life and activities of Wilhelm Wolff (#E918), his writing extends from June to Nov, with publ beginning July 1; for the republ of this work, see → 86:24.

JANUARY

2. POLITICAL AFFAIRS. **Jan 22:** E gives a speech (#E767) at a meeting celebrating the anniversary of the Polish uprising of 1863, chaired by Wróblewski.

FEBRUARY

3. POLITICAL AFFAIRS. **Feb 7:** M&E speak at the 36th anniversary meeting of the London GWEA; M treats the history of the assoc and the principle of internationalism.

4. GERMAN MOVEMENT. **Feb:** E writes the essay "Prussian Schnaps in the German Reichstag" (#E645), a thrust at Junkerdom; section I is pubd in Volksstaat, Feb 25, 27.

5. *CAPITAL*. **Feb M:** M drafts a passage on "Differential rent and rent as mere interest on capital incorporated in the soil" (which E will later insert into Vol. 3, Ch. 44).

MARCH

6. POLITICAL AFFAIRS. **Mar 17** (rec'd Apr A): Sorge writes M about the state of the US movement and his own activity. **Mar 28:** Leo Frankel (in Budapest) reports to M on his arrest in Vienna and his coming trial for participating in the Paris Commune.

7. W&P. **Mar 1:** Volksstaat pubs section II of E's "Prussian Schnaps [etc.]" (#E645) [← :4]; the entire essay is then pubd as a pamphlet (which the government bans). **Mar 17:** The letter by Sorge (see ← :6) urges M to check over the trans of the Com Manifesto by

Hermann Meyer, which he had given M in 1872, and to write something supplementary so that it can be pubd in America (Sorge will repeat this request 1876–80, without success) [→ :11]. **Mar D:** Mrs. M writes her second article of theatrical reportage, "The London season," for *Frankfurter Ztg und Handelsblatt;* pubd Apr 4 [← :43.5; → :37].

8. FRIENDS. **Mar 11:** Pfänder dies in London. **Mar:** Schorlemmer visits E in London for a few days.

9. STUDIES. **Mar to May:** M studies a number of works on physiology: Schleiden, *Physiologie der Pflanzen und Tiere;* J. Ranke, *Grundzüge der Physiologie des Menschen;* a work by Hermann; et al.

APRIL

10. POLITICAL AFFAIRS. **Apr 4:** Replying to Sorge [← :6] about his complaint against dirty dealings in the movement, M paraphrases Chernyshevsky from memory: "Whoever goes down historical roads must not be afraid of getting dirty" (Chernyshevsky: "The road of history is not the sidewalk of the Nevsky Prospekt.... Whoever is afraid of ... getting his boots dirty should not meddle in social activity.")

11. W&P. **Apr 4:** In his letter to Sorge (see ← :10), M agrees to prepare a new edn of the *Com Manifesto* but says the time has not yet come to add an "appendix," i.e., a supplement to bring the *Manifesto* up to date. M also mentions that he possesses none of his *NYDT* articles, and asks for the file which Weydemeyer left to the late Hermann Meyer.

12. CAPITAL. **Apr 4:** In his letter to Sorge (see ← :10), M requests American book catalogs from 1873 to the present, for his studies on American agriculture and landed property relations, as well as on "credit (panics, money, etc.)," for Vol. 2. **Apr:** The second edn of J. Most's condensation of *Capital* (ST/51) [← 75:29] is pubd in Chemnitz (*KMC* dating: May A) [→ :18]. **Apr-May:** M plans to study land ownership in Hungary, and obtains the relevant literature in German through Frankel [→ :14].

MAY

13. GERMAN MOVEMENT; DÜHRING. **May 16:** Liebknecht sends E the ms of an article by J. Most, submitted to *Volksstaat,* lauding Dühring, esp his philosophy; Liebknecht again urges E to write a critique of Dühring. **May 24:** E (in Ramsgate) sends the Most ms to M, with some mordant remarks on Liebknecht's incompetence as editor, and raises the question of whether the time has come to settle matters with Dühring. **Mar 25:** M agrees that an all-out critique of Dühring is necessary. **Mar 28:** E reluctantly accepts the task; in a letter to M, he outlines the course he will take.

14. CAPITAL. **May c.24:** M receives a letter from Frankel [← :12] with info on land ownership in Hungary. **May 28:** E's letter (see ← :13) incidentally notes that M is studying "ground rent in general and Russian agrarian conditions in particular." **May-June:** M studies forms of *Allmende* (*Almeinde*)—common land—and reads works by the historian G. L. von Maurer (SOURCE: *MEW Daten;* cf *KMC* entry under June).

15. POLITICAL AFFAIRS. **May c.20:** M is visited by the Danish socialist Pio. Before Pio leaves London May 22, M receives—by telegram and letter to Pio—an invitation to attend the June 6 congress of the Danish SDWP in Copenhagen. (M declines.)

16. W&P. **May 30:** Bracke writes E with a proposal for M: a new edn of *Herr Vogt* (#M372).

17. PERSONAL. **May 10:** A new grandson is born to M: Jenny Longuet's Jean Laurent Frederick ("Johnny"), the first of M's grandchildren who will survive childhood. **May c.20 to June 2** (or perhaps to June M): E and his companion, Lizzie Burns, are on holiday in Ramsgate.

JUNE

18. CAPITAL. **June 14:** M sends Sorge his revisions of Most's condensation of *Capital* (ST/51) [← 75:29], mentioning that he has made changes in re value, money, wages, and many other passages, but since much is still wrong with it, he forbids any use of his name [→ 77:47]. **June:** M begins an intensive study of the forms of primitive communal property among various peoples, esp the Slavs; i.a. he rereads Maurer's *Geschichte der Fronhöfe* and his *Geschichte der Dorfverfassung* [etc.] (cf ← :14 for the *MEW Daten* entry) (SOURCE: *KMC;* see → :40).

19. W&P. **June:** E begins writing his series on Wilhelm Wolff (#E918) [→ :22]. **Prob June:** E writes the study "The part played by labor in the transition from ape to man" (#E223), as introduction to a projected essay (see the *Register*); later the ms will be assigned to the work-in-progress *Dialectics of nature* (#E221).

20. PERSONAL. **June M to June c.30:** E and his companion go to Heidelberg to visit Mary Ellen Burns [← 75:40; → :25].

JULY

21. ANARCHIST BLANDISHMENTS. **July 3:** Two days after Bakunin's death, his funeral serves as the occasion for his colleagues (the anarchist rump of the IWMA) to talk of unity with the Social-Democrats. **July M:** Liebknecht writes E asking what M&E think of the Bakuninists' attempts at rapprochement; but in *Volksstaat* (July 15) Liebknecht treats the idea favorably. E replies (letter not extant) warning sharply against falling for the anarchists' solicitations. **July 25–26:** M&E exchange letters lamenting Liebknecht's political incompetence as usual, and stressing the dangers of accepting the anarchists into the organization.

22. W&P. **July 1 to Nov 25:** E's series on W. Wolff (#E918) [← :19] is pubd in *Die Neue Welt*, in 11 installs.

23. PERSONAL. **July 18–23:** M visits his wife, who is taking the waters in Brighton. **July 24 to Sep 1:** E and his companion, Lizzie Burns, sojourn in Ramsgate.

AUGUST

24. MARX'S TRIP TO CARLSBAD. **Aug 13:** M and Eleanor depart for Carlsbad to take the waters (his third trip there). **Aug 13–14:** Night stopover in Cologne. **Aug 14:** A few hours' stop in Nuremberg. **Aug 15:** Ditto in Weiden, and arrival in Carlsbad. **Aug 15 to Sep 15:** M and Eleanor sojourn in Carlsbad, at the same hotel as before [← 75:31]. **Aug c.19:** M receives from Lavrov his essay in *Vperyod* on "The state element in the future society," which M puts aside to be read "in the future." **Aug 19:** M discusses politics with the physician Prof. Friedberg of the U. of Breslau, esp on Eduard Lasker's *Erlebnisse einer Mannes-Seele* (1873). **Aug c.20:** M receives a request for an article from the NY *Labor Standard*. **Aug D to Sep 15:** Among other people whom M talks with in Carlsbad are the physicians Dr. Fleckles and Dr. W. A. Freund, also H. Graetz, author of a history of the Jews, with whom he has a long talk i.a. about Russian czarism [→ :26].

25. ENGELS' TRAVELS. **Aug A:** E and his companion go to Heidelberg to visit Mary Ellen Burns [← :20]. **Aug 5:** They leave Heidelberg. **Aug 11:** They stop over in Cologne. **Aug 12:** They return to England via Vlissingen, changing in London direct for Ramsgate. **Aug 12 to Sep 1:** E remains in Ramsgate; on Aug 15 he goes to London and finds Schorlemmer visiting M.

SEPTEMBER

26. MARX'S TRIP (CONCLUSION). **Sep AB:** M and Eleanor are in Carlsbad (see ← :24 for contacts there). **Sep 15:** They leave Carlsbad. **Sep 16:** They stop over in Prague; M visits Max Oppenheim. **Sep c.19–20:** They stop in Bingen and in Kreuznach, to show Eleanor

where her parents spent their honeymoon. **Sep 21:** They stop in Liège, visiting Utin; depart Sep 22. **Sep 22:** M and Eleanor arrive back in London.

27. POLITICAL AFFAIRS. **Sep 8:** Glaser de Willebrord sends M a report on the state of the movement in Belgium. **Sep 23:** M writes Bracke proposing he publish a German edn of Lissagaray's history of the Paris Commune, mentioning J. Grunzig as possible translator. (Lissagaray has authorized M to make arrangements for a German trans; the French edn is still to appear in autumn.) **Sep 30:** In response to Bracke's concern (letter of Sep 27) about a history of the Commune being written by B. Becker, M argues that it cannot be favored over Lissagaray's firsthand account.

28. ENGELS. **Sep 1:** E returns to London. **Sep:** E begins working on the first part of *Anti-Dühring* (#E23) [← :13; → 77:4]. For his preparatory writings, see #E24.

OCTOBER

29. ANARCHIST BLANDISHMENTS. **Oct A:** In view of the unity blandishments being offered by the anarchists [← :21] in connection with their forthcoming Bern congress (Oct 26–30), to which the German party is sending Vahlteich as unofficial representative, M warns Liebknecht against rapprochement with this rump of the anarchist movement. **Oct 9:** Leo Frankel, now editor of the Budapest *Arbeiter-Wochen-Chronik*, asks M for advice on attitude toward the anarchists' attempt at rapprochement with the Social-Democracy. **Oct 26–30:** The anarchist international congress in Bern proposes calling a Universal Socialist Congress in 1877, i.e., uniting the disintegrating remnant of the anarchist movement with the growing socialist movement.

30. RUSSIAN AFFAIRS. **Oct A:** In connection with the Serbian uprising, M spurs Liebknecht to write an article attacking Russia's role and Bismarck's foreign policy, and gives him advice on it. (Liebknecht's article appears in *Volksstaat* Oct 13.) **Oct 21:** M writes Lavrov about the projected establishment of a new periodical on Russian affairs in English, to influence British public opinion, ed by P. D. Golochvastov and Prince Meshchersky. (M's letter is partly pubd in Lavrov's *Vperyod* Nov 1.)

31. POLITICAL AFFAIRS. **Oct M:** M replies to Barry's request of Oct 11 for advice on his leading article on foreign affairs in *Morning Advertiser*.

32. *CAPITAL.* **Oct 7:** M points to Laveleye's critique of *Capital* in *Revue des Deux Mondes* (Sep 1, article on German socialism) as an example of "the idiocy of our bourgeois 'thinkers' " (letter to Lavrov). **Oct 20:** M will resume work on Vol. 2 in a few days—so E writes to Kugelmann. "If you wanted to correct all the silly things that circulate in academic circles about M, you would have your work cut out for you."

NOVEMBER

33. POLITICAL AFFAIRS. **Nov A:** M sends Collet, at his request, info on Gladstone's Russian policy, for use in the *Diplomatic Rev*. **Nov 20:** E approves J. P. Becker's position on rejecting anarchist overtures [← :29]; building a strong class party in a country is more important right now than international org⟨...⟩izn; meanwhile, at this juncture of relative p⟨...⟩ce, M&E are giving priority to producing the necessary scientific works. **Nov 25:** M asks Carl Hirsch (in Paris) to send him reports on the French movement. **Nov:** M drops Grunzig as a possible translator of Lissagaray [← :27], and later this month entrusts the trans to Isolde Kurz [→ 77:1].

34. W&P. **Nov 25:** The last installment of E's series on W. Wolff (#E918) [← :22] is pubd.

35. PERSONAL. **Nov c.10–30:** M suffers badly from rheumatism and bronchitis.

DECEMBER

36. POLITICAL AFFAIRS. **Dec AB:** M gets several visits from Kovalevsky. On Dec 12, the two of them visit E. **Dec 18:** Writing to his brother Hermann, E analyzes the situation in the Balkans and comes to the conclusion that a Russo-Turkish war is bound to break out. **Dec 21:** In a letter to J. P. Becker, E criticizes both the current English TU movement, which is absorbed in petty economic issues, and the unity maneuvers of the Bakuninist remnant of anarchism—"with them, no peace is possible."

37. W&P. **Dec 7** (rec'd c.18): The NY *Labor Standard* (McDonnell) once more requests M to contribute articles. **Dec D:** Mrs. M writes her third article on the London theater [← :7] for the *Frankfurter Ztg und Handelsblatt*, "Shakespearean studies in England"; pubd Jan 3.

38. READING AND STUDY. **Dec:** M reads a number of works on common property and land ownership forms in Spain and other countries (for details, see → :40).

39. PERSONAL. **Dec D:** J. C. Juta, M's brother-in-law, and his son Henry, of Cape Town, visit M in London.

YEAR APPENDIX

40. M's reading and study on early forms of common property are assigned by KMC to June and by *MEW Daten* to Dec; see these entries. M reads and makes notes on the following authors i.a.: G. Hanssen, Demelić, Utješenović, Cárdenas, and Cremazy.

1877

CONSPECTUS

1. *Broad-dated Entries*. Engels' work on *Anti-Dühring* (#E23) extends throughout the year; for relevant dates, see the *Register*. For E's preparatory writings, see #E24. For one of these, "Infantry tactics . . ." (#E25), note that it is here entered under June-July but (cf *Register*) may have been written at some other time between Jan A and Aug M. —For another broad-dated entry, see → :19 for E's notes on the Russian army in the Russo-Turkish war. —Extending over the year is M's work in promoting a German trans of Lissagaray's *Histoire de la Commune*, and then helping to revise it, both in ms and in galley proofs. At first M tries to use Kurz as translator [← 76:33] but then, in consultation with Bracke, decides her work is unusable; in Oct the job is given to W. Blos. The German edn is finally pubd by Bracke before the end of the year (see → :46, here entered under c.Dec). —Under "Jan to Dec" *MEW Daten* reminds that M is continuing his study of socioeco-nomic developments in Russia, esp agrarian relations after the abolition of serfdom (for details, see → :48).

JANUARY

2. GERMAN MOVEMENT. **Jan 10:** In the Reichstag elections the German party's vote goes up 40%; the number of deputies increases from 9 to 12. **Jan 21:** In three letters written today (to Bracke, Dr. Fleckles, Dr. Freund) M expresses great satisfaction over this electoral victory, noting esp that the bourgeoisie in England and other countries is scared and impressed [→ :6].

3. POLITICAL AFFAIRS. **Jan 9:** On the basis of info from Utin (letter of Dec 17), M writes Kovalevsky (in Moscow) with a plea to help get a lawyer for the husband (I. M. Davydovsky) of E. L. Tomanovskaya (Dmitriyeva); he is in danger of being sent to Siberia.

4. *ANTI-DÜHRING*. **Jan 3:** *Vorwärts* begins the serial publ of Part I (#E23) [→

18]. **Jan 9:** E sends Liebknecht the last batch of ms for Part I.

5. EASTERN QUESTION. **Jan M:** In connection with the Russo-Turkish conflict, M takes up intensive reading on the Eastern Question, e.g., Slade.

5.5. MRS. M AS THEATER CRITIC. **Jan 3:** Her third article of reportage on the London theater [← 76:37] is pubd in *Frankfurter Ztg und Handelsblatt* [→ :8.5].

FEBRUARY

6. POLITICAL AFFAIRS. **Feb-Mar:** M pumps his anti-Gladstone critique into Barry, who is now a correspondent of the *Standard*, and uses him to get an exposé of Gladstone's Russophile foreign policy into the conservative press, in articles on the Eastern Question. For example, on Feb 3 the *Whitehall Rev* pubs an article by Barry which M had helped him write; this article is reprinted in several other papers [→ :9]. **Feb A:** E writes a note (#E527) about page 29 of Lissagaray's history of the Commune, dealing with Thiers's armistice of Oct 30, 1870, and sends it to Lissagaray. **Feb 8:** Lissagaray sends E his thanks for the "brilliant note." **Feb 10 or 13:** E writes a report (#E436) for Bignami on the S-D party victory in the Reichstag election [← :2]; it is read at the Second Congress of the Northern Italian Federation, Milan, Feb 17–18; pubd in *La Plebe* Feb 26.

7. CONTACTS. **Feb 1:** Prof. H. Graetz [← 76:24] writes M a thank-you note, full of esteem, for the copy of *Capital*, photos, and other things sent by M. **c.Feb-Mar:** M gets a number of visits by Utin's wife. **Feb to Apr:** M and Lavrov meet and correspond a number of times (during this period, eight letters by M to Lavrov).

8. PERSONAL. **Feb c.20 to Mar c.14:** E stays in Brighton with his companion, who is ill.

8.5. MRS. M AS THEATER CRITIC. **Feb 1:** Her fourth article of theater reportage [← :5.5], "Shakespeare's *Richard III* in London's Lyceum Theater," is sent in to *Frankfurter Ztg und Handelsblatt*; pubd Feb 8 [→ :20.5].

MARCH

9. RUSSIAN AFFAIRS. **Mar 3, 10:** *Vanity Fair* pubs an anti-Gladstone article written by Barry with M's help [← :6]. **Mar 7:** Writing to E, M describes his influence on Barry's writings. **Mar 16:** For the benefit of the Irish M. P., K. O'Clery, whom M has agitated on the subject of Russian persecutions and atrocities esp in Poland, M asks Lavrov to write a piece surveying this topic in recent years [→ :13]. **Mar 22:** Danielson asks M to write an

article on Russian land ownership for the *Otechestvenniye Zapiski*.

10. W&P. **Mar c.2:** Hirsch and Castelnau (in Paris) ask M to write for their projected workers' paper; M declines, for lack of time. (The paper does not materialize, anyway.) **Mar 5, 7:** M sends E the first part of the chapter he is writing for *Anti-Dühring* (Ch. 10 of Part II) criticizing Dühring's conceptions on the history of polit eco [→ :30]. **Mar 6–14:** At M's urging (letter of Mar 3), E writes an article, "In Italy" (#E373), on the need for a workers' party as against anarchism: "behind the preachment of anarchy and self-rule lay hidden the claim by a few wire-pullers to take dictatorial command over the whole working-class movement" (pubd in *Vorwä▮▮Mar* 16).

11. CAPITAL. **Mar D:** M res▮▮▮▮ work on Vol. 2; he makes excerpts from his earlier mss.

12. CONTACTS. **Mar 4:** Collet's son and daughter visit M. **Mar 22:** Prof. Beesly visits M; Beesly agrees to Lavrov's writing for the *Fortnightly Rev*.

APRIL

13. RUSSIAN AFFAIRS. **Apr 14:** Lavrov's article on Russian persecutions, written at M's request [← :9], is pubd in *Vanity Fair* in French, "La justice en Russie" [→ :16]. **Apr 21:** Writing to Bracke three days before Russia's declaration of war against Turkey, M expresses the fear that Prussia has made a secret agreement with Russia, and complains that the movement pays too little attention to the Eastern Question and the danger of war.

14. CAPITAL. **Apr 18:** G. M. Calberla sends M his just-pubd work on him, together with a request for M's opinion of it.

15. ANTI-DÜHRING. **Apr 11:** E writing to Liebknecht and M writing to Bracke, both object strongly to the way in which E's *Anti-Dühring* (#E23) is being pubd in *Vorwärts*: as space-filler, in dribs and drabs, disconnectedly.

MAY

16. RUSSIAN AFFAIRS. **May 3, 14:** The info on Russian persecutions supplied by Lavrov and M [← :9] is used by O'Clery in two speeches in the House of Commons.

17. NYDT COLLECTION. **May c.12:** M receives from Sorge the *NYDT* articles written by himself and E; this collection is from Weydemeyer's papers.

18. ANTI-DÜHRING. **May 13:** Part I of #E23 ends publ in *Vorwärts* after 20 installs [→ :21].

19. ENGELS: MILITARIA. **May to Dec:** E makes notes on the composition and distribution of the Russian army in the Russo-Turkish war.

20. PERSONAL. **May:** M, suffering from insomnia and nerves, plans to take a curative trip to Neuenahr, since Carlsbad is too expensive. **May CD:** E and his sick companion stop in Brighton.

20.5. MRS. M AS THEATER CRITIC. **May 22:** She writes her fifth (last) article of theater reportage [← :8.5] for the *Frankfurter Ztg und Handelsblatt*, "From the London theater"; pubd May 25.

JUNE

21. *ANTI-DÜHRING*. **June to Aug:** E writes Part II (Polit Eco) of #E23; for the chapter written by M, see ← :10 (pubd → :27). **July:** E drafts the passage on "Infantry ta . . ." (#E25), later replaced by a shorter passage. (For date, cf *Register*.)

22. W&P. **June M:** At Bracke's request, E writes a short biographical sketch of M for an almanac (#E406); pubd in 1878.

JULY

23. GERMAN MOVEMENT. **July 1:** While in France the conflict sharpens between the republicans and the monarchists, with danger of a monarchist coup by MacMahon, Liebknecht's line in *Vorwärts* is that monarchy or republic makes no difference to the working class; an article by Hasenclever is even entitled "Down with the republic!" **July 2:** E writes to Liebknecht in criticism of this line: it is best for the workers' movement to develop under the bourgeois republic; the return of monarchy would push republicanism to the fore instead of socialism. **July 11–20:** Liebknecht pubs a series of articles "Reds vs Blues" which, in M&E's view, repeats Hasenclever's nonsense. **July 23–24:** M&E exchange letters lamenting the position being taken by "stupid Wilhelm" [Liebknecht]. M reports that Hirsch is furious at the *Vorwärts* position.

24. POLITICAL AFFAIRS. **July 23–29:** Carl Hirsch, visiting from Paris, meets several times with M during the week, and informs him on economic and political developments in France and on the situation in the German party. **July 25:** Writing to E, M greets the outbreak of a militant strike movement in the US and its clashes with the state; this may be the start of a "serious workers' party" which would ally itself with the blacks and the western farmers.

25. PUBL PLANS: *NEUE GESELLSCHAFT*. **July 9–10:** F. Wiede asks M (July 9) and E (July 10) to write for his planned periodical *Die Neue Gesellschaft*. **July 18:** M tells E he will decline because its prospectus shows it will be a bad journal; M would like to see a "really

scientific socialist journal" which i.a. would "expose the utter ignorance of professors." **July 25:** E writes Wiede declining on ground of lack of time; M also declines, July c.25–26.

26. PUBL PLANS: *ZUKUNFT* AND HÖCHBERG. **July 20:** The editors of *Zukunft*, which will start Oct 1, write M&E asking their collaboration, but sign no names. M refuses to answer this "anonymous circular." **July D:** Johannes Wedde visits M and renews the invitation. M is also asked by J. Most. M refuses, criticizing Höchberg's reform socialism and pro-Dühring tendency. **July 31:** E criticizes the *Zukunft* project in a letter to Liebknecht [→ :37].

27. *ANTI-DÜHRING*. **July 27:** Part II [← :21] begins publ in *Vorwärts* (until Dec 30). **July:** A pamphlet edn of Part I (only) is pubd in Leipzig; see *Register* for details.

28. READING AND STUDY. **July c.D:** M reads Mehring's brochure *Zur Geschichte der deutschen Socialdemokratie* (1877) and another on Treitschke (1875); he considers the latter "very tiresomely and shallowly written" but making some points of interest. **July–Aug:** M reads books by the Russian economist and statistician I. I. Kaufman and K. Knies' work *Das Geld*.

29. PERSONAL. **July c.4:** E goes to Manchester for a few days. **July 11 to Aug 28:** E and his sick companion sojourn in Ramsgate. **July 24:** E sends M £100 for his trip to Neuenahr.

AUGUST

30. *ANTI-DÜHRING*. **Aug A:** E begins writing Part III; he will finish this Mar/Apr of next year. (For publ, see → 78:16.) —To help E on the section "Socialism," M goes through and excerpts six pamphlets by Owen and four years of his organ *The Crisis*, also Macnab's *The new views of Mr. Owen of Lanark* (SOURCE: *KMC*; see → :44). **Aug 8:** M writes E about his efforts to find other material by Owen and material by and about the French utopians. —M sends E the second part of the chapter he is doing for *Anti-Dühring* (Ch. 10 of Part II) [← :10]. He also sends along Quesnay's *Tableau Economique* with some annotations of his own.

31. LINGENAU LEGACY. **Aug 4:** J. K. F. Lingenau, a German socialist, 1849 emigrant to the US, dies in St. Louis, leaving a legacy of $7000 in cash to the German Social-Democratic party; the executors named are five party leaders and M. Since the executors want to give Sorge full powers, while the Bismarck government works to quash the legacy (eventually successfully), M will be involved with this affair for the next two years [→ 79:47].

32. *CAPITAL.* **Aug 15:** Uriele Cavagnari (in Naples) writes M asking for authorization for his Italian trans.

33. MARX'S TRIP. **Aug 8:** M, accompanied by his wife (who is ill) and daughter Eleanor, departs for Neuenahr, to take the waters (till Sep c.26). **Aug:** In Neuenahr, staying at the Hotel Flora, M gets acquainted with Dr. Richard Schmitz, who agrees with M's own opinion that his medical trouble is "of a nervous nature," and recommends the Black Forest. **Aug c.23–24:** Schorlemmer visits M. **Aug 24:** M, who has been in touch with Barry about attending the World Socialist Congress (Ghent, Sep 9–15), writes Bracke to introduce Barry to the German delegates.

SEPTEMBER

34. MARX'S TRIP. **Sep c.26:** Until about this date M remains in Neuenahr with his wife and Eleanor [← :33]. (On Sep 27 M is again dating correspondence from London.) Note: *KMC* has M sojourning in the Black Forest Sep 4–20, but its references do not support this claim, which is not accepted in *MEW Daten*.

35. RUSSIAN AFFAIRS. **Sep 27:** In a letter to Sorge, M opines that Russia is on the threshold of an epochal upheaval, hastened by the Russo-Turkish war crisis: "This time the revolution begins in the East. . . ."

36. ENGELS IN SCOTLAND. **Sep 5 to c.21:** E and his companion are in Scotland; as for their whereabouts, a later letter shows that on Sep 20 they are in the Edinburgh area. **Sep:** Lizzie Burns's health begins to decline drastically, presaging her death [→ 78:35].

OCTOBER

37. GERMAN MOVEMENT. **Oct 19:** Writing to Sorge, M describes his dissatisfaction with the "rotten spirit" advancing in the leadership of the German party, stemming from the rotten compromise of 1875 with the Lassalleans: an influx of intellectuals is diluting program and theory; Höchberg and his *Zukunft* [← :26] represent this tendency. **Oct 23:** In a letter to Bracke, M again laments the "miserable program" of Höchberg's *Zukunft*, its idealist phrases, future-society-mongering, etc.; it is a case of a bourgeois (Höchberg) buying his way into party influence. **Oct 27:** Franckenberg, for the Deutsche Handwerkerverein in Porto Alegre, Brazil, sends M a report on the activity of the local S-D group, and asks him to establish connections with the German party.

38. LISSAGARAY TRANSLATION. **Oct 23:** After much labor trying to save Kurz's German trans [← 77:1], M writes Bracke that it is too error-filled to be usable; revision of the German version should be handed over to W. Blos.

39. *CAPITAL.* **Oct 19:** M sends Sorge a list of changes to be made in the text of Vol. 1, intended for K. D. A. Douai who is supposed to be working on an English trans; some of the changes are indicated in the German edn, others marked in the French trans.

40. RUSSIAN AFFAIRS. **Oct:** In no. 10 of the periodical *Otechestvenniye Zapiski* (St. Petersburg)—sent to M by Danielson—Mikhailovsky's essay "KM before the tribunal of Mr. Zhukovsky" ascribes to M the view that to attain socialism Russia must first destroy the peasant common property of the village community and enter on the road to capitalist development [→ :41].

NOVEMBER

41. RUSSIAN AFFAIRS. **c.Nov:** M drafts a rejoinder (#M464) to Mikhailovsky [← :40] in the form of a letter to the *Otechestvenniye Zapiski*: he denies that the analysis of western European capitalism in *Capital* automatically applies to every other country and part of the world; for Russia, history is still open-ended; the historical sketch of capitalist development in *Capital* is not "a general historico-philosophical theory whose supreme virtue consists in being suprahistorical." But he does not sent the letter [→ 84:20].

42. POLITICAL AFFAIRS. **Nov 10:** In a letter to W. Blos, M comments on Blos's statement (letter sent to M on Nov 6) that M&E are "more popular figures" in Germany than they may be aware. We don't give a fig for popularity, writes M; because of "aversion to any cult of personalities" during the period of the International, expressions of appreciation were ignored or rebuked. Back in the Communist League "everything tending to further the superstition of authority" was removed from the by-laws, the very opposite of Lassalle's practice.

43. CONTACTS. **Nov 29:** M sends a thank-you letter, on behalf of himself and E, to Moses Hess's wife Sibylle, who sent them copies of Hess's posthumous work *Dynamische Stofflehre*. (M previously acknowledged the gift on Oct 25.)

44. READING AND STUDY. **Nov-Dec:** M studies the works of Robert Owen (SOURCE: *MEW Daten*; cf the similar entry under Aug A from *KMC*; these prob refer to the same notebook material).

45. *CAPITAL.* **Nov:** M begins preparing the first chapter of Vol. 2 for the printer (*MEW* dating: Nov to next July). *KMC*, under Oct 26, has the following entry: "M begins making a clean copy of the first chapter (three pages)."

Then, under Nov-Dec, KMC also states: "M works up a small part of the ms of Volume 2 (17 pages) so that it is almost ready for printing." **Nov 3:** Writing to S. Schott, M explains that the order in which he has drafted *Capital*, beginning with the "third, historical part" (*Theories of surplus value*), is the reverse of the order presented to the public.

DECEMBER

46. W&P. **Dec 2:** Jaclard sends M an invitation to write articles on the German and English movements for the journal *Slovo*, scheduled to appear in St. Petersburg in Jan. **Dec 30:** Part II of *Anti-Dühring* (#E23) ends serial publ in *Vorwärts* [← :27]. **c.Dec** (around the end of this year): The German trans of Lissagaray's book, on which M has

spent much time [← :1], is pubd in Brunswick.
47. *CAPITAL.* **Dec 30:** The *Labor Standard* (NY) begins serial publ of Weydemeyer's English trans of J. Most's abridgment of *Capital* (ST/51), which M helped revise [← 76:18] serialization ends Mar 10 [→ 78:30].

YEAR APPENDIX

48. In connection with M's study of socio-economic developments in Russia (see ← :1) *MEW Daten* gives books by the following authors as examples of his reading: A. I Vassilchikov, M. V. Neruchev, P. A. Sokolovsky. KMC notes for this year that M also studies Russian history, reading Kostomarov's historical monographs (in Russian) and making many excerpts from the essay on Stenka Razin.

1878

CONSPECTUS

1. *Broad-dated Entries.* For the period 1878–1882 M occupies himself extensively with mathematical studies, in particular algebra. He studies and excerpts treatises by Lacroix, Maclaurin, Euler, and Potts, and keeps special notebooks on the subject, with a large number of notes. Continuing mathematical studies begun in the 1860s, he studies and makes notes on books i.a. by Boucharlat, Hind, and Hemming; and he writes a sketch of the history of the differential calculus; cf #M499 (SOURCE: *MEW Daten*). —Re M's relations with people, note the broad entry for Thomas Allsop (→ :21) and for M. Barry (→ :23). —E's work on *Anti-Dühring* (#E23) extends through this year, as in 1877; see the *Register* for a summary of the dates. Note that on finishing this work, E returns to his *Dialectics of nature* (#E221); cf the entry under Aug.

2. *Indefinite Entries.* Re *Capital*, see ← 77:45, which has M working on preparing the first chapter of Vol. 2 for printing until July of this year (SOURCE: *MEW Daten*). On the other hand, cf the KMC entry (→ :26). —For an early exchange of correspondence between M and Jules Guesde, see → 79:6; but this perhaps dates from the end of 1878. —E's biographical article on M (#E406), written ← 77:22, is pubd sometime this year in an almanac.

JANUARY

3. POLITICAL AFFAIRS. **Jan 11:** In a letter to J. P. Becker, E expresses gratification over

Swiss progress toward the formation of an independent workers' party, and presents two serious criticisms of the German party: its attitude toward the crisis of republicanism in France [← 77:23], and the dominance of ignorant intellectuals as its theoreticians, an "infantile disease" of the movement.

4. W&P. **Jan 12:** E sends Bignami a piece on the workers' movement in a number of countries (#E751); pubd in *La Plebe* Jan 22.

5. *DIALECTICS OF NATURE.* **c.Jan** (around beginning of year): E writes a study on "Natural science in the spirit world," which will become a part of his *Dialectics of nature* (#E221).

FEBRUARY

6. EASTERN QUESTION. **Feb 4, 11:** At Liebknecht's request (Jan 22) for articles on this subject, M sends two substantial letters dealing with a number of associated issues— support of Turkey against Russia in the war, counting on Russian defeat and revolution; the play of big-power politics; the impact on the British party system; etc. (Liebknecht uses parts of these letters, without M's name, as an appendix to the second edn of his brochure *Zur orientalischen Frage*, with his postscript note dated Feb 27; pubd Mar A.)

7. POLITICAL AFFAIRS. **Feb 6:** Hirsch (in Paris) sends M info on the French movement, the difficulties of publishing *L'Egalité*, etc.; he asks E to write for the paper.

8. W&P. **Feb M to Mar M:** E writes a long essay, "The workingmen of Europe in 1877"

#E922), a survey of the movement in a number of countries (pubd Mar 3–31; → :10).

9. PERSONAL. **Feb-Mar:** Mrs. M is ill; she goes to Manchester for several weeks for medical treatment.

MARCH

10. W&P. **Mar 3–31:** E's "Workingmen of Europe in 1877" (#E922) [← :8] is pubd in five parts in the *Labor Standard* (NY). **Mar 10:** The *Labor Standard* (NY) ends publ of J. Most's abridgment of *Capital* (ST/51) [← 7:47; → :30].

11. *ANTI-DÜHRING.* **Mar D to Apr:** E finishes writing the third and last part (pubd → 16).

12. READING AND STUDY. **Mar D to May:** M reads and excerpts I. I. Kaufman's *Teoriya i praktika bankovovo dela*, and Kaufman's essay in *Nachalo* on the Russian peasant commune. **Mar-Apr:** M corresponds with S. Schott (in Frankfurt), who sends him newly pubd material on the development of German industry and finance.

APRIL

13. GERMAN MOVEMENT. **Apr 15–20:** M&E meet with Liebknecht, who is visiting London. **Apr 30:** In a letter to Bracke, E sets forth his view of Bismarckian social reform and statification as a means of increasing the power of the existing state for reactionary ends; statification can be either reactionary or progressive.

14. *CAPITAL.* **c.Apr to May A:** For Vol. 2, M studies a number of works on the history and theory of money.

MAY

15. POLITICAL AFFAIRS. **May 12:** Kovalevsky visits M at home; they discuss the news of Hödel's assassination attempt (May 11) against the kaiser.

16. *ANTI-DÜHRING.* **May 5:** *Vorwärts* begins publ of the third and last part (until July 7). **c.May to June A:** E drafts a preface (#E222) for the first book edn of *Anti-Dühring* (which will appear in July); but this draft will be replaced [→ :20] and consigned by E to the materials for *Dialectics of nature.*

17. W&P. **May 29:** For the editors of *L'Egalité,* Labusquière writes M asking for an article for a planned special issue. (M is unable to comply because of illness.)

18. READING AND STUDY. **May:** Cf ← :12. **May 21 to May D:** For his work on *Capital* M makes a conspectus of statistical sources he has received from the US. **May D**

to June: As part of his study of agrochemistry and geology, M reads and excerpts works by J. B. Jukes and J. F. W. Johnston on agronomy and geology; also, J. G. Koppe and Hlubeck (*KMC* dating: May).

JUNE

19. GERMAN MOVEMENT. **June 2:** A Dr. Nobiling makes an unsuccessful assassination attempt on Kaiser Wilhelm; coming on top of Hödel's [← :15], this will give the Bismarck government the pretext for imposing the Anti-Socialist Law illegalizing the S-D party. This is the context for M's exposé (see next) of Bismarck's right-hand man Lothar Bucher and his "communist" past. **June 12:** M writes a letter to the London *Daily News* detailing Bucher's political record (#M370); pubd June 13; reprinted in Germany June CD. **Jun 20:** Bucher replies with a "Statement" in the *Norddeutsche Allgemeine Ztg.* **June 27:** M writes a rejoinder (#M739); pubd in Germany June 29 and July A.

20. *ANTI-DÜHRING.* **June 11:** E writes the preface (#E26) which will be pubd in the book edn of this work (pubd July).

21. CONTACTS. **c.June to Dec:** M sees Thomas Allsop often during this period.

22. READING AND STUDY. **c.June:** M again takes up the study of geology; he reads and excerpts i.a. J. B. Jukes's *Student's manual of geology.*

JULY

23. POLITICAL AFFAIRS. **July 19:** M receives a letter from Sorge on the SLP and German-American socialists and on American affairs in general. **July-Aug:** M has a number of talks with the journalist J. S. Glennie (introduced by Furnivall); he gives Glennie material on "socialism as one of the political powers of the present time" for Glennie's book *Europe and Asia* (pubd 1879). **c.July to Dec:** M sees Barry often, gives him advice on his articles and lectures about German socialism.

24. *ANTI-DÜHRING.* **July:** A pamphlet edn of Parts II and III is pubd in Leipzig (for Part I, see ← 77:27). **July c.8:** The first book edn of the work as a whole (#E23) is pubd in Leipzig, with the new preface (#E26) [← :20].

25. W&P. **July A:** The July issue of the *Nineteenth Century* appears with an article by George Howell giving a (distorted) history of the IWMA. M writes a reply (#M520). **July 10:** M sends the reply to the magazine's editor, Sir James T. Knowles, who rejects it July 21 [→ :29]. **July 22:** The editors of

Nachalo, writing to E, invite M to write for their publ.

26. CAPITAL. July 2: M begins his last revision of the first chapter of Vol. 2, for publ (seven pages) (SOURCE: KMC).

27. PERSONAL. July 4: Another grandson is born to M: daughter Jenny's son Harry Michel Longuet (also called Henri and "Harra") [→ *83*:13]. **July D:** Mrs. M's liver and stomach ailment becomes markedly worse.

AUGUST

28. DIALECTICS OF NATURE. Aug: E, having finished with *Anti-Dühring*, goes back to his work on *Dialectics of nature* (#E221); he plans a systematic revision of the material and to this end drafts a plan of work.

29. W&P. Aug 4: M's reply to Howell (#M520) [← :25] is pubd in the *Secular Chronicle*, ed by Harriet Law.

30. CAPITAL. Aug: The English version of J. Most's abridgment of *Capital* [← :10] is pubd as an unsigned brochure (cf ST/51) [→ :34].

31. POLITICAL AFFAIRS. Aug 23: Hember of the London Dialectical Society sends M an invitation to give a lecture at the society on the principles of "democratic socialism."

SEPTEMBER

32. GERMAN MOVEMENT. Sep 16–17: The Reichstag begins to debate the Anti-Socialist Law proposed by Bismarck. Bracke sends M the stenographic report of the debate for these first two days. **Sep 23:** M begins to make excerpts constituting a conspectus of the Reichstag debate (#M179). **Sep 24:** M writes E that he has a mind to write the material up for the English press, possibly the *Daily News*. **Sep D:** M does not continue the unfinished conspectus, nor write an article on the material.

33. POLITICAL AFFAIRS. Sep 15: Kovalevsky visits M. **Sep 23:** Moritz Kaufmann, an English clergyman, asks M to check his article on M's life and works, which is also intended for inclusion in a book on socialist history [→ :36].

34. CAPITAL. Sep 4: M writes Sorge acknowledging receipt of the J. Most abridgment [← :30], opines it is not good enough to distribute in England, but plans a "somewhat amended edition" with a short preface, all under Weydemeyer's name. (This plan will not be realized.)

35. PERSONAL. Sep 4–14: M sojourns in Malvern, taking the waters; his wife has preceded him by a few weeks. Daughter Jenny is also staying there. **Sep 11:** As Lizzie Burns

is on her deathbed and urgently desires legalization of their union, E accedes to her wish for a formal marriage ceremony, held in the evening. **Sep 12:** Lizzie Burns dies. E sends a note on her death to *Vorwärts* (#E533); pubd Sep 18. **Sep 16:** E goes to Littlehampton, and stays there for a while (at least until Sep 25).

OCTOBER

36. POLITICAL AFFAIRS. Oct 3, 10: M sends Moritz Kaufmann [← :33] a number of criticisms and suggestions on his ms [→ :44].

37. GERMAN MOVEMENT. Oct 19: The Anti-Socialist Law is adopted by the Reichstag; it goes into force Oct 21. **Oct 27:** *Vorwärts* suspends publ as the organ of the German party. **Oct D:** M&E advise Liebknecht that the party should publish an illegal party organ in Switzerland, for secret distribution in Germany.

38. CAPITAL: READING AND STUDY. Oct-Nov: M reads, excerpts, and comments on books on the history of the banks and money circulation by Pietro Rota, A. Ciccone, K. D. Hüllmann, L. Cossa, Ch. A. Mann, A. Walker, et al.

NOVEMBER

39. CAPITAL. Nov AB: M gets info from Kovalevsky about a lively controversy in the Russian press over *Capital*. **Nov 15, 28:** In letters to Danielson concerning a new Russian edn of Vol. 1, M points to changes that should be made in the text. He directs attention esp to the development of monopolies and to industrial crises, and predicts that the US will be unable to throw off the power of the monopolies. He stresses that the outcome of the Civil War has indeed freed the blacks but "has enslaved the white producers." **Nov CD to Dec:** In work relating to Vols. 2 and 3, M studies sources on the history of agricultural relations; also in French history (for details, see → :46).

40. RUSSIAN AFFAIRS. Nov c.26: From Lopatin, who has just returned from an illegal sortie into Russia, E gets info on the situation there after the end of the Russo-Turkish war and on the activity of the Narodniks.

41. POLITICAL AFFAIRS. Nov A: Through Barry, M gets Liebknecht a position as correspondent for the *Whitehall Rev*. **Nov 25:** Lessner, writing to E, proposes that M give lectures to the London GWEA. **Nov c.D:** Paul Singer visits M.

42. READING AND STUDY. Nov 12: M begins reading and excerpting Avenel's *Lundis révolutionnaires* (on the French Revolution).

DECEMBER

43. INTERVIEW. Dec A: M is interviewed, allegedly "twice or thrice," by a correspondent of the *Chicago Daily Tribune* who signs his article "H." His report of the interview(s) is datelined Dec 18 (#M415) (pubd → :10).

44. PUBLICATION. Dec: Moritz Kaufmann's article on M [← :36], revised after M's suggestions, is pubd in the magazine *Leisure Hour*, Dec issue. (It will also be included in Kaufmann's 1879 book, *Utopias*.)

45. READING AND STUDY. Dec: M reads works on natural science and mathematics, by and about Leibniz and Descartes; see → :46 (KMC dating: c.Nov to c.Jan). **Dec to Jan:** M studies material on problems of finance and banking, esp on the Continent; for details, see → :46 (KMC dating: c.Nov to c.Jan). He makes

extensive excerpts and comments on part of this reading.

YEAR APPENDIX

46. The following authors are listed by KMC for M's study of early societal development and various problems in polit eco: **1878 as a whole:** J. R. Dakyns, J. K. Ingram, and P. A. Sokolovsky. **c.Apr to May A:** J. P. Gassiot, K. D. Hüllmann, Ch. A. Mann, Poor, P. Rota. **Nov CD to Dec:** G. Hanssen, S. Jacini, Van Enschut; and the *Annual report of the Commission of the General Land Office...* (Washington, D.C., 1871). **Dec:** O. Caspari, E. Du Bois-Reymond; also Leibniz's and Descartes's works on natural science and mathematics. **Dec to next Jan:** O. von Diest-Daber, J. P. Gassiot, J. L. Rey, Bonnet.

1879

CONSPECTUS

1. During a good part of this year M&E are closely involved with two questions concerning the German movement, which pervade their correspondence. Following is a summary of the background for the references in the entries below.

2. *Party Organ Question.* M&E see this as vital to ensuring the revolutionary character of the new German party organ which now has to be set up in illegality because of the Anti-Socialist Law. During the summer the party Exec moves to put the extreme right-winger Höchberg, with his colleagues Eduard Bernstein and C. A. Schramm, in charge of a supervisory board over the paper in Zurich, esp because Höchberg's money is largely financing the enterprise. From July to Sep in particular, letters fly about among four cities: Leipzig (Bebel, Liebknecht, the party Exec), Zurich (the Höchberg trio), Paris (Carl Hirsch, whom M&E think should be editor), and London (M&E). Liebknecht's letters are esp slippery since he wants to gloss over Höchberg's role while taking his money. This situation leads to E's letter to Bebel of Aug 4, and from there to the political high point represented by M&E's Circular Letter of Sep 17–18 (#ME29), one of the basic documents of M's political theory. A compromise is effected when the *Sozialdemokrat* begins publ Sep 28, at first under the editorship of Vollmar. But in fact M&E will keep their distance from the paper until 1881 (for the turning point, see → 80:44).

3. *Tariff Question; J. Most.* This issue raises the question for M&E of the revolution-

ary character of the party's Reichstag Fraction (group of deputies), esp when the Fraction permits one of its members, Kayser, to make a speech favoring Bismarck's tariff program, even though the Fraction itself remains officially silent. M&E attack Kayser's speech repeatedly. Related to this is the role played on the "left" by the anarchist Johann Most, publishing *Freiheit* in London since the beginning of the year. From Jan to Sep, Most repeatedly visits M, and in the first months takes a temporizing attitude toward him. On the other hand M more and more comes out against Most's type of propagandistic fustian as being the other side of the coin of Höchberg's pink parliamentarism.

4. *Broad-dated Entries (Continuing).* Re M's mathematical studies (#M499), see ← 78:1. —Re E's *Dialectics of nature* (#E221): there is only one passage dated to this year in the list drawn up by IML; see ST/E14 (DN) 449 or *MEW* 20:694.

5. *Broad-dated Entries (New).* Under Oct (→ :42), note two entries dated c.Oct to next Oct (1880), viz.: M's studies on Kovalevsky's work, and his *Notes on Indian history* (#M579) (ST/M77). —M's notes on Adolph Wagner's textbook (#M578) are dated c.July (1879) to Nov 1880.

6. *Indefinite Dates.* There is a question about the dating of an early exchange of correspondence between M and Jules Guesde, reflecting Guesde's break from anarchism and his rapprochement with M's views. (M's letter is not extant; all we have are excerpts from Guesde's reply, describing his growing agreement with key features of M's ideas; see *MEW* 34:505.) *MEW* dates this exchange "end of

1878 or beginning of 1879." In *MEW Daten* an apparently similar letter by Guesde is described under the date "not later than Apr [1879]." According to the biography of M by Fedoseyev et al, M's letter was written in Jan 1879 and Guesde's in "spring." —During this year an Italian abridgment of *Capital*, Vol. 1, by Carlo Cafiero, *Il Capitale de Carlo Marx, brevemente compendiato*, was pubd in Milan. For M's thank-you letter to Cafiero, see → :29.

7. *Reading and Study*. For details on polit eco read by M during the year, see → :53.

JANUARY

8. GRANT DUFF. **Jan 31:** M has a three-hour luncheon at the Devonshire Club with Sir Mountstuart Elphinstone Grant Duff, accompanied by Leonard Montefiore (who arranged the meeting). Grant Duff had requested to meet M because of an inquiry about him made by the Crown Princess Victoria [→ :13].

9. BIOGRAPHY. c.Jan (around the beginning of the year): M sends biographical material on himself to Arnold Kerdijk, who had requested it for his book *Karl Marx*.

10. W&P. **Jan 21:** F. J. Ehrhart, of J. Most's *Freiheit*, writes E inviting M&E to write for the paper. **Jan 5:** The interview, signed "H." (#M415) [← 78:43], is pubd in the *Chicago Daily Tribune*.

11. PERSONAL. **Jan A:** M's nephew, Henry Juta of Cape Town, visits M.

12. POLITICAL AFFAIRS. **Jan 30:** In a letter to J. P. Becker, E chortles over the news that Bakunin's lieutenant Guillaume has now split from the Bakuninist Jura Federation: "The anarchists would not be worthy of their name unless anarchy broke out in their own ranks." **Jan:** For the exchange of correspondence between M and Jules Guesde, see ← :6.

FEBRUARY

13. GRANT DUFF. **Feb 1:** Grant Duff writes a long letter-report (#M184) to the Crown Princess Victoria on his conversation with M [← :8].

14. RUSSIAN AFFAIRS. **Feb 5:** Danielson sends M a survey of and materials on the financial situation and finance policies of Russia in the last 15 years (*KMC* dates this Mar 17, perhaps referring to a second communication).

15. PERSONAL. **Feb to Apr:** Mrs. M is very ill. M's health declines; at times he is entirely unable to work.

MARCH

16. GERMAN MOVEMENT. **Mar 1:** Writing to Liebknecht, E expresses satisfaction over the German party's electoral progress evi-

denced in a Breslau by-election despite the Anti-Socialist Law, and in general over what M&E see as Bismarck's inevitable "self-ruination." **Mar 21:** E writes an article for *Le Plebe* on the German socialists' progress despite the antisocialist repression, and also on the progress toward revolution in Russia (#E29); pubd Mar 30.

17. RUSSIAN AFFAIRS. **Mar 17:** See ← :14. **Mar 21:** See ← :16. **Mar CD:** M reads the Russian journal *Slovo* and makes notes on Kovalevsky's articles about the draft of the Bulgarian constitution.

18. FRENCH MOVEMENT. **Mar or Apr:** For the correspondence with Guesde, see ← :6.

APRIL

19. CAPITAL. **Apr 10:** In a longish letter to Danielson, M explains why Vol. 2 has been delayed; in the course, he discusses the features of the economic crisis in Europe, the importance of the railway system for capitalism, a comparison of America with Russia, etc. —See also → :20.

20. POLITICAL ECONOMY. **Apr:** In a letter to Kovalevsky, M gives his views on the significance of the Physiocrats in the history of economics, apropos of a criticism of a newly pubd book by N. I. Kareyev.

21. FRENCH MOVEMENT. **Apr or before:** See ← :18.

MAY

22. R. MEYER. **May 27:** Rudolph Meyer, in London, writes M a flattering letter asking to meet him. **May 28:** M agrees, suggesting the next day. **May 31:** Meyer suggests June 8 [→ :25].

23. INVITATION. **May 29:** J. Gugenheim, secy of the London GWEA (now called Communist Workers Educational Assoc) writes E inviting him to give a "scientific lecture" (i.e., on a question of theory) [→ :24].

JUNE

24. GERMAN MOVEMENT. **June-July:** M&E are closely concerned with helping the German party prepare to publish an illegal organ for distribution in Germany [← :2], to be named the *Sozialdemokrat*. Through Hirsch, M is kept au courant; M comes out strongly in favor of naming Hirsch as editor. **June 16:** E declines Gugenheim's invitation to lecture [← :23] because the Assoc's organ *Freiheit*, ed by J. Most, has since May been publishing virulent attacks on the German party's Reichstag Fraction in connection with the tariff debate. Although E disagrees with the Fraction's behavior [← :3] he does not wish to solidarize himself with the kind of public attack on the

party which *Freiheit* is now making. **June**
to Sep: From here on M&E criticize the
anarchoid position of the so-called left voiced
by Most in his *Freiheit*, incl his repudiation of
using a parliament as a revolutionary tribune.

25. R. MEYER. June 8: M is visited by
Meyer [← :22], who lends M his recent book,
banned in Germany, *Politische Gründer und
die Corruption in Deutschland.* **June M to
Aug A:** M&E read and excerpt Meyer's book
(later used by E for #E758).

26. TRADE-UNIONISM. June 17: In a letter
to Bernstein, E criticizes the narrowness of the
English TUs, which confine themselves to
economic issues and bar political action, and
also the mistake of the *Freiheit* in inflating the
significance of the limited strike movement.

JULY

27. GERMAN MOVEMENT. July 19: Bebel
writes M asking him to contribute to the
planned party organ. **July 25:** In E's reply to
Bebel, M&E agree to write for the paper. M
asks Hirsch to accept the editorship.

28. RUSSIAN AFFAIRS. July 26 (rec'd Aug
A): Danielson sends M a survey based on
zemstvo statistics of the situation of finances
and agriculture in Russia—productivity, etc.

29. CAPITAL. July 29: M writes Cafiero of
his general approval of the latter's popular
condensation of *Capital,* just received. —
See also → :30.

30. POLITICAL ECONOMY. c.July: M begins drafting a number of critical remarks on
Adolph Wagner's recent textbook (#M578) [←
:5].

AUGUST

31. MARX'S TRAVELS. Aug c.8: M and
daughter Eleanor go to the Isle of Jersey. At
Waterloo Station they run across Harney and
converse briefly. En route M reads Carleton's
Traits and stories of the Irish peasantry, Vol. 1
(which he reviews for E, letter of Aug
14). **Aug c.8–15:** They stay in St. Aubin
(Trafalgar Hotel). **Aug 15:** They quit this
hotel because of its bad food, and move to
Saint Helier (Hôtel de l'Europe). **Aug 19:** M
learns by telegram of the birth of Jenny's son
in Ramsgate (see → :36). **Aug 20:** M and
Eleanor leave Jersey, and, via London, arrive
in Ramsgate on Aug 21. **Aug 21 to Sep 17:** M
and Eleanor sojourn in Ramsgate; see → :37.

32. ENGELS' TRAVELS. Aug c.5–7: E goes
to Eastbourne, accompanied by Schorlemmer.
Aug 28: E returns to London.

33. GERMAN MOVEMENT. Aug: There is
confusing crisscrossing correspondence over
the German party-organ issue among four
cities (see ← :2). Adding to the uncertainty is

M's shifting location during this month (see ←
:31). For the background at this point, see esp
section II of M&E's Circular Letter (#ME29),
on M&E's endorsement of C. Hirsch for editor
of the forthcoming *Sozialdemokrat* and their
agreement with his criticisms of the party
leadership's goings-on. **Aug 4:** After receiving from Hirsch copies of preceding Leipzig-
Zurich-Paris correspondence on the party-organ issue, E (on behalf of both M&E) writes
Bebel withdrawing their previous agreement
to write for the paper [← :27] and stipulating
that their names are not to be used as
collaborators. E explains that the paper will
apparently be controlled by Höchberg's Zurich trio, which has already in *Zukunft* shown
its antirevolutionary, "social-philanthropist"
position; this would make "split and disorganization" inevitable. **Aug 20:** Writing to
M, E summarizes his correspondence with
Liebknecht (Aug 14, 20—not extant), illustrating Liebknecht's slipperiness, and sympathizing with Hirsch's problem. —Bebel writes E,
urging arguments for M&E's collaboration
with the paper. —Hirsch, who was arrested
in Paris Aug M and expelled from France,
visits M's home in London, finds him away,
and leaves his card. **Aug 23:** Hirsch writes E
(in Eastbourne) about his expulsion from
France and his present situation, and also
sends a packet of correspondence bearing on
the party-organ issue. **Aug 25:** E informs M
(in Ramsgate) about Hirsch's situation; he
reports that instead of appointing Hirsch as
editor, the party leadership has named Vollmar as temporary editor. **Aug 26:** Replying
to a letter from Höchberg (Aug 24) urging
M&E's collaboration, E explains that their
(M&E's) opinion has been based not on
Hirsch's allegations but on the body of correspondence on the issue. —E, who up to now
has been uncertain of M's exact address in
Ramsgate, now sends him a packet of accumulated documents and correspondence about
the party-organ issue. E notes that it appears,
from Bebel's letter of Aug 20, that Liebknecht
has failed to show E's last letter to Bebel,
despite an express injunction. (This fact will
affect M&E's issuance in Sep of their views in
a "circular letter," so that Liebknecht cannot
suppress it.) **Aug 28:** M receives a letter from
J. Most, asking support against attacks on him
and urging opposition to the Höchberg group.
(M sends Most's letter to E, but delays answering.)

34. VISITS. Aug c.1: R. Meyer visits M
again [← :25]. **Aug 22:** Dana, in London,
comes to visit M, who is away; Dana leaves his
card.

35. CAPITAL: STUDIES. Aug c.25: M receives from Sorge statistical publications of
the State Labor Departments of Pennsylvania,

Ohio, and Massachusetts; also the 1874–79 reports by the head of the Massachusetts Labor Statistics Bureau, Wright (forwarded to M in Ramsgate by E).

36. PERSONAL. Aug 18: M's third grandson: daughter Jenny gives birth to a son, Edgar Marcel Longuet (called "Wolf"), in Ramsgate.

SEPTEMBER

37. MARX'S TRAVELS (END). Sep AB: M continues [← :31] to sojourn in Ramsgate (at 62 Plains of Waterloo). **Sep A:** M visits Borkheim (who is ill) in Hastings, and returns to Ramsgate. **Sep 10:** M unexpectedly runs into Rudolph Meyer, who is on his way to Margate and Edinburgh. **Sep 17:** M returns to London.

38. GERMAN MOVEMENT. Sep 8: In a letter to J. P. Becker, E summarizes the party-organ issue, emphasizing that the *Jahrbuch* article (ST/31.5) just pubd by Höchberg's Zurich group means "it is high time to come out against the philanthropic big bourgeois and petty bourgeois, the students and academics, who are pushing their way into the German party. . . ." **Sep 9:** E writes M about the contents of the just-pubd *Jahrbuch* article (a copy of which was left for M by Kovalevsky): it proposes that the movement should have a nonworking-class, peaceful-reformist character under the leadership of bourgeois intellectuals. E promises to draft a letter to Bebel, replying to his letter of Aug 20. **Sep 10:** M replies: "I entirely share your opinion that no time is to be lost in making known our opinion of the *Jahrbuch* drivel *bluntly* and *pitilessly.* . . ." He says the party organ will have to be publicly disavowed if it is like this drivel. **Sep 13:** Höchberg pays a surprise visit to London, but finds only E at home; E tells him bluntly what M&E think of his proposal to bourgeoisify the German party into a reform-parliamentary movement (as reported by E to J. P. Becker, Sep 15). **Sep M:** E drafts a political statement in the form of a Circular Letter (#ME29) addressed to Bebel and the party Exec; he prob starts work after the Sep 9–10 exchange with M. **Sep 17–18:** The final version of the Circular Letter (#ME29) is completed after M's return to London (see ← :37). The first two sections deal with "The negotiations with C. Hirsch" and "The proposed position of the paper"; they defend Hirsch both in general and in regard to the tariff debate in the party. The third section, "The manifesto of the three Zurichers," deals with the *Jahrbuch* article (ST/31.5); it stresses the need of a break "with people who openly state that the workers are too uneducated to emancipate themselves and must be freed from above. . . ." **Sep 19:** In a

letter to Sorge, M summarizes the dispute over the party-organ issue and the Höchberg group, incl the Circular Letter just sent. **Sep 28:** The first number of the new party organ, *Sozialdemokrat*, appears in Zurich, under the editorship of Vollmar.

39. RUSSIAN AFFAIRS. Sep: M begins study of Russian financial conditions on the basis of the materials sent by Danielson [← :28]. **Sep or Oct:** M studies and makes notes (#M567) on Kovalevsky's book (ST/37), sent him recently by the author, on communal land ownership in Russia and its decline [→ :42].

40. DIALECTICS OF NATURE. Sep (or later): E writes the chapter "Dialectics" (part of #E221).

OCTOBER

41. GERMAN MOVEMENT. Oct 21: Liebknecht and Fritzsche write a letter to E, on behalf of the party's Reichstag Fraction, replying to the Circular Letter [← :38] and denying any connection with the views of the Höchberg group's *Jahrbuch* article. **Oct 23:** A letter by Bebel to E condemns the *Jahrbuch* article, makes excuses for Höchberg's influence, and defends Kayser's Reichstag speech in the tariff debate. —Vollmar, now editor of *Sozialdemokrat* and still known as a leftwinger, writes E that he will editorially follow the line of the M–E Circular Letter.

42. STUDIES: INDIA, RUSSIA. c.Oct to next Oct: M draws up a chronology of the history of India from 664 to 1858 (#M579) (ST/M77). —M's study of Kovalevsky [← :39] is part of his ongoing study of land rent and agricultural problems in general, esp the source literature on the *obshchina* (Russian communal village formation).

43. POLITICAL AFFAIRS. Oct M: M&E receive from Cuno (in the US) the request to express their views on the political and financial program of the Greenback-Labor party, and to persuade the German-American socialists to drop their sectarian attitude toward the workers' movement.

44. NOVELS. Oct 25: In a letter to Bertha Augusti, M expresses his pleasure in reading her novel, just serialized in the *Kölnische Ztg.* He describes himself as "a great heretic with respect to German novels" but very "spoiled" by the "best French, English, and Russian novelists."

NOVEMBER

45. GERMAN MOVEMENT. Nov 14, 24: In two lively follow-up letters to Bebel, E sharpens his criticism of the German party's Reichstag Fraction and its role in the tariff debate.

He discusses the conditions under which socialist deputies can take a "positive" stand on proposals, and emphasizes the principle (applying to tariffs, statification, etc.) that the party's representatives must never "grant anything that strengthens the power of the government as against the people."

46. LORIA. **Nov 23:** Achille Loria (in Mantua) sends M his book *La rendita fondiaria e la sua elisione naturale* (just off the press, dated 1880), along with a letter expressing fulsome admiration [→ :50].

47. LINGENAU LEGACY. **Nov 14:** After complicated legal entanglements devised by the Bismarck government to prevent the German party from getting the legacy [← 77:31], and after Bracke has sent M on Oct 27 the legal document with the German executors' signatures, M is finally able to send Sorge the documents which will enable him to collect. (But in fact the Bismarck government will eventually prevent this.)

48. PERSONAL. **Nov-Dec:** M is prevented from working by a bad cold as well as his wife's illness.

DECEMBER

49. GERMAN MOVEMENT. **Dec 16:** E writes Bebel denouncing the latest Höchberg product, a *Sozialdemokrat* article which regrets the Revolution of 1848 since it was violent. E stresses that M&E cannot be in the same party as people who publish such views,

impugning "all of proletarian socialism." In conclusion he discusses the possibility of a European war which may "bury the *present* German party" and perhaps set the world back temporarily; but the new party to emerge in all countries would "be free from a lot of hesitations and petty things that now everywhere hamper the movement." **Dec 19:** Writing to J. P. Becker, E summarizes the attitude taken by M&E on the *Sozialdemokrat* issue.

50. LORIA. **Dec 3:** M replies to Loria [← :46] with a brief thank-you note. **Dec 15:** Loria writes again, pressing for M's opinion of his book [→ 80:33].

51. RUSSIAN STUDIES. **c.Dec to Jan:** M reads N. I. Kostomarov's *Istoricheskiye monografii i issledovaniya*, making excerpts and comments, esp on the uprising of Razin (*MEW* dating is, actually, end of 1879 to beginning of 1880).

52. OTHER STUDIES. **c.Dec to Jan:** M studies the history of ancient Rome. (For details, see → :54.)

YEAR APPENDIX

53. *KMC* lists the following authors for M's reading and study in polit eco for the year as a whole: Alexander Redgrave, J. F. Reitemeier, F. W. Rowsell, J. Guesde, and Höchberg (ed.), *Staatswissenschaftliche Abhandlungen*.

54. On ancient Rome (see ← :52), it lists: R. von Jhering, L. Lange, L. Friedländer, K. Bücher.

1880

CONSPECTUS

1. *Broad-dated Entries (Continuing).* E, who has resumed work on *Dialectics of nature* (#E221), writes some chapters for it, also a number of lesser passages; for the passages dated to 1880–81, see ST/E14 (DN) 449 or *MEW* 20:694. —For M's mathematical studies (#M499), see ← 78:1. —M's notes on Adolph Wagner's textbook in polit eco (#M578) come to a halt in Nov [← 79:30]. —M's chronology, *Notes on Indian history* (#M579) [← 79:42], comes to a halt in Oct.

2. *Broad-dated Entries (New).* Leo Hartmann's association with M [→ :11] will continue until June 1881. —Regarding *Capital*, an entry in *MEW Daten* for the year summarizes as follows: "M works on Vols. 2 and 3; writes a new version of Part III of Vol. 2; reads and excerpts works on polit eco, esp questions of land ownership, rent, agriculture, and finance." See also → :37, for the entry Oct to Mar 1881. —Regarding French affairs, M's

growing involvement with the new French Workers party ("Guesdists") is evidenced, esp after the Communard amnesty [→ :23]. Cf M's report in his letter to Sorge of Nov 5. *KMC* has an unexplained entry for the year as a whole: "M in personal association with Lafargue"; its reference is only to Guesde's letter to Lafargue of Dec 31. From this year on it is E who will maintain close relations with Lafargue, both political and personal. Note that E's work on *Socialism: Utopian and scientific* (#E759) is closely related to the needs of the French party; see → :4, 8, 16. —Individual Relations: Under Sep and Oct there are broad entries relating to individuals, Annenkov (c.Sep to Nov), Collet (Sep-Oct), R. Banner (Sep-Dec), Hyndman (Oct to May).

3. *Reading and Study.* Under the year as a whole, *KMC* lists a number of miscellaneous works. (For the list, see → :51.) —The readings which are excerpted in M's "ethnological notebooks" (see #M298) are of uncertain date. The notebook on Morgan's *Ancient society*

(#M570) may have been begun this Dec; the notebook on Maine (#M569), ascribed to c.May-June 1881, may have been done in 1880–81.

JANUARY

4. SOCIALISM: UTOPIAN AND SCIENTIFIC. **Jan:** At Lafargue's suggestion for a work of socialist propaganda, E starts work on adapting three chapters of *Anti-Dühring* (#E23) into an independent work (#E759) [→ :8].

5. LORIA. **c.Jan:** M reads and makes notes on Loria's book [← 79:50].

6. RUSSIAN AFFAIRS. **Jan 10:** In a letter to Liebknecht, E chortles over the alliance Bismarck has recently (Oct 1879) made with Austria-Hungary: it places the Russian regime before the alternatives of war or revolution, and the forthcoming Russian revolution will immediately change the character of all Europe.

FEBRUARY

7. W&P. **Feb D:** E writes the article "The socialism of Herr Bismarck" (#E758) for *L'Egalité* [→ :9].

MARCH

8. SOCIALISM: UTOPIAN AND SCIENTIFIC. **Mar M:** E finishes work on this adaptation [← :4]; it is translated by Lafargue (#E759). **Mar 20:** *Revue Socialiste* begins publ in three installs [→ :16].

9. W&P. **Mar 3, 24:** *L'Egalité* pubs E's "Socialism of Herr Bismarck" (#E758) [← :7]. **Mar D:** M writes an introductory note (#M682) for the serial republication of his *Poverty of philosophy* (#M681) in *L'Egalité* [→ :13].

10. FRENCH AFFAIRS. **Mar c.M:** In a letter to M, Guesde avows that he agrees with M's views, reports on the French movement, and says he will visit M in London.

11. VISITORS. **Mar c.A:** Paul Brousse visits M. **Mar 28:** The Viennese physician Dr. Bernhard Kraus has dinner at M's house. **Mar D:** Leo (Lev Nikolaevich) Hartmann, a Russian revolutionist arrested in Paris and expelled from France Mar A, moves to London and gets acquainted with M. (He will frequent M until he emigrates to the US on June 3, 1881.)

12. LONDON GWEA. **Mar 25:** H. Meyer, a member of the Assoc—now called the Communist Workers Educational Assoc—writes E about the split that has taken place as a result of anarchist domination; the socialists have formed a parallel assoc, using the same name; Meyer invites E to the opening of its clubhouse, Mar 27. **Mar D:** E explains to Meyer

that he received the invitation too late to attend, and that he cannot support either side without inquiry, since he disapproves of the Zurich *Sozialdemokrat* as much as of Most's *Freiheit*.

APRIL

13. W&P. **Apr 7:** M's introduction (#M682) to *Poverty of philosophy* (#M681) is pubd in *L'Egalité* as the editor's preface to republ of the work. **Apr AB:** At the request of Malon, editor of *Revue Socialiste*, M drafts a questionnaire for workers on their conditions of labor, etc. (#M994) (KMC dating: Mar c.M). **Apr 20:** The questionnaire is pubd in the magazine as "Enquête ouvrière." (It is also printed separately and distributed in France in 25,000 copies.)

14. GERMAN MOVEMENT. **Apr 1:** In a letter to J. P. Becker, E takes a dark view of the German party: while Most's *Freiheit* goes in for "empty screaming" of the word *revolution*, the *Sozialdemokrat* is beset by "narrow philistinism," and the party is too tightly disciplined in subordination to the Reichstag Fraction, which treats opponents as "heretics."

MAY

15. FRENCH AFFAIRS. **May A:** E's house in London sees a discussion by M&E with Lafargue and Jules Guesde to work out the terms of the program of the new French Workers party. M formulates the brief preamble ("Considérants") of the program (#M683) (KMC dating: Apr c.A). (The party program here discussed, plus later revisions, will be pubd in *L'Egalité* June 30, in other French periodicals in July, and will be adopted at the congress in Le Havre in Nov.) **May D** (after May 21): M edits the ms of Lafargue's manifesto for the French party (SOURCE: *MEW Daten*).

16. SOCIALISM: UTOPIAN AND SCIENTIFIC. **May 4 or 5:** After consultation with E, M writes a foreword (#M322) to the planned pamphlet publ of E's work (#E759), to be signed with Paul Lafargue's initials. **May 5:** *Revue Socialiste* ends the serial publ of the work [← :8]. **May D:** It is pubd in Paris as a separate pamphlet.

17. W&P. **May 20:** Julius Kräcker (in Breslau) writes E asking for M's consent to republishing his *Wage-labor and capital* of 1849 (#M968).

18. GERMAN MOVEMENT. **May A:** In a letter to Bebel, E stresses that despite the party's shortcomings, the powers of the bourgeois world are willy-nilly working to strengthen the revolutionary movement.

JUNE

19. CAPITAL. **June 19:** Nieuwenhuis (in
The Hague) asks M if he is willing to check
over his (Nieuwenhuis') ms for a popular
condensation of *Capital* in Dutch. **June 27:**
M replies that he cannot do so because his
Dutch is not good enough as well as because
of poor health, but he encourages the project
[→ 81:6].

20. W&P. **June 30:** The French party program, with (M's) preamble (#M683), is pubd
in *L'Egalité* [← :15].

21. PERSONAL. **June D:** Because of extreme exhaustion, M is forbidden by his
doctor to do any work for an indefinite time;
he cannot go to the Continent to take the
waters because of Mrs. M's advancing illness.

JULY

22. EDUCATION. **July AB:** Minna K. Gorbunova writes E about her work as a trade-
school teacher in Moscow and inquires about
trade-school systems in other countries, esp
for material on English trade schools. **July
22:** In reply, after consultation with M, E
summarizes what he knows about the English
system, which he thinks inferior to the Continent's, refers the correspondent to the government reports on the subject, and also comments on adult workers' education. **July 25:**
Gorbunova writes that before establishing a
trade school in Russia, she wants to answer
for herself some questions about its relation to
the economic development of the country [→
:26].

23. FRENCH AFFAIRS. **July 11:** The
French government's amnesty for Communards goes into effect, changing the conditions
for the building of a new socialist movement
in the country, and opening up the return of
M's sons-in-laws (and daughters) to France.

24. HYNDMAN. **July:** Hirsch takes H. M.
Hyndman with him on a visit to M and
introduces him (dating by *KMC*) [→ :36].

25. PERSONAL. **July D:** M and his wife go
to Manchester to consult Dr. Gumpert about
her illness.

AUGUST

26. RUSSIAN AFFAIRS. **Aug 5:** Replying to
Gorbunova [← :22] E stresses that the *obshchina* form is decaying, along with peasant
petty industry, but may still play a role in the
"next upheaval." **Aug M:** Some Russian Narodniks ask M to send his photograph, as a
token of sympathy. M has it sent through Hartmann, Aug 25. **Aug 21:** Danielson writes M
asking him for a magazine article on the Russian economy after the reform, in interpretation of material previously sent M by Daniel-

son on Russian agriculture [→ :31]. —N. A.
Kablukov (in St. Petersburg) sends E (for M&E)
his book on the collection of statistics by the
Moscow regional government in 1877–79.

27. TRAVELS. **Aug A:** M and his family go
to Ramsgate; the party includes Mrs. M,
daughters Laura and Jenny and their hus-
bands, and Jenny's sons, also E for part of the
time. M stays until Sep 13. **Aug M to Aug 27:**
E goes to join the M family in Ramsgate. **Aug
27:** E returns to London for a short time, then
goes to Bridlington Quay (Yorkshire), until
Sep 18/19.

28. CONVERSATION WITH SWINTON. **Aug
M:** While M is in Ramsgate, John Swinton,
who is traveling around Europe, interviews
him (#M418) [→ :34].

SEPTEMBER

29. GERMAN MOVEMENT. **Sep AB:** Writing to Liebknecht, who says that he and Bebel
are planning to come to London, E informs
him that both he and M will be available in
London from Sep 19 on. **Sep 22:** Bebel
writes E asking for a statement by M&E for
publ against J. Most, who is claiming that
M&E agree with his *Freiheit*. Bebel excuses
himself for being unable to come to London
with Liebknecht as planned. **Sep D** (last
third of month): Liebknecht comes to London
on a visit, and sees M&E about party problems, esp the editing of *Sozialdemokrat*.
When E later (Oct 12) reports Liebknecht's
visit to J. P. Becker, he mentions only that
Liebknecht promised that the *Sozialdemokrat*
will return to its previous (revolutionary) line.

30. FRENCH AFFAIRS. **Sep 30:** Hirsch (in
Paris) writes M reporting on the state of the
French WP and the Guesde–Malon dispute,
also the forthcoming publ of *L'Emancipation*
in Lyons, etc. (*MEW* dates M's receipt as Oct
c.3).

31. RUSSIAN AFFAIRS. **Sep 12:** M replies
to Danielson [← :26] with the advice that he
should himself publish the statistical material
on the economic development of Russia; he
gives permission to use the contents of his
letters to Danielson. He also discusses the
peculiarities of the present industrial and
agricultural crisis in England. **c.Sep to Nov:**
M reads the memoirs of the 1840s pubd in
Vestnik Yevropy by Annenkov, and makes
marginal comments on it.

32. CONTACTS. **Sep-Oct:** At Collet's request (Aug 14) M sends him considerable info
on the diplomatic and economic history of the
19th century. **Sep to Dec:** M corresponds
with Robert Banner (in Edinburgh), who
wants to translate and spread M&E's writings;
the correspondence also deals with the question of building a socialist workers' party in

Scotland. —M corresponds and socializes with the biologist Ray Lankester.

33. LORIA. **Sep 14:** Loria [← :5] writes to M asking his help in getting a journalist job for himself in London in order to study English conditions—perhaps, he suggests, as M's private secy [→ :41].

34. SWINTON. **Sep 6:** Swinton [← :28] pubs "A visit with KM," about his interview, in the NY *Sun* (#M418).

35. PERSONAL. **Sep:** M and his family [← :27] leave Ramsgate Sep 13; E [← :27] returns to London Sep 18/19. **Sep 12:** In his letter to Danielson (see → :31), M openly speaks of his fear that the turn for the worse in his wife's illness portends her death. **Sep 29:** In writing her own medical report on her illness, in answer to a questionnaire sent by Dr. Fleckles (at M's request), Mrs. M adds remarks on her state of mind: she clearly knows that her illness (which is a form of cancer) is getting worse and that she faces death; the removal of her married daughters to France [← :23] is a source of great distress; she would like to live a little longer, she confesses, even by clutching at straws if necessary: "It is strange—the closer one nears the end, the more one hangs on to this 'earthly vale of tears.' "

OCTOBER

36. ENGLISH AFFAIRS. **Oct to next May:** M meets often with Hyndman (July, according to *KMC* dating—see ← :24). They discuss politics, Hyndman's writings in the press (e.g., on England in India), the question of an English workers' party, etc. (SOURCE: *MEW Daten*).

37. CAPITAL. **Oct A:** In a letter to Charles Darwin, M asks him to accept the dedication of Vol. 2. **Oct 13:** Darwin politely declines: he does not want to offend his family's religious feelings, and does not want to seem to approve without knowing the subject. **Oct to next Mar:** M, continuing his work on subjects involved in Vols. 2 and 3, studies a great number of official publications (Blue Books) and much literature on the economic development of the US, esp California, on which Sorge sends him material. He reads Henry George's *The Kearny agitation in California.*

38. STUDIES: INDIA. **Oct:** This marks the end of M's period of work on his chronology *Notes on Indian history* (#M579) [← 79:42].

NOVEMBER

39. INTERNATIONAL AFFAIRS. **Nov 4:** M addresses a letter to Swinton thanking him for the *Sun* article [← :34] but mainly to propose that he establish a fund collection for the Social-Democratic victims of Bismarck's Anti-Socialist Law. M also discusses the relation of the Irish question to England. **Nov 5:** In a long informational letter to Sorge, M writes of the German party and the political need for its financial support against the strains of the Anti-Socialist Law; of the progress of the French movement toward becoming the "first real workers' party in France"; of his discovery of the foul articles that J. Most is publishing in the Russian press besmirching the German movement, as well as of the "miserable" line still being taken by the party's organ *Sozialdemokrat;* and of the success of *Capital* in Russia, together with a characterization of the Narodnaya Volya party in that country. M asks Sorge for material on California, since he wants to follow the unusually speedy process of capitalist centralization in this area. **Nov 27:** M&E send greetings, also signed by Lafargue and Lessner, to the international meeting called for Nov 29 in Geneva on the 50th anniversary of the Polish revolution of 1830 (#ME185); it is read to the meeting on Nov 29 (pubd in 1881 in a Polish pamphlet) [→ :46].

40. RUSSIAN AFFAIRS. **Nov 6:** The Exec Comm of Narodnaya Volya sends M a letter expressing a high opinion of the significance of *Capital* and other scientific works by M, and also gratification at his interest in the Russian revolutionary movement; they ask him to use his influence to arouse sympathy for this movement in the West. The party's representative abroad, Leo Hartmann, is to keep England and America informed.

41. LORIA. **Nov 13:** Replying to Loria's request [← :33], M says he can do little for him, but will see some people about it.

42. READING AND STUDY. **Nov:** M ceases work on his critique of A. Wagner's polit eco textbook (#M578), leaving it unfinished; see ← :1 and 79:30. —M reads Murray O'Brien's articles in the Oct and Nov *Fortnightly Rev,* and makes excerpts.

43. SQUARE ROOT OF MINUS ONE. **Nov 6:** H. W. Fabian (in the US) writes M objecting to E's use of $\sqrt{-1}$ in *Anti-Dühring.* (E is going to refer to this letter more than once; see *MEW* 20:628, n.12.)

DECEMBER

44. GERMAN MOVEMENT. **Dec 4:** Bebel again writes E asking M&E to collaborate on the *Sozialdemokrat.* **Dec 9–c.16:** Bebel comes to London with Bernstein in order to effect a change in M&E's view of Bernstein (who is slated to become editor of *Sozialdemokrat* in Jan) and toward *Sozialdemokrat* itself, as well as to discuss problems of the movement in general. (Paul Singer also comes to London, after Bebel.) Bebel is successful in convincing M&E that Bernstein has broken politically with the Höchberg tendency and is now a reliable revolutionary socialist. Moreover M&E, meeting Bebel for the first time, are extremely impressed by his intelligence and ability. (Bebel's autobiography calls this trip "Going to Canossa.")

45. RUSSIAN AFFAIRS. **Dec A:** The Russian narodnik N. A. Morozov comes from Geneva to meet M; he visits twice. Morozov reports on the split in the Zemlya i Volya party and the state of the movement in general, and asks M, on behalf of Narodnaya Volya, to collaborate with the publications of the "Russian Social-Revolutionary Library" (publisher's series) which will appear in Geneva. M agrees to write an article on the Russian village community. (*KMC* dating: c.Jan 1881.) **c.Dec** (i.e., end of year): M reads the book by Saltykov-Shchedrin, *Ubeshishche mon repos,* esp about landowner–peasant relations and the class struggle in the Russian village.

46. POLISH AFFAIRS. **Dec 5:** The editors of the Polish *Równość,* in a letter sent by S. Mendelson, write M that they disagree with the line of his letter to the Polish meeting of Nov 29 [← :39]: they are against the demand of national independence for Poland; socialists should be independent of the nationalist movement; they counterpose "Workers of the world, unite!" to the watchword "Long live Poland!"

47. REVOLUTION AND LEGALITY. **Dec 8:** In a letter to Hyndman, M discusses the problem of evolution and revolution (or violent revolution) in England and Germany, in particular the difference in working-class policy in a bourgeois democracy and a despotism.

48. *CAPITAL.* **Dec D to Jan A:** M gets several requests from one Edouard Fortin (in Paris), who wants M to correct monthly résumés of *Capital* which Fortin is making with a view to eventual publ (cf M to Longuet, Jan 4, 1881).

49. READING AND STUDY. **c.Dec:** At this time M prob begins working on his notes on Morgan's *Ancient society* (#M570) [→ 81:7]; perhaps also working on other ethnological notebooks; see ← :3.

50. PERSONAL. **Dec 31:** Hirsch has New Year's Eve dinner with the M family. (We have M's invitation to Hirsch; perhaps M also invited others.)

YEAR APPENDIX

51. *KMC* mentions a few specimen titles of M's reading during the year; cf ← :3. The authors' list is as follows: H. C. Irwin, R. B. O'Brien, A. Ronna, Ch. Letourneau, and Richard Bennet.

1881

CONSPECTUS

1. *Background: Engels' Letters to Bernstein.* With Bernstein's accession to the editorship of the German party's organ *Sozialdemokrat* in Jan, E delightedly begins to recognize that the paper is at last being edited as a militantly revolutionary organ. By Mar 12 E begins writing a series of letters to Bernstein—going on for years—which are virtually a correspondence school in Marxian politics as seen by E. This year there are only six such letters (extant); there will be many more in succeeding years. Because of Bernstein's later political relapse, it should be kept in mind that E is here treating Bernstein as a revolutionary disciple who has to be trained up to the task and who requires special attention because of his key position as editor of the party's voice. Essentially, "letter to Bernstein" should be understood as "letter to the editors of *Sozialdemokrat.*"

2. *Broad-dated Entries (Continuing).* E's work on *Dialectics of nature* (#E221) continues, from time to time. For passages dated to 1880–81, see ST/E14 (DN) 449 or *MEW* 20:694. There is another passage dated to 1881–82. —For M's mathematical studies (#M499), see ← 78:1. (In this connection, for this year see esp → :45.) —The period 1881–82 covers E's work on the history of the German people, incl his notes "On the ancient history of the Germans" (#E542) and his notes on "The Frankish epoch" (#E289)—neither of which appears below under any specific date. E's work in this field is also reflected in parts of E's *Origin of the family* (#E573) and "The mark" (#E468). —Two sets of notes which begin "end of 1881" and go over to 1882 are entered under Dec. These are M's notes on the Russian reform of 1861 (#M586) and his "Chronological excerpts" on world history (#M141). M's synopsis of Green's history (#M872.5) may also belong to 1881–82.

3. *Broad-dated Entries (This Year).* E's series of popular articles in the London *Labour Standard* (#E40) will be found entered under the months from May to Aug. —An entry concerning M's studies in Russian affairs, covering Jan to June (i.e., first half of year), will be found entered under Jan.

JANUARY

4. POLITICAL AFFAIRS. Jan 4: M sends Longuet an extensive account of Bradlaugh's career, with suggestions for an article on him for *La Justice*. —M has a conversation with Hyndman on the political situation in England, Ireland, and India; personal relations between the two are still good. **Jan 6:** Nieuwenhuis poses a question to M which the Dutch intend to raise at the forthcoming Zurich international socialist conference: after socialists take power, what legislative measures should they introduce to safeguard the victory of socialism? [→ :9]. **Jan 13:** Hermann Greulich (in Zurich) writes M about setting up a correspondence agency for English and American papers. **Jan c.20:** M meets with Viereck and Fritzsche, who are on their way to America. **Jan to Mar:** A KMC entry states: "In the rapprochement that is beginning between English workers' leaders (Hyndman and trade unionists) and members of Parliament (Jos. Cowen, Butler-Johnstone, etc.), M more than once gives both sides, at their own request, advice on political policy." KMC's references are to letters to M by the aforementioned figures.

5. RUSSIAN AFFAIRS. Jan: M is visited by two Russian economists, Profs. Ziber and Kablukov. **c.Jan to Feb A:** M reads Danielson's "Sketches on the Russian economy after the reform" in *Slovo* [→ :10]. **Jan to June:** M studies a number of books on the socioeconomic development of Russia after 1861, incl works by A. I. Skrebitzky, A. A. Golovachov, Skaldin, Y. E. Yanson, and N. F. Danielson, making notes on them. He rereads Chernyshevsky's *Pisma bes adressa* and summarizes its contents under the heading "On the Russian emancipation of the serfs." (SOURCE: *MEW Daten.*)

6. CAPITAL. Jan 8: Nieuwenhuis (in The Hague) [← 80:19] sends M a copy of his just-pubd popularization of Vol. 1, in Dutch, *Karl Marx. Kapitaal en arbeid*, which bears a flattering dedication to M [→ :11].

7. ETHNOLOGICAL NOTES. Jan to Mar: M's notebook on L. H. Morgan's *Ancient society*, prob begun last month [← 80:49], continues during the first quarter of 1881 (#M570).

FEBRUARY

8. GERMAN MOVEMENT. Feb 2: In a letter to Bernstein (who in Jan became editor of *Sozialdemokrat*), E praises the change in the paper's approach and tone; this marks a reversal of the negative attitude which M&E have been taking to the paper. E points to the NRZ of 1848–49 as a model revolutionary

organ. **Feb 4:** W. Blos sends E a report on the state of the German movement.

9. POLITICAL AFFAIRS. Feb 1: Replying to Kautsky's letter of Dec 4, which asked for criticism of his recent book *Der Einfluss der Volksvermehrung auf den Fortschritt der Gesellschaft*, E postpones most discussion until Kautsky comes to London [→ :15], but offers a few comments on the book's subject, overpopulation and social progress. **Feb 22:** In response to Nieuwenhuis' query [← :4], M replies that the question is too abstract; questions about future policy can be answered only on the basis of concrete circumstances; in this connection he also comments on the Paris Commune. M opines the time has not yet come to establish a new international organizn. **Feb 24:** In reply to an inquiry from Marx's daughter Jenny, E sends her a long account of some moot points in the history of Irish-English relations.

10. RUSSIAN AFFAIRS. Feb 16: Vera Zasulich writes M asking, in the name of her group of Russian socialists, for his views on the perspective of socioeconomic development in Russia, esp on the fate of the Russian village community (*obshchina*) [→ :13]. **Feb 19:** In a long letter to Danielson, M comments on his recent article [← :5] and goes on to discuss problems of harvest periodicity in Russian agriculture, the English economic crisis, the railway boom in Europe and the US, British superexploitation of India. Referring to the "boycotting" of Danielson's work in Russia, he comments that the same has happened to himself: when a man's thought leaves the rutted ways, the routiniers have only one defense—they ignore you. **Feb D to Mar A:** In an effort to reply to Zasulich's query, M writes four drafts of a letter in order to generalize his studies about the Russian village community (cf #M469) [→ :13].

11. CAPITAL. Feb: M wants to draw up a list of changes and corrections for Nieuwenhuis' book [← :6], looking to a second edn, but he is unable to do so because of personal difficulties—this he tells Nieuwenhuis in his letter of Feb 22. (Nieuwenhuis will in fact publish a second edn in 1889.)

12. PERSONAL. Feb to June: Mrs. M's health deteriorates; M suffers from chronic colds, which interfere with his sleep. He is forbidden all night work.

MARCH

13. RUSSIAN AFFAIRS. Mar 8: After drafting and abandoning four versions of a reply to Zasulich [← :10], M sends a short letter (#M469) leaving open the possibility that Russia might bypass capitalist development under certain circumstances. **Mar 13:** Czar

Alexander II is assassinated by Narodnaya Volya terrorists. **Mar 21:** M&E send greetings (#ME174) to a Slavic meeting in London in celebration of the 10th anniversary of the Paris Commune, with Leo Hartmann in the chair, held in Upper Marylebone Street; they have a good word for the czar's assassins [→ :20]. **Mar D:** M associates in London with the Russian revolutionary N. V. Tchaikovsky, introduced to him by Leo Hartmann; Tchaikovsky gives him info on the czar's assassins. (See also the J. Most case, → :14.) **Mar to c.Apr:** M reads brochures by P. F. Alisov and M. P. Dragomanov, and makes notes on them.

14. JOHANN MOST CASE. **Mar 30:** J. Most is arrested for his Mar 19 article in *Freiheit* (London) greeting the assassination of the czar. **Mar 31:** M&E send a letter to the London *Daily News* (#ME176) in defense of Most, pubd Apr 1 [→ :20].

15. GERMAN MOVEMENT. **Mar 12:** In a letter to Bernstein, E again [← :8] expresses satisfaction with *Sozialdemokrat*, and sharply criticizes a Mar 6 article by Kautsky on state socialism. E denounces the view that "every interference of the state in free competition" is socialism and "that the state equals socialism." He also writes about the impact of the Irish liberation struggle on England. **Mar CD:** Kautsky arrives in London, to stay a while.

16. *CAPITAL.* **Mar CD:** When the newly arrived Kautsky tells M that the new generation of socialists in Germany are impatient to read the rest of *Capital*, M replies "Me too." Asked if he plans to publish a complete edn of his works, M answers, "These works have to be written first."

17. POLITICAL AFFAIRS. **Mar 4** (rec'd c.15): Viereck, who is on a fundraising tour of America in behalf of the German party, sends M a request from the editors of the NY *Irish World* for articles on the agrarian question in Germany. **Mar 30:** E sends Bebel a report (gained from Viereck) on Viereck's and Fritzsche's fundraising tour in the US, incl a Mar 6 Boston mass meeting at which a speech by Wendell Phillips gave advance approval to the czar's assassination (seven days before the fact).

18. ETHNOLOGICAL NOTES. **c.Mar-Apr** (prob date): M makes notes on Phear's *Aryan village* (#M571).

APRIL

19. GERMAN MOVEMENT. **Apr 11:** In a letter to daughter Jenny, M gives an unfavorable view of the personality and ability of young Kautsky, who is now [← :15] frequenting M's house. **Apr 14:** E writes Bernstein to dissuade him from his intention of leaving the editorship of *Sozialdemokrat*, arguing that

Kautsky is not suitable and no replacement is in sight. He explains that he and M may soon start writing for the paper. **Apr 28:** On behalf of M as well, E congratulates Bebel on his best speech so far, in the debate on Bismarck's accident insurance bill Apr 4.

20. J. MOST AND THE CZAR'S ASSASSINATION. **Apr 1:** M&E's letter to the *Daily News* on Most (#ME176) [← :14] is pubd. **Apr AB:** M closely follows the trial of the czar's assassins (Apr 7–10) in St. Petersburg. **Apr c.9:** M sends a contribution to the defense fund for Most's *Freiheit* against the English government's persecution. **Apr 11:** In his letter to daughter Jenny (see ← :19), M writes with great admiration of the conduct of the Narodnaya Volya assassins at their trial, and comments that their modus operandi is "a specifically Russian and historically inevitable mode of action, about which there is no more reason to moralize—for or against—than about the earthquake in Chios." M also comments on the attempt by Randolph Churchill ("a cheeky Tory youngster") to link Most up with the English Radicals.

21. ENGLAND AND IRELAND. **Apr 11:** In his letter to Jenny (see ← :19), M makes suggestions for an article by Longuet on Gladstone's Irish land bill as a form of robbery. **Apr 29:** Again to Jenny, M remarks that the Irish land problem is so difficult that "the only possible way to solve it is to give Home Rule to the Irish and thus force them to solve it themselves. But John Bull is too stupid to grasp this."

22. LORIA. **Apr 16:** Loria again asks M to find a job for him in London.

23. HENRY GEORGE. **Apr-May:** M reads George's *Progress and poverty* (KMC dating: May). M has received a copy from both Swinton and Willard Brown; later (June), another from Sorge [→ :33].

24. PERSONAL. **Apr c.27:** Fourth grandson: M's daughter Jenny gives birth to a son, Marcel Charles Longuet (called "Par"), in Argenteuil. **Apr 29:** In a letter to Jenny, M comments on this event: children born now "have before them the most revolutionary period that people have ever lived through. It's a bad thing now to be so old that one can only foresee, not see."

MAY

25. THE *LABOUR STANDARD* SERIES. **May 1–2:** E begins writing a series of popular articles for workers (#E40), for the *Labour Standard* (London), pubd as leading articles without signature. His first is "A fair day's wage . . ." (#E266); pubd May 7. **May 15–16:** E writes the second article, on "The wages system" (#E894); pubd May 21. **May c.20:** E writes two articles on "Trades unions" (#E870); pubd May 28, June 4.

26. ETHNOLOGICAL NOTES. c.May-June (prob date): M makes notes on H. S. Maine's book on the early history of institutions (#M569).

27. HENRY GEORGE. May: See ← :23.

28. JOHANN MOST CASE. May 2: Most [← :14, 20] is tried and convicted for his *Freiheit* article, contrary to M's expectation. (In June he will be sentenced to 16 months in prison; in 1882 he will emigrate to the US.)

29. VISITOR. May-June: M gets frequent visits, about weekly, from Sorge's son Adolph.

30. PERSONAL. May D: Mrs. M, although very ill, is anxious to visit her daughter Jenny and her grandsons in France, and persuades her doctor to permit the journey. M so informs E on May 27, who writes Jenny Longuet on May 31.

JUNE

31. THE *LABOUR STANDARD* SERIES. June 4: E's second article on "Trades unions" (#E870B) is pubd. **June M:** E writes the fifth article in the series, "The French commercial treaty" (#E295); pubd June 18. **June CD:** E writes the sixth article, "Two model town councils" (#E880); pubd June 25. **June D:** E writes the seventh article, "American food and the land question" (#E16); pubd July 2.

32. AMERICAN AFFAIRS. June 2: A day before his friend Leo Hartmann sails for NY, M sends a number of recommendatory letters about him to friends in the US. **June 20:** Viereck, returned from America [← :17], visits M and reports on the movement there. **June:** M studies the development of American large-scale industry (for details, see → :64; see also → :33, 34).

33. HENRY GEORGE. June 2: Writing to Swinton to introduce Hartmann (see ← :32), M comments on George's *Progress and poverty* [← :23]: it is objectively "a last attempt to save the capitalistic regime," prefigured by the Ricardian socialists and already discussed in M's book on Proudhon (#M681). **June 20:** Writing to Sorge, M gives a longer account of the economic ancestry of this "panacea monger" [→ :61].

34. LINGENAU LEGACY. June c.17: Kautsky visits M in connection with this affair.

35. BRITISH AFFAIRS. June A: Hyndman's *England for all* is pubd with two chapters plagiarized from *Capital* (with errors) without mentioning M's name. In letters to M (e.g., June 5) Hyndman gives various excuses [→ :38]. **June 3:** Robert Banner writes M about a forthcoming congress of Scottish socialists, and asks his advice and help in building a socialist party.

36. PERSONAL. June 5: A family friend, Lina Schöler, arrives unexpectedly, and stays with the M family for about a month; her presence is very good for Mrs. M, whose condition is deteriorating (as reported June 17 by E to Jenny Longuet). **June D to July c.20:** M and his wife go to stay in Eastbourne.

JULY

37. THE *LABOUR STANDARD* SERIES. July 2: E's seventh article, "American food ..." (#E16), is pubd. **July A:** E writes the eighth article, "The wages theory of the Anti-Corn Law League" (#E895); pubd July 9. **July M:** E writes the ninth and tenth articles, "A working men's party" (#E921) and "Bismarck and the German working men's party" (#E81); both pubd July 23. **July D:** E writes the 11th article, "Cotton and iron" (#E187); pubd July 30.

38. HYNDMAN. July 2: In a letter to Hyndman, M dissects his excuses [← :35] in objective fashion, assuming continued personal relations. (But in fact a personal estrangement begins here.)

39. ELEANOR MARX. July 5: E attends a theatrical performance at the Dilettante Club theater with Eleanor in the cast. E observes (letter to M, July 7) that she is "very good in the passionate scenes," but too obviously takes Ellen Terry as her model; she will soon "strike out a line of her own."

40. PERSONAL. July c.20: M and his wife return from Eastbourne [← :36]. **July 26:** With the permission of Mrs. M's doctor, M takes his wife to visit their daughter Jenny at the Longuet home in Argenteuil, near Paris. (For this visit, see → :43.)

41. ENGELS ON HOLIDAY. July 28 to Aug 22: E sojourns in Bridlington Quay, Yorkshire.

AUGUST

42. THE *LABOUR STANDARD* SERIES. Aug 1–2: E writes his 12th (and last) article in the series, "Social classes—necessary and superfluous" (#E753); pubd Aug 6. **Aug 10, 15:** When editor Shipton objects to a mild article by Kautsky as too strong for his readers, E writes Shipton terminating his own series. E's main reason (E to M, Aug 11) is disappointment at the lack of response to his articles and the absence of any effect on the rest of the paper; the British workers need a shaking-up by the loss of Britain's "industrial monopoly."

43. MARX FAMILY IN FRANCE. Aug: Since July 26, M and his wife are staying at the Longuets in Argenteuil, near Paris. Mrs. M's condition fluctuates; M urges her to return home, without avail. For this period, *MEW Daten* states: "M makes notes on land ownership, artisanry, guilds, and finances, also in the situation of the French peasant on the eve of the French Revolution. He reads and excerpts Fleury's book on 1789." **Aug 3–8:** M stays in nearby Paris; meets with Lavrov and Hirsch. **Aug 7:** M takes his wife on a ride through Paris. **Aug 8:** Jaclard visits M and informs him about the French movement and the coming parliamentary elections. **Aug 9:** Lissagaray visits M, discussing similar topics. **Aug 16:** M receives word that daughter Eleanor is very ill and is refusing to see a doctor. **Aug 17:** M returns hurriedly to London to go to Eleanor. (Mrs. M will follow in a few days.) **Aug 18:** M reaches Eleanor's bedside and immediately makes arrangements for a doctor's examination, etc.

44. GERMAN MOVEMENT. **Aug 17:** E sends Bernstein a number of comments on articles in the *Sozialdemokrat* and praises his editorship in general and his articles on intellectuals and on Bismarckian statification. Since on July 23 Kautsky, via Bernstein, had sent E a sample packet of current anti-Semitic literature, E discusses its socially reactionary roots and how to fight it. E adds a "thirdhand" report on the feeble anarchist congress held in London July 14–19 (the "R-r-revolutionary congress").

45. STUDIES. **Aug 17–18:** E studies M's mathematical mss, esp his explanation of the differential calculus, and writes M (Aug 18) enthusiastically about the value of his exposition. **Aug 27:** Writing to Kautsky, E urges a German trans of a talk at an international medical congress by John Simon ("State medicine," *Nature,* Aug 18). **Aug c.D to Sep:** M finishes making a list of the Russian books and sources he possesses, mainly material on the socioeconomic development of Russia after 1861; the list is titled "Russisches [Russian material] in my bookshelf." **c.Aug to Sep:** M interests himself in the history of colonial peoples; he excerpts and annotates G. Manis's *Java* and Phear's *The Aryan village* (this according to *MEW Daten,* but see ← :18 for Phear).

46. POLITICAL AFFAIRS. **Aug 30:** H. Rackow of the London GWEA asks E for advice on policy at the international socialist conference in Chur (Switz.) Oct A.

47. ENGELS ON HOLIDAY. **Aug 22:** E returns [← :41] from Bridlington Quay. **Aug D to Sep 18:** E is back again in Bridlington Quay.

48. PERSONAL. **Aug:** Again in debt because of so much illness in the family, M turns as usual to E (Aug 3), who helps out with £50 (Aug 6, 11).

SEPTEMBER

49. POLITICAL AFFAIRS. **Sep 9:** The London correspondent of the NY *Herald* sees M

about Leo Hartmann: Russian agents are claiming that the Hartmann in NY [← :32] is not the same man as the well-known revolutionary; M attests to his identity. The *Herald* reports this, Sep 10. **Sep 23:** J. P. Becker writes E asking if he or M will come to the international socialist congress opening in Chur (Switz.) on Oct 2 [→ :53].

OCTOBER

50. FRENCH MOVEMENT. **Oct 20:** Bernstein sends E a letter (actually dated Oct 14) asking about the movement in France, since Lafargue has asked him to write for *L'Egalité.* **Oct 25:** E replies with a long survey, for general background: on the many weaknesses and mistakes of the French movement and its feuding leaders, personal antagonisms, anti-German chauvinism (masked as anti-M hostility), and the influence of M's ideas.

51. AMERICAN AFFAIRS. **Oct 1:** Apropos of an American socialist visiting in London, M remarks (letter to Kautsky) that "I always have a certain *prima facie* suspicion of Yankee socialists, and in particular I know that the type Shipton [← :42] is connected with is very crotchety [faddist] and sectarian." **Oct D:** Leo Hartmann [← :49] returns to London from America, and sees M often (until Dec D).

52. ENGLISH AFFAIRS. **Oct:** The *Contemporary Rev* appears with an article by John Rae on "The socialism of KM and the Young Hegelians" (cf M to Sorge, Dec 15).

53. INTERNATIONAL AFFAIRS. **Oct 13:** J. P. Becker reports to E that the international socialist congress [← :49] went off well, "free from all school-socialists, anarchists, sectarians, and other panacea inventors" [→ :56].

54. *CAPITAL.* **Oct 22:** Pub'r Meissner asks M to prepare a third edn of Vol. 1. (M is not so inclined, since he wants to work on Vol. 2.)

55. PERSONAL. **Oct c.13 to Dec AB:** M is very ill (pleurisy, bronchitis, incipient pneumonia), critically so during Oct. Since returning from France, Mrs. M is bedridden and weakening daily.

NOVEMBER

56. GERMAN MOVEMENT. **Nov 4:** Writing to J. P. Becker, E explains his disinclination to attend the Chur conference [← :53]; he esp enthuses over the German party's vote (over 300,000) in the Oct 27 election, in the face of illegality and harassment, most particularly not the number of seats won but the increase of party strength in the big cities. **Nov 30:** Writing to Bernstein about the Oct 27 election, E is esp joyful over the shift in the party's strength from Saxony to the big industrial cities; but he is worried about the character of the elected deputies, esp without Bebel.

57. FRENCH MOVEMENT. **Nov 30:** In his letter to Bernstein (see ← :56), E reports on the French party, esp its Rheims congress (a "humbug," representing fewer forces than claimed). E points out that Malon's "Marxophobia" did not prevent him from asking Lafargue to get M to write a preface for his history of socialism.

58. ENGLISH AFFAIRS. **Nov 30:** M (and also Mrs. M, three days before her death) sees the Dec 1 issue of *Modern Thought* with an article by E. B. Bax, "Leaders of modern thought. XXIII—Karl Marx." M thinks it is the first English publ to express real enthusiasm for the "new ideas," in spite of the article's mistakes (M to Sorge, Dec 15).

DECEMBER

59. DEATH OF MRS. JENNY MARX. **Dec 2:** Mrs. M dies, of cancer of the liver. **Dec 4:** E writes the obituary (#E399) for the *Sozialdemokrat;* pubd Dec 8. **Dec 5:** At the funeral in Highgate Cemetery, E gives an obituary talk (#E766); pubd in *L'Egalité* Dec 11. M is barred by doctor's orders from attending the funeral. **Dec 7:** M writes a letter to his daughter Jenny about her mother's end, correcting some biographical misstatements, etc. **Dec 17:** In another letter to Jenny, M writes of the numerous letters of condolence he has received that are not merely conventional notes; e.g., Liebknecht's (Dec 12) on Mrs. M's help in the exile days. **Dec 29:** M goes to take the waters in Ventnor (Isle of Wight), with Eleanor [→ 82:3]. —E receives Nieuwenhuis' inquiry about a rumor that M is on his death bed, and replies that it is an invention. (In general, the end of 1881 sees many press reports about M's imminent death.)

60. CAPITAL. **Dec 13:** In a letter to Danielson, M says that, in reply to Meissner's proposal of a third edn [← :54], he will propose making as few changes as possible this time, lowering the press run from 3000 to 1000, and when the edn is exhausted, doing a thorough revision of the book, a revision such as he would do now if the circumstances were different. **Dec 15:** In a long postscript to Sorge, M summarizes the attention recently paid to *Capital* in England—by Rae [← :52], Bax [← :58], and Hyndman [← :35].

61. HENRY GEORGE. **Dec 15:** In his letter to Sorge (see ← :60), M comments that George—who had come on a trip to Ireland and England in late Oct—"reveals himself more and more as a humbug" [← :33].

62. SCIENCE. **c.Dec:** M is greatly interested on hearing of Marcel Deprez's experimental work on the long-distance wire transmission of electrical energy (which can revolutionize the organizn of industry), and asks Longuet to obtain relevant publications [→ 82:47].

63. STUDIES. **End of 1881 to 1882:** M writes up notes on the Russian reform of 1861 (#M586), and works on systematizing his material on Russia. He also continues his study of the development of US capitalism. (SOURCE: *MEW Daten.*) **About end of 1881 to end of 1882:** M works on his "Chronological excerpts" (#M141), a survey of world historical events.

YEAR APPENDIX

64. M's reading in the history of early society—besides the works written up in his "ethnological notebooks" (#M298)—includes the following authors: W. B. Dawkins, R. Sohm, E. B. Tylor, J. W. B. Money, L. Gumplowicz. Under June, M's reading in the development of US big industry incl the following authors: H. D. Lloyd, E. H. House, W. B. Grohmann, and T. E. Cliffe Leslie; also articles in the *Atlantic Monthly* on the American silk industry and child labor. (The KMC date for this reading is Apr-May.)

1882

CONSPECTUS

1. *Broad-dated Entries.* See ← 81:2 for E's continuing work, from time to time, on *Dialectics of nature* (#E221), and for M's mathematical studies; also for E's work on the history of the German people during 1881–82, and M's notes on the Russian reform of 1861 (#M586) and his "Chronological excerpts" (#M141), also #M872.5.

2. *Reading and Study.* For M's reading ascribed to this year, without specific date, see → :55.

JANUARY

3. MARX IN VENTNOR. **Jan AB:** M and Eleanor stay on [← :59] in Ventnor (Isle of Wight) until Jan 16, despite bad weather which worsens M's condition. Eleanor is in a distressed nervous state. M gives E (Jan 12) a sympathetic account of her desire for a theatrical career. There is considerable M–E correspondence during this period.

4. GERMAN MOVEMENT. **Jan 6:** Writing to Bernstein, whose *Sozialdemokrat* has been in a power fight with the right-wing Reichstag

Fraction, E gives strong support to the *Sozialdemokrat*'s views [→ :11]. **Jan 15:** M writes E that it was a great victory when Bismarck confessed in the Reichstag (Jan 9) that the German workers had rejected "his state socialism." **Jan 25** (sent Jan 31): In a letter to Bernstein, E castigates the opportunism dominant in the party leadership (which under the Anti-Socialist Law is constituted by the Reichstag Fraction). **Jan:** The current controversy between C. A. Schramm and K. Bürkli on interest-bearing paper money in relation to M's views is discussed in various letters: M to E, Jan 12; E to Bernstein, Jan 25/31.

5. FRENCH MOVEMENT. **Jan 6:** E's letter to Bernstein (see ← :4) includes a report on the petty factional fights of Malon, Brousse, etc. (the future Possibilists) against Guesde, Lafargue, and the party leadership. E gives this report also to M in a letter of Jan 13; and a further report to Bernstein on Jan 25. **Jan D:** Lafargue, in London, spends time with M; also Hepner, who is on his way to America.

6. ENGLISH AFFAIRS. **Jan 23:** In a letter to Lavrov, M surveys the scene: new interest in *Capital* [← :60]; new class struggles stirring; and a new periodical *The Radical* has been vainly urging M to write for it.

7. DIETZGEN. **Jan 3:** Dietzgen writes M about his study of Hegel, esp the *Phenomenology*. **Jan 5:** M comments to E that Dietzgen seems to be developing in the wrong direction.

8. W&P. **Jan 21:** At Lavrov's request, M&E write a new preface (#ME37) for a Russian edn of the *Com Manifesto*, translated by Plekhanov. M sends the ms to Lavrov on Jan 23 [→ :13].

FEBRUARY

9. ON NATIONALISM. **Feb AB:** The nationalist uprising in Bosnia and Herzegovina, breaking out in Jan against Austrian rule, reaches a high point; the czarist regime embraces it in the name of Pan-Slavism. The *Sozialdemokrat*, like other western European socialists, expresses sympathy for the revolt. In a letter to editor Bernstein, E warns against un-thought-through partisanship for Bosnia and Herzegovina, in order not to play into the hands of Pan-Slavism and czarist power, and in order to guard against a European or world war breaking out around the Balkan imbroglio. (This letter is not extant and its exact date is not known; prob sent to Bernstein about the same time as E's letter to Kautsky, next entry.) **Feb 7:** In a long letter to Kautsky, E makes a thoroughgoing statement of his viewpoint on the claims of nationalism in Europe,

esp but not only in East Europe, and its relationship to socialist revolution. **Feb 22–25:** In a second letter to Bernstein on nationalism, E analyzes nationalism in the Slavic Balkans, esp Serbia, its relation to czarist Pan-Slavism, proletarian revolution, and the coming European war.

10. INTERNATIONAL AFFAIRS. **Feb 1:** J. P. Becker writes E proposing that a new international workers' organizn should be set up after the model of the IWMA, now that the anarchist international has collapsed. **Feb 10:** E replies that "we" (M&E) have given thought to the proposal but the time has not yet come; but it is approaching. E surveys a number of countries to explain the reasons; conditions will mature for the establishment of an International that will not be a mere propaganda society but an organizn for action.

11. GERMAN MOVEMENT. **Feb 16:** The *Sozialdemokrat* pubs a statement by the Reichstag Fraction in which the right wing [← :4] is forced to acknowledge the paper as the voice of the party, and hence independent of the Fraction.

12. AMERICAN AFFAIRS. **Feb c.5:** E receives a letter from Cuno on the successful propaganda for M&E's ideas in the Knights of Labor.

13. W&P. **Feb 5:** *Narodnaya Volya* pubs M&E's new preface (#ME37) to a Russian edn of the *Com Manifesto* [← :8; → :17].

14. MARX'S TRIP. **Feb A:** M decides, on doctor's advice, to take a curative trip to Algeria (Italy being out of bounds because of the danger of arrest), stopping off first at the Longuets. **Feb 9–16:** M, accompanied by Eleanor, stays with daughter Jenny in Argenteuil, near Paris. **Feb c.13:** M visits J. Mesa, in Paris. **Feb M:** In Paris, M has a long talk with Guesde, Deville, and Mesa on problems of the French movement. **Feb 16:** M, without Eleanor, leaves Argenteuil. **Feb 17:** M stops over in Marseilles, to take a steamer in the morning. **Feb 18–20:** Steamship from Marseilles to Algiers. **Feb 20 to May 2:** Marx sojourns in Algiers (see → :15).

MARCH

15. MARX IN ALGIERS. **Mar-Apr:** During M's stay (in toto Feb 20 to May 2) his health worsens amid bad weather, incl the onset of pneumonia; he is treated by a Dr. Stephann; he suffers from lack of appetite, insomnia, depression. He spends time with a judge, Albert Fermé, a friend of Longuet, banished from France by Napoleon III; Fermé gives him info on Arab property relations and on the colonial suppression of the native population by the French, English, and Dutch.

APRIL

16. MARX IN ALGIERS. Apr to May 2: See ← :15.

17. W&P. Apr 10: E sends Lavrov corrected proofs of the M–E preface (#ME37) to the Russian edn of the *Com Manifesto*, for the pamphlet edn [→ :21]. **Apr 13:** The *Sozialdemokrat* pubs a German version of the preface, retrotranslated from the Russian since the original ms is not found. **Apr CD:** E writes the essay on "Bruno Bauer and early Christianity" (#E105); pubd May 4, 11.

18. RICHARD WAGNER. c.Apr (or sometime in spring): In a letter of this period (not extant), presumably to E, M sharply criticizes the view of early society embodied in Wagner's Nibelungen operas. (Its content is summarized by E in *Origin of the family*, #E573; see *MEW* 21:43f.)

MAY

19. MARX'S TRAVELS. May 2: On Dr. Stephann's advice, M leaves Algiers. **May 5–6:** M stops over in Marseilles and Nice, on the way to Monte Carlo, where he arrives May 6. **May 6 to June 3:** In Monte Carlo, M meets a Swiss Dr. Delachaux who strongly recommends staying there for the climate; he does. While looking over the casino, M encounters Zhukovsky. M puts himself under treatment by a Dr. Kunemann [→ :23].

20. GERMAN MOVEMENT. May 10: In a letter to Bernstein mostly discussing bimetallism, E attacks a growing problem, the party intellectuals [*Literaten*], who "think they have the privilege of learning nothing and pontificating on everything." **May 11, 31:** Kautsky writes E two long letters inquiring about his views on the colonial question; Kautsky opines that possession of India by an English proletarian regime would be advantageous for both countries [→ :36]. **May 14:** E meets with Paul Singer, who is visiting from Germany; E is unable to shake Singer's favorable attitude toward the Bismarckian state-socialist program, since Singer sees "a semisocialist measure . . . in any statification whatever" (so E writes Bebel on May 16).

21. W&P. May 3: E writes the article "On the concentration of capital in the US" (#E547); pubd in *Sozialdemokrat* May 18. **May 4, 11:** *Sozialdemokrat* pubs E's article on early Christianity (#E105) [← :17]. **May D:** The new Russian edn of the *Com Manifesto* is pubd in Geneva (with the new preface, #ME37).

22. ENGLISH AFFAIRS. May 3: In a letter to Bernstein, E informs him that Hyndman's group is "of no account whatever," and that Gladstone's Irish policy has foundered.

JUNE

23. MARX'S TRAVELS. June 3: M leaves Monte Carlo, marveling that he has spent almost a month in this haunt of idlers, lumpenproletarians, and ex-pirates (the Grimaldi rulers). **June 3–5:** M stops over in Cannes, for a medical rest before continuing on to Argenteuil. **June 6:** M is back in Argenteuil with the Longuets (until Aug 22), taking daily sulfur baths at Enghien, from June 17 on. **June c.24/25:** Helene Demuth arrives at Argenteuil.

24. GERMAN MOVEMENT; FRANCE. June 20, 21: In letters to Sorge and Bebel, E thinks there will eventually be a right-left split in the German party in view of the right-wing intellectuals' efforts to turn the movement toward tame, belly-crawling meekness in face of the Anti-Socialist Law. E also informs Bebel of the split in the French party by the Malon–Brousse right wing, which wants an alliance with "radical bourgeois intellectuals."

25. W&P. June c.3: E gets the new Russian edn of the *Com Manifesto* [← :21] from Lavrov [→ :29]. **June 22:** Since Hepner (in NYC) asked E (May 3) for permission to reprint M&E's writings in a "workers' library" series, M (after the delay due to traveling) advises E to reply: let them reprint without special authorization so that we do not bear the responsibility [→ :29].

26. STUDIES. June to next Jan: M works on the subject of organic and inorganic chemistry (SOURCE: *MEW Daten*).

JULY

27. MARX IN ARGENTEUIL. July: M continues staying at the Longuets' [← :23]. **July D:** Daughter Eleanor comes to stay at Argenteuil too. **July D to Aug A:** M reads two new brochures sent by Loria; M's opinion of the author sinks even lower.

28. MEHRING. July 2: F. Mehring (at this point hostile to the German Social-Democrats) pubs an article, inspired by C. Hirsch, stating that M has had nothing to do with the German party or the *Sozialdemokrat* since the Anti-Socialist Law. **July 15:** E reacts to this "Mehringiad" by suggesting it be answered indirectly, by pointing out that a signed article by E (#E105) had recently appeared in the paper, and that "M and I always execute our public acts by prior agreement." But "Mehring has put out so many lies about us" that a direct refutation of this one is inadvisable. **July 27:** A *Sozialdemokrat* editorial lambastes Mehring on this point.

29. W&P. July 25: E informs Hepner [← :25] that he can reprint M&E writings but without special authorization. **July 31:** E sends Lavrov delayed thanks for the Russian edn of the *Com Manifesto* [← :25].

AUGUST

30. MARX'S TRAVELS. **Aug:** M stays with the Longuets in Argenteuil [← :23] until Aug 22. **Aug 2:** M has lunch with Guesde, Deville, and J. Mesa, along with Lafargue, discussing movement problems; Deville discusses the condensation of *Capital* he has begun. **Aug A:** See ← :27 re Loria. **Aug 21:** Just before M's departure, Longuet brings that "poor devil" Roy (translator of *Capital*) to meet M. **Aug 22:** M, accompanied by his daughter Laura, leaves Argenteuil. **Aug 23:** After an overnight in Dijon, they arrive in Lausanne and stay for a few days. **Aug 27:** M and Laura leave for Vevey (Switz.), where they stay until Sep 25. **Aug D:** M visits J. P. Becker in Geneva.

31. GERMAN MOVEMENT. **Aug 9:** In a letter to Bernstein, E promises to work on a German version of *Socialism: Utopian and scientific* (#E759). E also makes clear that Liebknecht has been misusing his (E's) letters by publishing parts of them without regard to circumstances (see #E3.5); hence Bernstein is no longer to let Liebknecht keep any copy of a letter by E.

32. NATIONALISM. **Aug 9:** In his letter to Bernstein (see ← :31), E criticizes the party press for being too uncritically favorable to the leadership of the Egyptian Nationalist party (Arabi Pasha); such nationalist leaders in peasant countries usually fight imperialist exploitation in order to substitute their own exploitation; we can take sides with the oppressed fellahin without sharing their illusions, and can support their military struggle against the "English brutalities" without declaring our (political) solidarity with temporary military leaders.

33. PERSONAL (E). **Aug 11 to Sep 8:** E sojourns in Great Yarmouth. **Aug 20:** In a letter to a nephew, E makes clear that business matters are to be addressed to his friend, the barrister Sam Moore, a "model Englishman, with all the good characteristics of his nation without a single bad one."

SEPTEMBER

34. MARX'S TRAVELS. **Sep:** M, accompanied by his daughter Laura, stays in Vevey, Aug 27 to Sep 25. For M's talks with Laura here, see her account in a letter to E, June 20, 1883. **Sep c.2:** M is visited by the pres of the Paris city council, Songeon, who had been a revolutionary refugee in London in 1849–50. **Sep 16:** M is shocked by the (false) newspaper report of the death of Bebel, whom

he calls "a unique phenomenon in the German, indeed the European, working class." **Sep 26–27:** On the way to France, M stops off in Geneva to see J. P. Becker. **Sep 28 to Oct A:** M spends a few days with the Longuets in Argenteuil, before returning to London. During this time he visits Paris a few times. **Sep 30:** Writing to E, M remarks that if the police knew he was in France, he would be in trouble from both socialist congresses taking place at that moment—both the "Marxist" and the "anti-Marxist," he explains (that is, the Guesdist and Possibilist).

35. PERSONAL. **Sep 16:** Jenny (Marx) Longuet gives birth to her first daughter, Jenny (called Mémé)—M's first granddaughter.

36. COLONIALISM. **Sep 12:** In a delayed reply to Kautsky's inquiry [← :20], E discusses the colonial policy of a socialist government: independence as soon as possible; we "can force no blessings" on a foreign nation without undermining our own victory.

37. GERMAN MOVEMENT. **Sep 13:** E considers Bernstein's proposal for a preface to *Socialism: Utopian and scientific* (#E759) dealing with "Bismarckian socialism," but thinks it too long a subject to cover in a preface. He proposes to do a series of articles on it, each independent in itself, later pubd as a brochure: Part 1 on Bismarckian socialism (articles on tariffs, railway statification, tobacco monopoly, workers' insurance laws); Part 2 on Lassallean state-socialistic nostrums: more important than Part 1. He asks Bernstein to send relevant material [→ 83:7]. Finally, E again inveighs against the intellectual element in the party leadership, which believes that the workers must not emancipate themselves but be emancipated by them.

38. W&P (E). **Sep A:** E does a German verse translation of the English ballad "The vicar of Bray," with a commentary to point up its political meaning for Germany (#E886); pubd in *Sozialdemokrat* Sep 7, where it arouses much interest. **Sep 14–21:** E prepares the German text of the first German edn of his *Socialism: Utopian and scientific* (#E759), and writes a preface for it (#E760). (The pamphlet will be printed in 1882 but not pubd until next Mar.) —E decides to add a special supplement "The mark" (#E468), on the early form of German land ownership and communal organizn, directed to the rural working classes [→ :51]. **Sep CD to Dec AB:** In connection with his work on "The mark," E rereads books by Maurer, *Einleitung zur Geschichte der Mark-, Hof-, Dorf- und Stadt-Verfassung und der öffentlichen Gewalt*, and *Geschichte der Dorfverfassung in Deutschland*, on which he makes notes and excerpts; he compares Maurer with other sources [→ :51].

OCTOBER

39. MARX: BACK IN ENGLAND. **Oct A:** M returns to London from Argenteuil [← :34]. **Oct M to Oct D:** M stays in London for about three weeks. He has some visitors: Loria (Oct M or somewhat later), Alessandro Oldrini (Oct 21). **Oct 27:** On M's behalf, E writes Bernstein asking for material on Swiss and German factory legislation needed for M's work on the third German edn of *Capital*, Vol. 1; M promises to write on the subject for the *Sozialdemokrat* (but will not do so). **Oct 30:** M goes to Ventnor (Isle of Wight); despite the onset of a cold and limited working time, he devotes himself to the third edn of *Capital*. He is visited by Eleanor M and by the Longuets' boy Jean (Johnny). **c.Oct-Nov:** M studies the history of early societies, esp notes and excerpts on Lubbock's *Origin of civilisation* (#M568, latest of M's "ethnological notebooks"). He also makes notes on articles on Egypt: M. G. Mulhall, in *Contemporary Rev*; W. S. Blunt, in *Nineteenth Century*.

40. FRENCH SPLIT. **Oct 20:** E gives Bernstein his view of the definitive split in the French party (Sep 25, at Saint-Etienne Congress), in which the Malon–Brousse "Possibilists" have formed their own right-wing party. E stresses Malon's background in Bakuninist tactics, which "justify any means—lies, calumny, secret intrigues" to rule or ruin a movement; every workers' party develops only through internal struggle. **Oct 28:** Further on the French split, to Bebel, E says the issue is the class character of the party, which the Possibilists want to sacrifice for votes: "Unity is a good thing as long as it works, but there are things that stand above unity. And when, like M and myself, all our lives long, one has done more fighting against self-styled socialists than against anyone else (for we regarded the bourgeoisie only as a *class* and almost never got into individual fights with bourgeois), one can't be very grieved that the unavoidable struggle has broken out." **Oct 30:** E urges Lafargue to keep Bernstein informed, for the *Sozialdemokrat*: "Do remember from time to time that Paris is no longer the capital of the world (which has no capital any more). . . ." —During the next few days E arranges a regular exchange of papers between the French and German party editors.

41. ENGLISH AFFAIRS. **Oct 27:** Writing to Bernstein, E advises caution about articles by the *Sozialdemokrat*'s London correspondent, Garcia, who is associated with the Hyndman group, "a little clique which for 20 years, under various names and forms, has remained the same nullity," while posing as an important party. E himself has recently refused to give a talk at Garcia's branch.

42. W&P. **Oct D:** E writes an article for *Sozialdemokrat*, "How Pindter tells fibs" (#E361), on the antisocialist slanders of a Bismarckian organ, *Norddeutsche Allgemeine Ztg*; pubd Nov 2.

NOVEMBER

43. FRENCH MOVEMENT. **Nov 3:** Writing to Bernstein in a critical vein about the leadership of the French party (Guesde, Lafargue, etc.), E for the first time mentions a quip made by M (destined for fame): "What's certain is that *I* am no Marxist." **Nov 4, 28:** E sends Bernstein lengthy letters on the antics going on in the French movement, esp since Bernstein (as editor) is bombarded by letters from pro-Possibilists. E's Nov 28 letter deals esp with Malon's distorted history of the French movement. **Nov 11:** M&E exchange letters on the French doings, critical of Guesde and Lafargue for their many mistakes and ineptness and Lafargue's propensity for "childish braggadocio" and verbal revolutionism. (There are similar passages in other M–E letters this month.)

44. GERMAN MOVEMENT. **Nov 4:** Discussing the Bernstein–Vollmar plan to launch a discussion for a new party program, E tells Bernstein this is tactically untimely, as long as the Anti-Socialist Law is still in force, since only the right wing can propagandize legally now. **Nov 14:** In a letter to E, Bebel discusses how the downfall of the Anti-Socialist Law may come about; he can see only two possibilities: either an economic crisis or a European war, the second being unlikely because the powers know it means a European revolution [→ :50].

45. DIALECTICS OF NATURE. **Nov 11:** Kautsky asks E to write an article on Darwin for the forthcoming first number of the party's new theoretical organ, *Neue Zeit*. **Nov 15:** E telegraphs "Impossible," and writes that he has to finish his "big work" (*Dialectics of nature*, #E221) before age overtakes him, despite the press of international correspondence; hence he must limit his journalistic articles to urgent ones only. **Nov 23:** In a letter to M, E likewise mentions that "I must finish the *Dialectics of nature* quickly."

46. W&P. **Nov 2:** *Sozialdemokrat* pubs E's article on Pindter (#E361) [← :42].

47. SCIENCE AND MATH. **Nov 8:** Writing to E, M again [← 81:62] brings up his interest in Deprez's experiments in electric power transmission; he is again trying to get literature on the subject, promised by Longuet. He reads i.a. two books by Hospitalier. **Nov 21:** E sends M a study by Sam Moore on the differential calculus and algebra. **Nov 22:** M, in reply, discusses i.a. the different approaches to calculus: mystical (Newton, Leibniz), rationalist (d'Alembert, Euler), algebraic (Lagrange).

48. RUSSIAN STUDIES. **Nov D:** M reads V. Vorontsev's book on "The fate of capitalism in Russia" (in Russian).

49. MARX IN VENTNOR. **Nov-Dec:** M remains in Ventnor [← :39] until Jan 12.

DECEMBER

50. GERMAN MOVEMENT. **Dec 4, 22:** M&E discuss Bebel's view on the fate of the Anti-Socialist Law [← :44]. M (Dec 4) doubts that an economic crisis can come soon. E writes Bebel (Dec 22) on the various possibilities (incl Bismarck's "death or departure") short of war or crisis; discusses the possibilities of a crisis; and in response to Bebel's simplistic equation of war with revolution, stresses that a European war would be a misfortune, to begin with. **Dec 8:** Writing to E, M opines that *Sozialdemokrat* should provide "*detailed material* on the treatment of workers in Prussian state mines, etc., in order to show up the Wagener-Bismarckian state-socialism."

51. ENGELS' "THE MARK." **Dec AB:** For this essay (#E468) [← :38] E pursues further research on early society, esp in Bancroft's histories and Maurer's works. He tells M (Dec 8) he has rewritten it two or three times and will send it for M's perusal. **Dec 15:** E sends his last draft to M; he stresses his view on a "second serfdom" reintroduced in the mid-15th century, and its meaning for German history. **Dec 16:** E, evidently concerned about M's reaction, continues his discussion about the history of serfdom and his view of its near-disappearance in the 13th or 14th century before the "second edition" of serfdom in the 15th. **Dec 18:** M returns the ms with the sole comment "Very good!" (E demurs as to the praise, Dec 19). **Dec 20:** E sends the ms to Zurich for publ in the German edn of *Socialism: Utopian and scientific*

(#E759) (re publ, see ← :38). **Dec 22:** E tells M he is glad they agree; in his view "serfdom or bondage is not a peculiarly medieval-feudal form" but arises regularly wherever conquerors let a conquered people cultivate the land for them. —Writing to Bebel, E observes that this essay is the "first fruit" of his years-long study of German history.

52. *CAPITAL* AND *POLIT ECO.* **Dec 4:** M mentions to E a controversy over his theory of value which is raging in *La Plebe* (Oct-Nov), in articles by R. Candelari, Malon, and Cafiero; M's comment is that they are all talking nonsense. **Dec 14:** M refers with gratification to recent evidence of his influence in Russia, and comments (in his own English), "Nowhere my success is to me more delightful."

53. OPINIONS. **Dec 16:** Writing to J. P. Becker, E comments on the anarchist sects as "pure pretence and public fakery" which harms only workers who take them seriously. **Dec 19, 22:** Writing to M, E criticizes an essay by S. Podolinsky in *La Plebe* of 1881 (to be reprinted in *Neue Zeit* in 1883) which purports to demonstrate that physical forces themselves (like solar energy) bespeak the truth of socialism. E thinks Podolinsky is confusing physics and economics.

54. PERSONAL. **Dec:** M remains in Ventnor [← :39; → 83:3].

YEAR APPENDIX

55. Regarding M's reading of "the latest literature on socioeconomic relations in Russia," dated Jan to Dec, *MEW Daten* mentions works by V. I. Semevsky, A. A. Isayev, G. Mineyko, and V. P. Vorontsev. *KMC* lists some of these for c.Jan, specif on Russian agrarian relations, and adds A. Skrebitzky and A. Engelhardt.

56. On Egypt and other subjects, *KMC* lists books by Keay, "Peter the Hermit," and Brousse; also *Diplomatic Fly-Sheets* (reprinted from *Vanity Fair*), and articles in the *North American Rev.*

1883

CONSPECTUS

1. The death of Marx drastically changes Engels' priorities; above all, E drops his sporadic work on *Dialectics of nature* (#E221) to devote himself to sorting out and preparing M's literary remains and, in particular, finishing *Capital* from M's mss and notes. His immediate task is to see the third German edn of Vol. 1 through the press; this occupies E into Oct (*MEW* gives the dates June to Oct M). For E's work on M's mss of *Capital* and his

correspondence, *MEW* gives the dates May to Dec. For the date of publ of the third German edn, see → 84:2.

JANUARY

2. DEATH OF JENNY LONGUET. **Jan A:** Although M's daughter Jenny has been very ill since last Apr—in pain from a bladder disease (perhaps cancer), increasingly worn out by household work, beset by money troubles, and disheartened by family problems—it is only now that Laura and Paul Lafargue realize that her condition is critical. **Jan 10:** On the basis of a letter from Lafargue (to E, Jan 6) M believes Jenny is improving. **Jan 11:** Jenny dies, about 5 P.M., at home in Argenteuil. **Jan 13:** Her funeral is attended by many French socialists and representatives of foreign socialist papers. —E writes an obituary (#E398) for *Sozialdemokrat*; pubd Jan 18.

3. MARX'S ILLNESS. Jan 9–10: The last exchange of letters between M&E (E on Jan 9, M on Jan 10) deals i.a. with Hepner's insistence (Dec 14) on getting a new preface for a US edn of the *Com Manifesto*, which they decline to do. **Jan 10:** M's letter of this date to E and one to Eleanor are his last (known) letters. Although M thinks Jenny's condition has improved (see ← :2), he reports that Jenny's danger has worsened his own "nervous upset." His last words to E are that "I think that I can soon get back on the track with patience and meticulous self-control." **Jan 12:** On hearing of Jenny's death, M returns to London from Ventnor; his health begins to deteriorate visibly. **Jan M:** M develops a case of bronchitis and laryngitis which makes speaking and swallowing difficult.

4. POLITICAL AFFAIRS. Jan 5: Tullio Martello (in Venice) sends M his work on the economics of money. **Jan 9:** In a letter to Eleanor (his next to last) M sharply denounces a speech by English Radical M. P. Joseph Cowen (Jan 8, Newcastle) which justifies England's conquest of Egypt and its repression of the nationalist movement.

5. GERMAN MOVEMENT. Jan 18: Continuing his indoctrination of *Sozialdemokrat* editor Bernstein in the sins of the right wing, E counsels (apropos of the Reichstag discussion on renewal of the Anti-Socialist Law) that the socialists should always aggressively attack the government, not "wail that we are revolutionaries only in a Pickwickian sense," as the opportunists do. They should say that the whole Reichstag is the result of a revolution: "all legality . . . is nothing more than the product of countless revolutions made against the will of the people. . . ."

FEBRUARY

6. MARX'S ILLNESS. Feb: While M's bronchitis-laryngitis may be improving, he develops a lung abscess. **Feb 8:** E reports (to Bernstein) that Ventnor's constant rain has hurt M's health, already hard hit by Jenny's death; during the three weeks since his return he has been able to speak only a little; the third German edn of *Capital* will be

delayed. **Feb 16/17:** E reports (to Laura) that M has somewhat improved, signalized by his reading novels (e.g., Frédéric Soulié) instead of publishers' catalogs; he has even begun to drink milk, which he could never stand even to see. **Feb 27/Mar 1:** In his letter to Bernstein, E reports that M is still reading French novels.

7. GERMAN MOVEMENT. Feb 8: E tells Bernstein he thinks sympathy for Bismarckian state socialism is dying down, making unnecessary the brochure [← 82:37] he was planning to do; but its projected Part 2 on Lassalleanism is still needed. —Against the demand for a stock exchange tax as an economic panacea, E discusses the role of the stock exchange in the concentration of capital. (He continues this subject in his letter of Feb 10.) **Feb 27:** E informs Bernstein about a "swinish" trick perpetrated by Viereck on E's old friend Prof. Schorlemmer, involuntarily involving E, an affair which compels him to break personally with Viereck. (More on this in E's letter of Feb 27/Mar 1.) **Feb 28** (in letter of Feb 27/Mar 1): E objects to being called "Genosse" (comrade) in *Sozialdemokrat* on the ground it implies he is a member of the German party, whereas "we" (M&E) belong to no single national party but rather are representatives of international socialism. —E repeats his criticism of Liebknecht as one who pampers bourgeois-minded intellectuals joining the party for their own reasons; but one must combat the traditional German tendency to philistine petty-bourgeois servility, which is endemic to intellectuals and esp to student elements washed out by examinations.

8. CRITIQUES OF KAUTSKY. Feb 8: Writing to Bernstein, E remarks that Kautsky has sent his recent essay on "overseas food competition," in which he argues that America produces more food than Europe and America can consume; this refutes his 1880 book [← 81:9] where he defended the Malthusian thesis. **Feb 10:** E writes the same criticism to Kautsky; he adds that the rejection of Malthusian ideology does not impugn the use of birth-control methods for economic or health reasons—in fact, "I myself have recommended what you call the 'Raciborski method'. . . ." —In this letter E also criticizes the first of a series of articles by Kautsky on "The origin of marriage and the family" in *Kosmos* (Stuttgart), which maintains that monogamy has always existed, motivated by "jealousy" (i.e., motivated psychologically) [→ :10].

9. VERSE TRANSLATION. Feb 16/17: E gives Laura (Marx) Lafargue a detailed critique of the English trans she has made of a German poem by Chamisso.

MARCH

10. German Movement. Mar: The first German edn of E's *Socialism: Utopian and scientific* (#E759) is pubd as a brochure (imprinted 1882) [→ :41]. **Mar 1:** In his letter to Bernstein of Feb 27/Mar 1, E stresses that the application of electrical energy to industry [← 82:47] is "enormously revolutionary," in expanding productive forces, abolishing the town/country antithesis, etc. **Mar 2:** Responding to Kautsky's second article on marriage and the family [← :8] in which he has somewhat modified his position, E returns to the attack with a further refutation. **Mar 7:** Writing to Bebel, E compares the Bismarckian era in Germany with the course of Bonaparte's Second Empire in France.

11. Death of Marx. Mar 7: In his letter to Bebel, E reports that M's health is still not improving, as stormy weather hangs on. **Mar 10:** To Laura, E reports that Dr. Donkin, as of yesterday, thinks M is better than a fortnight ago, though still getting weaker. **Mar 14:** M dies, at his home, about 2:45 or near 3 P.M.—after a sudden collapse of strength in the morning, "then simply a falling asleep" (E). —E devotes the afternoon and evening to sending out letters, telegrams, cables of notification, incl a telegram to Bebel's home (where Mrs. Bebel receives it) and letters to Bernstein and Liebknecht; cables to Sorge (in the US) and the *New Yorker Volkszeitung* (where it is pubd Mar 15—cf #E860); telegram to Longuet; et al. **Mar 15:** E sends letters on M's death to Sorge (with a summary of M's health problem since 1881: "Mankind is shorter by a head"); also to J. P. Becker and Lessner. **Mar 16:** E sends a telegram (#E860) to the *New Yorker Volkszeitung* with details on M's death, which is, however, rewritten and garbled by the editors when they publish it Mar 17 [→ :16].

12. Funeral and Memorials. Mar 17: M is buried in Highgate Cemetery, London, with his wife, in a small grave marked by a flat stone. At the funeral, which begins about noon, E gives the main speech (#E317; draft, #E230). Lemke lays two wreaths, for the *Sozialdemokrat* staff and for the London GWEA; then E gives his speech; Longuet reads messages in French from Lavrov for the Russian socialists, Lépine for the Paris branch of the French WP, Mesa for the Spanish party; Liebknecht speaks in German. Other persons present: Eleanor M, Paul Lafargue, Lessner, Lochner, Aveling, Schorlemmer, E. R. Lankester, Ernest Radford —The august London *Times* pubs a short notice of M's death, beginning "Our Paris correspondent informs us ..." with a factual error in every sentence. **Mar c.18:** E writes an account of

the funeral for the *Sozialdemokrat*, incl the text of his own speech (#E317); pubd Mar 22. **Mar 18:** A memorial meeting in the Brooklyn Labor Lyceum is addressed by A. Douai and C. Pattberg; in Cleveland a memorial speech on M is made at the Paris Commune commemoration meeting. **Mar 20:** A memorial meeting at Cooper Union, New York City, sees a packed house with thousands turned away; it is sponsored by the Central Labor Union of the city; speeches are made in several languages, by Swinton, Douai, J. Most, et al, with P. J. McGuire in the chair; a letter is read from Henry George. —Eleanor M receives a telegram, sending a wreath for the grave, from the students of the Petrovskoe Academy, Moscow. **Mar 25:** A memorial meeting is held in Chicago by the SLP, with speakers Paul Ehmann and J. Vahlteich. **Mar 31:** Lavrov (in Paris) sends money for a wreath on behalf of other Russian student groups.

13. Grandson Dies. Mar 21: M's grandson, Harry (Henri) Longuet, dies at the age of four and a half [← 78:27]. (He will be buried in the M family grave.)

14. "Moor." Mar 16 (rec'd c.29): Cuno (in the US) writes E to verify that M's nickname was "Moor" (*Mohr*), since Hepner insists this is untrue and would harm the party. (The unstated reason is that *Mohr* more or less equals "nigger.") **Mar 29:** E assures Cuno that M has been called *Mohr* (or *Der Mohr*), since university days, by family and close friends, never "Karl" or "Marx."

15. Capital. Mar 25: Among M's papers, Helene Demuth finds his ms of over 500 pages for Vol. 2 [→ :17].

APRIL

16. Death of Marx: Follow-up. Apr CD: Students of Odessa ask *Sozialdemokrat* to have a wreath laid on M's grave in their name. **Apr 18:** E writes the *New Yorker Volkszeitung* correcting the distorted facts in its version of his cable [← :11]. **Apr 28:** E sends *Sozialdemokrat* the first part of his article "On the death of KM" (#E551); pubd May 3. **Apr 30:** E writes Bebel, re proposals for a memorial stone, that the M family is strongly opposed to any monument on the grave.

17. Capital. Apr: E interrupts other work [← :1] to begin his labors on M's mss and papers; he examines the material left by M for *Capital* (what is now Vols. 2 and 3). **Apr 2:** Writing to Lavrov, E reports he has now [← :15] found about 1000 pages of ms for Vols. 2 and 3, all in M's first draft. "It is a question above all of a sketch on dialectics which he always wanted to do." (E also reports this to Bernstein, Nieuwenhuis, et al.) **Apr D:** Having received from Loria his latest essay on M, E hauls him over the coals for his slanderous statements alleging dishonesty by M, without the least evidence. (E inserts this letter exposing Loria into his article in *Sozialdemokrat*, #E551; and he will return to Loria in his preface to *Capital*, Vol. 3, #E606.) **Apr 30:** Writing to Bebel, E says of Vol. 2 that the ms was written before 1873, as shown by its German-alphabet handwriting (← 73:5) and prob before 1870.

18. A CASE OF CHUTZPAH. Apr 7: James Knowles, editor of *Nineteenth Century*, writes E requesting him to furnish Knowles with a condensed presentation of *Capital* in English so that he can write an article on *Capital* in his magazine. **Apr 17:** E replies that this is an unusual request, and suggests Knowles might read *Capital* if he wants to write on it; he also mentions that in 1878 [← 78:25] Knowles's magazine had pubd Howell's slander but refused to publish M's reply (#M520), and remarks that in general English reviewers had garbled and falsified M's views and actions. However, he suggests Samuel Moore as a knowledgeable writer on *Capital*, and mentions the existence of his own synopsis (#E799). **Apr 18:** Knowles expresses interest in publishing E's synopsis under certain conditions (as part of an article by another). **Apr 20:** E replies he will consider conditions when the synopsis is found (it is among M's papers). E also informs Knowles he is not "Dr. Engels" but a retired cotton manufacturer.

19. OTHER WRITINGS BY MARX. Apr 11: Writing to Laura (M) Lafargue, E says he is willing to cooperate on a French trans of the *Com Manifesto* with a Russian woman named Nikitina suggested by Laura; but "it's no child's play, you know." **Apr 24:** To Sorge, who wanted (Mar 19) permission to publish excerpts from M's letters on Henry George, E replies that it would be better to wait till he prepares for publ M's marginal notes on George's book *The Irish land question*, and publish it all together (these notes are still unpubd) [→ :27]. **Apr 30:** Writing to Bebel about Liebknecht's idea of a collected edn (*Gesamtausgabe*) of M's writings, E points out it would have to appear outside of Germany.

20. POLITICAL AFFAIRS. Apr 2: P. Van Patten, secy of the Central Labor Union of NY, writes E that J. Most is claiming to be M's disciple; he asks about M's views on anarchism. (Most's speech at Cooper Union [← :12] was in this vein.) **Apr 18:** E replies with a concise critique of anarchism; he explains M's opposition to Bakunin and the falsity of Most's pretensions. (E pubs his letter as part of #E551.) **Apr 30:** In response to Bebel's query (Mar 17) whether now, after M's death, E would return to Germany and work in the

movement, E gives several reasons for staying in England.

21. ENGELS-VS-MARX MYTH. Apr 23: Writing to Bernstein, E makes a wry reference to recent attacks on M&E by the French Possibilist Paul Brousse: "Innumerable times since 1844, the bit about the evil Engels who corrupted the good Marx has alternated with the other bit about Ahriman-Marx who seduced Ormuzd-Engels from the path of virtue."

22. POLITENESS. Apr 28: For the first time (after almost four years of correspondence) E addresses the *Sozialdemokrat* editor as "Dear Bernstein" instead of "Dear Mr. Bernstein," saying, "I think we should put aside the tedious *Herr*" (cf E on "Genosse"; ← :7) [→ 84:8].

MAY

23. GERMAN MOVEMENT. May 10/11: In a confidential letter to Bebel, E reviews the leaders of the party right wing, plus a longer portrait of Liebknecht's weaknesses as party leader. E states he will break with the party if the Reichstag Fraction permits any deputy to vote for the Bismarckian legislative program of state socialism; a split in the party would be unfortunate but may be necessary. **May 22:** Writing to J. P. Becker, E gives a rather optimistic account of the new "splendid young fellows" in the German party now, since (he says, optimistically) the Anti-Socialist Law got rid of the intellectuals who want to "schoolmaster the workers from the top down, with their ignorant university-type confusion. . . ."

24. CAPITAL, ETC. May 10: E writes Liebknecht on the legal and other circumstances for the third German edn of Vol. 1 and for a new edn of E's *Condition of the working class* (#E171). **May 22:** To Laura Lafargue, E describes the problem posed by the mss for *Capital*, Book 2, as left by M; he suggests he can put together a third vol. from the 1858–62 mss. Sam Moore (who has been visiting E in London, until May 21) has discovered that unauthorized translations of Vol. 1 cannot be stopped. E is busy with preparing to incorporate into the third German edn of Vol. 1 those changes from the French edn "which I know Mohr [M] intended inserting. . . ." E has also been sorting out the letters of 1841–62. —In a letter to J. P. Becker, E repeats some of this. He adds he is surprised that M saved almost all papers, letters, mss "even from pre-1848 days"—material basic to the biography of M that E intends to write as well as to histories of the *NRZ*, the 1848–49 Rhenish movement, the IWMA, etc.

25. W&P. May 3: *Sozialdemokrat* pubs

the first part of #E551 [← :20]. **May 12:** E writes the second part; pubd May 17. **May D:** E, having found in M's papers a poem by G. Weerth, writes an article in memory of Weerth to go with its publ in *Sozialdemokrat* (#E327); pubd June 7.

JUNE

26. *CAPITAL.* **June 2:** E reports (to Laura Lafargue) that Kegan Paul & Co may publish an English edn of Vol. 1; Sam Moore to translate. **June AB:** E negotiates with Kegan Paul (SOURCE: *MEW Daten*). **June 12–29:** In a number of letters E gives some account of the mss left by M and the enormous labor they will require, in the first place to do the forthcoming third German edn of Vol. 1, plus further vols. of *Capital*; this in letters to Bernstein, Laura Lafargue, and Sorge. To Sorge (June 29) E writes that M rewrote the beginning of Vol. 2 at least four times from before 1870 to 1878.

27. MARX'S PAPERS. **June:** Much of E's correspondence is about material in and problems about M's papers, mss, etc. (literary remains, *Nachlass*). **June 2:** E tells Laura Lafargue of finding the ms of a "sassy" pre-1848 work—meaning the *German ideology* (#ME66)—which he rereads with great pleasure. **June 12:** In a letter to Bernstein, E reports that he has enjoyed rereading the M–E letters of 1841–62; E himself has M's letters only since 1849. —E sends, as a gift, an original page of the draft for the *Com Manifesto* (see #ME35) discovered in M's papers. —In a June 13 postscript, E mentions the newfound *German ideology* and suggests publ of a part of it in the *Sozialdemokrat* feuilleton. (He repeats this suggestion on June 22, but on Aug 27 says the suggestion is jocular.) **June 20, 24:** In an exchange of letters with E, Laura gives an account of M's conversations with her in Vevey in 1882 [← 82:30] about plans for disposal of his research papers; M had talked i.a. of turning the IWMA material over to Laura. E says he is willing to do so, although it would be vital to his planned biography of M. **June 29:** In a letter to Sorge, E reviews the situation concerning M's mss. He reverses his opinion [← :19] about publishing M's letters on Henry George immediately, without waiting for the marginal notes on George's book.

28. MATHEMATICAL MSS. **June 20:** The importance M assigned to his mathematical studies is attested by Laura Lafargue's account (see ← :27) of M's conversations in Vevey; she stresses two of his greatest concerns: "his work in mathematics and his forthcoming third German edn of *Capital*." **June 24:** E mentions (to Laura) that M, in talking to

Eleanor about being a literary executor, mentioned two things in particular: Vol. 2 of *Capital* and his mathematical studies. **June 29:** Writing to Sorge, E mentions that M's math studies are in "three-four notebooks"; "I once showed your [son] Adolph an example of M's new foundation for the differential calculus."

29. W&P. **June 7:** *Sozialdemokrat* pubs E's article on Weerth (#E327) along with Weerth's poem. **June 12:** E sends Bernstein another poem by Weerth he has just found in M's papers. (It will be pubd in *Sozialdemokrat* on July 12.) **June 12, 19:** Martignetti sends E the ms of his Italian trans of *Socialism: Utopian and scientific* (#E759), made from the French version. E sends him corrections and additions based on the fuller German edn. (The Italian edn will be pubd in Benevento in July.) **June 28:** E writes a new preface for a new German edn, to be pubd in Zurich, of the *Com Manifesto* (#E612) [→ :31].

30. GERMAN MOVEMENT. **June 12:** In his letter to Bernstein, i.a., E reemphasizes that a split with the right wing is inevitable, though not preferable while the Anti-Socialist Law is still in force unless *they* reject party discipline (in which case a split could take place now). —Discussing the difficulties faced by Bismarck, E inserts a denunciation of the Lassallean phrase "one reactionary mass."

JULY

31. W&P. **July:** The "third authorized edn" of the *Com Manifesto* is pubd in Zurich with a new preface by E (#E612), in a press run of 10,000; this is the first edn produced by the German party for general distribution. — Possibly this month, E works on his article on "The Book of Revelation" (#E93); see → :35. **July 30:** Martignetti [← :29] informs E that 12 copies of the Italian edn of *Socialism: Utopian and scientific* (#E759) are on the way.

AUGUST

32. GERMAN MOVEMENT. **Aug 27:** E tells Bernstein that the *Sozialdemokrat*'s handling of the question of the republic in France (defense of the republic against monarchist restoration) is "not clear." E stresses the importance of the democratic republican state as the arena of class struggle. **Aug 30:** Writing to Bebel—who on June 29 was elected to the Reichstag in a Hamburg by-election—E showers praises on the principled character of the electoral campaign carried on.

33. ENGLISH AFFAIRS. **Aug 30:** In his letter to Bebel, E criticizes the manifesto

"Socialism made plain" of Hyndman's Democratic Federation: though the group has perforce adopted "our theoretical program," Hyndman is a chauvinist careerist and there is no real proletarian movement in England—only "confused sects." The workers will start moving as a class when England's "world monopoly" is broken.

34. *CAPITAL.* **Aug 10:** Deville sends E his ms of a popularized condensation of *Capital* [← 82:30] and asks his criticism. **Aug 11:** E finishes work on preparing the ms on the third German edn of Vol. 1 [→ :38]. **Aug 12:** E acknowledges receipt of Deville's ms and promises to go over it while in Eastbourne (see → :37, 38]. **Aug M:** E receives from Sam Moore the first part of his English trans of Vol. 1, and (Aug CD) begins editing it. (He will continue working on Moore's drafts, as Moore passes them on, for the next three years or so, along with other work.)

35. W&P. **Aug:** E's article on "The Book of Revelation" (#E93) is pubd in the Aug issue of *Progress* (London).

36. HOW TO LEARN A LANGUAGE. **Aug 22:** Responding to a query (June 25) from Martignetti [← :29] on how to learn German, E gives his general recipe: don't worry about grammar, but use a dictionary to read the most difficult classical author. E began Italian with Dante, Petrarch, and Ariosto; Spanish with Cervantes and Calderón; Russian with Pushkin; and for German one should start with Goethe's *Faust;* next: read newspapers, etc.

37. HOLIDAY. **Aug 17 to Sep 14:** E sojourns in Eastbourne.

SEPTEMBER

38. *CAPITAL.* **Sep 18:** Writing to Kautsky, E mentions that the largest part of Vol. 2 dates from before 1868. **Sep 19:** E reports (to Laura Lafargue) that he has just begun working on Deville's ms; that he will start work on Vol. 2 when finished with Deville; that he is now reading proofs of the third German edn and will be finished by Dec; and that Moore's specimen translations are encouraging [← :34]. **Sep CD:** E begins work on Vol. 2 [SOURCE: *MEW Daten*).

39. GERMAN MOVEMENT. **Sep 14:** Kautsky sends E a leaflet issued by party right-wingers raising the "right to work" as an independent slogan in a purely reformist way, and urges E to write an article for *Sozial-demokrat* combating this tendency. **Sep 18:** E declines to do so, partly for lack of time, partly for lack of close knowledge of the concrete situation, and partly out of reluctance to mix publicly into party affairs except in special cases [→ :46].

40. POLITICAL AFFAIRS. **Sep 18:** In his letter to Kautsky, E praises his *Neue Zeit* article on colonialism, esp "colonialism in the interest of stock exchange swindles" as in Tunisia and Tonkin by France and other recent cases. —E also makes some further remarks on Kautsky's series on marriage and the family [← :8, 10] and on the general problem of training people to produce good theoretical work. **Sep 19, 23:** Lopatin visits E; in conversation E opines that Russia is nearing a new social upheaval as the democratic revolution matures (Lopatin quotes him in a letter) [→ 93:26].

41. W&P. **Sep 19:** E reports (to Laura) on the German edn [← :10] of *Socialism: Utopian and scientific* (#E759): two edns have been exhausted, and a third is on the press [→ :44].

OCTOBER

42. *CAPITAL.* **Oct 3:** E sends Deville (via Laura Lafargue) the first 123 pages of the ms [← :38] with detailed criticisms (which are summarized in E's letter to Laura) [→ 84:3]. **Oct 15:** E reports he is working on the proofs of the third German edn. **Oct M:** Lessner writes E asking for some copies of Vol. 1 to disseminate among German workers in London.

43. RUSSIAN AFFAIRS. **Oct c.D to Nov A:** E gets a letter from Vera Zasulich about the formation of the Russian "Emancipation of Labor" group (Marxist) in Geneva; she sends its first programmatic statement, a flysheet on the publ of a "Library of modern socialism."

44. W&P. **c.Oct:** E prepares a new edn of "The mark" as a pamphlet directed to peasants, with a new title (see #E468B). **Oct:** A third German edn of *Socialism: Utopian and scientific* (#E759) is pubd [← :41]; it is the third since Mar.

45. ILLNESS. **Oct A to Dec 17:** E suffers an attack of rheumatism of the legs; he takes to bed Oct 10.

NOVEMBER

46. POLITICAL AFFAIRS. **Nov 8:** In a letter to Bernstein, E praises Bernstein's article of Oct 25 on the "right to work" issue [← :39]. —Re the "international" conference of right-wing elements held in Paris Oct 29 by the Possibilists, E denounces their alliance with "the betrayers of the English workers' movement, the official representatives of the trade unions."

47. *CAPITAL* AND OTHER WRITINGS. **Nov 7:** E writes the preface (#E603) to the third German edn of Vol. 1. **Nov 10:** Responding to E's inquiry (Nov 8) about a Max Quarck who offered to translate M's *Poverty of philosophy* (#M681), Bernstein says he would like to translate it himself. **Nov 13:** E gladly accepts Bernstein's proposal and makes arrangements to cooperate [→ :49]. —E thanks Zasulich, who had written letter of Oct/Nov) about plans for a Russian edn of Vol. 2 of *Capital*, had sent a Russian edn of M's *Wage-labor and capital* (#M968), and reported that a Russian edn of E's *Socialism: Utopian and scientific* (#E759) is on the press. However, E postpones decisions about a Russian edn of Vol. 2. He expresses the belief, in view of the tense situation in Russia, that possibly freedom of the press may be won in Russia sooner than in Germany.

48. PERSONAL. Nov: E remains confined to bed all this month [← :45]. **Nov 28:** E, celebrating his birthday, is visited by Kautsky, who has just come to England (until Dec A).

DECEMBER

49. W&P. Dec: E takes on the task of editing the German version of M's *Poverty of philosophy* (#M681) which is being translated by Bernstein and Kautsky [← :47; → 84:5]. —E sends the just-pubd edn of his *Socialism: Utopian and scientific* (#E759) [← :44] to Kovalevsky. **Dec 13:** E reports (to Laura Lafargue) that the third German edn of *Capital*, Vol. 1, is now "fully printed" and promises to send a copy. (Re its publ date, see → 84:2.)

50. PERSONAL. Dec 13: Writing to Laura, E reports he is still confined to bed but expects to be up soon. He has been reading mostly Balzac: "There is the history of France from 1815 to 1848. . . . And what boldness! what a revolutionary dialectic in his poetical justice!" **Dec 17:** E is allowed to get out of bed; convalescing.

1884

CONSPECTUS

1. From M's death to his own, E's activity centers on two tasks: (1) preparation of M's writings for publ—above all, the vols. of *Capital*, and also various edns of previously pubd writings, all of this entailing much work in editing, translating, revising, correcting proofs, etc.; and (2) a voluminous correspondence with socialist leaders and friends in a number of countries. In 1884, as later, E's attention is largely taken up by four countries: Germany, France, England, and the US; but increasingly, as national parties develop elsewhere, there will be more calls on his time. In addition there is the continual task of organizing the papers, mss, and letters left by M. This labor of sorting is dated Jan to Mar by MEW *Daten*, where it refers to a concentrated task, but in fact this work keeps going on. MEW *Daten* assigns the date Jan to Aug A to E's activity in following the course of the struggle inside the SDF (Hyndman's group) and then notes that Nov-Dec brought even more activity since the SDF finally split.

2. The date of publ of the third German edn of Vol. 1 of *Capital* seems to be uncertain. The imprint says 1883, and MEW says "winter," but it does not seem to have appeared in the "winter of 1883," which literally means Dec D. E's letters (cf Dec 13, 1883; and Jan 23, 28, Mar 7, 1884) indicate that the best guess for the date of publ is 1884: c.Feb. (MEW *Daten* has an entry for Feb A saying that the vol. "goes to press.")

JANUARY

3. CAPITAL. Jan 9: To Kautsky who wants (letter of Dec 29) to do a German version of Deville [← 83:42], E sends a critical evaluation of Deville's condensed *Capital* (which was pubd in 1883). E recommends doing a popularization of *Capital* that would be half the size and restrict itself to the theory of surplus value, not necessarily following M's chapters; suggested title "Unpaid labor and its transformation into capital," or something like that. (Kautsky will eventually take E's advice; cf his *Economic doctrines of KM*, 1887, in German.) [But → :11.] **Jan 28:** E gives permission for publ of a Polish trans of *Capital* to L. Krzywicki (Leipzig), who is editing a trans already made by a number of hands. (Its first part will appear later this year; cf → 90:1.) —Writing to Lavrov about his task with respect to M's mss, E stresses that he wants to publish further vols. so that they are "really a work by M," i.e., not rewritten by E. Of Vol. 2 he says that, for the major part, constituting the beginning and end, a version exists from 1875 and later; for the middle part, there are no fewer than four versions from before 1870 (cf E's statement to Sorge, June 29, 1883). As for most of Vol. 3, he says, there are two versions from before 1869.

4. GERMAN MOVEMENT. Jan 18: In a letter to Bebel, E says he is ready to publish an article in *Sozialdemokrat* on the "right to work" issue [← 83:39] if the party rightwingers offer an opportunity. "These good-for-nothing students, clerks, etc., are the curse of the movement. . . ." E also has great praise for Bebel's book *Woman and socialism*; in particular E discusses the book's views on the industrial development of Germany.

5. POLITICAL AFFAIRS. Jan 1: E replies to queries by Bernstein: he will add a note to the German edn of M's *Poverty of philosophy* (#M681) on the economics of American slavery (cf *MEW* 4:132); and he expounds the passage in the *Manifesto* preface (#ME36) about the lesson of the Paris Commune on the state, i.e., the revolutionary need to smash and recast the state machine. **Jan 28:** Writing to Bernstein, E provides an answer to a *New Yorker Volkszeitung* article (Jan 3) which claimed that M made "concessions" to anarchism by coming out for the dying away of the state and the end of (class) rule in society. E advises Bernstein to anticipate quoters by himself citing two passages in M: one from *Poverty of philosophy* (#M681) (cf *MEW* 4:182) and another from the *Com Manifesto* (cf *MEW* 4:482).

6. ENGLISH MOVEMENT. Jan 1: E reports (to Bernstein) that two periodicals have switched to socialism, *To-Day* and *Progress*; he characterizes some of the figures involved (Bax, Aveling, Joynes, Hyndman). **Jan 25:** Charles Fitzgerald, editor of Hyndman's new organ *Justice*, asks E to write for it. **Jan c.26–28:** E declines politely, citing lack of time. (E explains his real thought in a letter of Jan 28 to Bernstein.)

7. MARX'S LIBRARY. Jan 28: E tells Lavrov that after sorting out M's collection of Russian books, he and Eleanor M want to donate most of it to the Russian émigré library [→ :16].

8. POLITENESS. Jan 9: E proposes to Kautsky to stop "bothering with the *Herr*," i.e., using the salutation "Dear Kautsky" (cf ← 83:22).

9. GERMAN TASTE. Jan 7: Paul Lafargue writes E: "You have always sneered at German taste and their 'nasty goods,' " well, the French now admire German toys and other imported products. **Jan 14:** E explains the superiority of German toys: besides their cheapness, "they are invented by *peasants;* townspeople will never be fit to invent for children, least of all French townspeople who hate their own children"; bourgeois taste is so bad even the Germans can satisfy it.

10. PERSONAL. Jan 1: E writes that he expects to be back at work in a week. Eleanor M writes that E looked well on New Year's Day.

FEBRUARY

11. *CAPITAL.* Feb (prob date): The third German edn of Vol. 1 [← :2] is pubd in Ham-

burg. **Feb 2:** Kautsky informs E that he and Bernstein will translate the Deville condensation [← :3]; he wants E to check it over before publ. **Feb 4:** E replies he is willing to do this for the theoretical part only. As for the descriptive part, Deville's main fault is that "he poses M's propositions as absolute, whereas in M they hold only under conditions which Deville omits, and hence come out false." (E comments along the same lines to Lavrov, Feb 5; for further comment on Deville, see E to Lafargue, Aug 11.) **Feb 5:** E confesses (to Lavrov) how worried he is about the task of doing Vol. 2, which he cannot begin before Mar M, because of the sorting-out labor still to be done. This oppresses him because he is "the only person alive" who can decipher M's handwriting. **Feb 16:** Writing to Laura Lafargue, E reports he has found the "first version" of *Capital*, i.e., notebooks of 1861–63, and several hundred pages on the theories of surplus value, which may make a Vol. 3. (He also reports this to Kautsky, same day.) (In *MEW Daten*, E's study of these mss is dated Feb to Mar.)

12. OTHER WRITINGS BY MARX. Feb 5: In response to Lavrov's query (Jan 30) about unavailable writings by M (e.g., his #M148), E discusses some of his difficulties in trying to make these available. He points out he has nearly a thousand book pages worth of old mss (by M&E) from 1845–48; re #M148, he possesses only two numbers of the *NRZ-Revue* and is looking for the rest. **Feb 16:** E reports (to Kautsky) that he has found M's notes on L. H. Morgan's *Ancient society* (#M570), and remembers how enthusiastically M praised the work, which E has not yet obtained. He would like to do an article on it, but not now [→ :21]. **Feb 21:** Having received from Bernstein (by request of Feb 5) a copy of M's 1865 letter on Proudhon (#M593), E has immediately translated it into French, for the planned new French edn of M's *Poverty of philosophy* (#M681)—so he reports to Laura Lafargue. (E's trans will be ed by Lafargue and pubd in the edition, which however will not in fact appear until 1896.) **Feb D to Mar A:** E reads Morgan's book and is further spurred to write it up along the lines contemplated by M.

13. W&P. Feb 14: Kautsky writes E about the new vogue in Germany for counterposing Rodbertus against M. **Feb 16:** E replies that he is writing a preface to a new French edn of M's *Poverty of philosophy* (#M681) where he will take up the "Rodbertus myth"; he summarizes its contents. (Actually, this discussion will be pubd in E's preface, #E608, to the first German edn of *Poverty of philosophy;* see → :53.) **Feb M to Mar A:** E writes an article for the first anniversary of M's death, "M and the *NRZ*" (#E469) [→ :19].

14. GERMAN MOVEMENT. **Feb 14:** E sends J. P. Becker an optimistic report on party progress in Germany, with emphasis on the revolutionary training of the rank and file in the struggle with the police. **Feb 16:** In his letter to Kautsky, E points to J. W. B. Money's 1861 book on Java and its Dutch colonial regime as an analogue of Bismarckian state socialism, to be used in propaganda.

15. INTERNATIONAL AFFAIRS. **Feb 7–26:** In an exchange of correspondence with H. Nonne (in Paris), who presents vague ideas about opening up negotiations for new international unity, E makes reserved comments on the practical side, but states (letter of Feb M) that he is ready for a "cartel" with noncommunists but not an "alliance"; one can have good relations with socialists of various hues short of a principled or tactical falling-out. (Nonne will be revealed in Sep to be a Prussian police agent.) **Feb c.20:** E receives a letter from Sorge with info on the American situation; Dietzgen will move to the US.

16. MARX'S LIBRARY. **Feb 5:** E writes to Laura Lafargue and Bernstein (perhaps others) on the disposition of M's surplus books. French books, incl a collection on the French Revolution, will go to the Lafargues; Bernstein (*Sozialdemokrat* office) will get dictionaries not taken by Eleanor M, and also "the editorial copy of the *NRZ*"; the Blue Book collection will go mostly to Samuel Moore, for use in the English trans of *Capital*; a few "popular" things, to the London GWEA. (Re Russian books to Lavrov, see ← :7.) **Feb D to Mar A:** E ships these packages to the Lafargues (Feb 29) and to Lavrov, prob also to Bernstein for the *Sozialdemokrat*.

17. VERSE TRANSLATION. **Feb 2:** Bernstein informs E of his plan to publish a collection of socialist poems; he asks E if he has any for the book. **Feb 5:** E suggests including his old German trans of the Chartist poem "The steam king," which appeared in *Condition of the working class* (#E171) (cf *MEW* 4:474). **Feb 28:** *Sozialdemokrat* repubs this piece.

18. VISIT. **Feb D to Mar A:** Bernstein, on a visit to London, stays with E for a few days.

MARCH
19. ABOUT MARX. **Mar c.5:** E sends G. Gross of the U. of Vienna, at his request, some facts about M's life for a biographical sketch in the *Allgemeine Deutsche Biographie*. **Mar 11:** How to translate M: E sends Lafargue a point-by-point criticism of the latter's trans of #M593 [← :12], ending, "Try to be more faithful to the original. . . ." **Mar 13:** E's article on "M and the NRZ" (#E469) [← :13] is

pubd in *Sozialdemokrat*. **Mar 16:** On the Sunday after the anniversary of the Paris Commune and of M's death, a rally of 5000–6000 goes to Highgate Cemetery to lay a wreath on M's grave; a strong line of police prevent them from entering the cemetery; they go to a nearby hillock and hold the rally there.

20. RUSSIAN AFFAIRS. **Mar 2:** Vera Zasulich, on behalf of her Russian group in Geneva, writes E asking permission to publish a Russian edn of M's *Poverty of philosophy* (#M681) plus E's preface (#E608). **Mar 6:** E enthusiastically promises full cooperation with Zasulich's plan; he also sends her the ms he has found in M's papers of M's unsent letter to *Otechestvenniye Zapiski* (#M464) [← 77:41; → :29]. Writing of the tense situation in Russia, E summarizes the forces leading to a probable "palace revolution."

21. "ORIGIN OF THE FAMILY." **Mar 2:** Kautsky [← :12] suggests that E do a piece on Morgan's book for *Neue Zeit*. **Mar 7:** Writing to Sorge, E enthuses over Morgan's disclosures on primitive communalism and his rediscovery of M's theory of history. **Mar 24:** Replying to Kautsky, E provisionally promises to do the essay for *Neue Zeit*, incl M's notes on Morgan (#M570), provided it is offprinted as a separate brochure [→ :26]. **Mar D:** E begins work on the essay (which will eventually be pubd as a booklet) (#E573; for a draft passage not eventually used, see #E544) [→ :31].

22. *CAPITAL.* **Mar:** E negotiates with pub'r Meissner on the publ of Vol. 2. **Mar 7:** Writing to Sorge, E says he will start on Vol. 2 in two weeks. **Mar 24, 31:** Writing to Kautsky and Laura Lafargue, E reports Meissner's agreement to publish Vol. 2 in two parts, separately: first half comprising Book II ("Circulation"), second half comprising Book III plus "Theories of surplus value."

23. GERMAN MOVEMENT. **Mar 24:** Writing to Bernstein about his Mar 20 article on the People's party, E criticizes his fuzzy treatment of the "concept of democracy," i.e., bourgeois democracy, and of the democratic republic (as against the liberal constitutional monarchy) as the "logical" form of bourgeois rule. **Mar 31:** E tells Laura Lafargue that the right-wing Reichstag Fraction would oust Bernstein from *Sozialdemokrat* "if they could and dared"; the leaders "have become a sorry lot" due to the influx of petty-bourgeois.

APRIL
24. FRENCH MOVEMENT. **Apr 2:** Laura Lafargue sends E a brief report on the success of the party congress at Roubaix. **Apr 10:** Paul Lafargue sends a more detailed report. **Apr 18:** E replies to Paul with congratulations.

25. *CAPITAL.* **Apr 18:** In a letter to Laura

Lafargue, E describes how *Capital* is being translated into English, not only by Moore [← 83:38] but also by Aveling's apprentice efforts, with Eleanor M checking on original citations in English. E proposes to Laura that she become one of the translators [→ :30]. In a letter to Paul Lafargue, E makes clear that he has *not* yet started on Vol. 2.

26. W&P. Apr 7: Bernstein raises the question of a second edn of *Anti-Dühring* (#E23). **Apr 11:** E, replying favorably, notes that the book has had an "unexpected impact" even in Russia, as "an encyclopedic survey of our conception of philosophic, scientific, and historical problems." **Apr 28:** E informs Kautsky that his essay on Morgan's book (which will become #E573) cannot conform to legal publ in *Neue Zeit* but will have to be a booklet only; it will be important for understanding "our overall outlook" from new points of view. **Apr-May:** E tells correspondents (Apr 18, 26, May 23) that he plans to do a complete revision of his *Peasant war in Germany* (#E579) [→ :57].

MAY

27. GERMAN MOVEMENT. May 23: Writing to Bernstein, E discusses two political problems. One (just discussed with Paul Singer, who is visiting London) is the question of supporting nonparty candidates on the second ballot in the two-stage Reichstag election; E would admit the possibility under certain circumstances. The other is the "right to work" slogan: why it is wrong "as a *separate* demand" abstracted from the social order.

28. FRENCH MOVEMENT. May 9: Paul Lafargue sends E a report on the results of the May 4 Paris municipal elections. **May 10:** E approves the French party's "electoral tactics" in general. He also praises recent lectures by Lafargue on Darwinism and Deville on polit eco, while suggesting criticisms.

29. RUSSIAN AFFAIRS. May: See #M464 (M's letter to *Otechestvenniye Zapiski*) for possible publ at this time [→ 86:2].

30. CAPITAL. May 26: E reports to Laura Lafargue on the progress of the English trans; he presses her to participate [← :25].

31. W&P. May 22: E sends the ms of *Origin of the family* (#E573)—excepting the last (ninth) chapter—to Zurich for publ as a booklet. **May 26:** E finishes the last chapter of this work. —In a letter to Laura Lafargue, E describes his working schedule: daytimes, on Vol. 2 of *Capital;* evenings, on revision of translations in progress. He will not be able to do any more independent work "for some time to come."

32. PERSONAL. May 29 to June 4: E is a guest at S. Borkheim's house in Hastings.

JUNE

33. GERMAN MOVEMENT. June 5: In a letter to Bernstein, E gives his fullest exposition of his proposed policies and tactics vis-à-vis the inevitable split in the party with the right wing. **June 6:** Writing to Bebel on the same subject, E is less explicit; he again condemns the right wing for falling for Bismarck's state socialism. Discussing political prospects in France, E stresses that the masses must go through a process of disillusionment with the left or liberal bourgeois parties. **June 21:** E receives the ms of Kautsky's article on Rodbertus (who is being trumpeted in Germany as against M), and begins studying it. **June 26:** E sends Kautsky a number of detailed criticisms of the article, urging emphasis on the similarity between Rodbertus and Proudhon.

34. W&P. June 29: E finishes work on editing a new edn of M's *Wage-labor and capital* (#M968), with a short prefatory note (#E616), and sends it to Zurich for publ [→ :53].

35. RUSSIAN AFFAIRS. June 26: In a letter to the Russian émigré Eugenie Papritz (in London), E praises Chernyshevsky, Dobrolyubov, and the left historical school in Russia as superior to the French and Germans in this field; he also praises the Russian left émigrés for their pubd translations of M. E objects to reprinting his own old article of 1844 on polit eco (#E576) as too full of errors.

36. PERSONAL. June: E's pain [← 83:45] recurs in chronic form, as a result of his desk work. **June M:** E engages a secy, Eisengarten, to whom he dictates his decipherment of the ms of Vol. 2 of *Capital*, from 10 A.M. to 5 P.M.

JULY

37. GERMAN MOVEMENT. July 11: E points out to Kautsky that a recent article in *Neue Zeit* by Schippel speaks of the "Rodbertus–Marx theory" in polit eco, without even an ed note on it. **July 16:** Kautsky informs E that NZ pub'r Dietz wants to suspend publ over money troubles. **July 19:** E responds that suspension of NZ would be no misfortune because most party writers are right-wing opportunists who fill their stuff with "philanthropy, humanitarianism, sentimentality" and assorted "antirevolutionary vices" as substitutes for revolutionary analyses. **July D** (after 21): Writing to Bernstein, E urges the need to reserve the safest electoral districts for the party's best candidates, like Bebel, rather than right-wingers. —In another letter this month (no date) to Bernstein, E criticizes recent *Neue Welt* articles by the right-wingers Blos and Geiser, the latter's being an attack on atheism; E agrees that some abstract atheism

:an be a "religion" too, if it is a simple
₁egation of religion without positive content.

38. *ORIGIN OF THE FAMILY.* **July 11:** Writ-
ng to Kautsky, E complains of the delay by
)ietz (in Stuttgart) in publishing his work
#E573). **July 16:** Kautsky reports that the
₁rinting of this work has been transferred to
he party press in Zurich. **July D to Oct 3:** E
,vorks at correcting proofs of the booklet [→
52].

39. FRIENDS. **July 16:** E visits the Russian
₃migré Stepniak. **July 22:** E writes support-
vely of Eleanor M's decision to live with
₁veling as his wife, this in a letter to Laura
₌afargue (who has been informed by Eleanor
₁n June 18).

AUGUST

40. W&P. **Aug 1 to 11:** After Paul Lafargue writes him (July 25) about Leroy-Beau-
₁ieu's book *Le collectivisme* and its critique of
M, E reads the book, and goes over Lafargue's
₁raft of an article-review. **Aug 11:** E sends
₌afargue a detailed criticism of his draft,
₌overing many points, e.g., the definition of
"capitalist." (Lafargue's article will be pubd
₁n the *Journal des Economistes* later this
year.) **Aug 13–20:** E gives permission for a
₱olish edn of his *Origin of the family* (#E573)
by Maria Jankowska-Mendelson (S. Leono-
wicz) of Geneva. **Aug 22:** E sends Kautsky a
criticism of the Kautsky–Bernstein German
₁rans of M's *Poverty of philosophy* (#M681).
—E says he will divide his polemic on the
₱odbertus issue [← :13] into two parts, one in
₁ preface to *Capital*, Vol. 2 (#E604), the other
in a preface to the German edn of *Poverty of
philosophy* (#E608).

41. *CAPITAL.* **Aug 22:** E accepts Bernstein's suggestion (Aug 18) for a Bernstein–
₭autsky index to *Capital*, but suggests they
wait till all volumes are pubd—surely next
year, says E.

42. POLITICAL AFFAIRS. **Aug A:** E receives a letter from J. P. Becker on the Swiss
workers' movement and the remnants of
anarchist influence.

43. LEARNING ECONOMICS. **Aug 13:** In response to an inquiry by Vollmar (Aug 6), E
describes the low level of the teaching of
economics in English schools, and suggests
that a course of self-study is preferable.

44. PERSONAL. **Aug c.5 to Sep 1:** E sojourns in Worthing, on the southern coast.

SEPTEMBER

45. GRONLUND. **Sep AB:** E reads the
popular book *The co-operative commonwealth* by the American, L. Gronlund, sent to
him by Sorge. **Sep 14:** Writing to Bernstein,

E condemns the book as philistine future-
mongering.

46. ENGLISH AFFAIRS. **Sep 14, 20:** E tells
Bernstein, then Kautsky, that *To-Day*, recently
taken over by Hyndman, has become a general
"symposium"-type magazine, no longer a
socialist one; it plans to publish a criticism of
Capital [by Wicksteed] but E has refused to
write a reply, i.e., to write for the magazine.

47. RODBERTUS. **Sep M:** E reads Kautsky's draft reply to C. A. Schramm's defense of
Rodbertus against M. **Sep 20:** Writing to
Kautsky, E praises the draft as very good but
suggests some changes.

48. *ORIGIN OF THE FAMILY.* **Sep:** NZ carries an editorial article announcing the publ of
E's new book (#E573) and citing excerpts
from the preface.

OCTOBER

49. GERMAN MOVEMENT. **Oct 11:** Writing
to Bebel, E looks forward to the Oct 28
Reichstag election, which may spur the entire
European movement and strike a blow against
the "caricature-anarchists à la Most" and the
American sects; but there is also the problem
of the "bourgeois-inspired" wing of the party
which pushes to the fore in the electoral
process. E then repeats his perspective of a
party split [← :33]. **Oct 15:** Writing to J. P.
Becker, E includes one of his several passages
of admiring praise for Bebel as party
leader. **Oct 28:** The S-D party scores a great
success in the election, despite the restrictions of the Anti-Socialist Law. **Oct 28–29:** E
writes to a number of English and French
correspondents apprising them of the German
victory. **Oct 29:** Bebel sends, and E receives,
a telegram on the party's victory. In a letter to
Bebel, E jubilates: the number of seats is of
slight importance; the main thing is the proof
of the advance of the movement.

50. ON MARX. **Oct 15:** E writes to an old
friend, J. P. Becker: "The trouble is that, since
we lost M, I have to substitute for him. All my
life I have done what I was made for, namely,
play second fiddle, and I think I have done my
thing quite passably. And I was glad to have
such a splendid first fiddle as M. But now
when suddenly I have to take M's place in
respect to theory and play first fiddle, I cannot
carry it off without making blunders, and
nobody feels this more than I do." E goes on to
say that M had the ability to see the right thing
to do on the decisive point esp in revolutionary times.

51. *CAPITAL.* **Oct 11, 15:** E informs Bebel
and Becker that Vol. 2 has been all deciphered
and copied, nearly ready for printing; he has
also revised the first three-eighths of the
English trans of Vol. 1.

52. *ORIGIN OF THE FAMILY.* **Oct 2:** In connection with the coming Reichstag election (see ← :49), the *Sozialdemokrat* pubs an excerpt on the proletariat's use of universal suffrage to carry on revolutionary struggle. **Oct c.3:** E's work (#E573) is pubd in Zurich. **Oct 11–14:** E sends copies to Bebel, J. P. Becker, Lavrov, and others. **Oct c.30 to Dec 30:** E exchanges letters with Martignetti about an Italian edn.

53. W&P. **Oct 1:** E suggests to Schlüter (Zurich party press) that M's 1848 speech on free trade (#M836)—about which Schlüter was inquiring—be appended to the coming German edn of M's *Poverty of philosophy* (#M681). **Oct 22:** E sends his copy of this speech on free trade to Zurich. **Oct 23:** E finishes, and sends to Zurich, his preface (#E608) to the *Poverty of philosophy*, dealing with Rodbertus [→ 85:4]. **Oct:** The new edn of M's *Wage-labor and capital* (#M968) [← :34] is pubd in Zurich with a short prefatory note by E (#E616).

NOVEMBER

54. GERMAN MOVEMENT. **Nov 8, 11:** In letters to Kautsky and Bernstein resp, E continues to offer his views on the new opportunities created by the party's success in the Oct 28 election, esp the prospects and tasks of the party in face of the Anti-Socialist Law. **Nov 18:** In a letter to Bebel which is essentially an outline for an essay or speech to be made, E takes up the new bourgeois cry that the Social-Democrats, to be legalized again, must abjure revolution, force and violence, etc. He answers with a historical account of the right to revolution and of revolution as the real origin of the status quo; he ridicules the demand that socialists swear that "in no circumstances will we resort to force"; no one has ever really renounced the right to armed resistance, in certain circumstances. But the party cannot resort to force until the army is neutralized.

55. ENGLISH MOVEMENT. **Nov:** A split develops in Hyndman's SDF between the Hyndman dictatorship and a dissident group headed by William Morris which includes Eleanor M and Aveling. Under Nov-Dec, *MEW Daten* says that E "meets regularly" with the members of this group; in any case, E no doubt keeps in touch through Eleanor and Aveling and sees others now and then. (See → :59.) **Nov 21:** E attends a benefit for the SDF in which Eleanor M and Aveling perform a playlet which is "more or less their own history," Bax plays the piano, and William Morris recites his poetry. **Nov 28:** J. L. Mahon makes E's acquaintance: having written in advance (Nov 26) for an appointment,

he visits E to discuss the SDF split situation [→ 87:27].

56. CAPITAL. **Nov 11:** E writes Bernstein that "tomorrow" he will begin the "complicated final editing" of Part III of Vol. 2.

57. W&P: PLANS. **Nov-Dec:** In letters to Bernstein and Sorge (Nov 11, Dec 31), E says he is still [← :26] planning to do a complete rewriting of his *Peasant war in Germany* (#E579); this peasant war was the "turning point" of all German history. In connection with his plans, around the end of this year E drafts notes on the subject (#E282); prob also related are E's notes on the decay of feudalism (#E210).

DECEMBER

58. GERMAN MOVEMENT. **Dec 7, 14:** E is visited by Paul Singer, who, E finds, is singing a more optimistic tune about revolutionary prospects, under the impress of the party's gains [← :49]. **Dec 11:** E continues his exposition, to Bebel, of the socioeconomic basis, in the nature of delayed industrial development in Germany, for the party's prospects; he repeats his fears about the right-wing intellectuals and his faith in the rank-and-file's militancy. He criticizes Bebel's views on "pure [i.e., bourgeois] democracy," and discusses the propensity for all antirevolutionary forces to get behind the leftmost wing of the bourgeoisie in order to defeat revolution. **Dec 11–31:** In a number of letters to Bebel and Liebknecht and in conversation with Singer (see above), E discusses party policy in face of Bismarck's proposals for a government subsidy to private shipping companies, which strengthens Bismarckian state socialism and German colonialism; as against the Bismarck program he proposes what is in effect the concept of a "transitional demand" (not yet so named), and outlines a set of concrete planks to implement it. This proposal is also part of E's letter to Liebknecht of Dec 29 [→ 85:5].

59. ENGLISH MOVEMENT. **Dec:** E heartily supports and approves the anti-Hyndman struggle in the SDF by Morris, Eleanor M, et al (who will shortly form the Socialist League) [← :55]. The SDF split takes place in a series of clashes at meetings, culminating Dec 27. **Dec 27:** In the morning Aveling and Morris visit E, at E's suggestion, to discuss their plans. E urges modest beginnings for whatever new group they plan, esp monthly publ of their organ *Commonweal*. At the evening SDF Exec meeting the Morris group collectively resigns from the SDF. **Dec 29, 31:** In a detailed report to Bernstein, and a shorter one to Sorge, E recounts the course of the fight inside the SDF and its inevitable outcome in a split.

60. *CAPITAL.* **Dec 31:** E describes (to Sorge) his schedule for *Capital:* the editing of Book 2 will be finished in 10 days; then revision of the text; it will go to press in Jan. Then he will work on Book 3, after some urgent intervening work. And then Book 4 ("Theories of surplus value"), which is still untouched. The English edn of Vol. 1 is over half finished.

61. REVOLUTION. **Dec M:** In a passage in a letter to Paul Lafargue (context not extant) E emphasizes that modern revolution starts with the army; decisive in Germany and France is the large number of soldiers and noncoms in the armed forces who belong to the socialist party, while the number of socialist conscripts increases.

Dec 21: Lafargue includes this passage, or its content, in his article in *Lyon Socialiste* directed against the anarchist cry for a street putsch.

62. PERSONAL. **Dec 1:** E receives a telegram announcing the death of his brother Emil. To Emil's wife, Charlotte, E writes explaining that the German police make it impossible for him to attend the funeral—as proved by the recent police harassment of Schorlemmer on a visit to Darmstadt, despite his eminence as a scientist.

63. W&P. **Dec:** Florence Kelley Wischnewetzky (in the US) sends E her trans of his *Condition of the working class* (#E171), which he will revise for publ in America; it is received by E before Jan 1 [→ 85:4].

1885

CONSPECTUS

1. E is still planning, or hoping, to do a thorough revision of his *Peasant war in Germany* (#E579) [← 84:57]; and he mentions this in letters to Schlüter (party press in Zurich) from Jan 1 to Dec 7. But this hope is going to fade before the press of other work, esp the onerous work on the third vol. of *Capital.*

2. E makes some additions to his mss on *Dialectics of nature* (#E221), which he had dropped when M died. For two passages dated to 1885, see ST/E14 (DN) 450 or MEW 20:694.

3. *Capital.* Sometime in 1885, a so-called secret edn of the French version of *Capital,* Vol. 1, is publ in France by H. Oriol. With interest in *Capital* quickened by Deville's popular abridgment, Oriol has—already in 1884—finished printing some copies left incomplete by Lachâtre, and in 1885 carried out a reprinting job of the entire volume, using several printshops. His edn, not registered with the Bibliothèque Nationale, can be distinguished esp by the imprint "Librairie du Progrès," Paris, n.d. Oriol prints at least 5000 copies, perhaps many more. E is aware of this operation and evidently raises no objection.

JANUARY

4. W&P. **Jan A:** E's preface (#E608) to the German edn of M's *Poverty of philosophy* (#M681) is publ in NZ as "M and Rodbertus." Later this month M's work is publ as a book. **Jan 13:** In reply to Schlüter (of the party press), who has raised the question (Jan 10) of reprinting M/E articles from the NRZ-

Revue, E replies that he has no full set, only no. 3 and no. 5/6; besides he takes a dim view of reprinting from it. **Jan 25:** E writes an article for *Sozialdemokrat* suggesting that recent terrorist bombings in London were done by Russian agents to influence English public opinion against political émigrés (#E326); pubd Jan 29. **Jan c.25:** E writes along the same lines in a letter to Paul Lafargue, excerpts from which are pubd in an article by Guesde in *Le Cri du Peuple,* Jan 31. **Jan:** E works on the second German edn of his *Anti-Dühring* (#E23). **Jan to Feb 4:** E edits part of Mrs. Wischnewetzky's translation (#E171) [← 84:63].

5. GERMAN MOVEMENT. **Jan 8:** On the ship-subsidy issue [← 84:58], an article by Liebknecht summarizes E's proposal on what to counterpose to Bismarck's scheme, in particular the plan for workers' cooperatives on the land. **Jan 15:** Bernstein writes E that he disagrees with this proposal; he counterposes flat "principled" opposition to the ship subsidy.

FEBRUARY

6. *CAPITAL.* **Feb 11:** E writes Danielson agreeing to send him proof sheets of Vol. 2 in order to speed the trans into Russian. **Feb 23:** E finishes work on the last part of Vol. 2, and sends it to the printer. **Feb D:** E begins working on the ms of Vol. 3—work that will go on for another decade—beginning with decipherment of M's ms. **Feb to June A:** E works at correcting the proofs of Vol. 2 as they come from the printer.

7. W&P. **Feb 4:** E sends back to Mrs. Wischnewetzky the corrected ms of her trans

(#E171) [← :4]; he advises dropping the old preface and dedication, and promises to write a new preface. **Feb M:** In connection with this forthcoming American edn, E writes the essay "England in 1845 and in 1885" (#E242) [→ :11].

8. GERMAN MOVEMENT. Feb 4: Commenting acidly on a couple of intellectuals recently sent to him by Liebknecht, E writes him reproving his weakness for the petty-bourgeois intellectuals who are spoiling the party: "If this goes on, there will be a split in the party, you can bet on that."

9. PERSONAL. Feb 14: Since Kautsky, editor of NZ, is now living in London (until 1888), E sends him an invitation to Sunday dinner tomorrow, and a standing invitation for any other Sunday.

MARCH

10. CAPITAL. Mar 8: Having started work on Vol. 3 [← :6], E feels (in a letter to Laura Lafargue) that it is "almost inconceivable" that M, with such "tremendous discoveries" and a "complete scientific revolution in his head," could keep them there for 20 years without publishing. E also refers to Vol. 2, "which he [M] wrote last and which alone he touched after 1870." Of Vol. 3 he says it was written before and at the same time as Vol. 1; the essential part was already contained in the mss of 1860–62.

11. W&P. Mar 1: E's essay "England in 1845 and in 1885" (#E242) is pubd in *Commonweal* [→ :24]. **Mar 3:** E helps Aveling write a reply to a letter in the Feb 26 *Sozialdemokrat* by Varenholz which defends the SDF and Hyndman (against a Jan 15 article prob by Eleanor M). The reply, signed by Aveling, is pubd Mar 26.

12. ABOUT MARX. Mar 21: Stegemann writes E asking for an "authentic characterization" of M, for a book about *Capital*. **Mar 26:** In reply, E excuses himself from this task, but suggests that Stegemann work on the assumption that "M was in every respect just the opposite of a German philistine." **Mar 29:** Stegemann renews his plea for E to send him a vindicatory personal piece on M, esp since it is alleged that M died friendless [→ :20].

APRIL

13. GERMAN MOVEMENT. Apr 2: As a result of the conflict over the ship-subsidy issue [← 84:58], the right-wing Reichstag Fraction majority, abetted by Liebknecht, pressures the *Sozialdemokrat* into publishing a statement conceding control of the paper to the Fraction. The same day, though he does not know this, E writes Becker of his fear that the right wing wants to get the "upper hand"

in the party; but beyond a certain point, writes E, "I'll say *Good-by, gentlemen*." **Apr 4:** Seeing the Apr 2 statement, E writes Bebel in indignation that the right wing is moving to take over power in the party; if they take over the *Sozialdemokrat*, he (E) will cease to defend the German party in the international movement. **Apr 5:** In Germany, Bebel threatens to take the fight against the Reichstag Fraction majority to the party rank-and-file; the right wing thereupon backs off. **Apr 16–17:** Writing to Paul Lafargue, E repeats his view that the right wing is showing its hand and he expects a split. **Apr 23:** The *Sozialdemokrat* carries a "compromise" statement in the direction of the paper's independence of the Fraction. The same issue carries a denunciation of the right wing by the Frankfurt party. (E will take this compromise as a de facto victory for Bebel and the left.)

14. CAPITAL. Apr 23: Writing to Danielson, E is exuberant about Vol. 3: it is the crowning part which will put Vol. 1 in the shade; it is the most amazing piece of work he has ever seen. E mentions he expects Vol. 2 to appear May D.

15. W&P. Apr 11: E acknowledges receipt of Martignetti's Italian trans in ms of the *Origin of the family* (#E573), sent Mar 24; he promises to check it over [→ :19].

16. RUSSIAN AFFAIRS. Apr 23: Writing to Zasulich, who sent him Plekhanov's *Our differences* (in Russian) and wants (letter of Feb 14) to know his opinion of it, E replies that he has so far read only part; in any case he declines to make judgments on political tactics in Russia. Russia, he adds, is a tinderbox of revolution—an exceptional case where a handful can "make" a revolution since the whole structure is already tottering; here Blanquism has a unique place; but the explosion will then sweep the handful away.

MAY

17. GERMAN MOVEMENT. May 10: Paul Singer visits E; they argue i.a. over the April conflict on the ship-subsidy issue. **May 15:** E writes to Bernstein on tactics in the fight against the party right wing, incl how to end Liebknecht's "double-dealing." E points out that although the right-wingers have exposed their hand, Bebel is ill and depressed, E is overwhelmed with work on *Capital*, and it is up to the editors (Bernstein, Kautsky) to keep the party press secure from right-wing control. **May 19:** Writing to Paul Lafargue, E knows the fight is not over; as often, he condemns Liebknecht's behavior; he repeats that he would be for "an open split" if the Anti-Socialist Law did not make this course disadvantageous at the moment.

18. *CAPITAL.* **May 5:** E finishes his preface (#E604) to Vol. 2, dealing with Rodbertus, and dates it "On M's birthday. . . ." **May 19:** E's letter to Lafargue reports that Vol. 3 is over half deciphered, but two parts (Parts 5, 6) are still in a mixed-up state; he thinks it will take at least another year. He mentions that the mss of Vol. 3 on ground rent date from 1865.

19. W&P. **May 19:** E writes Martignetti [← :15] that he has already sent him the edited ms of his Italian trans of *Origin of the Family* (#E573). Included by E is the text of a footnote which he wants added to Ch. 7 (see #E573.5). **May D to June:** E works on the proof sheets of the third German edn of M's *18th Brumaire* (#M267), and during this period writes a new preface for it (#E607) [→ :24]. **May to Nov:** E works on the proof sheets of the second German edn of his *Anti-Dühring* (#E23).

20. ABOUT MARX. **May 5:** E replies to Stegemann [← :12] with a considered but firm no. As for the need to answer falsehoods about M: "An enormous amount of lies were told about M without his taking the trouble to answer them."

21. SOCIALIST VERSE. **May 13:** Schlüter (party press) asks E for examples of poems that played a role in the movement of the Reformation, Chartism, or 1848, for a verse collection to be pubd. **May 15:** E refers him to a few specimens he knows of in the periods mentioned.

JUNE

22. GERMAN MOVEMENT. **June:** In letters to cothinkers (June 3 to Sorge, June 15 to J. P. Becker, June 22 to Bebel) E writes of the inevitable coming split in the party, on the background of recent events. In his letter to Bebel, E counsels care to hold on, in a split, to the three key posts now held by the left: the Zurich party press, the *Sozialdemokrat*, and the *NZ*.

23. *CAPITAL.* **June 3:** In letters to Danielson and to Sorge, E discusses the task ahead of putting Vol. 3 together. To the former he mentions that Vol. 3 was written by 1864–66. **June 25:** Danielson, acknowledging receipt of E's preface to Vol. 2 (#E604) on Rodbertus, suggests that E write a modified preface for the Russian edn since Rodbertus is not well known in Russia [→ :29].

24. W&P. **June c.13:** E promises to write an article on Feuerbach for *NZ*. **June 16:** E writes Schlüter (party press) that he approves, and is willing to cooperate with, the publ of a number of writings by M, incl the defense speeches in the 1849 trials (#M947) and M's 1852 pamphlet on the Cologne Communist trial (#M762). **June:** *NZ* pubs E's German

trans of his article "England in 1845 and in 1885" (#E242) [← :11]. **c.June:** M's *18th Brumaire* (#M267), third German edn, is pubd with a new preface by E (#E607) [← :19].

JULY

25. *CAPITAL.* **July A** (by July 10): Vol. 2 is pubd—first German edn (#M133), ed by E, with his preface (#E604). **July 24:** E reports (to Bebel) that the ms of Vol. 3 has finally been all set down in a clear copy, all deciphered.

26. W&P. **July 1:** E writes a preface (#E600) to a pamphlet edn of the speeches at the 1849 trial of M and other *NRZ* defendants in Cologne (see #M947) under the title in German, *KM Before the Cologne Jury* [→ :36]. —E writes to Schlüter about his plans: to start Sep A on a preface and notes to #M762, and to a collection of M–E articles pubd in the *NRZ* in 1848 on the June revolt in France. (The latter is never realized.) In response to Schlüter's proposal of June 24, E greets the idea of reprinting W. Wolff's essay *Schlesische Milliarde* plus other material about Wolff by E. **July:** E agrees to check over a French trans of M's *18th Brumaire* (#M267) being made by Fortin (E will correspond with Fortin about this until at least Sep M, and will remain concerned about it later) [→ 87:19].

27. GERMAN MOVEMENT. **July 24:** In a letter to Bebel, E has significant comments on two men: Kautsky is weak as a party theoretician; his bad academic training has spoiled him for "really scientific work"; and as for Mehring (who was sympathetic to the Social-Democracy in one period but then reverted to attacking the movement in the liberal press): "The fellow has much talent and an open mind, but he is a calculating scamp and a betrayer by nature; I hope that this is kept in mind if he comes over to us again, which he will certainly do as soon as the times change."

28. EQUALITY FOR WOMEN. **July 1:** Gertrud Guillaume-Schack writes E asking about the French Guesdist party program calling for equal pay for equal work. **July c.5:** E replies that all socialists demand equal pay for equal work for both sexes; but women need special protective laws to guard the health of the new generation; upper-class women champion the right of women to be as grossly exploited as men because they are for the capitalist exploitation of both sexes. Real equality requires the abolition of capitalism and the transformation of private housework into a public industry.

AUGUST

29. *CAPITAL.* **Aug 8:** E replies to Danielson's proposal [← :23] that he is not in a position to write a new preface for Vol. 2; he suggests that the Russian edn simply drop the section on Rodbertus in (#E604 (which will in fact be done). **Aug c.21:** E learns from Danielson that the Russian trans of Vol. 2 is finished, but that because of censorship E's preface (#E604) has to take some cuts.

30. W&P. **Aug 25:** On Danielson's suggestion, in a note to the *Severny Vestnik* (#E837) E offers the hitherto unpubd letter by M to the *Otechestvenniye Zapiski* (#M464) [← 84:20]. (But this periodical will not publish it.) **Aug 29 to Nov 7:** Laura Lafargue's French trans of the *Com Manifesto* is pubd in *Le Socialiste* in 11 weekly installs [→ :32].

31. PERSONAL. **Aug A:** E meets the novelist Minna Kautsky (Karl's mother), who is visiting London; he recommends that she study Balzac [→ :42]. **Aug 14 to Sep 14:** E sojourns on the Isle of Jersey; he corrects the proof sheets of the second German edn of *Anti-Dühring* (#E23) (SOURCE: MEW *Daten*).

SEPTEMBER

32. W&P. **Sep A to Oct:** E works on revising Laura Lafargue's French trans of the *Com Manifesto* [← :30] with a view to pamphlet publ [→ :36]. **Sep 23:** E finishes his preface (#E27) to the second German edn of *Anti-Dühring* (#E23); pubd 1886 (see → 86:2).

33. ENGLISH AFFAIRS. **Sep 22:** Eleanor M and Aveling, who are in the thick of a free-speech fight in the East End, visit E to consult on policy.

OCTOBER

34. FRENCH AFFAIRS. **Oct 8:** In a letter to Bernstein, E analyzes the situation created by the defeat of the Opportunist party in the Oct 4 first ballot in the parliamentary election, which creates a favorable situation for the socialists. (*Sozialdemokrat* pubs unsigned excerpts from this letter, Oct 15.) **Oct 12:** E writes to Paul Lafargue along the same lines. **Oct 17:** *Le Socialiste* pubs a part of E's letter of Oct 12 under the title "La situation" (#E435), without E's knowledge. **Oct 21:** E sends *Le Socialiste* a letter (#E830) with corrections and modifications of formulations in the excerpt printed on Oct 17, in view of the fact of its publ. **Oct 28:** In a letter to Bebel, E gives another overall view of the way socialism is developing in France, esp its lack of theoretical maturity.

35. ENGLISH AFFAIRS. **Oct 28:** E's letter to Bebel opines that the coming crisis will end the old TU craft system based on skilled and privileged workers.

36. W&P. **Oct A:** The pamphlet presenting *KM before the Cologne Jury* (#M947) [← :26] is pubd, with a preface by E (#E600). E's

preface is pubd in shortened form in *Sozialdemokrat*, Oct 15. **Oct 8:** E finishes, and sends to Zurich, his essay on the history of the Communist League (#E557) as preface to the third German edn of M's pamphlet on the Cologne Communist trial (#M762). The pamphlet edn is pubd later this month [→ :40]. **Oct 9:** E promises Schlüter to begin "tomorrow" to write an intro to the planned pamphlet edn of Wolff's *Schlesische Milliarde* [← :26]—an intro which will take up the historical development of the Prussian peasantry (cf #E558). MEW *Daten* therefore dates its writing Oct 10 to Nov 24; but the early date is dubious: cf MEW 36:798 n.449 [→ :40]. **Oct M:** E sends Laura Lafargue a number of comments and corrections on her French trans of the *Com Manifesto* [← :32]. In one letter (Oct 13) he remarks that the *Manifesto* is the most untranslatable of all documents.

37. CAPITAL. **Oct:** The English periodical *To-Day* pubs excerpts from *Capital* translated by Hyndman using the pen name John Broadhouse. E writes an article "How not to translate M" (#E360) on the many mistakes in this trans [→ :40].

38. RUSSIAN AFFAIRS. **Oct CD to Dec:** A MEW *Daten* entry reads as follows: "As the war between Serbia and Bulgaria sharpens the European situation and leads to growing antagonisms over the Bulgarian question, E studies the economic and financial situation of Russia, and concludes that Bismarck, promoting the German bank loan to the czarist government, is playing a provocatory role in the Balkan conflict and at the same time using czarism to suppress the revolutionary movement" [→ :43]. **Oct 22:** In a letter to S. Faerber, E makes explicit a changed attitude toward Russian affairs: while he always said that Russia is the bulwark of reaction, "in the last 20 years much has changed"—specif the development of a revolutionary peasantry and advancing industrialization, i.e., a new revolutionary potential.

NOVEMBER

39. GERMAN MOVEMENT. **Nov to Dec 2:** E reads G. Adler's recent book on German socialist history (sent to him in Oct by Kautsky) and gives Kautsky comments and notes on it for a critical review of the book's falsification of the history of the Communist League. (Kautsky's review will be pubd in NZ next Feb.) **Nov 17:** In a letter to Bebel, E reviews his position on the ship-subsidy issue [← 84:58], reporting on an exchange of letters with G. Schumacher. At greater length he reviews the mounting war danger: he weighs the consequences of a great destructive war in throwing the movement back and in accelerating revolution.

40. W&P. **Nov 7:** E tells Laura Lafargue he is willing to write a new preface for her French trans of the *Com Manifesto* [← :36] but wants to know why the "old preface" of 1872 (#ME36) is not suitable for the French public. **Nov 12– 26:** E's history of the Communist League (#E557) is pubd in *Sozialdemokrat* [← :36]. **Nov 13:** E thanks Danielson for sending extracts from M's letters of 1879–81; he refers to his aim of publishing M's collected letters, esp on questions of theoretical importance. —Paul Lafargue writes E requesting details on the May 1849 uprisings in Germany, to be used in a biographical sketch of E in *Le Socialiste*. **Nov 14:** E's letter to Lafargue complies with this request. **Nov 21:** Lafargue pubs a section, based on E's letter, in the sketch of E in *Le Socialiste*, unsigned, under the heading "The May uprising of 1849" (#E474). **Nov 24:** E finishes, and dates, his essay on the history of the Prussian peasantry (#E558) [← :36] (for publ, see → 86:24). **Nov:** E's article "How not to translate M" (#E360) is pubd in *Commonweal*.

41. *CAPITAL.* **Nov 13:** Writing to Danielson, E reports he has finished transcribing (deciphering) Vol. 3; he thinks three-quarters of the ms can be printed as-is. The English trans is nearly complete, he says. **Nov 29:** John Swinton, in his *John Swinton's Paper*, supplements his previous memoir on M [← 80:34] with an article emphasizing the importance M ascribed to the French trans of *Capital* and the many changes that M introduced there.

42. NOVEL WRITING. **Nov 26:** In a letter to Minna Kautsky [← :31] E praises her new novel *Die Alten und die Neuen*, and adds a caution against tendentious preaching. He criticizes the hero as too idealized; there is no need for a novelist to take sides openly, with explicit solutions of social problems; the "socialist problem novel" need merely give a faithful portrayal of the real relations in society (like Balzac).

DECEMBER

43. RUSSIA AND GERMANY. **Dec:** In response to Liebknecht's request (Nov 26) for material on the German bank loan to Russia [← :38], E sends him letters (Dec 1, 5, 28) with info. (Liebknecht will use E's material in a Reichstag speech next Feb 8.)

44. ENGLISH AFFAIRS. **Dec 7:** E reports (to Bernstein) on the scandal in the SDF about Hyndman's taking Tory money in the Nov 3 election campaign; E discusses the conditions under which taking money may be admissible. E also writes to Paul Lafargue on the same lines. E on Hyndman: "completely indifferent about the kind of means he uses, even when they do *not* lead to the end, as long as something profitable to Hyndman comes of it."

45. GERMAN MOVEMENT. **Dec 7:** Bebel, after a considerable hiatus, explains to E what his objections are to E's position on the ship-subsidy issue [← :5; → 86:3].

46. W&P. **Dec c.2:** The second German edn of *Anti-Dühring* (#E23) is pubd in Zurich, with the imprint 1886.

1886

CONSPECTUS

1. *Broad-dated Entries (Continuing).* Through most of this year E is immersed in the work of editing and revising the English trans of *Capital*, Vol. 1; see esp → :11, 34, 50. —E makes one or more additions to his mss on the *Dialectics of nature* (#E221), but he will not return to it again. For one passage in his *Dialectics of nature* file dated to 1886, see ST/E14 (DN) 450 or MEW 20:694; but this comprises unused passages from E's *Ludwig Feuerbach* (#E457).

2. *Indefinite Dates.* Sometime during the first months of this year Laura Lafargue's second version [← 85:36] of her French trans of the *Com Manifesto* is pubd in the appendix of the book *La France socialiste* by "Mermeix" (G. Terrail); it embodies many revisions suggested by E. —During this

year, M's 1877 letter to the *Otechestvenniye Zapiski* (#M464), discovered by E among M's papers [← 84:20], is pubd in the Russian émigré press. (For the uncertain date, see the Register.) —The second German edn of *Anti-Dühring* (#E23) bears the imprint 1886 but it actually came out at the end of 1885 [← 85:46].

JANUARY

3. GERMAN MOVEMENT. **Jan 7:** E writes Liebknecht that both Bebel and he should go on the planned tour of America to raise electoral-campaign funds for the German party [→ :13]. **Jan c.M:** E sends Bernstein suggestions on how to reply to C. A. Schramm's book *Rodbertus, Marx, Lassalle* (pubd end of 1885). E's points are used in

Bernstein's four-part article on Schramm in *Sozialdemokrat*, Jan 21 to Feb 12. **Jan 20–23:** E replies at length to Bebel's letter [← 85:45] criticizing his position on the ship-subsidy issue; he explains his view in detail, esp its nature as a transitional program. He also discusses the disintegration of German liberalism and the questions raised by the coming crisis as it becomes a chronic one. He urges Bebel to go on the US tour with Liebknecht [→ :13]. **Jan:** At Liebknecht's request, E sends him advice on his propagandist activity and Reichstag speeches, and on the struggle in the party against the right wing (SOURCE: MEW *Daten*).

4. W&P. **Jan 7 to Feb 25:** E edits Mrs. Wischnewetzky's trans of his *Condition of the working class* (#E171) for an American edn, and drafts a preface for it [→ :10]. **Jan 26:** E. R. Pease (Fabian Society) invites E to write a short Fabian tract on "What socialism is," as a concise presentation of socialist demands. **Jan 27:** E replies with a polite refusal grounded on lack of time; but he adds that "the party [tendency] I belong to" has no hard-and-fast, ready-made proposals of this sort to put forward. **Jan to Mar** (prob date): E drafts his essay *Ludwig Feuerbach* (#E457) [→ :15].

5. *CAPITAL*. **Jan D:** From Moore and Aveling E receives the complete ms of their trans of Vol. 1. From Danielson he receives the Russian edn of Vol. 2, just pubd.

6. RUSSIAN AFFAIRS. **Jan:** E receives from Danielson remarks on the economic situation in Russia.

FEBRUARY

7. ENGLISH AFFAIRS. **Feb 8:** A tumultuous demonstration of the unemployed takes place in Trafalgar Square, with speeches by Hyndman and the SDF in a leading role, winding up in uncontrolled hooliganism. E regards the affair as irresponsible adventurism by Hyndman. **Feb 9:** Writing to Sorge and to Laura Lafargue, E says that "the SDF leaders committed the most horrible idiocy in the streets." **Feb 15:** Writing to Bebel, E includes a detailed criticism of Hyndman's policy in the Trafalgar Square demonstration. He also writes of Hyndman's attempted deals with the Tories and with Chamberlain.

8. FRENCH AFFAIRS. **Feb 16:** Writing to Paul Lafargue, E greets the "historic event" in the Chamber of Deputies: three workers' deputies of the Radicals' labor wing have broken with the party on the issue of supporting the miners' strike in Decazeville; they move toward independent class action instead of clinging to the Radicals.

9. AMERICAN AFFAIRS. **Feb 3:** In a letter to Mrs. Wischnewetzky, E predicts that Amer-

ica will smash England's industrial monopoly but cannot succeed to it; capitalist crisis will mark an epoch in the political development of the working class. —E is impressed by the differences in American English: "What a splendid future must there be in store for a language which gets enriched and developed on two sides of an ocean. . . ."

10. W&P. **Feb 25:** E finishes, and sends off to Mrs. Wischnewetzky, his proposed preface (#E172) to the American edn of his *Condition of the working class* (#E171). In this essay E wholly incorporates his 1885 article, #E242. (As a result of the delay in publishing the edn, this preface will be converted to an Appendix, giving way to a new preface [→ :51].) In a letter, E explains to Mrs. Wischnewetzky that the "semi-Hegelian language" of passages in the book (#E171) is both untranslatable and largely meaningless now, hence his modernization of these passages in the English trans. Also, he strongly objects to steps taken to have the book pubd under the SLP's auspices or finances.

11. *CAPITAL*. **Feb 23 to Aug 5:** E works at editing and revising the Moore–Aveling English trans of Vol. 1 [← :5], using i.a. written suggestions made by M in 1877 in connection with an attempt at a trans in America.

12. SELF-GOVERNMENT. **Feb 4:** E congratulates Nieuwenhuis on his new book about Dutch government: since Holland did not go through the absolute monarchy in the 16th to 18th centuries, it retained some local self-government, "without a real bureaucracy in the French or Prussian sense"; this will make possible "the free self-government of the working people, with a few changes, and this must be our best tool for the transformation of the mode of production."

MARCH

13. EUROPEAN AFFAIRS. **Mar 6:** Bebel explains to E why he cannot go on the US tour with Liebknecht (throat trouble) [← :3]. **Mar 15:** In a letter to Laura Lafargue, E repeats his optimistic analysis [← :8] of the emergence of an independent group of workers' deputies in the French Chamber; the French WP's policy of patiently supporting united action of all proletarian elements is bearing fruit. E is sending the French deputies' speeches to Bebel, to alert the German party to the importance of the event. **Mar 18:** Again denouncing the Hyndman–SDF tactics of Feb 8, E tells Bebel that Hyndman has followed up with much empty "shouting about revolution"; all he has done is identify socialism with looting, in the public mind.

14. *CAPITAL*. **Mar AB:** E negotiates with Kegan Paul for publ of the English edn of

Capital; the pub'r accepts E's terms "in principle," but since he is "extremely slippery" (says E) this means little. E expects publ in Sep.

15. W&P. Mar 12: E receives the first part of Martignetti's Italian trans of M's *Wage-labor and capital* (#M968). Being busy with the English trans of *Capital,* he hopes to review the ms in April. **Mar 15:** On request, E writes a message to the French socialists on the 15th anniversary of the Paris Commune (#E432); pubd in *Le Socialiste,* Mar 27. **Mar 31:** E thanks Zasulich for sending the Russian edn of M's *Poverty of philosophy* (#M681), just pubd in her trans. **Mar:** E prob finishes writing his essay on *Ludwig Feuerbach* (#E457) [← :4; → :19].

APRIL

16. EUROPEAN MOVEMENT. Apr 12: E applauds the speeches made by Bebel (Mar 30–31) and Liebknecht (Apr 2) in the Reichstag debate on prolongation of the Anti-Socialist Law, and is glad that the party's right wing did not take the floor. Writing to Bebel, he sees the left turn in France [← :8] as exercising a revolutionizing influence on the German party, e.g., on Liebknecht. **Apr 28, 29:** In letters to Laura Lafargue and Sorge, E laments the incompetence of Bax and Morris as socialist leaders, in part because of anarchist influence in their Socialist League; it is a good thing that the working class takes no notice of these crotchets called out of courtesy English socialism. (E will write along the same lines to Liebknecht on May 12.) **Apr 29:** E's letter to Sorge is a general report on the state of the movement, esp in Germany and France. He also comments on the welcome transformation of German sentence structure, abandoning the classical pattern of putting "ten miles" between subject and end-verb.

17. REFUTING BISMARCK. Apr AB: Since in a Reichstag speech of Mar 31 Bismarck said that F. Blind, who tried to assassinate him in 1866, was a "pupil" of M's, E gets M's daughter Eleanor to write a statement refuting the charge against M. **Apr 14:** The statement, signed by both Eleanor and Laura, is sent to Bismarck (text: see *MEW* 36:820 n.607). **Apr 15:** The statement is pubd in *Sozialdemokrat* and (Apr 24) *Le Socialiste,* as well as in *Commonweal* (May 1).

18. AMERICAN AFFAIRS. Apr M: E sees a J. T. McEnnis of St. Louis, sent to him by Stepniak, presumably to discuss advice on labor legislation. Later E will discover he is a reporter for the *Missouri Republican;* McEnnis breaks his pledge to have E review his article. **Apr 29:** E writes to Sorge, enclosing the text of a statement (cf #E778) repudiating

McEnnis, to be pubd if McEnnis pubs anything [→ :29]. **Apr D to Sep:** *MEW Daten* summarizes as follows: E follows the mass struggle for the eight-hour day in the US, incl the work stoppage on May 1 and demonstrations in many cities; in letters to Sorge, Bebel, and others, he stresses the great international impact of this movement; he repeats his conviction that further struggles will overcome the weaknesses of the movement—anarchist influence, lack of clear program and aims, weak dissemination of scientific-socialist theory.

19. W&P. Apr-May: E's *Ludwig Feuerbach* (#E457) [← :4] is pubd in NZ.

20. CAPITAL. Apr 28: E describes to Laura Lafargue how the English trans is being made, with corrections going back and forth between Moore–Aveling and E, with E finally having to reread everything for final form, incl Eleanor M's work in finding the original English citations. **Apr 29:** In a letter to Sorge, E discusses M's instructions in two cases on what to take over from the French version.

21. PERSONAL. Apr to July: E is ill during this period; he is unable to do much walking.

MAY

22. FRENCH AFFAIRS. May 7: E congratulates Paul Lafargue on the success of the socialist candidates in the Paris municipal elections of May 2, exemplifying the tendency of the Paris workers toward a break with the Radical party. **May 12:** E writes Liebknecht on France along the same lines.

23. CAPITAL. May 22: E and Aveling meet with the publishing firm of Swan Sonnenschein and come to an agreement for publ of the English edn; the contract is to be signed in a few days. However, the work of revising the ms is still going on.

24. W&P. May A: E sends Martignetti (in Italy) the NZ publ of his essay on Feuerbach (#E457) [← :19] as well as the pamphlet edn of Wolff's *Schlesische Milliarde.* Wolff's pamphlet contains an intro by E (cf #E395.5) in two parts: a biographical sketch of Wolff (cf #E918), and E's essay on the history of the Prussian peasantry (#E558). The publ date of this pamphlet can be taken as May A, possibly Apr. **May 8–14:** E writes an item on the Lyons glass workers' strike, for *Commonweal* (#E570); pubd May 15. **May 10:** The Hamburg pub'r Nestler & Melle proposes to E that he become general editor of a series of publications on "social economy," to be written by various hands. **May 13:** E declines for lack of time, and recommends Kautsky. **May D to June 13:** E reads proof sheets of the American edn of his *Condition of the working class* (#E171) [← :10].

JUNE

25. AMERICAN AFFAIRS. June 3: In a letter to Mrs. Wischnewetzky, E stresses that the events of the last six months have broken the illusion "that America stood *above* class antagonisms and struggles."

26. CHARTISM. June 3: E promises Schlüter that, as soon as his work on the English edn of *Capital* permits, he will help him with his project on the Chartist preacher J. R. Stephens [→ :53].

27. J. P. BECKER. June 22: Becker (in Geneva) writes E with an urgent request: he has to discuss with E, orally only, a plan connected with his making his will. Becker proposes meeting halfway, in Paris, this year [→ :30].

28. PERSONAL. June c.25 to July 7: E sojourns in Eastbourne, taking the waters; he is visited by Schorlemmer.

JULY

29. McENNIS AFFAIR. July 8: E's statement repudiating McEnnis's interview (#E778) is pubd in the *New Yorker Volkszeitung,* on Sorge's initiative [← :18; → :33].

30. J. P. BECKER. July 9: Replying to Becker's proposal [← :27], E explains that his illness makes him immobile [← :21]; he asks Becker to come to London, preferably in Oct, at E's expense.

31. PERSONAL. July 26: E reports (to Kautsky) that his health is improving daily; he can now walk some distance [← :21; → :35].

AUGUST

32. EUROPEAN AFFAIRS. Aug 18: E's letter to Bebel (his first in some months [← :16]) reviews the scene; the two big events of this year were the upsurge of a class movement in America and the turn in France [← :13]. In England, where there are "as many sects as there are heads," E as usual condemns the SDF and Socialist League as meaningless sects. To begin with, however, he comments on the Freiberg court verdict which is sending Bebel (and other party leaders) to prison for some months: this "sudden persecution furor" reflects the rage of the "ruling clique" over the failure of the Anti-Socialist Law to repress socialism. **Aug CD to Oct:** *MEW Daten* entry: E studies the international situation with its increasingly tense Great Power rivalries over the Balkans, French *revanchisme,* German militarism, English colonialism, etc., with a view to the danger of a European war to the workers' movement, on the one hand, and on the other, the probability of its leading to a revolutionary crisis [cf → :36, 40].

33. W&P. Aug 3: E receives from Sorge a copy of the article pubd by McEnnis [← :29]. **Aug 9:** Kautsky asks E to check over his ms for his book on *The economic doctrines of KM.* **Aug 11:** E agrees to do what he can [→ :39]. **Aug 13–14:** Writing to Mrs. Wischnewetzky, E discusses why socialist books should be pubd in the regular book trade by commercial publishers, rather than as party literature which soons becomes unobtainable. **Aug 20:** E gives Schlüter (of the party press) his assent to a new edn of his *Housing question* (#E358), and also recommends publishing a new edn of a pamphlet by S. Borkheim (cf ST/6), who died last Dec; E promises to supply a biographical sketch of Borkheim as intro (cf #E391) [→ 87:48].

34. CAPITAL. Aug 5: E finishes the work of editing and revising Moore and Aveling's English trans of Vol. 1. **Aug 13–14:** In his letter to Mrs. Wischnewetzky (see ← :33), E suggests a series of pamphlets giving a popular version of the content of *Capital;* the first should to be on the theory of surplus value. **Aug to Nov:** E works on the galley proofs of the English edn of Vol. 1.

35. PERSONAL. Aug 7 to Sep 4: As the result of a relapse in health [← :31] E goes to Eastbourne [→ :38]. **Aug 29:** E leaves Eastbourne for a day to meet Liebknecht in London [→ :38]; in London E also meets with Harney. **Aug 31:** Eleanor M and Aveling sail from Liverpool for NY, to begin their American tour (which will eventually involve E) [→ :37].

SEPTEMBER

36. INTERNATIONAL AFFAIRS. Sep 5–13: E meets several times with the leaders of the Socialist League, Bax and Morris, to discuss the critical situation in the group. **Sep 13–14:** In a long letter to Bebel, E gives a detailed analysis of the tense international situation and the danger of war [cf ← :32; → :40]. **Sep 16:** E writes Sorge that the Socialist League is in the hands of "faddists and sentimental socialists." In America, Dietzgen has overreacted against the "contemptible" behavior of the SLP leaders regarding the Haymarket anarchists: he is now writing that no distinctions should be made between anarchists and socialists/communists; this means he is forgetting dialectics.

37. AMERICAN TOURS. Sep 10 to Dec 25: Eleanor M and Aveling are on tour in America under the auspices of the SLP; as a result of Aveling's open criticism of the SLP leadership, the tour will result in SLP charges against Aveling of mishandling party money. (Around the same time, and partly with the Avelings, Liebknecht is on a fundraising tour of America, Sep 13 to Nov 27.) For the aftermath of these tours, see → 87:1.

38. VISITORS. **Sep A:** Before sailing for America on Sep 4, Liebknecht [← :35] spends four days with E in Eastbourne. **Sep 17 to c.27/28:** J. P. Becker [← :30], visiting from Geneva, is E's guest in London (from where he goes to the Lafargues', near Paris). (For one subject of discussion, see → :41.)

39. KAUTSKY. **Sep c.5–11:** E reads the ms of Kautsky's book on M's economics [← :33] and makes suggestions for change. (The book will be pubd in 1887.)

OCTOBER

40. INTERNATIONAL AFFAIRS. **Oct 9, 22:** In letters to Bernstein, E discusses the tense Great Power situation and the danger of war, along the same lines as to Bebel [← :36], though more briefly. **Oct 25:** E sends Paul Lafargue a long letter on the Great Power maneuverings leading to war, and the prospect of revolution. Lafargue converts this letter into an article [→ :48].

41. J. P. BECKER. **Oct 8, 9:** In letters to Bebel and Bernstein, E urges the German party to give financial support to Becker to enable him to write his memoirs, as an important source of the history of the movement [→ :52].

42. BERNSTEIN AS THEORETICIAN. **Oct 9:** E responds to a three-page letter by Bernstein (Sep 17) giving "painstaking considerations" on the subject of why he is thinking of getting married. E has read this document with amazement and hearty laughter: "If all proletarians were as dubiously reflective, the proletariat would die out or propagate only through illegitimate children, and to the latter mode we will indeed come en masse when there is no longer any proletariat in existence. . . . So give my best to your bride and jump forthwith into the marriage bed with both feet."

43. GERMAN MOVEMENT. **Oct 23:** Writing to Bebel, E approves the Oct 21 party statement that henceforth the *Sozialdemokrat* is not its official organ—a decision enforced by the recent government persecution [← :32] but which will facilitate the paper's struggle against the party's right wing.

44. FRENCH AFFAIRS. **Oct 2:** E responds to a Sep 30 letter from Paul Lafargue crowing over the recent (Sep 24) jury acquittal of Lafargue, Guesde, and Susini, on a charge of subversion, after a political trial. E cautions Lafargue against drawing overoptimistic conclusions about recruiting petty-bourgeois elements to socialism, even though the contradictions between sectors of the bourgeoisie are useful.

45. MENGER. **c.Oct:** Prof. Anton Menger pubs a book *Das Recht auf den vollen Arbeitsertrag* which gains some notoriety for its claim that M's *Capital* plagiarized the Ricardian socialists, esp William Thompson. **Oct:** E arranges to have a critical review of Menger's book appear in *NZ*, either as an unsigned article or under Kautsky's signature, but he plans to write most of it himself; Kautsky agrees to collaborate. **Oct 30:** Laura Lafargue writes E from Paris about Menger's claims, thinking to alert him [→ :49].

NOVEMBER

46. ENGLISH MOVEMENT. **Nov D:** In at least three letters (Nov 24 to Laura Lafargue, Nov 26 to Schlüter, Nov 29 to Sorge) E indicates he is upgrading his view of the SDF's role (though not of Hyndman); this will turn out to be temporary.

47. AMERICAN AFFAIRS. **Nov 24, 29:** In letters to Laura Lafargue and to Sorge, esp the latter, E again expounds the significance of the new class movement in America, esp the Knights of Labor and the NY labor party movement which ran H. George for mayor— "the first formation of a real American working men's party," with a confused program, to be sure, but no matter as long as it is a distinctly class party. The SLP sectists cannot grasp that the working class is in motion; as doctrinaires, their theory is "a credo, not a guide to action" [→ 87:4].

48. W&P. **Nov 4, 26:** Schlüter asks E if he has any objection to the publ of a separate pamphlet comprising the three chapters of *Anti-Dühring* (#E23) on the "force theory" (Part II, Chs. 2–4). E replies that he is willing in principle; but he suggests adding Chs. 9–10 of Part I (on Morality and Law) to make a larger whole; this would revolve around the "materialist-economic conception of history," under a title like "On law and power in world history." (E will later change his plan; see #E705.) **Nov 6:** E's letter to Paul Lafargue on the international situation [← :40], somewhat adapted, is pubd by Lafargue in *Le Socialiste* as an article, "Political situation in Europe" (#E593); pubd in a NY German paper, Nov 20, 27 [→ :54]. **Nov 13:** *Commonweal* pubs a brief reply by E to a letter to the editor; see #E665.5.

49. MENGER. **Nov to Dec A:** E works on a critical review of Menger's book [← :45], but ill health forces him to have the article finished by Kautsky, with E's aid and suggestions (SOURCE: *MEW Daten* and notes). **Nov 2:** E tells Laura Lafargue that he is already aware of Menger's book, "and I shall give Kautsky notes enough to enable him to smash the cheeky devil." **Nov 24:** E informs Laura that "I have given Kautsky the necessary materials and partly worked them out myself as far as necessary." (For publ of the article, "Lawyers' socialism," #E429, see → 87:15.)

50. *CAPITAL.* **Nov 5:** E finishes the preface (#E601) to the English edn [→ 87:6]. **Nov 9:** E informs Danielson that the sales of Vol. 2 up to last Mar amount to 1300; and he comments on some reviews. Of the English trans he remarks that it has been a hard job because in the final analysis it is he (E) who must bear responsibility for the text (i.e., not Moore and Aveling). **Nov 29:** E delivers the last part of the preface (#E601) to the English edn to the printer.

DECEMBER

51. AMERICAN AFFAIRS. **Dec 10:** Mrs. Wischnewetzky asks E to write a new preface for the American edn of his *Condition of the working class* (#E171) because of the changed scene since Feb [← :10] when E wrote the preface (#E172), particularly because of the need to do a critique of Henry George [→ 87:7]. **Dec 28:** Replying to Mrs. Wischnewetzky, E explains what he will take up in the new preface (#E174)—a trenchant version of

what he has long been writing about the US movement: the expansion of the class movement is far more important than that it proceed "on theoretically perfectly correct lines"; the Knights of Labor ought "not to be poohpoohed from without but to be revolutionized from within"; anything that delays the crystallization of a workers' party is a mistake; and so on.

52. J. P. BECKER. **Dec 9:** Becker having died Dec 7, E writes an obituary article on this old revolutionist [← :41] (#E401); pubd in *Sozialdemokrat,* Dec 17.

53. CHARTISM. **c.Dec to Mar:** In line with his promise [← :26], E reads the ms of Schlüter's work, whose subject has now broadened to *Die Chartistenbewegung in England;* E draws up a Chartist chronology and suggests changes and additions [→ 87:32].

54. W&P. **Dec 12:** E's article on the "Political situation in Europe" (#E593) [← :48] is pubd in German in *Sozialdemokrat.*

55. VISITORS. **Dec 5–10:** Liebknecht (returned from his US tour) and his wife are E's guests in London. **Dec 6:** E is also visited by Paul Singer. **Dec c.23 to Jan M:** Paul and Laura Lafargue stay in London as E's guests.

1887

CONSPECTUS

1. *Aveling Affair (Background).* This episode sprawls through the first half of the year, and is not noticed in detail in the following pages, since E's connection, while time-consuming, is peripheral. It involves the aftermath of the US tour by Eleanor M and Edward Aveling (usually called "the Avelings" at this time since they are living together as husband and wife); for the tour, see ← 86:37. The Avelings return to London on Jan 4. Beginning Jan A, the American SLP leadership—which E has been criticizing for years as a clutch of sectists ruining the movement, and which Aveling openly criticized on the tour itself—launches a campaign of vilification against Aveling around the charge that he has defrauded the party of expense moneys. The SLP leaders begin by leaking the story to the bourgeois press, which makes an antisocialist scandal out of it. By Mar there are a spate of statements—replies by Aveling and rejoinders by the SLP, continuing into Apr and May. By Apr D, Hyndman takes up the cry in England. In May, Liebknecht (who was on an American tour at about the same time) issues a statement defending Aveling. In correspondence, E comes vigorously to Aveling's defense immediately; for his first

long analysis of the SLP's case, see his letter of Feb 7 to Mrs. Wischnewetzky (who is eventually convinced, and later expelled from the SLP). E continues his argumentation in letters to Sorge (Feb 12; Mar 3, 16; Apr 6), and in other correspondence. E also helps Aveling to formulate his replies. For an account of the affair, esp through E's letters, see ST/35.5 (Kapp) 2:171–91.

2. Another entry that extends over the first months of 1887 revolves around the fact that, on returning from America, both of the Avelings throw themselves—in consultation with E—into effective propaganda work among the Radical workers' clubs of the East End, with the aim of developing a workers' political movement independent of the Liberals. The Avelings are already planning this in Jan [see →:5] and E writes friends about it, esp Mar CD to May.

3. W&P. During 1887, from July on there are various republications—in French, German, and English—of E's piece on "The labor movement in America," for which see #E174.

JANUARY

4. AMERICAN AFFAIRS. **Jan 27:** E continues his series of letters to Mrs. Wischnewetzky counterposing the need for an open class movement against the doctrinaire sectarianism of the SLP; the great danger, E says, is the consolidation of political differences into separate sects, each holding a mechanically repeated dogma. Against this he cites the examples of M&E's tactics in 1848 and in the International, on how to "work along with the general movement of the working class at every one of its stages without giving up or hiding our own distinct position or even organizn. . . ."

5. ENGLISH MOVEMENT. **Jan 28:** Writing to Paul Lafargue, E notes that the Avelings, who are giving lectures on their American tour, are using these lectures to campaign for an independent labor party after the American example [← 86:47] among the East End Radical clubs [→ :17].

6. *CAPITAL.* **Jan A:** The English edn of Vol. 1 is pubd in London by Swan Sonnenschein, with a preface by E (#E601) [← 86:50], in an edn of 500 copies; the volume is in two physical books.

7. W&P. **Jan 10:** E finishes, and dates, his preface (#E359) to the second edn of his *Housing question* (#E358); pubd in *Sozialdemokrat,* Jan 15, 22 [→ :19]. **Jan 26:** E finishes, and dates, his new preface (#E174) [← 86:51] to the American edn of his *Condition of the working class* (#E171), replacing the previous draft [← 86:10] which now becomes an appendix (#E172).

8. RETROSPECTIVE. **Jan 9:** Martignetti (in Italy) writes E that he can no longer work in Italy as a minor government official because of harassment: can E help him get a job in America or elsewhere? **Jan 26:** E replies with advice, and adds that in 1844 and 1849 M&E too ran into such economic difficulties: ". . . how often did M and I regret that we had not learned any kind of manual work. . . ."

9. PERSONAL **Jan to July:** Because of eye trouble (conjunctivitis), E is forced to limit his working time at reading or writing.

FEBRUARY

10. GERMAN ELECTION. **Feb 24:** Writing to Laura Lafargue, E is pleased by the results of the Feb 21 Reichstag election, gained despite intensified police harassment: although the number of seats decreased, this is of no account; the important thing is the shift of party strength from the Saxon weavers (moribund trade) to the cities and rural industrial districts [→ :16].

11. INTERNATIONAL FETE. **Feb A:** As an organizing comm of socialist émigrés in Paris prepares an International Fête for Feb 19 to protest the war danger, Ossip Zetkin on its behalf invites E to send greetings. **Feb 13** (or 16/17?): E sends a letter of greetings to the organizing comm (#E446). (Dated Feb 13 according to *MEW,* but cf letter of E to Paul Lafargue, Feb 16.) **Feb 19:** E's letter is read to the Paris meeting; pubd in *Le Socialiste,* Feb 25 [→ :19].

12. DANIELSON. **Feb 12:** E sends Danielson the English edn of *Capital,* and (Feb c.12) receives from him a copy of Saltykov-Shchedrin's *Tales.*

13. ROUMANIA. **Feb AB:** E studies the Roumanian language as he reads an article of his (#E593) pubd in the *Revista Socială.* For E's comments on the language, see his letter to Paul Lafargue, Feb 16.

14. ROOT OF EVIL. **Feb 9:** In connection with the "Aveling affair" and the SLP charges [← :1], E comments that because such charges were so common in the movement, he and M always avoided "any money dealings with the party" in any country.

15. W&P. Feb: The Engels–Kautsky article on Menger (#E429) [← 86:49] is pubd in NZ.

MARCH

16. GERMAN ELECTION. **Mar 3:** Writing to Sorge, E repeats [← :10] his delight over the election results of Feb 21, and opines that Liebknecht's weaknesses are not vital as long as Bebel keeps him straight. —E repeats his views on the election in letters to Mrs. Julie Bebel (Mar 12) and Schlüter (Mar 19).

17. ENGLISH MOVEMENT. **Mar CD:** About this time E begins stressing and praising (cf his letter to Laura Lafargue, Mar 21) the propaganda campaign by Aveling, soon joined by Eleanor M, among the workers' East End Radical clubs; cf ← :2, 5 [→ :23].

18. *CAPITAL.* **Mar A:** By this time the first edn of the English trans (500 copies) has sold all but about 50 copies, almost half in America; a second printing is in preparation [→ :24].

19. W&P. **Mar AB:** E's *Housing question* (#E358), in a complete pamphlet edn for the first time, is pubd in Zurich, with E's new preface (#E359) [← :7]. **Mar 4:** *Sozialdemokrat* pubs an excerpt from *Anti-Dühring* under the title "Wie die Gleichheitsidee entstand" [How the idea of equality arose]. **Mar 11:** E's letter to the Paris International Fête (#E446) [← :11] is pubd in *Sozialdemokrat;* also in NY *Sozialist,* Mar 19. **Mar 18:** E sends brief Paris Commune anniversary greetings to the Paris organization of the French party (#E848); pubd in *Le Socialiste,* Mar 26. **Mar 21:** Re Fortin's French trans of M's *18th Brumaire* (#M267) [← 85:26], E reports to Laura Lafargue that he has received all of Fortin's ms, but will not be able to check it over immediately because of eye trouble. (It will be pubd in 1891 as a book, first in *Le*

Socialiste, Jan-Nov.) **Mar c.D:** E checks over the Danish trans of his *Origin of the family* (#E573). **Mar-Apr:** Sam Moore drafts an English trans of the *Com Manifesto,* under E's supervision. E's work—checking, editing, revising, annotating—is delayed by his eye trouble [→ 88:2].

APRIL

20. EUROPEAN AFFAIRS. **Apr 6:** Writing to Sorge, E discusses the bad state of the Paris movement. **Apr 9:** To Sorge, E comments on the Mar 13 attentat against Czar Alexander III and the resultant executions: these actions cap the climax; the crisis in Russia is deepening; and E ends with "Hurrah." **Apr D to May A:** E corresponds with the Spanish socialist leader Mesa, who writes him about the elimination of anarchist influence and the growth of the movement in Spain. Mesa sends the issues of *El Socialista* of 1886 containing the first Spanish trans of *Socialism: Utopian and scientific* (#E759).

21. COLLECTING MARX. **Apr 7:** Danielson sends two packets containing M's letters to him; rec'd by E, Apr c.24.

22. AMERICAN EDITION. **Apr:** The SLP delays publ of the American edn of E's *Condition of the working class* (#E171), even though all work on it has been finished and E has sent in [← :7] his new preface (#E174); E becomes increasingly suspicious. **Apr 9:** E complains (to Sorge) about the delay, which he believes is due to the SLP leadership's disapproval of what the preface says. E also becomes increasingly irritated with Mrs. Wischnewetzky: "she translates like a machine," leaving the real work to E; and so on. **Apr 10:** Without E's knowledge, the *New Yorker Volkszeitung* pubs a German trans of the preface (#E174) by A. Jonas, full of errors besides. **Apr 23:** Writing to Sorge, E is furious at this unauthorized and garbled publ and at Mrs. Wischnewetzky for making it possible; he threatens to cut relations with her. He sends a formal letter of protest to the paper itself [→ :25].

23. ENGLISH MOVEMENT. **Apr 9 to May 5:** In a number of letters, E admiringly reports the effective propaganda campaign by the Avelings among the Radical workers' clubs of the East End [← :17] for an independent labor party [→ :26].

24. *CAPITAL.* **Apr:** Swan Sonnenschein issues the second (stereotyped, hence cheaper) printing of Vol. 1, English edn, in 500 copies [← :18].

MAY

25. AMERICAN EDITION. **May 4:** Writing to Sorge about the delay in publishing his *Condition of the working class* (#E171) [← :22], E is still steaming at Mrs. Wischnewetzky's handling of the book: she "has bungled everything she has handled up to now. . . ." **May 7:** E has now heard from Sorge that in NYC the Wischnewetzkys have openly attacked the "dissimulations and suppressions" of the SLP Exec in the Aveling affair; he writes Mrs. Wischnewetzky that he is glad of this and will not return to the controversy. (E's relations with her will now improve; by July she will be expelled by the SLP bureaucracy.) E is also glad to hear that the book will not be pubd by the SLP. He explains his general opposition to publishing party literature on a narrow basis. **May A:** The American edn of the book (#E171) is finally pubd in NYC.

26. ENGLISH MOVEMENT. **May 4, 5:** In letters to Sorge and Bernstein about the Avelings' work among the East End Radical clubs [← :23], E stresses the direct prospect of "an English labor party with an independent class program" which would push the sects (SDF, Socialist League) into the background. **May 29:** At the third annual conference of the Socialist League, William Morris and the anarchist wing put through a policy of principled antiparliamentarism ("policy of abstention") against a minority (incl Eleanor M) whose position is put forward in a resolution by J. L. Mahon. Mahon's resolution may have been drafted with E's help; it gives electoral work its place in a socialist program.

JUNE

27. ENGLISH MOVEMENT. **June 4, 7:** In letters to Sorge and Laura Lafargue, E reports the victory of antiparliamentarism in the Socialist League [← :26] and opines that the minority (Eleanor M, Aveling, Bax, Mahon, etc.) may as well quit a group that is only a hindrance to a class movement. **June 14:** Mahon (in Newcastle) [← 84:55] sends E a copy of the Principles and Program of the North of England Socialist Federation (founded over a month ago in Northumberland), reports on the movement, and urges the founding of a new socialist party through amalgamation. **June 22:** E returns the program to Mahon with marginal notes giving suggested changes (#E788). **June 23:** In another letter to Mahon, E says that his organizn plan is premature, the "provinces" have to be organized first in order to bring pressure on London. **June 24:** Mahon says the suggestions came too late to be incorporated; he continues the discussion on problems of the movement [→ :33].

28. W&P. **June 3:** *Sozialdemokrat* pubs a German trans of M's 1877 letter to the *Ote-*

chestvenniye Zapiski, on Russian social development (#M464) [← 86:2]. **June 10, 17:** E's preface (#E174) to the American edn of the *Condition of the working class* (#E171) [← :25] is pubd in *Sozialdemokrat*, in E's own German trans, as an article on "The labor movement in America." **June 24:** E (in a letter to Harney) expresses his intention to write a biography of M.

JULY

29. W&P. **July 9–23:** E's preface (#E174) to the *Condition of the working class* (#E171) [← :28] is pubd in French in *Le Socialiste*.
30. AMERICAN AFFAIRS. **July 20:** E returns to Mrs. Wischnewetzky the copies of reviews of *The condition of the working class* which she had sent him. **July 20, 27:** Sorge informs E that Mrs. Wischnewetzky and her husband have been expelled from the SLP for criticizing the leadership on the Aveling affair [→ :38]. **July:** E's preface (#E174) is pubd in NYC as a separate pamphlet in German and also in English, with a new title (see *Register*).
31. BIOGRAPHY. **July:** E checks over the ms of Kautsky's biographical sketch of him, written for the *Österreichischer Arbeiter-Kalendar für das Jahr 1888*; he corrects and supplements some passages.
32. CHARTISM. **July:** E reads the proof sheets of Schlüter's brochure *Die Chartistenbewegung in England* [← 86:53]. (The brochure will be pubd in Zurich Oct A, unsigned, with acknowledgment of E's aid.)
33. J. L. MAHON. **July 19:** This young socialist [← :27] visits E for a discussion, i.a. about Aveling. **July 21, 26:** In an exchange of letters, E tries unsuccessfully to get Mahon to say why he refuses to deal with Aveling (on July 31, Aveling himself elicits only an evasive reply from Mahon, who refuses to state a reason) [→ 88:3].
34. BOULANGER. **July:** The Boulanger crisis in France is heralded by the first big demonstration in Paris (July 8, Gare de Lyon) in favor of Gen. Boulanger. Paul Lafargue writes E: "The Parisians have gone mad . . ." (July 11; followed by further reports). E advises: the socialists should "demand . . . the arming of the people as the only guarantee" against caesarist aims by popular generals (July 15) [→ 88:12].
35. PERSONAL. **July 23 to Sep 2:** E sojourns in Eastbourne.

AUGUST

36. ABOUT HONORS. **Aug 20:** Bruno Schoenlank, who is having a book pubd on the mirror-making industry, asks permission to dedicate it to E as the "founder of descrip-

tive economics." **Aug 29:** E declines this dedication, and also rejects the "founder" appellation as inaccurate: "M and I, from way back, have had a certain aversion to such honorific testimonials which are more or less dragged in by the hair"; besides, E thinks that his own services to the movement are presently being overestimated, at the cost of M's.
37. KAUTSKY. **Aug CD:** At Kautsky's request, E reads the galley proofs of his book *Thomas More and his utopia*, and makes comments on it.
38. AMERICAN AFFAIRS. **Aug 8:** In response to Sorge's news of Mrs. Wischnewetzky's expulsion by the SLP [← :30] E comments that a "gang of pure louts" is getting control of the American movement.
39. VISITORS. **Aug A:** At Eastbourne [← :35] Bax stays with E for at least a week, conversing and asking questions. **Aug 13:** Since Bebel is getting out of jail tomorrow, E invites him to come to London for a restorative junket, at E's expense [→ :43].

SEPTEMBER

40. AMERICAN MOVEMENT. **Sep 15, 16:** Writing to Mrs. Wischnewetzky and Sorge, E is glad that Henry George's United Labor party of NY has excluded the SLP, which was supporting it; now the socialist movement will not be saddled with the George sect as its leadership. To Mrs. Wischnewetzky he writes that he is indifferent to the SLP press's boycott of his writings and similar "chicanery."
41. WAR DANGER. **Sep 16:** In his letter to Sorge, E opines that the danger of war is not yet immediate because everyone hesitates to begin, the cost being so immense; the danger is that the war will break out without their wanting it to.
42. LOPATIN. **Sep 3:** On getting the (false) news of Lopatin's death, E writes Lavrov that he plans to send an obituary notice to *Sozialdemokrat*.

OCTOBER

43. BEBEL IN LONDON. **Oct CD:** Bebel [← :39] visits as E's guest.
44. PENALTY OF FAME. **Oct 8:** J. Weiss, a friend of Conrad Schmidt otherwise unknown to E, writes E asking for a "loan" to complete his medical studies. **Oct c.10:** E politely declines, mentioning that he gets an increasing number of requests for money.

NOVEMBER

45. EUROPEAN MOVEMENT. **Nov 22:** E writes on the growing bourgeoisification of the party, in a letter to Paul Lafargue: "That is the tragedy of all extreme parties as soon as the day for them to become 'possible' draws near. But ours, in this respect, cannot go beyond a certain limit without betraying itself, and in my view we have reached that point in France as in Germany."

46. W&P. **Nov D to Dec A:** E negotiates with the London pub'r Reeves on distributing the American edn of the *Condition of the working class* (#E171) and on separate publ of its preface (#E174) in England.

47. BIRTHDAY. **Nov 28:** E's birthday is informally celebrated: after a private theatrical performance by Eleanor M and Aveling in a local pub, the gathering goes to E's house for a party.

DECEMBER

48. W&P. **Dec 3:** E promises Mrs. Wischnewetzky, not for the first time, that he will check over her trans of M's speech on free trade (#M836) and that he will write an introduction. **Dec 7:** E agrees to Schlüter's proposal to publish a collection of his "minor essays of 1871–75," under the title *Kleinere Aufsätze von FE aus den Jahren 1871–1875.* E's outline of the planned contents lists #E571, 660, 662, 754, 59. (This project will

not be realized.) **Dec A:** Having revised his work on *Ludwig Feuerbach* (#E457) from its NZ version [← 86:19], E sends the ms to party pub'r Dietz, along with the text of M's *Theses on Feuerbach* (#M878), all for publ as a brochure [→ 88:19]. **Dec 15:** E writes an intro (#E391) to a second edn of Borkheim's brochure *Zur Erinnerung für die deutschen Mordspatrioten, 1806–1807* (ST/6), which on E's recommendation is being pubd as no. 25 of the party press's Social-Democratic Library series. The subject of E's intro is the danger of a European war and its revolutionary consequences [→ 88:2]. **Dec D to Mar:** E works on the project which later (unfinished) will be titled *The role of force in history* (#E705). At this point his plan is to write a fourth chapter, on Bismarckism, to be added to the three chapters of *Anti-Dühring* (#E23) on the force theory of history [← 86:48; → 88:4].

49. OBERWINDER. **Dec 29:** E sends Paul Lafargue an account of the political record and character of H. Oberwinder, an Austrian Lassallean, whom the *Sozialdemokrat* now reports to have been a Prussian agent.

50. ROUMANIA. **Dec to Jan:** E studies the Roumanian language [← :13] esp using Roumanian translations of his own writings.

1888

JANUARY

1. WAR POLICY. **Jan 4:** In a letter to the Roumanian socialist Nădejde, of *Contemporanul* (which pubs it in its Jan issue), E discusses the looming European war, and concludes: "Let us hope that there is no war; in such a war, one could sympathize with none of the belligerents, on the contrary one would wish that *all* be defeated if that were possible. It would be a frightful war. But come what will, it is certain that in the end everything would end in favor of the socialist movement and would hasten the taking of power by the working class. . . . A revolution in Russia at the present moment would save Europe from the misfortune of a general war and would be the beginning of revolution in the whole world." **Jan 7:** In a letter to Sorge, E again harks back to the danger of a European war— its devastation, etc. He stresses that the war will be long and perhaps settle nothing quickly; if it were fought to a finish without revolution, Europe would be prostrated and American industry would take over. **Jan-Feb:** Under this date *MEW Daten* has the following general statement: "E pays close attention to the international situation and the war danger."

2. W&P. **Jan 15:** *Sozialdemokrat* pubs the second part (only) of E's introduction (#E391) to Borkheim's pamphlet [← 87:48]. The pamphlet itself, with the whole of E's intro, is pubd later this year [→ :22]. **Jan 30:** E writes a preface (#E611) to the English edn of the *Com Manifesto*, on which Sam Moore has now finished his translation work [→ :13].

3. ENGLISH MOVEMENT. **Jan 14:** J. L. Mahon [← 87:33] writes E reporting on his work in the north of England [→ :20].

4. STUDIES. **Jan 2–4:** E orders a copy of a work on the Russian peasant community by the economist Keussler. **Jan to Mar:** During his work on *The role of force in history* (#E705) [← 87:48], E reads the new book by the German historian Bulle, *Geschichte der neuesten Zeit, 1815–1885,* Vol. 4, and from it makes chronological extracts on German history after 1871.

5. PERSONAL. **Jan to May:** E's eye trouble forces him once again to limit his working time.

FEBRUARY

6. WAR DANGER. **Feb 7:** Writing to Paul Lafargue, E reports that the war danger has turned him back to his military studies. In case of war, "I hope that the Russians will be soundly beaten," but without a decisive result on the French front—"in which case there will be a chance of reconciliation" (between the French and Germans). **Feb 22:** In a letter to Sorge, E analyzes the chances of the countries in a war; but war or no war, a crisis is approaching; an "instinctive socialism" is taking hold of the masses.

7. GERMAN MOVEMENT. **Feb 23:** E writes that the Reichstag debate on extending the Anti-Socialist Law (during Jan-Feb, with Bebel and Singer most prominent) "was the greatest triumph we have yet gained on the parliamentary arena" even though the law was extended.

8. RELIEF WORK. **Feb D:** E helps to collect aid for the widow of his old comrade Karl Pfänder.

9. ENGLISH MOVEMENT. **Feb 22, 23:** E's letters report on the successful work being carried on among the East End Radical clubs [← 87:2] for independent workers' political action, using the example of the NY electoral campaign of Nov 1886.

10. W&P. **Feb 13–25:** E corrects the galley proofs of the English edn of the Com Manifesto [→ :13]. **Feb 21:** E writes the foreword (#E458) for the book publ of his Ludwig Feuerbach (#E457) [→ :19].

MARCH

11. GERMAN AFFAIRS. **Mar 17, 19:** In letters to Schlüter and to Paul Lafargue, E discusses the unstable situation created in Germany by the death (Mar 9) of Kaiser Wilhelm I. Lafargue uses E's letter as the basis for his own article in L'Intransigeant, May 26.

12. FRANCE: BOULANGER. **Mar 18–21:** In an exchange of letters, E and Paul Lafargue discuss the outbreak of mass enthusiasm for Gen. Boulanger [← 87:34]; Lafargue poohpoohs fears about Boulanger; E (Mar 19) warns that Boulanger is not a "cipher."

13. W&P. **Mar A:** The "authorized English translation" of the Com Manifesto, translated by Samuel Moore and edited (and revised) by E, is pubd in London, with a new preface by E (#E611) [← :2]. **Mar:** E leaves unfinished [← 87:48] his draft essay on The role of force in history (#E705; cf also #E706–07).

APRIL

14. NOVEL WRITING. **Apr A:** On reading Margaret Harkness's novel City girl (sent by the author), E writes her his praise but criticizes her treatment of the working class as a "passive mass," helped only "from without, from above," as a violation of realism.

15. INTERNATIONAL CONGRESS. **Apr 16:** E advises Liebknecht that an international congress should not be initiated by the German party nor held in London; he proposes that it be called by the French socialists for the centennial of the 1789 revolution.

16. BOULANGER. **Apr-May:** Paul Lafargue's letters to E continue [← :12] to put forward the line that Boulanger is not a danger but rather "useful" to the movement, and should not be attacked by socialists [→ :21].

17. W&P. **Apr to May A:** E edits and revises Mrs. Wischnewetzky's English trans of M's speech on free trade (#M836) [→ :31]. He also writes an introduction (#E394) to the American pamphlet edn [→ :19].

18. PERSONAL. **Apr-May:** E is still allowed to write only two hours a day, because of his eye trouble—so he reports in letters Apr 11, May 2.

MAY

19. W&P. **May 2:** E sends Mrs. Wischnewetzky the finished ms of the English trans of M's speech on free trade (#M836) as revised by himself [← :17]. **May 16:** E sends her the last part of his intro (#E394) to this speech [→ :26]. **May AB:** E's essay Ludwig Feuerbach (#E457), revised from its NZ version [← 86:19], is pubd as a brochure, with a new foreword by E (#E458).

20. MAHON. **May 10:** Through Eleanor M, E sends Mahon [← :3] an open invitation to visit and discuss problems [→ 89:16].

JUNE

21. BOULANGER. **June 3:** Writing to Laura Lafargue, E criticizes Paul Lafargue's view of Gen. Boulanger [← :16] and stresses the chauvinist, Bonapartist character of his movement: "What I want our people to do is to show that there is a real third issue [way out]" besides the choice between Boulanger and his bourgeois-democratic opponents.

22. W&P. **June:** E's intro to Borkheim's pamphlet (#E391) [← :2] is pubd as a separate pamphlet.

23. VISITOR. **June 17:** Schlüter, visiting London, has dinner at E's.

JULY

24. BOULANGER. **July 15:** In another letter to Laura Lafargue [← :21] E stresses two elements in the case against supporting Boulanger: this chauvinist movement points to a European war; and it shows the power of Bonapartism in France.

25. VERSE TRANSLATION. **July 6 to Aug A:** In response to Kautsky's request (June 20), E makes a German verse trans from Shelley for the article "Shelley als Sozialist" by E. Aveling and Eleanor M; pubd in *NZ*, Dec.

26. W&P. **July:** NZ pubs E's own German trans of his intro (#E394) to the American edn of M's speech on free trade [← :19], under the title "Protective tariff and free trade."

27. PERSONAL. **July 11:** E informs Sorge confidentially that he may take a trip to the US, Aug c.M or a bit later. **July 22:** E entertains at supper the newly arrived contingent of "Zurichers" and their wives, i.e., the staff of the *Sozialdemokrat* recently (Apr) expelled from Switzerland and now relocating in London, incl Bernstein, Schlüter, Motteler.

AUGUST

28. AMERICAN TOUR. **Aug 8:** E, together with Eleanor M, Edward Aveling, and Prof. Schorlemmer, sails for NYC from Liverpool on the steamer *City of Berlin*; the ship puts in at Queenstown (Cobh), Aug 9. **Aug 17:** E's ship arrives in NYC. **Aug 18–26:** E spends several days in the NY area, also visiting in Hoboken with Sorge. **Aug 27:** E goes to Boston, by railway. **Aug 28:** In Cambridge, E visits the Harneys, but finds only Mrs. Harney; her husband is visiting London. **Aug 30:** E visits Concord; he is impressed by a progressively managed prison (as he reports to Sorge) [continue → :30].

29. W&P. **Aug:** The *Labor Standard* (NY) pubs E's intro (#E394) to M's speech on free trade [← :19].

SEPTEMBER

30. AMERICAN TOUR (CONT'D). **Sep 1:** E leaves Boston, by railway, for Niagara Falls, arriving the next morning, Sep 2, and staying about five days. **Sep c.6–7:** E leaves via steamer on Lake Ontario for Toronto; then via the lake and St. Lawrence River to Port Hope and Kingston. **Sep 9:** E arrives in Montreal. **Sep 10:** In the evening E leaves for Plattsburgh (NY), arriving there on Sep 11, on Lake Champlain; at 1 P.M. he takes an excursion into the Adirondacks (Lake Placid), returning to Plattsburgh on Sep 12. **Sep 13:** E sails down Lake Champlain and Lake George to Albany; then down the Hudson River, arriving Sep 15 (evening) in NYC. **Sep 18:** The steamer *City of New York* takes on passengers, to sail the next day. **Sep 19:** Before sailing, E is interviewed for the *New Yorker Volkszeitung* by his old comrade T. Cuno (this is the sole contact with American socialists that E permits). The interview (#E389) is pubd in the paper, Sep 20 [→ :37]. **Sep 19–29:** During this return trip on board the *City of New York*, E writes some fragmentary travel sketches intended for *NZ* (#E18), but they

remain unfinished and unpubd. He also writes (Sep 27) a letter to his brother Hermann reporting on Adirondack scenery, American beer, California wine, and his improved health.

31. W&P. **Sep:** The American edn of M's speech on free trade (#M836), with E's intro (#E394), is pubd, with an 1889 imprint (ST/M41).

OCTOBER

32. BOULANGER. **Oct to Dec:** In correspondence with Paul Lafargue, who writes (Oct 15) on his advocacy of an electoral coalition with the Boulangists, E attacks this policy and advocates an independent electoral line by the socialists, condemning both the Boulangists and the liberal supporters of the status quo. (For more info, see → :39.)

33. POLITICAL ECONOMY. **Oct 15:** In a letter to Danielson, E discusses the state of polit eco in England and Germany.

34. *CAPITAL.* **Oct to Jan A:** E prepares the first part of Vol. 3 for the press, establishes the structure of the parts and the chapter titles, writes Chs. 1–3 according to M's indications, and writes all of Ch. 4 (of which M left only the title) (SOURCE: *MEW Daten*).

35. WEITLING. **Oct 25:** In response to a request (Oct 15) from Bebel, who is planning to write a book on Weitling and the movement of the 1840s, E gives him some pointers and suggestions.

36. LOUISE VS KARL KAUTSKY. **Oct:** Learning on his return from America that Kautsky has left his wife Louise for another woman (who, however, quickly swaps him for his brother Hans), E energetically takes Louise's side in the imbroglio, with a number of letters; he writes Louise (Oct 11) of his admiration for her conduct; reports the story (Oct 13) to Laura Lafargue; writes Kautsky himself (Oct 17) along the same lines, esp regarding the unfairness of such a situation to the woman; and gives his opinion in a letter (Oct 25) to Bebel.

37. W&P. **Oct 13:** *Sozialdemokrat* pubs E's interview with Cuno (#E389) [← :30].

NOVEMBER

38. INTERNATIONAL CONGRESS. **Nov 17:** E meets with Barry, who gives him an account of the international workers' congress in London, which decided to call a world congress in Paris in the summer of 1889, organized by the French Possibilists. **Nov D to Dec:** The Lafargues inform E of the steps taken by the Guesdist-led TU congress in Bordeaux to schedule an international workers' congress in Paris for July 1889, as against the

Possibilist-sponsored congress; they warn of the Possibilists' aim of involving the German party by flattering relations with Liebknecht.

DECEMBER

39. BOULANGER. **Dec 4:** Continuing an interchange of letters with Paul Lafargue [← :32], E directly accuses him: "You coquetted and flirted with the Boulangists. . . . You were not compelled to choose between these two follies [Boulanger or the status-quo liberals]; you could pillory both alike. . . ." Instead, E

charges, Lafargue was soft on Boulangism, whereas he should have taken the position that "both stink." **Dec 27:** Whereas Paul Lafargue (Dec 6) continues to argue against E's position, Laura Lafargue writes E that Paul's letters represent his own opinion, not that of the party or Guesde.

40. CAPITAL. **Dec 15:** E confesses (to Sorge) that Vol. 3 involves more work than he expected.

41. W&P. **c.Dec:** Lee & Shepard publish a pamphlet edn of M's speech on free trade (#M836) [← :31] in England.

1889

CONSPECTUS

1. M's 1865 lecture on "Wages, price and profit" (#M971) gets its first publ this year, in German trans, in NZ. (The English original will be pubd in 1898.)

2. *Indefinite Dates.* E's conspectus (historical synopsis) of G. von Gülich's work on German history (#E181) is assigned by *MEW Daten* to the period c.Oct 1873 to Feb 1874. But when E's notes were pubd in ST/ME67 (Über Dt), they were given a much later date by the editors, namely, "prob the end of the 1880s or beginning of the 1890s." —Some time in 1889 (prob date), E works up a list of his own publications—see #E240.5; the dating is approximate, and the purpose unknown. E will supplement the list at the end of 1892.

JANUARY

3. INTERNATIONAL CONGRESS. **Jan 5, 14:** Concerned about the situation in which two rival congresses are scheduled for Paris in the summer [← 88:38], under the aegis resp of the Possibilists and the Guesdists (Marxists), E tries to coordinate the policies of the German and French Marxists so as to frustrate the plans of the Possibilist right-wingers; to this end he corresponds with Bebel and Paul Lafargue.

4. BOULANGER. **Jan 2:** Writing to Laura Lafargue, E expresses gratification at her assurance [← 88:39] that Paul's viewpoint is a minority in the party; he reiterates that "the Boulangists should be treated as bourgeois enemies quite as much as the Cadettists [liberals]," and repeats that "both stink." **Jan 3:** Paul Lafargue repeats his line of anti-anti-Boulangism, but (Jan 27) Boulanger wins a big electoral victory in Paris which panics the left, including Lafargue; from now on he will begin to speak in terms of "fighting" Boulanger for the first time.

5. CAPITAL. **Jan 11, 12:** In letters to Schmidt and Sorge, E reports on the status of Vol. 3: Part I is finished, and Parts II and III are in process; but the work is taking longer than expected, because of E's eye trouble, etc. **Jan 28:** E proposes to Kautsky that he take over the work on "Vol. 4," i.e., *Theories of surplus value* (#M877), first of all taking on the work of deciphering M's ms and making a clear copy [→ 90:23].

6. W&P. **Jan AB:** E receives from Lee & Shepard (Boston pub'r) a bundle of 500 copies of the *Free Trade* pamphlet (#M836) [← 88:31], a part of which is to go to the London pub'r Reeves for distribution.

FEBRUARY

7. INTERNATIONAL CONGRESS. **Feb 11:** Writing to Laura Lafargue, E reports that the Possibilists, echoed by Hyndman, are falsely claiming that the German party will participate in their congress [← :3]. **Feb CD:** E is active in preparing the Feb 28 conference of socialist parties in The Hague, held to discuss the coming international congress.

8. BOULANGER. **Feb 4:** Taking advantage of Boulanger's Jan 27 victory [← :4] to reemphasize his position, E tells the Lafargues that the Boulanger movement is a "revival of Bonapartism" and an augury of war. He attacks Paul Lafargue's line as follows: "if we are not to go *against* the popular current . . . what in the name of the devil *is* our business?"

9. FRENCH REVOLUTION. **Feb 14–20:** E reads proofs of Kautsky's NZ article on "class antagonisms of 1789" and sends him (Feb 20) a number of comments, incl remarks on the plebeian mass as the driving force of the revolution, and on why the Terror of the Jacobins became "absurd" and "untenable."

10. CAPITAL. **Feb 10:** E finishes work on

Part IV of Vol. 3; he is about a third of the way through the total ms.

11. NICOTINE. **Feb 15:** In a letter to Harney (not extant), E must have mentioned that he has given up or will give up smoking, for Harney replies (in a few days) that Nim (Helene Demuth) "will think you [are] getting ready for the Kingdom of Heaven, when you have given up smoking" [→ :22].

MARCH

12. INTERNATIONAL CONGRESS. **Mar to July 14:** E actively helps to prepare and support the international congress called by the French Guesdist party, as against the right-wing (Possibilist) rival congress, esp through a lively correspondence with socialist leaders in various countries. In this connection he also criticizes the sectarian attitudes and tactical blunders of his French comrades, in letters to Paul Lafargue (e.g., Mar 12, 21, 23, 25, 27) [→ :15]. **Mar 17–22:** E collaborates with Bernstein as the latter drafts a reply to a Mar 16 attack in *Justice* (organ of Hyndman's SDF) on the German party, in connection with this issue; E edits and revises Bernstein's draft. **Mar c.23:** This reply (#E387) is pubd as a pamphlet in English, signed by Bernstein. **Mar 30 to Apr 6:** *Sozialdemokrat* pubs a German version of it [→ :17].

13. BOULANGER. **Mar 5, 23:** Paul Lafargue [← :4] has drastically changed his tune as he now writes to E in terms of fighting Boulangism. **Mar 25:** E makes two more points for Lafargue's education: he replies to Lafargue's hope that a Boulanger-initiated war will usher in revolution, and he stresses that Boulanger in power will crush the socialist movement.

14. CAPITAL. **Mar to Aug:** Esp because of his involvement in preparing the international congress, E finds it impossible to spend any time on Vol. 3 [→ :30].

APRIL

15. INTERNATIONAL CONGRESS. **Apr:** E keeps straightening out problems of tactics in the relations between the French and German Marxists, with evident exasperation at their blunders; cf his letters to Paul Lafargue on Apr 1, 10, 30, and to Liebknecht on Apr 4, 5, 17 [← :12]. **Apr D:** In reply to the claim in *Justice* (Apr 27) that the right-wing congress is supported by a majority of organized workers in France, E drafts a letter to be signed by Charles Bonnier, sent for publ to the *Labour Elector* (#E443) [→ :17].

16. MAHON'S CLUB. **Apr 17:** J. L. Mahon [← 88:20] invites E to become one of the vice-presidents of the club Mahon is now associated with, the Central Democratic Club,

whose president is Cunninghame Graham. (E must have sent in a subscription to membership in the club, for Mahon sends him a receipt on May 22.)

MAY

17. INTERNATIONAL CONGRESS. **May:** As before [← :12], E is heavily involved in congress preparations; cf 11 (extant) letters to the Lafargues alone. For an overall view, see E's letter to Sorge, May 11: "The writing and running about in connection with the damned congress leave me hardly any time for anything else.... nothing but misunderstandings, squabbles, and vexation on all sides. . ; ." E also describes Liebknecht's sorry role in connection with the conniving of the right wing. **May 4:** The letter signed by Bonnier (#E443) [← :15] is pubd in *Labour Elector*. **May 7–10:** On Paul Lafargue's request, E makes a German trans of the French party's invitation to the international congress in Paris, also arranges for its trans into English, for publ in a number of German and English socialist papers. **May 14:** Lafargue sends E the text, drafted by himself and Guesde, of a Call to the International Socialist Workers' Congress in Paris, by the organizing comm. **May CD to June A:** E arranges for this Call to be translated into various languages, printed, mailed out, and signed by socialists of various countries. **May D to June 1:** In response to a Hyndman manifesto in *Justice* (May 25), E again [← :12] collaborates with Bernstein on a reply (#E388) [→ :19].

18. RUHR STRIKE. **May D** (not later than May 27): E writes a note on the Ruhr miners' strike begun on May 4, in the form of a letter to the editor of the *Labour Leader*, Keir Hardie (#E490) [→ :20].

JUNE

19. INTERNATIONAL CONGRESS. **June 1:** E and Bernstein finish, and date, the second reply to *Justice* [← :17] on the question of the international congress. **June c.8:** It is pubd as a pamphlet in English (#E388), again signed by Bernstein. **June 8:** In a letter to Sorge, E gives an overall account of the battle over the congress with the right wing, which is trying to build a reformist International hostile to Marxism. **June 15:** Excerpts from the second pamphlet (#E388) are pubd in German in *Sozialdemokrat*, and in English in *Labour Elector*.

20. RUHR STRIKE. **June:** E's letter on the Ruhr miners' strike (#E490) [← :18] is pubd in *Labour Leader*.

21. CAPITAL. **June 15:** Sam Moore leaves England to go to the Niger region as a judge, agreeing with E to translate Vol. 3 while he is in Africa. (But he will not carry out this aim.)

22. NICOTINE. **June 8:** In his letter to Sorge, E announces he has been forced to give up almost all smoking, "for my nerves," though he expects to go back to smoking next year [cf ← :11].

JULY

23. INTERNATIONAL CONGRESS. **July 14–20:** The International Socialist Workers Congress meets in Paris (rue Petrelle) with about 400 delegates from 22 countries; this is regarded as the founding congress of the Second International. A Possibilist-dominated congress meets at the same time (rue Lancre), but it is overshadowed. **July 17, 20:** In letters to Sorge, E reports his view of the "brilliant success" of the "Rue Petrelle congress," and his satisfaction that the "reconciliation bubble" has burst, because of the Possibilists' rejection of merger terms.

AUGUST

24. INTERNATIONAL CONGRESS. **Aug A:** E writes an article on "Possibilist credentials" (#E598) dealing with the right-wing congress in Paris [← :23]; pubd in *Labour Elector*, Aug 10. **Aug 17:** In response to Liebknecht's protest against E's criticism of his (Liebknecht's) role in recent events, E specifies his objections to Liebknecht's conduct.
25. FRENCH AFFAIRS. **Aug D to Oct A:** E follows French politics and Guesdist party activities in the course of correspondence with Paul Lafargue, who keeps him informed. As before, E presses for a completely independent electoral policy by the French party. **Aug 27:** Writing to Laura Lafargue, E attacks the pro-Boulangist wing of the Blanquists, who think they can win a couple of parliamentary seats by supporting Boulanger.
26. LONDON DOCKERS. **Aug D to Sep A:** E is enthusiastic about the strike of the London dock workers as an augury of a new labor movement, and writes in this sense to a number of correspondents in various countries. **Aug 31:** An excerpt from a letter by E along these lines—prob written (Aug c.20–26) to Eleanor M—is pubd in *Labour Elector* (#E562), and partly also included in the *Sozialdemokrat*'s leading article of this day.
27. PERSONAL. **Aug c.8 to Sep c.6:** E stays in Eastbourne. **Aug:** Finding that the cocaine tincture which he has been using for his eye trouble has weakened in effectiveness, E switches to using zinc chloride.

SEPTEMBER

28. ENGLISH MOVEMENT. **Sep:** In a number of letters, E enthuses over the victory of the dock strike—for example, in a letter to Kautsky (Sep 15) he says it is the greatest event in England in recent years, the beginning of a revolutionary transformation of the London working-class movement. **Sep D to Oct A:** E writes an article on "The abdication of the bourgeoisie" (#E2) [→ :31].
29. VISITORS. **Sep c.6:** Liebknecht and Singer visit E in London; E notes that Liebknecht has now dropped his illusions about the Possibilists.
30. CAPITAL. **Sep CD to Oct:** After neglecting Vol. 3 [← :14], E now finds he has to work on preparing the fourth German edn of Vol. 1 for the press; he overhauls citations, corrects errors, and adds explanatory notes. (For publ, see → 90:44.)

OCTOBER

31. ENGLISH MOVEMENT. **Oct 5:** E's article "The abdication of the bourgeoisie" (#E2) [← :28] is pubd in *Sozialdemokrat*, and (Oct 12) in English in *Labour Elector* (a bit shortened); also in other German and Austrian papers during this month. **Oct to Dec:** E closely follows and supports the organizing work by Eleanor M, along with Aveling and other socialists, among London's unskilled workers, as part of the new labor movement (the New Unionism) which is coming into being.
32. FRENCH AFFAIRS. **Oct:** In letters to Laura Lafargue (Oct 8, 29) and Liebknecht (Oct 3), E interprets the results of the French election (Sep 22 to Oct 6) as a "relative success" though Lafargue and the French party are downcast; E stresses that Boulangism and monarchism have been defeated, the republic firmly established. **Oct-Nov:** Writing to Laura Lafargue (Oct 29), E urges that the party have nothing to do with the "Boulangeo-Blanquists" who have won seats in the parliament as Boulangists. Writing to Guesde (Nov 20), E stresses: "I am very glad that the socialist workers' party, in accordance with its slogan 'Neither Ferry [bourgeois liberal] nor Boulanger,' has closed its doors to the renegades and traitors of *both camps*."
33. HISTORY. **Oct 22:** In response to a query (Oct 19) from M. Hildebrand about Max Stirner, E jots down his recollections of Stirner and the Young Hegelian circle of 1842. **Oct 29:** In response to a query (Oct 26) from Liebknecht about Gottschalk, E summarizes his 1848 view of Gottschalk's politics, character, and role.

NOVEMBER

34. CAPITAL. **Nov:** E returns to work on Vol. 3, incl work on checking the associated economic literature.

35. VERSE TRANSLATION. Nov: E, delighted with Laura Lafargue's translation of Béranger into English verse (Nov 16), urges (Nov 18) her to undertake translation of Heinrich Heine's poetry: "Heine is in fashion at the moment—and the translations are so British!" Laura informs E (Nov D) that she is translating Pottier's songs (pubd in *Commonweal* during 1889–90) [→ 90:8].

DECEMBER

36. ENGLISH MOVEMENT. Dec 7: In a letter to Sorge, E reports on Eleanor M's notable organizing work in the Gas Workers and General Labourers Union, as part of the "New Unionism" now under way.

37. EUROPEAN MOVEMENT. Dec 7: In his letter to Sorge, E also reports on the favorable situation of the party in Germany, the increase in the French parliamentary fraction to eight deputies, the growth of the movement in Austria under Victor Adler, and the death of anarchism. **Dec 8:** Gerson Trier (in Copenhagen) writes E of the Danish party's expulsion of two left-wingers for opposing a bloc with the radical-bourgeois party. **Dec 18:** E explains to Trier why it is incorrect to exclude any and all collaboration with other parties on principled grounds, but he agrees with Trier in condemning the expulsion. He criticizes past party "dictatorships" (Lassalleans, American SLP, O'Connor in the Chartist movement): "The workers' movement rests on the sharpest criticism of existing society; criticism is its vital element; how can it itself wish to avoid criticism or forbid debate?"

38. FRENCH REVOLUTION. Dec 4: In a letter to V. Adler, E strongly recommends two books by Avenel, incl one on Anacharsis Cloots, as the best source on the critical 1792–94 period of the French Revolution. E also discusses some basic features of the revolution, incl why the Terror was intensified to "a pitch of insanity."

39. W&P. Dec: E begins work on a major essay, "The foreign policy of Russian czarism" (#E284), at the request of the Russian *Sotsial-Demokrat* [→ 90:9].

1890

CONSPECTUS

1. *Capital.* At various times during this year E works on the ms of Vol. 3, a task that will take him till early 1894. During this year E completes some parts of the volume, writes new passages and chapters, and edits the text.—*Polish Edition:* This year sees the publ of the first complete Polish trans of Vol. 1: cf → :44. Parts of the volume had previously been pubd, in Leipzig, in 1884, 1886, 1889 [← 84:3].

2. *War Danger.* A general entry in *MEW Daten*, dated Jan to Mar, highlights E's concern with the danger of war: "Europe sees a sharpening of the antagonisms between France and Germany and a rapprochement between France and Russia. The war danger grows. E studies the foreign policy situation. . . ." This note, of course, will recur in E's correspondence much more frequently.

3. *Origin of the family.* See → :26 for a broad-dated entry about E's work on the fourth edn (#E573), extending to June 1891.

4. *Communist Manifesto* (Yiddish). It is possibly in 1890 that E writes a preface for a planned Yiddish trans of the *Manifesto*, and mails it to NYC for A. Cahan of the Yiddish socialist monthly *Di Zukunft*—only to have the ms lost in NY. Or perhaps this happens in autumn 1891. For the details, see #E615.5; also see → 91:44.

JANUARY

5. ENGLISH MOVEMENT. Jan 11: E's letter to Schlüter gives his enthusiastic view of new developments in the labor movement, a view he will repeat often in the coming months: the "New Unionism," based on the organization of the unskilled, and abandoning craft-union exclusiveness, unites TUs in a common struggle against capitalism, even if it is not directly socialist; it will revolutionize the movement. **Jan D:** E reads the newly pubd *Fabian Essays*, received from S. Webb [→ :12].

6. AMERICAN MOVEMENT. Jan-Feb: E greets the evidences of disintegration following last fall's split in the SLP, in letters to Schlüter (Jan 11), Bebel (Jan 23), and Sorge (Feb 8); he keeps repeating that the SLP "must be smashed up as such, it is the worst obstacle . . ." a fossilized sect of obsolete Lassalleans.

7. EUROPEAN MOVEMENT. Jan 8: E makes explicit what has been implicit in his letters to the Lafargues: of all the comrades in France, it is Laura Marx Lafargue who, in E's opinion, has the clearest political head. **Jan D to Feb M:** E keeps informed through news reports and letters on the German political situation, on the eve of the Reichstag elections of Feb 20 [→ :10]. **Jan c.28 to May c.25:** E gets several letters from Danielson on the Russian economic situation.

8. MORE ON VERSE TRANSLATION. **Jan 8:** Sending Laura Lafargue the original text of a Walther von der Vogelweide poem for her to translate into English, E states his agreement with the principle that verse translation should preserve the original meter and rhyme [← 89:35].

9. W&P. **Jan 3:** E sends the first chapter of his essay on "The foreign policy of Russian czarism" (#E284) [← 89:39] to Stepniak, for forwarding to the Sotsial-Demokrat editors in Geneva.

FEBRUARY

10. GERMAN VICTORY. **Feb 21 to Apr 12:** In response to the huge success of the Social-Democrats in the Reichstag election of Feb 20–Mar 1, E stresses in a number of letters that socialist victory is so close that the rulers will try to provoke premature riots and fighting in order to crush the party by violence before it gets too strong and well prepared (letter to Laura Lafargue, Feb 26). So far the party has only one soldier out of three, four, or five: "that is why we must come out for the time being for legal action" (letter to Paul Lafargue, Mar 7). If we avoid bloodletting now, then "in three years, we can win over the rural workers, Prussia's main prop, and then—fire!" (letter to Laura Lafargue, Mar 14). The Prussian generals must be eager to precipitate a massacre in order to put us out of action, "So if our party apparently adopts a somewhat peaceful attitude in Germany in the near future . . . you know the reasons" (letter to Sorge, Apr 12). But to Liebknecht, who is making speeches "against violence in any form and under all circumstances," E writes (Mar 9) that he is wrong and moreover "no opponent will believe this—they are not that stupid"; what is correct is "that for now we have to behave as peacefully and legally as possible" and avoid any pretext for a premature collision. **Feb 21 to Mar 1:** E writes two articles dealing with the German election, one for a Newcastle paper (#E335), and one asking "What now?" for the Sozialdemokrat (#E917) [→ :14].

11. FRENCH AFFAIRS. **Feb 17:** Writing to Bebel, E comments on the results of the Feb parliamentary election in Paris, where Boulangists won seats: this is due to the corruption of the Paris workers by chauvinism.

12. FABIANS. **Feb 8:** Having read Fabian essays [← :5], E describes the Fabians as "a well-meaning band of 'eddicated' bourgeois" whose "main aim is . . . to convert the bourgeois to socialism and thus introduce the thing peacefully and constitutionally."

13. W&P. **Feb D:** E finishes his essay "The foreign policy of Russian czarism"

(#E284) [← :9]; the first chapter is pubd in the Feb issue of the Russian Sotsial-Demokrat [→ :17].

MARCH

14. ARTICLES ON GERMANY. **Mar 3:** E's article on the German election [← :10] for the Newcastle Daily Chronicle (#E335) is pubd in that paper [→ :24]. **Mar 8:** E's article "What now?" (#E917) is pubd in Sozialdemokrat, reprinted Mar 14 in the Vienna Arbeiter-Ztg.

15. ITALIAN CORRESPONDENTS. **Mar 26:** Martignetti sends E a proposal by Antonio Labriola (pubd Mar 15) on the utilization of uncultivated land in colonies like Eritrea, under the title "Land to those who till it"; he asks E's opinion. **Mar 30:** E's reply advocates the demand that such land be given to small peasants for their own cultivation and not to monopolists or exploitive companies (pubd → :24). —E thanks Labriola for sending two of his brochures: Del socialismo (1189), already read, and I problemi della filosofia della storia (1187), still to be read; in return E sends Labriola his book Ludwig Feuerbach (#E457).

16. BIOGRAPHY. **Mar 20–31:** E revises the text of the biographical sketch of him contained in Vol. 6 of the Brockhaus Conversationslexikon, 13th edn, the revision to be used in the 14th edn.

APRIL

17. ARTICLE ON RUSSIAN CZARISM: BOWDLERIZATION. **April:** Neue Zeit for this month (actually out Mar D) pubs the first two chapters of E's essay "The foreign policy of Russian czarism" (#E284) [← :13], with arbitrary editorial changes made without E's knowledge to soften references to Russian and Prussian rulers. The changes have been made not by the publisher Dietz, as E thinks, but by W. Blos, to whom Dietz handed the editorial work. **Apr 1:** E writes both Dietz and editor Kautsky, protesting the changes in the article and forbidding publ of the rest of the article unless the ms is faithfully followed [→ :26]. **Apr A:** E sends Stepniak the proofs and ms of Chs. 2–3, for publ in the next issue of the Russian Sotsial-Demokrat [→ :35]. **Apr 3:** E writes Zasulich that it is important to publish the article in English, since the Liberals' belief in czarist emancipation has been shaken by recent exposés (such as George Kennan's); since a revolutionary movement has arisen in Russia itself, czarist diplomacy is no longer sure of success. **Apr 4:** E warns Sorge that the falsified version in the April Neue Zeit should not be reprinted; the May issue will republish the article correctly.

Apr: E collaborates on making an English translation of the article for the monthly *Time*, which pubs the first installment in its April issue [→ :26].

18. RUSSIAN MOVEMENT. **Apr AB:** E notes that the *Sozialdemokrat* has pubd (Apr 5) an article by a Russian populist, G. Beck, attacking the Russian Marxist group; he tells Bernstein he would not have pubd this "nonsense" but agrees that it provides the Marxists with an occasion to present their viewpoint. **Apr 17:** E writes V. Zasulich along these lines; he advises her group to contribute actively to *Sozialdemokrat* and *Neue Zeit*; but the German party organs are bound to publish the views of all wings of foreign socialist parties. (Zasulich's reply to Beck appears in *Sozialdemokrat*, Apr 26.)

19. GERMAN MOVEMENT. **Apr 11:** E discusses the proposal for Kautsky and *Neue Zeit* editorial work to move to Stuttgart so as to work directly with the party press establishment there; he stresses the importance of retaining control over NZ and the advantage of acquiring influence over the party press. **Apr 12:** In a letter to Sorge, E discusses German party policy in this period (for this, see ← :10), and rejects Sorge's request for the file of Miquel's old letters to M, which are now useful for "exerting pressure" on him.

20. ENGLISH MOVEMENT. **Apr 19:** Writing to Sorge, E gives a detailed report on the TU upsurge in England, the good work being done by Eleanor M and others, the futility of the sects (SDF and Socialist League); also the shallowness of the Fabians, who "condescend to emancipate the workers" if the workers docilely obey. **Apr 30:** Also to Sorge, E describes preparations for a May Day demonstration in London, in accordance with the decisions of the International Socialist Congress of 1889, under the watchword of the eight-hour day. (Part of this letter is pubd by Sorge in the *New Yorker Volkszeitung*, May 10, and in the NY *Workmen's Advocate*.)

21. FRENCH MOVEMENT. **Apr 16:** E writes Laura Lafargue that the strength of Boulangism among Paris workers is due to chauvinism, esp since no French party has ever fought chauvinism. This is the third wave of Bonapartism that has blanketed Parisian revolutionism—"an appeal to a savior who is to destroy the vile bourgeois. . . ."

22. ANTI-SEMITISM. **Apr 19:** In response to an inquiry (Mar 21) from an Austrian bank employee for his views, E analyzes anti-Semitism as a feudal remnant, and refutes its claims of anticapitalist content, as well as listing some socialist leaders of Jewish birth, incl M (#E537) [→ :26].

23. *CAPITAL.* **Apr 9:** Writing to Nieuwenhuis, E reports he is working on Part V of Vol.

3, and expects little trouble in doing Parts VI and VII. **Apr 12:** To C. Schmidt, E mentions that Kautsky has already made a clear copy of part of the ms for Vol. 4 (*Theories of surplus value*, #M877), and is still working on it [← 89:5].

24. PUBLICATION. **Apr 6:** *Berliner Volksblatt* pubs a German trans of E's article on the German elections (#E335) [← :14], edited for legality. **Apr 16:** The essential part of E's letter to Martignetti (#E572.5) [← :15] is pubd in the Italian *Cuore e Critica*.

MAY

25. LONDON MAY DAY. **May 4:** E participates in the May Day demonstration [← :20] and enthusiastically describes his impressions in letters (May 9, 10) to Bebel and Laura Lafargue. **May 5–21:** E writes an article on the London May Day action (#E473) for the Vienna *Arbeiter-Ztg*; pubd May 23; repubd in Germany, May 29, 31.

26. W&P. **May:** *Neue Zeit* pubs the whole of E's article on Russian foreign policy (#E284) [← :7], this time unaltered. (But see the note appended to #E284.) *Time* pubs the second part of the English translation. **May 1:** E writes, and dates, the preface (#E613) to the fourth German edn of the *Com Manifesto* [→ :35]. **May 9:** E's letter on anti-Semitism (#E537) is pubd in the Vienna *Arbeiter-Ztg* as a letter to an unnamed correspondent [← :22]; repubd in Germany, May 13, 28. **May D to June 1891:** E works, with interruptions, on the fourth edn of his *Origin of the family* (#E573), reading new publications on the subject, revising passages (esp in Ch. 2), and correcting mistakes [→ 91:34]. Among his readings are the books by the Russian sociologist M. M. Kovalevsky, *Tableau des origines et d'évolution de la famille et de la propriété* and *Modern custom and ancient law in Russia*.

JUNE

27. HISTORICAL MATERIALISM. **June 5:** Since Paul Ernst, who has gotten into a literary polemic with Hermann Bahr on the subject of Ibsen and the women's movement, asks E (May 31) to support him publicly, E replies that he cannot do so, i.a. because he is not acquainted with the Scandinavian movement nor "to what extent Ibsen can be held responsible for the more or less hysterical effusions of bourgeois and petty-bourgeois women careerists." Mainly E proceeds to criticize Ernst's own analysis of Norwegian conditions, in which "the materialist method is turned into its opposite when used, not as a guideline in historical investigation, but as a

ready-made pattern on which to tailor historical facts."

28. DANIELSON. **June 10:** In a letter to
Danielson, E expresses his sympathy on the
death of N. G. Chernyshevsky; reports that
Eleanor M has typed a copy of the Marx–
Danielson file of correspondence, which is
now being mailed back; and discusses the
confusion in economic literature between
"rent" and "tribute."

29. *CAPITAL.* **June 10:** E reports he is
engaged in reading proof sheets of the fourth
German edn of Vol. 1. **June 25:** E writes the
preface (#E602) to the fourth edn (pubd →
:44).

JULY

30. NORWEGIAN TOUR. **July 1–26:** E and
his friend Prof. Schorlemmer take a steamer to
the west coast of Norway: up the Hardanger
Fjord to Odda, up the coast to Trondheim
(July 7–8), then past the Svartisen glacier to
Tromsö (where Laplanders and reindeer are
encountered), and so up to the midnight sun
at Nordkapp; then more fjords on the way
south, finally taking the railway from Voss
(Vossevangen) to Bergen.

31. WRÓBLEWSKI. **July c.9 to Sep c.22:** E
corresponds with the Polish general and Communard Walery Wróblewski, and sends financial aid. (These dates come from *MEW Daten;*
but note that on July 9 E is far north in
Norway.)

AUGUST

32. PARTY DEMOCRACY. **Aug:** A faction
fight is developing in the German party
looking to the Halle Congress (Oct 12–18),
from groups of new intellectuals ("*Literaten*"), incl a *Jungen* (youth) faction. Liebknecht and Bebel, in E's opinion, are reacting
with unwise heat and talk of "throwing 'em
out." **Aug 9:** Writing to Sorge, E summarizes
the problem and his advice to Bebel and
Liebknecht: oppositions are unavoidable; "the
party is so big that absolute freedom of debate
inside it is a necessity"; even the "appearance" of a Schweitzer-type dictatorship must
be avoided. E says he will try to talk Bebel and
Liebknecht out of their present tactics. **Aug
10:** Writing to Liebknecht esp about the new
draft by-laws, E lists several bad provisions
(incl control over the party Exec by the
Reischstag Fraction), and warns: "Make no
unnecessary martyrs; demonstrate that freedom of criticism rules; and if there are any
expulsions, then only in cases where there are
altogether striking and fully provable acts—
overt acts—of dirty work or betrayal! This is
my opinion. More orally" (that is, when

Liebknecht visits London). **Aug 27:** E sends
Paul Lafargue a political portrait of the *Jungen*
faction.

33. THEORY. **Aug 5:** In an important letter to C. Schmidt on the meaning of historical
materialism, E emphasizes that the primacy of
material factors does not preclude ideological
effects; the theory is not an artificial construct
à la Hegel to invent a neat system, nor is
theory an excuse for not studying the facts of
history. **Aug 21:** In reply to O. von Boenigk's
inquiry about socialist society, E emphasizes
that the obstacle is not the "ignorance of the
masses" but the ignorant bourgeois intellectuals who think they are able to tutor the
masses.

34. PLANS. **Aug 5:** E promises *Neue Zeit*
an article "On the history of early Christianity" for early 1891. (It will actually not be
written until June 1894; cf #E556.)

35. W&P. **Aug A:** The fourth German edn
of the *Com Manifesto* with E's preface
(#E613), is pubd with a press run of 5000.
(Subsequent German edns will be made from
the same plates till 1909.) **Aug:** The Russian
Sotsial-Demokrat pubs the second part (Chs.
2–3) of E's essay "The foreign policy of
Russian czarism" (E284) [← :13].

36. PERSONAL. **Aug c.14 to Sep 12:** E
sojourns in Folkestone.

SEPTEMBER

37. INTERNATIONAL CONGRESS. **Sep 9:**
Ch. Bonnier writes E about the call to the 1891
congress sent out by the Belgian party, which
has been charged with this function only by
the Possibilist (right-wing) congress of 1890.
Sep 10–15: E, drafting a reply to Bonnier,
finds his statement elaborating into a fuller
memo on policy re the 1891 congress (#E386),
for private circulation only. **Sep 15:** E writes
Paul Lafargue with the gist of this policy,
giving reasons for proposing a merger of the
two congresses being prepared. E also suggests that a preliminary conference take place
at the (German) Halle Congress in Oct. **Sep
19, 27:** E writes again along the same lines to
Paul Lafargue and to Sorge.

38. HISTORICAL MATERIALISM. **Sep 3:**
Joseph Bloch's letter to E asks whether in the
materialist conception of history economic
conditions *alone* are the decisive factor or are
only to some extent the foundation of all
other conditions, which, however, also have
their own effects. **Sep 21–22:** In another
important statement of the question [← :33] E
replies that the economic element is not the
only factor in history; he explains its relation
to superstructural elements, and their interaction.

39. ON THE *JUNGEN AND ALTEN.* **Sep c.6:**

E drafts a reply to an editorial statement by the *Jungen* faction pubd (Aug 31) in the Saxon party paper which they control, since the *Jungen* imply that their position on parliamentary socialism is the same as E's; E rejects political solidarity with this faction and criticizes their distorted version of "Marxism." For the first draft, see #E668. **Sep 7:** E finishes, and dates, his reply to the *Jungen* (#E667), and sends it to a number of party newspapers (pubd Sep 13 in the *Sozialdemokrat*, and Sep 14–19 in other papers). **Sep 12–18:** E writes a "farewell letter" to *Sozialdemokrat* readers (#E272) for the last issue of the illegal paper (which is being suspended now that the Anti-Socialist Law is defunct); he lauds the paper as an organ of revolutionary policy. In a letter to Kautsky (Sep 18) E makes clear that his article is implicitly aimed at the right wing of the party, as counterpoise to the previous attack on the "leftist" *Jungen* faction (pubd in *Sozialdemokrat*, Sep 27; repubd on the Continent, Sep D and Oct).

40. ENGLISH AFFAIRS. Sep A: E follows the course of the TU Congress in Liverpool Sep 1–6, and sees the growing influence of the "New Unionism" in the endorsement of an eight-hour-day law against opposition by the TU leadership (SOURCE: *MEW Daten*). **Sep 18:** E comments (to Kautsky) on the irony of Brentano's presence on the platform while the TUs refute his pet thesis, that the English TUs are the best bulwark against socialism.

41. PERSONAL. Sep 23: E lays down an ultimatum to his house landlord: either a new kitchen range and a new hot-water bathtub, or no renewal of the lease. (The landlord capitulates immediately.)

OCTOBER

42. GERMAN AND FRENCH AFFAIRS. Oct 1: In reply to an article (Sep 16) by Paul Ernst, a leader of the *Jungen* faction [← :39], which again tries to cover its own viewpoint with E's authority, E writes a "Reply to Herr Paul Ernst" (#E666); pubd Oct 5. **Oct 7:** In response to Liebknecht's request that he contribute to the new party central organ *Berliner Volksblatt* (which will become *Vorwärts* on Jan 1), E writes that he will do so insofar as he has time, but on two conditions: signed articles are not to be altered without his permission [← :17], and any payment is to go to the party treasury as E's contribution. **Oct CD:** E follows the course of the German party congress at Halle (Oct 12–18) through news reports and letters from Liebknecht, Eleanor M, Fischer, etc. His letters (e.g., to Laura Lafargue, Oct 19) express satisfaction with the outcome. —Ditto for the simultaneous congresses in France: French Workers party at

Lille, Oct 11–12; TUs at Calais, Oct 13–18. E's letters (Oct 18 to Sorge, Oct 19 to Laura Lafargue) esp welcome the coeval split in the Possibilist (right) wing between Brousse and Allemane.

43. HISTORICAL MATERIALISM. Oct 27: the third and longest of his 1890 letters on this subject, addressed to C. Schmidt, E again stresses the interaction of primary and secondary factors in history, refuting any "one factor" theory; he discusses the relation of state power to productive forces, the development of law, and the "realms of ideology" (cf ← :33, 38).

44. CAPITAL. Oct c.25: E receives a copy of the Polish trans of Vol. 1 from Ludwik Krzywicki. **c.Oct:** The fourth German edn of Vol. 1 is published, with E's new preface (#E602) [← :29].

45. MARX'S LETTERS. Oct. c.12–19: E sorts and arranges "about four cubic feet" of M's correspondence files of 1836–64, mostly letters addressed to him.

NOVEMBER

46. HELENE AND LOUISE. Nov 4: Helene Demuth ("Lenchen," "Nim") dies this afternoon, after a brief and painful illness. E informs various friends, Nov 4–5. **Nov 9:** E writes to Louise Kautsky (Vienna, divorced from Karl) urging her to come to London to take charge of his household as housekeeper-secretary. **Nov 18:** Louise arrives in London and is installed. (She will agree, Dec M, to remain on permanently.)

47. 70TH BIRTHDAY. Nov 27: Leaders of the German party, Bebel, Liebknecht, and Paul Singer, arrive in London to stay at E's, in honor of his birthday. E makes arrangements for them to meet some English workers' leaders before they return—John Burns, Will Thorne, Cunninghame Graham, as well as Eleanor M. **Nov 28** (birthday): "Letters and telegrams en masse" pour in from various countries, also some gifts. In the evening E has a party with the visitors (incl visitors from the GWEA, etc.) until 3:30 A.M. [→ :48].

DECEMBER

48. 70TH BIRTHDAY: Dec 2–5: E is busy replying to many birthday greetings [← :47]: with formal letters for publ (to *Berliner Volksblatt*, National Council of French Workers party, and the Hungarian party organs—see #E833, 858, 832) and to individual friends (A. Goegg, Schorlemmer, E. Vaillant, Lavrov, and prob many others not extant). **Dec 8–11:** The congress of the German workers' provident societies, meeting in Berlin, votes to send greetings to E; its chairman, G. Blume, sends them on Dec 18; E sends a warm letter of thanks, Dec 27.

49. MARX'S PAPERS: Dec 13: In a letter to Kautsky, E mentions for the first time that he has finally found a copy of M's *Critique of the Gotha program* (#M207) of 1875, and that it is "extremely timely and of topical interest." He will write a foreword to it (#E285). During this month E prepares M's critique for publ [→ 91:6]. **Dec 18:** E objects to Liebknecht's plan to publish the Marx–Ruge correspondence of 1843 (#M471) unless this is done as a part of a Collected Works project; he says this "confused" correspondence, in "Hegelianized language," is incomprehensible without explanation; besides, M had said more than once that Ruge had prepared it for publ and "had inserted all kinds of nonsense." **Dec AB:** E complies with Fortin's request for publ of his French trans of M's *18th Brumaire* (#M267) in *Le Socialiste* (pubd 1891, Jan to Nov). He declines to permit publ of M's *Poverty of philosophy* (#M681) in the *Revue Socialiste* ed by the Possibilist Malon.

50. BRENTANO. Dec 4: The *Deutsches Wochenblatt* (Berlin) pubs a note citing Gladstone's approval of Brentano's charge against M [← 72:30, 39]; Liebknecht sends it to E. **Dec 4–13:** E writes a comment on the *Deutsches Wochenblatt* piece (#E374), and sends it to Kautsky for *Neue Zeit* (pubd early next year, in no. 13). **Dec:** Probably around the same time E begins work on a brochure giving a longish account of the controversy with Brentano and appending a number of articles (#E375) [→ 91:12]. During 1890 Brentano had pubd a book *Meine Polemik mit KM*.

51. FRANCE AND PARTY UNITY. Dec 23: Leo Frankel, now a leader of the Hungarian Social-Democracy, writes E from Paris lamenting the split in France between Guesdists and Possibilists. **Dec 25:** E replies with an extensive discussion of the dynamics of party unity and split, comparing the French split with the struggle of Lassalleans and Eisenachers in Germany; he points to eventual unity through political defeat of the right wing. E reviews the mistake of the Gotha unity of 1875 and points to M's critique (see ← :49), not yet pubd.

1891

CONSPECTUS

1. *MEW Daten* lists some broad-dated entries whose main content is included below under more specific dates. Thus under Feb to Oct it says: "E regularly reads *Vorwärts*, the SPD organ since Jan 1. In letters to Bebel and other party leaders, E criticizes the editors for opportunist waverings and mistakes." This generality can be repeated every year. In point of fact the editor of *Vorwärts* is Wilhelm Liebknecht; and following the dust-up in which Liebknecht (with others) tries to surpress publ of M's *Critique of the Gotha program* (see → :6, 11), E recurs again and again in correspondence to this theme: Liebknecht is incompetent, muddleheaded, unreliable, and, in short, a disaster as a socialist leader (see, e.g. → :22). Most of these passages are not noted below. (See *Liebknecht in Glossary.*)

2. Another broad entry in *MEW Daten* is under Feb to Apr: "E closely follows the development of the socialist movement in England and gives regular help to Eleanor M, Aveling, and other English socialists in their struggle to create a political party of the working class." The dates given refer to specific letters by E, but in fact this work went on for a whole period. For Eleanor M's extensive work as a movement organizer, see ST/35.5 (Kapp), Vol. 2.

3. A broad entry for Mar to Nov refers to Italy and E's concern with the work of forming a Marxist party in that country, also to E's correspondence with P. Martignetti on publ of his writings in Italian. Under Mar 4 to Oct 2, an entry lists E's help on a French edn of his *Origins of the family* (#E573); it will be found below under Mar 4 [→ :18].

4. *MEW Daten* is mistaken in its assertion that in Nov-Dec "E works intensively on preparing Vol. 3 of *Capital* for the press," and in a similar statement under Dec 3; indeed, it says the same under Sep c.29. In point of fact E's letters make clear that he did not achieve his wish of getting back to steady work on Vol. 3 by the end of this year; statements suggesting otherwise are merely anticipatory. —*Oct 29–31:* E writes Danielson that he will "begin again with Vol. 3" on Nov 1. —*Nov 1:* E writes in a letter to C. Schmidt that he will go to work on Vol. 3 "next week." —*Dec 3:* E writes Kautsky that "I am coming to the most difficult part, the last chapters (about six to eight) on money capital, banks, credit, etc." (*MEW Daten* misquotes this.) —*Dec 27:* E tells Kautsky that he "will again attack Vol. 3 as soon as possible. . . ." Meanwhile E is getting more and more impatient of constant interruptions and demands on his time; he will get back to Vol. 3 in the coming year [→ 92:54].

5. There are two indefinite dates of publ to

be mentioned. The new (third German) ed of M's *Civil war in France* (#M143)—augmented by two IWMA addresses on the war (#M318, 813) and by a new intro (#E392)—must have been pubd in the spring; it is aimed at the Paris Commune anniversary, Mar 18, but apparently does not make it on time. The fourth German edn of E's *Socialism: Utopian and scientific* (#E759) is pubd sometime during the second half of the year.

JANUARY

6. CRITIQUE OF THE GOTHA PROGRAM. **Jan 6:** E finishes, and dates, his foreword (#E285) to M's critique of the Gotha program of 1875 (#M207) [← 90:49]. He sends his foreword along with M's ms to Kautsky for *Neue Zeit*. **Jan 7:** In a letter to Kautsky, E makes clear that if M's document is not pubd in NZ, he will have it pubd by the Vienna party press. **Jan 15:** In another letter to Kautsky, E writes that he has written his foreword in soothing terms (with "tranquilizing morphine and sedative") to assuage the expected cries of pain. Liebknecht, who at the Halle party congress (Oct 1890) used excerpts from the 1875 critique without mentioning its existence, will "move heaven and earth to prevent its publ." —E also writes to Bebel, informing him about M's critique for the first time (since in 1875 Liebknecht deliberately kept it from him). **Jan 17:** E tells Sorge that "In no. 17 of *Neue Zeit* there will be a bombshell: M's critique of the draft program of 1875. You will be glad, but among many in Germany there will be anger and indignation." **Jan 21:** Bebel writes E that he never heard of M's critique in 1875, even though as late as May D or June he had written Liebknecht that the draft program was defective. **Jan D:** M's critique (#M207), along with E's foreword (#E285) and two contemporaneous letters, is pubd in *Neue Zeit*. (For the resultant uproar, see → :11.)

7. MAY DAY. **Jan D to Apr:** E discusses the preparation of the coming May Day demonstrations in a wide correspondence with socialist leaders in several countries. **Jan 31:** Writing to Paul Lafargue, E gives a detailed defense of the policy of the German party in celebrating on Sunday (May 3) instead of calling for mass work stoppages thereby inviting a shattering contest of strength and premature defeats on a big scale; each party must decide this itself.

8. FRENCH MOVEMENT. **Jan 31:** In a letter to Paul Lafargue, E fully endorses the policy of the Guesdists vis-à-vis the Allemanists (split-off from the Possibilists; cf ← 90:42): practical cooperation but no merger—just what M proposed in 1875 vis-à-vis the Lassalleans

(*MEW Daten* enters this under date Jan 31 to Apr 22) [→ :23].

9. AMERICAN AFFAIRS. **Jan:** From Sorge and other sources E learns of the conflict between the SLP and the AFL (Gompers) over the SLP's demand to affiliate to the TU federation as a political body. E also receives a letter from Gompers on this issue. **Jan 29:** Writing to Schlüter, E rejects the SLP's position and says that Gompers is right in refusing SLP affiliation.

10. MENDELSON. **Jan A to Feb 1:** E meets several times (incl dinner Jan 15) with the Polish émigré Stanislaw Mendelson and his wife Maria, who have been expelled from France. On E's advice, Mendelson addresses a letter to *Justice* (SDF)—edited and checked over by E—warning against provocations by two Russian agents who have turned up in London; letter pubd Jan 24.

FEBRUARY

11. FUROR OVER THE CRITIQUE. **Feb-Mar:** The *NZ's* publ of M's 1875 critique [← :6] produces an outcry of rage from some sections of the German party leadership—against M, against E for making it known, and against NZ and Kautsky for publishing it. Denunciations come esp from the right wing (led by the Reischstag Fraction majority) and "old Lassallean" elements, while favorable comments and congratulations are pubd in the press from party members, also in Austria. A leading part in attacking the publ is played by Liebknecht, whose role in suppressing the M critique in 1875 is being exposed (also his lies to the party about his role). Party leaders like Bebel and Paul Singer are scared by the outcry for fear of party unity, and at first blame E for jeopardizing the party [→ :22]. In England, Hyndman utilizes the situation to launch a campaign of vilification against E as the head of the "Marx clique." During this period E's correspondence frequently alludes to the uproar, in a shoulder-shrugging tone, and explains why the document had to be pubd—e.g., in letters to Kautsky, Sorge, Schlüter, Paul Lafargue, later Bebel. But E decides to make no public answer to the attacks and let it blow over. By Mar D/Apr A, the Bebel–Singer party leadership will abandon its "boycott" of E (E's term) and resume relations [→ :22]. **Feb 1, 3:** M's critique (#M207) is reprinted in *Vorwärts*, without E's foreword. **Feb 2:** Until the NZ arrives today, E wonders whether the party leadership, esp Liebknecht, has after all succeeded in suppressing publ. **Feb 3:** Writing to Kautsky, E says he is making clear to Bebel that he (E) takes responsibility for the publ, since he threatened Austrian publ if the NZ refused [← :6]. **Feb**

6–12: M's critique is reprinted in the *Sächsische Arbeiter-Ztg* in four installs. **Feb 10:** E reports (to Paul Lafargue) that the publ "excited great anger in the Central Comm . . . and much praise in the party itself. There was an attempt to suppress that whole edn of NZ. . . ." **Feb 11:** E writes Sorge that there is anger on top but joy below, in the party: "Liebknecht of course is furious, since the whole specific critique was directed at him and he was the father that begat that rotten program [of 1875] together with that bum-bugger Hasselmann." —Writing to Kautsky, E stresses that the party members "have to finally stop eternally treating the party officials, their own servants, with kid gloves, and stop standing before them, as before infallible bureaucrats, so very obediently instead of critically." **Feb 13:** *Vorwärts* pubs a statement by the Reichstag Fraction, written by Liebknecht, with a queasy attack on M's critique and on its publ, incl falsifications (in E's view) of M's 1875 opinions. **Feb 23:** In a letter to Kautsky, E recalls that he partially "forced your hand" to ensure publ [← :6], and argues that this episode shows the public how strong the party is. He discusses the "Lassalle legend" and the need to expose it in the party; the Reichstag Fraction's demands for "censorship" over NZ smack of the Fraction's former "dictatorship" over the party under the Anti-Socialist Law (1878–90). **Feb 28:** In the Reichstag, a right-wing Social-Democratic deputy, Grillenberger, publicly denounces M's reference in the critique to the "dictatorship of the proletariat."

12. W&P. **Feb 20:** E receives from Kautsky, and reads, an article Paul Lafargue had sent NZ on "M's theory of value and surplus value and the bourgeois economists"; E agrees with Kautsky that the article should not be pubd [→ :18]. —R. Fischer writes E that the German party Exec has decided to publish new edns of 10,000 each of E's *Socialism: Utopian and scientific* (#E759), M's *Civil war in France* (#M143) and *Wage-labor and capital* (#M968); he wants E's permission, and new prefaces to these works (E agrees, Feb c.27). **Feb 21:** Labriola writes E that Mackay, the Stirnerite-anarchist poet, would like to read the ms of M&E's *German ideology* (#ME66). **Feb 27:** E declines to make the unpubd, unedited ms available. **Feb:** E finishes putting together the material for the case against Brentano [← 90:50], to be pubd as a brochure (#E375) [→ :24].

MARCH

13. FUROR OVER THE CRITIQUE. **Mar 4:** E tells Sorge that the outcries of indignation [← :11] are still going on in the German

party. **Mar 14:** For E's challenge to the "Social-Democratic philistine," see → :17. **Mar 17:** E writes Kautsky that the publ of M's critique provoked indignation only among "the Berlin gentlemen" [party leaders] and not in the party ranks. **Mar 30:** Bebel writes E that he has been refraining from correspondence because immediately after the publ he was angry over the "form" of publ; he claims that "no one" objected to the publ as such [→ :22].

14. MAY DAY ISSUE. **Mar-Apr:** The argument [← :7] over whether to celebrate May Day on May 1 (with work stoppages, advocated by the French) or on Sunday, May 3 (advocated by the English and Germans), continues, with E arguing that the matter should be decided by the specific national situation, in letters to Sorge (Mar 4), Paul Lafargue (Mar 6), and others.

15. INTERNATIONAL AFFAIRS. **Mar 21:** E thanks Schlüter for info on the situation in the American SLP; he criticizes the latter for its sectarian attitude toward the Knights of Labor and other mass workers' organizations. **Mar 25 to May 15:** E corresponds with Labriola (in Italy), who sends material on the labor movement and the spread of Marxism, and on the May Day clash with police in Rome (SOURCE: *MEW Daten*). **Mar 28:** J. Wierzjeski (in Nice) informs E that W. Wróblewski is ill and needy, and requests his letter be forwarded to Stanislaw Mendelson (which E does, Mar 31).

16. STATIFICATION. **Mar 24:** E writes M. Oppenheim that "as long as the possessing classes remain at the helm, every statification means not the abolition of exploitation but a change in its form—in the French, American and Swiss republics no less than in monarchist Central Europe or despotic East Europe."

17. W&P: GERMAN. **Mar 4:** As E tells Sorge, he faces three tasks for publ [for which, see ← :12], and he is engaged in writing, or planning, new intros to M's *Civil war in France* (#M143) and *Wage-labor and capital* (#M968). **Mar AB:** E writes the intro (#E392) to *The civil war in France*, which is scheduled for the 20th anniversary of the Paris Commune. **Mar 14:** E finishes the intro, and sends it to the *Vorwärts* press in Berlin (R. Fischer), though it is dated Mar 18, the Commune anniversary. In the last paragraph E hits at the right-wing furor over the publ of M's *Critique of the Gotha program* [cf ← :11], writing: "Of late, the Social-Democratic philistine has been filled with wholesome terror at the term dictatorship of the proletariat"—well, the Paris Commune was the dictatorship of the proletariat. **Mar M:** The *Vorwärts* editors alter "Social-Democratic" to "German" without consulting E. Evidently E spots this in the proofs, and protests, for— **Mar 17:** R. Fischer's letter to E makes clear that the change was made in Berlin without E's approval. (However, E allows the change to go through without making a furor over it.) **Mar D:** E's intro (#E392) is pubd in *Neue Zeit*. —The new edn of M's work (third German edn) is pubd this spring, perhaps Mar D or Apr.

18. W&P: FRENCH. **Mar 4 to Oct 2:** E edits Ravé's French trans of a part of his *Origin of the family* (#E573) and checks Laura Lafargue's trans of the rest. **Mar 6:** E explains to Paul Lafargue what is wrong with the latter's article for *NZ* [← :12]. **Mar 17:** E sends a letter of greetings to French workers for the 20th anniversary of the Paris Commune (#E343); pubd in *Le Socialiste*, Mar 25.

19. W&P: ITALIAN. **Mar 6, 7:** In letters to Martignetti and Turati, E gives his Italian correspondents general permission to translate M/E's writings for *Critica Sociale* or a planned "Socialist Library" (pamphlet series), and expresses special interest in publ of a good trans of the *Com Manifesto*. E's letter to Turati is pubd in *Critica Sociale*, Mar 10 (#E431.5). **Mar 18:** Publisher Fantuzzi sends E copies of an Italian pamphlet edn of the *Com Manifesto*, in a poor, defective, unauthorized trans by P. Gori (prob pubd Feb c.M). **Mar 21:** E sends a copy of this Italian edn to Sorge.

20. W&P: SPANISH. **Mar 24:** At Mesa's request, E sends him a letter authorizing his Spanish edn of M's *Poverty of philosophy* (#M681). E's letter (#E437) will be pubd as preface to the edn [→ :40], stressing that Proudhonism is still an ideological source of counterfeit socialism.

21. MARX'S PAPERS. **Mar-Apr:** Louise Kautsky works at sorting out the file of M's correspondence.

"precisely" those that M proposed in 1875 on Lassallean-Eisenacher unity as against the Gotha Congress unification on unprincipled grounds. **Apr 8:** In his letter to Sorge, E expounds a dietary-nutrition theory of the cause of gout and rheumatism. **Apr 30:** Writing to Kautsky, E stresses the difference between a real militia system and the US National Guard, which is in practice nothing but a civil guard for the bourgeoisie against the workers and utterly useless against foreign foes; a real militia means a rifle and 100 good bullets in every worker's home. **Apr 30, May 29:** Writing to Kautsky, who had pubd Paul Lafargue's "Myth of Adam and Eve" in *NZ*, E rejects Lafargue's theories as untenable; writing to Lafargue himself, E diplomatically says that the essay is witty, has "some truth in it," but goes too far in interpretation.

24. W&P. **Apr A:** Responding to Ravé's query about Kautsky's book on Thomas More, E says it is "generally correct and in many respects original," and is worth translating into French. **Apr 9:** Having received an invitation (of Apr 2) from the organization committee for an international meeting in Milan on the "right to work" (right to a job), E sends a letter of greetings (#E861); it is read to the meeting on Apr 12, but unpubd. **Apr before 10:** E's brochure against Brentano (#E375) [← :12] is pubd. **Apr 10–15:** E sends copies to Sorge, Fischer, Nieuwenhuis, and other friends and correspondents. **Apr 30:** E writes an intro (#E395) for a new, revised edn of M's *Wage-labor and capital* (#M968), explaining how he has revised M's work [→ :29]. **c.Apr:** After many interruptions in his revision of his *Origin of the family* (#E573), now enters on a final period of work on it [→ :34].

25. VISITOR. **Apr A:** Schorlemmer spends about a week as E's guest.

APRIL

27. FUROR OVER THE CRITIQUE. **Apr A:** The "boycott" of E by the German party leadership peters out (first evidenced by Bebel's letter, ← :13). Paul Singer (Apr 2) writes E to be sure to send Bebel greetings on his silver wedding anniversary; E's letter of greetings to Bebel stresses his personal regard [→ :26]. **Apr 8:** Writing to Sorge, E reports this easing of the situation. In this letter E gives his most cutting and contemptuous characterization of Liebknecht as a party leader—a note that will appear frequently in his correspondence (cf ← :1). **Apr 25:** Another letter from Bebel shows the old tone of friendship.

23. OPINIONS. **Apr 3, 7:** In letters to Paul Lafargue and Kautsky, E repeats [← :8] his thesis that the policies now being pursued by the French party vis-à-vis the Possibilists are

MAY

26. END OF THE FUROR. **May 1:** With friendly relations restored [← :22], E replies to Bebel's letters of Mar 30 and Apr 25 with an exposition of his views. He replies to the claim that "no one opposed publ" [← :13] by surveying Liebknecht's bad role in the recent furor and also his lying and unprincipled conduct in 1875. E discusses what a correct unity position should have been in 1875. Finally, he strongly attacks the antidemocratic efforts of the party leadership to throttle the *NZ*, to "statify and censor" it, and to scuttle freedom of discussion in the party.

27. MAY DAY. **May 2:** Writing to Bebel, E surveys the success of the demonstrations in Vienna and France. **May 3:** E participates in the London demonstration. **May 4:** E reports (to Laura Lafargue) on the London affair, the organizing role of Eleanor M and Aveling, the sect role of the SDF. He criticizes the tactics of the French party on relations with other socialist groups. **May c.6:** E receives from Fischer a report on the success of demonstrations in Berlin and other German cities.

28. OTHER INTERNATIONAL AFFAIRS. **May CD:** At the request of Anseele (in Belgium), E helps to get aid from English TUs for the striking dock workers of Belgium; he corresponds with TU leaders John Burns and E. Klemm. **May c.20:** From Schlüter, E receives reports on the US movement, incl on the miners' struggle for the eight-hour day; also on the dissemination of the English edn of *Capital*.

29. W&P. **May 12:** E writes a short preface (#E761) for the fourth German edn of his *Socialism: Utopian and scientific* (#E759), which will be pubd in the second half of this year. **May 13:** E's new intro (#E395) to M's *Wage-labor and capital* [← :24] is pubd in *Vorwärts* [→ :34]. **May c.21:** Complying with the request of Prof. Ludwig Elster, E sends biographical info and a bibliography of his writings for an article in the *Handwörterbuch der Staatswissenschaften*, which will appear in Vol. 3 of this work (Jena, 1892).

30. WORK IN PROGRESS. **May:** Working on his planned revision of his *Origin of the family* (#E573), E reads Giraud-Teulon and asks Paul Lafargue (May 29) to check on his claims.

31. MARXISM AND SECTISM. **May 4:** Writing to Laura Lafargue, E highlights a phenomenon much in his mind (cf → :35): the British SDF and American SLP both exemplify people who have "the correct theory as to the dogmatic side of it" but who have become "a mere sect" because they do not understand "working with the working class at every possible stage of its development," who treat theory as "a conjuror's formula."

32. *CAPITAL*: YANKEE KNOW-HOW. **May 11:** Schlüter informs E that a pirated serial edn of *Capital* (in English), pubd by Humboldt (NY) in 1890 in 5000 copies, is now exhausted; Humboldt had sent out an advertising circular to bank officials saying that M taught "how to accumulate capital"; bankers had hastened to subscribe in order to learn the secret.

JUNE

33. GERMAN PARTY AFFAIRS. **June 1:** Vollmar makes a speech at a Munich public party meeting openly advocating gradualist reform in domestic and foreign policy (for E's reaction, see June 29, below). **June 10:** E writes Sorge confidentially that the German

party leadership (meaning mainly Bebel and Singer) now sees Liebknecht as discredited, an empty phrasemonger and incompetent editor of *Vorwärts*. **June 18:** Fischer, on behalf of the party Exec, sends E material for the coming (Oct) Erfurt Congress: program drafts, incl the latest draft by the Exec. **June 18–29:** E writes a critique of the Erfurt draft program (#E198) and sends it to the Exec. (It will not be pubd till 1901; his criticisms are considered for the new Exec draft pubd July 4.) **June 29:** E writes Kautsky that he has not had the time to reformulate the preamble; his critique of the political part of the program has given him an opportunity to attack "the conciliatory opportunism of the *Vorwärts* [Liebknecht]" and the theory that the capitalist system will "grow into a socialist society" by itself. E also attacks Vollmar's June 1 speech, esp his assurance that the party will join in the defense of the fatherland if it is attacked, "hence will help to defend the annexation of Alsace-Lorraine." He proposes that the Exec state that Vollmar cannot speak for the party (in fact such a statement is issued June 30 and pubd July 1) [→ :37].

34. W&P. **June 13:** E finishes drafting a preface (#E574) to the fourth German edn of his *Origin of the family* (#E573), surveying the tendencies of research in this field. Writing to Laura Lafargue, he describes his reading and research [← 90:26]. **June 16:** E puts finishing touches to the preface, and dates it. It is pubd by itself in the June issue of *NZ* [→ :59]. **June 26:** E writes a letter of greetings (#E345) to the second congress of the Austrian party (Vienna, June 28–30)—drafted first as a letter to V. Adler [→ :40]. **June D:** The new, revised edn of M's *Wage-labor and capital* (#M968B) is pubd in Berlin, with E's new intro (#E395).

35. MARXIST THEORY. **June 10:** Writing to Sorge, E repeats [← :31] that in America and England the "orthodox Marxists" have become a "pure sect" by turning their theory into a "rigid dogma." **June:** E reads Paul Barth's *Die Geschichtsphilosophie Hegel's und der Hegelianer bis auf Marx und Hartmann*, and condemns its distorted view of Marx's theory of history [→ :38].

36. PERSONAL. **June 26 to Aug c.24:** E is on holiday—with interruptions—in Ryde, Isle of Wight; Schorlemmer and Harney come as guests.

JULY

37. INTERNATIONAL AFFAIRS. **July 12:** Re Alsace-Lorraine and French chauvinism, E objects (in a letter to Laura Lafargue) to making the fate of Europe (i.e., the question of war) dependent on liberating this province.

(For the other side of the coin, cf ← :33.) **July:** E disagrees with the plan of Guesde and Bonnier to restore the "old International with a Central Council" now; this is premature and would create interparty antagonisms (letter to Laura Lafargue, July 20). —To aid the Austrian party, E instructs pub'r Dietz to turn over to its treasury half the proceeds from the new edn of *Origin of the family* (#E573); he so informs V. Adler on July 22 [→ 92:9].

38. THEORY. July 1: E criticizes Barth's book on Hegel and Marx [← :35] in a letter to C. Schmidt: Barth invents a theory of history for M, and then accuses M of contradicting himself because he does not find it in M's writings! Barth is a *Korinthenscheisser* (one who turns everything into trivia).

39. *CAPITAL*. July 8: To J. G. Vogt, whose letters of June 20 and July 5 proposed that someone rewrite the text of *Capital* in more easily understood language, E replies that everyone concerned would reject the idea. (This does not concern the idea of a new summary or exposition.)

40. W&P. July 3: The Vienna *Arbeiter-Ztg* pubs E's greetings to the Austrian party congress (#E345) [← :34]. **July D:** E finishes work on revising his *Origin of the family* (#E573) for the fourth German edn [→ :59]. **July-Aug** (i.e., summer): The Spanish edn of M's *Poverty of philosophy* (#M681) [← :20] is pubd, ed by J. Mesa.

AUGUST

41. BRUSSELS CONGRESS. Aug 16–22: The International Socialist Congress in Brussels is a definite success from E's standpoint, as he gets letters on it from Eleanor M, Lessner, et al. **Aug 17:** Writing to Laura Lafargue, E repeats his view [← :37] on the inadvisability of setting up a restored International at this time. **Aug CD:** E's letters to correspondents on the congress express satisfaction with its work [→ :44]. **Aug c.25 to c.27:** Bebel and V. Adler, coming from Brussels, visit E in London, and discuss the work of the congress.

42. ITALIAN MOVEMENT. Aug A: From Turati, E receives an Italian propaganda brochure based on E's new intro (#E395) to M's *Wage-labor and capital* [← :34]. **Aug 3–18:** From Labriola, E receives a report on the situation in Italy—jailings after the May Day demonstration and other political trials, the Workers' Congress in Milan Aug 2–3, etc.

43. ENGLISH MOVEMENT. Aug 9–11: In a letter to Sorge, E reports on the sad collapse of the dockers' union as the result of reactionary policies; also on other European affairs.

SEPTEMBER

44. AFTER THE BRUSSELS CONGRESS. Sep 2: In letters to Paul Lafargue and Sorge esp, E gives a very favorable estimation of the congress results: exclusion of the anarchists; inclusion of the British TUs on a class-struggle basis; rejection of Nieuwenhuis's phrasemongering on a "general strike against war"—indeed, a victory for the "Marxists" in principles and tactics adopted. **Sep c.3:** E is visited by American delegates to Brussels: Abraham Cahan, Jewish-American socialist leader and editor (NYC), and one MacVey. (Re Cahan, cf ← 90:4.) **Sep 12:** Most of E's letter to Paul Lafargue of Sep 2 is pubd in *Le Socialiste* (#E106); repubd in *Vorwärts*, Sep 16.

45. WAR QUESTION. Sep 23: Laura Lafargue, on behalf of French party, asks E to write a contribution for a planned "Socialist almanac," suggesting the subject "Progress of socialism in Germany." (E will use this opportunity to discuss war policy; → :52.) **Sep 29:** In a letter to Bebel, E discusses at some length questions of policy in case of war, incl the tactics of a socialist Germany in a war of, say, France and Russia versus Germany.

46. GERMAN MOVEMENT. Sep 24–28: E reads the new draft program for the Erfurt Congress drawn up by the NZ editors, pubd Sep 14. **Sep 28:** E sends Kautsky comments on and criticisms of this draft, which he says is far better than the Exec's [← :33].

47. WOMEN'S MOVEMENT. c.Sep: E works with Louise Kautsky and Eleanor M in London, and with Laura Lafargue in Paris, in preparing articles for the coming new organ of the Austrian socialist women, *Arbeiterinnen-Ztg*. They look to the new paper as a counterweight against the standpoint of the Berlin women dominated by elements like Gertrud Guillaume-Schack (Countess Schack), i.e. radical women who want to separate feminism from workingwomen's class struggle [→ :54].

48. ENGLISH MOVEMENT. Sep 14, 30: In letters to Sorge, E expresses satisfaction over the results of the congress of the English TUs in Newcastle (Sep 7–12), in particular the defeat of the "bourgeois labor" (conservative) wing of the union movement.

49. PERSONAL. Sep 8 to c.23: E goes on a tour of Ireland and Scotland with Mary Ellen Rosher and Louise Kautsky.

OCTOBER

50. GERMAN PARTY: ERFURT CONGRESS. Oct 6: *Vorwärts*, reprinting the NZ draft program [← :46], adds the Lassallean phrase that, as against the proletariat, all others form "one reactionary mass." **Oct 14:** In a letter to

Kautsky, E strongly criticizes this insertion. (It will not appear in the adopted program.) **Oct 14–21:** The party congress meets in Erfurt. **Oct 24, 25:** In letters to Sorge and Kautsky, E expresses well-nigh complete approval of the work of the congress and the program adopted, from which "the last trace of Lassalleanism" has been removed. Ditto in letter to Bebel (Oct 24–26), and other correspondence of Oct D to Nov A.

51. FRENCH ELECTION. Oct 27: E congratulates Paul Lafargue on his lead in the first ballot (Oct 25) for a parliamentary seat from Lille; Lafargue at this point has been a political prisoner since July [→ :56].

52. WAR QUESTION. Oct 9: Bebel informs E that in the German party leadership there are differences on appraisal of the war danger [← :45]. **Oct 13:** In a letter to Bebel, E discusses the possibilities of war and revolutionary policy in war: if Germany is attacked from east and west (Russia and France) and its national existence is at stake, then one should demand revolutionary means of defense; socialists may come to power then. **Oct 13–22:** E writes an article for the French party's Almanac [← :45] on "Socialism in Germany" (#E757A) [→ :62]; it deals esp with policy in war. **Oct 24–26:** Writing to Sorge (Oct 24) and Bebel (Oct 24–26), E summarizes his views from the article "Socialism in Germany," and reports that the French party leaders like the article very much. In his letter to Bebel, E discusses a problem of socialist society: getting enough reliable elements with technical training to administer the new social order.

53. AMERICAN AFFAIRS. Oct 24: E's letter to Sorge reviews his opinions on the situation of the US movement: its backwardness is due to higher living standards, effects of immigration, etc.; another negative element is the socialist sects with their "supercilious Germans" who want to be workers' schoolmasters and commanders; but things will move fast once they start.

54. WOMEN'S MOVEMENT. Oct 1: E warns Bebel (part of letter of Sep 29/Oct 1) that the coming publ of the Vienna *Arbeiterinnen-Ztg* [← :47] will irk the Berlin group of Social-Democratic women, because the Austrian women want to build a workingwomen's sector of the workers' movement, not a separate feminist movement. The Vienna paper will be the first to defend this standpoint. **Oct 2:** Writing to Laura Lafargue, E opines that the coming articles by Laura, Eleanor M, and Louise Kautsky in the Vienna paper will "create a sensation" among the women who want to divorce women's rights from the workers' class struggle ("*Frauenrechtlerinnen*" in Socialist terminology, or "women's

rights women" in E's English terminology); the "reign" of the Berlin feminists (of the Guillaume-Schack type) will soon be over, for workingwomen are now coming into the women's movement.

55. PUBLICATION. Oct c.3 to Dec 1: E negotiates with pub'r Swan Sonnenschein over a British edn of the Wischnewetzky trans of his *Condition of the working class* (#E171) [→ 92:20] and corresponds on the matter with the translator. **Oct 25:** According to a letter by E to Kautsky for a notice in *NZ*, Swan Sonnenschein will also publish Aveling's trans of his *Socialism: Utopian and scientific* (#E759) and Eleanor M's trans of Bernstein's essay on Lassalle (pubd in German as an intro to Lassalle's writings and in English as a book *Ferdinand Lassalle as a social reformer*).

NOVEMBER

56. FRENCH AFFAIRS. Nov 8: Paul Lafargue wins the Lille parliamentary seat on the second ballot [← :51], a great victory for the French party. **Nov 9–14:** In letters to Bebel, Sorge, and others, E expresses great satisfaction over this significant success for the French party's policies. Lafargue is released from prison on Nov 10. **Nov 23 to Dec 1:** As the result of a Reuters dispatch allegedly quoting Lafargue as implying that German socialists committed treasonous acts in the 1870–71 war, letters fly back and forth between the Lafargues and E, who fears the whipping-up of a major antisocialist scandal by the German press; E also acquaints Bebel with the dangerous possibilities. E and Lafargue make preparations to scotch the report, but the danger blows over.

57. HEGEL. Nov 1: To C. Schmidt who has written (Oct 25) that he is going to prepare a work on M and wants to treat the influence of Hegel's dialectic on M's method in *Capital*, E gives a deal of advice on how to study Hegel and on the difference between Hegel's method and M's [→ 92:10]. **Nov to Dec 3:** E reads Plekhanov on the 60th anniversary of Hegel's death in *NZ* and (Dec 3) calls the essay "outstanding."

58. *CAPITAL*. Nov–Dec: See ← :4.

59. W&P. Nov A: The fourth German edn of E's *Origin of the family* (#E573), dated 1892, is pubd, with a new preface by E (#E574) [← :34]. **Nov 13:** Responding to the invitation (Nov A) from the Austrian Social-Democratic organ *Volksfreund* to attend a Nov 22 celebration of its 10th anniversary in Brünn (Brno)—which would also be a protest against Austrian press restrictions—E replies, declining, with greetings (#E838); pubd Nov 25. (The Nov 22 affair is banned.) **Nov 17:** Reading a garbled account of the Pyrenees episode [← 71:43] in the *Daily Chronicle*, E sends in a letter correcting the tale (#E421); pubd Nov 26. **Nov 28:** On hearing that the GWEA Choral Society plans to honor him with a serenade on his 71th birthday, E asks the assoc to cancel it (#E818): he and M, he explains, have always opposed hero-worshiping demonstrations in honor of individuals without a larger purpose.

60. OBITUARY. Nov 11: Oscar Heidfeld (in Liverpool) informs E of the death of Ernst Dronke.

DECEMBER

61. LASSALLE. Dec 3: Writing to Kautsky, E stresses the value and significance of Bernstein's just-pubd essay on Lassalle (intro to the new three-vol. edn of Lassalle's writings and speeches) [← :55], because the movement's enemies "live on the antithesis between the nationalist Lassalle and the fatherlandless Social-Democrats." E thinks it unfortunate that Bernstein's notorious footnote (saying that Lassalle "prob" had chronic syphilis) has caused a to-do; the Berlin party "censors" should have caught it before publ.

62. W&P. Dec A: E's essay "Socialism in Germany" (#E757A) is pubd in the French party's Almanac [← :52]. **Dec to Jan:** E drafts an enlarged verson of this essay (#E757B) for publ in German [→ 92:5].

63. PERSONAL. Dec M: E goes to Ryde (Isle of Wight).

1892

CONSPECTUS

1. Overshadowing E's activities is his frustrated desire to get to work on the mss of Vol. 3 of *Capital* [← 91:4]; when he finally resumes work on the volume in Oct, he has to keep explaining to correspondents that he must cut out all responsibilities in order to concentrate his time. As background, we can cite E's letter of Mar 5, written to Sorge: "You should see the pile of German, French, Italian, Spanish, Polish, Russian, Danish, American, English, and sometimes Roumanian newspapers that come to me and that I must at least look at in order to stay *au courant* with the movement. In addition, real jobs of work, which eat away the rest of my time. And the correspondence! I have accumulated enough for a week. And then Volume 3 is supposed to be finished. It's a shame. But still it will be carried out."

2. At some time, thought to be the end of 1892, E supplemented the list of his published works which he had jotted down in 1889 [← 89:2]. For more details, see #E240.5 (cf also #E471).

JANUARY

3. WOMEN'S MOVEMENT. Jan 1: The first issue of the Vienna *Arbeiterinnen-Ztg* appears [← 91:54] with articles by Laura Lafargue and Louise Kautsky. **Jan 6:** E compliments Laura on her article and encourages more writing. **Jan 20:** E passes on, to Laura, Louise Kautsky's urging of more contributions.

4. BOOKS. Jan: E reads Julius Wolf's article on M's economic theory, which he will later attack in his preface to *Capital*, Vol. 3. He also reads C. Schmidt's reply to Wolf in the same journal [→ :10]. **Jan 28:** In reply to a query from Kautsky, E agrees it is worthwhile to translate T. Rogers' book *Six centuries of work and wages* (1886).

5. W&P. Jan 11: E writes a preface (#E175) to the new British edn of his *Condition of the working class* (#E171) [→ :20]. **Jan 16, Feb 1:** *Critica Sociale* pubs an Italian trans of E's essay "Socialism in Germany" (#E757A). **Jan 19:** E finishes doing the German version of his essay "Socialism in Germany" (#E757B)—with additions at beginning and end—and sends it to Bebel; pubd Feb in NZ.

6. FRIENDS. Jan to Mar: E makes repeated visits to Harney (in Richmond), corresponds with him, and gives him financial aid.

7. AMERICAN AFFAIRS. Jan 6: Writing to Sorge, E discusses the dim immediate prospect of a third party and the factors that may produce it; farmers cannot form a strong, stable party. He also reports on Gompers' efforts to enlist him as arbitrator between the AFL and SLP, but he will decline this role.

FEBRUARY

8. GERMAN MOVEMENT. Feb 19: E's letter to Bebel discusses the danger of a turn to the right and to antisocialist persecution on the part of the German government, in order to smash the advancing movement.

9. GIFT TO AUSTRIANS. Feb 19: E instructs publisher Dietz to turn over all payments due him to the party treasury of the Austrian Social-Democrats; E so informs V. Adler [← 91:37; → :26].

10. THEORY. Feb 4: In a letter to Schmidt, E discusses Wolf's article on the average rate of profit in Marx, and Schmidt's reply to Wolf

[← :4]. E also again [← 91:57] gives advice on how to study Hegel.

11. W&P. **Feb 1:** For publ of an Italian trans of "Socialism in Germany" (#E757A), see ← :5. **Feb 2:** Turati sends E a copy of *La Tribuna* (Rome) with an article by G. Bovio criticizing this essay, i.e., its first part (pubd Jan 16), and asks E to reply to it. Bovio claims that the German socialists lay no store by the form of the proletariat's political rule. **Feb 6:** E writes a reply to Bovio (#E669) and sends it to Turati; pubd in *Critica Sociale*, Feb 16. **Feb 10:** Complying with the request of the Polish socialist émigré Stanislaw Mendelson, E writes a preface (#E615) for a Polish edn of the *Com Manifesto;* he sends it to Mendelson on Feb 11 (pubd Feb 27 in the journal *Przedświt*, and then in the *Manifesto* brochure) [→ :20]. **Feb M to Apr:** E works at editing Aveling's trans of *Socialism: Utopian and scientific* (#E759), and writes an intro to the English edn (#E762). **Feb c.20 or earlier:** On request (Jan D) from Dietz for the Reichstag Fraction, E drafts an address greeting Bebel on the 25th anniversary (Feb 22) of his entrance into parliamentary activity; see #E341.5. (The Fraction does not use E's draft, and it is not extant.) **Feb:** E's essay "Socialism in Germany" in its enlarged German version (#E757B) [← :5] is pubd in NZ.

MARCH

12. GERMAN AFFAIRS. **Mar A:** E is visited by the Social-Democratic miner August Siegel, who emigrated from Germany because of government harassment; E gives him financial aid and helps him look for work. **Mar 5:** E returns the ms of *Das Erfurter Programm* to Kautsky and apologizes for being able to read only the first 16 pages (most of which he recommends dropping). **Mar 8:** In a letter to Bebel, E discusses the economic situation in Germany.

13. FRENCH MOVEMENT. **Mar 5, 14:** In letters to Paul Lafargue, E involves himself in working out the French party's policy toward both wings of the Blanquists, the Boulangist-Blanquists (Granger group) and the traditional group (Vaillant group). E strongly attacks any alliance with the Granger group, who committed "treason" to the movement [→ :22]. **Mar 17:** For the 21st anniversary of the Paris Commune E writes a greeting to the French workers (#E344); pubd in *Le Socialiste*, Mar 26.

14. ENGLISH MOVEMENT. **Mar-Apr:** E works with Eleanor M and Aveling, who are involved in May Day preparations on behalf of the Legal Eight Hours and International Labour League, trying to achieve unity of action by all socialist and workers' groups. In a

number of letters (Mar 14 to Laura Lafargue, Mar 16 to Bebel, Apr 20 to Kautsky) E describes the "play of intrigues" and maneuvers by the SDF, TU Council, etc.

15. AMERICAN AFFAIRS. **Mar 30:** In a letter to Schlüter, E reviews the reasons why the movement is retarded in the US, esp the playing-off of native vs immigrant and various immigrant groups against each other.

16. RUSSIAN AFFAIRS. **Mar 15 to Sep c.25:** E corresponds with Danielson on the economic situation in Russia and its prospects; he gets material from Danielson on the subject, incl economic journals and books, i.a. Vol. 1 of *Itogi statistiko-ekonomicheskikh issledovani, proisvedyonnykh zemstvami.* E emphasizes the growth of capitalist relations in Russia, the transformation of the peasant community (*obshchina*) and the proletarianization of a large part of the peasantry. In his letter of Mar 15 he states flatly: "We shall have to treat the *obshchina* as a dream of the past, and reckon, in future, with a Capitalist Russia" [→ :29, 48].

17. ITALIAN MOVEMENT. **Mar c.10:** From Labriola, E receives the program of the Italian workers' party based on decisions of the Milan Congress, also material on the unemployed movement in Rome, and info on the situation in Italy generally.

18. MEHRING: PRO AND CON. **Mar 8:** In a letter to Bebel, E reports that Mehring is so put out by neglect of his book on Eugen Richter in NZ and *Vorwärts* that he has written Bernstein he is thinking of withdrawing from politics (i.e., leaving the party). E defends the practice of the socialist press—so different from the bourgeois literary world in which Mehring developed—of not publicizing books just because they are written by a comrade; better no publicity than advertisements for every piece of "party trash." E has also just read Mehring's *Deutsche Sozialdemokratie* (third edn of 1879), and comments on the passages in which Mehring discusses his anti–Social-Democratic turn of 1876. **Mar 16:** Again to Bebel, E discusses Mehring's essay on the "Lessing legend" in NZ; this he praises enthusiastically: at last historical materialism, which for 20 years has been a swaggering phrase, is finally used properly, as a guideline to the study of history.

19. DUELING. **Mar 30:** Responding to a query (Mar 26) from P. Martignetti, E opines that accepting a challenge to a duel (from an army officer yet) is a mistake; there may be cases where a duel is unavoidable, but it is senseless to undertake or provoke a duel.

20. W&P. **Mar 29:** E writes the preface (#E609) to the second German edn of M's *Poverty of philosophy* (#M681) [→ :31]. **Mar D:** The British edn of the Wischnewetzky trans of *Condition of the working class* (#E171) is pubd, with a new preface by E (#E175). **Prob Mar:** The Polish edn of the *Com Manifesto* is pubd, with a new preface by E (#E615).

21. PERSONAL. **Mar 14:** On the anniversary of M's death, writes E to Laura Lafargue, "we" have visited the grave in Highgate Cemetery: a small cypress has been planted by Eleanor M; crocuses are blooming; and ivy from Ulrich von Hutten's grave—planted by Motteler—is well rooted. **Mar c.20–26:** E is on holiday in Ryde.

APRIL

22. INTERNATIONAL AFFAIRS. **Apr 1:** E is interviewed by a correspondent of *L'Eclair*, E. Massard, mainly on the international situation. **Apr 3:** E revises Massard's notes on the interview. **Apr 6:** The interview (#E390) is pubd in *L'Eclair*. **Apr 16:** It is reprinted in *Le Socialiste*, except the last two sections. **Apr M:** The Russian populist N. S. Rusanov visits E; they discuss the economic situation in Russia and the prospects of capitalist development (cf ← :16). **Apr 19:** In a letter to Laura Lafargue, E continues his discussion [← :13] of policy vis-à-vis the two Blanquist groups in France; this letter is the longest and most thorough analysis. **Apr 20:** In a letter to Kautsky, E continues his account of maneuvers on May Day preparations in London (cf ← :14).

23. W&P. **Apr 20:** E finishes, and dates, his intro (#E762) to the English edn of *Socialism: Utopian and scientific* (#E759), dealing with problems of historical materialism [→ :31]. **Apr 20–27:** In correspondence with Dietz, who has acquired Wigand's rights to E's *Condition of the working class* (#E171), E agrees to a new German edn with minimum additions; he agrees to do a new preface (#E176) and some explanatory notes [→ :36].

MAY

24. MAY DAY. **May 1:** E participates in the May Day demonstration in London, which is esp huge, since May 1 falls on Sunday. E is with Platform 14, which he describes as "the international platform," incl many foreigners as well as Britishers. **May 2:** The *Daily Chronicle* runs a caricature sketch of the scene around Platform 14, showing the enormous crowd before it and some of the speakers on the platform; Stepniak, Aveling, and Mrs. Cunninghame Graham are named; E and Eleanor M are prob among the other figures shown. (See reproduction in *MEW* 38: opp. 336.) **May 3:** In a letter to Laura Lafargue, E enthusiastically reports the "triumph" of "our" two platforms among the throng. He adds that he is glad that May Day went quietly everywhere: "The idea that the 1st of May is to be a day of rows and riots is a mere trap set by the bourgeois. . . . We want to show our strength, that's all"—and at times of our own choosing. (E also gives Bebel a brief report, May 7.) **May c.5:** From Labriola, E receives info on the May Day demonstrations in various Italian cities. **May:** From Stanislaw Mendelson, E receives Polish flysheets issued for May 1 in Lvov and Cracow.

25. FRENCH MOVEMENT. **May 2–10:** E follows the course of the municipal elections (May 1, 8), and greets the party's successes in the campaign. **May 27:** Since the party is planning to publish a daily paper, E urges that it must have an international news editor who can report on the English and German movements—and Laura Lafargue is "the only person in toute la belle France" who can do this. But E insists that in this capacity Laura must be made a regular editorial board member, and paid accordingly. "Paul is too much of an hidalgo to think of, or to press, such matters," hence Laura must insist on it.

26. AUSTRIAN MOVEMENT. **May 19:** On behalf also of Bebel and Singer (who are visiting in London), E makes a proposal to Victor Adler, who they know is in bad financial straits. Since E has already arranged that his publishers' payments be turned over to the Austrian party [← :9], E now wants them to go to Adler, so as to ensure his services to the Austrian movement. **May 31:** E sends greetings (#E813.5) to the third congress of the Austrian party; pubd in the Vienna *Arbeiter-Ztg*, June 10.

27. GERMAN MOVEMENT. **May 15 to June 1:** Bebel and Paul Singer are in London on a visit, Bebel staying with E, Singer with Bernstein; they jointly discuss problems of the German movement [→ :29].

28. FRIENDS. **May 17 to June:** Schorlemmer is fatally ill; at 58 he is "dying of senile marasmus while his mother is still alive and in perfect health!" E corresponds with his friend's brother and doctors, and visits him in Manchester [→ :30]. **May to July:** Since Karl Kautsky (May 13) wants E to persuade Louise Kautsky to stop using this name and change to "Strasser-Kautsky," E gets involved in a three-month polemical exchange on the subject (letters of May 17, June 25, July 5) in which he, as usual, takes Louise's side, explaining why Louise does not want to drop the name which is becoming somewhat known in the party.

JUNE

29. MOVEMENT AFFAIRS. **June 9–17:** E is visited several times by a delegation of German mine workers who are attending an international mine workers' congress in London; they discuss problems of the German miners' struggles. **June M to July 25:** E follows the course of the parliamentary campaign and election in England (July 7–24), and discusses the problems of the movement for an independent workers' party, in correspondence (e.g., June 20 to Bebel) before the election takes place [→ :32]. **June 18:** E reports to Sorge on his discussions with Bebel and Singer [← :27]. In confidence he relates that both see Liebknecht as a worn-out figure, "a positive hindrance for the party," a man who failed to develop, a very bad editor of *Vorwärts*. E recommends pensioning him off somehow, but it is difficult to get him out. — In a letter to Danielson [← :16] E continues his argument that Russia's capitalist development of industry was an unavoidable necessity after the Crimean War: "All governments, be they ever so absolute, are in the final instance but the executors of the economic necessities of the national situation."

30. SCHORLEMMER. **June 2–4:** E goes to Manchester to visit Schorlemmer, who is dying [← :28]. **June 9–20:** E writes to various friends (Laura Lafargue, Kautsky, Bebel) to acquaint them with Schorlemmer's condition. **June 27:** Schorlemmer dies; autopsy shows cancer. **June 29 to July 2:** E is in Manchester for the funeral [→ :34].

31. W&P. **June A:** The second German edn of M's *Poverty of philosophy* (#M681) is pubd, with a new preface by E (#E609). **June A** (by June 11): E makes a German trans of his intro (#E762) to the English edn of *Socialism: Utopian and scientific* (#E759) (he sends it to Kautsky for NZ, July 5) [→ :49]. **June 10:** E's greetings to the Austrian party congress (#E813.5) [← :26] are pubd.

JULY

32. ENGLISH AFFAIRS. **July 5:** In a letter to Bebel, E criticizes a *Vorwärts* article (July 2) on the English election [cf ← :29], esp its thesis that the Tories are more favorable to the workers than the Liberals; refuting this, he analyzes the class role of both parties and three types of "workers' candidates."—In a letter to Kautsky, E opines that an independent labor party is on the way; hopefully, this is the last election fought out only between the two official parties. **July 7–25:** In a number of letters (to Bebel, Laura Lafargue, Bernstein) E waxes ever more hopeful and enthusiastic about the result of the election, esp the victory of three real workers' candidates (Keir Hardie, John Burns, J. H. Wilson).

33. GERMAN MOVEMENT. **July 23:** E writes a monitory letter to Bebel about Voll-

mar's advocacy of state socialism; he opines that there will prob have to be a break with him this year or next. E gives three points of advice on how to deal with his maneuverist intrigues in the party, esp the need to go over from defense to offense.

34. SCHORLEMMER. **July 1:** E attends Schorlemmer's funeral [← :30] in Manchester. He writes an obituary on him (#E125). **July 2:** E returns to London. **July 3:** The obituary is pubd in *Vorwärts*.

35. G. B. SHAW. **July 7:** E suggests to Bebel that when he writes Shaw, he should refer him to C. Schmidt's recent refutation in NZ of the "Austrian theory of value" (similar to W. S. Jevons's). Note: The previous month the Fabians pubd Shaw's "Fabian Election Manifesto, 1892" calling suddenly for a working-class party—a temporary aberration on the Fabians' part. Apparently this has aroused some hope for Shaw in E's breast; he recalls that in 1887 Shaw had come out in a series of articles as a champion of Jevons' economics [→ :44].

36. W&P. **July 21:** E finishes, and dates, the preface (#E176) to the second German edn of his *Condition of the working class* (#E171) [→ :41].

37. PERSONAL. **July 27 to Sep 6:** E sojourns in Ryde. Originally intending to stay till Aug 8/9, he remains here on account of illness [→ :43].

AUGUST

38. ENGLISH AFFAIRS. **Aug 19–23:** With great satisfaction, in various letters (to Bebel, Sorge, Louise Kautsky, Adler) E reports the successes of English socialists in the eight-hour-day movement, esp among the Lancashire textile workers who have endorsed an eight-hour law by a great majority.

39. FABIANS, BERNSTEIN, KAUTSKY. **Aug 8:** Kautsky writes E explaining why the NZ article on the English election by Eleanor M and Aveling has been shorn of its passages criticizing the sectarianism and opportunism of the SDF and the Fabians: he cites lack of space. **Aug 12:** Writing to Kautsky, E expresses dissatisfaction with this episode, and stresses the importance of the article's criticism of the SDF and Fabians—of the former's futile sectarian ossification of Marxism into dogma and the latter's futile reformism. To force labor candidates on the Liberals, one must, like Keir Hardie, "keep them at the point of the sword, and not, like the Fabians, fawn on them under false pretences" [→ :44]. **Aug 14:** Writing to Bebel, E is dubious about Kautsky's explanation; part of the reason for striking the passages about the Fabians may be Bernstein's "funny respect for the

Fabians. . . ." **Aug 20:** To Bebel, E writes of
the nervous disorder which besets Bernstein;
he thinks its root lies in Bernstein's *Fabian-
schwärmerei* (enthusiasm for the Fabians):
"Neurasthenics are mistrustful, and I am of
the opinion that the Lassalle trouble was not
only the first symptom of his illness but
definitely also the occasion of its outbreak. . . .
Also, I consider overestimation of the Fabians
to be responsible for his illness. . . ." (The
"Lassalle trouble" was the attack on Bernstein
for his essay on Lassalle, with its notorious
footnote; cf ← 91:61. Thus E diagnoses Bernstein's faltering nerves as a failure of nerve in
the face of political pressure from the right.)
[→ :57]

40. INTERNATIONAL AFFAIRS. **Aug c.2:** E
receives info on the Danish movement from
Gerson Trier. **Aug 4 to Sep 3:** Labriola keeps
E informed on the preparation of and course
of the founding congress of the Italian
workers' party, Genoa, Aug 14–15.

41. W&P. **Aug M:** The second German
edn of E's *Condition of the working class*
(#E171) is pubd, with a new preface (#E176)
[← :36].

42. STUDIES. **Aug:** E goes back to his
study (begun in the 1840s) of the history of
early Christianity; he reads the works of
Renan (whom he finds to be quite unreliable
as a historian) and the Bible.

43. TOUR ABORTED. **Aug 6:** In Ryde [←
:37] E suddenly has a relapse of an old
complaint from which he suffered in 1883–
87, producing lameness from time to time,
viz., low-back pain or lumbago. He has to
cancel a trip planned to start Aug c.12, which
was to take him first to Zurich, then to Saint
Gall to pick up Bebel, then with Bebel to
Stuttgart, Munich, Vienna (to pick up Louise
Kautsky), Berlin, and back to London. **Aug
8–9:** E visits London to put his house in
order; sees the Avelings (Eleanor M); and
returns to Ryde to start a regimen of bed rest
and abstinence from alcohol [→ :51].

SEPTEMBER

44. FABIANS, TUs, ILP. **Sep 4:** E again [←
:39] cautions Kautsky not to overestimate the
Fabians, who are still preaching dependence
on the Liberals—incl "the paradoxical belle-
trist Shaw," who is talented, witty and honest
but "absolutely useless as an economist and
politician"; the Fabian leadership is a clique
of bourgeois socialists "united only by their
fear of the threatening rule of the workers" [cf
← :35; → :57]. **Sep 5–10:** The TU Congress
(in Glasgow) rejects an invitation to the
International Socialist Congress in Zurich in
1893 and counterposes an international congress on the eight-hour question, in order to

hinder union contact with the socialist
movement. **Sep 11–26:** In letters to various
European socialist leaders, E proposes the
policy of rejecting the eight-hour congress and
working to get individual TUs to come to
Zurich. For such a letter to the Spanish party
(Sep 16), see #E857; he writes to the German,
Austrian, and French socialists as well (not
extant). He checks over Bebel's article on this
question for *NZ*, written on his advice, and
revises some passages. **Sep 26:** In a letter to
Kautsky, E opines that the Glasgow organizational meeting for an Independent Labour
party held under the chairmanship of Keir
Hardie is not to be taken seriously; he regards
it only as the sect product of the columnist
Autolycus (J. Burgess). (For his change in
viewpoint, see → 93:2.)

45. FRENCH MOVEMENT. **Sep 5:** E gives a
characterization and evaluation of Ch. Bon-
nier, Guesde's collaborator, in a letter to
Kautsky. **Sep CD:** E follows the work of the
TU congress (Marseilles, Sep 19–23) and the
Workers Party Congress (Sep 24–28), both of
which follow the policy proposed by E on the
British plan (cf ← :44).

46. GERMAN MOVEMENT. **Sep 12:** In response to C. Schmidt, who writes him on the
negative role of the former *Jungen* faction
(now called the Assoc of Independent Socialists), E agrees that the group has proved it is
worthless and has nothing to say: "In Germany they are as dead as everyone who
separates himself from the big movement." He
counsels Schmidt not to be influenced by
personal friendship: "One can remain good
friends personally in spite of a political
separation."

47. THEORY AND JUDGMENTS. **Sep 4:** E
warmly praises Bernstein's *NZ* article on
Proudhon: "I am esp glad to see that he is again
the old Bernstein" [cf ← :39]. **Sep 12:** E hails
Schmidt's article in *NZ* (cf ← :35) on "The psy-
chological current in modern political economy" as an answer to the Jevons–Menger view
now spreading in the Fabian Society; it should
be translated into English. Rogers's book *The
economic interpretation of history* has useful
material but it is not M's conception. **Sep 28:**
E criticizes Mehring's opinion that the materialist conception of history is to be traced to
"the Prussian romanticists of the historical
school." In this letter to Mehring, E also discusses the relationship between economic
order and state form.

48. RUSSIAN FRIENDS. **Sep 22:** E sends
Danielson a long discussion of the dynamics
of industrial development in Russia as that
country necessarily takes the path of capitalist
development [← :29]. —In London, Stepniak visits E [→ :61]. **Sep CD:** Kovalevsky
visits E several times.

49. W&P. Sep 12: E writes a ms fragmentary note "On certain peculiarities of England's economic and political development" (#E540), prob intended for a new German edn of his *Condition of the working class* (#E171). **Sep 17/18 to Dec 24/25:** An Italian trans of the *Com Manifesto*, by P. Bettini, is pubd in 11 installs, in *Lotta di Classe* [→ 93:19]. **Sep:** The English edn of E's *Socialism: Utopian and scientific* (E759) is pubd, with a new intro (#E762). —E's own German trans of this new intro (#E762) is pubd in *NZ*, under the title "On historical materialism."

50. MARX LIBRARY COLLECTION. Sep-Oct: E corresponds with Dr. Kugelmann, i.a. about getting copies of some rare books and publications by M, incl *Herr Vogt* (#M372), *Knight of the noble consciousness* (#M429), *Palmerston, What has he done?* (#M474).

51. PERSONAL. Sep 4: Writing to Kautsky about his personal plans, E mentions he is still unable to travel [← :43]; he must spend another two weeks of rest, lying down. **Sep 6:** E returns to London from Ryde, and remains "housebound." **Sep 14:** Louise Kautsky, who has been sojourning in Austria, returns to London and the E household.

OCTOBER

52. FRANCE, GERMANY, AND WAR. Oct 6: Paul Lafargue asks E's help in getting material for his speech in the Chamber on the antiwar record of the German Social-Democrats; for since Liebknecht's Sep 25 speech at the party congress in Marseilles on internationalism, the press and government are on an anti-German and antisocialist spree. **Oct 7:** E requests Bebel to send documentation and citations on the antiwar stand of the Germany party 1870–71, Bebel's speeches since then, etc. (Bebel complies, and E forwards the material to France, Oct 14.) **Oct 14:** In a letter to Laura Lafargue, E writes that he is glad the French are taking up the war danger; the Continental movement must be Franco-German, not French- or German-led. "If the Germans taught the French how to use the suffrage and how to organize strongly, the French will have to penetrate the Germans with that revolutionary spirit which the history of a century has made traditional in them." **Oct M:** Having read the new pamphlet *Chauvins et réacteurs* by Eugène Protot, the Boulangist-Blanquist, E writes Bonnier (who found it to be "well-written") that it is a "pile of lies and falsifications" in its denigration of the German movement. E discusses socialist participation in a defensive war, whether in France or Germany. **Oct 24:** E replies to a letter from Bonnier (Oct 21), who

claims the French party is strong enough to prevent a war no matter from what side it threatens. E shows this is empty bluster: the czar and kaiser can precipitate a war and the boulevardier-patriots cannot prevent it. "If war breaks out, the ones who suffer a defeat have the possibility and the duty of carrying through the revolution—that's all."

53. GERMAN BLUSTERERS. Oct 7: Having read the new brochure by Hans Müller (Jungen faction, now called Independents) on *The class struggle in the German Social-Democracy*, E writes Bebel that it is empty, even in attacking the party right wing. Müller "works himself up to the assertion that force is revolutionary under all circumstances, never reactionary"; but this ass does not see that if there is no such thing as reactionary force, there is no need for revolutionary force. "This is the impotent fury of the chest-thumping students, literati, and ex-workers who want to be literati. . . ." Our party, writes E, is now so strong that it need not fear degeneration.

54. *CAPITAL*. Oct to Dec: At last, after long absence from the ms, E resumes work on Vol. 3, devoting most of his time to it. In order to concentrate on *Capital*, he tries to reduce his correspondence and all other calls on his time to the minimum.

NOVEMBER

55. GERMAN MOVEMENT. Nov 6: E writes Bebel that the attack on the right-winger Vollmar was carried out ineptly, too much centered on abstract terminological discussion of the term *state socialism*, when the point is Vollmar's kowtowing to the government and cringing before the kaiser and chancellor. In connection with the polemic against Hans Müller [← :53], E stresses that "it is absolutely necessary for the party to criticize its own past" in order to learn to do better. **Nov 19:** In a letter to Bebel, E criticizes the ongoing (Nov 14–21) party congress in Berlin. While he warmly praises its resolutions on state socialism and anti-Semitism, he feels that other actions make it inferior to the last congress. He esp disagrees with what he calls its "statification" of the socialist press (i.e., papers must be official organs). There must be a movement press that is not directly dependent on the Exec, that is free to criticize. The party is too large for rigid discipline; the first need is for a "formally independent party press." "M and I agreed, from way back, that we would never take such a position [editing a paper dependent on a party], that we could have only a paper financially independent from even the party." (On the congress, see also → :56.)

56. MAY DAY ISSUE. Nov 19, 22: E discusses the mistake of the Berlin congress (see ← :55) in deciding on a policy for May Day 1893 (evening demonstrations, without a work stoppage) which violates the decision of the 1891 International Socialist Congress in Brussels (work stoppages on May 1 except where "impossible") for which the Germans voted. E himself still strongly believes that each party should decide on the basis of national conditions, and that the imposition of international uniformity is senseless; but he urges that the German party must make clear its own position at the international (Zurich, 1893) congress and stick to it. This view he expresses at length to Bebel, and more briefly to Paul Lafargue [← 91:14].

57. ENGLISH AND GERMANS. **Nov 6:** Writing to Bebel, E explains that the English socialist groups hate and "boycott" the German socialists out of "pure English chauvinism"; besides, the German party goes from victory to victory using methods repudiated by the English; e.g., the Fabians see the Germans winning despite opposing all the bourgeois radicals. **Nov 19:** E reports (to Bebel) on the latest about the Fabians: in May, Shaw was telling the Germans that if they did not work with the Liberals they would meet "defeat and disgrace"; now he gives a speech recounting that the Fabians have been disgracefully duped by the Liberals, and have gained nothing but—defeat and disgrace, etc. "And these people want to teach you 'practical politics'!" This should act on Bernstein (and his "Fabian enthusiasm") like a cold shower [← :39].

58. FRANCE: PANAMA SCANDAL. **Nov 16:** The scandal (corruption in the Panama Canal project, extending through business into government) breaks in the press. **Nov 21:** The first questions about it are raised in the parliament. **Nov 22:** From London, E alerts Paul Lafargue to the potentialities of the scandal for the socialist movement [→ :63].

59. THEORY AND REVOLUTION. **Nov 3:** In a letter to Paul Lafargue, E draws attention to the "ghastly effects" of the new (melinite) bullets and shells; the government looks to this new weapon to curb revolutionaries. "The era of barricades and street fighting has gone for good"; if the army intervenes, revolutionary resistance is impossible; we need to "find new revolutionary tactics." **Nov 12:** E lectures Paul Lafargue on the value of universal suffrage—if only one knows how to use it. It is slower and more boring than issuing calls to revolution, but it is surer: "it indicates with the most perfect accuracy the day when a call to armed revolution has to be made." It will prob drive the ruling class to abandon legality, "that is, put us in the most favorable position to make the revolution."

60. W&P. **Nov 9–15:** E writes an article for *Vorwärts* on the American presidential election (#E17); pubd Nov 16. **Nov 9–25:** E writes a biographical sketch of M for the *Handwörterbuch der Staatswissenschaften* (#E470; cf also #E471), erroneously titled "Marx, Heinrich Karl." (It will be pubd before the end of this year in Vol. 4.) **Nov 15:** E writes a reply to a series of unsigned articles (Aug 6 to Dec 24) in *Berliner Volks-Tribüne* on the history of the International from the Bakuninist standpoint, incl standard Bakuninist distortions of the role of the GC and M. (The author is the Swiss, Louis Héritier.) The 10th installment (Nov 10) is so bad that E is moved to respond (#E834); E's reply is pubd Nov 19 [→ :68]. **Nov D to Dec 4:** E writes an article on "A recently discovered case of group marriage" (#E655), based on a report in a Russian journal in Oct by the ethnographer Shternberg; pubd in NZ for Dec. This article is usually treated as an appendix to E's *Origin of the family* (#E573).

61. FRIENDS. **Nov 17:** Stepniak [← :61] visits E for dinner and discussion. **Nov 27:** On the Sunday preceding his birthday, E celebrates with a gathering of friends: Sam Moore, Bax, Eleanor M, Aveling, the Bernsteins and Mottelers, Volkhovsky (Russian émigré), two GWEA workers, and Inka Fischer (daughter of Richard F., visiting England), plus the E household members (Louise Kautsky, etc.). The party makes merry till after midnight with food and potent drink.

DECEMBER

62. MAY DAY: FRENCH AND GERMANS. **Dec 2:** Bonnier (who from Oxford acts as Guesde's representative in England) writes E a hot letter on the May Day decision of the German party congress [← :56]. **Dec 3:** E replies coolly, and writes Bebel a summary of this exchange. He explains Bonnier's situation: isolated in Oxford but chafing, Bonnier wants to direct the European movement from "the sole piece of the real Middle Ages extant in Europe" (Oxford); one difficulty is that there is no one in the Paris leadership who can read German. **Dec 5:** In a letter to Paul Lafargue, E tries to straighten him out on his prejudices against Bebel, absorbed from Bonnier and Liebknecht (who has recently been in France). E explains that Bonnier hates Bebel, and Liebknecht says whatever will make his immediate audience cheer. **Dec M:** Bonnier visits E in London, and they discuss May Day; E thinks his explanations have had an effect in quieting Bonnier (so he writes Dec 20, 22, to Laura Lafargue and Bebel).

63. FRANCE: PANAMA SCANDAL. **Dec:** All

month, from Dec 1 (letter to Liebknecht) to Dec 31 (letter to Sorge) and in many letters, E keeps stressing the revolutionary potential of the Panama scandal, first for France and also for lighting a fuse in Europe. He alerts the Germans to cover it in the press: "We're back in 1847" when similar exposures in Girardin's *La Presse* shook the regime. In other letters he points to similar corruption and looming scandals in England and on the Continent.

64. PERSPECTIVE. Dec: As the year ends, E repeats, in a number of letters (Dec 3–28) that a group of political crises are maturing in Europe: in France over the Panama scandal (see ← :63), in Germany over the government's military bill for a greatly increased budget, in England over Gladstone's bill for Irish home rule. In more than one letter E indicates that 1894 may see a revolution which begins in Paris, spreads to Germany, shakes England, and leads to "revolutionary war" against czarism.

65. NEUE ZEIT. Dec 3–4: In letters to Bebel and Kautsky, E discusses the proposal to change the *Neue Zeit* (which, having become a weekly, has lost circulation) into a popular political-literary-art magazine with restricted theoretical contents. He argues that such a magazine cannot fulfill the function of a theoretical organ, and that therefore an additional monthly or quarterly journal would have to be established.

66. PROSTITUTION. Dec 22: E congratulates Bebel on his Reichstag speech (Dec 15) pillorying the hypocrisy of bourgeois legislation against prostitution, and goes on to a longish analysis of what the socialist position should be. He stresses that the first concern is "the girl herself" and her "complete freedom from all special laws," being the victim of the social order, not the offender. He also compares legislation in England and Germany, the farce of medical inspection, etc.

67. CAPITAL. Dec to July: While still working on Vol. 3 (which in Dec he tells friends is "over the hump"), E also has to work on a second German edn of Vol. 2. **Dec 24:** E asks Kautsky to return the ms of M's Vol. 4 (*Theories of surplus value*), via Bebel, who is coming to England [← 90:23; → 93:6].

68. W&P. Dec 24: At the end of his last (13th) installment of his pro-Bakuninist history of the International [← :60] Héritier signs his name and gives a reply to E's refutation (#E834). **Dec 25:** Héritier also sends a letter to E denying that he has falsified history [→ 93:4]. **Dec:** E's article "A recently discovered case of group marriage" (#E655) is pubd in NZ. **Dec D:** E sends a New Year's greeting (recipient unknown) in deathless doggerel: "Hail to eighteen ninety three!/ Hope and joy dawn with it newly./ Bright and happy may it be/ To the end, prays Yours most truly"— signed F. E. (#E808.5).

1893

CONSPECTUS

1. Capital. E continues working on the mss of Vol. 3 all year, off and on. (For the last entry, see → :54.) MEW *Daten* has a misleading entry to this effect dated Jan to May.

JANUARY

2. ILP. Jan 18: Writing to Sorge, E is glad of the formation of the Independent Labour party at Bradford (Jan 13–14)—"quite a good thing," "something can come of it"—esp because it is already stronger in the industrial north than the existing sects (SDF, Fabians); Aveling was right to accept a seat on its Exec. E adds a biting portrait of the Fabians, as a band of careerists who fear revolution and class struggle above all, and want to permeate the Liberal party with their municipal socialism; but they have produced some good propaganda writings [← 92:57]. **Jan 24:** Writing to Bebel, E cites indications that impugn Keir Hardie's leadership of the new party, incl the suspicion he wants to dominate it "dictatorially."

3. CAPITAL. Jan to July: E continues working on the second German edn of Vol. 2 [← 92:67] as well as on Vol. 3.
4. W&P. Jan A: In response to the invitation (Dec D) of the Hungarian Social-Democratic party to attend its second congress (Budapest, Jan 6–8), E sends a letter of greetings (#E844) which, by hoping the congress will avoid a split, politely counsels against the Exec's expulsion of the left-wing group supporting Paul Engelmann. Since the congress has to confirm the Exec's expulsion, E's letter is suppressed—not made known to the congress and not pubd afterward. **Jan 7:** To Turati, who wants E to write a preface for the new Italian trans of the *Com Manifesto* which ran in *Lotta di Classe* Sep to Dec (and which E praises), E answers that all this preface writing puts him in a quandary: what is there to say that is new? **Jan c.8:** Maria Mendelson (Polish socialist émigré) writes E about the arrest of five Polish revolutionists in Paris. **Jan 10:** E writes this case up as an article for *Vorwärts* (#E561); pubd Jan 13. **Jan 20:** E sends Héritier [← 92:68] a

personal letter of reply, stressing that Héritier knows and uses only Bakuninist documents, but should do more thorough and less partisan research. Jan 26–29: On the basis of documents and material received from Labriola, on the financial machinations by big Italian banks connected with influential politicians, E writes an article "On the Italian Panama [scandal]," leaving it unsigned in order not to incriminate his source (#E560); pubd in Vorwärts, Feb 1–3.

5. FRENCH AFFAIRS. Jan: In correspondence with Paul Lafargue (not extant), E raises the question of why the socialist deputies remain silent in the Chamber on the Panama scandal [← :63]. Lafargue replies (Jan 3, 26) with reasons: it would line them up with Rightist attacks on the corruption, and the people are unconcerned [→ :8]. (Note: This issue raised by E gains in importance in the light of the future policy of the French Guesdists of remaining aloof from the Dreyfus fight.)

6. PERSONAL. Jan c.3–10: Bebel, visiting England, stays at Engels' house. He brings with him the ms of Theories of surplus value which Kautsky is returning [← 92:67]. **Jan 23:** E participates in a soirée (concert and dance) on the anniversary of the GWEA. **Jan D to Feb:** E finds that the German, Austrian, and American press is printing reports that he is dead or dying; the source of this rumor is not discovered.

FEBRUARY

7. GERMAN MOVEMENT. Feb 3–7: Since the Reichstag budget debate has given rise (Jan D) to attacks on the socialists for criticizing the status quo without putting forward their alternative, Bebel takes the floor (Feb 3) for a presentation on the "future socialist state." This opens a debate on the subject for five days; Bebel speaks again on Feb 6; also Liebknecht and Frohme. The majority hastily shuts down debate on Feb 7. (The entire debate is then pubd as a brochure, Bebel's Feb 3 speech as a separate pamphlet.) **Feb 9–25:** In letters to Bebel and others, E hails this debate (the first parliamentary debate on the subject ever held) as a triumph, esp enthusiastic about Bebel's speech ("masterpiece").

8. FRENCH AFFAIRS. Feb 10: Unlike Paul Lafargue [← :5], whose letters to E on the Panama scandal stress the nonrevolutionary mood of the people, Laura Lafargue writes E that France is in ferment and "on the eve of other and vaster events." But E's pressure has had results: Paul did want to speak in the Chamber, but the socialist group did not let him. **Feb 12:** E continues to urge socialist intervention in the Chamber. **Feb 16:** La-

fargue finally takes the floor with a Chamber speech on the Panama scandal, and claims to E (Feb 25) that he has "seized the first opportunity." **Feb 25:** E comments that it is better late than never: it is a disgrace that the Right has led in the exposé. **Feb D:** E follows the preparation for new elections to the Chamber. He begins (Feb 25) hammering away at Lafargue on maintaining the independent freedom of action of the party in making any electoral agreements with the Radicals or anyone else, esp since he expects gains for the Guesdists (Workers party).

9. ENGLAND: ILP. Feb 9, 25: In letters to Bebel and Paul Lafargue, E follows the beginnings of the ILP [← :2], which is still in embryo but already scaring the government into concessions; he looks to it to become the independent party of the working class. But he is very critical of Keir Hardie's acts in Parliament—suspicious about his independence from the Tories as well as Liberals—and increasingly suspicious also of John Burns's direction away from the movement.

10. RUSSIAN AFFAIRS. Feb 24: In a long letter, E replies to Danielson's letters of last Oct 3 and Jan 27, in which the latter argued for the Narodnik thesis about bypassing capitalist development; E summarizes his case on this question [← 92:16].

11. WRITER'S AID. Feb c.2: At the request of the Russian Jewish socialist "Progress" group of émigrés (London), E sends several books on socialist theory and history. **Feb 4:** E proposes to Harney that he write a history of Chartism, since people who have been active in the movement should preserve its history. (Harney replies on Feb 24, explaining why he is unable to do this.) **Feb 7:** In response to a request (Feb 4) from the Russian émigré Shmuilov for help in writing a biography of M for a Russian publisher, E explains he cannot send the copious notes Shmuilov requests, but gives references for M's activity 1844–49, and for the period of the IWMA (recommending only Eichhoff's work, all others being "lies and legends"). He sends two brochures by M&E on the International (#ME 5, 6).

12. W&P. Feb 1: E writes a preface (#E614) to the new Italian edn of the Com Manifesto [→ :19]. **Feb 1–3:** E's article "On the Italian Panama" (#E560) [← :4] is pubd in Vorwärts in three installs. **Feb M:** In response to Bebel's letter of Feb 11 asking what attitude the party Reichstag Fraction should take in the debate on the military budget [← 92:64], E writes a long essay, "Can Europe disarm?" (#E118), for Vorwärts, discussing the war danger, arms race, and German and European militarism [→ :19].

MARCH

13. ENGLISH MOVEMENT. **Mar 13:** E writes a May Day greeting (#E852) to German workers (to be pubd May 1; see → :24) which is almost entirely devoted to a note of triumph about the progress of the English movement: socialism is no longer merely a matter of sects; a class-conscious socialistic mass is in motion. **Mar 18:** E tells Sorge that so far the ILP [← :2] is the best expression of the movement, despite the parliamentary habits of most of its leaders; great progress is to be expected; Hyndman is finished in the SDF, and the Fabian rank-and-file are outgrowing the Webb–Shaw leadership. —At an anniversary celebration of the Paris Commune held by the "Communist Workingmen's Club" (GWEA) and the Bloomsbury Socialist Society, E gives a talk reviewing the progress of socialism; he urges socialists to join the ILP (reported in the *Workman's Times*, Mar 25). **Mar 20:** E tells Kautsky that the ILP will serve to scotch the danger of the sects (SDF and Fabians); the first meeting of its Exec, with Aveling attending, has been very satisfactory.

14. GERMAN PERSPECTIVE. **Mar 18:** E writes Sorge that still greater gains are due in Germany: "I should prefer winning to proceed peacefully until 1895, when we should create an altogether different effect. . . ."

15. AMERICAN AFFAIRS. **Mar M:** E replies to Henry Demarest Lloyd who, on behalf of the 1893 Chicago Exposition, has asked him (Feb 3, Mar 9) to send a paper to be read before a labor congress at the Exposition. E politely declines, citing lack of time, but sends copies of the *Com Manifesto* and *Socialism: Utopian and scientific* (#E759) in English, for the edification of the delegates.

16. MARX ANNIVERSARY. **Mar 14:** From a memorial affair on the 10th anniversary of M's death, held in Geneva by socialists of various countries, E receives a telegram signed by Plekhanov and others. **Mar M:** E reads Lessner's memoir on M in the Mar issue of *NZ*, and finds it good. **Mar 15:** The leadership of the Austrian party sends E a telegram on this anniversary.

17. OPINIONS. **Mar 14:** E replies to a letter (Jan 29) from one F. Wiesen of Texas, who asks for a statement condemning running candidates for president since "we" want to abolish the office; hence such a campaign denies revolutionary principle. E replies that he rejects this "principle"; anyway, there can be legitimate difference of opinion on ways and means of struggling for political power without leading to differences in principle.

18. *CAPITAL.* **Mar 14, 20:** Vol. 3 is "as good as ready"—only two relatively easy

sections remain to be done: so E writes to Laura Lafargue and Kautsky.

19. W&P. **Mar 1–10:** E's long essay "Can Europe disarm?" (#E118) [← :12] is pubd in *Vorwärts* in eight installs; also Mar 20–30 in *Der Wähler*; also Mar D as a separate pamphlet, with an added foreword dated Mar 28. **Mar 13:** E writes May Day greetings to German workers (#E852)—for content, see ← :13 [→ :24]. **Mar 17:** E's biographical article on "Marx, Heinrich Karl" (#E470) [← 92:60], is repubd in the Vienna *Arbeiter-Ztg.* **Mar 20:** E suggests (to Kautsky) that Dietz should reprint the entire file of the *NRZ-Revue* (which, incidentally, E himself does not possess complete at this time). **Mar 21:** E expresses satisfaction over the info (sent him on Mar 18 by A. Radimsky) that the Czech Social-Democrats will publish the *Com Manifesto* in the Czech language, as a brochure. **Mar CD:** The *Com Manifesto*, in a new Italian trans by Turati and Anna Kuliscioff, is pubd as a pamphlet, with a new preface by E (#E614) [← :12]. **Mar to Apr A:** E writes "To the Austrian workers for May 1 . . ." (#E814) [→ :21].

20. OTHER ACTIVITIES. **Mar c.1–17:** E sojourns in Eastbourne. **Mar 18:** E is one of the speakers at a Paris Commune celebration held jointly by GWEA and the Bloomsbury Socialist Society. (At any rate, four days before, he writes Laura Lafargue that he is going to do this.) **Mar c.28 to Apr 4:** Bebel— who has been attending the preconference in Brussels (Mar 26) to prepare the coming International Socialist Congress in Zurich— comes to London to visit with E. The Lafargues come to stay at E's about the same time (exact dates uncertain). E discusses with Bebel i.a. Singer's proposal to publish M&E's works as individual publications; with the Lafargues he takes up problems of the French movement. E is eager to have Paul Lafargue meet Bebel personally [cf ← 92:62]. On March 31, when John Burns visits E, this marks (as E notes in a letter) "the first time in the history of the world" that three socialist deputies from three major countries meet in one place.

APRIL

21. MAY DAY GREETINGS. **Apr 8:** As requested by Krapka, editor of the Czech party's organ, E writes greetings to the party's May Day celebration, with a reminiscence about M's trip to Vienna in 1848 (#E824) [→ :24]. **Apr 14:** E writes May Day greetings to the French workers, for *Le Socialiste* (#E13); pubd Apr 23. **Apr M:** In response to a request from Iglesias (whose letter, Apr A, reports on the Spanish movement and its struggle against the anarchists and bourgeois republicans), E replies—chiding Iglesias for using the formal *you* rather than the intimate form—and sends May Day greetings (#E867) [→ :24]. **Apr CD:** E's May Day greetings to Austrian workers (#E814) [← :19] are pubd in *Arbeiter-Ztg,* prob about this time.

22. FRIENDS. **Apr 24:** E attends the Manchester funeral of his friend, the physician Dr. Gumpert (who died Apr 20). **Apr to July A:** On Plekhanov's recommendation, the Russian socialist A. M. Voden visits E a few times; they discuss economic and philosophical problems, the situation of Russia, etc. When Voden reports that Plekhanov's view of the "dictatorship of the proletariat" is that "when 'we' come to power, of course 'we' would allow freedom to no one but 'ourselves,' " and that the "monopolists of freedom" would be "comrades who correctly understand Marx's teachings," Engels responds that this view would turn the Russian party into a sect or split the movement.

23. MEDITATIONS. **Apr 16:** In a letter to G. W. Lamplugh, E reflects that "Nature is great . . . but History seems even greater than Nature to me. It took Nature millions of years to produce conscious beings, and now it takes these conscious beings thousands of years to act together consciously. . . ." (*MEW* dates this letter Apr 11.)

MAY

24. MAY DAY. **May 1:** E's greetings to German workers (#E852) [← :19] appear in the May Day journal pubd by the *Vorwärts* press. —E's greetings to Spanish workers (#E867) [← :21] are pubd in *El Socialista.* **May c.1:** E's greetings to Czech workers (#E824) [← :21] are pubd in the Czech party's May Day journal; also in *Arbeiter-Ztg,* May 12. **May c.5:** E is informed by letter from Iglesias on the course of the May Day demonstrations in Spain, and asked to represent the Spanish party at the London demonstration on May 7. **May c.6:** E receives Plekhanov's and Zasulich's message to English workers for the London demonstration; Plekhanov reports on the course of the May Day demonstration in Geneva. **May 7:** E attends the May Day demonstration in London (the Sunday after May 1). Although the total attendance is near a quarter million, he thinks it is becoming routine. As he reports (to Sorge, May 17), "we—the Eight-Hour Committee" [← 92:14]—had a bigger affair than the sects and TU Council; our "international" platform (one out of 12) had many foreign speakers.

25. INTERVIEW. **May 8:** E is interviewed by a correspondent of the Paris *Figaro;* he surveys the international situation (#E185).

May 13: The interview is pubd in *Figaro;* reprinted in *Le Socialiste,* May 20. **26.** RUSSIAN AFFAIRS. **May c.25:** From Lavrov, E receives a collection *Osnovy teoreticheskovo sotsializma i ikh prilosheniye k Rossii,* recently pubd in Geneva, which contains a letter by Lopatin reporting on his conversation with E in 1883 [← 83:40]. **May 27:** E replies to I. A. Hourwich (in Gurwich), a Russian economist now in America, who had sent him his new book *The economics of the Russian village* (NY), requesting a comment on the peasant problem. E declines to express an opinion, says something nice about the book, and remarks that M's writings have been interpreted by Russian émigrés "in the most contradictory ways, exactly as if they had been texts from the classics or from the New Testament."

27. CAPITAL, ETC. **May 17:** Writing to Sorge, E says he is working on the last chapter of Vol. 3, and expresses his intention of writing a history of the First International.

JUNE

28. INTERNATIONALISM. **June 17:** In response to a "patriotic" antisocialist hysteria being whipped up by the bourgeois establishment, the French Guesdist ("Marxist") party publishes a manifesto on "Socialism and patriotism" which meets it head on. Also, an interview with Guesde on this issue is pubd in *Figaro.* **June 20, 27:** Briefly on June 20, but at length on June 27, E writes the Lafargues a long analysis of the party manifesto, which he approves in general, in order to highlight some criticisms and to stress the principle of "equality of nations" in the international struggle. This letter is a strong statement on the danger of chauvinistic influences.

29. GERMAN AFFAIRS: **June CD:** E comments with satisfaction on the Reichstag elections of this month, in which the S-D party has won another big victory. E concludes that liberalism in Germany has abdicated, there is no real opposition outside the Social-Democrats (June 27, to Paul Lafargue).

30. OPINIONS. **June 1:** Informed by Kautsky (May 19) that Brentano has pubd an article attacking his *Origin of the family* (#E573), E discounts it because Brentano defends Westermarck's *History of human marriage* (1891), which E rejects.

31. CAPITAL. **June 6:** In response to Turati's request (June 1), E gives his criticism of Deville's abridgement (ST/M89), of which an Italian trans is being prepared. **June c.12:** From Turati, E receives an Italian trans of Vol. 1, based on the French edn.

32. W&P. **June 9:** Through the Bulgarian émigré Nokov, who has acted as intermediary, E sends a letter of greetings to the Bulgarian *Sotsial-Demokrat* (#E835). He notes i.a. that the international movement is growing so much that now "in my old age I must learn even Roumanian and Bulgarian if I want to follow the progress of socialism eastward and southeastward"; pubd in no. 3 of the journal. **June D:** E gives an interview (#E290) to a correspondent of the liberal *Daily Chronicle*, on the German election (see ← :29); pubd July 1.

33. FRIENDS. **June 13:** E sends a telegram of best wishes to Lavrov on the latter's 70th birthday, signed also by Louise Kautsky and the Avelings.

JULY

34. THEORY. **July 14:** E thanks Mehring for sending his *Lessing legend* (which he praises), and writes a long letter which is one of his basic discussions of historical materialism and its place in Marxist theory; also comments on Prussian history (Mehring's subject). He mentions incidentally that he still plans to revise his *Peasant war in Germany* (#E579) and/or the "historical introduction" to it (cf #E282). **July 19:** E replies to a letter (June 22) from the economist Rudolph Meyer, criticizing Bebel's book *Women and socialism* and arguing that the socialist transformation of agriculture is impossible. E refutes Meyer at some length, and stresses that the town–country antithesis can be eliminated only on the basis of socialized agriculture.

35. CORRESPONDENCE. **July c.5:** E receives a report from N. Petersen on the economic situation in Denmark.

36. *CAPITAL*. **July 15:** E writes, and dates, his preface (#E605) to the second German edn of Vol. 2 [→ :43].

37. W&P. **July 1, 15, 16:** E's interview in the *Daily Chronicle* (#E290) [← :32] is pubd in that paper, then in France and Italy.

38. PERSONAL. **July 21–28:** E rests in Eastbourne, in preparation for his European tour of Aug. **July 29:** E makes a new Will (#E801), since an old one named M as heir [→ 94:47].

39. FRIENDS. **July 27:** E sends Liebknecht a letter of congratulations on his silver wedding anniversary (July 30); also a letter to Natalie Liebknecht, who (July 24) has sent E a photograph of his Barmen birthplace, taken in June.

AUGUST

40. EUROPEAN TRIP. **Aug 1 to Sep 29:** E makes a trip to Germany, Switzerland, and Austria-Hungary, incl a visit at the last session of the International Socialist Congress in Zurich on Aug 12 (it had begun Aug 6). —E leaves London on Aug 1, with Louise Kautsky, and goes via the Hook of Holland to Cologne, where he meets the Bebels. They travel together to Mainz (a one-night stop, where, as in Cologne, E is struck by the tremendous industrial transformation), to Strasbourg (where he notes esp the use of French or German by the Alsatians), and on to Zurich. Then E goes to visit his brother Hermann in Thusis, a village in the Swiss canton of Graubünden (Grisons), where he stays a week. On Aug 12 he returns to Zurich, for the congress's closing session: as "honorary chairman," closing the congress, he gives a short speech ("in English, French, and German," says *MEW Daten*) (#E166, pubd in *Vorwärts*, Aug 15)—all amid great acclaim. He stays in Zurich till Sep 4, during part of this time staying at the home of his cousin Anna Beust; in Zurich (Aug M), he makes a number of visits to talk to V. Zasulich and Axelrod of the Russian Marxist group. For six days he, with Bebel and the Pole S. Mendelson, spend time in the Berner Oberland (Alpine region), on Aug 30 going up on the Uetliberg. From Zurich Aug 16, he writes his brother Hermann a letter which mentions the congress only to enthuse over the pretty Russian and Viennese women met there (as he does also in a letter of Aug 21 to Laura Lafargue). [Continued → :42]

41. FRENCH MOVEMENT. **Aug 31:** Having read the text of Guesde's letter of thanks on his election, E writes Laura Lafargue (in vain) that he hopes *Le Socialiste* will not publish it, because of its "grotesque" chauvinist tone.

SEPTEMBER

42. EUROPEAN TRIP (CONT'D). **Sep 4:** Continuing his trip [← :40] E leaves Zurich for Munich. **Sep 6 or 7:** He leaves Munich for Salzburg; then on to Vienna for six days. In Vienna, the party puts on two events. **Sep 11:** E is guest of honor at a social evening, sponsored by the party with 600 in attendance. **Sep 14:** At a party meeting of about 2000 for a report on the Zurich congress, with speeches by V. Adler and Bebel, E is persuaded to give a speech also—on the growing world influence of socialism (#E765); pubd Sep 22. From Vienna, E goes to Prague for one day (meeting Rudolph Meyer i.a.); then via Carlsbad to Berlin, arriving Sep 16. In Berlin (Sep 16–28), E stays with the Bebels; visits Liebknecht's apartment in Charlottenberg; attends (Sep 17) a theatrical performance at the workers' Freie Volksbühne (Lessing Theater). **Sep 22:** He is honored at a party meeting in the Concordia Festsälen, with a select 4000 present; besides a speech of greetings to E given by Liebknecht, E himself gives a talk (#E764); pubd Sep 26. In Berlin, E meets Dr. Kugelmann; they discuss i.a. problems of putting together a collected edn of M's works. From Berlin, via Rotterdam, E returns to London, Sep 29 morning. The next day E writes Laura Lafargue about the enormous impression made on him by the rank-and-file of the German and Austrian parties, esp the latter: the Austrians, he warns Laura, esp because of their mixed-race (German, Celtic, Slavic) qualities, may well outclass the French as the revolutionary people of Europe.

43. *CAPITAL.* c.Sep-Oct: The second German edn of Vol. 2 is pubd, with a preface by E (#E605) [← :36].

OCTOBER

44. EUROPEAN AFFAIRS. **Oct 10:** Paul Lafargue reports, in a letter to E, on the course of the 11th national congress of the French party, in Paris, Oct 7–9. **Oct 11, 12, 14:** In letters to Adler, Bebel, and Laura Lafargue, E hails the "brilliant victory" scored by the Austrian socialists' campaign for universal suffrage, as the Taaffe government introduces (Oct 10) a bill to extend the suffrage significantly. In his letter to Adler (Oct 11) E congratulates him on his Oct 2 speech against the anti-Czech law imposed by Taaffe, and adds an extensive discussion of the Austrian situation and the party's tasks. **Oct M:** E writes Bebel (Oct 12) and others on the struggle of the Midlands (English) miners, since July D, against a lockout, and on the miners' partial victory. **Oct c.24 to Dec c.23:** From Labriola, E gets reports on the political situation in Italy and the movement, esp in Sicily (the "Fasci" movement).

45. TRANSLATION. **Oct 14, 18:** In letters to Laura Lafargue, E discusses Fortin's plans to translate M's 1844 critique of Hegel (#M205) and E's three chapters on the force theory in *Anti-Dühring* (#E23), for publ in *L'Ere Nouvelle.* E insists that a trans of M's article would be "almost impossible," and in any case could be accomplished by no one in France but Laura.

46. RUSSIAN AFFAIRS. **Oct 17:** E sends Danielson his opinion of his new book on Russian economy since the 1861 reform, and of Struve's articles on it. E argues that a communistic order cannot develop in Russia directly out of the old village community formation—unless communism as a model has first developed elsewhere. At the same time he criticizes Struve for idealizing capitalism. **Oct 22–31:** On Lavrov's recommendation, the then Narodnik Rappoport visits E several times; they discuss problems of historical theory, the Russian movement, etc. (SOURCE: *MEW Daten).*

47. MARRIAGE. **Oct 12:** On hearing that Schlüter's wife Anna had left him, E remarks (to Bebel) that "it is always gratifying to hear that a woman whom one knows has had the courage to go independent. . . . But what a prodigal waste of energy is bourgeois marriage. . . ."

48. EX-FRIENDS. **Oct D:** Ferdinand Wolff, of the old Com League, now at Oxford, writes E a peculiar, murky letter with obscure threats. E drafts a reply (perhaps also sends it) spurning Wolff, and (not yet aware that Wolff, at 81, is mentally ill) suggests that he is "in a state of nervous strain" [→ :56].

NOVEMBER

49. FABIAN SOCIETY. **Nov 1:** The Fabian Society publishes a manifesto "To your tents, O Israel!" attacking the Liberal party for refusing to be "permeated," and in general expressing its frustration at the failure of its recipe for socialist success via Liberalism. **Nov 10, 11:** In letters to Adler and Sorge, E gleefully points to this development—discussed by "Autolycus" (Burgess) in the current *Workman's Times*—as demonstrating the bankruptcy of the Fabian line: it is a confession of dismal failure by these bourgeois "who would graciously deign to emancipate the proletariat from above if it would only be sensible enough to realize that such a raw uneducated mass cannot emancipate itself. . . ."

50. GENERAL STRIKE. **Nov 3:** In a letter to Kautsky, E discusses the tactic of the general strike as political weapon: its possibilities, potentiality, dangers, and relation to the possibility of barricade fighting even in modern times.

51. READING. **Nov 6–12:** E reads Rudolph Meyer's *Der Capitalismus fin de siècle.*

52. PERSONAL. **Nov 28:** E receives best wishes on his 73rd birthday from socialist leaders and groups in various countries; the Avelings (Eleanor M and Aveling) and the Bernsteins spend the evening with him sharing liquid cheer.

DECEMBER

53. INTERNATIONAL AFFAIRS. **Dec 2:** In a letter to Sorge, E returns to the question of why the American movement is retarded as compared to Europe, giving a somewhat more systematic analysis than in previous letters. **Dec 4:** Writing to Kautsky, E discusses the "artificial equilibrium" of the Austro-Hungarian monarchy, quoting the Humpty Dumpty verse in Latin and English. **Dec 19, 30:** In letters to Laura Lafargue and Sorge, E comments caustically on the antic instability of the self-styled socialists, or even "Marxists," in the French Chamber of Deputies—incl an unknown number "suddenly converted to what they call socialism"—and how they are split up.

54. *CAPITAL.* **Dec 19, 30:** E informs Laura Lafargue and Sorge that the first third of Vol. 3 has been packed for shipment (by the 30th), that he expects press work to begin in Jan, and publ in Sep.

55. W&P. **Dec 19:** Invited to the International Congress of Socialist Students (Geneva, Dec 22–25), E instead sends a message of greetings (#E856) [→ 94:12]. **Dec 20:** E sends Liebknecht, for *Vorwärts*, an article on Italy, based on info supplied by Labriola. Discovering he has misunderstood Labriola's instruc-

tions in some way, on Dec 21 E notifies Liebknecht not to publish the article at this time. (It is not clear what article this incident refers to, if it was pubd later, or if it is extant.) **Dec:** E checks over Laura Lafargue's French trans of the first half of E's *Ludwig Feuerbach* (#E457), and sends her his comments.

56. PERSONAL. **Dec 1:** E sends a letter of thanks (#E853) to the London GWEA for its birthday greetings [← :52]. **Dec 1–4:** E sends out personal letters of thanks for birthday greetings, i.a. to Natalie Liebknecht and Kautsky. **Dec AB:** On hearing of Ferdinand Wolff's bad health [← :48], E visits him in Oxford, and Dec 19 reports to Laura Lafargue that the "poor devil" is "quite cracked again."

1894

CONSPECTUS

1. E finishes his work on Vol. 3 of *Capital* [→ :21], and is relieved to see it come off the press [→ :46]. In a letter to Laura Lafargue near the end of the year (Dec 17), he describes the work he faces, in a passage which portrays the usually unmentioned background of E's life in these last years: "I have to follow the movement in five large and a lot of small European countries and the U.S. [of] America. For this purpose I receive 3 German, 2 English, 1 Italian *dailies*, and from Jan, 1 [1895] the Vienna daily, 7 in all. Of *weeklies* I receive 2 from Germany, 7 Austria, 1 France, 3 America (2 English, 1 German), 2 Italian, and 1 each in Polish, Bulgarian, Spanish and Bohemian, three of which are in languages I am still gradually acquiring. Besides this, calls of the most varied sorts of people . . . and an ever-increasing crowd of correspondents, more than at the time of the International! many of whom expect long explanations and all of them taking away time. With all this and the 3d volume, I have not, even during the proof-sheet time, that is the whole of 1894, been able to read *more than one book*."

2. E then lists tasks remaining: (1) publ of Lassalle's letters to M, with a preface; (2) revised version of the *Peasant war in Germany* (#E579); (3) the "chief chapters" of M's life—the International (most important) and 1842–52; (4) collected edn of M's "smaller writings"—e.g., NRZ articles, and the same for E's writings; (5) Vol. 4 of *Capital* (*Theories of surplus value*).

3. E does not know at this point that cancer gives him less than a year to live. He will open the new year (Jan 3, 1895) by telling a friend that "my health is again good. . . . for

my age I'm right sturdy and hope to live out this year and the next. . . ." But his desire to "take a peep" into the 20th century will not be fulfilled.

JANUARY

4. EUROPEAN AFFAIRS. **Jan 3:** E sends Paul Lafargue his comments, criticisms, and revision proposals on Vaillant's bill for disarmament, and the proposal for a disarmament conference of socialist deputies from France, Germany, and Italy; he discusses the militia plan, and sends Lafargue his own essay "Can Europe disarm?" (#E118). **Jan 19:** Turati and his wife Anna Kulisciov ask E his views on Italian party policy in view of the movement's growth and prospects of revolution. **Jan 26:** E sends his reply (in French), which Turati translates for publ in *Critica Sociale* under the title "The future Italian revolution and the Socialist party" (#E319) [→ :12]. **Jan to Mar:** E follows the struggle for universal suffrage in Austria. In letters to Adler (Jan 11), Sorge (Feb 23, Mar 21), and Iglesias (Mar 26) i.a., E stresses the importance of this struggle for the development of the movement.

5. W&P. *INTERNATIONALES* . . . **Jan 3:** Since the *Vorwärts* press is publishing a pamphlet reprint of some of E's articles of 1870–75 (#E383), E writes a new preface (#E384) to introduce the collection. **Jan A:** E writes a new prefatory note (#E60) for one of the reprinted essays, "Bakuninists at work" (#E59). **Jan AB:** E writes an Afterword (#E756) for another of these essays, "Social questions in Russia" (#E754), on the development of capitalism and the *obshchina* in Russia. **Jan D:** The reprint collection is pubd as a pamphlet *Internationales aus dem "Volksstaat" (1871–75)*; see #E383 for more info.

6. CAPITAL. **Jan 4:** In a letter to Lavrov, E makes arrangements for initiating a Russian trans of Vol. 3 when it appears. **Jan 9:** E sends out two announcements of the coming publ of Vol. 3, plus a word on its contents—one to Kautsky for *NZ* (#E548), another to *Vorwärts* (#E806). The *NZ* announcement (pubd in the Jan issue) gives the autumn as date of publ; the *Vorwärts* note (pubd Jan 12) gives Sep. **Jan AB:** E sends the first four parts of Vol. 3—20 chapters, or one-third of the ms—to publisher Meissner (Hamburg).

7. IDEAS. **Jan 3:** G. Canepa (in Italy) asks E to suggest a motto—to be used for his weekly *L'Era Nuova* planned for Mar in Geneva—which will concisely express the basic idea of the coming socialist era, as against the old era characterized by Dante with the saying that some rule and some suffer themselves to be ruled. **Jan 9:** In reply, E suggests a sentence from the *Com Manifesto*: "In place of the old bourgeois society, with its classes and class antagonisms, we shall have an association in which the free development of each is the condition for the free development of all." **Jan 25:** In response to a request (Jan 19) from a Breslau student, W. Borgius, E writes one of his most systematic and concise summaries of the meaning of the materialist conception of history: the meaning of "economic relations," the place of technology and science, political and ideological factors, the role of accident in historical causation, etc. (This letter was formerly labeled a letter to H. Starkenburg, who indeed pubd it in Oct 1895 in the socialist student journal *Der sozialistische Akademiker*.)

8. FRIENDS. **Jan A:** The English geologist Lamplugh sends E a copy of Robert Burton's *Anatomy of melancholy* (1621), with which E was previously unacquainted. **Jan 10:** Having read a part of the book, E writes Lamplugh of his great pleasure in it. **Jan D:** Paul Lafargue is a guest at E's house, and there meets John Burns. **Jan-Feb:** E corresponds with Harney and sends him money.

FEBRUARY

9. ENGLISH AFFAIRS. **Feb 23:** E analyzes the scene (to Sorge) as a crisis for both Liberals and Tories. The Liberals, instead of proposing concessions to the workers, are pushing measures designed to give the bourgeoisie more power as against the House of Lords. The Liberals may split into a pro-Chamberlain wing and "a bourgeois-democratic party with pro-labor tendencies," under working-class pressure.

10. RUSSIAN AFFAIRS. **Feb D to May:** E reads two vols. sent to him by Danielson, with statistical material on the economic development of Russia (SOURCE: *MEW Daten*).

11. "COMMUNISM." **Feb 7:** In connection with the plan by Kautsky and Bernstein for a series of books on the history of socialism, Kautsky asks E if it should rather be called a "history of communism." **Feb 13:** E replies that today the term *communism* is not generally appropriate; it should be reserved for cases where precision is needed, and even then requires explanation, for in the past 30 years it has practically gone out of use.

12. W&P. **Feb 1:** E's letter to Turati on "The future Italian revolution . . ." (#E319) is pubd in *Critica Sociale* [→ :30]. **Feb 18:** E's message of greetings to the international students' congress [← 93:55], or most of it, is pubd in German in *Vorwärts* (#856) [→ :16].

13. PERSONAL. **Feb A:** Louise Kautsky, who has been E's secy and household manager, unexpectedly marries Dr. Ludwig Freyberger, a Viennese physician in London, in a secret wedding. (The couple will live in the E household, and Louise—now Louise Freyberger—will continue her functions for E.) **Feb c.9 to Mar 1:** E, again beset by lameness, goes to Eastbourne; he is accompanied by the Freybergers on honeymoon.

MARCH

14. MOVEMENT AFFAIRS. **Mar 6:** E reads the speech made (Feb 17) in the French Chamber by Jaurès for the socialist group's bill proposing a state monopoly on grain imports (which would aid the peasants at the expense of the workers); also the supporting speech by Guesde (Feb 19). E writes Paul Lafargue that Jaurès's speech is "astounding" and "regrettable": it is a form of "state socialism," which is "one of the infantile diseases of proletarian socialism"—no better because proposed for a bourgeois-democratic republic, where the capitalists still hold power. **Mar 20, 21:** In letters to Adler and Sorge, E continues [cf ← :9] his analysis of party politics in England—the crisis of Liberals and Tories in particular. **Mar 26:** In a letter to Iglesias (Spanish party), E expresses satisfaction over socialist growth in the Basque region as well as in Galicia and Asturias, and over the self-destruction of the anarchist "fools and police agents."

15. SOCIALIST LITERATURE. **Mar 9:** In response to an inquiry from A. Momberger (in Wiesbaden), E supplies a short bibliography of socialist publications available in English; his list—incomplete, obviously hasty—includes titles from a more or less Marxist standpoint: headed by Morris and Bax, *Social-*

ism, its growth and outcome. (Incidentally, on Mar 21, E sends Sorge a copy of the Morris–Bax book.) **Mar 20:** E thanks the Roumanian socialist P. Muşoiu for sending (Feb 24) new Roumanian editions of the *Com Manifesto* and *Socialism: Utopian and scientific* (#E759), but declines to write new prefaces for planned second edns of these works.
    16. GREETINGS. **Mar 18:** On the 23d anniversary of the Paris Commune, E sends brief greetings to the French party (#E859); pubd in *Le Socialiste*, Mar 25. **Mar 22:** Invited to the fourth congress of the Austrian party (Mar 25–31), E instead sends greetings (#849), hailing the struggle for universal suffrage [→ :19]. **Mar 27:** E receives greetings sent him by the Austrian party congress. **Mar D:** E's greetings to the international students' congress (#E856) [← :12] are pubd in French in Brussels and Paris socialist organs.
    17. CAPITAL. **Mar 20:** E sends Danielson the first proof sheets of Vol. 3, to be translated into Russian. **Mar 21:** E tells Sorge that his work on Vol. 3 is now about two-thirds finished.

APRIL

    18. MOVEMENT AFFAIRS. **Apr 3, 16:** On receiving invitations—first from J. H. Watts, then secy H. W. Lee—to give a lecture for the SDF, E declines citing lack of time, but adding this: for years the SDF's *Justice* has thrown vague charges against him, never spelled out, never proved, never withdrawn, and so he will have nothing to do with the group. **Apr 11:** Continuing his attack on the Jaurès "state-socialist" proposal [← 14] in a letter to Laura Lafargue, E points out that a Junker-sponsored bill in the Reichstag is almost exactly the same as Jaurès's—openly in the interest of the German landed aristocracy: is this "socialistic" too?
    19. GREETINGS. **Apr:** E's greetings to the Austrian party congress (#E849) [← :16] are pubd in the congress proceedings.
    20. FRIENDS. **Apr 24:** E sends thanks, via C. Eberle, to the Barmen comrades who sent him an album with views of his hometown.

MAY

    21. CAPITAL. **May 11:** E sends the last part of the ms of Vol. 3 off to publisher Meissner (Hamburg): finished at last (but correction of proof sheets will still occupy E) [→ :46].
    22. ENGLISH MOVEMENT. **May 12:** In a letter to Sorge, E discusses how the Liberal party, though itself on the decline, is trying to kill the nascent independent workers' party. The English SDF and the American SLP are

"the only parties that have contrived to reduce the Marxist theory of development to a rigid orthodoxy." They remain mere sects, "and, as Hegel says, come from nothing through nothing to nothing." **May 21:** Writing to Plekhanov, E considers it probable that in England it is the TUs that will get workers into Parliament—"still, it is a step forward. Let us first smash the enslavement of the workers to the two big bourgeois parties. . . ."
    23. W&P. **May 15:** E sends greetings to the third congress of the Hungarian Social-Democratic party (#E845); pubd May 18. **May 23:** E writes a new preface (#E28) for the third German edn of *Anti-Dühring* (#E23) [→ :30].
    24. VISITOR. **May 6–7:** E is visited by A. Delcluze of the French party.

JUNE

    25. MOVEMENT AFFAIRS. **June 1:** E thanks Danielson for sending a copy of the first Russian edn of *Origin of the family* (#E573), recently pubd in St. Petersburg, with some mutilation by the censorship; E considers the translation good. **June 2:** E says that the trouble with French socialism is its division into several wings besides Marxism; and "phrasemongers like Jaurès" are likely to predominate. The first revolutionary battles may be fought in France—"but to ensure victory . . . you will need the active support of a much stronger, more numerous, more tried, and more conscious socialist party than you have at your command." The German movement may, then, well be decisive in the European revolution. **June M:** E is informed by Sorge on the strike movement of the American mine workers. **June c.18:** The Hungarian socialist M. Deák informs E that a Hungarian trans of the *Com Manifesto* is being prepared.
    26. W&P. **June 19 to July 16:** E works on the essay "On the history of early Christianity" (#E556) [→ :30].
    27. CAPITAL. **June 19:** E offers Kautsky two chapters of Vol. 3 (Chs. 23–24) for advance publ in NZ. **June 27:** He sends them to Kautsky [→ :30]. **June:** During this period E is "literally overwhelmed by proof sheets" since those coming from Meissner for Vol. 3 are in poor condition, while at the same time Dietz is printing the third German edn of *Anti-Dühring* (#E23) [→ :30].
    28. PERSONAL. **June 2:** In a letter to Paul Lafargue, E reveals that he permits no photo of his profile, since it makes him "look like an ass." **June c.19 to July 2:** E is frequently visited by Liebknecht, who is sojourning in London. **June 25:** E, Louise (Kautsky) Freyberger, and the Avelings attend a Handel

Festival at the Crystal Palace and hear the *Messiah*.

JULY

29. INTERNATIONAL AFFAIRS. **July 17:** Writing to Adler on Austria, E stresses the importance of the electoral reform (universal suffrage) issue but adds it is only the push that sets things rolling for other gains too. The Austrian party may have the historic mission of forming the vanguard of the European proletariat. In this letter E also gives an extensive analysis of the problems of the French movement. **July 19 to Aug 2:** In response to a request from the Scottish mine workers' strike committee, E writes to the German party Exec and the London GWEA for material aid to the strikers; he also contributes money himself. **July 28:** E explains to Kautsky why in America he cannot find a single able correspondent for NZ except Sorge or Schlüter. The German-American socialists of the SLP see only the mistakes of American labor, look down on the "stupid" Americans and rant at them, brag of their own orthodox superiority, repel the native workers instead of drawing them in; hence they remain only a small impotent sect and their writers understand nothing. **July 30 to Aug 6:** At Iglesias's request (July 27) E sends out invitations to continental and English socialists to send greetings to the Spanish party congress (Aug 29–Sep 1) [→ :32].

30. W&P. **July 12:** E's letter to Turati on "The future Italian revolution . . ." (#E319) is pubd in German in *Sozialdemokrat* (Berlin) [← :12]. **July 16:** E finishes and sends Kautsky his essay "On the history of early Christianity" (#E556) [← :26; → :36]. **July 28:** In a letter to Kautsky, E discusses some problems raised in this essay. **July:** NZ pubs two chapters (Chs. 23–24) from Vol. 3 of *Capital* in its no. 42 [← :27]. —The third German edn of *Anti-Dühring* (#E23) is pubd, with a new preface (#E28) [← :23]. **July c.26:** E sends a copy to Labriola.

AUGUST

31. ANTI-SDF CAMPAIGN. **Aug 5–6:** The SDF congress makes two basic decisions which appall E: (1) it rejects any electoral collaboration with the ILP, since the SDF alone is truly revolutionary; (2) since the coming International Socialist Congress of 1896 will include TU organizations too, the SDF proclaims for a "purely socialist" International, and calls a "pure" congress just before the scheduled one. **Aug:** E sends out letters to Continental parties alerting them to the SDF's moves and explaining its fossilized sectism and "incomprehensible stupidity":

Aug AB, to Iglesias (Spain); Aug 14, to Bernstein (in Germany); Aug 16, to Turati (in Italy); Aug 22, to Paul Lafargue (in France). Among other things he relates that in its 14 years of existence the SDF has gained and lost one million members, who passed through it as though through a revolving door; it now claims 4500. It says: if you are socialist, you belong in our group; if you refuse and form a different group, you are ipso facto no socialist. That is, it proclaims the policy of the Caliph Omar in burning the books at Alexandria: if a book is contrary to the Koran, burn it; if it is the same, it is superfluous—burn it.

32. INTERNATIONAL AFFAIRS. **Aug 6:** E sends the Spanish party's invitation [← :29] to a list of English groups (#E841). **Aug 15–30:** Labriola sends E reports on the situation in Italy, also on the efforts by Loria and his supporters to attack M's economic doctrines in the press. (E receives such info in subsequent months also.) (SOURCE: *MEW Daten*.)

33. BUSTS. **Aug 2:** Turati sends E a photo of a bust of M available in Florence, and asks Eleanor M to give her opinion on its resemblance. **Aug 16:** E replies that his friends do not admire it: "It has too little of M and too much of Garibaldi." Anyway, there is sales competition: a big medallion of M is sold in Paris; in Germany, Austria, and Switzerland there are plaster busts of M in profusion.

34. PERSONAL. **Aug 14 to Sep 18:** E sojourns in Eastbourne, with the Freybergers.

SEPTEMBER

35. INTERNATIONAL AFFAIRS. **Sep CD:** E reacts to the peasant program just adopted by the Nantes congress (Sep 14–16) of the French party: he writes Laura Lafargue rejecting the Preamble, which says that socialists have the duty of preserving peasant property, including that of employers of farm labor [→ :39]. —E comments on the outbreak of the Sino-Japanese War in letters to Kautsky (Sep 23) and Laura (Sep CD): however it turns out, it will collapse the traditional order of old China, impel modernization and the export of coolie labor, which will intensify the crisis in Europe. Irony of history: Capitalism has only China left to conquer, and once it does so, it makes itself impossible at home. (*MEW Daten* lists this under date Sep to Nov.)

36. W&P. **Sep 6:** In response to an invitation (Aug 30) from Dell'Avalli, É sends greetings (#E868) to the Socialist Party of Italian Workingmen for its coming congress (Imola, Sep 7–9). But the congress is banned: E's greetings are read to the CC on Sep 10; pubd in *Lotta di Classe*, Sep 22–23. **Sep c.9:** E hears from Martignetti about the latter's Italian trans of *Origin of the family* (#E573) and other works by E, and about the difficulty of getting them pubd. **Sep 26:** In response to a request (Sep 18) from the editor of the Sicilian *La Riscossa Socialista* for greetings to the coming new organ *Giustizia Sociale*, E sends greetings (#E346) to the socialists of Sicily—not immediately pubd since the new organ is suppressed [→ 95:35]. **Sep D/Oct A:** E's essay "On the history of early Christianity" (#E556) is pubd in *NZ* [← :30]. **Sep to Nov:** *L'Ere Nouvelle*, in three monthly installs, pubs a revised version [← 86:2] of Laura Lafargue's French trans of *Com Manifesto*—this revision also by Laura [→ 95:2; → :45].

37. FERRI. Sep 22: E receives a collection of Enrico Ferri's recent writings from the author. **Sep 23:** E evaluates Ferri's new book *Socialismo e scienza positiva (Darwin, Spencer, Marx)*, in a letter to Kautsky: the book by "the muddlehead Ferri" is "terribly confused, shallow rubbish."

38. PERSONAL. Sep 18: E returns from Eastbourne [← :34].

OCTOBER

39. INTERNATIONAL AFFAIRS. Oct CD: E is elated by the big victory of the Belgian Labor party in the parliamentary election (Oct 14, 21); in a letter to Vandervelde, he congratulates the Belgian party, and stresses that the smaller states often provide invaluable laboratories of experience for all Europe. **Oct 21–27:** At the German party congress (Frankfurt), which takes up the question of a party program addressed to the peasantry, Vollmar (leader of the Bavarian party) presses for an openly opportunist-reformist platform designed to catch peasant votes—even to the right of the Nantes Preamble in France [← :35]. E reacts not only to this challenge but esp to Vollmar's public claim that E has approved of the Nantes program [→ :43]. **Oct:** E gets reports and letters from Iglesias on the Spanish textile workers' strike in Malaga; he is enthused by the strikers' courageous struggle.

40. CAPITAL. Oct 4: E finishes, and dates, his preface (#E606) to Vol. 3 [→ :50].

41. W&P. Oct 27: At Turati's request (Oct 24), E writes a letter to *Critica Sociale* replying to recent attacks on Marxism in the Italian press (#E385) [→ :45].

42. PERSONAL. Oct: E moves from 122 Regent's Park Road [← 70:53] to a larger house at no. 41 on the same road, nearer the gate to Regent's Park; this is his last residence. **Oct 26:** E resumes inviting house guests. **Oct-Nov:** E gets a number of visits by Plekhanov, who is temporarily living in London after his expulsion from Switzerland. Plekhanov wants to look over E's files of *NRZ* and *NRZ-Revue*, a difficult thing to do just now.

NOVEMBER

43. GERMAN PARTY FIGHT ON THE PEASANT QUESTION. Nov 10: E writes Sorge that peasant vote catching is affecting the French and German party, that Vollmar even proposes to win big peasant exploiters of labor, unprincipledly. **Nov 12:** E receives a detailed report on the Frankfurt congress [← :39] from Bebel (Nov 10), and learns of Vollmar's effort to cover his line with E's authority; Bebel asks E to counteract Vollmar. —Writing to Laura Lafargue, E warns her that since Vollmar has forced him to speak up fully, he must now also speak out on the Nantes congress [← :35]. —E sends an open letter to *Vorwärts* (#E444) sharply rejecting Vollmar's statements on the peasant question; pubd Nov 16. **Nov 14:** At a party meeting in Berlin, Bebel breaks it open by publicly attacking Vollmar and his Bavarian right wing on the peasant question; his speech is pubd in *Vorwärts* on Nov 16. **Nov 15:** E begins writing his long programmatic essay, "The peasant question in France and Germany" (#E578), for *NZ*, criticizing the Nantes program and the Vollmar position and expounding his views on how to win peasants to socialism. **Nov 22:** E finishes this essay and sends it to Kautsky. Having read Bebel's "beginning of a polemic" against the right wing, E tells Kautsky, "it's high time." The attitude in *Vorwärts* (i.e., by Liebknecht) is to hush things up, E writes, but this only helps Vollmar. —E writes Paul Lafargue, and in a friendly but measured tone bluntly tells him that the Nantes program leaned too much "toward the opportunist tendency." Bebel has taken up the challenge, and says the party is going bourgeois. "This is the misfortune of all extreme parties when the time approaches for them to become 'possible.'" But beyond a certain limit, the party betrays itself—and "in France as in Germany we have now reached that point." **Nov 23 to Dec 1:** Polemic in the press: first a series of articles by Vollmar attacking Bebel, then four articles by Bebel in reply. **Nov 24:** E tells off Liebknecht, who has written him (Nov 16) criticizing Bebel for attacking Vollmar and asking E to cool Bebel down. In reply, E backs Bebel 100%, and advises Liebknecht that even a party editor should not try to smooth things over if he is also a real party leader like Bebel. E criticizes a Liebknecht editorial which in effect repudiated Bebel's speech, in unprincipled fashion. E explains the factional course of the Bavarian group, its threats of split, and abuse of left-wingers; the danger of a split comes from Vollmar, who is not a real socialist, and not from Bebel, who is calling things by the right name; the way to party harmony is not to hush up and cover up internal disputes. (E writes Liebknecht another letter about this time—not extant—perhaps in reply to Liebknecht's letter of Nov 29 in which he whitewashes the Bavarian party and denigrates Bebel.) **Nov D:** E's essay on the peasant question (#E578) is pubd in NZ.

44. INTERNATIONAL AFFAIRS. **Nov 10:** Writing to Sorge, E repeats his views on the sectism of the SDF and SLP, and reports that the ILP is "extremely indefinite in its tactics" under the "supercunning Scot," Keir Hardie; he gives political portraits of Hardie and John Burns. **Nov 23:** E writes a letter of thanks to an Armenian student, Atabekyanc, for translating *Socialism: Utopian and scientific* (#E759) and the *Com Manifesto*, but declines to write a new preface for the *Manifesto*. The liberation of Armenia from both Turkey and Russia, he says, depends on overthrowing Russian czarism. **Nov 24:** E declines to let Danielson cite his views on Russian affairs from private letters, in a planned critique of Struve. He explains that he is constantly beset by pleas from Russians that he intervene in Russian arguments over M and other subjects; that he has steadily refused to be drawn in; and that he cannot let it happen indirectly by citation of letters.

45. W&P. **Nov 1:** E's letter to *Critica Sociale* (#E385) [← :41] is pubd under the title "International socialism and Italian socialism." **Nov 12:** E, having examined the Sep-Oct numbers of *L'Ere Nouvelle* with Laura Lafargue's revised French trans of the *Com Manifesto* [← :36], greets it as "the first French trans of the old Manifesto I have read with undivided pleasure." He also writes Laura that he must now do what he has long planned: an account of M's activity in the International.

46. *CAPITAL.* **Nov 22:** Because of a statement in *Vorwärts* that Vol. 4 (*Theories of surplus value*) will not be pubd, E writes a short note denying this report (#E554), anonymously; pubd in NZ in a few days. **Nov D:** Vol. 3, with a preface by E (#E606), comes off the press in Hamburg (Meissner); but apparently E does not receive it until Dec A.

47. WILL AND TESTAMENT. **Nov 14:** E draws up a Supplement to his Will (#E803) [← 93:38] giving certain instructions to the

executors. He also writes a letter to Laura Lafargue and Eleanor M explaining two provisions.

DECEMBER

48. GERMAN PARTY FIGHT. **Dec 4:** Writing to Sorge, E summarizes the party situation, esp the extreme right-wing and aggressively factional line of the Bavarian party under Vollmar, and Liebknecht's sorry role as conciliator. Writing to Turati, E commends him for publishing Bebel's anti-Vollmar speech [← :43] in *Critica Sociale* (Dec 1). **Dec 12, 14:** Writing to Adler and (again) Sorge, E reports that "Bebel has won" over Vollmar—in the press debate [← :43] and in appeals to the Exec and Reichstag Fraction; at the next congress, Bebel will have a big majority. E also recalls Vollmar's two previous right-wing campaigns: to support Caprivi as "government socialists" [← 91:33] and to advocate state socialism [← 92:33]. Liebknecht, remarks E, "is becoming more and more embarrassing."

49. MOVEMENT AFFAIRS. **Dec 6:** The German government introduces an antisubversive bill, allegedly to prevent a coup d'état, really to control the socialist movement—in substance a new Anti-Socialist Law; this serious threat to the S-D party will provide the background for the party's bowdlerization of E [→ 95:16]. **Dec 27:** Since the Vienna *Arbeiter-Ztg* will appear as a daily on Jan 1, E sends greetings to the Austrian movement on this achievement (#E342) [→ 95:9].

50. W&P. **Dec AB:** E sends out copies of Vol. 3 of *Capital* [← :46] to friends: Plekhanov (Dec 11), Sorge and Schlüter (Dec 12), etc. **Dec 17:** In a letter to Laura Lafargue, E lists the many tasks that face him now that Vol. 3 is out: see ← :1, 2. **Dec 29:** E arranges for a preface to the planned publ of Laura Lafargue's French trans of the *Com Manifesto* [← :45] by asking Laura herself to draft part of it, which he will then supplement and revise. (This preface will never be done.)

51. PERSONAL. **Dec 6:** E writes a letter to the London GWEA with thanks for its birthday greetings (#E854). **Dec 31:** At a New Year's eve gathering at E's house, with many friends present, V. Zasulich discusses problem of revolutions with E, and next day sends a report on the conversation to Plekhanov.

1895

CONSPECTUS

1. This is the last year of E's life.
2. *Indefinite-date Entry.* Laura Lafargue's

third and last version of her French trans of the *Com Manifesto* [← 94:36] is pubd as a pamphlet, prob around the beginning of the year, benefiting from E's suggestions. It will go through many reprintings during the following years.

JANUARY

3. GERMAN MOVEMENT. **Jan:** Since the German government has introduced an anti-subversive bill in the Reichstag aimed against the socialist movement [← 94:49], the party is mobilizing to fight it. E (Jan 12) approves the speech made against the bill by "Nazi" (nickname of Ignaz Auer, a party secy). **Jan 3:** In a letter, E analyzes the reasons for the right-wing pressures building up in the party, esp the influx of nonproletarian elements attracted to the "only really progressive party." But he is sure the proletarian rank-and-file will defeat this right wing, which will not split off. **Jan 19:** Writing to Laura Lafargue about the European scene, E makes the point that in Germany, unlike France or England, the parliament is not the supreme power: "A similar power our men in Germany [the S-D party] can get by a revolution only. . . ." **Jan 30:** Richard Fischer, party secy overseeing the *Vorwärts* party press, writes E about the plan to publish M's *Class struggles in France* (#M148) as a book by Mar; he asks E to write an intro [→ :11].

4. INTERNATIONAL AFFAIRS. **Jan 1:** Writing to Schlüter about England, E appears unhappy not only with the sects but also with the ILP [← :44]: there is no real party, he says of the English movement. He explains how parliamentary democracy is made so expensive that only the two official parties can afford it. **Jan 16:** Writing to Sorge about the US, E reflects on the decline of the American movement. **Jan 28:** In a letter to Adler about the coming appearance of the Austrian party's daily, E discusses editorial problems and promises his aid.

5. RESEARCH ASSISTANT. **Jan 12:** Requested by Adler (Dec 27) to supply info on M's 1848 trip to Vienna [← 48:57, 58] for an article, E sends a summary about M's trip taken from *NRZ*. **Jan 19:** Requested (Jan M) by Bebel, who is gathering ammunition against the antisubversive bill (see ← :3), for material on how England deals with riots without special repressive laws, E researches the subject and sends the info to Bebel.

6. OPINIONS. **Jan 24:** For F. Tönnies, who has sent E a couple of his writings, E discusses one of Tönnies's subjects, Comte, in some detail. **Jan 28:** In a letter to Adler, E cries "Bravo, Clara!"—approving Clara Zetkin's side in her recent (Jan) polemic with *Vorwärts*: as head of the German socialist women's movement Zetkin wants a hard line of opposition against the politics of the bourgeois feminists.

7. *CAPITAL.* **Jan 1:** E sends copies of Vol. 3 to Lavrov and to Adler. **Jan to Mar:** Labriola informs E that Loria and his group are again attacking M, in particular the points made in E's preface to Vol. 3 (#E606). Labriola sends the Italian trans of this preface pubd in *La Rassegna* for Jan.

8. *GESAMTAUSGABE.* **Jan:** E is taking steps to prepare the contents of a collected edn of M's works, as well as his own. In letters to Kugelmann (Jan 1, 9, 25) E discusses getting a complete file of the *NYDT* articles, articles of 1842–52, etc. **Jan 27:** Fischer proposes to E the idea of publishing the works of M&E in small fascicules [→ :25].

9. W&P. **Jan 1:** *Arbeiter-Ztg* pubs E's greetings (#E342) [← 94:49].

10. FRIENDS. **Jan AB:** Learning of Wróblewski's bad financial plight, E writes to Vaillant and Paul Lafargue, urging that they provide aid for this hero of the Commune through a public appeal. **Jan 31** (or Feb 1): E is visited by V. Zasulich.

FEBRUARY

11. INTRODUCTION TO *THE CLASS STRUGGLES IN FRANCE.* **Feb 2:** In response to Fischer's request [← :3] for an intro to M's *Class struggles in France* (CSF) (#M148), E asks for further details. He grumbles because this will force the shelving of his Lassalle correspondence project [← 94:2]. **Feb 12, 13:** E proposes to constitute M's work (#M148) out of its three original articles plus a section of #ME136—as will in fact be done. **Feb 14:** E starts work on his intro (#E393), with the lowering situation in Germany much in mind. **Feb 26:** Writing to Paul Lafargue, E explains what is in his mind about this intro (which is mostly finished). The threat of a new Anti-Socialist Law [← :3] hangs over the German party: "We are facing a crisis coming on apace. . . . What is certain is that for our friends there will be a new period of persecution." The Right may be preparing a coup d'état, besides.

12. INTERNATIONAL AFFAIRS. **Feb 2:** In response to a query about the proposal to name the coming international congress (London, 1896) "International Socialist Labor and TU Congress," E replies that he favors it for this congress, since the English TUs are the greatest mass of the organized workers here, and besides we should encourage the TU trend toward the socialist camp. **Feb c.20:** From Willie Burns (in the US, a nephew-in-law) E receives material on the American socialist movement and strikes, esp the Brooklyn streetcar strike. **Feb 26:** Writing to Plekhanov, E remarks that Danielson is hopeless about "the spontaneous communistic mission distinguishing Russia from profane peoples."

"It is altogether impossible to discuss with this generation of Russians to which he belongs" (i.e., the Narodniks).

13. W&P. **Feb A:** E shelves his project of producing an edn of Lassalle's letters to M, at least for the nonce [← 3, 11]. **Feb 26:** E returns the ms of Laura Lafargue's French trans of his essay "On the history of early Christianity" (#E556), with enthusiastic approval (plus a few suggestions for revision).

14. READING. **Feb:** E receives Plekhanov's new book *The development of the monist view of history* (St. Petersburg, signed N. Beltov) from V. Zasulich. E thanks Plekhanov (Feb 8) but only begins the reading. (*MEW Daten* is in error.)

15. FRIENDS. **Feb 2–26:** Plekhanov informs E that Zasulich is ill and suggests that Dr. Freyberger examine her; Freyberger finds bronchitis. E arranges to take care of Zasulich: better diet; loan of money (disguised by E as coming from Plekhanov); a stay at a watering place for her recovery.

MARCH

16. INTRODUCTION TO *CSF*: BOWDLERIZATION. **Mar 5, 16:** In letters to Vaillant and Iglesias referring to this intro, E mentions that it has to be done fast, since the German party wants to hasten the publ of all works in preparation because of the danger of a new Anti-Socialist Law [← :11]. **Mar 6:** E finishes, and dates, his intro (#E393) to M's *Class struggles in France* (#M148). —There is a dating problem here—perhaps E sent it off a couple of days before—for in a letter itself dated Mar 6 (cf *MEW* 39:605, n.455), Richard Fischer, on behalf of the party Exec, objects to the too revolutionary tone of the piece and asks E to weaken it, because of the danger of provoking the feared Anti-Socialist Law. **Mar 8:** Replying to Fischer, E is willing to accept some changes even where he thinks the motivation is silly; but then he digs in his heels: he cannot accept subscribing "body and soul to absolute legality—legality under all circumstances. . . ." True, *Vorwärts* often disavows revolution, but he cannot go along with this. No party anywhere renounces "the right to resist illegality with arms in hand. . . ." He concludes: "Legality as long and as far as suits us, but no legality at any price, not even in phrases!" **Mar 11:** A letter from Bebel puts extreme pressure on E from the standpoint of not making himself responsible for a disaster to the party. Bebel writes: "We do not ask you to say something that you do not wish to say—or may not say—but we ask you *not* to say something which, if said at this time, would be embarrassing for us. . . ." **Mar 25:** Kautsky telegraphs E for

permission to publish the intro in *NZ*. E replies, "With pleasure," and follows with a letter, saying: "*My* text has suffered somewhat from the hesitations of our Berlin friends [party Exec] out of fear of the antisubversive bill, and indeed I had to take them into account under the circumstances." **Mar 28:** Writing to Laura Lafargue, E repeats that the intro "has suffered somewhat from the, as I think, exaggerated desires" of the party leaders to say nothing that might help the antisubversive bill. "Under the circumstances, I had to give way." Discussing the German situation, he opines that it is "decidedly becoming critical." The young kaiser, with caesarist hankerings, may resort to a reactionary coup d'état. **Mar 30:** Without E's consultation or knowledge, *Vorwärts* (Liebknecht) pubs a leading article "How revolutions are made nowadays," in which chopped-out extracts from E's intro are quoted tendentiously to give the impression of a policy of unqualified legalism and pacifism [→ :24]. Note: This falsification by *Vorwärts* (Liebknecht) is often confused with the bowdlerization of the intro by the party Exec; there are two different presentations involved here.

17. PERSPECTIVE. **Mar 5:** Writing to Vaillant with a survey of the international scene, E concludes: "The end of the century is taking on a decisively revolutionary turn."

18. ENGLISH MOVEMENT. **Mar 5, 28:** In letters to Vaillant and Laura Lafargue, E attacks the policy of the ILP and SDF in the London County Council election, in refusing to continue supporting as before the Progressive (Fabian-Liberal) candidates, thereby helping bring about a right-wing victory. E writes that Webb and the Fabians are "muff" as socialists, but are "really doing very good work municipally," in maintaining London self-government and making it easy for the working class to conquer this capital base.

19. FRENCH AFFAIRS. **Mar 5:** In response to a query (Jan 8) from Vaillant about bills introduced into the Chamber by socialists, E gives his opinion; he approves i.a. a bill for an eight-hour day and minimum wage for government workers, and one to set up a separate Ministry of Labor, explaining his grounds. **Mar c.12:** E hears from Laura Lafargue about the May Day preparations in France.

20. *CAPITAL*. **Mar 5:** In response to a query from Danielson (Jan 29) about M's studies for *Capital* on Russian landed property—mentioned by E in his preface to Vol. 3 (#E606)—E replies that M's papers do not show what he was planning to do with these studies; in none of them did M include remarks of his own; they are simply extensive excerpts from Russian statistical and general economic sources. **Mar 11, 12:** In response to pubd reviews of Vol. 3 by Werner Sombart and Conrad Schmidt, E writes to each of them criticizing their mistakes and erroneous interpretations of M [→ :26]. **Mar 16:** Since V. Adler wants to study Vols. 2 and 3 in jail, E sends him "a few hints" as a guide to study, pointing esp to the key sections. **Mar 28:** Writing to Laura Lafargue that the German situation imperils future publication plans, E reports: "I am taking up Volume IV [*Theories of surplus value*]," checking on the ms as partly copied out by Kautsky [← 90:23] and planning to have Eleanor M continue the copying work.

21. READER-CRITIC. **Mar c.18:** E reads Carl Hirsch's articles in *Sozialpolitische Centralblatt* on the shorter-workday struggle, at the author's request, and sends his comments. **Mar 25:** E writes to Kautsky about the collective project for a history of socialism, Vol. 1 of which has just been pubd, with Kautsky's study on "From Plato to the Anabaptists" and Bernstein's on the Cromwellian revolution. E has not yet received the book, but he comments on some available sources; also on sources for the history of the International which Kautsky may do [→ :31]. **Mar D to Apr A:** E reads Paul Lafargue's book *The evolution of property*, and writes Lafargue (Apr 3) with approval tempered by important criticisms.

22. W&P. **Mar 11:** E sends a letter to the London GWEA (#E842) apologizing for being unable to participate in its affairs because of illness.

23. PERSONAL. **Mar AB:** Dr. Freyberger diagnoses E's condition as cancer of the esophagus and larynx, but E is not informed (as far as we know). At this time E is aware of a swelling on the right side of his neck [→ :28] (SOURCE: ST/35.5 [Kapp] 2:588, and E to Laura Lafargue, May 14). **Mar 26:** E draws up a codicil (#E802) to his Will (SOURCE: ST/35.5 [Kapp] ibid.) [→ :36].

APRIL

24. INTRODUCTION TO CSF. **Apr 1:** E flares up on seeing the *Vorwärts* article [← :16], and writes to Kautsky: "To my astonishment, today I see in *Vorwärts* an extract from my Intro, printed without my knowing it and trimmed up so that I appear as a peaceable worshiper of legality *quand même* [under any circumstances]." He reiterates the need for NZ publ "to wipe out this disgraceful impression." He promises to give Liebknecht a piece of his mind for "distorting my views." **Apr 3:** E is still indignant as he writes to Paul Lafargue: "Liebknecht has just played me a fine trick. He has taken ... everything that could serve his purpose in support of peaceful

and antiviolent tactics at any price, which he has chosen to preach for some time now, particularly at this juncture when coercive laws are being drawn up in Berlin. But I preach those tactics only for the Germany of today and even then with many reservations." These tactics do not apply as a whole to other countries or to Germany tomorrow, he says. (Note: While E is writing about the Liebknecht falsification, his words qualify the Exec's bowdlerization.) **Apr A:** E's intro (#E393) is pubd in NZ. (This is the bowdlerized version, same as next.) **Apr AB:** The book edn of M's *Class struggles in France* (#M148) is pubd, with E's intro (#E393). **Apr c.15:** E sends this book to Lessner, Zasulich, Labriola, Vaillant, and other friends and socialist leaders. **Apr c.19:** Martignetti informs E that his intro (#E393) has been transd into Italian [→ :32].

25. GESAMTAUSGABE. **Apr 5:** Learning that publisher Baake is planning to publish a volume of M's RZ articles of 1842, E writes to Fischer to stop this for the sake of M's heirs (daughters). He urges that *Vorwärts* press immediately prepare to publish a collection—specif, three articles: on freedom of the press (#M216), wood-theft law (#M218), Moselle peasants (#M965)—with E's intro and notes (see Apr 18 below). **Apr 15:** E informs Fischer that the copyright on this material has lapsed. He proposes a title for the 1842 articles: "Karl Marx' literarische Erstlinge" (KM's literary first-born). The plan for a *Gesamtausgabe* (collected edn) should wait till the Anti-Subversive Law danger is settled, since it might cause "castration" of the writings. E wants a collected edn of M&E's smaller writings, not in fascicules [← :8] but whole volumes, perhaps by a publisher outside Germany. **Apr 17:** E reports (to Laura Lafargue) that Fischer is having the 1842 articles copied from the RZ file now found in the Berlin library; *Vorwärts* will announce the edn, thus stopping competition. **Apr 18:** E corresponds with Kugelmann on his efforts to gather M's writings. —E asks Fischer to check the RZ for other material by M, to be distinguished by his characteristic style—"short sentences expressed pointedly, as antitheses." E has also discovered M's other article on freedom of the press (#M156), and is looking for others to represent "M's presocialist period." **Apr D:** E thanks Mehring for offering his aid in ferreting out M's old writings. E then sketches out, from memory, the background of M's RZ period.

26. CAPITAL. **Apr A:** E makes plans to prepare Vol. 4 (#M877) for the press [← :20]. **Apr 6:** E continues his discussion of political economy with C. Schmidt [← :20]. **Apr 10:** E thanks S. Bauer for sending his monograph on Quesnay's Tableau Econo-mique, and agrees that M was the first to rescue the Physiocrats from obscurity; Vol. 4, he adds, will have much on this. **Apr-May:** E writes two supplements to Vol. 3 (cf #E791): the first, on the law of value and rate of profit (#E428), is motivated by the objections of Schmidt and Sombart [← :20]; the second (#E781) is left unfinished. These are the last pieces written by E for publ.

27. GREETINGS. Apr: E informs corre-spondents (incl Quelch on Apr 2, Rakovsky on Apr 13) that this year he is declining all requests to write greetings for the Paris Com-mune anniversary (Mar 18). To the ILP's invitation (Apr 16) to its May Day celebration he sends a letter (#E823) declining on medi-cal grounds.

MAY

28. ILLNESS. May AB: The first acute signs of cancer of the esophagus show up [← :23]. E is beset (May c.2–9) by extreme pain in the skull, plus insomnia, diminishing after about a week. But E knows, at least by May 14, that the source is a lump, causing a swelling, on the right side of the neck, pressing on a nerve; he gets ready for an operation.

29. GESAMTAUSGABE. May 9: Because of illness (see ← :28), E asks Fischer and Meh-ring to take care of details. In a letter to Mehring, he lists the agreed-on contents of the 1842 RZ collection [← :25]. He has received the ms copy of two articles (#M216, 218) sent by Fischer, May 6. **May 29:** E asks Fischer for a copy of the entire Moselle article (#M965), which will be used either for the collected edn or by the editor of the present-day Rheinische Ztg.

30. CAPITAL. May 21: E informs Kautsky he is "about to send" the first supplement to Vol. 3 (#E428) [← :26].

31. HISTORY-OF-SOCIALISM PROJECT. May 21: In a letter to Kautsky, who has asked him for material on the history of the International, E replies irritatedly because he has not been asked to collaborate on the project; he refuses Kautsky's request. He comments on Kautsky's essay [← :21] that the early section on Plato and the early church is inadequate, better on Münzer and Anabaptists.

32. W&P. May 1: The Italian trans of E's intro (#E393) [← :24] is pubd in Critica Sociale, shortened. **May c.18:** From a Czech socialist, Heller, E receives the Czech trans of M's Wage-labor and capital (#M968), pubd in Vienna.

JUNE

33. EASTBOURNE. June AB to July 24: E sojourns in Eastbourne; he is unable to work as his illness takes its course. Visitors include Eleanor M, Laura Lafargue, Aveling, Adler, and others. —Adler has been released from jail, on suspended sentence, in order to make this trip from Austria. MEW Daten states: "June c.14: Adler informs E about the political situation in Austria," apparently from Vienna. **June 29:** E thanks Fischer for sending the Moselle article [← :29], but puts off all work during his illness.

34. LETTER: ON CAPITAL, ITALY. June 28: E's letter to Turati is his only discussion letter of this period. Informed (June 19) that Labri-ola wants to do a résumé of the three vols. of Capital, E warns that this is "one of the most difficult tasks" possible, and can be done only by half a dozen persons in Europe—not incl Labriola. —In another connection, E com-ments that the Italian party, like others, "suffers from the locust-like invasion of that 'declassed bourgeois youth' Bakunin was so proud of. Consequence: pullulation of literary dilettantism, turning only too often into sen-sationalism, and necessarily followed by a coterie spirit dominating the press."

35. W&P. June 30: E's greetings (#E346) to Sicilian socialists in 1894 [← 94:36] are finally pubd in Palermo.

JULY

36. LAST DAYS. July 9, 23: E's last (ex-tant) letters are to M's daughters, Eleanor and Laura. In both, his last political comments are on the English socialist scene, about the incapacity of the ILP and SDF leaders to build a movement. **July 21:** Dr. Freyberger tells Sam Moore that E's condition is extremely precarious; E, however, is certain he will recover. **July 24:** E returns to London from Eastbourne [← :33]. **July 26:** E signs and validates a codicil (#E802) to his Will and Testament [← :23]. **July 28:** In spite of his bad condition, E has Eleanor M report to him on the situation in the ILP.

AUGUST

37. ENGELS' DEATH. Aug 1: Vienna Ar-beiter-Ztg reprints E's greetings to Sicilian socialists (#E346) [← :35]. **Aug 3:** E lapses into unconsciousness. **Aug 4:** According to one version, Eleanor M, having been told by Sam Moore of Freddy Demuth's paternity, insists on hearing it from E himself; E, unable to speak, affirms the account on a slate (cf ST/35.5 [Kapp] 1:292). (But this conflicts with the version which has it that E was already unconscious, not merely speechless.) **Aug 5:** Engels dies, without regaining consciousness, at 10:15 or 10:30 P.M. Dr. Freyberger certifies the immediate cause as "broncho-pneumonia for 1 day and 16 hours." **Aug 6–10:** Telegrams and letters from friends and leading socialists stream in with expressions of grief. **Aug 10:** About 80 people go from Waterloo Station to the Woking crematorium, where the cremation, postponed for three hours pending verification by the coroner, takes place soon after 4:15 P.M. Short speeches are made by a nephew G. A. Schlechtendahl, Sam Moore, Aveling, Liebknecht, Paul Lafargue, Bebel, Anseele (Belgium), Van der Goes (Holland). Present also are Hermann Engels, Eleanor M, Laura Lafargue, "Johnny" Longuet, the Roshers, the Freybergers, Lessner, Stepniak, Stanislaw Mendelson, Zasulich, Freddy Demuth. **Aug 27:** From Eastbourne, E's favorite resort, Eleanor M, Aveling, Lessner, and Bernstein row six miles out beyond Beachy Head and consign E's ashes to the sea.

Appendix

THE ROAD TO *CAPITAL*: A PERIODIZATION

For specific references in the *Chronicle* to each of Marx's economic writings, see the *Register*. But the evolution of *Capital* is too complex to be summed up that way. In the following index, the course of Marx's study and writing on political economy is divided into periods, with some classification under each period. Engels' work in the field is mentioned only in relation to M's development; E's work on polit eco is not covered here. Wherever necessary, a period begins with a note explaining what defines its time boundaries.

1. Paris Period: 1844 to early 1845

M resides in Paris from Oct D, 1843, to Feb 1845. In Oct-Nov 1843 E writes his seminal article on polit eco (#E576) for DFJ (→ 43:25); it has an important impact on M (→ 44:3, 4, 6).

M begins working on polit eco: → 43:29; 44:1, 3, 4, 10.
M works on his "Economic and philosophical mss" (#M261): → 44:14, 26, 30, 48–49.
M interrupts this work: → 44:33, 37.   —He resumes: → 44:46; 45:10.
Dealings with pub'r (Leske): → 45:10, 12, 14.
Meanwhile E in Manchester studies English conditions: → 44:2, 15.   —And E writes his book on the English working class (#E171), which see for references.

2. Brussels Period, I: 1845 to early 1847

M resides in Brussels from Feb 1845 to Mar 1848. The division between the two parts of his stay is not sharp, based only on the shift in his attention to the three tasks listed under the second part.

M's work on polit eco: → 45:2, 14, 19, 28, 49–50.
M's trip to England with E (July-Aug 1845): → 45:30–32, 51.
M resumes some work on polit eco: → 45:37, 44, 52.
Hiatus for German ideology (#ME66): → 46:3, 33.
M resumes work: → 46:33, 38, 49, 51–53; 47:2, 58.
Dealings with pub'r (Leske): → 45:29, 47; 46:12, 28, 33, 49; 47:12.

3. Brussels Period, II: 1847 to early 1848

In this last year of M's stay in Brussels, his work becomes concretized around specific projects: first, the polemic against Proudhon, which is mainly concerned with polit eco; then the free-trade congress of economists held in Brussels in Sep 1847.

M's work on his Anti-Proudhon (#M681): → 46:49; 47:2, 6, 9, 22, 24, 58.
The tariff question (for early attention, see → 45:40): → 47:3, 32, 33, 40; 48:3, 8.

Lectures and preparation of articles, on "wages," "wage-labor and capital": →
47:53; 48:8. (For aftermath, → 48:31.)

4. Cologne: 1849

As the revolution declines, M—in addition to his work as NRZ editor and in the
Cologne movement—becomes involved in the educational work of the Cologne
Workers Assoc: → 49:2, 9.

In Apr, M begins a series of NRZ articles on "Wage-labor and capital" (#M968),
broken off unfinished: → 49:18.

5. The *NRZ-Revue* Period, London: 1849 to Sep 1850

M arrives in London in Aug 1849 and begins work to establish his magazine, the
NRZ-Revue, the first issue of which is pubd in Mar. From Nov 1849 to next Sep, M
gives lectures on polit eco but does not get to write them up: → 49:41.

M resumes the study of polit eco: → 50:3, 24, 28.
He resumes giving lectures: → 50:8, 24, 28, 32.
As a result of his economic studies, he concludes that the European crisis has come
to an end: → 50:28.
This period can be regarded as ending with the suspension of the NRZ-Revue (cf →
50:36) and the collapse of the Communist League (cf → 50:34).

6. The Notebooks of 1850–53

This period extends roughly from the end of the NRZ-Revue and the Communist
League (see preceding period) to the onset of the Crimean War, when M's attention
turns more to the Continental politics of Europe. For M's notebooks of this period: →
50:3, 36, 50–51.

M studies polit eco: → 50:42, 47, 50–51; 51:3, 7, 12, 17, 22, 29, 33, 40, 52, 53, 61–
71.
During this time he is periodically prodded to get the work finished: → 50:7, 22, 26,
52.

Hiatus: Bonaparte's coup of Dec 1851 sets M working on his 18th Brumaire
(#M267) into Mar 1852; and beginning Aug 1852 he begins writing regularly for
NYDT; other projects and problems also pile up. However, for M's notebook of this
time, see → 52:57. For a couple of NYDT articles of 1852 on economic questions, see
→ 52:49.

M's efforts to get a pub'r in 1851–52: → 51:22, 33, 43, 47, 52, 58; 52:5, 8, 14, 21, 28,
32, 37, 53.
M continues work on polit econ: → 53:6, 36, 50–52.
More NYDT articles (1853) on economic questions: → 53:8, 26, 35, 40, 44, 46.
Suspension of work: → 53:37.

7. The Interim Fifties: 1854–57

During these years M's main journalistic focus is on the Crimean War, the struggle
of the Great Powers, European political crises; this is expressed esp in his work for
NYDT and NOZ (cf → 53:37).

Some of M's journalistic work is on economic questions: → 54:2; 55:3–4; 56:1, 24, 28, 36. (More below.)

He does some work on polit eco: → 54:51; 55:5, 28; 56:1.

Toward the end of 1856 and in 1857, with the appearance of an economic crisis, M turns more attention to this field. In journalistic articles: → 56:41–42; 57:11, 20, 25. In work on polit eco: → 56:1, 34, 37; 57:2, 5, 10.

8. The *Grundrisse* Notebooks: 1857–58

For the Grundrisse . . . see #M361, incl the boxed "Guide." For the background (M's renewed attention to the economic crisis): → 56:37; 57:2.

M's work on the Grundrisse notebooks and related work: → 57:30, 35, 40, 43, 44, 48, 49, 52; 58:1, 7, 12, 17, 20, 24, 29, 30, 36.

Journalistic articles on economic questions: → 57:39, 42, 47, 51; 58:6, 11, 23.

Efforts to get a pub'r: → 58:12, 17, 22, 24.

9. The First Critique of Political Economy, *CCPE:* 1858–59

This is the first book M publishes on polit eco, his Contribution to the critique of polit eco (#M181), reworking part of the Grundrisse mss; begun Aug 1858, pubd June 1859. It is labeled the first volume or part (Heft) of a larger work to come dealing with capital; it comprises only two chapters (on commodities and money), without getting to the subject of capital (cf → 59:10), which is to be taken up in the next volume (which we here dub "CCPE II").

M's work on the book, and related study: → 58:1, 36, 43, 46, 50; 59:1, 10, 13.

Final preparation and publication: → 59:18, 25, 36, 43.

Dealings with pub'r Duncker: → 58:17, 22, 24, 39, 43; 59:10, 13.

Reviews, comments, reactions: → 59:1, 43, 51, 54, 68, 73. (For subseq years, see the index list under #M181 in the Register; note → 60:30, 47; 62:22; cf 63:14, 30.)

Problem of translations and foreign editions: → 59:13, 18, 62.

M's journalistic articles on economic questions during this period: → 58:42; 59:15, 39, 57.

10. The First Period of *CCPE* II: 1859 to mid-1861

After the publ of CCPE (#M181) in June 1859, M sets about producing what he regards as the second volume of this work—which we here label "CCPE II." He will think of it in this wise until Dec 1862 (cf → 62:62). There is a possibility of numerical confusion: since the 1859 volume comprised two chapters, CCPE II might be called the third chapter or part. —For the dates of the whole period of CCPE II, see the next period.

M's plan for CCPE II: → 59:13.

M's work on CCPE II during this period: → 59:25, 62, 76–77.

M interrupts the work for Herr Vogt (#M372): → 60:1–2.

M continues with sporadic work on polit eco: → 60:9, 16, 39, 47, 65–66; 61:2, 27.

Efforts to get a pub'r: → 61:22, 31.

Journalistic articles on economic questions during this period: → 60:43, 48, 55.

11. The Notebooks of 1861–63: mid-1861 to mid-1863

This occupies the second period of CCPE II—with an overlap. Although it is at the end of 1862 that M abandons the CCPE plan and decides to begin again with a new work to be called Capital, he continues working on these notebooks for another half year, to mid-1863. Therefore we take this period as ending in mid-1863, when M starts a new set of notebooks (for which, see next period).

The notebooks: → 61:2 (cf also 61:27).

Work on the notebooks, and related study: → 61:34, 42, 45, 56; 62:5–8, 17, 22, 28–30, 38, 40, 50, 62; 63:1, 5, 14, 20, 27.

The changeover to Capital: → 62:5, 62; 63:1.

Efforts to get a pub'r: → 63:14.

Problem of translations: → 62:62.

Journalistic articles on economic questions during this period (last such articles in NYDT): → 61:44, 51.

12. The Undifferentiated Capital: Notebooks of 1863–65

In Aug 1863, M turns to some subjects not sufficiently elaborated in the notebooks of 1861–63, esp circulation of capital, forms of surplus value (which will be important for Vols. 2–3 of Capital). These notebooks, together with those of 1861–63, will be the quarry from which, first, M will shape Vol. 1; later, Engels will produce Vols. 2 and 3; and still later, the volumes of Theories of surplus value will be drawn. This period ends when M begins to make a final draft of Vol. 1 for publ. For background: → 63:1, 5, 26.

Work on the notebooks, and related study: → 63:30; 64:2, 16, 33, 41; 65:3, 20, 31, 35, 43–45, 48, 59, 61.

Efforts to get a pub'r: → 63:26, 41; 65:11, 20, 26.

Problem of translations: → 63:26; 65:43.

Related economic issues and activity: M's debate with Weston (cf #M971): → 65:33, 35, 38, 41. On Lassalle's economics: → 64:13, 17. Bismarck's offer: → 65:54.

For later undifferentiated references to Capital, see esp → 66:48; 67:12; 68:18, 29.

13. Volume 1 of Capital: 1866–67

M starts on this final draft of Vol. 1 by Jan or Feb 1866 (cf → 66:3); it is pubd Sep 1867. For the inception, see → 66:3, 8, 12.

M's work on Vol. 1: → 66:11, 12, 25, 33, 39, 41, 48, 52; 67:1, 5, 11, 14, 15, 17, 23, 27. On the Supplement to Vol. 1 (in the first edn): → 67:14, 15, 17, 23.

Publication of the first edn: → 67:27, 31.

Relations with pub'r (Meissner): → 66:3, 8, 12, 48, 52, 54; 67:1, 11–12, 14, 23.

Reactions and opinions, publicism: → 67:1, 12, 17, 27, 31.

Problem of translations: → 67:1, 14, 15, 17.

Related economic questions and activity: → 66:12, 33, 51; 67:3, 8.

14. Capital after Publication—Immediate Aftermath: late 1867 to mid-1870

The cutoff date given here, marking the outbreak of the Franco-Prussian War, is partly arbitrary; it is chosen because the war forms a useful dividing line, since M's attention and activity makes a sharp shift.

Reviews and publicism, reactions and opinions: → 67:1, 34, 37, 38, 43, 48; 68:2, 5, 10, 13, 20, 27, 33, 40, 43, 44, 48, 52; 69:6, 13, 27, 32.   Sales: → 69:13.   Marx's own views: → 68:5, 59.   Engels's synopsis (#E799): → 68:19.

Relations with pub'r (Meissner): → 68:13; 69:13, 59.

Problems of translations and foreign editions: → 67:1; 68:5, 52, 59; 69:33, 63, 73.

Related economic questions and activity: → 68:10, 13, 27, 37, 42.

M's continued work on Vol. 2: → 67:27, 39, 48; 68:3–4, 19, 27, 40, 59, 65, 72; 70:22.   On Vol. 3: → 68:3–4, 19, 40.   Undifferentiated references (incl general reading): → 69:3, 7, 13, 23, 33, 68; 70:5.

15. Marx and *Capital*—the Last Years: mid-1870 to 1883

References are to Vol. 1 unless otherwise stated; references to Vols. 2–4 and undifferentiated references are at the end.

New German edns of Vol. 1–2, revision, etc.: → 71:31, 60, 65; 72:2, 7, 18, 22, 32, 38, 45, 58; 73:2, 10, 15, 25, 29, 35, 40, 45, 48; 77:39; 81:54, 60; 82:39.   *See also* Abridgments, *below.*

Translations and foreign editions: → 75:27.   French: → 71:65; 72:2, 6, 7, 12, 18, 22, 29, 32, 38, 45, 54, 58, 64; 73:2, 20, 29, 32, 35, 53, 57; 74:2, 20, 30; 75:4, 9, 19, 41, 46, 48; 77:39; 82:30.   Russian: → 70:42, 63; 71:26, 31, 54, 60; 72:2, 18, 22, 29; 78:39.   English: → 77:39.   Italian: → 72:45, 58; 73:20; 77:32.   Spanish: → 72:58; 73:20.   Portuguese: → 72:38.   *See also* Abridgments, *below.*

Reviews and publicism, reactions and opinions: → 70:63; 71:22, 60; 72:45, 54, 68; 73:45, 48, 57; 75:26; 76:32; 77:14; 78:39; 79:46, 50; 80:39, 40; 81:60; 82:6, 52.   M's own views: → 77:41; 82:52.   Hyndman's plagiarism: → 81:35, 38.

Abridgments—German: → 73:2; 75:29; 76:12, 18; 77:47.   English: → 75:27; 78:30, 34.   Italian: → 79:6, 29.   French: → 80:48; 82:30.   Dutch: → 80:19; 81:6, 11.

Relations with pub'r (Meissner): → 71:60; 72:7, 18, 22, 32, 38; 73:10, 15, 25, 29, 48; 81:54, 60.

M's work on Vol. 2: → 71:4, 31; 72:68; 74:6, 11; 75:42; 76:12, 32; 77:11, 45; 78:2, 14, 26, 38, 39, 45–51; 79:19; 80:2, 37; 81:54.

M's work on Vol. 3: → 74:6; 75:23, 45; 76:5; 78:39; 80:2, 37.

M's work on Vol. 4 (TSV): → 77:45.

M's work on *Capital*, undifferentiated references, incl general reading: → 72:24, 31; 74:11, 16; 75:23, 47; 76:12, 14, 18, 40; 77:45; 78:12, 18, 38, 45–51; 79:7, 35, 53; 80:51; 81:16, 32, 63, 64.   Reading and study on Russian conditions: → 75:3, 22, 34, 42, 45; 76:14, 18; 77:1, 28, 48; 78:12; 79:14, 28, 39, 42, 51; 80:26, 31; 81:2, 3, 5, 10, 13, 45, 63; 82:1, 48, 55.   Cf also 95:20.

16. Engels and *Capital:* 1883–1895

References are to Vol. 1 unless otherwise stated; references to Vols. 2–4 and undifferentiated references are at the end.

New German edns, revision, etc.: → 83:1, 24, 26, 34, 38, 42, 47, 49; 84:2, 11; 89:30; 90:29, 44.

Translations and foreign editions: → 83:24; 85:37, 40.   English: → 83:26, 34, 38; 84:16, 25, 30, 51, 60; 85:37, 41; 86:1, 5, 11, 14, 15, 20, 23, 26, 34, 50; 87:6, 12, 18, 24; 89:21; 91:32.   French: → 83:24; 85:3, 41; 86:20; 93:31.   Russian: → 83:47; 85:6, 23, 29; 86:5; 94:6, 17.   Polish: → 84:3; 90:1, 44.   Italian: → 93:31; 95:7.   *See also* Abridgments, *below.*

Reviews, reactions, publicism, publications about *Capital:* → *83:17*, 18, 42; *85:12*, 37; *86:45*, 49; *91:32*; *94:27*, 30, 50; *95:7*, 20.

Abridgments and popularizations: → *91:39*.   French: → *83:34*, 38, 42; *84:3*, 11; *85:3*; *93:31*.   German: → *84:3*, 11; *86:33*, 39.   English: → *86:34*.   Italian: → *93:31*; *95:34*.

E's work on Vol. 2: → *83:17*, 24, 26, 28, 38, 47; *84:3*, 11, 22, 25, 31, 36, 40, 51, 56, 60; *85:6*, 10, 14, 18, 23, 25, 29; *86:5*, 50; *92:67*; *93:3*, 36, 43.

E's work on Vol. 3: → *83:17*, 24, 26; *84:3*, 60; *85:1*, 6, 10, 14, 18, 23, 25, 41; *88:34*, 40; *89:5*, 10, 14, 21, 30, 34; *90:1*, 23; *91:4*, 58; *92:1*, 4, 10, 54, 67; *93:1*, 3, 18, 27, 54; *94:1*, 6, 17, 21, 27, 30, 40, 46; *95:7*, 20, 26, 30.

E's work on Vol. 4 (TSV): → *84:11*, 22, 60; *89:5*; *90:23*; *92:67*; *93:6*; *94:2*, 46; *95:20*, 26.

E's work on *Capital*, undifferentiated references: → *83:1*, 26; *84:1*, 3, 41; *85:10*, 17; *95:20*, 26, 34.